DEADPOOL

FIRS

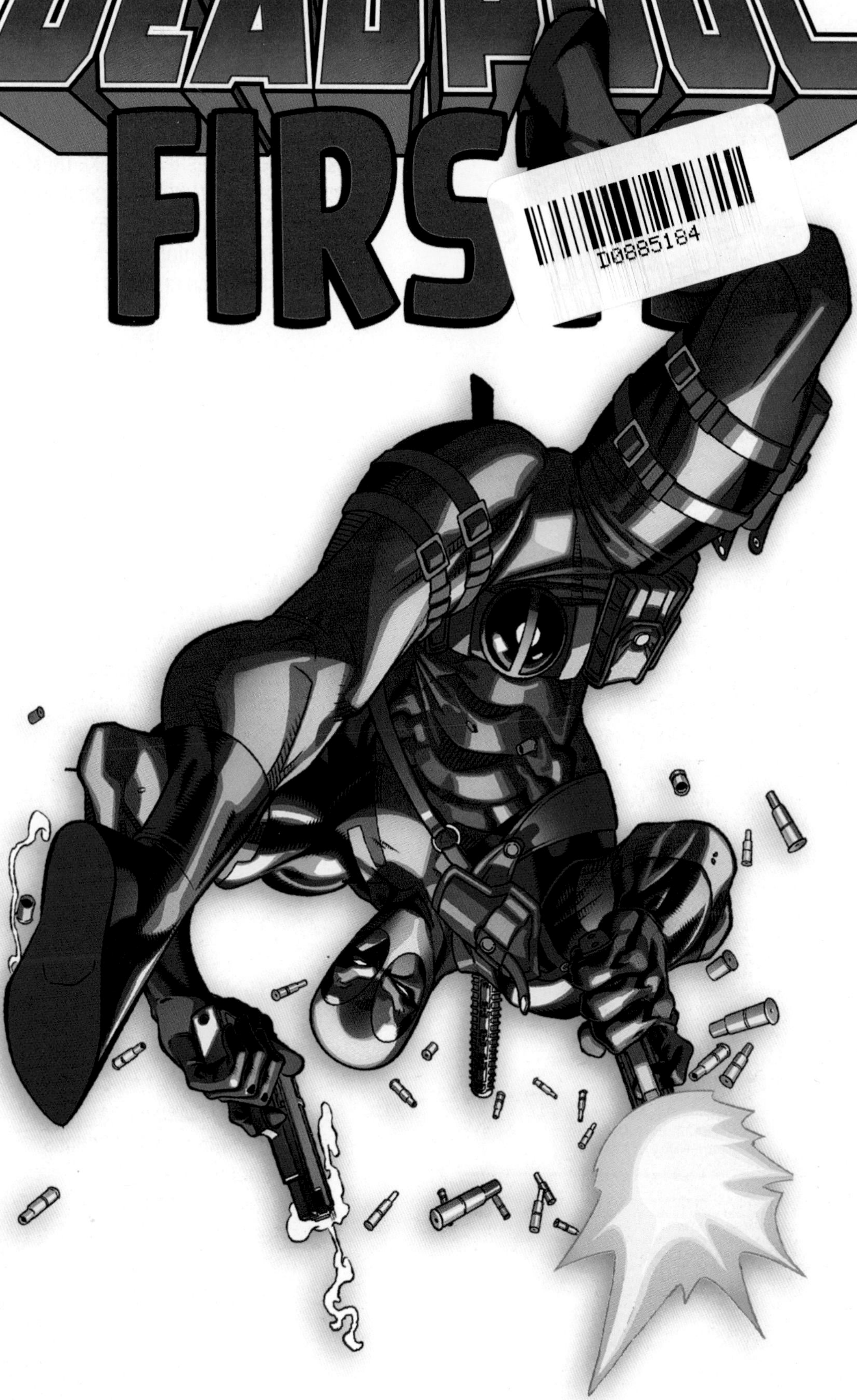

NEW MUTANTS #98
February 1991
"The Beginning of the End, Part One"
PLOTTER & ARTIST: ROB LIEFELD
SCRIPTER: FABIAN NICIEZA
COLORIST: STEVE BUCCELLATO
LETTERER: JOE ROSEN
ASSISTANT EDITOR: SUZANNE GAFFNEY
EDITOR: BOB HARRAS
COVER ART: ROB LIEFELD

DEADPOOL #1
August 1994
"If Looks Could Kill!"
WRITER: MARK WAID
PENCILER: IAN CHURCHILL
INKER: JASON MINOR
COLORISTS: DANA MORESHEAD & MIKE THOMAS
LETTERER: RICHARD STARKINGS & COMICRAFT
EDITOR: SUZANNE GAFFNEY
GROUP EDITOR: BOB HARRAS
COVER ART: IAN CHURCHILL

DEADPOOL: THE CIRCLE CHASE #1
August 1993
"The Circle Chase, Round 1: Ducks in a Row!"
WRITER: FABIAN NICIEZA
PENCILER: JOE MADUREIRA
INKER: MARK FARMER
COLORIST: GLYNIS OLIVER
LETTERER: CHRIS ELIOPOULOS
EDITOR: SUZANNE GAFFNEY
GROUP EDITOR: BOB HARRAS
COVER ART: JOE MADUREIRA

DEADPOOL #1
January 1997
"Hey, It's Deadpool! Or…Deadpool #1"
WRITER: JOE KELLY
PENCILER: ED MCGUINNESS
INKERS: NATHAN MASSENGILL WITH NORMAN LEE
COLORIST: CHRIS LICHTNER
SEPARATIONS: DIGITAL CHAMELEON
LETTERER: RICHARD STARKINGS
& COMICRAFT'S DAVE LANPHEAR
ASSISTANT EDITOR: PAUL TUTRONE
EDITOR: MATT IDELSON
COVER ART: ED MCGUINNESS, NORMAN LEE & LIQUID!

DEADPOOL CREATED BY ROB LIEFELD & FABIAN NICIEZA

COLLECTION EDITOR: MARK D. BEAZLEY
ASSISTANT EDITOR: SARAH BRUNSTAD
ASSISTANT MANAGING EDITOR: JOE HOCHSTEIN
ASSOCIATE MANAGING EDITOR: ALEX STARBUCK
EDITOR, SPECIAL PROJECTS: JENNIFER GRÜNWALD
SENIOR EDITOR, SPECIAL PROJECTS: JEFF YOUNGQUIST
RESEARCH & LAYOUT: JEPH YORK
BOOK DESIGNER: ADAM DEL RE
SVP PRINT, SALES & MARKETING: DAVID GABRIEL

EDITOR IN CHIEF: AXEL ALONSO
CHIEF CREATIVE OFFICER: JOE QUESADA
PUBLISHER: DAN BUCKLEY
EXECUTIVE PRODUCER: ALAN FINE

CABLE & DEADPOOL #1
May 2004
"If Looks Could Kill, Part 1: Face To Face"
WRITER: FABIAN NICIEZA
ARTISTS & COLORISTS: MARK BROOKS
& UDON'S SHANE LAW
UDON CHIEF: ERIK KO
LETTERER: VC'S CORY PETIT
ASSISTANT EDITORS: NICOLE WILEY & ANDY SCHMIDT
EDITOR: TOM BREVOORT
COVER ART: ROB LIEFELD

DEADPOOL FIRSTS. Contains material originally published in magazine form as NEW MUTANTS #98, DEADPOOL: THE CIRCLE CHASE #1, DEADPOOL (1994) #1, DEADPOOL (1997) #1, CABLE & DEADPOOL #1, DEADPOOL (2008) #1, DEADPOOL: MERC WITH A MOUTH #1, DEADPOOL TEAM-UP #899, DEADPOOL CORPS #1, DEADPOOL (2013) #1 and DEADPOOL (2015) #1. First printing 2016. ISBN# 978-0-7851-9531-3. Published by MARVEL WORLDWIDE, INC., a subsidiary of MARVEL ENTERTAINMENT, LLC. OFFICE OF PUBLICATION: 135 West 50th Street, New York, NY 10020. Copyright © 2016 MARVEL No similarity between any of the names, characters, persons, and/or institutions in this magazine with those of any living or dead person or institution is intended, and any such similarity which may exist is purely coincidental. **Printed in the U.S.A.** ALAN FINE, President, Marvel Entertainment; DAN BUCKLEY, President, TV, Publishing and Brand Management; JOE QUESADA, Chief Creative Officer; TOM BREVOORT, SVP of Publishing; DAVID BOGART, SVP of Operations & Procurement, Publishing; C.B. CEBULSKI, VP of International Development & Brand Management; DAVID GABRIEL, SVP Print, Sales & Marketing; JIM O'KEEFE, VP of Operations & Logistics; DAN CARR, Executive Director of Publishing Technology; SUSAN CRESPI, Editorial Operations Manager; ALEX MORALES, Publishing Operations Manager; STAN LEE, Chairman Emeritus. For information regarding advertising in Marvel Comics or on Marvel.com, please contact Jonathan Rheingold, VP of Custom Solutions & Ad Sales, at jrheingold@marvel.com. For Marvel subscription inquiries, please call 800-217-9158. **Manufactured between 12/11/2015 and 1/18/2016 by R.R. DONNELLEY, INC., SALEM, VA, USA.**

10 9 8 7 6 5 4 3 2 1

DEADPOOL #1

November 2008
"One of Us, Part 1"
WRITER: DANIEL WAY
PENCILER: PACO MEDINA
INKER: JUAN VLASCO
COLORIST: MARTE GRACIA
LETTERER: CHRIS ELIOPOULOS
ASSISTANT EDITORS: DANIEL KETCHUM & JODY LEHEUP
EDITOR: AXEL ALONSO
COVER ART: CLAYTON CRAIN

"One of Us, Part 1"
WRITER: RONALD BYRD
DESIGNER: RODOLFO MURAGUCHI
ASSISTANT EDITOR: ALEX STARBUCK
EDITOR: JEFF YOUNGQUIST

DEADPOOL: MERC WITH A MOUTH #1

September 2009
"Head Trip, Part One of Six"
WRITER: VICTOR GISCHLER
PENCILER: BONG DAZO
INKER: JOSÉ PIMENTEL
COLORIST: MATT MILLA
LETTERER: JEFF ECKLEBERRY
ASSISTANT EDITOR: SEBASTIAN GIRNER
EDITOR: AXEL ALONSO
COVER ART: ARTHUR SUYDAM

DEADPOOL TEAM-UP #899

January 2010
"Merc With a Myth"
WRITER: FRED VAN LENTE
ARTIST & COLORIST: DALIBOR TALAJIĆ
LETTERER: JEFF ECKLEBERRY
ASSISTANT EDITOR: SEBASTIAN GIRNER
EDITOR: AXEL ALONSO
COVER ART: HUMBERTO RAMOS & EDGAR DELGADO

DEADPOOL CORPS #1

June 2010
"Pool-Pocalypse Now, Part 1: Disrespect Your Elders"
WRITER: VICTOR GISCHLER
PENCILER: ROB LIEFELD
INKER: ADELSO CORONA
COLORIST: MATT YACKEY
LETTERER: VC'S CLAYTON COWLES
ASSISTANT EDITOR: SEBASTIAN GIRNER
EDITOR: AXEL ALONSO
COVER ART: ROB LIEFELD & MATT YACKEY

DEADPOOL #1

January 2013
"In Wade We Trust"
WRITERS: GERRY DUGGAN & BRIAN POSEHN
ARTIST: TONY MOORE
COLORIST: VAL STAPLES
LETTERER: VC'S JOE SABINO
EDITOR: JORDAN D. WHITE
SENIOR EDITOR: NICK LOWE
COVER ART: GEOF DARROW & PETER DOHERTY

DEADPOOL #1

January 2016
"Sumus Omnes Deadpool"
WRITER: GERRY DUGGAN
PENCILER: MIKE HAWTHORNE
INKER: TERRY PALLOT
COLORIST: VAL STAPLES
LETTERER: VC'S JOE SABINO
ASSISTANT EDITOR: HEATHER ANTOS
EDITOR: JORDAN D. WHITE
COVER ART: TONY MOORE

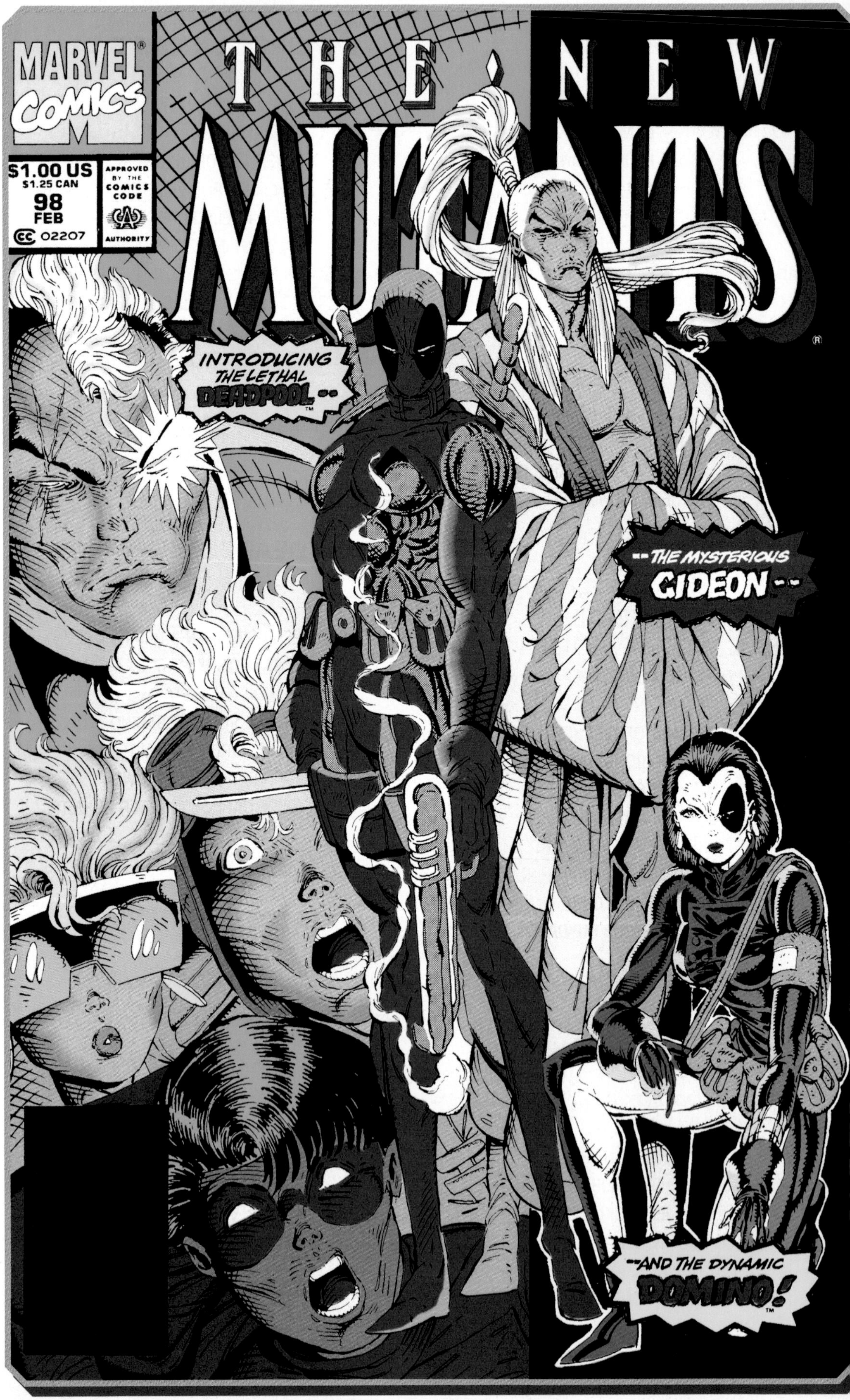
MARVEL COMICS
THE NEW MUTANTS
$1.00 US
$1.25 CAN
98
FEB
02207
APPROVED BY THE COMICS CODE AUTHORITY
INTRODUCING THE LETHAL DEADPOOL --
-- THE MYSTERIOUS GIDEON --
--AND THE DYNAMIC DOMINO!

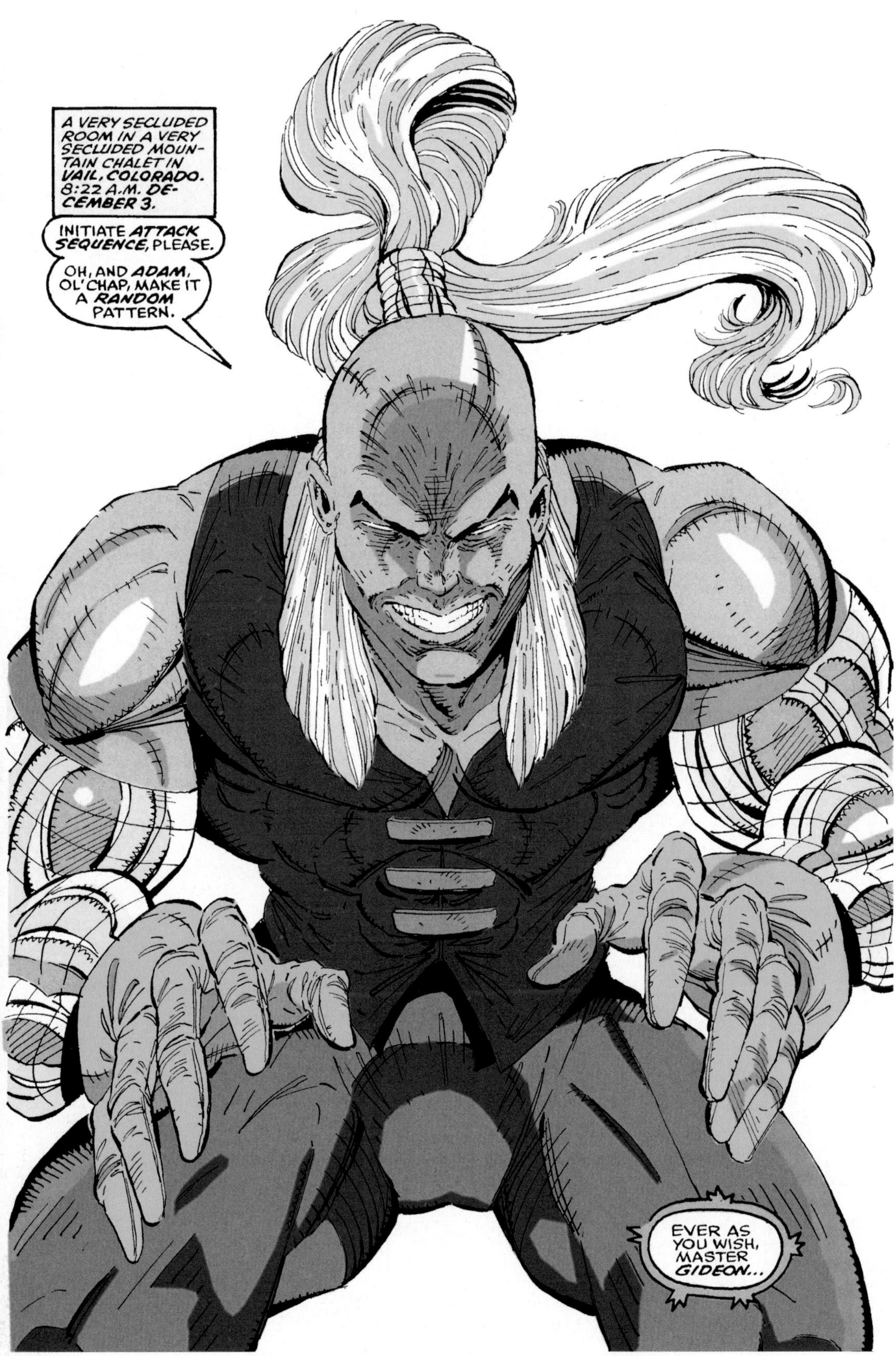
A VERY SECLUDED ROOM IN A VERY SECLUDED MOUNTAIN CHALET IN VAIL, COLORADO. 8:22 A.M. DECEMBER 3.
INITIATE ATTACK SEQUENCE, PLEASE.
OH, AND ADAM, OL' CHAP, MAKE IT A RANDOM PATTERN.
EVER AS YOU WISH, MASTER GIDEON...

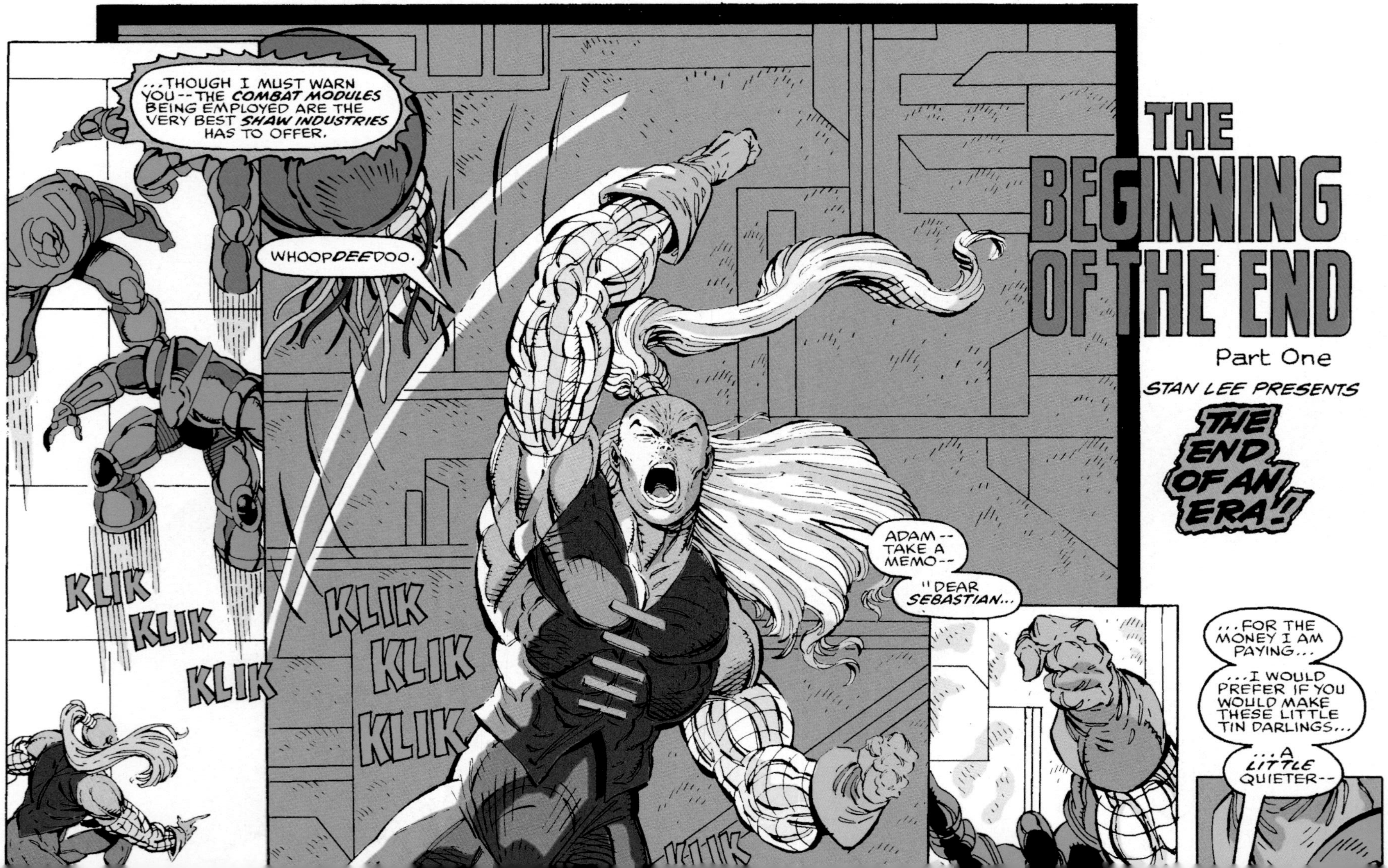
THE BEGINNING OF THE END
Part One
STAN LEE PRESENTS
THE END OF AN ERA!
...THOUGH I MUST WARN YOU--THE COMBAT MODULES BEING EMPLOYED ARE THE VERY BEST SHAW INDUSTRIES HAS TO OFFER.
WHOOPDEEDOO.
KLIK KLIK KLIK
KLIK KLIK KLIK
ADAM--TAKE A MEMO--
"DEAR SEBASTIAN...
...FOR THE MONEY I AM PAYING...
...I WOULD PREFER IF YOU WOULD MAKE THESE LITTLE TIN DARLINGS...
...A LITTLE QUIETER--

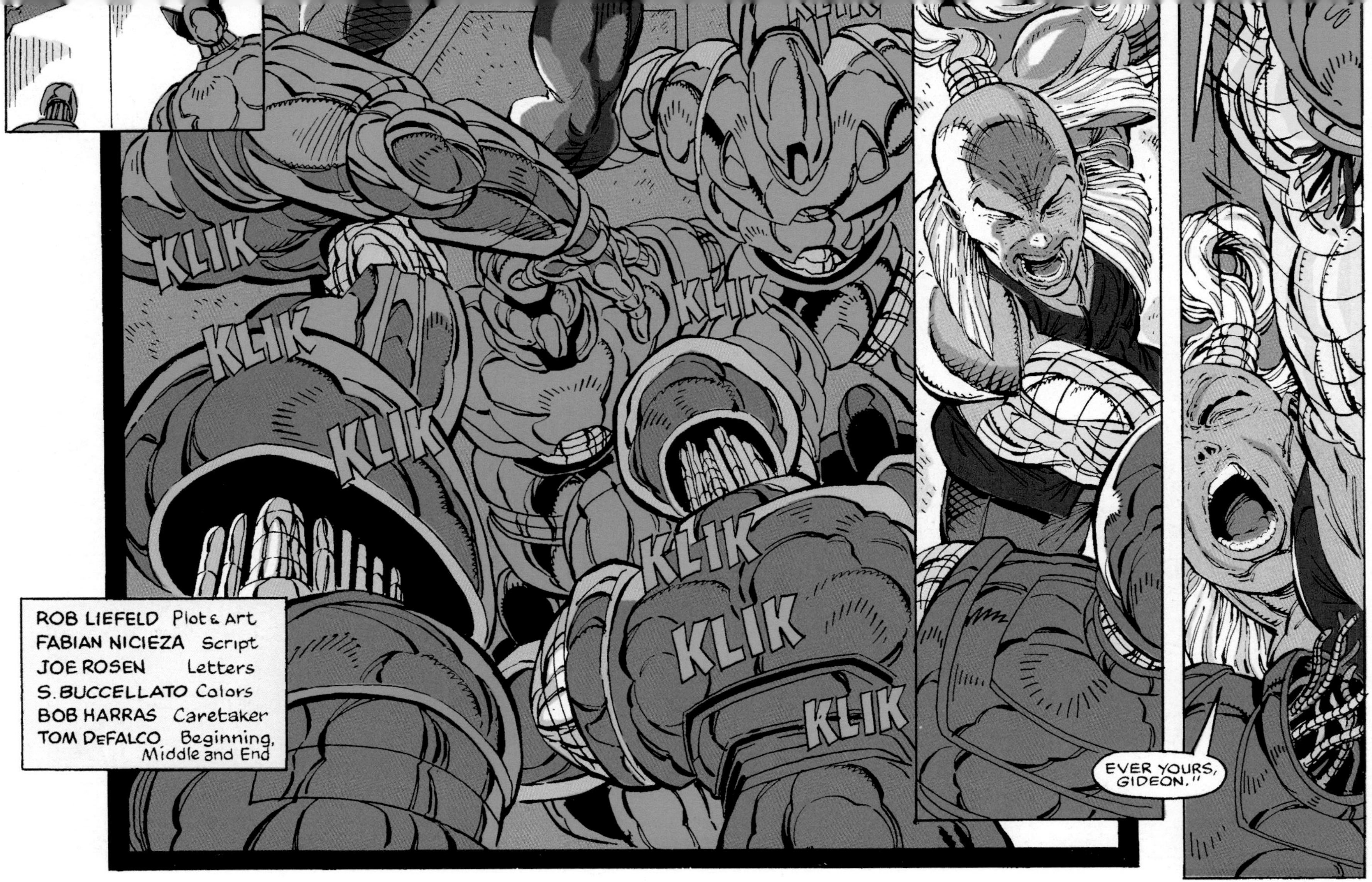
KLIK
KLIK
KLIK
KLIK
KLIK
KLIK
KLIK
ROB LIEFELD Plot & Art
FABIAN NICIEZA Script
JOE ROSEN Letters
S. BUCCELLATO Colors
BOB HARRAS Caretaker
TOM DeFALCO Beginning, Middle and End
EVER YOURS, GIDEON."

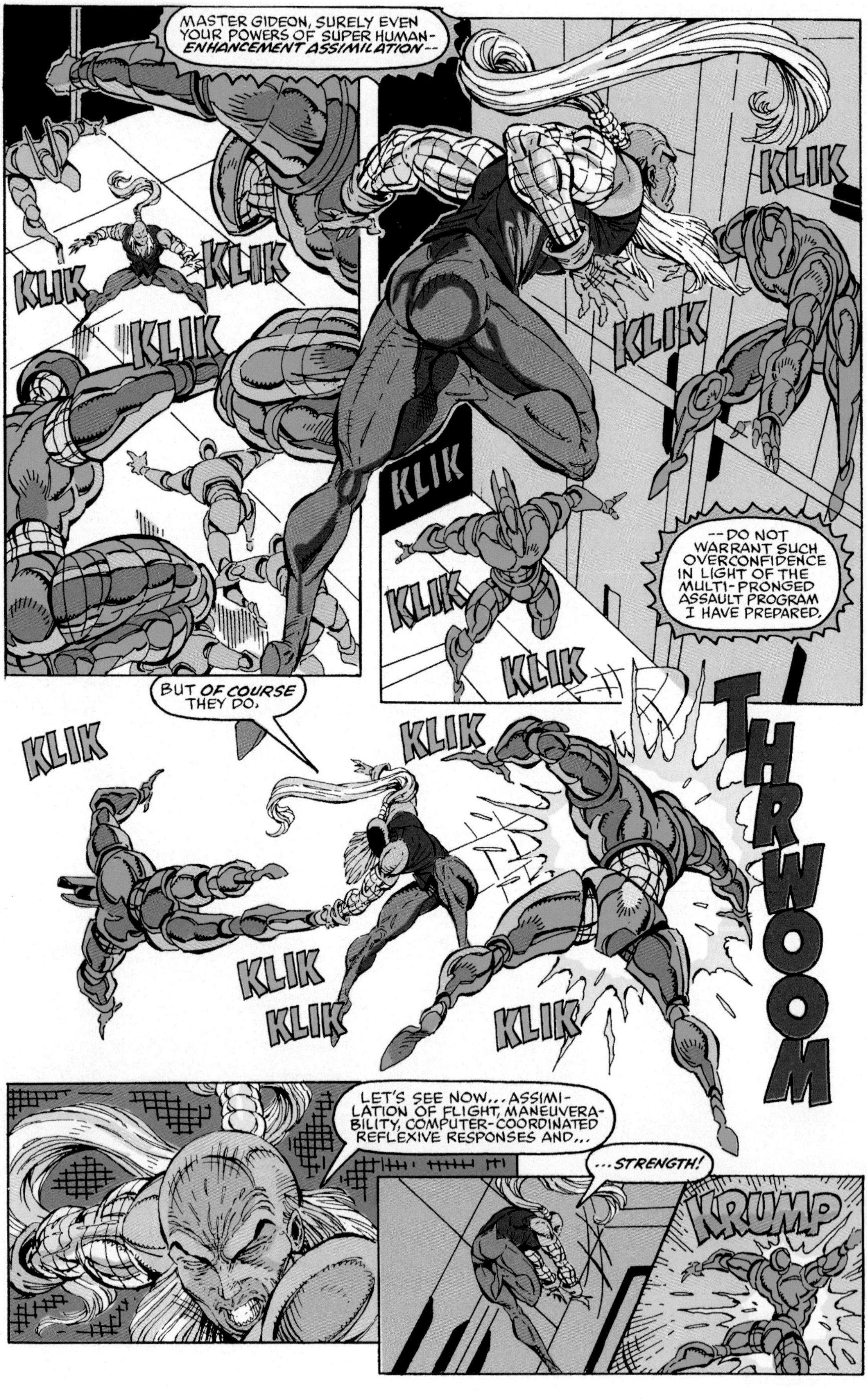
MASTER GIDEON, SURELY EVEN YOUR POWERS OF SUPER HUMAN-ENHANCEMENT ASSIMILATION--
KLIK
KLIK
KLIK
KLIK
KLIK
KLIK
--DO NOT WARRANT SUCH OVERCONFIDENCE IN LIGHT OF THE MULTI-PRONGED ASSAULT PROGRAM I HAVE PREPARED.
KLIK
KLIK
BUT OF COURSE THEY DO.
KLIK
KLIK
THRWOOM
KLIK
KLIK
KLIK
LET'S SEE NOW... ASSIMILATION OF FLIGHT, MANEUVERABILITY, COMPUTER-COORDINATED REFLEXIVE RESPONSES AND...
...STRENGTH!
KRUMP

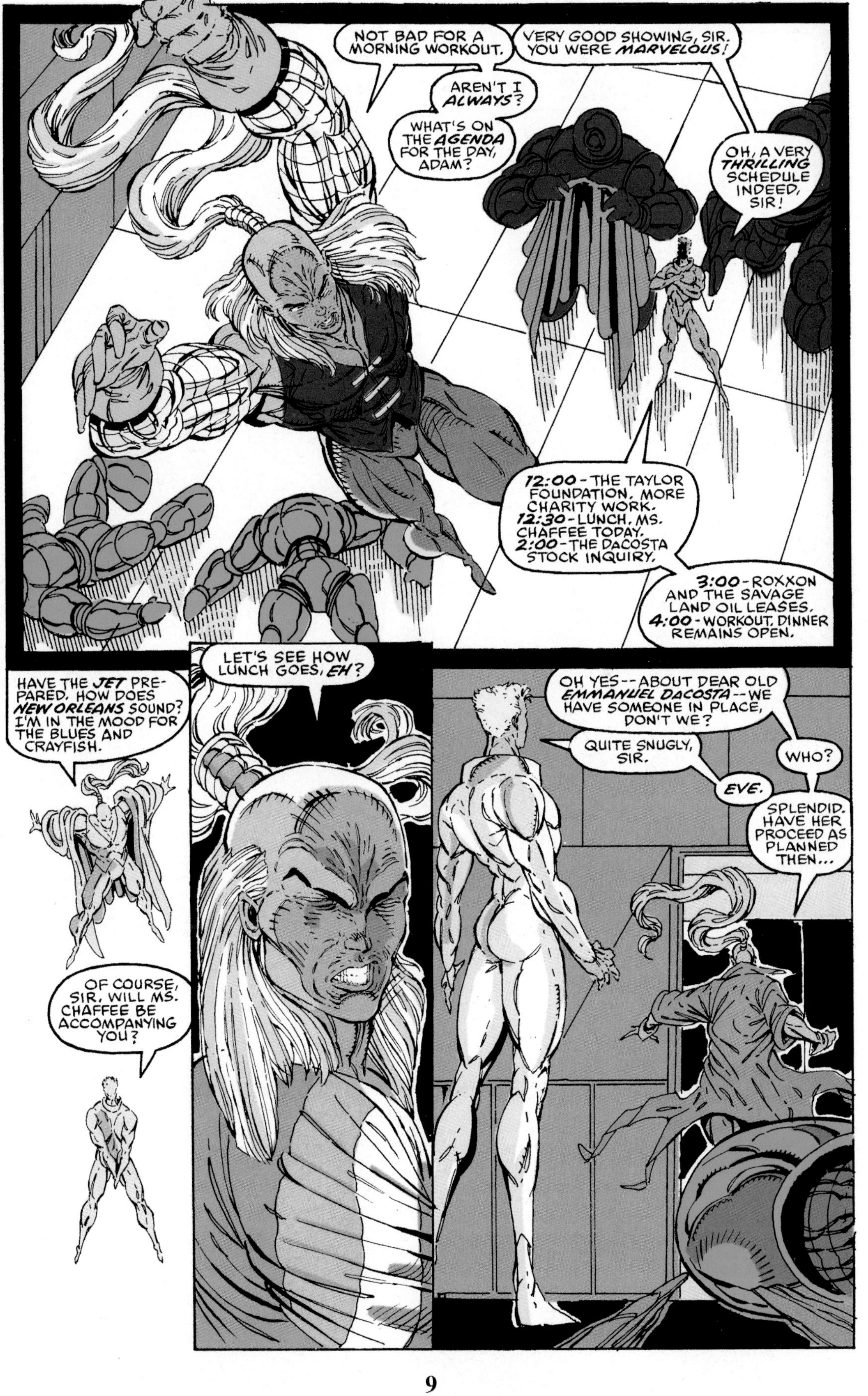
NOT BAD FOR A MORNING WORKOUT.
VERY GOOD SHOWING, SIR. YOU WERE MARVELOUS!
AREN'T I ALWAYS?
WHAT'S ON THE AGENDA FOR THE DAY, ADAM?
OH, A VERY THRILLING SCHEDULE INDEED, SIR!
12:00 - THE TAYLOR FOUNDATION, MORE CHARITY WORK.
12:30 - LUNCH, MS. CHAFFEE TODAY.
2:00 - THE DACOSTA STOCK INQUIRY.
3:00 - ROXXON AND THE SAVAGE LAND OIL LEASES.
4:00 - WORKOUT, DINNER REMAINS OPEN.
HAVE THE JET PREPARED. HOW DOES NEW ORLEANS SOUND? I'M IN THE MOOD FOR THE BLUES AND CRAYFISH.
OF COURSE, SIR, WILL MS. CHAFFEE BE ACCOMPANYING YOU?
LET'S SEE HOW LUNCH GOES, EH?
OH YES--ABOUT DEAR OLD EMMANUEL DACOSTA--WE HAVE SOMEONE IN PLACE, DON'T WE?
QUITE SNUGLY, SIR.
WHO?
EVE.
SPLENDID. HAVE HER PROCEED AS PLANNED THEN...

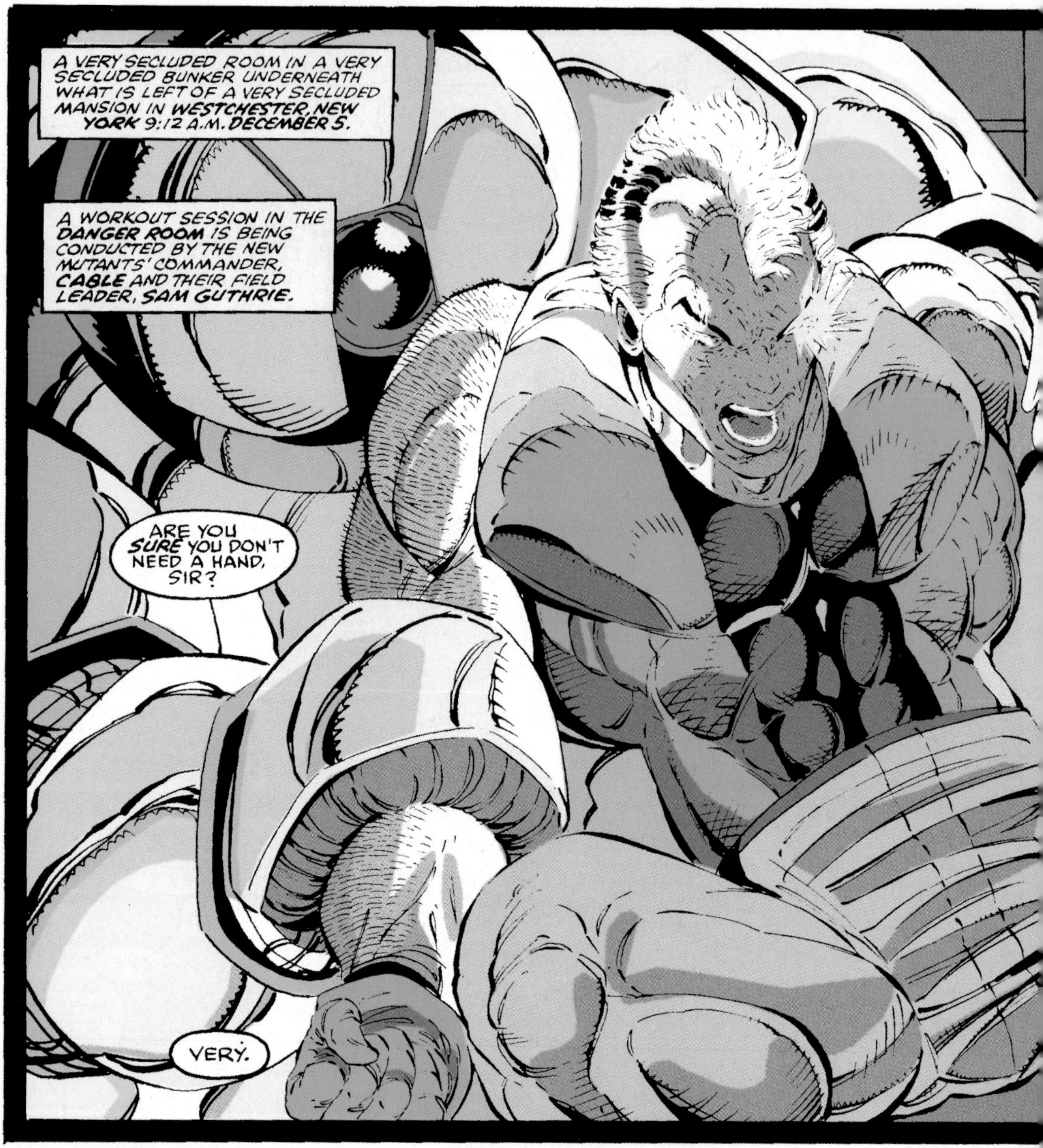
A VERY SECLUDED ROOM IN A VERY SECLUDED BUNKER UNDERNEATH WHAT IS LEFT OF A VERY SECLUDED MANSION IN WESTCHESTER, NEW YORK 9:12 A.M. DECEMBER 5.
A WORKOUT SESSION IN THE DANGER ROOM IS BEING CONDUCTED BY THE NEW MUTANTS' COMMANDER, CABLE AND THEIR FIELD LEADER, SAM GUTHRIE.
ARE YOU SURE YOU DON'T NEED A HAND, SIR?
VERY.

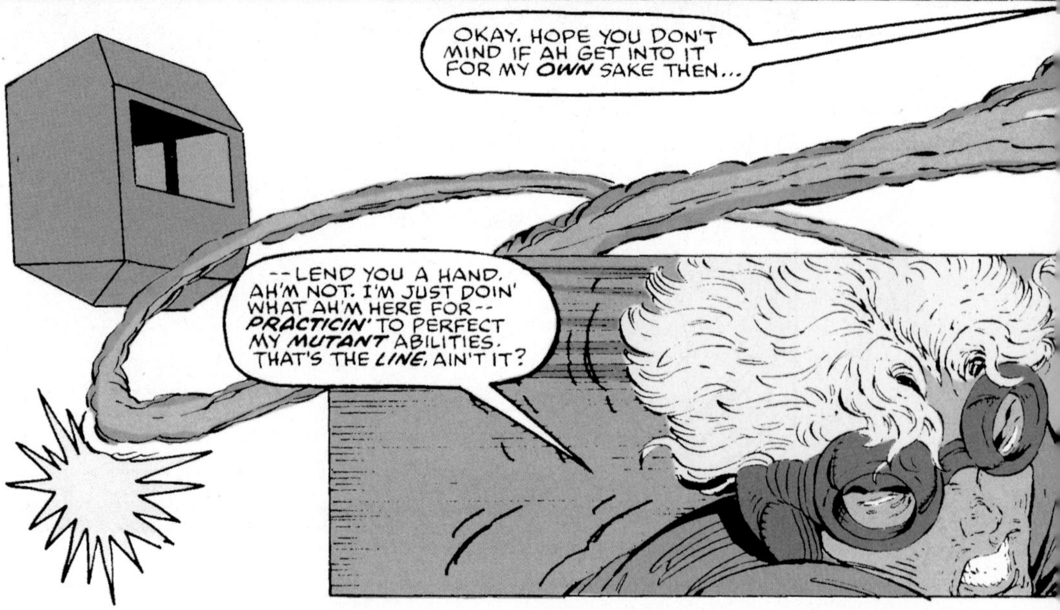
OKAY. HOPE YOU DON'T MIND IF AH GET INTO IT FOR MY OWN SAKE THEN...
--LEND YOU A HAND. AH'M NOT. I'M JUST DOIN' WHAT AH'M HERE FOR--PRACTICIN' TO PERFECT MY MUTANT ABILITIES. THAT'S THE LINE, AIN'T IT?

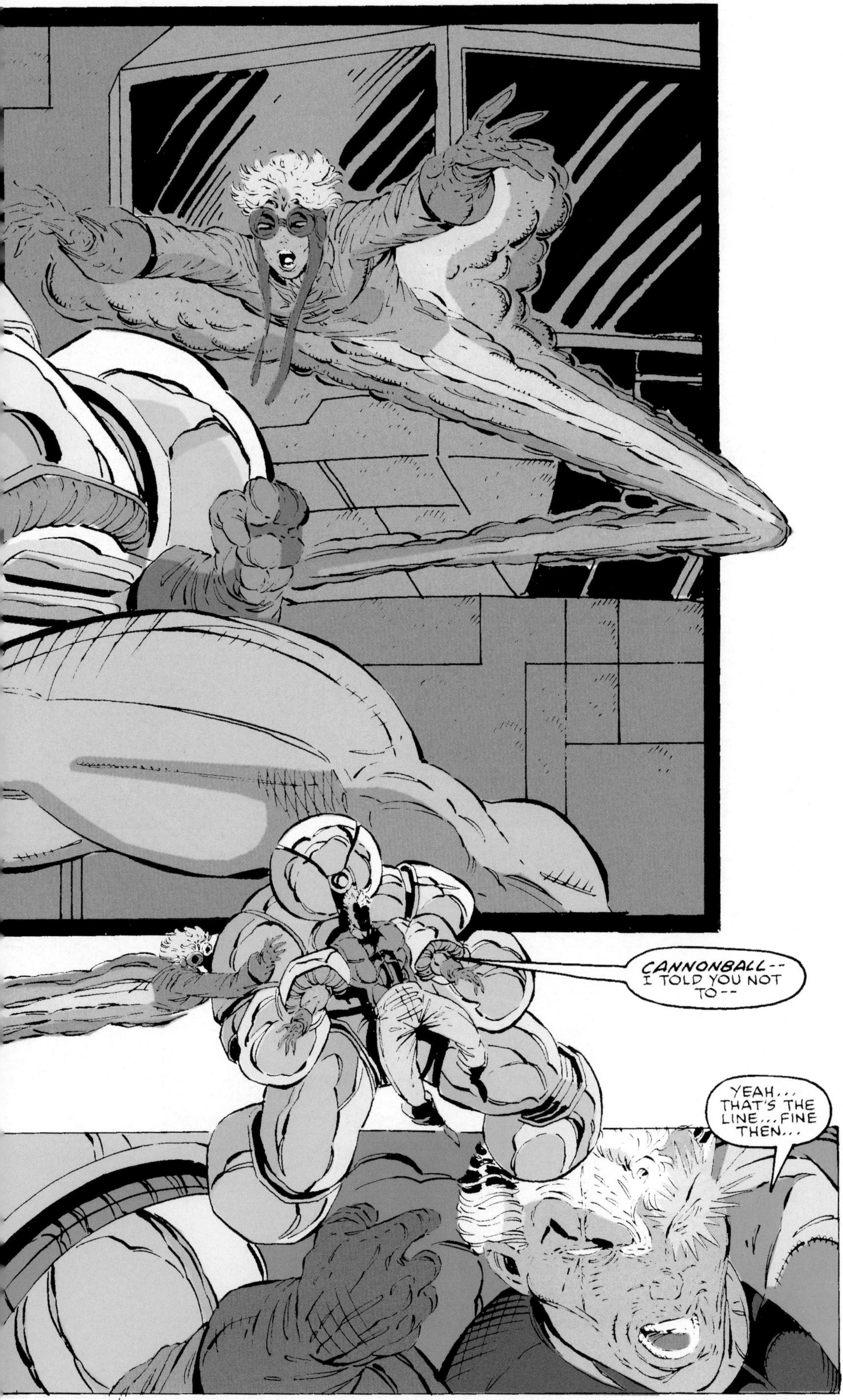
CANNONBALL-- I TOLD YOU NOT TO--
YEAH... THAT'S THE LINE... FINE THEN...

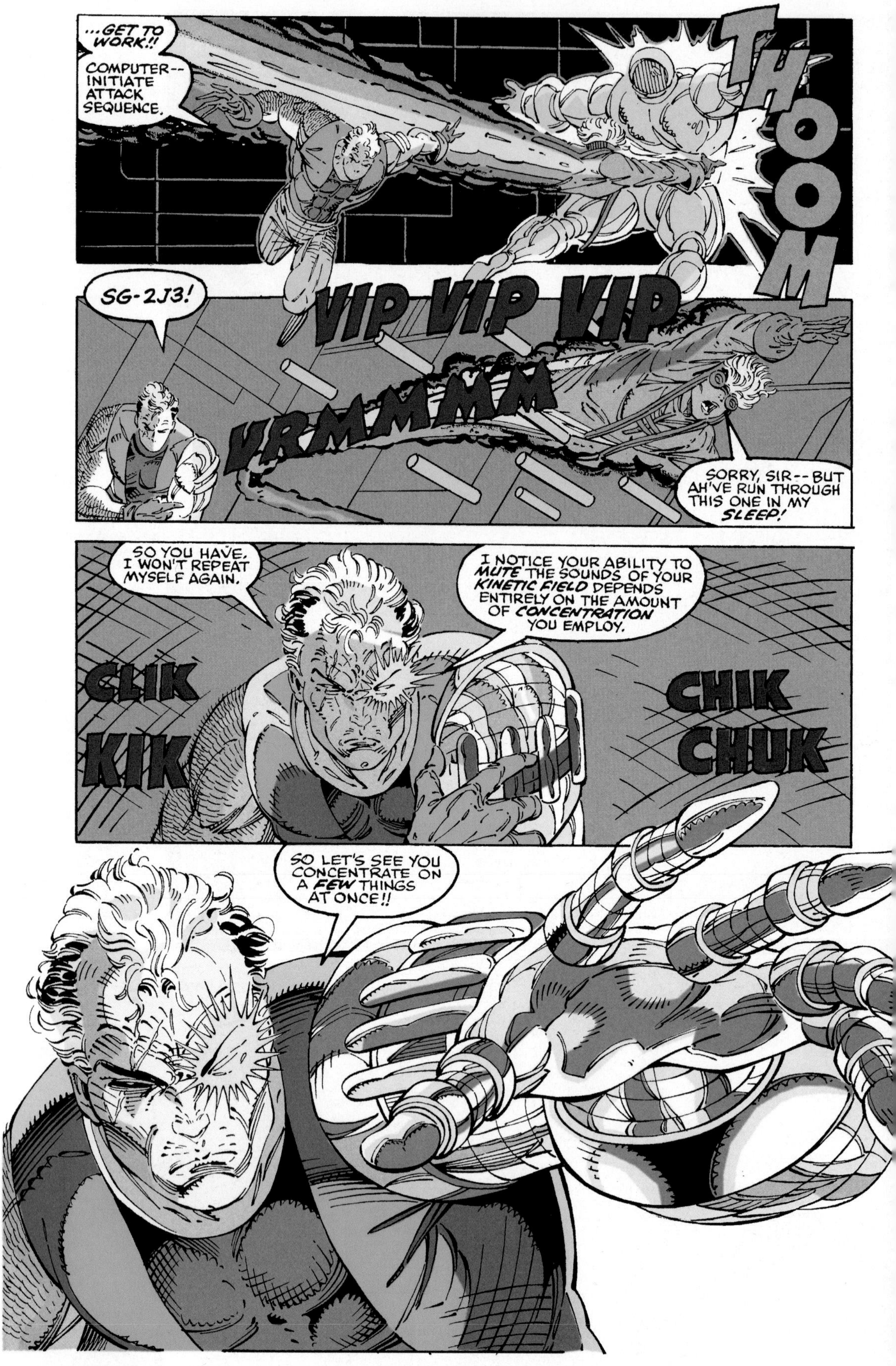
...GET TO WORK!!
COMPUTER-- INITIATE ATTACK SEQUENCE.
THOOM
SG-2J3!
VIP VIP VIP
VRMMMMM
SORRY, SIR--BUT AH'VE RUN THROUGH THIS ONE IN MY SLEEP!
SO YOU HAVE. I WON'T REPEAT MYSELF AGAIN.
I NOTICE YOUR ABILITY TO MUTE THE SOUNDS OF YOUR KINETIC FIELD DEPENDS ENTIRELY ON THE AMOUNT OF CONCENTRATION YOU EMPLOY.
CLIK KIK
CHIK CHUK
SO LET'S SEE YOU CONCENTRATE ON A FEW THINGS AT ONCE!!

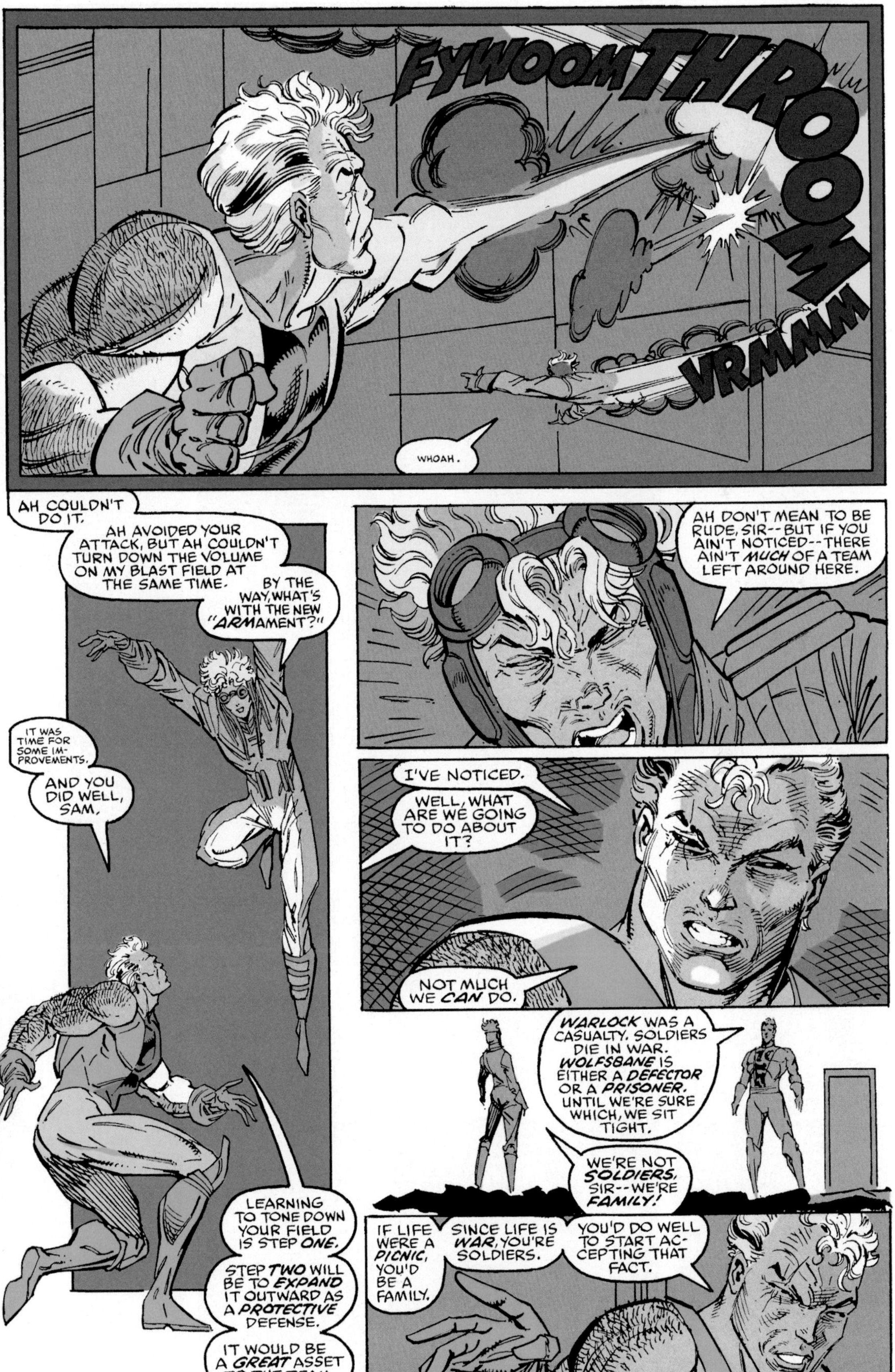
FYWOOM THROOM
VRMMMM
WHOAH.
AH COULDN'T DO IT.
AH AVOIDED YOUR ATTACK, BUT AH COULDN'T TURN DOWN THE VOLUME ON MY BLAST FIELD AT THE SAME TIME.
BY THE WAY, WHAT'S WITH THE NEW "ARMAMENT?"
IT WAS TIME FOR SOME IM-PROVEMENTS.
AND YOU DID WELL, SAM.
LEARNING TO TONE DOWN YOUR FIELD IS STEP ONE.
STEP TWO WILL BE TO EXPAND IT OUTWARD AS A PROTECTIVE DEFENSE.
IT WOULD BE A GREAT ASSET TO THE TEAM.
AH DON'T MEAN TO BE RUDE, SIR--BUT IF YOU AIN'T NOTICED--THERE AIN'T MUCH OF A TEAM LEFT AROUND HERE.
I'VE NOTICED.
WELL, WHAT ARE WE GOING TO DO ABOUT IT?
NOT MUCH WE CAN DO.
WARLOCK WAS A CASUALTY. SOLDIERS DIE IN WAR. WOLFSBANE IS EITHER A DEFECTOR OR A PRISONER. UNTIL WE'RE SURE WHICH, WE SIT TIGHT.
WE'RE NOT SOLDIERS, SIR--WE'RE FAMILY!
IF LIFE WERE A PICNIC, YOU'D BE A FAMILY.
SINCE LIFE IS WAR, YOU'RE SOLDIERS.
YOU'D DO WELL TO START AC-CEPTING THAT FACT.

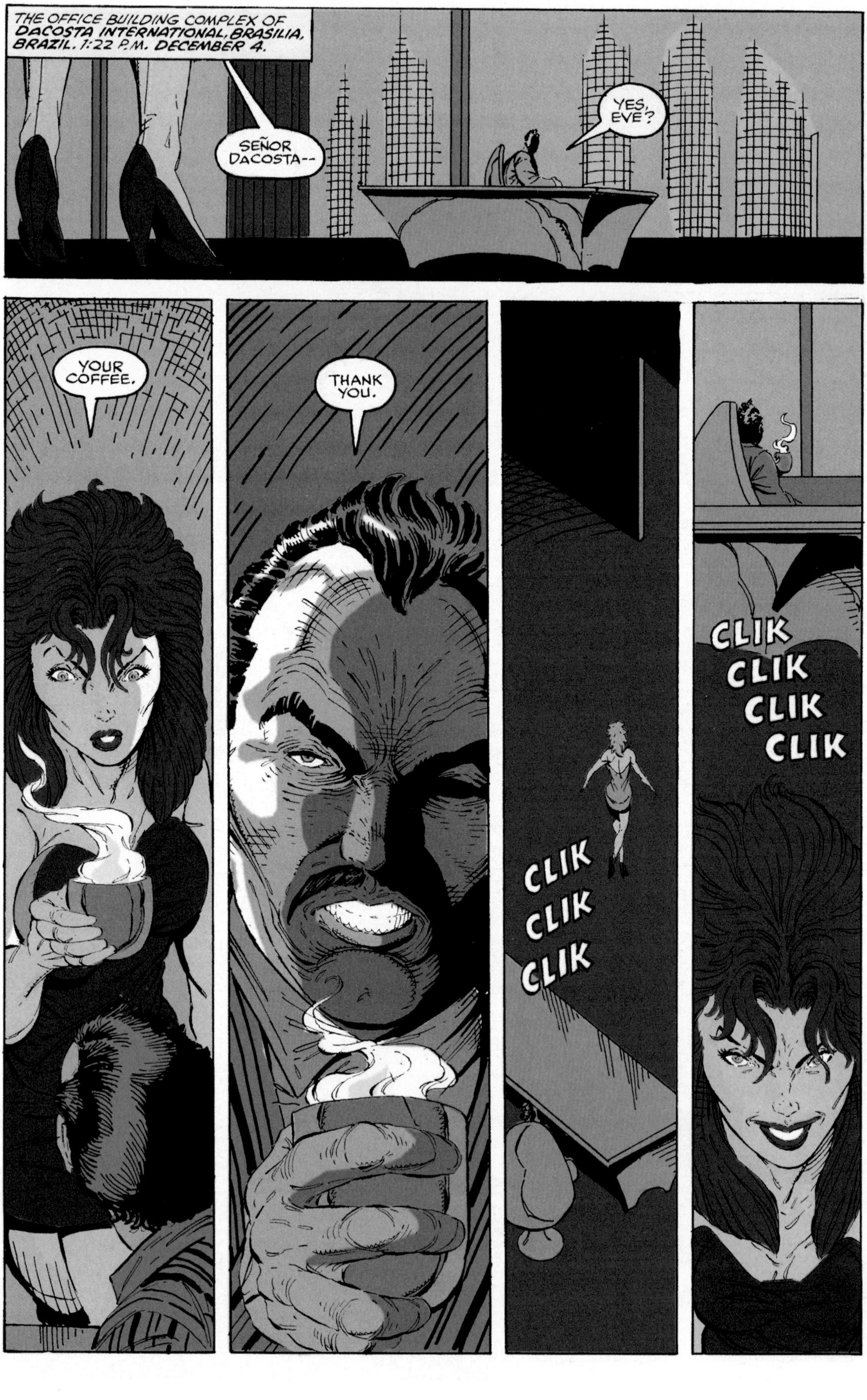
THE OFFICE BUILDING COMPLEX OF DACOSTA INTERNATIONAL, BRASILIA, BRAZIL. 1:22 P.M. DECEMBER 4.
SEÑOR DACOSTA--
YES, EVE?
YOUR COFFEE.
THANK YOU.
CLIK CLIK CLIK
CLIK CLIK CLIK CLIK

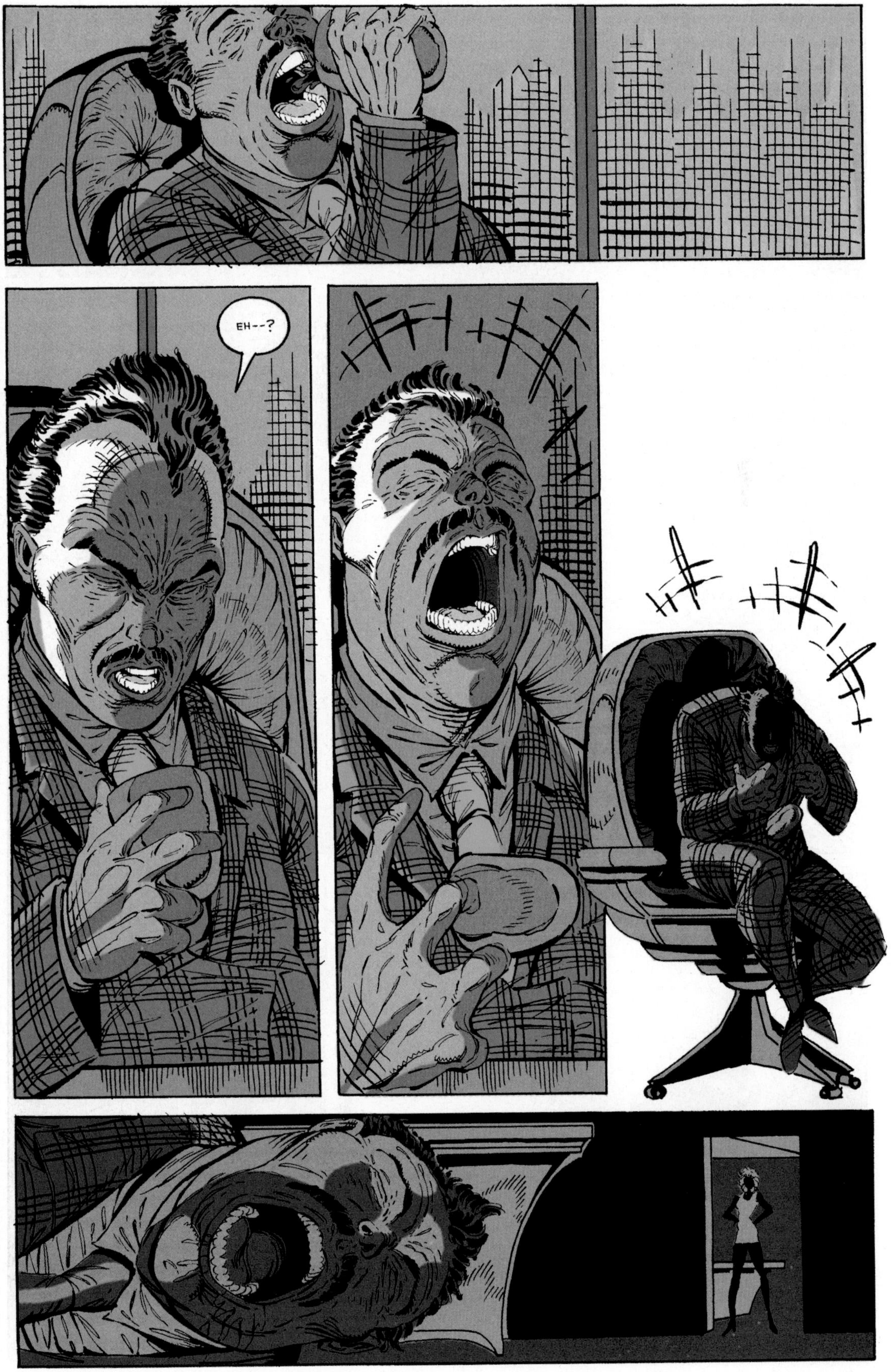
EH--?

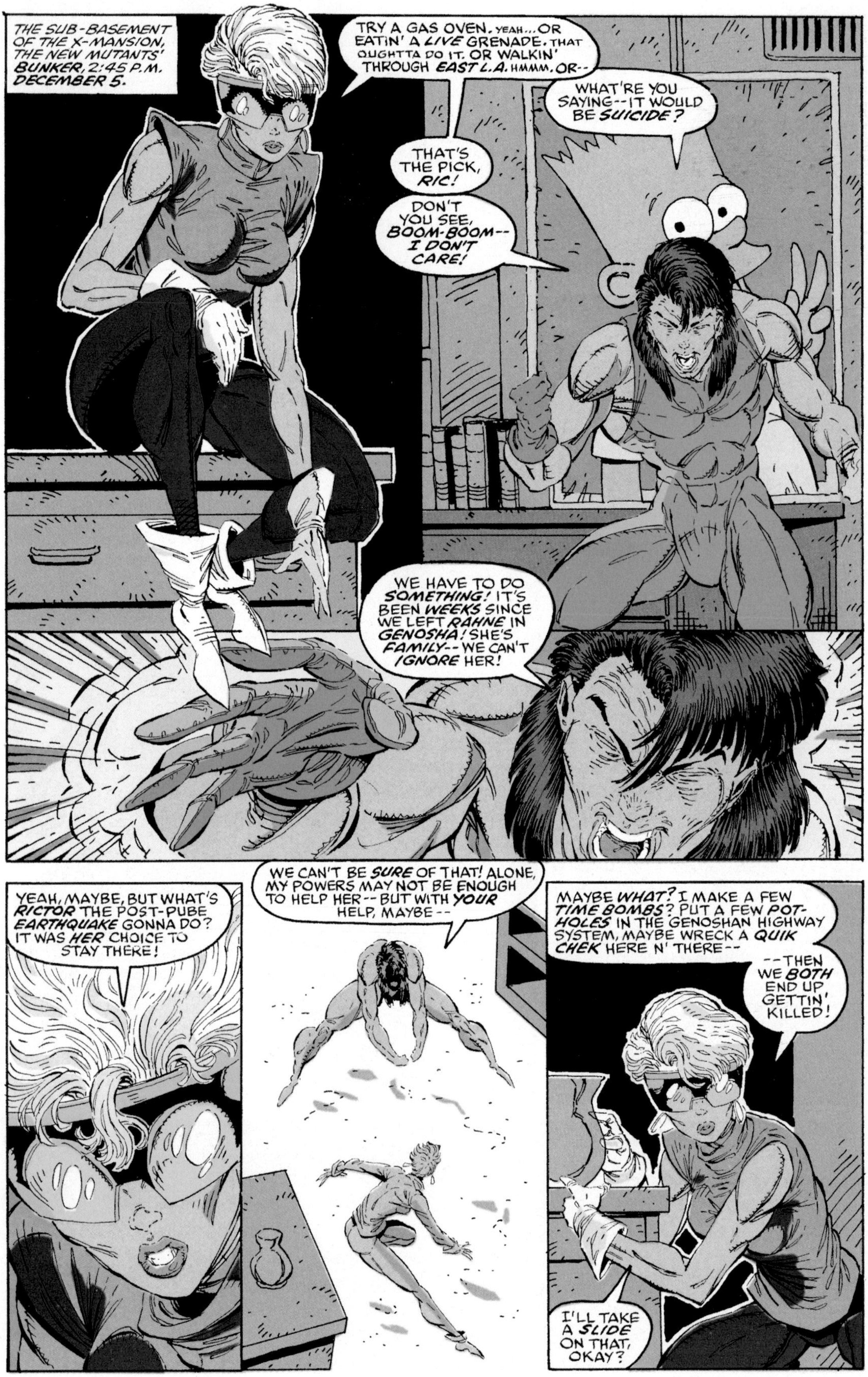
THE SUB-BASEMENT OF THE X-MANSION, THE NEW MUTANTS' BUNKER, 2:45 P.M. DECEMBER 5.
TRY A GAS OVEN. YEAH... OR EATIN' A LIVE GRENADE. THAT OUGHTTA DO IT. OR WALKIN' THROUGH EAST L.A. HMMM. OR--
WHAT'RE YOU SAYING--IT WOULD BE SUICIDE?
THAT'S THE PICK, RIC!
DON'T YOU SEE, BOOM-BOOM-- I DON'T CARE!
WE HAVE TO DO SOMETHING! IT'S BEEN WEEKS SINCE WE LEFT RAHNE IN GENOSHA! SHE'S FAMILY-- WE CAN'T IGNORE HER!
YEAH, MAYBE, BUT WHAT'S RICTOR THE POST-PUBE EARTHQUAKE GONNA DO? IT WAS HER CHOICE TO STAY THERE!
WE CAN'T BE SURE OF THAT! ALONE, MY POWERS MAY NOT BE ENOUGH TO HELP HER-- BUT WITH YOUR HELP, MAYBE--
MAYBE WHAT? I MAKE A FEW TIME BOMBS? PUT A FEW POT-HOLES IN THE GENOSHAN HIGHWAY SYSTEM, MAYBE WRECK A QUIK CHEK HERE N' THERE--
--THEN WE BOTH END UP GETTIN' KILLED!
I'LL TAKE A SLIDE ON THAT, OKAY?

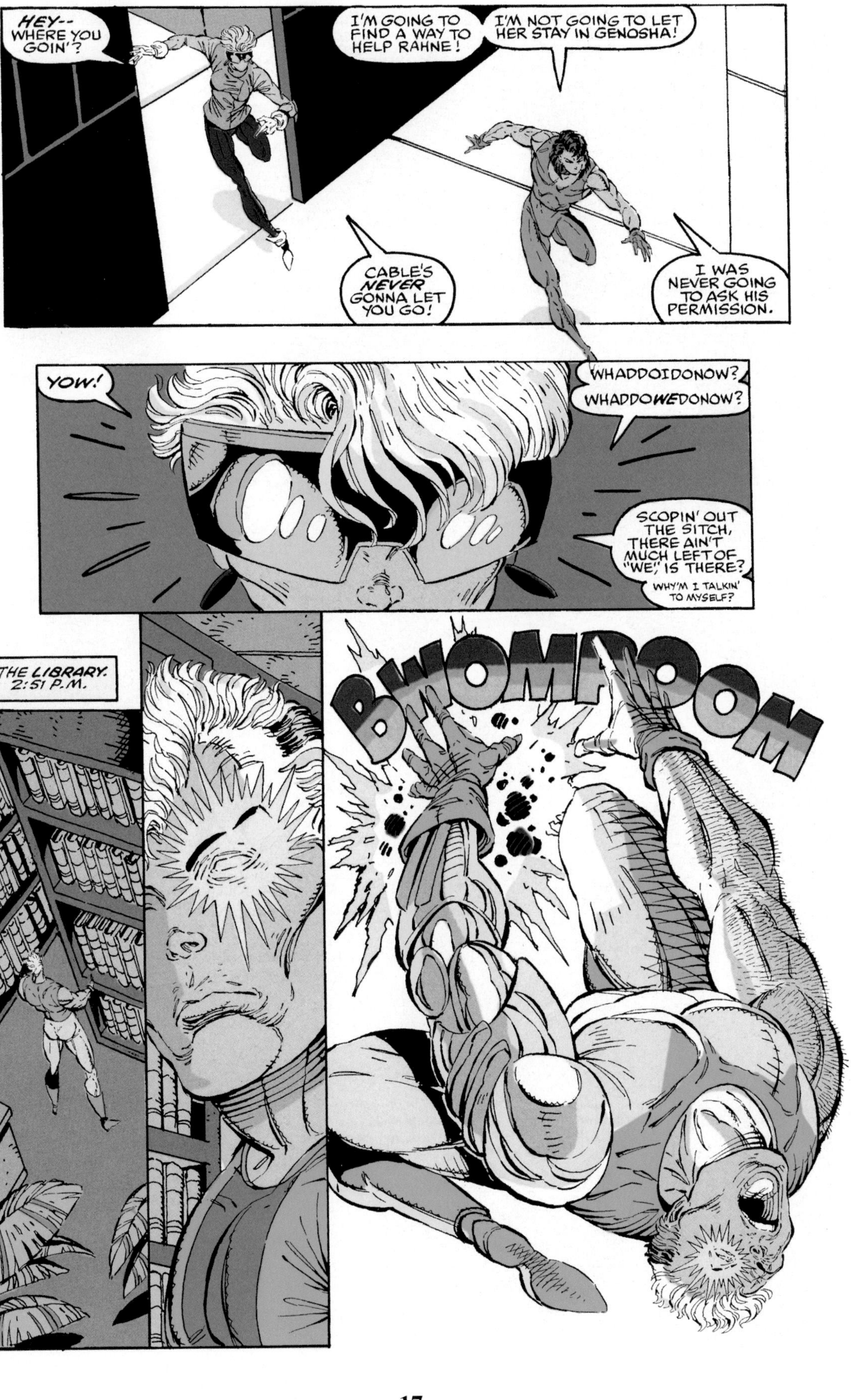
HEY-- WHERE YOU GOIN'?
I'M GOING TO FIND A WAY TO HELP RAHNE!
I'M NOT GOING TO LET HER STAY IN GENOSHA!
CABLE'S NEVER GONNA LET YOU GO!
I WAS NEVER GOING TO ASK HIS PERMISSION.
YOW!
WHADDOIDONOW?
WHADDOWEDONOW?
SCOPIN' OUT THE SITCH, THERE AIN'T MUCH LEFT OF "WE," IS THERE?
WHY'M I TALKIN' TO MYSELF?
THE LIBRARY. 2:51 P.M.
BWOMPOOM

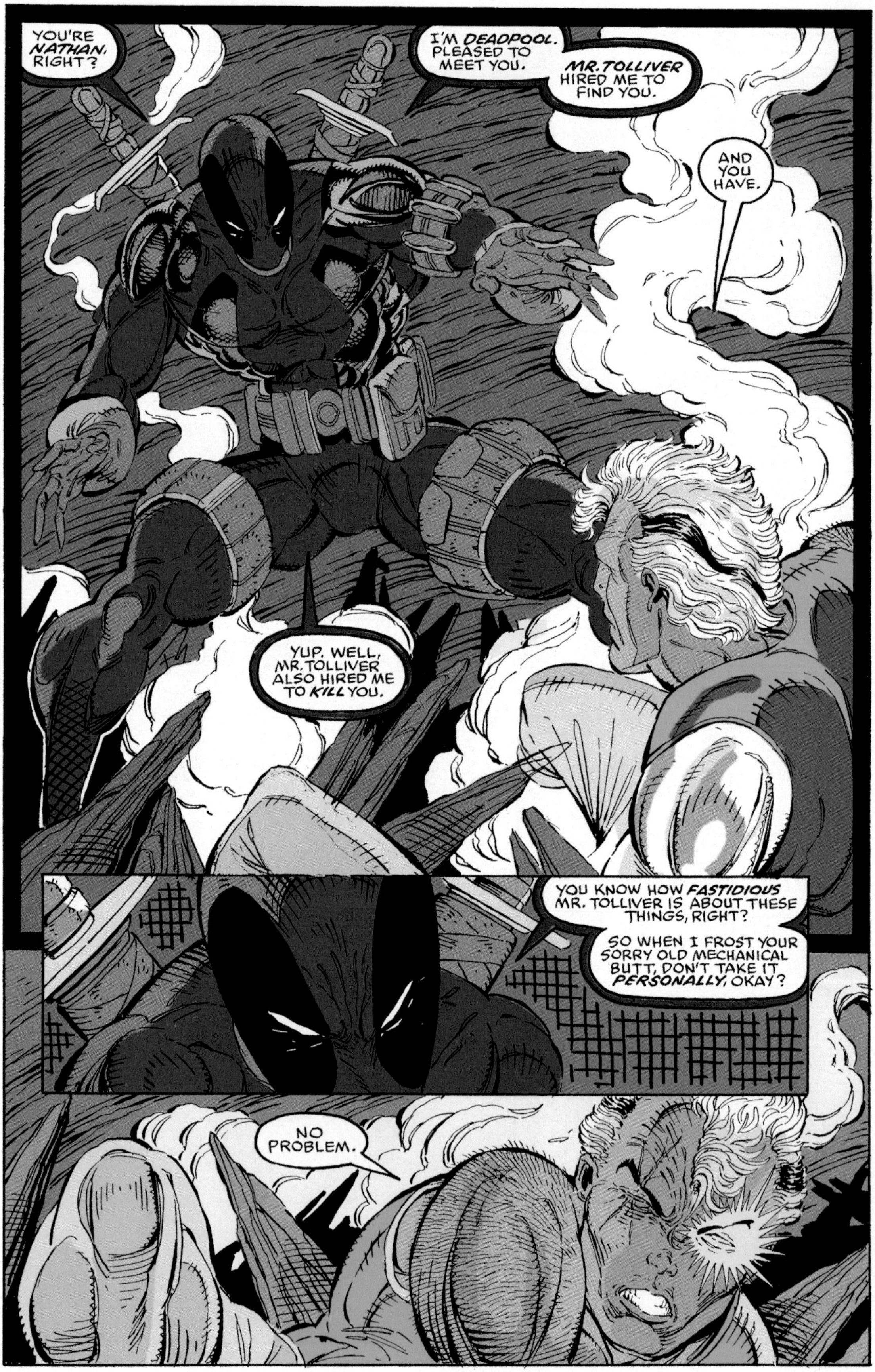
YOU'RE NATHAN, RIGHT?
I'M DEADPOOL. PLEASED TO MEET YOU.
MR. TOLLIVER HIRED ME TO FIND YOU.
AND YOU HAVE.
YUP. WELL, MR. TOLLIVER ALSO HIRED ME TO KILL YOU.
YOU KNOW HOW FASTIDIOUS MR. TOLLIVER IS ABOUT THESE THINGS, RIGHT?
SO WHEN I FROST YOUR SORRY OLD MECHANICAL BUTT, DON'T TAKE IT PERSONALLY, OKAY?
NO PROBLEM.

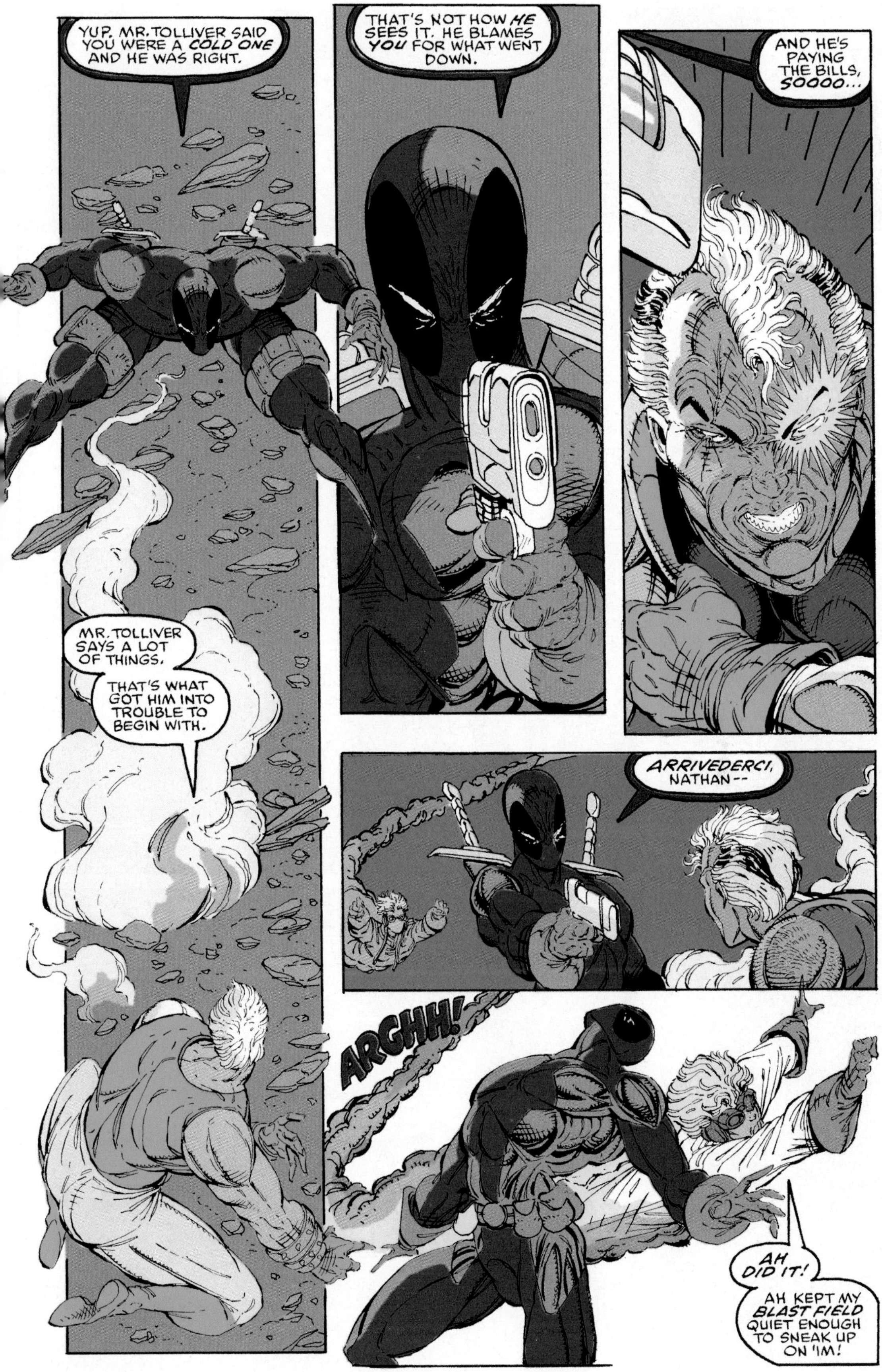
YUP, MR. TOLLIVER SAID YOU WERE A COLD ONE AND HE WAS RIGHT.
THAT'S NOT HOW HE SEES IT. HE BLAMES YOU FOR WHAT WENT DOWN.
AND HE'S PAYING THE BILLS, SOOOO...
MR. TOLLIVER SAYS A LOT OF THINGS.
THAT'S WHAT GOT HIM INTO TROUBLE TO BEGIN WITH.
ARRIVEDERCI, NATHAN--
ARGHH!
AH DID IT!
AH KEPT MY BLAST FIELD QUIET ENOUGH TO SNEAK UP ON 'IM!

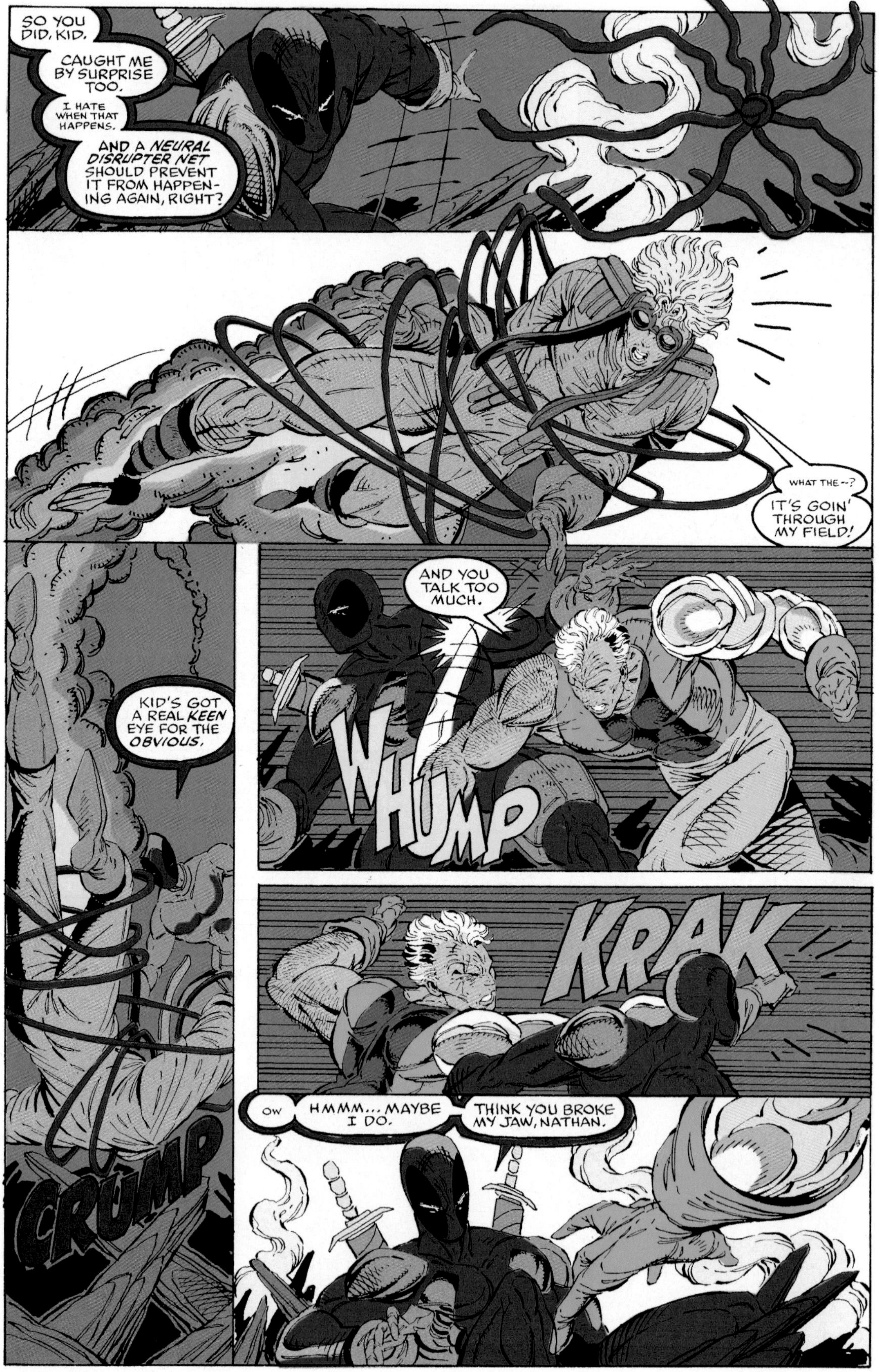
SO YOU DID, KID.
CAUGHT ME BY SURPRISE TOO.
I HATE WHEN THAT HAPPENS.
AND A NEURAL DISRUPTER NET SHOULD PREVENT IT FROM HAPPENING AGAIN, RIGHT?
WHAT THE --?
IT'S GOIN' THROUGH MY FIELD!
KID'S GOT A REAL KEEN EYE FOR THE OBVIOUS.
CRUMP
AND YOU TALK TOO MUCH.
WHUMP
KRAK
OW
HMMM... MAYBE I DO.
THINK YOU BROKE MY JAW, NATHAN.

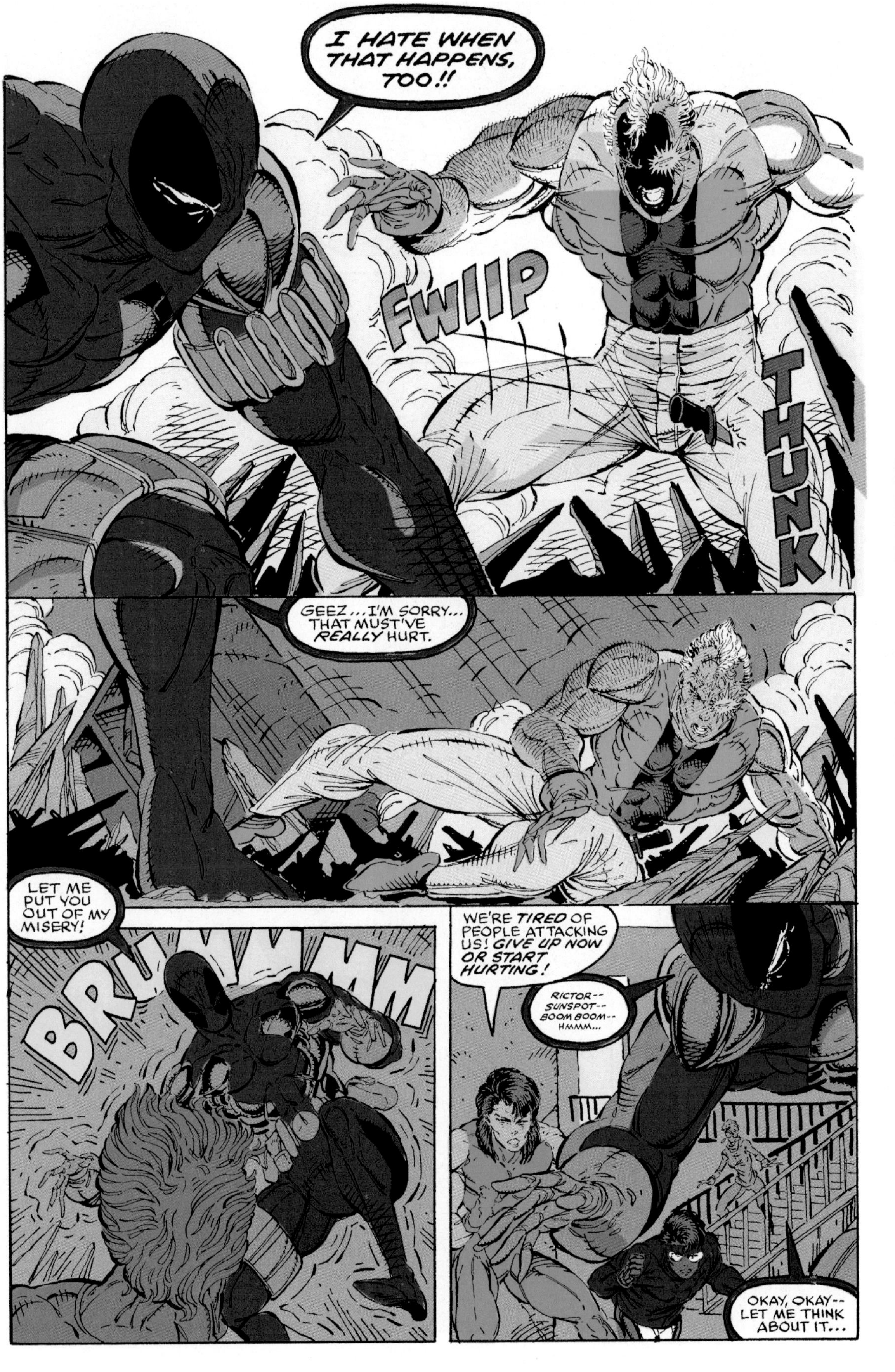
I HATE WHEN THAT HAPPENS, TOO!!
FWIIP
THUNK
GEEZ... I'M SORRY... THAT MUST'VE REALLY HURT.
LET ME PUT YOU OUT OF MY MISERY!
WE'RE TIRED OF PEOPLE ATTACKING US! GIVE UP NOW OR START HURTING!
RICTOR-- SUNSPOT-- BOOM BOOM-- HMMM...
OKAY, OKAY-- LET ME THINK ABOUT IT...

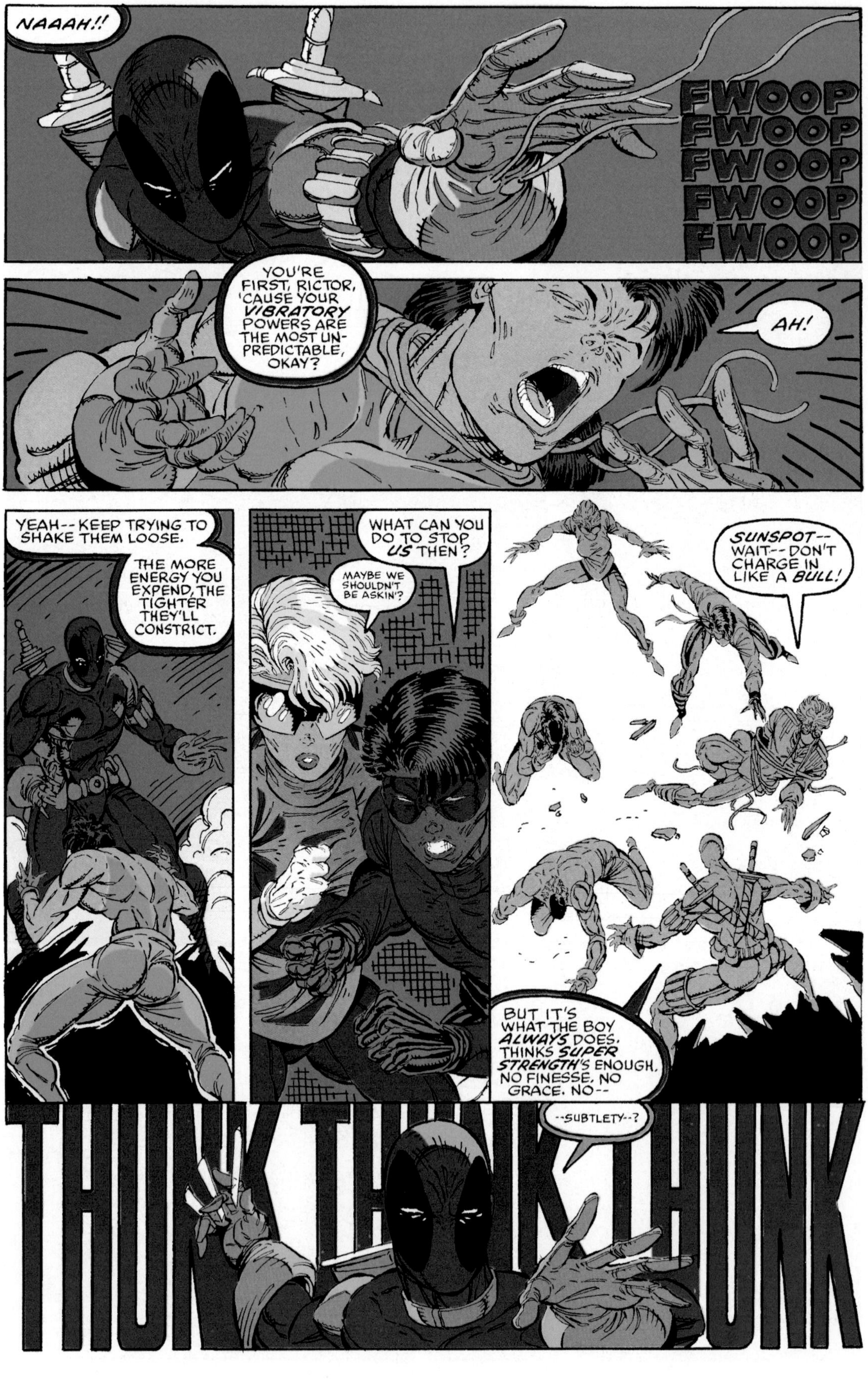
NAAAH!!
FWOOP FWOOP FWOOP FWOOP FWOOP
YOU'RE FIRST, RICTOR, 'CAUSE YOUR VIBRATORY POWERS ARE THE MOST UN-PREDICTABLE, OKAY?
AH!
YEAH-- KEEP TRYING TO SHAKE THEM LOOSE.
THE MORE ENERGY YOU EXPEND, THE TIGHTER THEY'LL CONSTRICT.
WHAT CAN YOU DO TO STOP US THEN?
MAYBE WE SHOULDN'T BE ASKIN'?
SUNSPOT-- WAIT-- DON'T CHARGE IN LIKE A BULL!
BUT IT'S WHAT THE BOY ALWAYS DOES. THINKS SUPER STRENGTH'S ENOUGH. NO FINESSE. NO GRACE. NO--
--SUBTLETY--?
THUNK THUNK THUNK

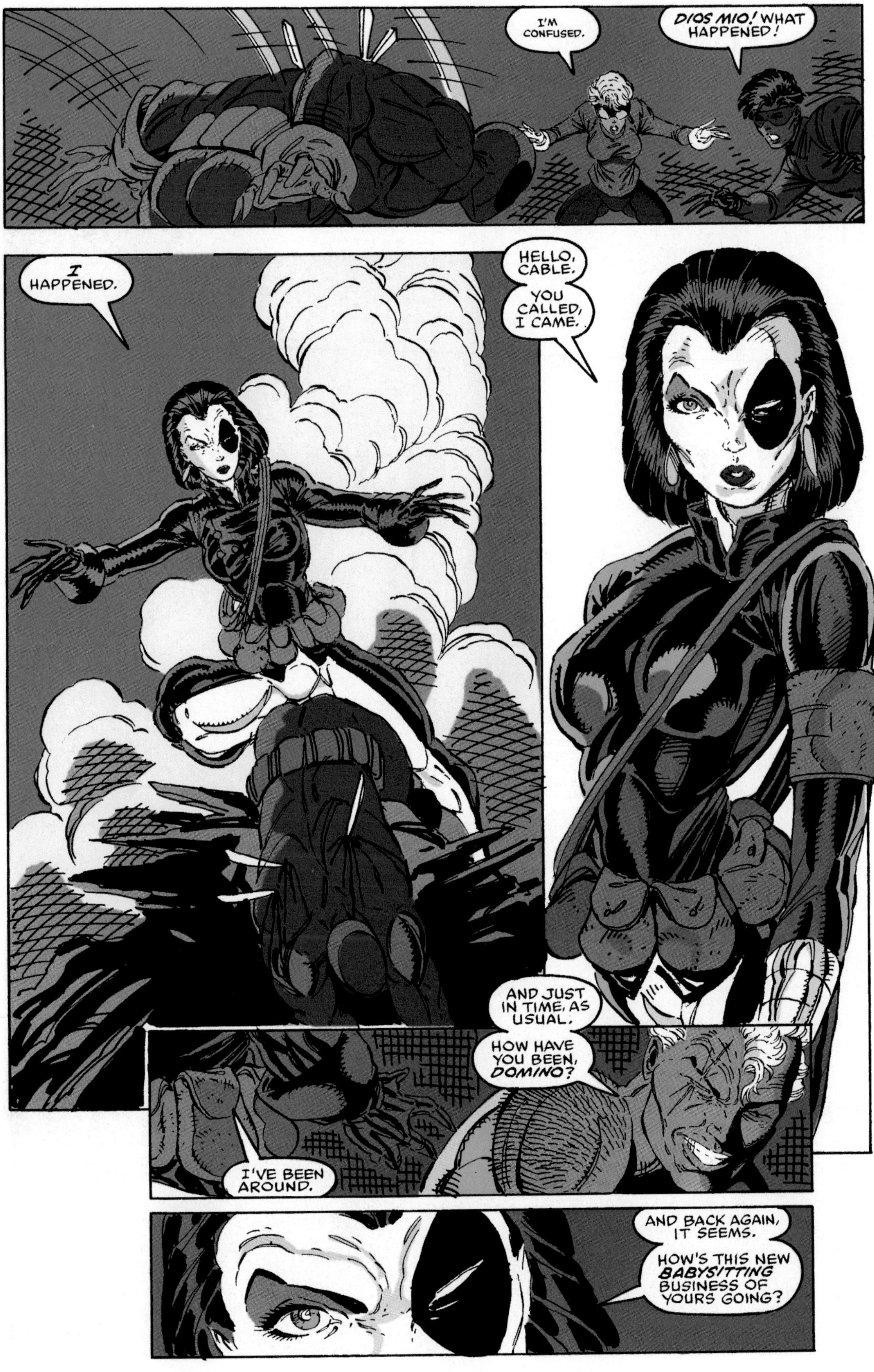
I'M CONFUSED.
DIOS MIO! WHAT HAPPENED!
I HAPPENED.
HELLO, CABLE.
YOU CALLED, I CAME.
AND JUST IN TIME, AS USUAL.
HOW HAVE YOU BEEN, DOMINO?
I'VE BEEN AROUND.
AND BACK AGAIN, IT SEEMS.
HOW'S THIS NEW BABYSITTING BUSINESS OF YOURS GOING?

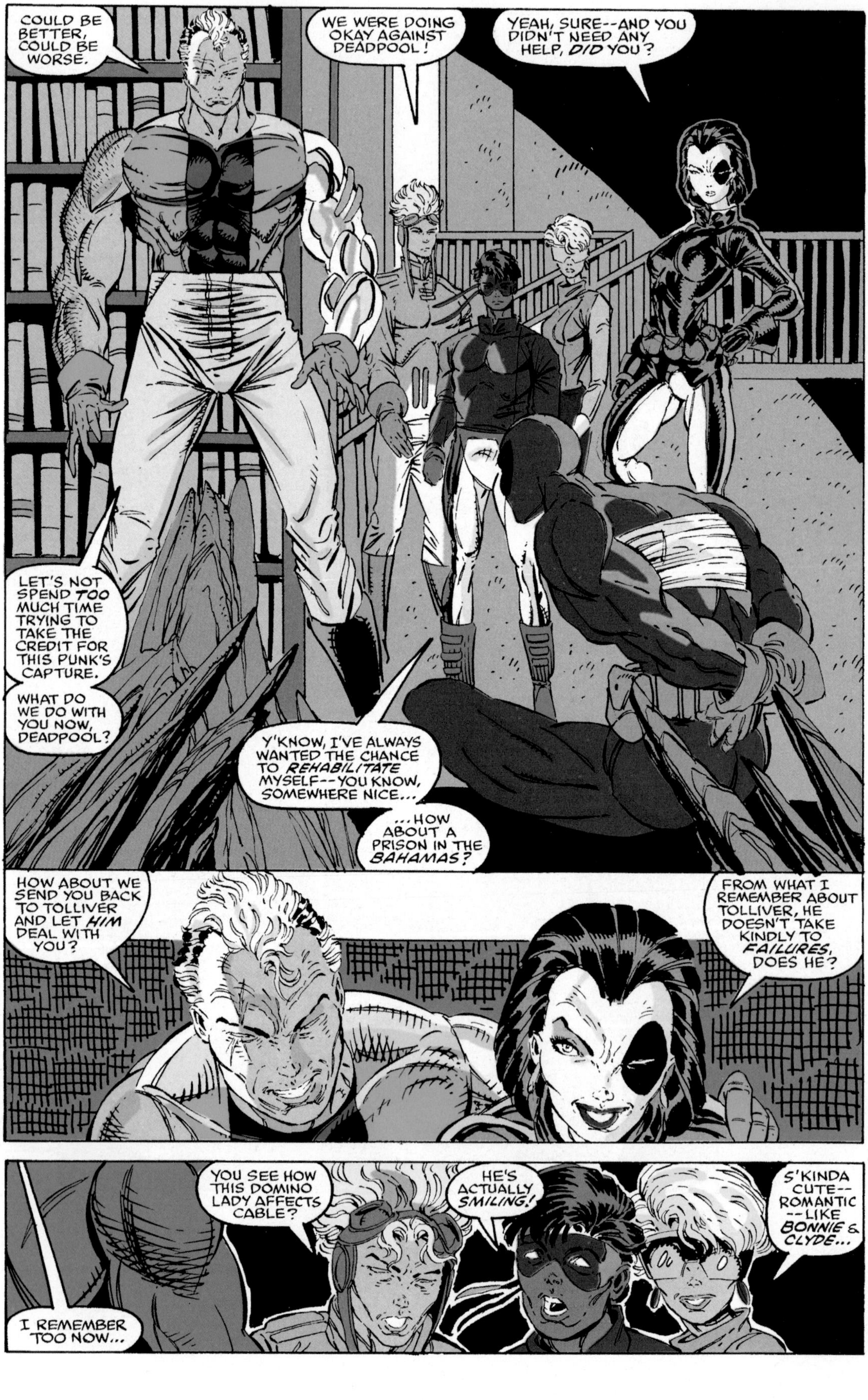
COULD BE BETTER, COULD BE WORSE.
WE WERE DOING OKAY AGAINST DEADPOOL!
YEAH, SURE--AND YOU DIDN'T NEED ANY HELP, DID YOU?
LET'S NOT SPEND TOO MUCH TIME TRYING TO TAKE THE CREDIT FOR THIS PUNK'S CAPTURE.
WHAT DO WE DO WITH YOU NOW, DEADPOOL?
Y'KNOW, I'VE ALWAYS WANTED THE CHANCE TO REHABILITATE MYSELF--YOU KNOW, SOMEWHERE NICE...
...HOW ABOUT A PRISON IN THE BAHAMAS?
HOW ABOUT WE SEND YOU BACK TO TOLLIVER AND LET HIM DEAL WITH YOU?
FROM WHAT I REMEMBER ABOUT TOLLIVER, HE DOESN'T TAKE KINDLY TO FAILURES, DOES HE?
YOU SEE HOW THIS DOMINO LADY AFFECTS CABLE?
HE'S ACTUALLY SMILING!
S'KINDA CUTE--ROMANTIC--LIKE BONNIE & CLYDE...
I REMEMBER TOO NOW...

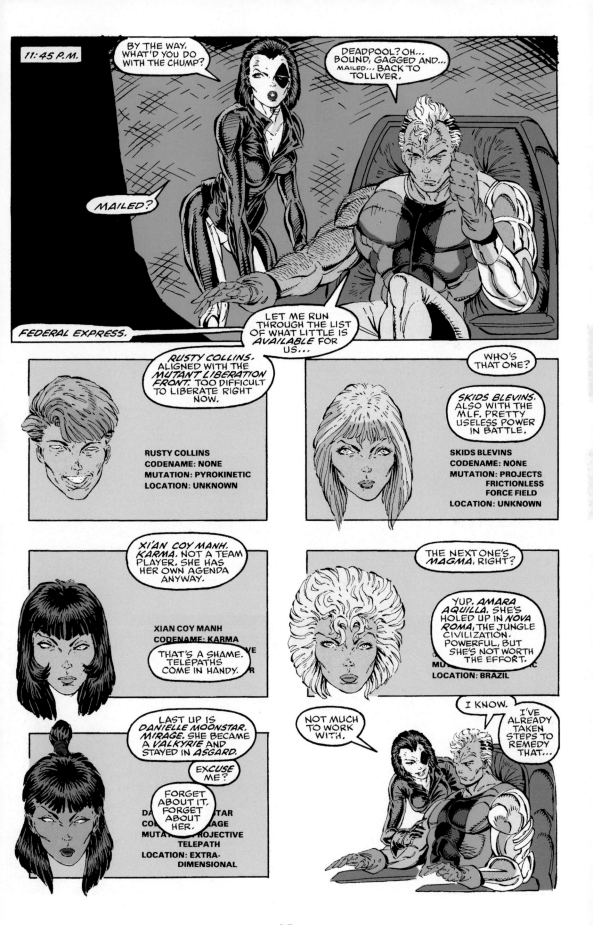

11:45 P.M.

BY THE WAY, WHAT'D YOU DO WITH THE CHUMP?

DEADPOOL? OH... BOUND, GAGGED AND... MAILED... BACK TO TOLLIVER.

MAILED?

FEDERAL EXPRESS.

LET ME RUN THROUGH THE LIST OF WHAT LITTLE IS *AVAILABLE* FOR US...

RUSTY COLLINS, ALIGNED WITH THE *MUTANT LIBERATION FRONT.* TOO DIFFICULT TO LIBERATE RIGHT NOW.

RUSTY COLLINS
CODENAME: NONE
MUTATION: PYROKINETIC
LOCATION: UNKNOWN

WHO'S THAT ONE?

SKIDS BLEVINS, ALSO WITH THE MLF. PRETTY USELESS POWER IN BATTLE.

SKIDS BLEVINS
CODENAME: NONE
MUTATION: PROJECTS FRICTIONLESS FORCE FIELD
LOCATION: UNKNOWN

XI'AN COY MANH, *KARMA.* NOT A TEAM PLAYER. SHE HAS HER OWN AGENDA ANYWAY.

XIAN COY MANH
CODENAME: KARMA

THAT'S A SHAME. TELEPATHS COME IN HANDY.

THE NEXT ONE'S *MAGMA*, RIGHT?

YUP. *AMARA AQUILLA.* SHE'S HOLED UP IN *NOVA ROMA*, THE JUNGLE CIVILIZATION. POWERFUL, BUT SHE'S NOT WORTH THE EFFORT.

MU...
LOCATION: BRAZIL

LAST UP IS *DANIELLE MOONSTAR, MIRAGE.* SHE BECAME A *VALKYRIE* AND STAYED IN *ASGARD.*

EXCUSE ME?

FORGET ABOUT IT, FORGET ABOUT HER.

DA...
CO...
MUTA... PROJECTIVE TELEPATH
LOCATION: EXTRA-DIMENSIONAL

NOT MUCH TO WORK WITH.

I KNOW. I'VE ALREADY TAKEN STEPS TO REMEDY THAT...

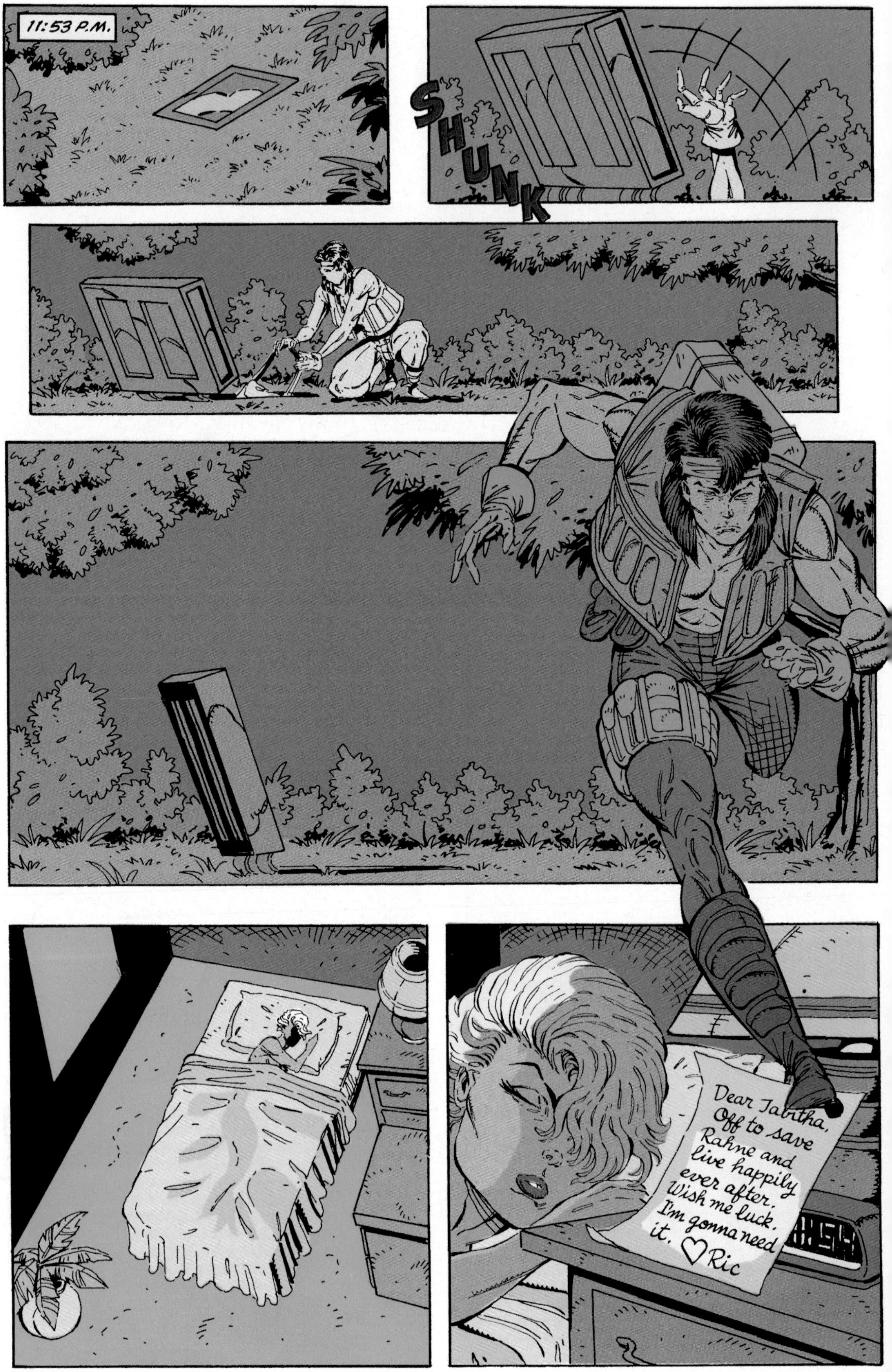
11:53 P.M.
SHUNK
Dear Jabitha,
Off to save
Rahne and
live happily
ever after.
Wish me luck.
I'm gonna need
it. ♡Ric

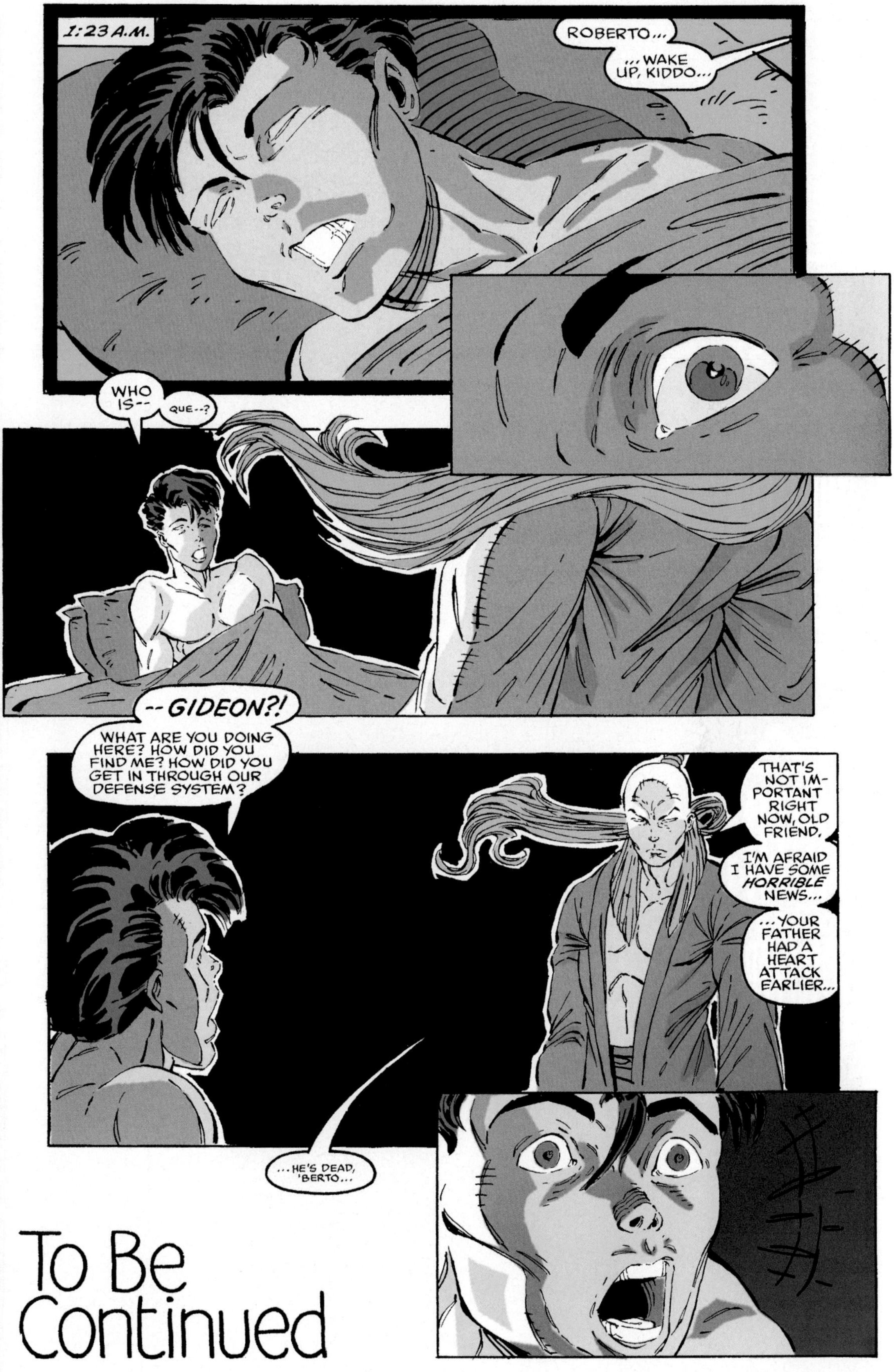
1:23 A.M.
ROBERTO...
...WAKE UP, KIDDO...
WHO IS--
QUE--?
--GIDEON?!
WHAT ARE YOU DOING HERE? HOW DID YOU FIND ME? HOW DID YOU GET IN THROUGH OUR DEFENSE SYSTEM?
THAT'S NOT IMPORTANT RIGHT NOW, OLD FRIEND.
I'M AFRAID I HAVE SOME *HORRIBLE* NEWS...
...YOUR FATHER HAD A HEART ATTACK EARLIER...
...HE'S DEAD, 'BERTO...

To Be Continued

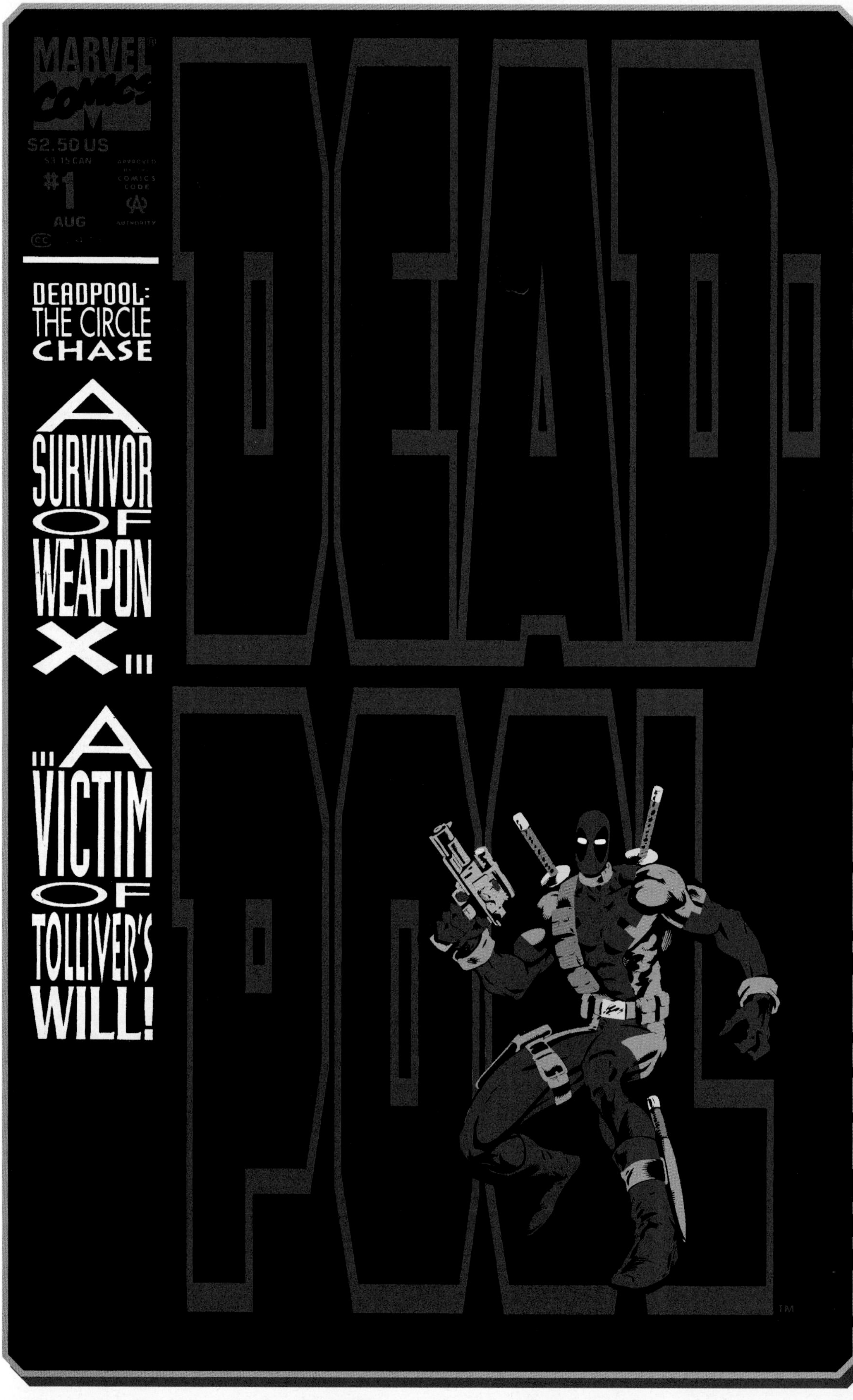

MARVEL COMICS
$2.50 US
$3.15 CAN
#1
AUG
DEADPOOL: THE CIRCLE CHASE
A SURVIVOR OF WEAPON X...
...A VICTIM OF TOLLIVER'S WILL!
DEAD-POOL

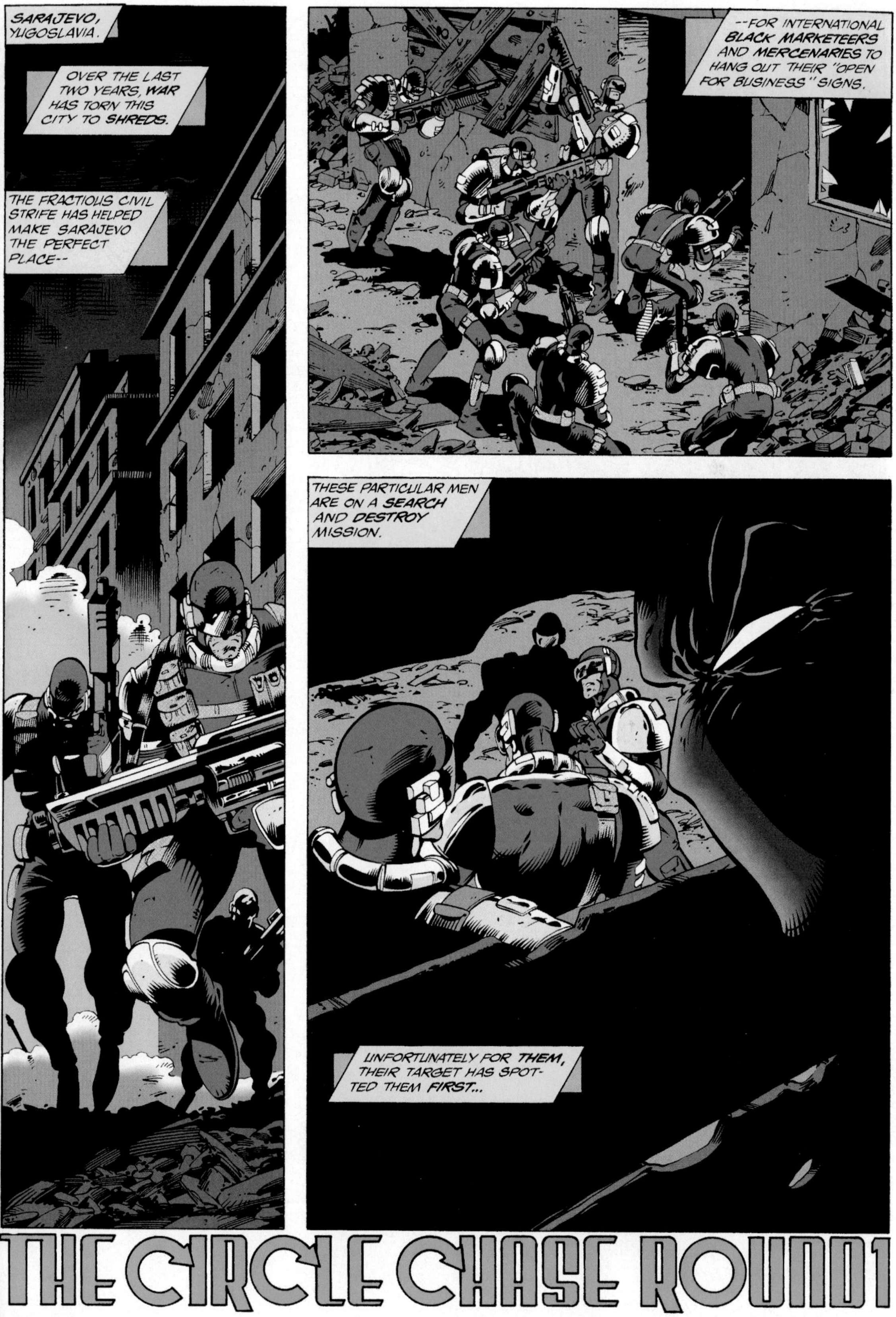
SARAJEVO, YUGOSLAVIA.
OVER THE LAST TWO YEARS, WAR HAS TORN THIS CITY TO SHREDS.
THE FRACTIOUS CIVIL STRIFE HAS HELPED MAKE SARAJEVO THE PERFECT PLACE--
--FOR INTERNATIONAL BLACK MARKETEERS AND MERCENARIES TO HANG OUT THEIR "OPEN FOR BUSINESS" SIGNS.
THESE PARTICULAR MEN ARE ON A SEARCH AND DESTROY MISSION.
UNFORTUNATELY FOR THEM, THEIR TARGET HAS SPOTTED THEM FIRST...
THE CIRCLE CHASE ROUND 1

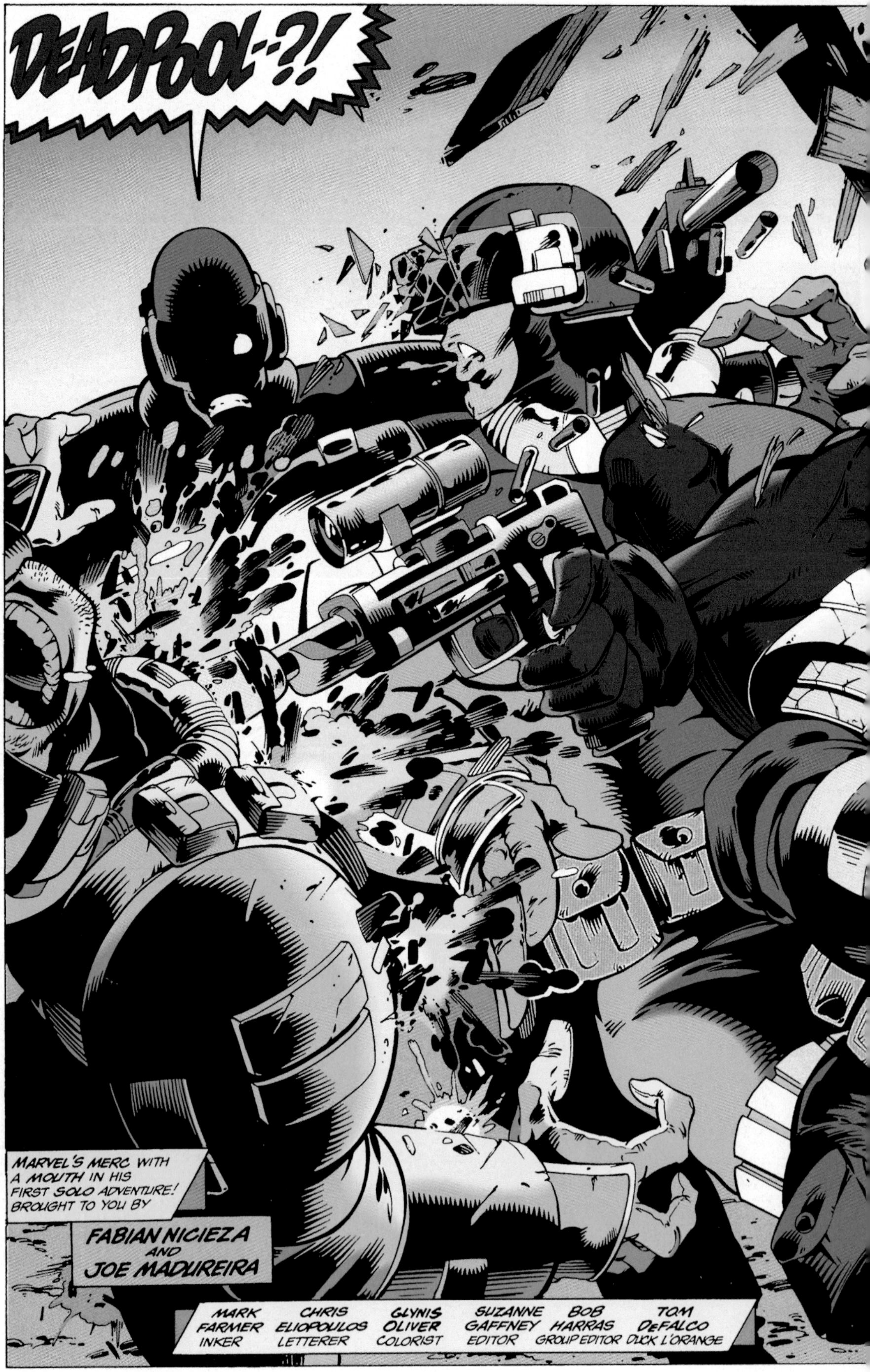
DEADPOOL--?!
MARVEL'S MERC WITH A MOUTH IN HIS FIRST SOLO ADVENTURE! BROUGHT TO YOU BY
FABIAN NICIEZA AND JOE MADUREIRA
MARK FARMER INKER
CHRIS ELIOPOULOS LETTERER
GLYNIS OLIVER COLORIST
SUZANNE GAFFNEY EDITOR
BOB HARRAS GROUP EDITOR
TOM DEFALCO DUCK L'ORANGE

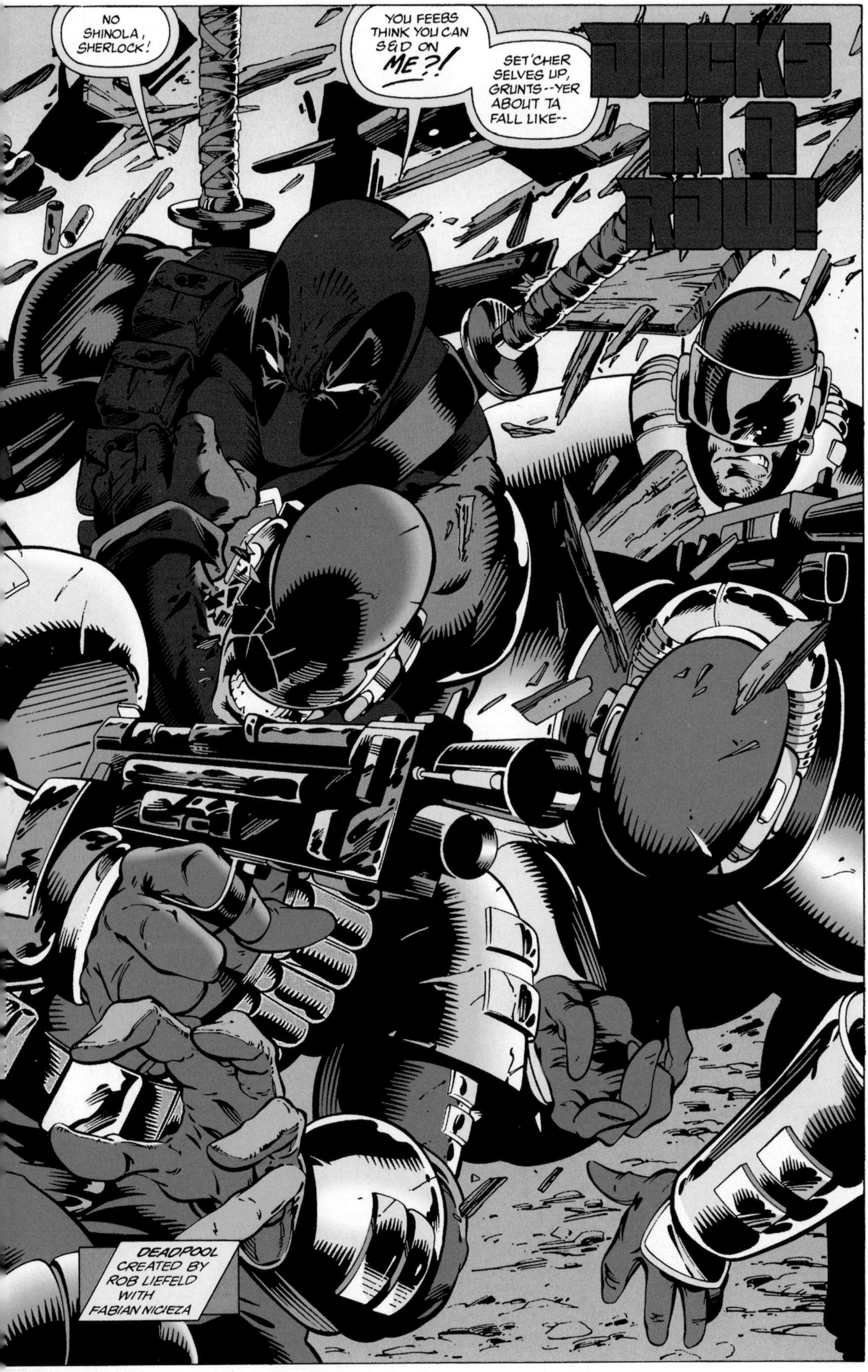
NO SHINOLA, SHERLOCK!
YOU FEEBS THINK YOU CAN S&D ON ME?!
SET'CHER SELVES UP, GRUNTS--YER ABOUT TA FALL LIKE--
DUCKS IN A ROW!
DEADPOOL CREATED BY ROB LIEFELD WITH FABIAN NICIEZA

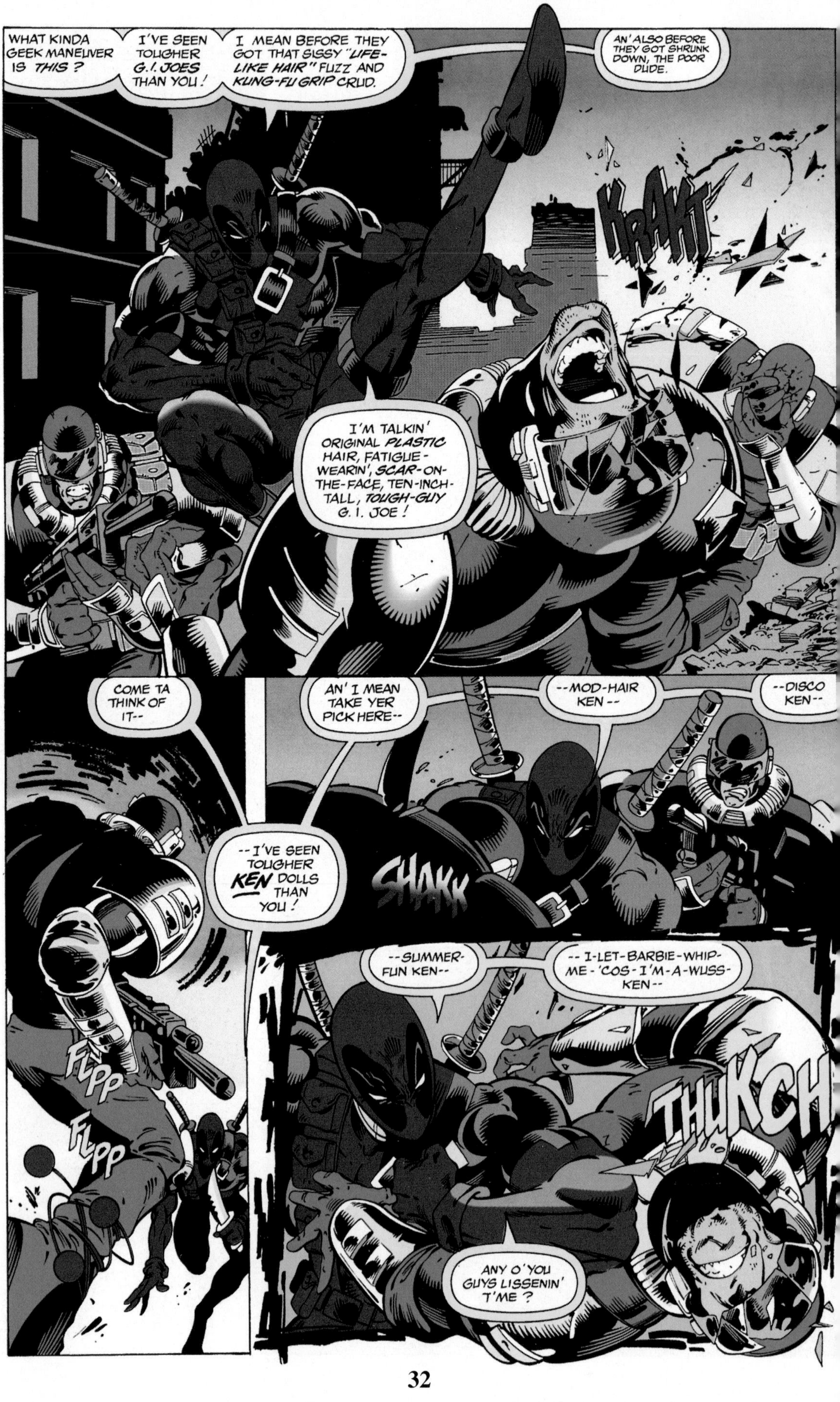
WHAT KINDA GEEK MANEUVER IS *THIS* ?
I'VE SEEN TOUGHER *G.I. JOES* THAN YOU !
I MEAN BEFORE THEY GOT THAT SISSY *"LIFE-LIKE HAIR"* FUZZ AND *KUNG-FU GRIP* CRUD.
AN' ALSO BEFORE THEY GOT SHRUNK DOWN, THE POOR DUDE.
KRAKT
I'M TALKIN' ORIGINAL *PLASTIC* HAIR, FATIGUE-WEARIN', *SCAR*-ON-THE-FACE, TEN-INCH-TALL, *TOUGH-GUY* G.I. JOE !
COME TA THINK OF IT--
AN' I MEAN TAKE YER PICK HERE--
--MOD-HAIR KEN --
--DISCO KEN--
--I'VE SEEN TOUGHER *KEN* DOLLS THAN YOU !
SHAKK
--SUMMER-FUN KEN--
-- I-LET-BARBIE-WHIP-ME -'COS-I'M-A-WUSS-KEN--
THUKCH
FLPP
FLPP
ANY O' YOU GUYS LISSENIN' T'ME ?

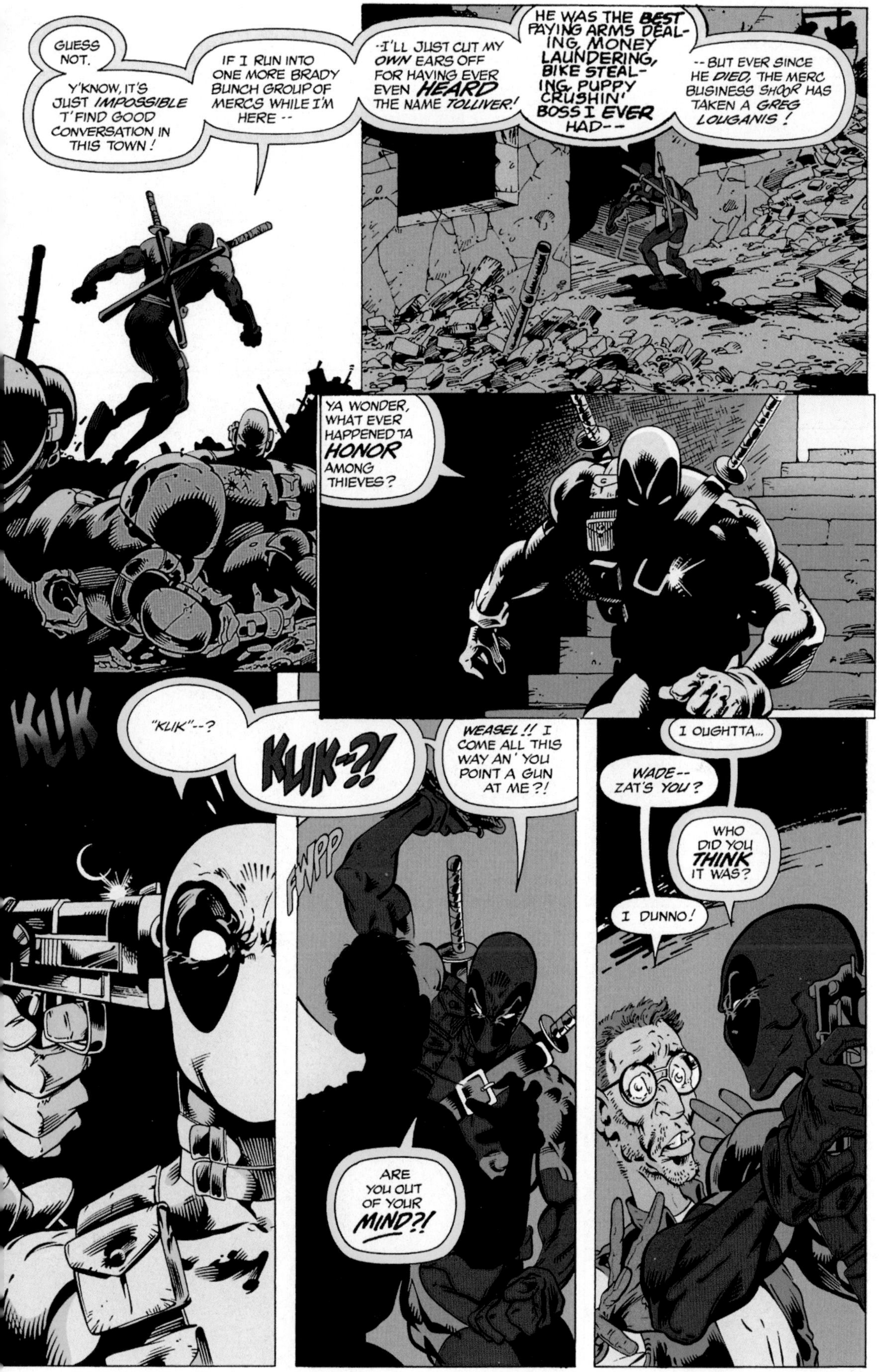

GUESS NOT.
Y'KNOW, IT'S JUST IMPOSSIBLE T'FIND GOOD CONVERSATION IN THIS TOWN!
IF I RUN INTO ONE MORE BRADY BUNCH GROUP OF MERCS WHILE I'M HERE --
--I'LL JUST CUT MY OWN EARS OFF FOR HAVING EVER EVEN HEARD THE NAME TOLLIVER!
HE WAS THE BEST PAYING ARMS DEALING, MONEY LAUNDERING, BIKE STEALING, PUPPY CRUSHIN' BOSS I EVER HAD--
--BUT EVER SINCE HE DIED, THE MERC BUSINESS SHOOR HAS TAKEN A GREG LOUGANIS!
YA WONDER, WHAT EVER HAPPENED TA HONOR AMONG THIEVES?
KLIK
"KLIK"--?
KLIK--?!
FWPP
WEASEL!! I COME ALL THIS WAY AN' YOU POINT A GUN AT ME?!
ARE YOU OUT OF YOUR MIND?!
I OUGHTTA...
WADE-- ZAT'S YOU?
WHO DID YOU THINK IT WAS?
I DUNNO!

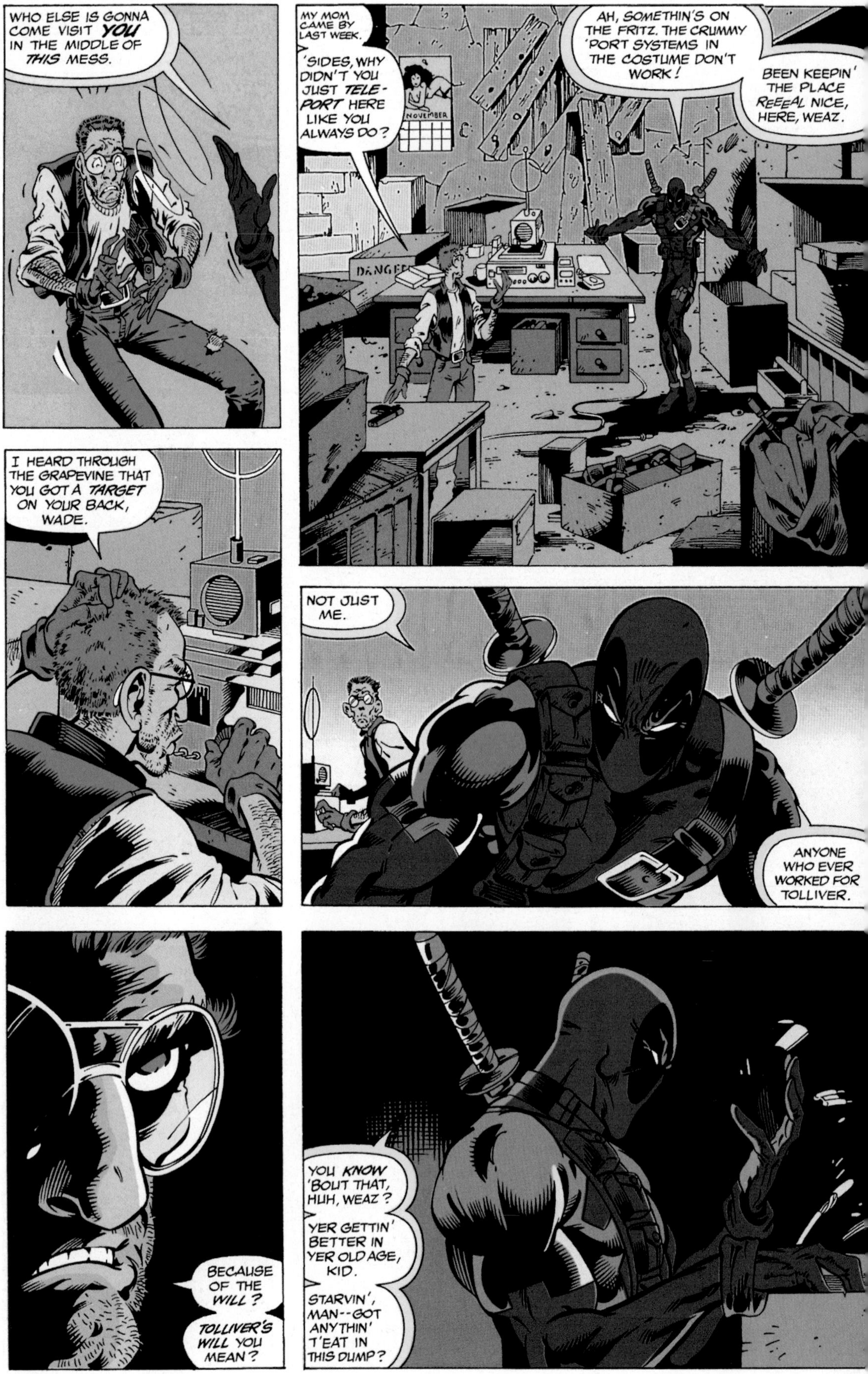
WHO ELSE IS GONNA COME VISIT YOU IN THE MIDDLE OF THIS MESS.
MY MOM CAME BY LAST WEEK.
'SIDES, WHY DIDN'T YOU JUST TELE-PORT HERE LIKE YOU ALWAYS DO?
NOVEMBER
DANGER
AH, SOMETHIN'S ON THE FRITZ. THE CRUMMY 'PORT SYSTEMS IN THE COSTUME DON'T WORK!
BEEN KEEPIN' THE PLACE REEEAL NICE, HERE, WEAZ.
I HEARD THROUGH THE GRAPEVINE THAT YOU GOT A TARGET ON YOUR BACK, WADE.
NOT JUST ME.
ANYONE WHO EVER WORKED FOR TOLLIVER.
BECAUSE OF THE WILL?
TOLLIVER'S WILL YOU MEAN?
YOU KNOW 'BOUT THAT, HUH, WEAZ?
YER GETTIN' BETTER IN YER OLD AGE, KID.
STARVIN', MAN--GOT ANYTHIN' T'EAT IN THIS DUMP?

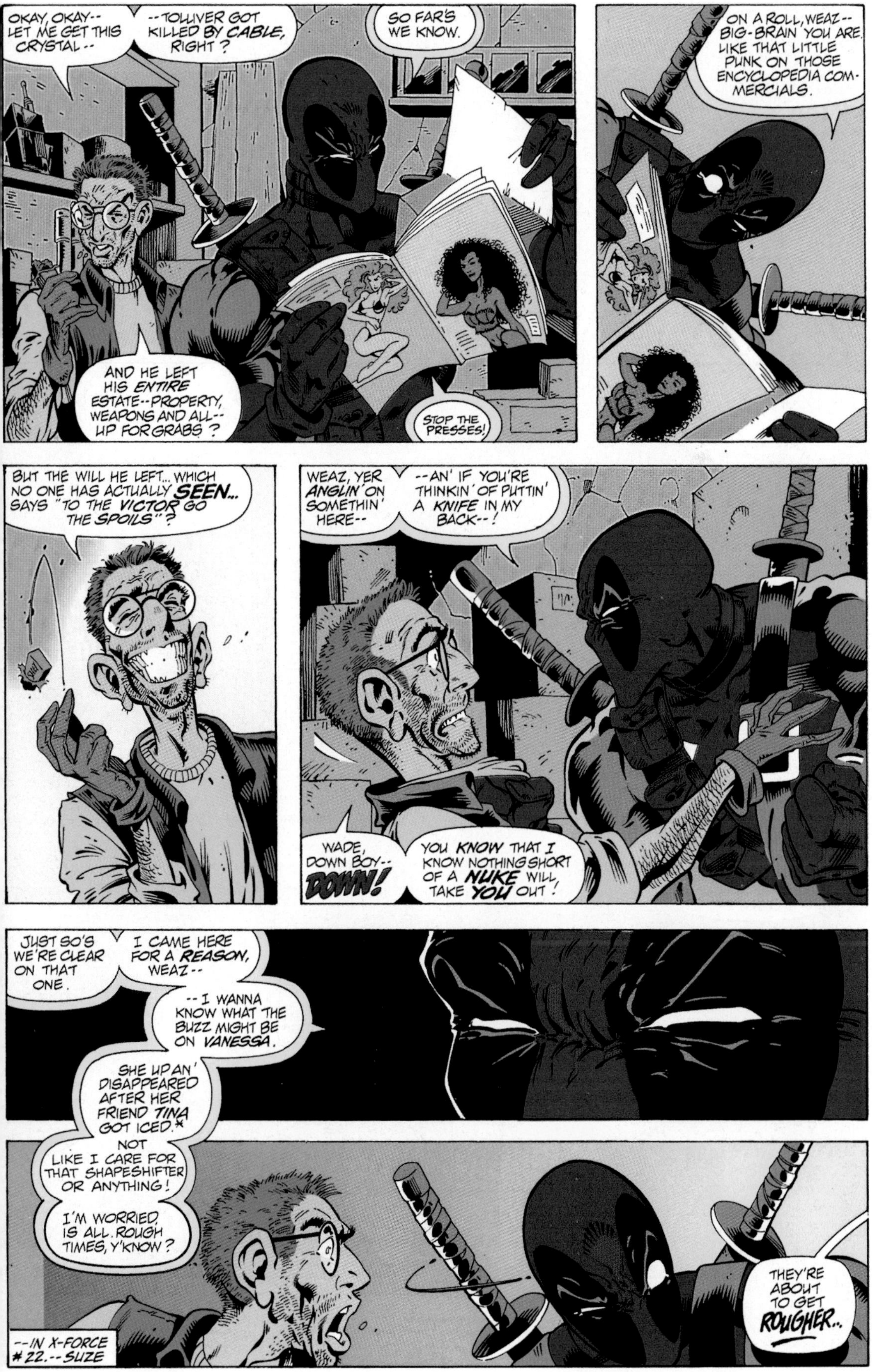
OKAY, OKAY-- LET ME GET THIS CRYSTAL--
--TOLLIVER GOT KILLED BY CABLE, RIGHT?
SO FAR'S WE KNOW.
AND HE LEFT HIS ENTIRE ESTATE--PROPERTY, WEAPONS AND ALL-- UP FOR GRABS?
STOP THE PRESSES!
ON A ROLL, WEAZ-- BIG-BRAIN YOU ARE. LIKE THAT LITTLE PUNK ON THOSE ENCYCLOPEDIA COMMERCIALS.
BUT THE WILL HE LEFT... WHICH NO ONE HAS ACTUALLY SEEN... SAYS "TO THE VICTOR GO THE SPOILS"?
WEAZ, YER ANGLIN' ON SOMETHIN' HERE--
--AN' IF YOU'RE THINKIN' OF PUTTIN' A KNIFE IN MY BACK--!
WADE, DOWN BOY-- DOWN!
YOU KNOW THAT I KNOW NOTHING SHORT OF A NUKE WILL TAKE YOU OUT!
JUST SO'S WE'RE CLEAR ON THAT ONE.
I CAME HERE FOR A REASON, WEAZ--
--I WANNA KNOW WHAT THE BUZZ MIGHT BE ON VANESSA.
SHE UP AN' DISAPPEARED AFTER HER FRIEND TINA GOT ICED.*
NOT LIKE I CARE FOR THAT SHAPESHIFTER OR ANYTHING!
I'M WORRIED, IS ALL. ROUGH TIMES, Y'KNOW?
THEY'RE ABOUT TO GET ROUGHER...
*--IN X-FORCE #22.--SUZE

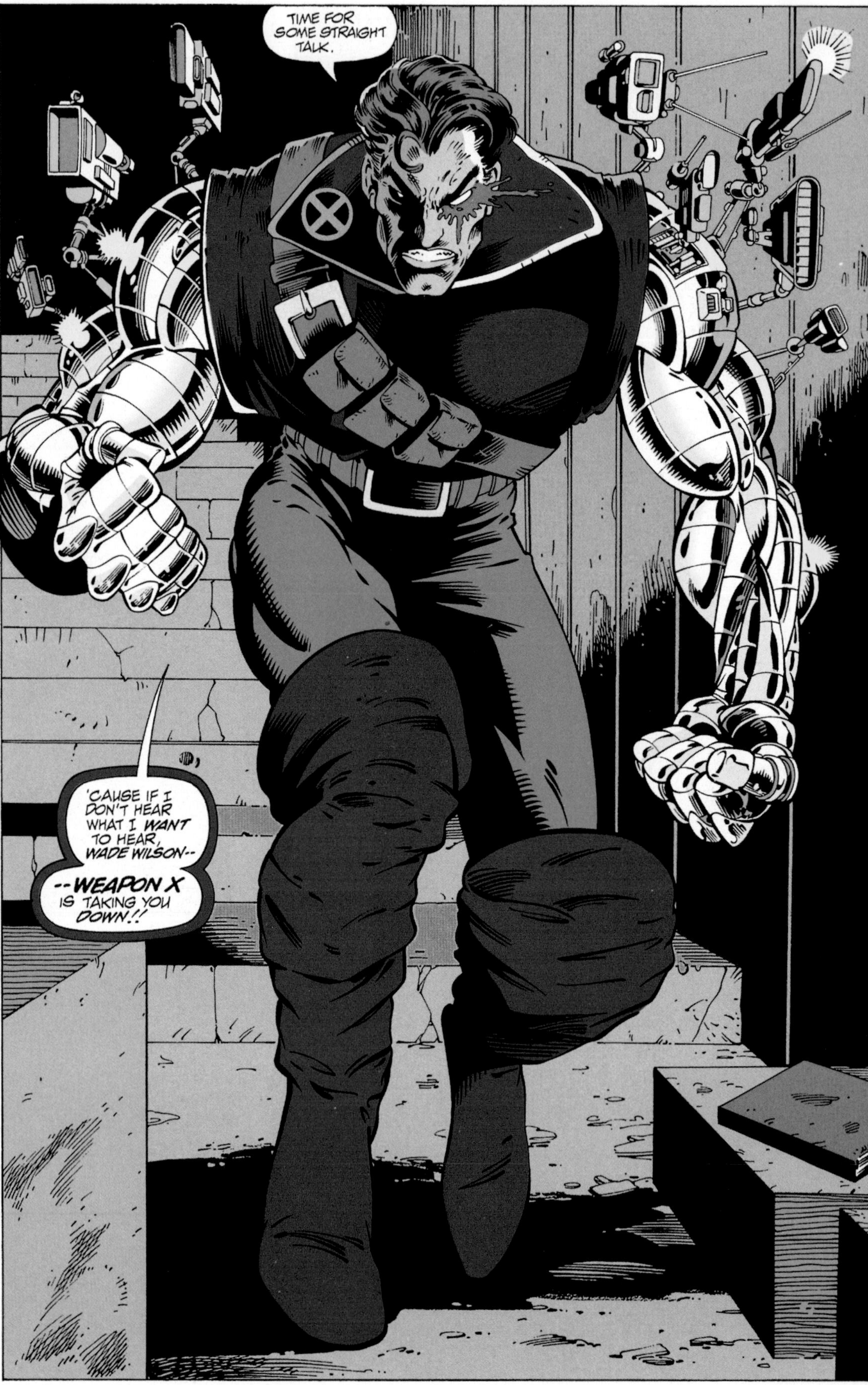
TIME FOR SOME STRAIGHT TALK.
'CAUSE IF I DON'T HEAR WHAT I *WANT* TO HEAR, *WADE WILSON*--
--*WEAPON X* IS TAKING YOU *DOWN*!!

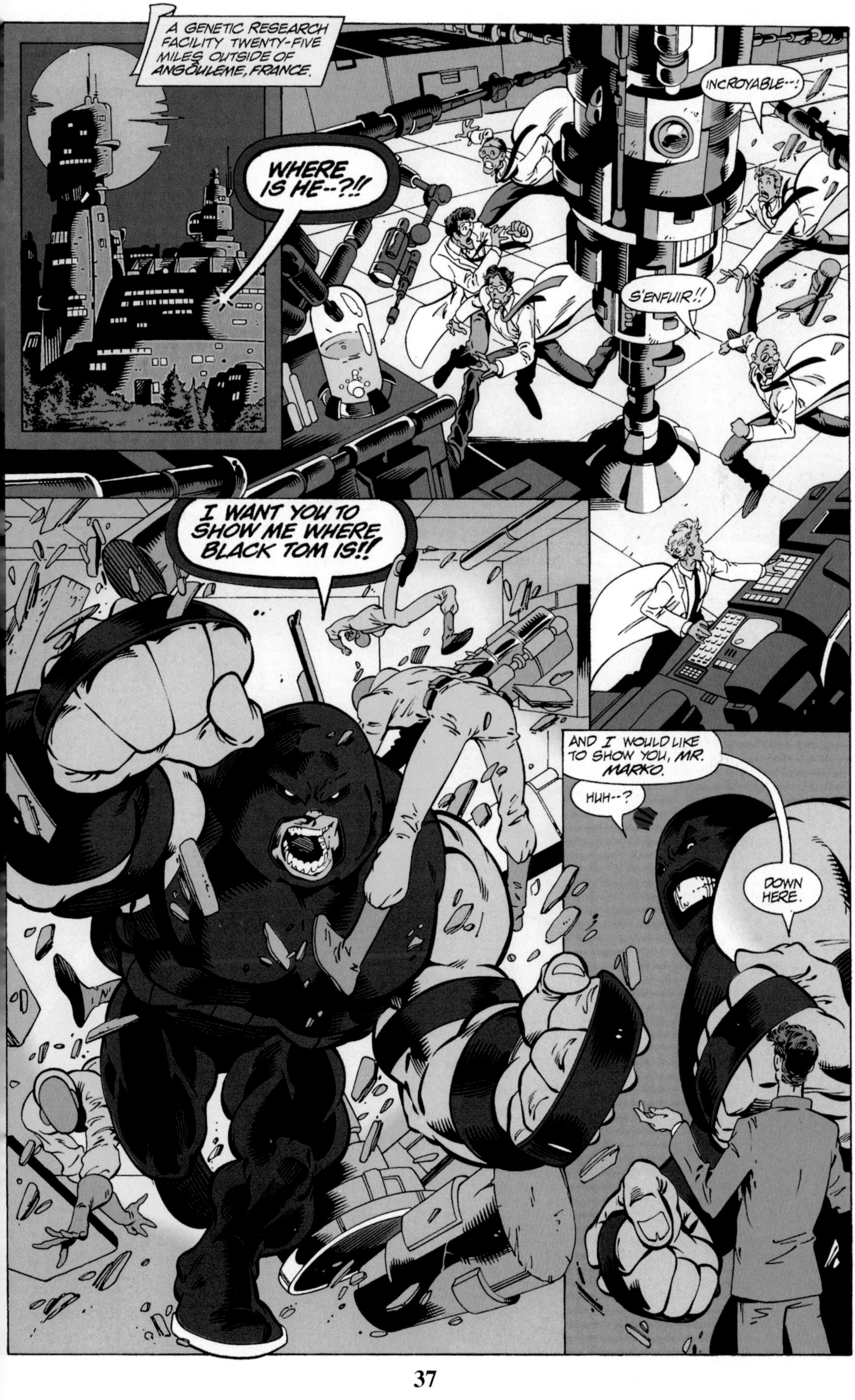
A GENETIC RESEARCH FACILITY TWENTY-FIVE MILES OUTSIDE OF ANGOULEME, FRANCE.
WHERE IS HE--?!!
INCROYABLE--!
S'ENFUIR!!
I WANT YOU TO SHOW ME WHERE BLACK TOM IS!!
AND I WOULD LIKE TO SHOW YOU, MR. MARKO.
HUH--?
DOWN HERE.

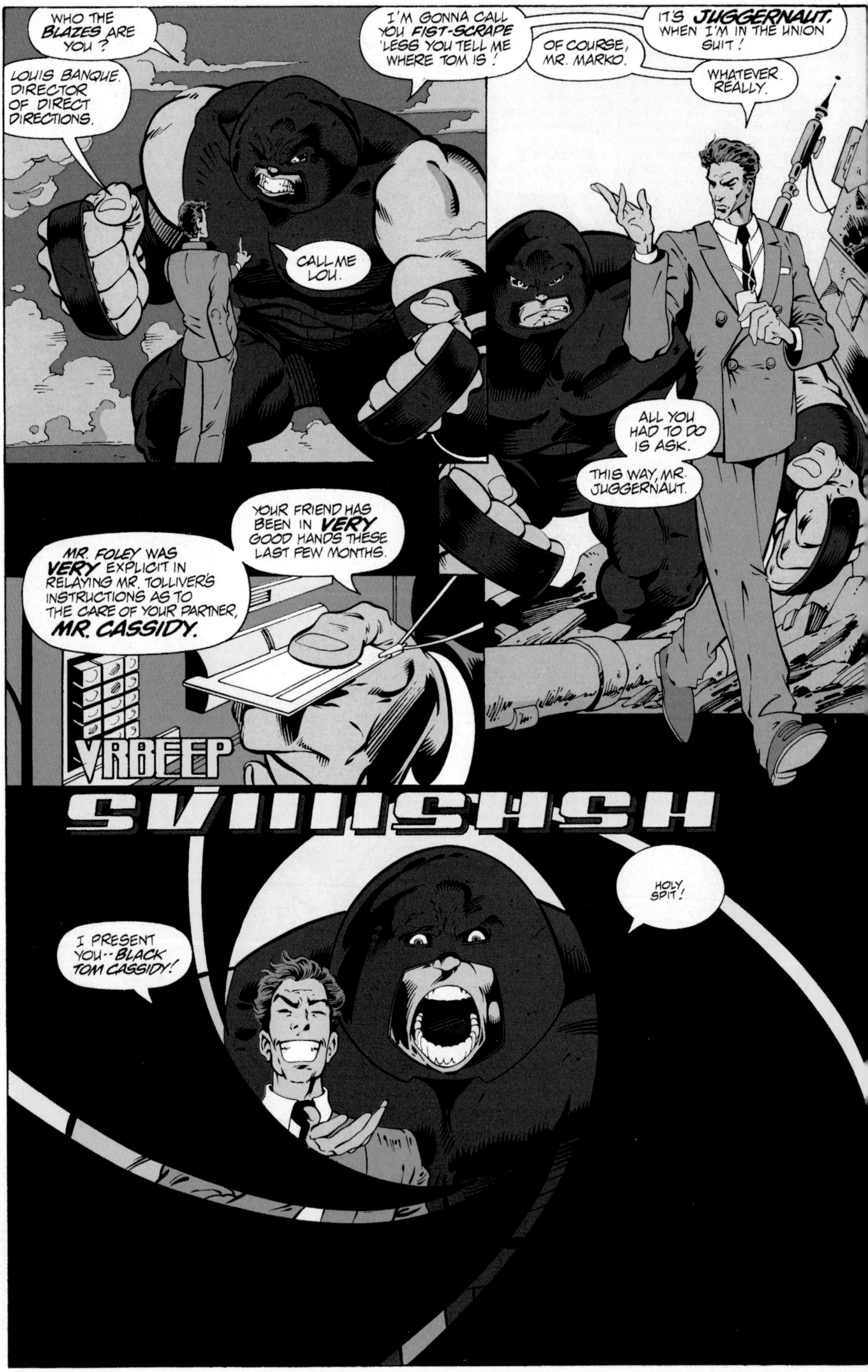

WHO THE BLAZES ARE YOU?
LOUIS BANQUE. DIRECTOR OF DIRECT DIRECTIONS.
CALL ME LOU.
I'M GONNA CALL YOU FIST-SCRAPE 'LESS YOU TELL ME WHERE TOM IS!
OF COURSE, MR. MARKO.
IT'S JUGGERNAUT, WHEN I'M IN THE UNION SUIT!
WHATEVER. REALLY.
ALL YOU HAD TO DO IS ASK.
THIS WAY, MR. JUGGERNAUT.
YOUR FRIEND HAS BEEN IN VERY GOOD HANDS THESE LAST FEW MONTHS.
MR. FOLEY WAS VERY EXPLICIT IN RELAYING MR. TOLLIVER'S INSTRUCTIONS AS TO THE CARE OF YOUR PARTNER, MR. CASSIDY.
VRBEEP
SVIIIISHSH
HOLY SPIT!
I PRESENT YOU--BLACK TOM CASSIDY!

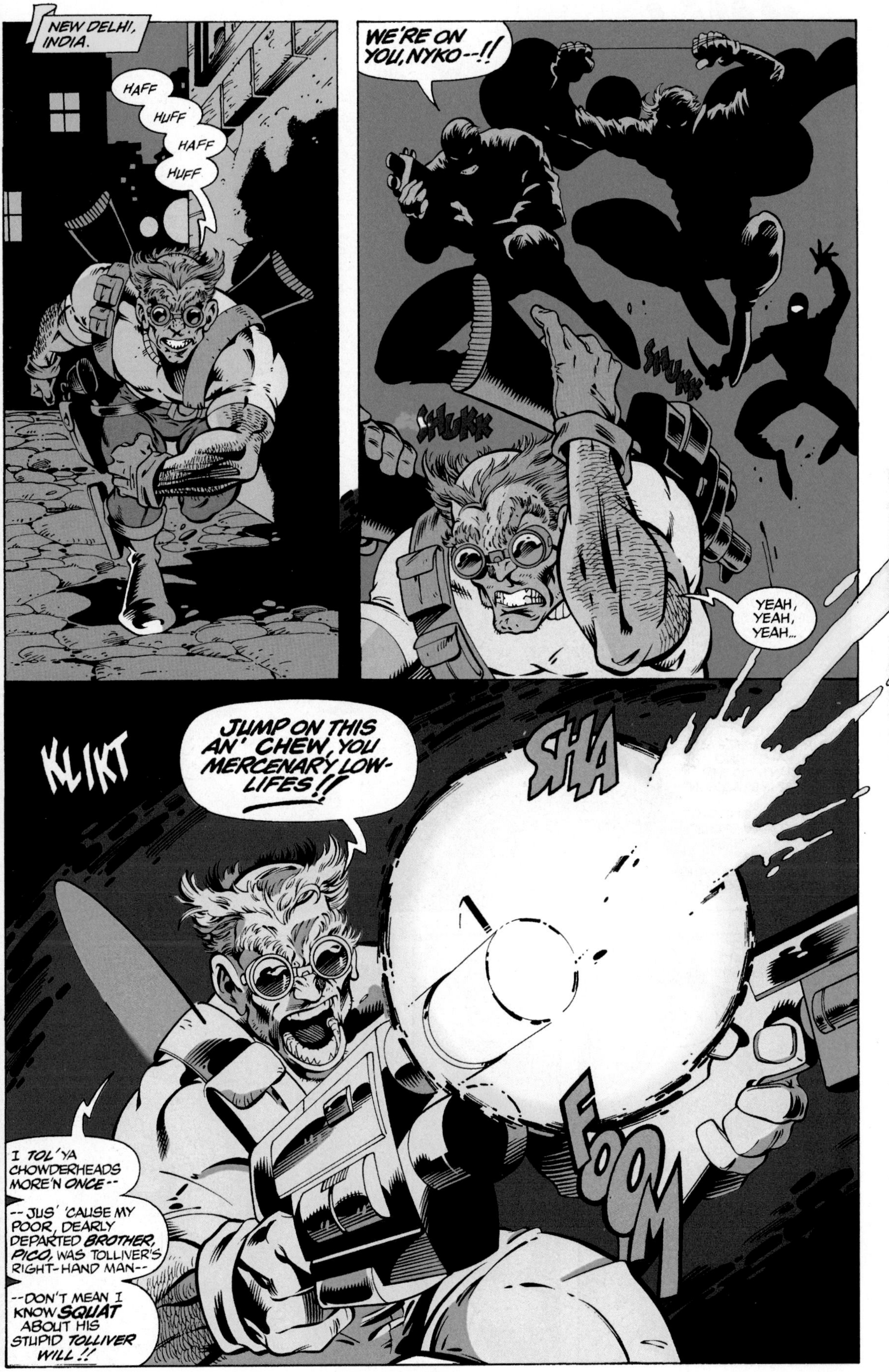

NEW DELHI, INDIA.
HAFF
HUFF
HAFF
HUFF
WE'RE ON YOU, NYKO--!!
SHUKK
SHUKK
YEAH, YEAH, YEAH...
KLIKT
JUMP ON THIS AN' CHEW, YOU MERCENARY LOW-LIFES!!
SHA
I TOL'YA CHOWDERHEADS MORE'N ONCE--
--JUS' 'CAUSE MY POOR, DEARLY DEPARTED BROTHER, PICO, WAS TOLLIVER'S RIGHT-HAND MAN--
--DON'T MEAN I KNOW SQUAT ABOUT HIS STUPID TOLLIVER WILL!!
FOOM

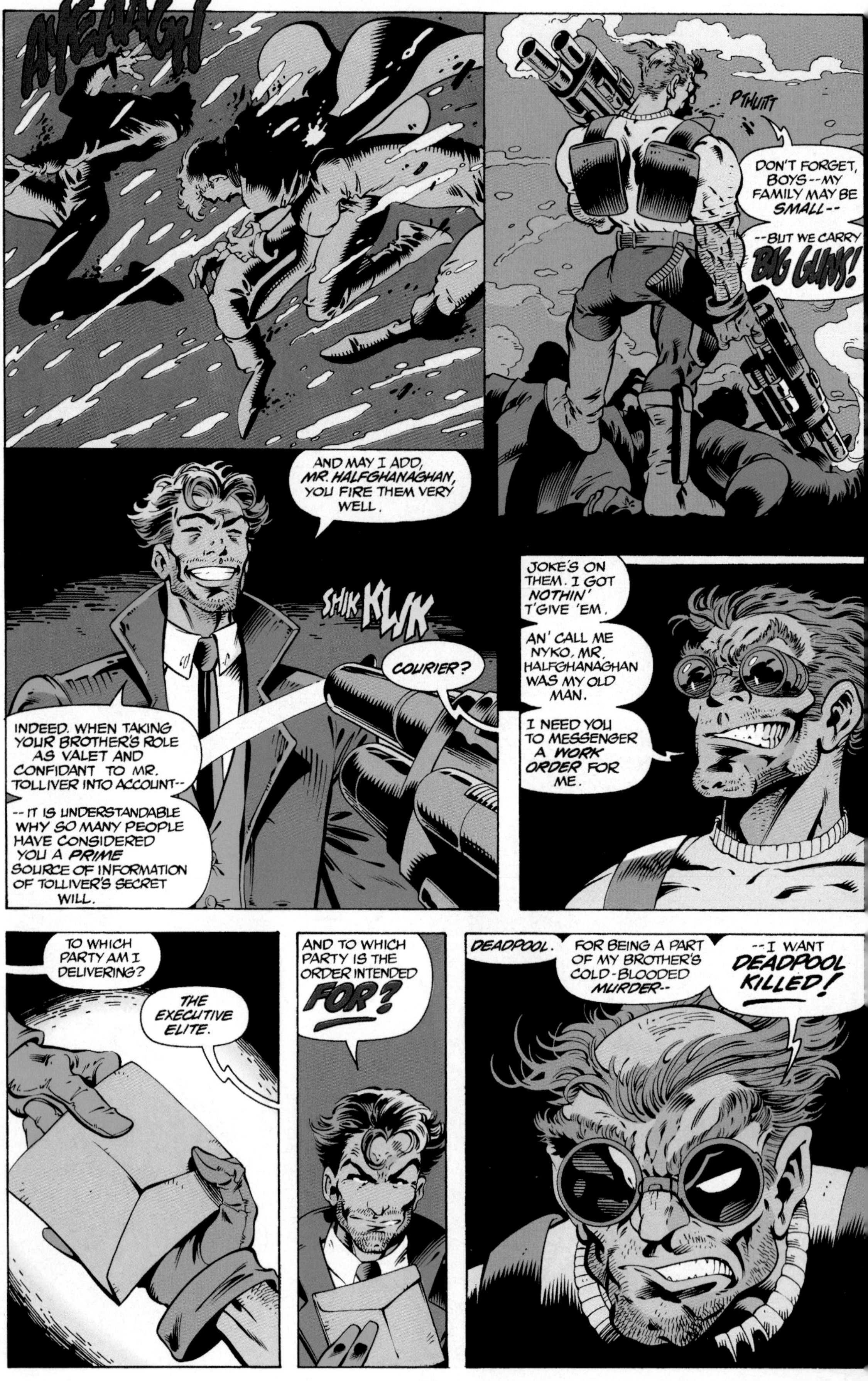
AYEAAAGH
PTHUTT
DON'T FORGET, BOYS--MY FAMILY MAY BE SMALL--
--BUT WE CARRY BIG GUNS!
AND MAY I ADD, MR. HALFGHANAGHAN, YOU FIRE THEM VERY WELL.
SHIK KLIK
COURIER?
INDEED. WHEN TAKING YOUR BROTHER'S ROLE AS VALET AND CONFIDANT TO MR. TOLLIVER INTO ACCOUNT--
-- IT IS UNDERSTANDABLE WHY SO MANY PEOPLE HAVE CONSIDERED YOU A PRIME SOURCE OF INFORMATION OF TOLLIVER'S SECRET WILL.
JOKE'S ON THEM. I GOT NOTHIN' T'GIVE 'EM.
AN' CALL ME NYKO, MR. HALFGHANAGHAN WAS MY OLD MAN.
I NEED YOU TO MESSENGER A WORK ORDER FOR ME.
TO WHICH PARTY AM I DELIVERING?
THE EXECUTIVE ELITE.
AND TO WHICH PARTY IS THE ORDER INTENDED FOR?
DEADPOOL.
FOR BEING A PART OF MY BROTHER'S COLD-BLOODED MURDER--
--I WANT DEADPOOL KILLED!

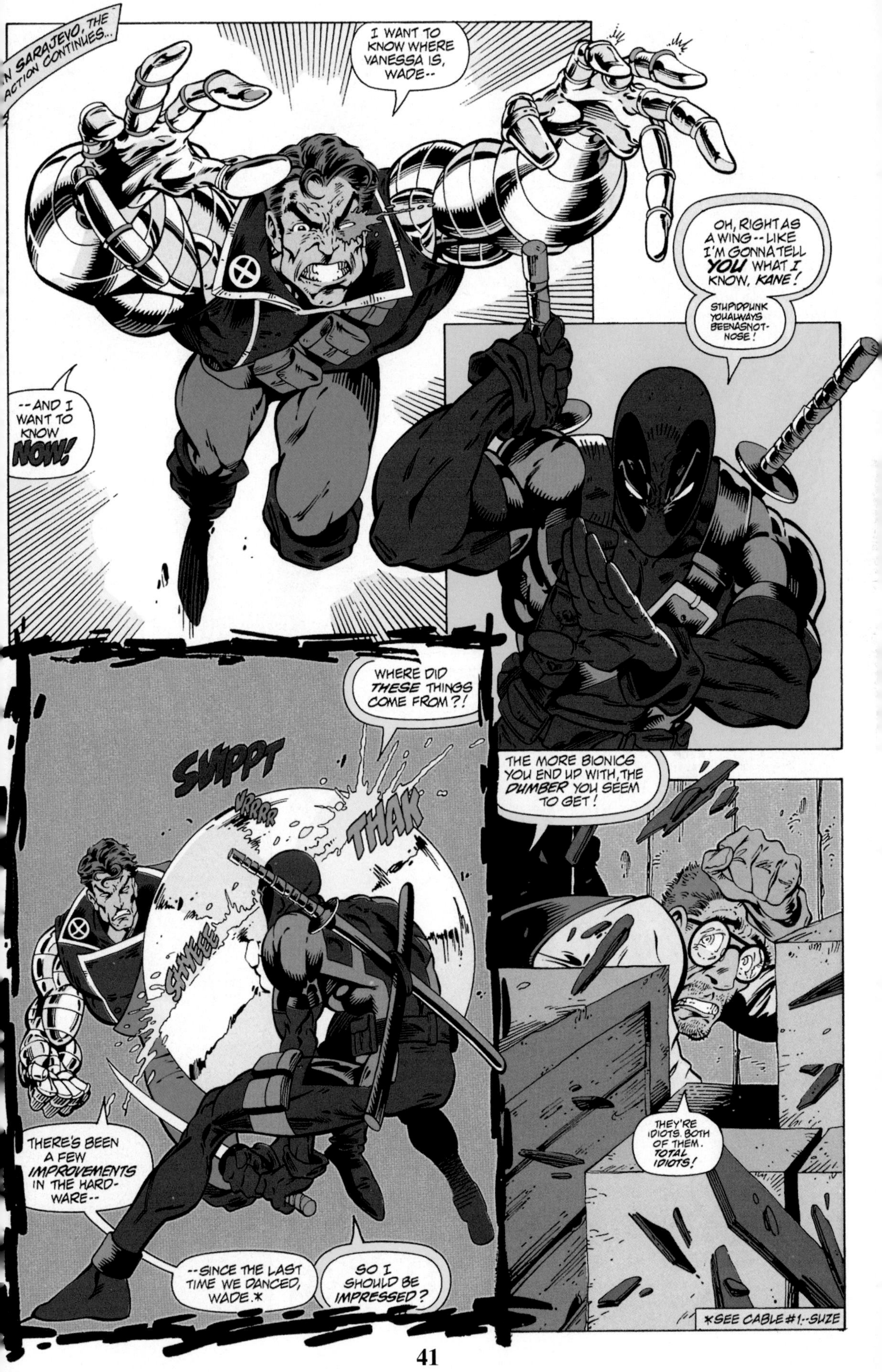
IN SARAJEVO, THE ACTION CONTINUES...
I WANT TO KNOW WHERE VANESSA IS, WADE--
OH, RIGHT AS A WING--LIKE I'M GONNA TELL YOU WHAT I KNOW, KANE!
STUPIDPUNK YOUALWAYS BEENASNOT-NOSE!
--AND I WANT TO KNOW NOW!
WHERE DID THESE THINGS COME FROM?!
SWIPPT
VRRRR
THAK
SHEEE
THERE'S BEEN A FEW IMPROVEMENTS IN THE HARD-WARE--
--SINCE THE LAST TIME WE DANCED, WADE.*
SO I SHOULD BE IMPRESSED?
THE MORE BIONICS YOU END UP WITH, THE DUMBER YOU SEEM TO GET!
THEY'RE IDIOTS. BOTH OF THEM. TOTAL IDIOTS!
*SEE CABLE #1.-SUZE

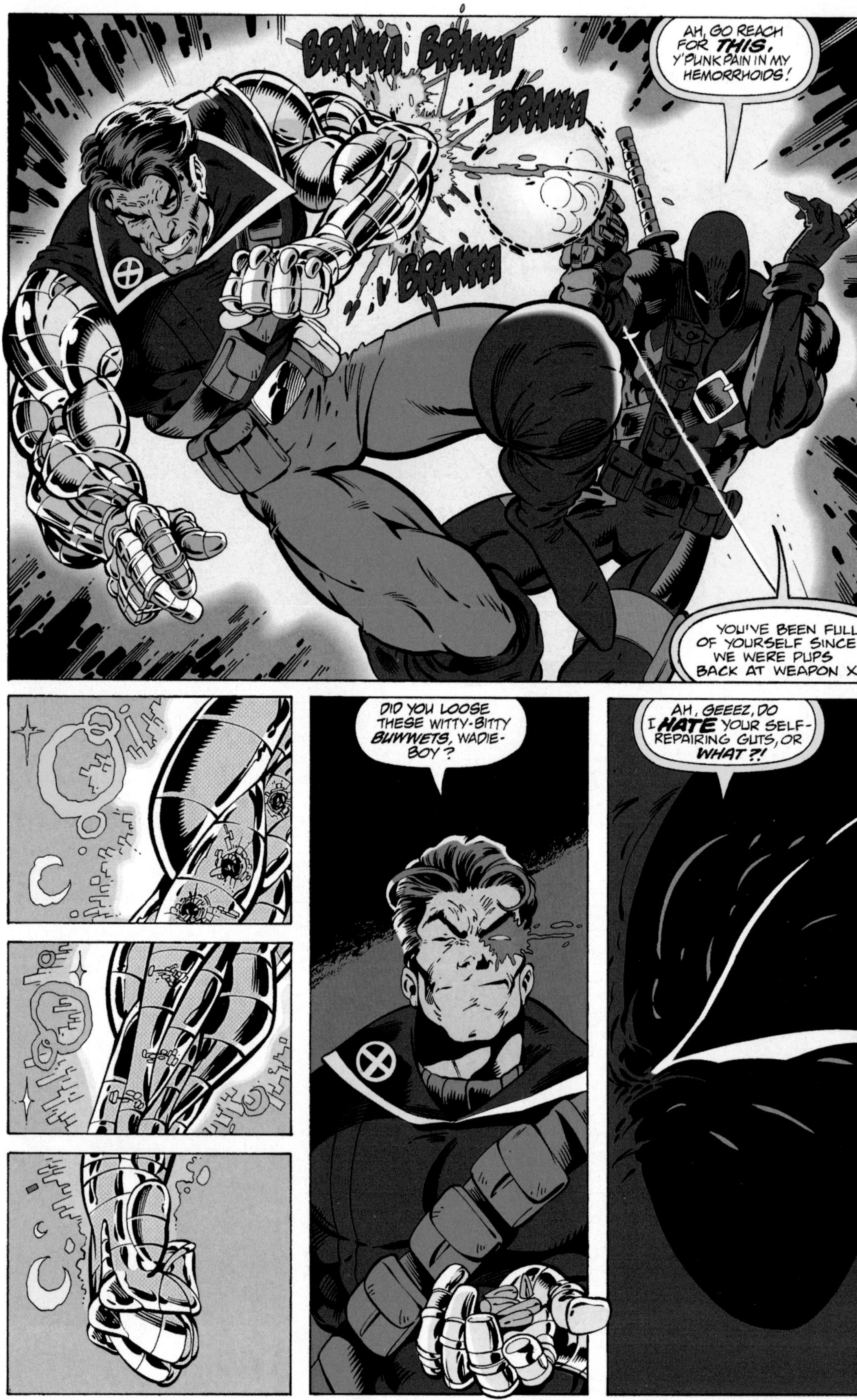
BRAKKA BRAKKA
BRAKKA
BRAKKA
AH, GO REACH FOR THIS, Y'PUNK PAIN IN MY HEMORRHOIDS!
YOU'VE BEEN FULL OF YOURSELF SINCE WE WERE PUPS BACK AT WEAPON X.
DID YOU LOOSE THESE WITTY-BITTY BUWWETS, WADIE-BOY?
AH, GEEEZ, DO I HATE YOUR SELF-REPAIRING GUTS, OR WHAT?!

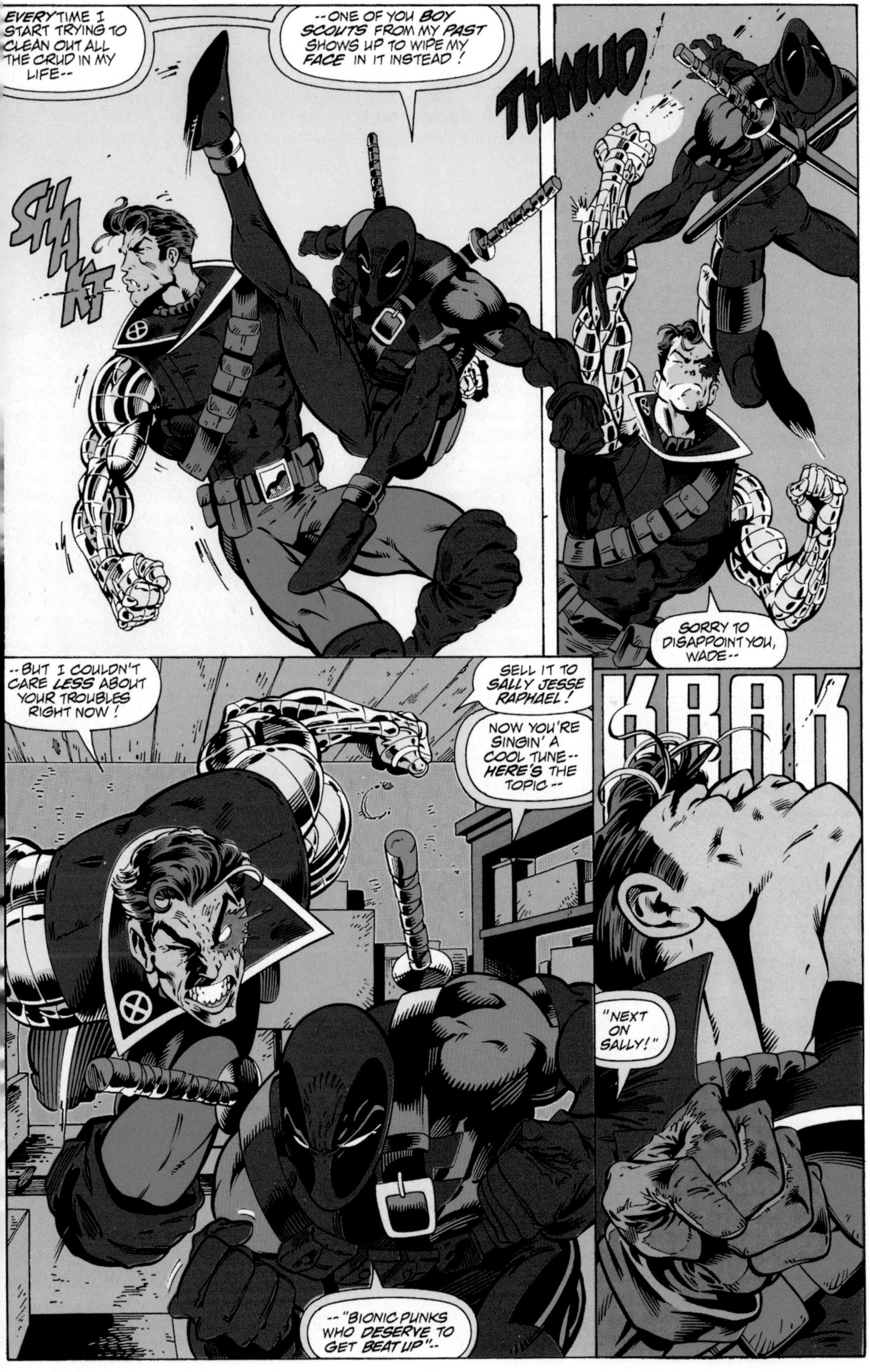
EVERYTIME I START TRYING TO CLEAN OUT ALL THE CRUD IN MY LIFE--
--ONE OF YOU BOY SCOUTS FROM MY PAST SHOWS UP TO WIPE MY FACE IN IT INSTEAD!
SHAKT
THWUD
SORRY TO DISAPPOINT YOU, WADE--
--BUT I COULDN'T CARE LESS ABOUT YOUR TROUBLES RIGHT NOW!
SELL IT TO SALLY JESSE RAPHAEL!
NOW YOU'RE SINGIN' A COOL TUNE-- HERE'S THE TOPIC--
--"BIONIC PUNKS WHO DESERVE TO GET BEAT UP"--
KRAK
"NEXT ON SALLY!"

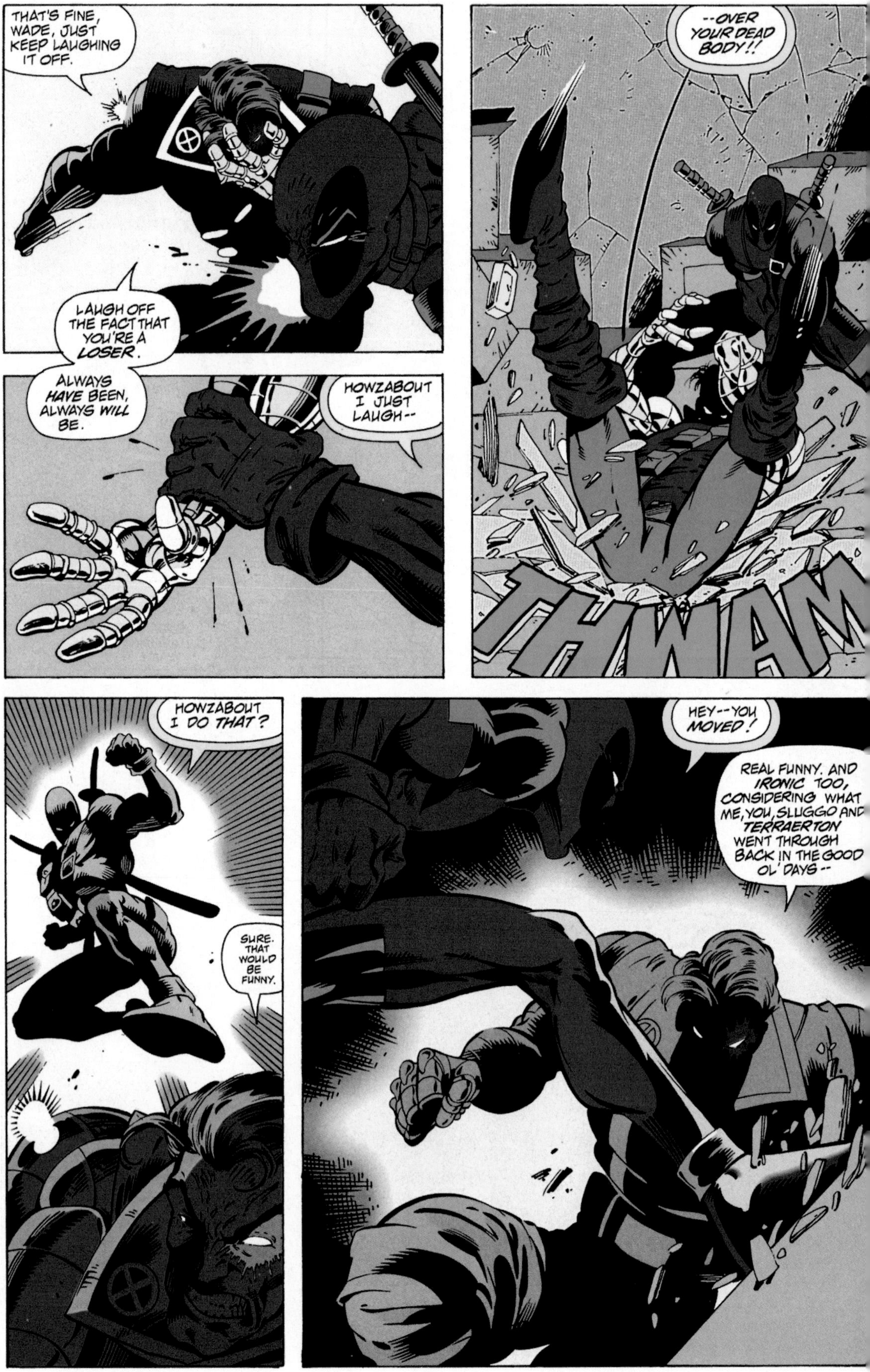
THAT'S FINE, WADE, JUST KEEP LAUGHING IT OFF.
LAUGH OFF THE FACT THAT YOU'RE A LOSER.
ALWAYS HAVE BEEN, ALWAYS WILL BE.
HOWZABOUT I JUST LAUGH--
--OVER YOUR DEAD BODY!!
THWAM
HOWZABOUT I DO THAT?
SURE. THAT WOULD BE FUNNY.
HEY--YOU MOVED!
REAL FUNNY. AND IRONIC TOO, CONSIDERING WHAT ME, YOU, SLUGGO AND TERRAERTON WENT THROUGH BACK IN THE GOOD OL' DAYS--

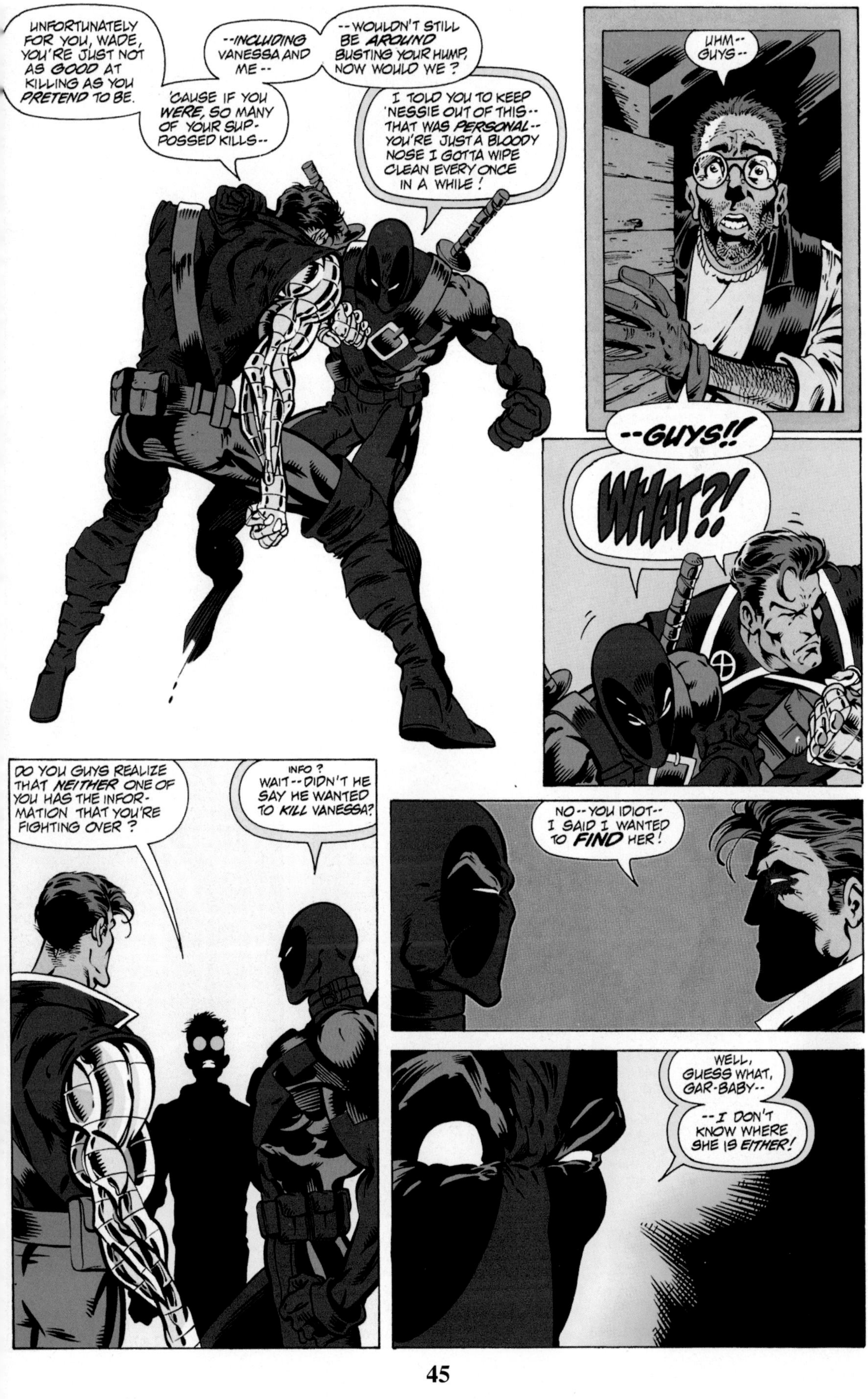
UNFORTUNATELY FOR YOU, WADE, YOU'RE JUST NOT AS GOOD AT KILLING AS YOU PRETEND TO BE.
'CAUSE IF YOU WERE, SO MANY OF YOUR SUP-POSSED KILLS--
--INCLUDING VANESSA AND ME--
--WOULDN'T STILL BE AROUND BUSTING YOUR HUMP, NOW WOULD WE?
I TOLD YOU TO KEEP 'NESSIE OUT OF THIS--THAT WAS PERSONAL--YOU'RE JUST A BLOODY NOSE I GOTTA WIPE CLEAN EVERY ONCE IN A WHILE!
UHM--GUYS--
--GUYS!!
WHAT?!
DO YOU GUYS REALIZE THAT NEITHER ONE OF YOU HAS THE INFOR-MATION THAT YOU'RE FIGHTING OVER?
INFO? WAIT--DIDN'T HE SAY HE WANTED TO KILL VANESSA?
NO--YOU IDIOT--I SAID I WANTED TO FIND HER!
WELL, GUESS WHAT, GAR-BABY--
--I DON'T KNOW WHERE SHE IS EITHER!

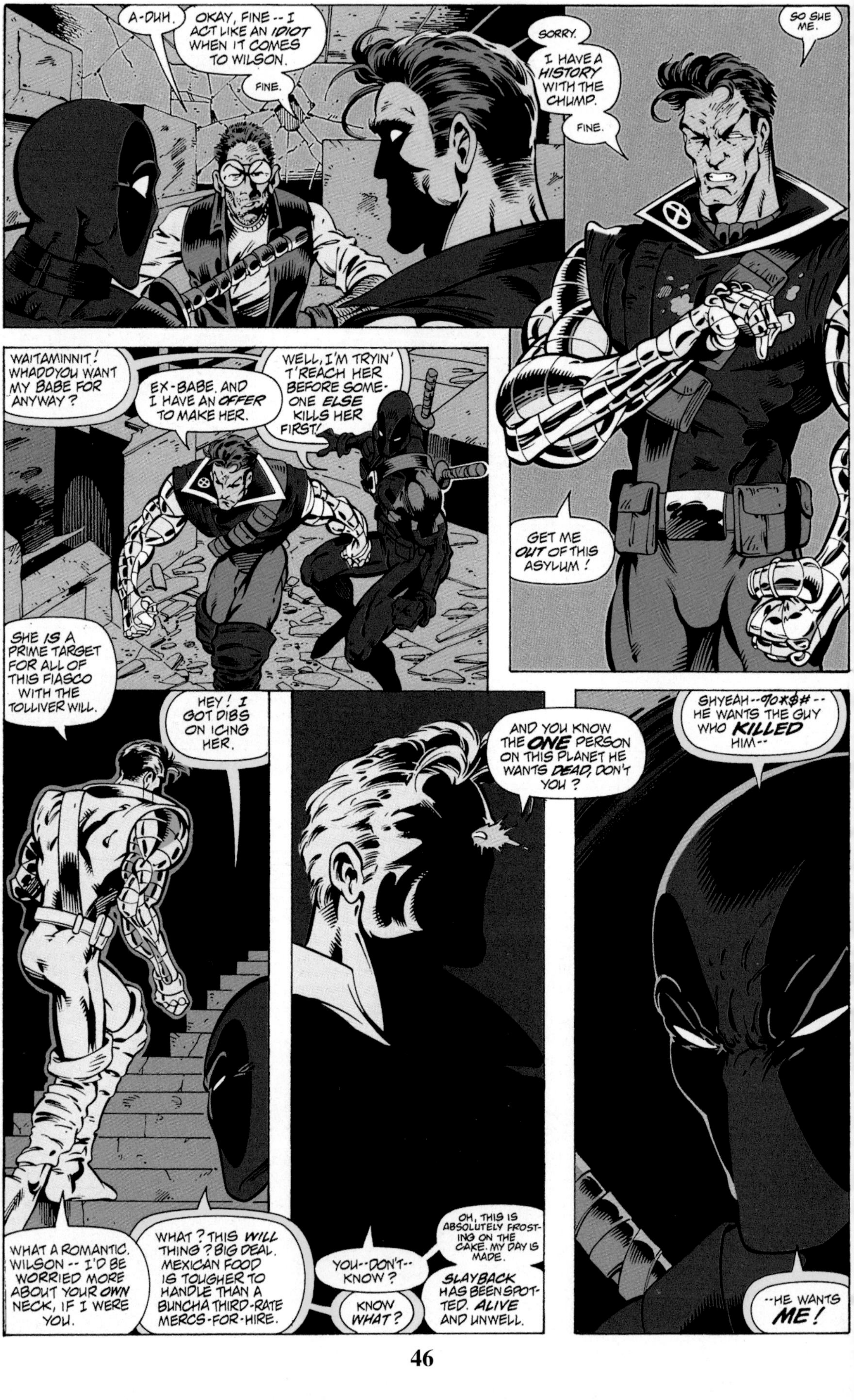
A-DUH.
OKAY, FINE -- I ACT LIKE AN IDIOT WHEN IT COMES TO WILSON.
FINE.
SORRY.
I HAVE A HISTORY WITH THE CHUMP.
FINE.
SO SHE ME.
GET ME OUT OF THIS ASYLUM!
WAITAMINNIT! WHADDOYOU WANT MY BABE FOR ANYWAY?
EX-BABE. AND I HAVE AN OFFER TO MAKE HER.
WELL, I'M TRYIN' T'REACH HER BEFORE SOME-ONE ELSE KILLS HER FIRST!
SHE IS A PRIME TARGET FOR ALL OF THIS FIASCO WITH THE TOLLIVER WILL.
HEY! I GOT DIBS ON ICING HER.
WHAT A ROMANTIC. WILSON -- I'D BE WORRIED MORE ABOUT YOUR OWN NECK, IF I WERE YOU.
WHAT? THIS WILL THING? BIG DEAL. MEXICAN FOOD IS TOUGHER TO HANDLE THAN A BUNCHA THIRD-RATE MERCS-FOR-HIRE.
YOU--DON'T--KNOW?
KNOW WHAT?
OH, THIS IS ABSOLUTELY FROSTING ON THE CAKE. MY DAY IS MADE.
SLAYBACK HAS BEEN SPOT-TED. ALIVE AND UNWELL.
AND YOU KNOW THE ONE PERSON ON THIS PLANET HE WANTS DEAD, DON'T YOU?
SHYEAH--%*$#--HE WANTS THE GUY WHO KILLED HIM--
--HE WANTS ME!

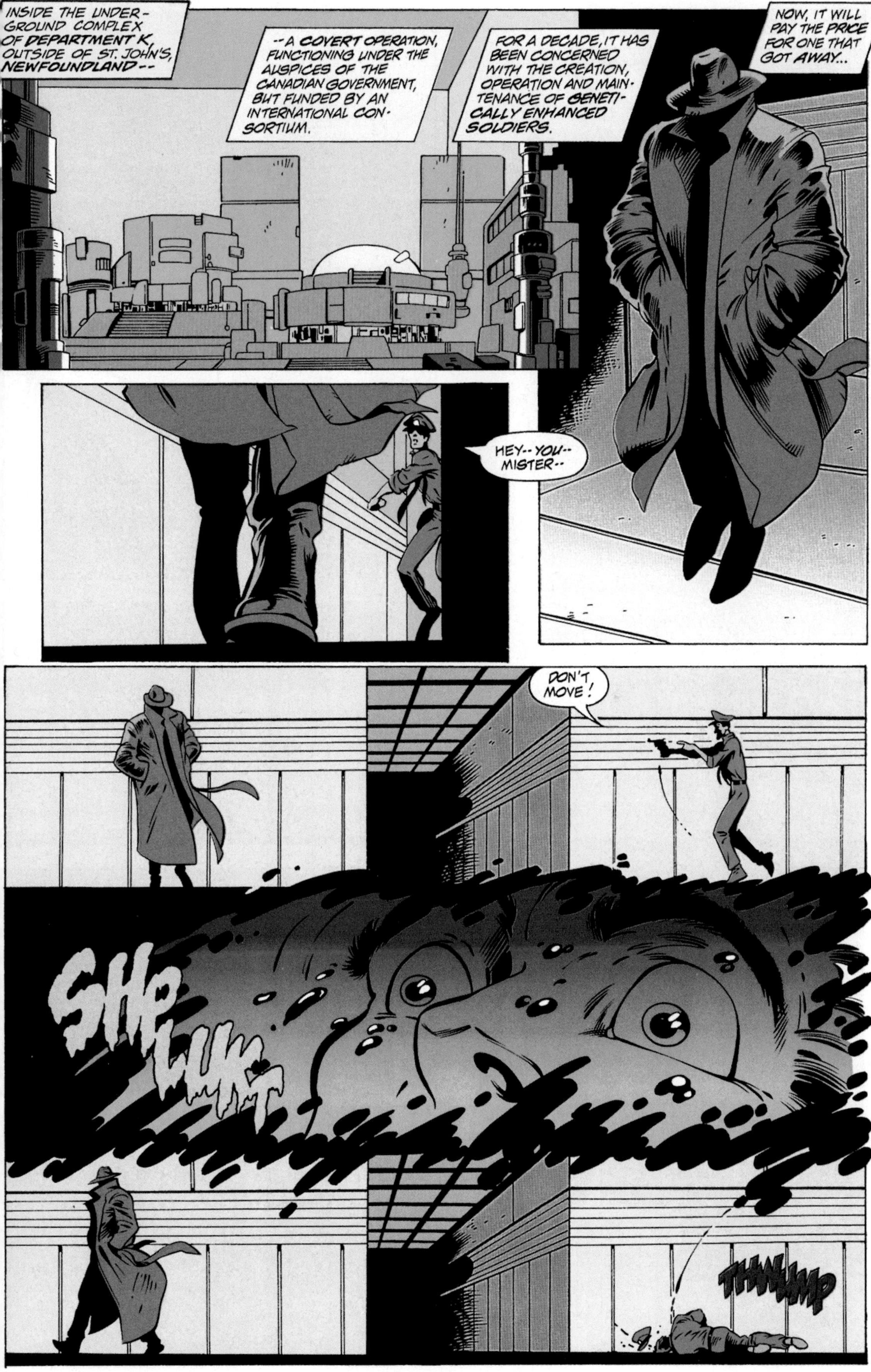
INSIDE THE UNDER-GROUND COMPLEX OF DEPARTMENT K, OUTSIDE OF ST. JOHN'S, NEWFOUNDLAND--
--A COVERT OPERATION, FUNCTIONING UNDER THE AUSPICES OF THE CANADIAN GOVERNMENT, BUT FUNDED BY AN INTERNATIONAL CON-SORTIUM.
FOR A DECADE, IT HAS BEEN CONCERNED WITH THE CREATION, OPERATION AND MAIN-TENANCE OF GENETI-CALLY ENHANCED SOLDIERS.
NOW, IT WILL PAY THE PRICE FOR ONE THAT GOT AWAY...
HEY--YOU--MISTER--
DON'T MOVE!
SHPLUNT
THWUMP

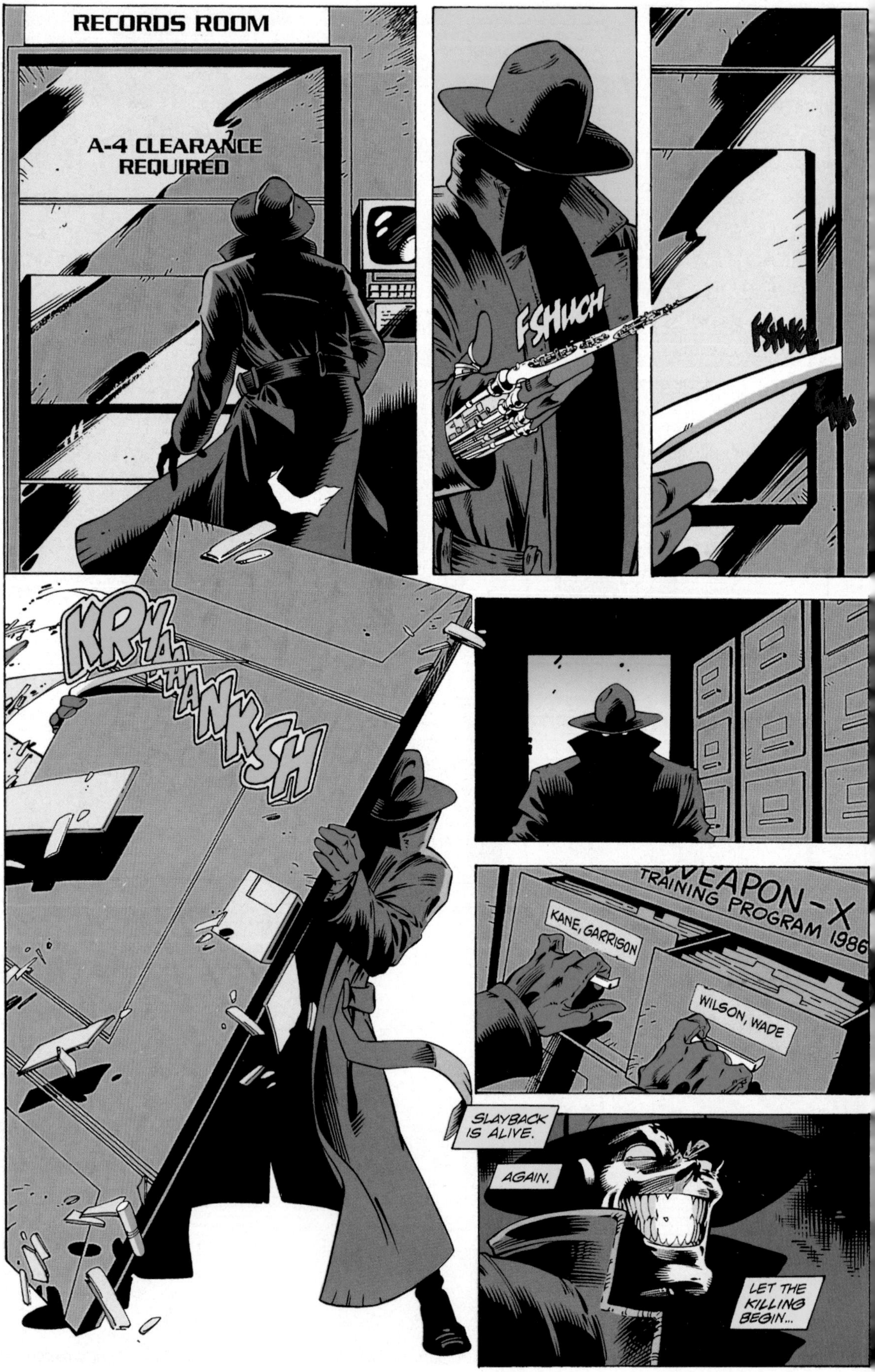
RECORDS ROOM
A-4 CLEARANCE REQUIRED
FSHUCH
KRYAAANKSH
WEAPON-X TRAINING PROGRAM 1986
KANE, GARRISON
WILSON, WADE
SLAYBACK IS ALIVE.
AGAIN.
LET THE KILLING BEGIN...

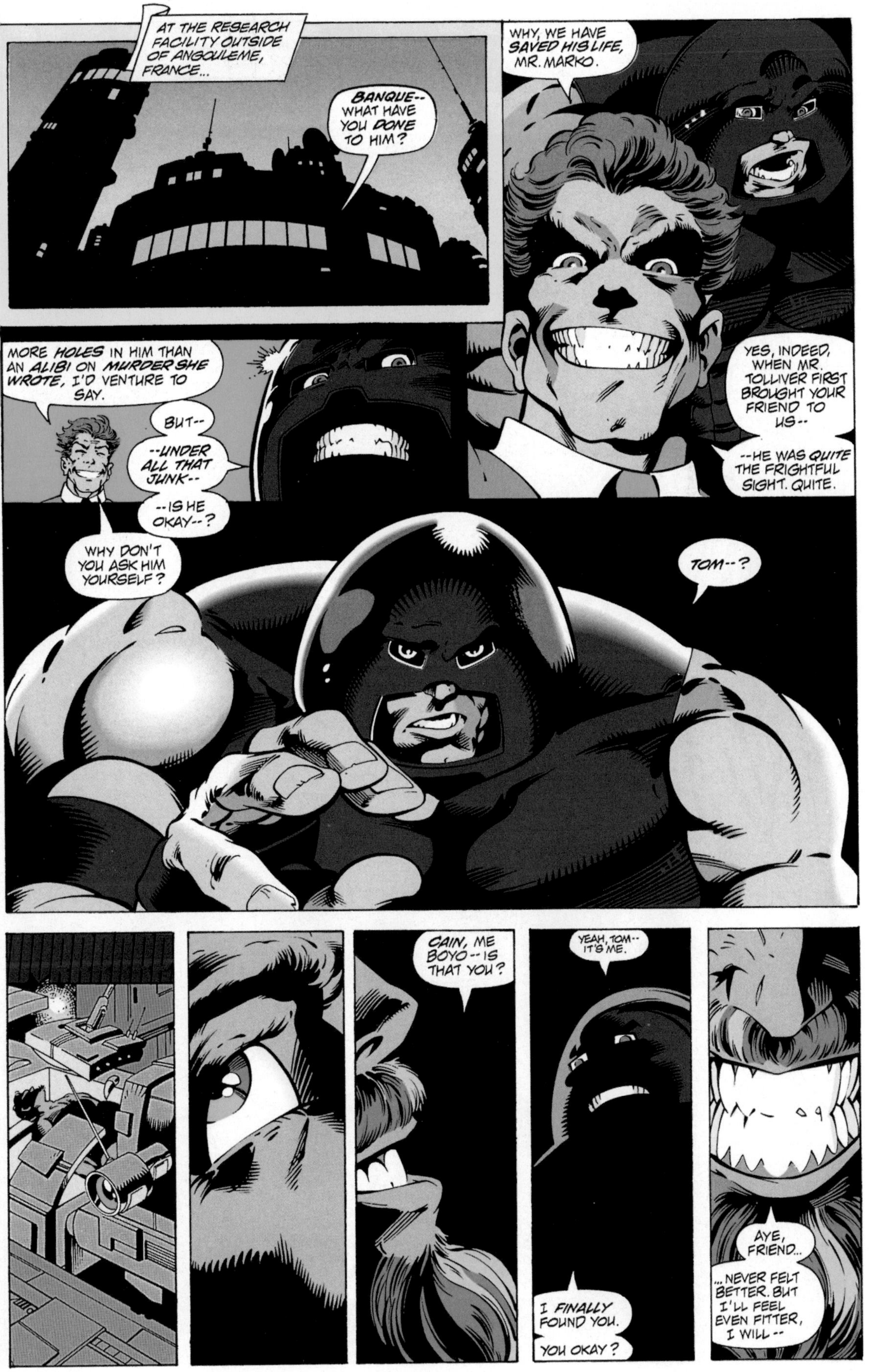
AT THE RESEARCH FACILITY OUTSIDE OF ANGOULEME, FRANCE...
BANQUE-- WHAT HAVE YOU DONE TO HIM?
WHY, WE HAVE SAVED HIS LIFE, MR. MARKO.
YES, INDEED, WHEN MR. TOLLIVER FIRST BROUGHT YOUR FRIEND TO US--
--HE WAS QUITE THE FRIGHTFUL SIGHT. QUITE.
MORE HOLES IN HIM THAN AN ALIBI ON MURDER SHE WROTE, I'D VENTURE TO SAY.
BUT--
--UNDER ALL THAT JUNK--
--IS HE OKAY--?
WHY DON'T YOU ASK HIM YOURSELF?
TOM--?
CAIN, ME BOYO--IS THAT YOU?
YEAH, TOM-- IT'S ME.
I FINALLY FOUND YOU.
YOU OKAY?
AYE, FRIEND...
...NEVER FELT BETTER. BUT I'LL FEEL EVEN FITTER, I WILL--

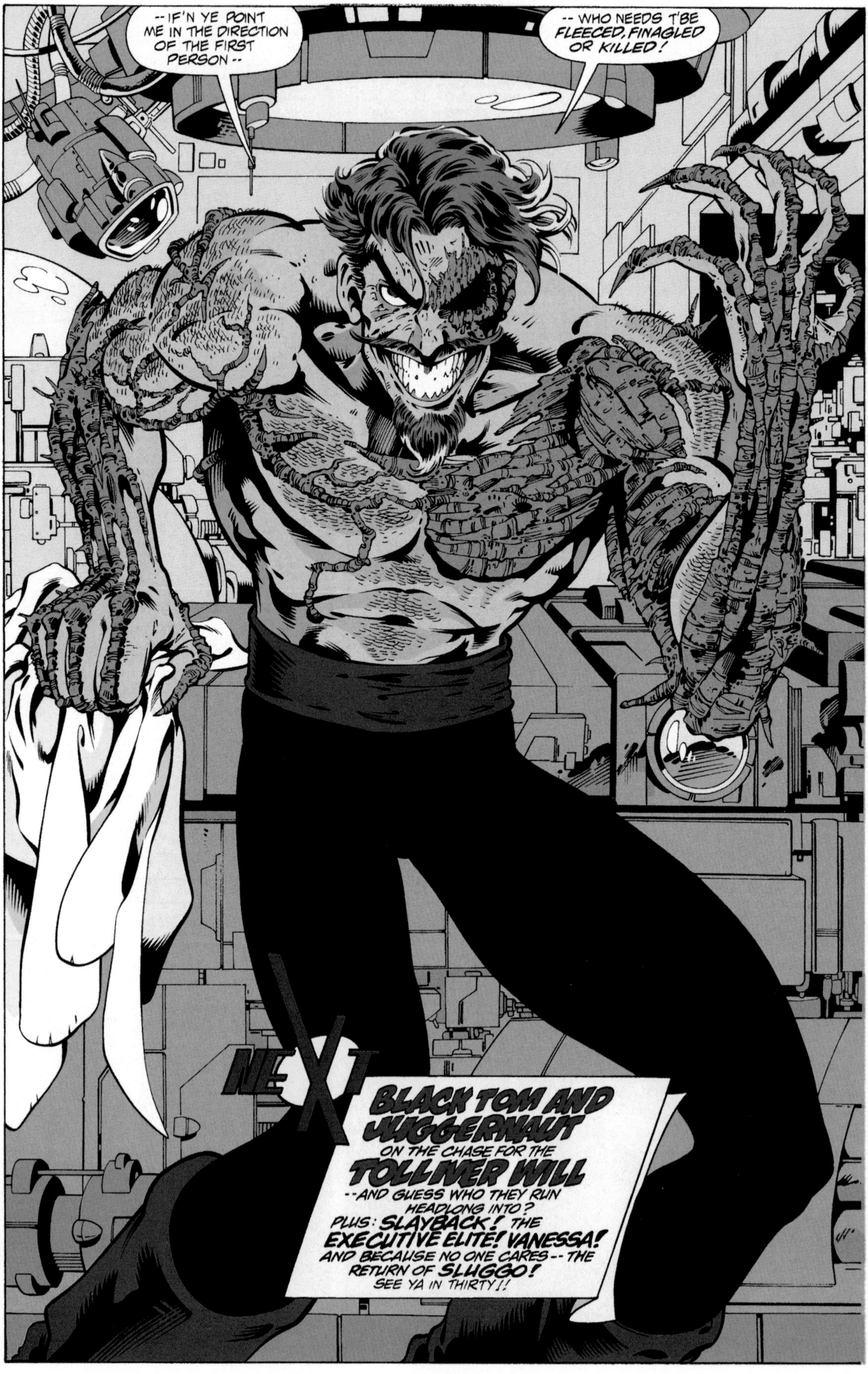
--IF'N YE POINT ME IN THE DIRECTION OF THE FIRST PERSON--
--WHO NEEDS T'BE FLEECED, FINAGLED OR KILLED!
NEXT
BLACK TOM AND JUGGERNAUT ON THE CHASE FOR THE TOLLIVER WILL --AND GUESS WHO THEY RUN HEADLONG INTO? PLUS: SLAYBACK! THE EXECUTIVE ELITE! VANESSA! AND BECAUSE NO ONE CARES--THE RETURN OF SLUGGO! SEE YA IN THIRTY!!

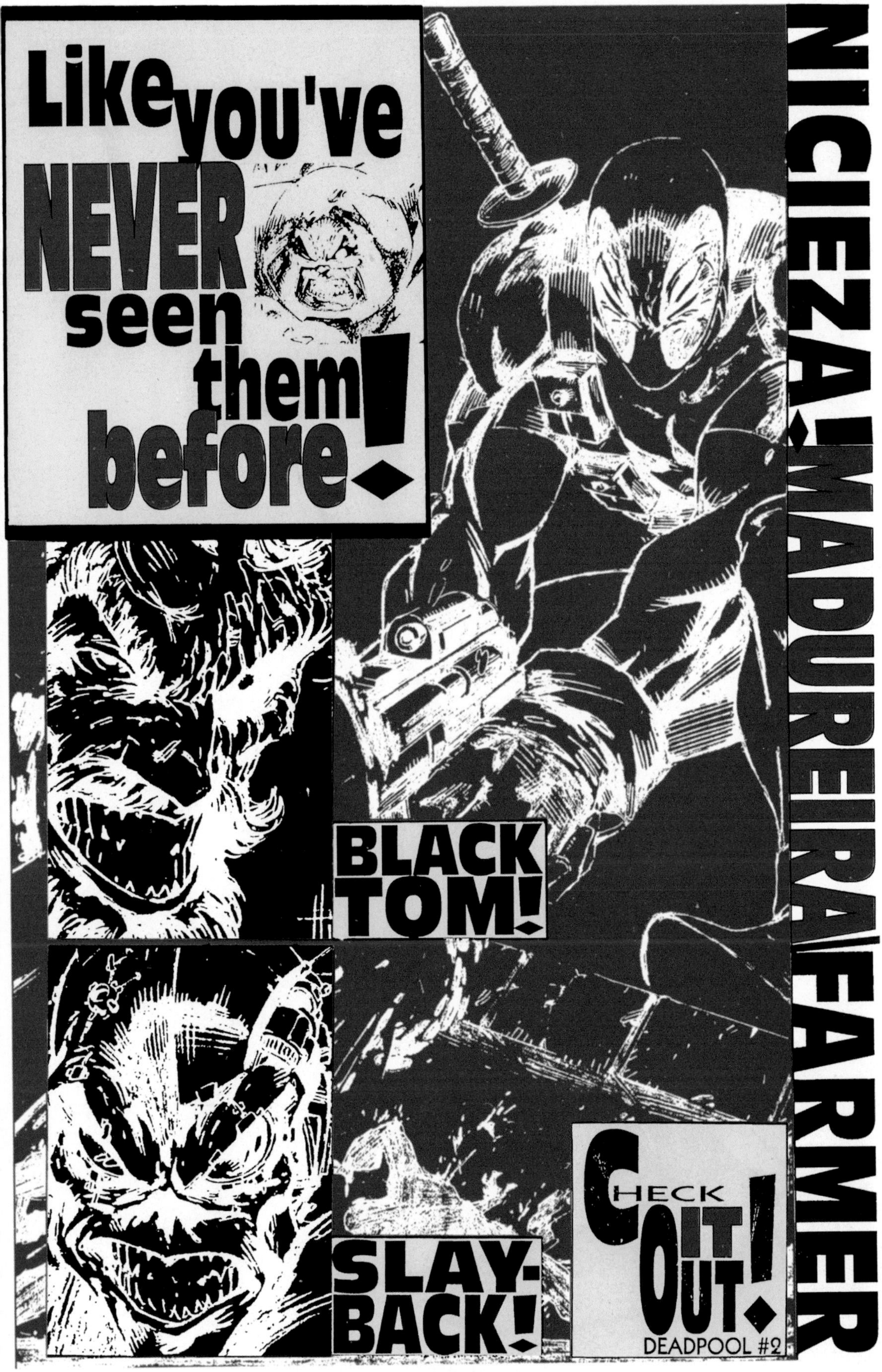
Like you've NEVER seen them before!
BLACK TOM!
SLAY-BACK!
CHECK IT OUT!
DEADPOOL #2
NICIEZA/MADUREIRA/FARMER

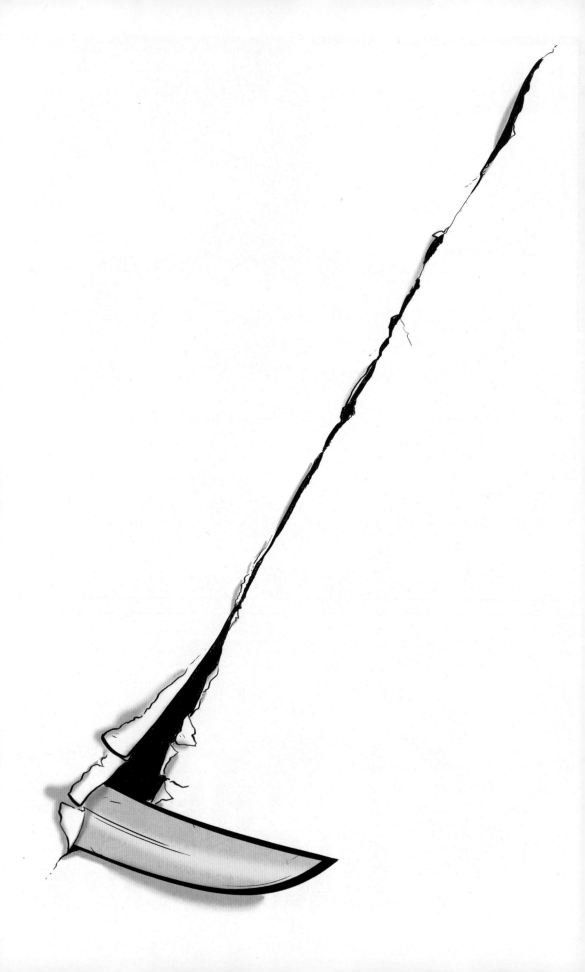

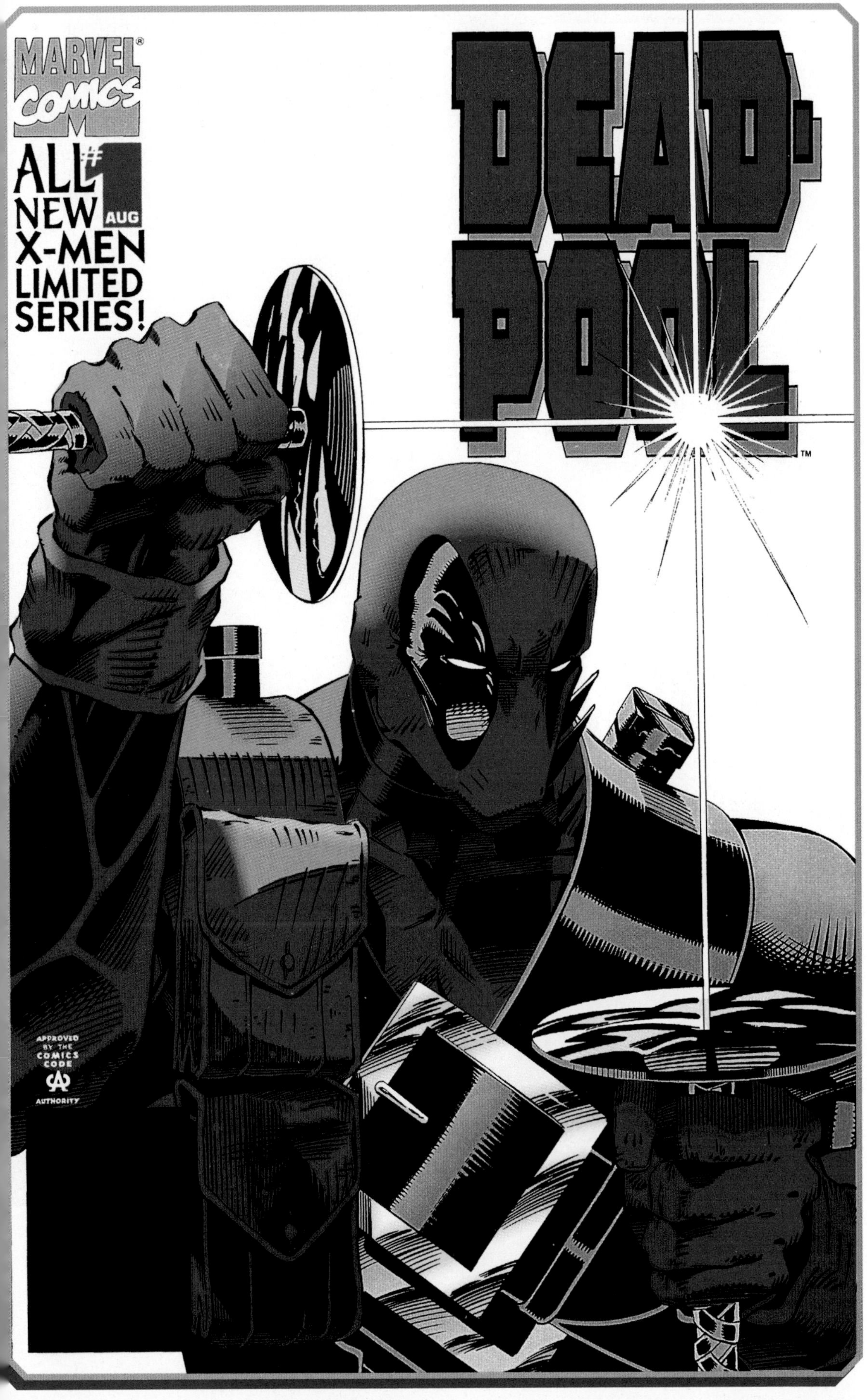
MARVEL®
COMICS
ALL NEW X-MEN LIMITED SERIES!
#1
AUG
DEAD-POOL™
APPROVED BY THE COMICS CODE AUTHORITY

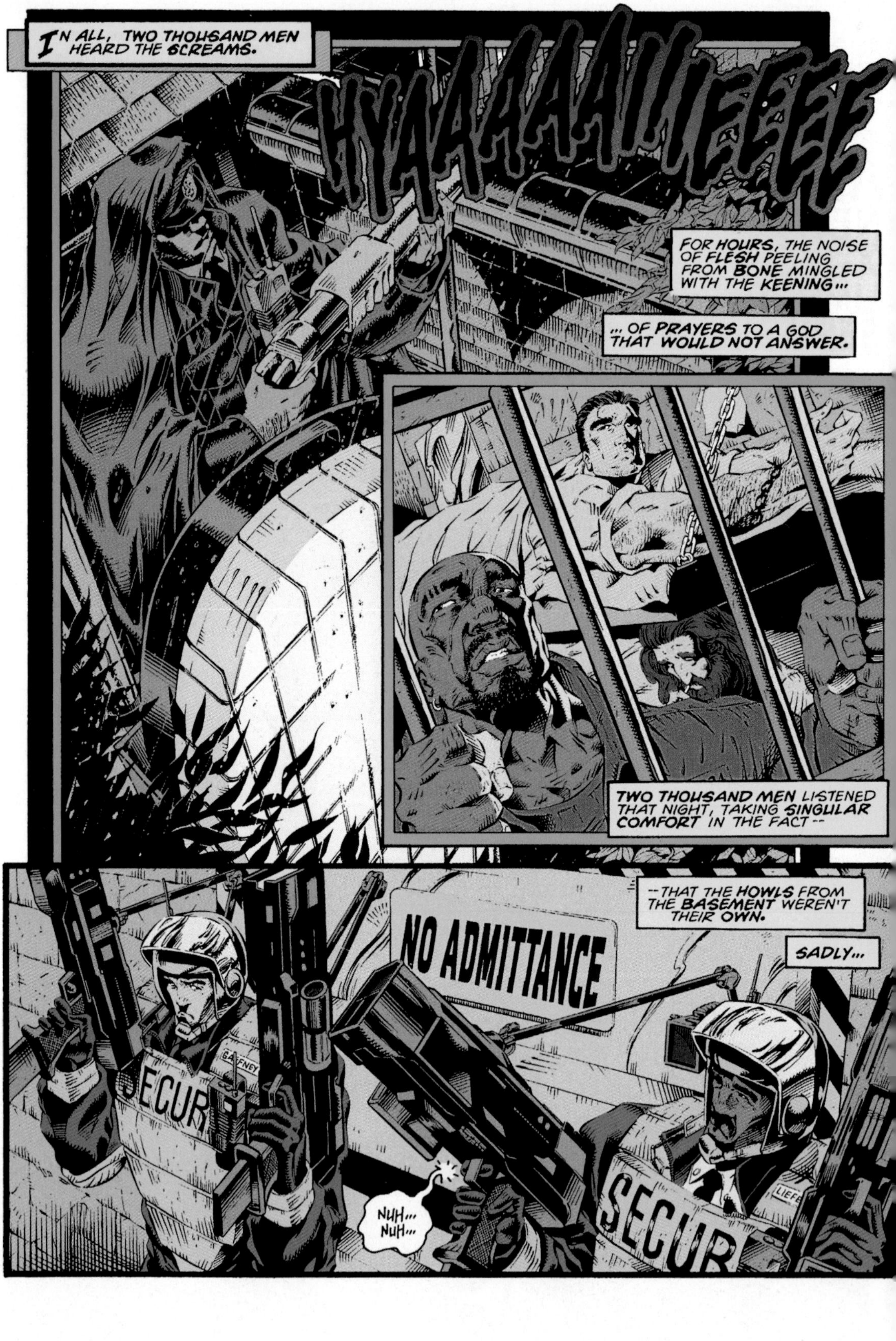

IN ALL, TWO THOUSAND MEN HEARD THE SCREAMS.
HYAAAAAAIIIEEEEE
FOR HOURS, THE NOISE OF FLESH PEELING FROM BONE MINGLED WITH THE KEENING...
...OF PRAYERS TO A GOD THAT WOULD NOT ANSWER.
TWO THOUSAND MEN LISTENED THAT NIGHT, TAKING SINGULAR COMFORT IN THE FACT--
--THAT THE HOWLS FROM THE BASEMENT WEREN'T THEIR OWN.
SADLY...
NO ADMITTANCE
NUH... NUH...

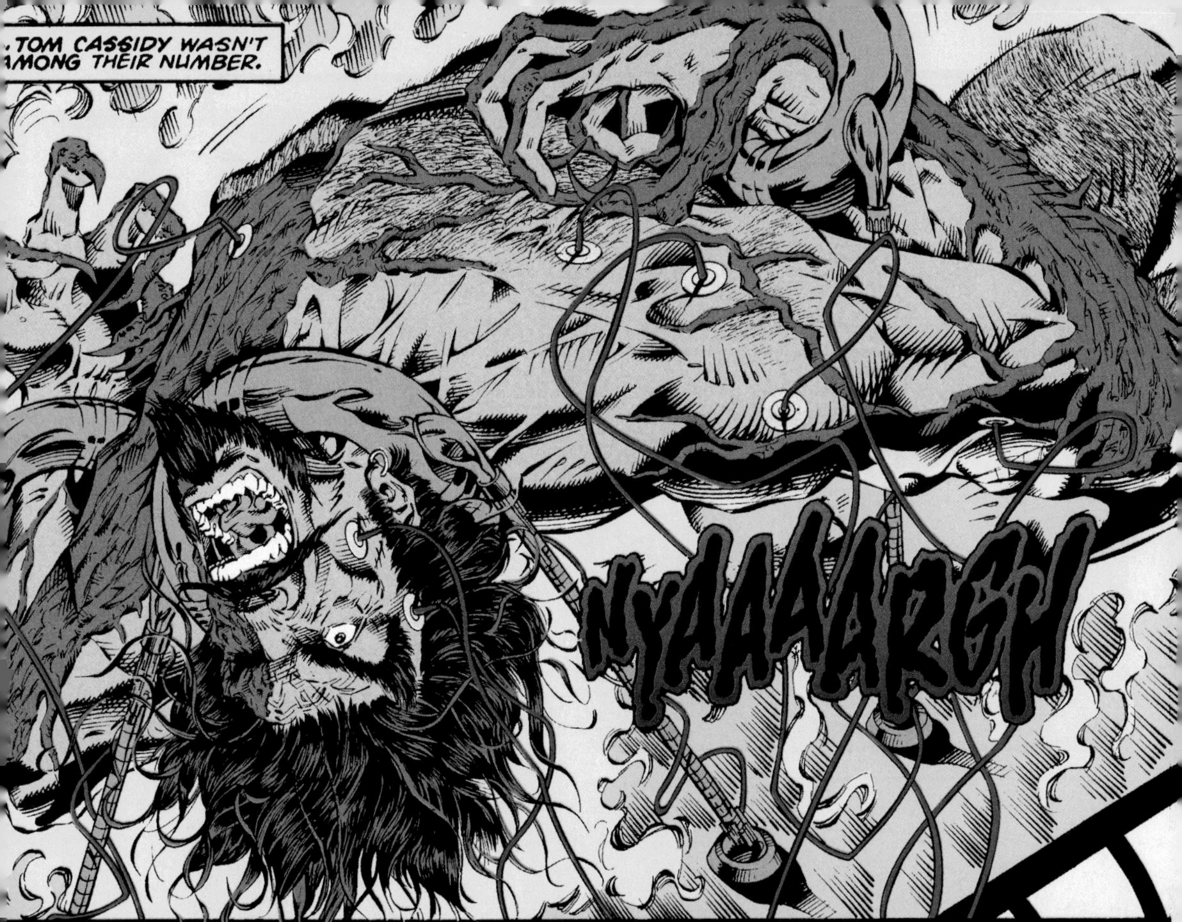
...TOM CASSIDY WASN'T AMONG THEIR NUMBER.
NYAAAAARGH

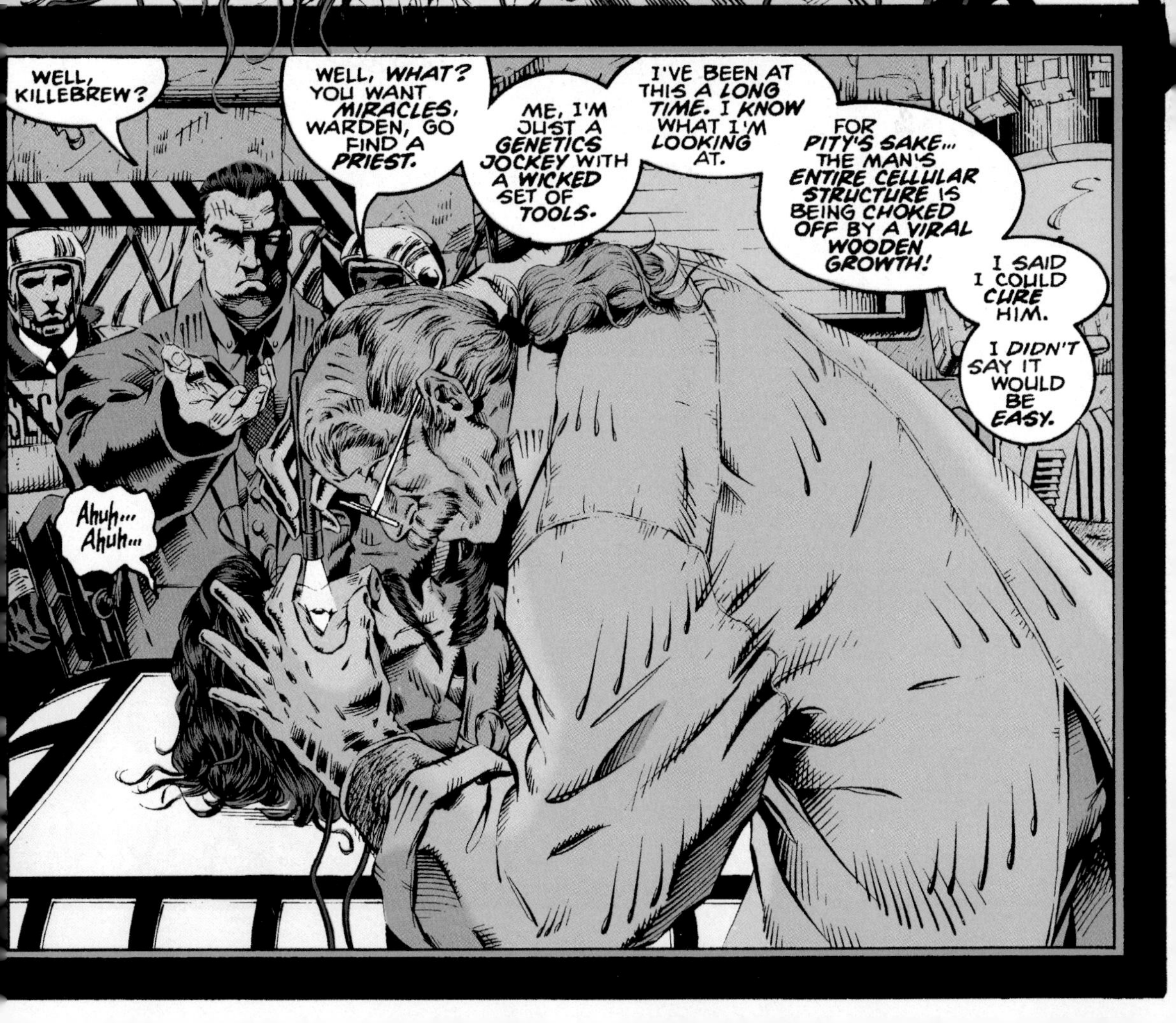
WELL, KILLEBREW?
WELL, WHAT? YOU WANT MIRACLES, WARDEN, GO FIND A PRIEST.
ME, I'M JUST A GENETICS JOCKEY WITH A WICKED SET OF TOOLS.
I'VE BEEN AT THIS A LONG TIME. I KNOW WHAT I'M LOOKING AT.
FOR PITY'S SAKE... THE MAN'S ENTIRE CELLULAR STRUCTURE IS BEING CHOKED OFF BY A VIRAL WOODEN GROWTH!
I SAID I COULD CURE HIM.
I DIDN'T SAY IT WOULD BE EASY.
Ahuh... Ahuh...

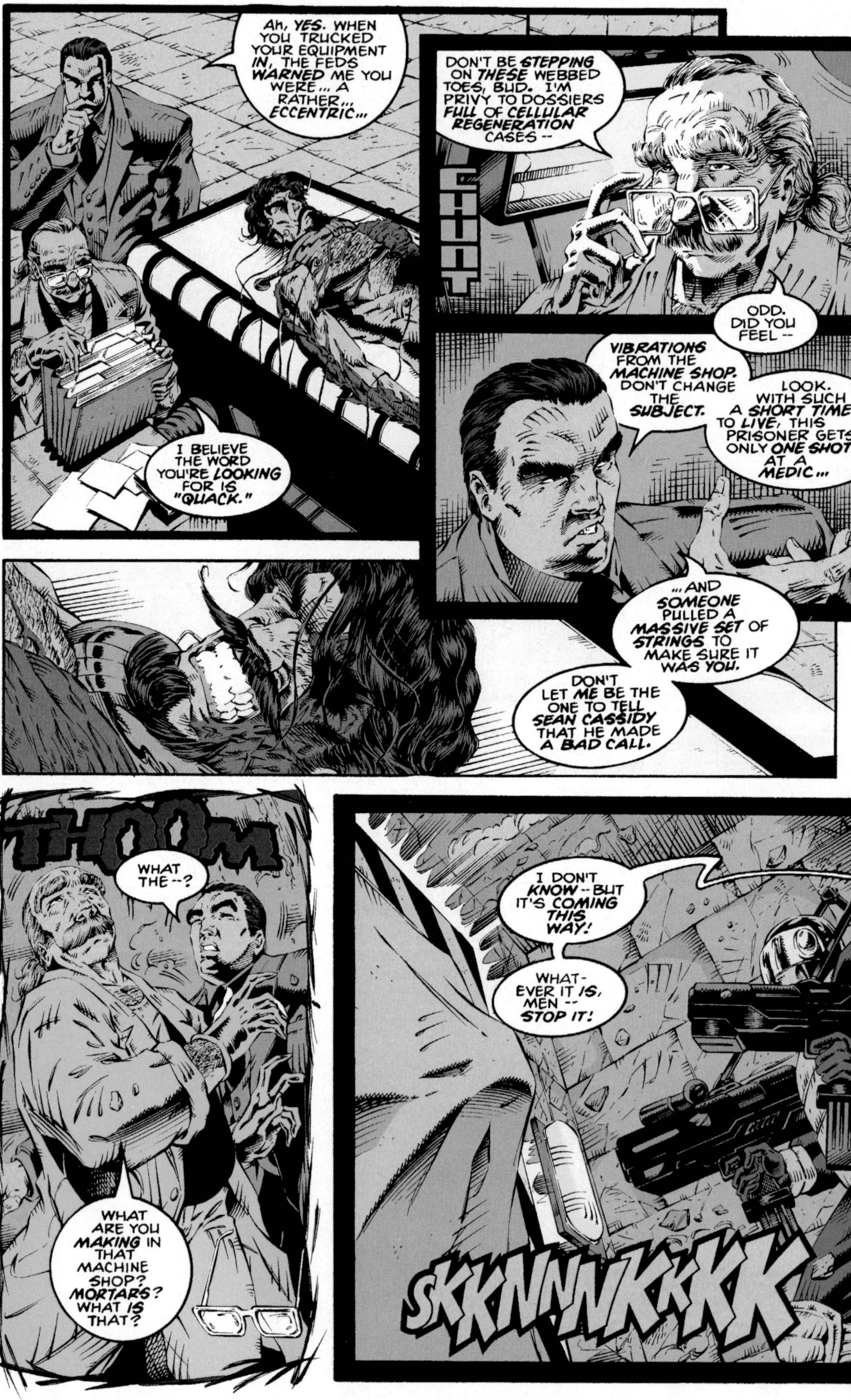
Ah, YES. WHEN YOU TRUCKED YOUR EQUIPMENT IN, THE FEDS WARNED ME YOU WERE... A RATHER... ECCENTRIC...
I BELIEVE THE WORD YOU'RE LOOKING FOR IS "QUACK."
CHUNT
DON'T BE STEPPING ON THESE WEBBED TOES, BUD. I'M PRIVY TO DOSSIERS FULL OF CELLULAR REGENERATION CASES --
ODD. DID YOU FEEL --
VIBRATIONS FROM THE MACHINE SHOP. DON'T CHANGE THE SUBJECT.
LOOK. WITH SUCH A SHORT TIME TO LIVE, THIS PRISONER GETS ONLY ONE SHOT AT A MEDIC...
...AND SOMEONE PULLED A MASSIVE SET OF STRINGS TO MAKE SURE IT WAS YOU.
DON'T LET ME BE THE ONE TO TELL SEAN CASSIDY THAT HE MADE A BAD CALL.
THOOM
WHAT THE --?
WHAT ARE YOU MAKING IN THAT MACHINE SHOP? MORTARS? WHAT IS THAT?
I DON'T KNOW -- BUT IT'S COMING THIS WAY!
WHAT-EVER IT IS, MEN -- STOP IT!
SKKNNNKKKK

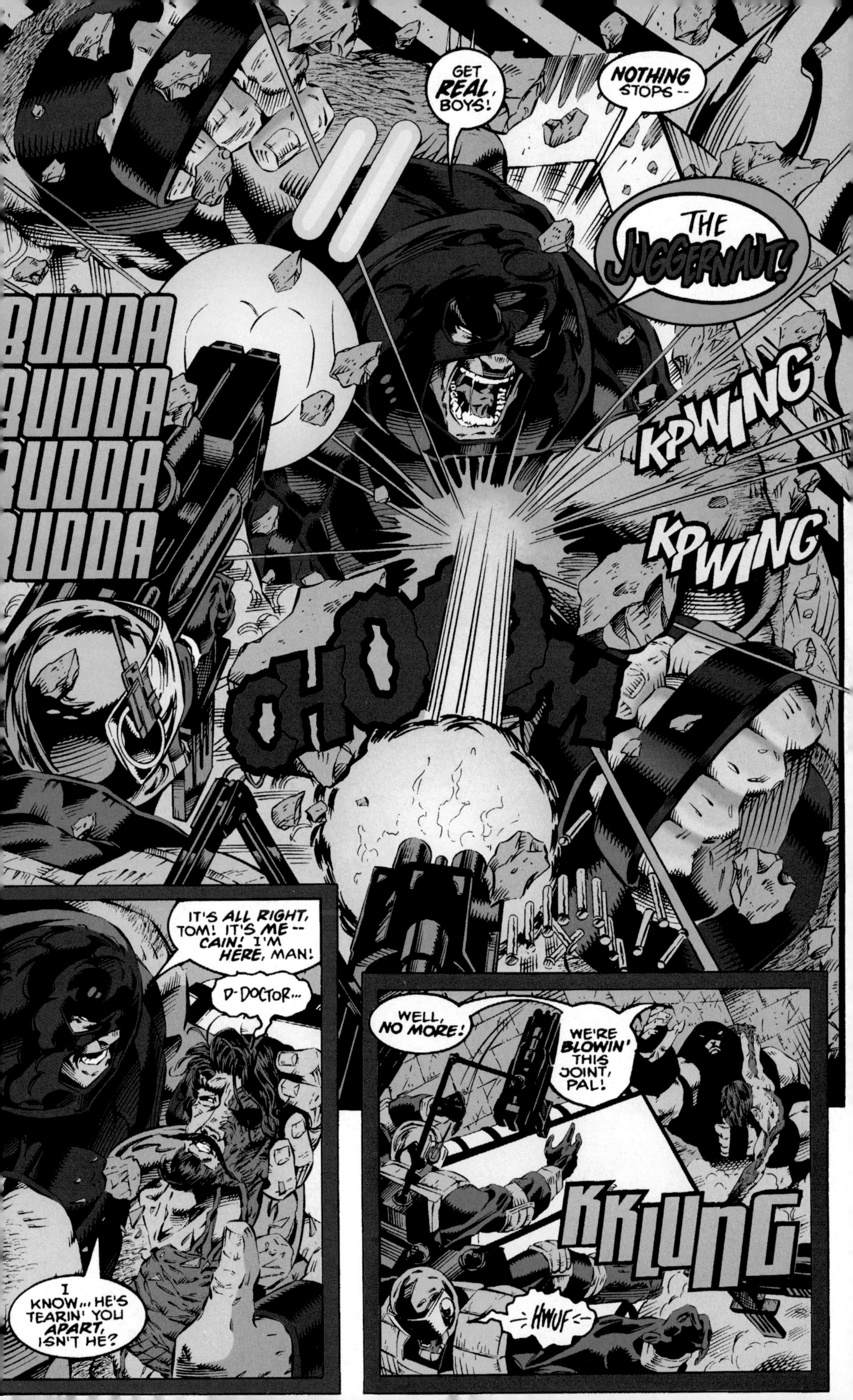
GET REAL, BOYS!
NOTHING STOPS --
THE JUGGERNAUT!
BUDDA BUDDA BUDDA BUDDA
KPWING
KPWING
CHOOM
IT'S ALL RIGHT, TOM! IT'S ME -- CAIN! I'M HERE, MAN!
D-DOCTOR...
I KNOW... HE'S TEARIN' YOU APART, ISN'T HE?
WELL, NO MORE!
WE'RE BLOWIN' THIS JOINT, PAL!
KKLUNG
HWUF

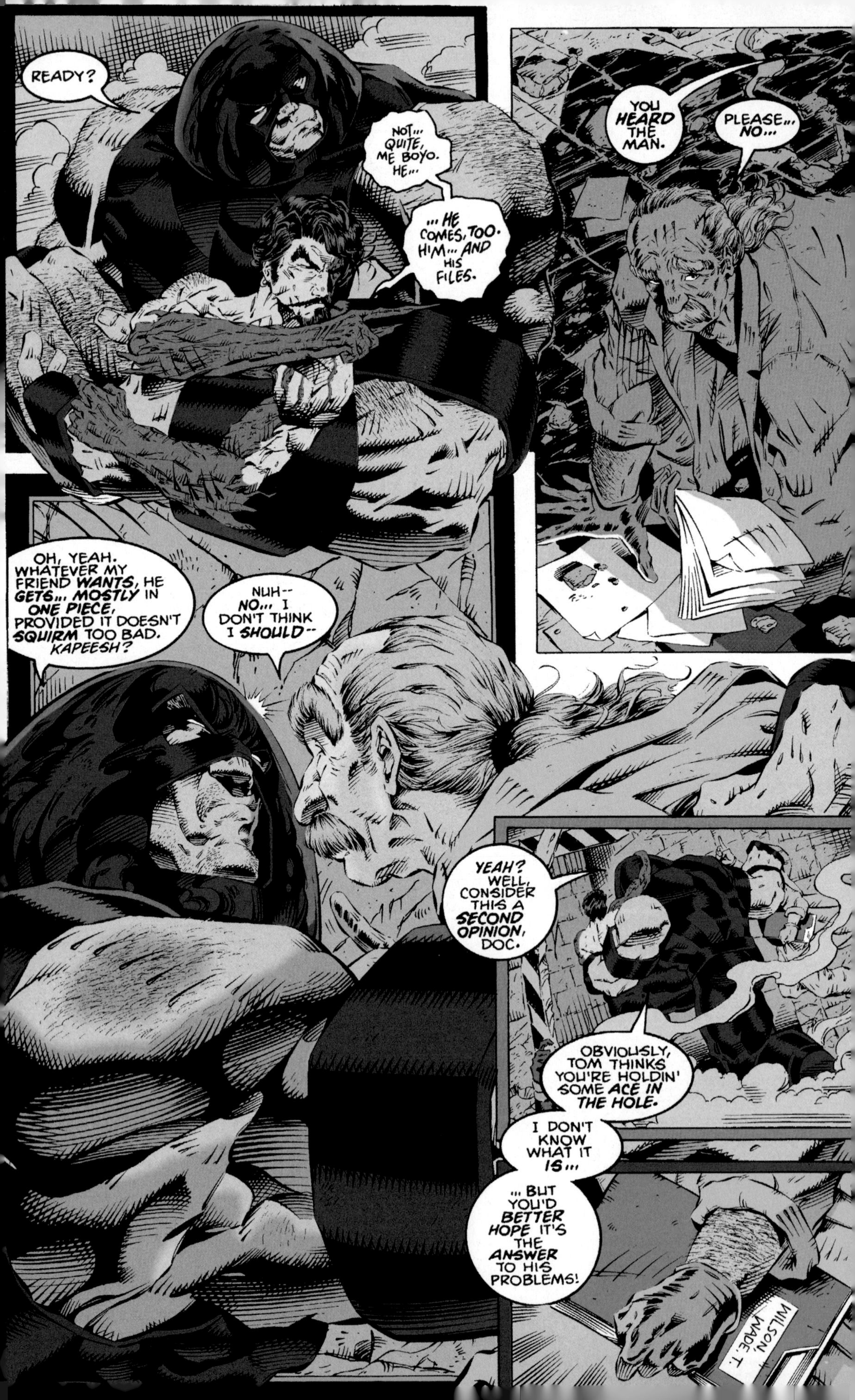

READY?
NOT... QUITE, ME BOYO. HE...
...HE COMES, TOO. HIM... AND HIS FILES.
YOU HEARD THE MAN.
PLEASE... NO...
OH, YEAH. WHATEVER MY FRIEND WANTS, HE GETS... MOSTLY IN ONE PIECE, PROVIDED IT DOESN'T SQUIRM TOO BAD. KAPEESH?
NUH-- NO... I DON'T THINK I SHOULD--
YEAH? WELL, CONSIDER THIS A SECOND OPINION, DOC.
OBVIOUSLY, TOM THINKS YOU'RE HOLDIN' SOME ACE IN THE HOLE.
I DON'T KNOW WHAT IT IS...
...BUT YOU'D BETTER HOPE IT'S THE ANSWER TO HIS PROBLEMS!
WILSON, WADE T.

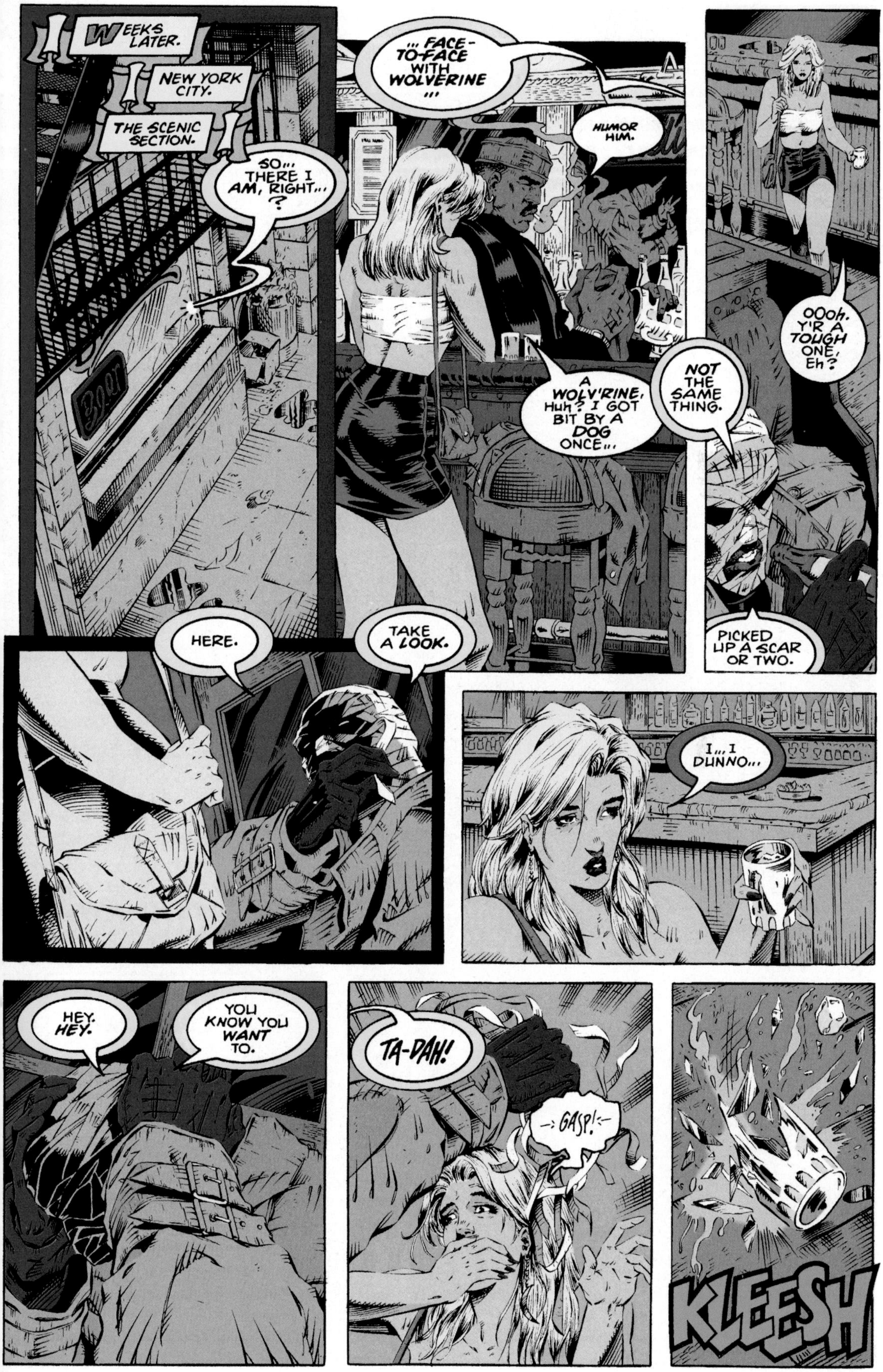
WEEKS LATER.
NEW YORK CITY.
THE SCENIC SECTION.
SO... THERE I AM, RIGHT... ?
... FACE-TO-FACE WITH WOLVERINE ...
HUMOR HIM.
A WOLV'RINE, Huh? I GOT BIT BY A DOG ONCE...
NOT THE SAME THING.
OOOh. Y'R A TOUGH ONE, Eh?
PICKED UP A SCAR OR TWO.
HERE.
TAKE A LOOK.
I... I DUNNO...
HEY. HEY.
YOU KNOW YOU WANT TO.
TA-DAH!
GASP!
KLEESH

IF LOOKS COULD KILL!

Marvel's MERC with a MOUTH returns, courtesy of

MARK WAID writer **IAN CHURCHILL** penciler **JASON MINOR** inke

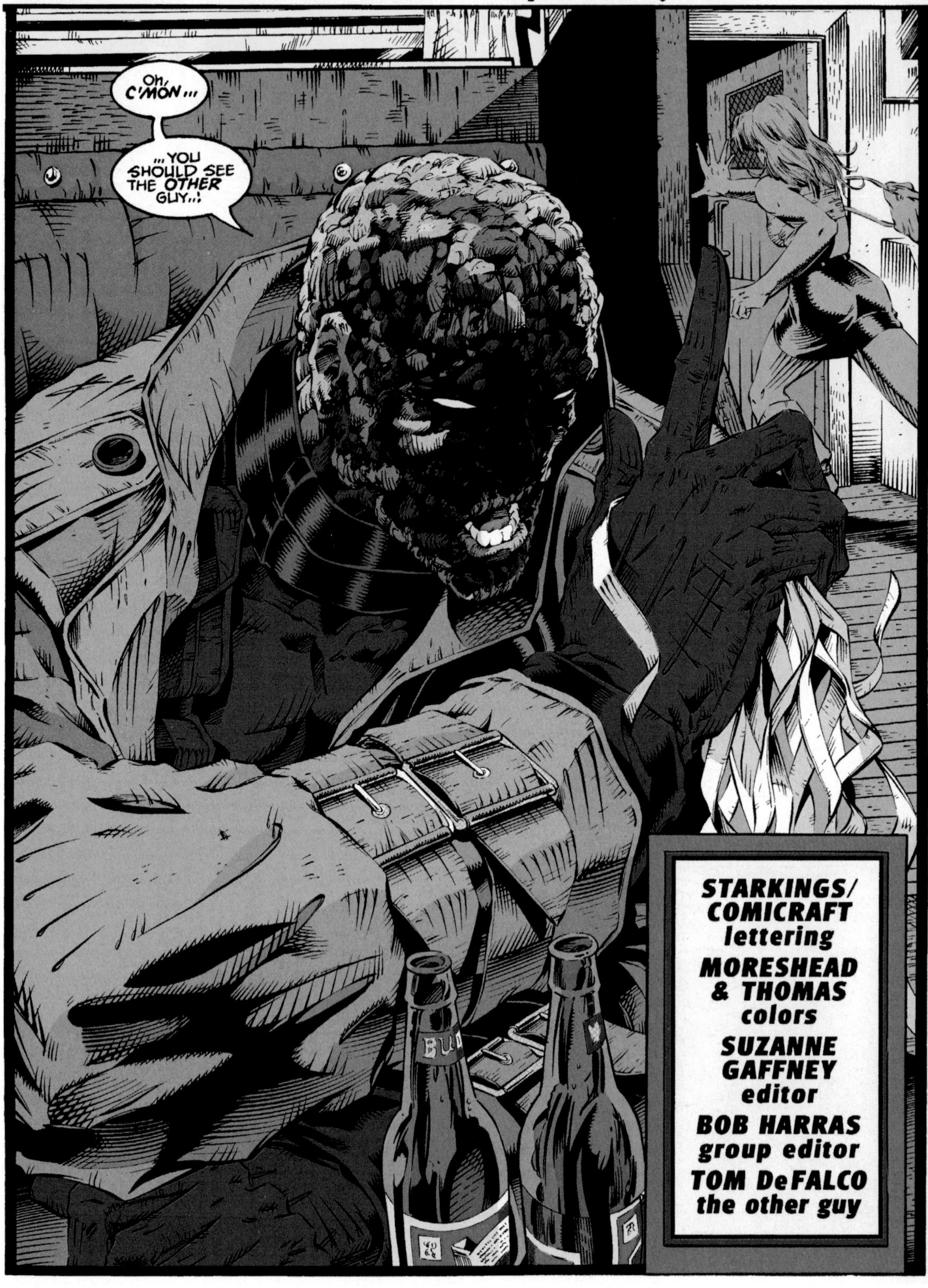

OH, C'MON...
...YOU SHOULD SEE THE OTHER GUY...!
STARKINGS/ COMICRAFT lettering
MORESHEAD & THOMAS colors
SUZANNE GAFFNEY editor
BOB HARRAS group editor
TOM DeFALCO the other guy

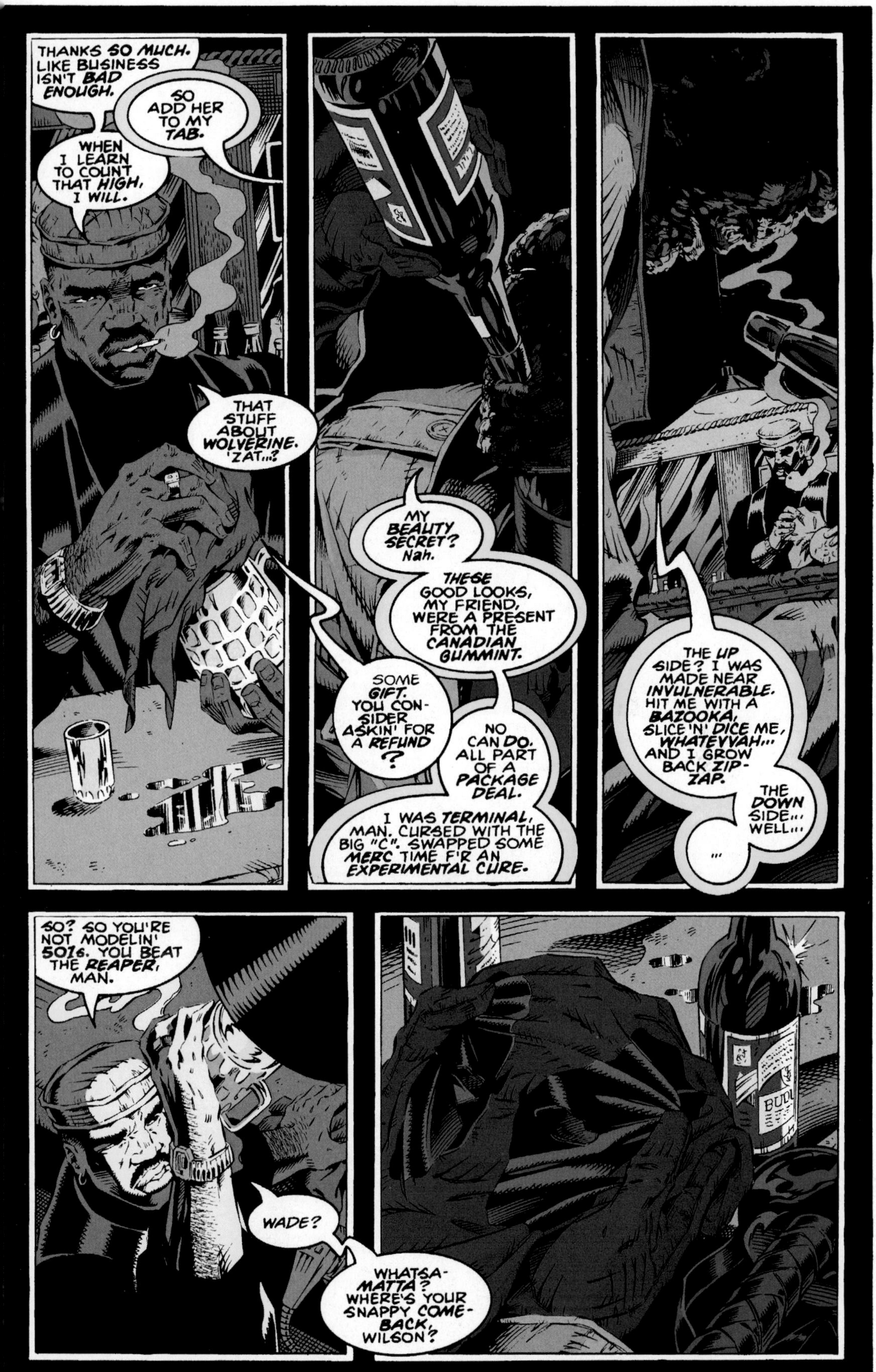
THANKS SO MUCH. LIKE BUSINESS ISN'T BAD ENOUGH.
SO ADD HER TO MY TAB.
WHEN I LEARN TO COUNT THAT HIGH, I WILL.
THAT STUFF ABOUT WOLVERINE. 'ZAT...?
MY BEAUTY SECRET? Nah.
THESE GOOD LOOKS, MY FRIEND, WERE A PRESENT FROM THE CANADIAN GUMMINT.
SOME GIFT. YOU CONSIDER ASKIN' FOR A REFUND?
NO CAN DO. ALL PART OF A PACKAGE DEAL.
I WAS TERMINAL, MAN. CURSED WITH THE BIG "C". SWAPPED SOME MERC TIME F'R AN EXPERIMENTAL CURE.
THE UP SIDE? I WAS MADE NEAR INVULNERABLE. HIT ME WITH A BAZOOKA, SLICE 'N' DICE ME, WHATEVVAH... AND I GROW BACK ZIP-ZAP.
THE DOWN SIDE... WELL...
...
SO? SO YOU'RE NOT MODELIN' 501s. YOU BEAT THE REAPER, MAN.
WADE?
WHATSA-MATTA? WHERE'S YOUR SNAPPY COME-BACK, WILSON?

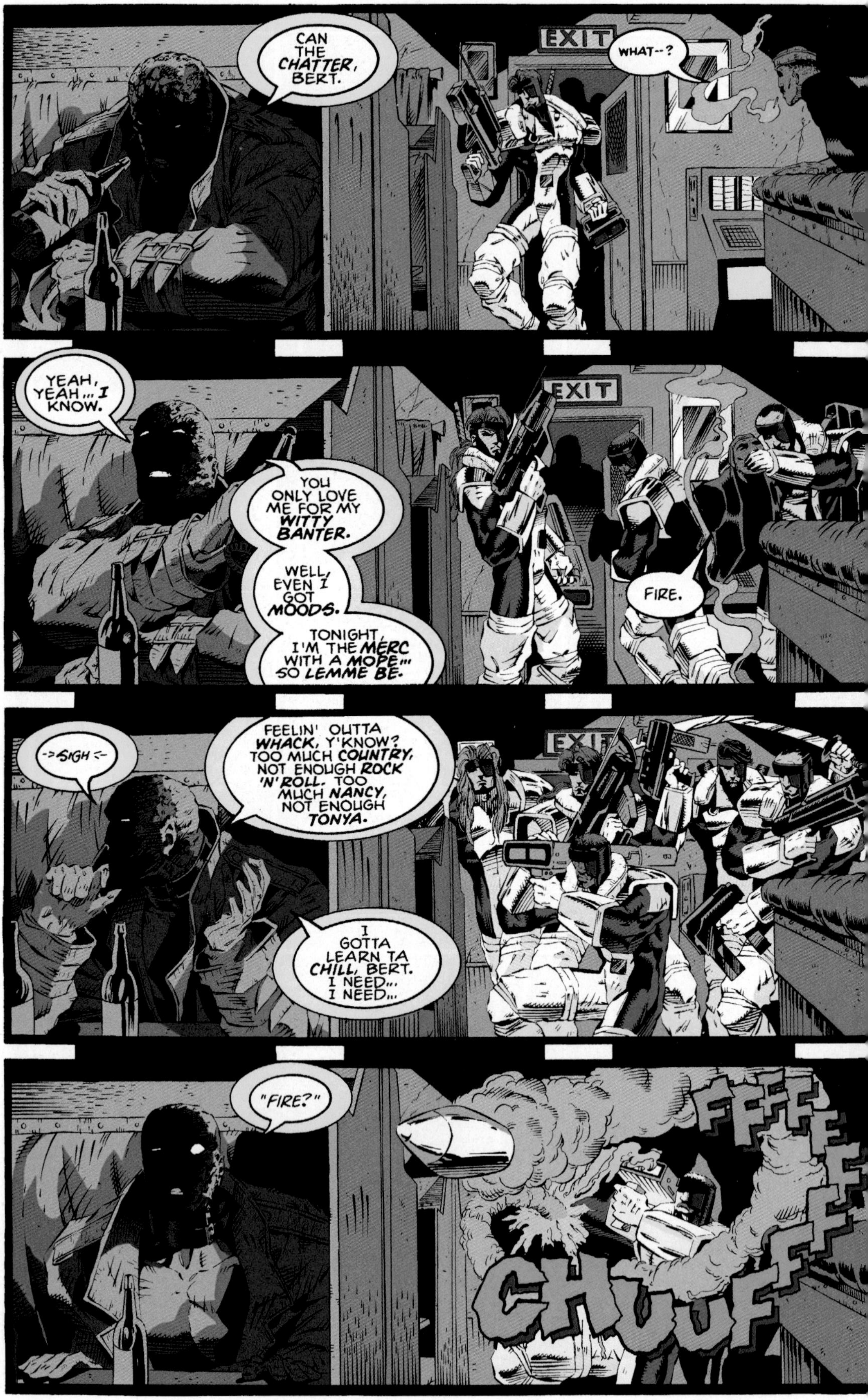
CAN THE CHATTER, BERT.
WHAT--?
YEAH, YEAH... I KNOW.
YOU ONLY LOVE ME FOR MY WITTY BANTER.
WELL, EVEN I GOT MOODS.
TONIGHT, I'M THE MERC WITH A MOPE... SO LEMME BE.
FIRE.
-> SIGH <-
FEELIN' OUTTA WHACK, Y'KNOW? TOO MUCH COUNTRY, NOT ENOUGH ROCK 'N' ROLL. TOO MUCH NANCY, NOT ENOUGH TONYA.
I GOTTA LEARN TA CHILL, BERT. I NEED... I NEED...
"FIRE?"
FFFFFFFFF
CHUUFF

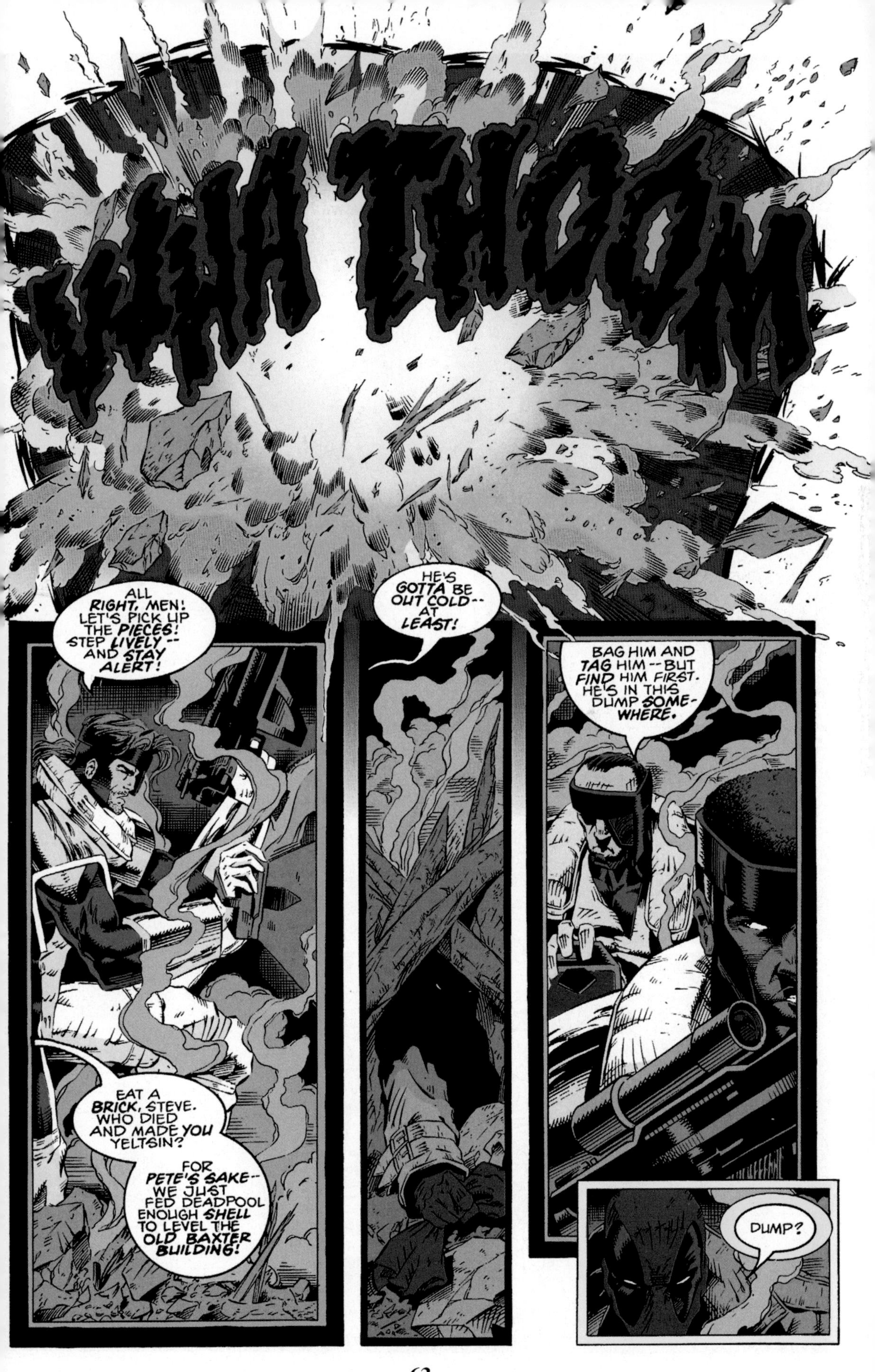
WHA THOOM
ALL RIGHT, MEN! LET'S PICK UP THE PIECES! STEP LIVELY -- AND STAY ALERT!
EAT A BRICK, STEVE. WHO DIED AND MADE YOU YELTSIN?
FOR PETE'S SAKE-- WE JUST FED DEADPOOL ENOUGH SHELL TO LEVEL THE OLD BAXTER BUILDING!
HE'S GOTTA BE OUT COLD-- AT LEAST!
BAG HIM AND TAG HIM --BUT FIND HIM FIRST. HE'S IN THIS DUMP SOMEWHERE.
DUMP?

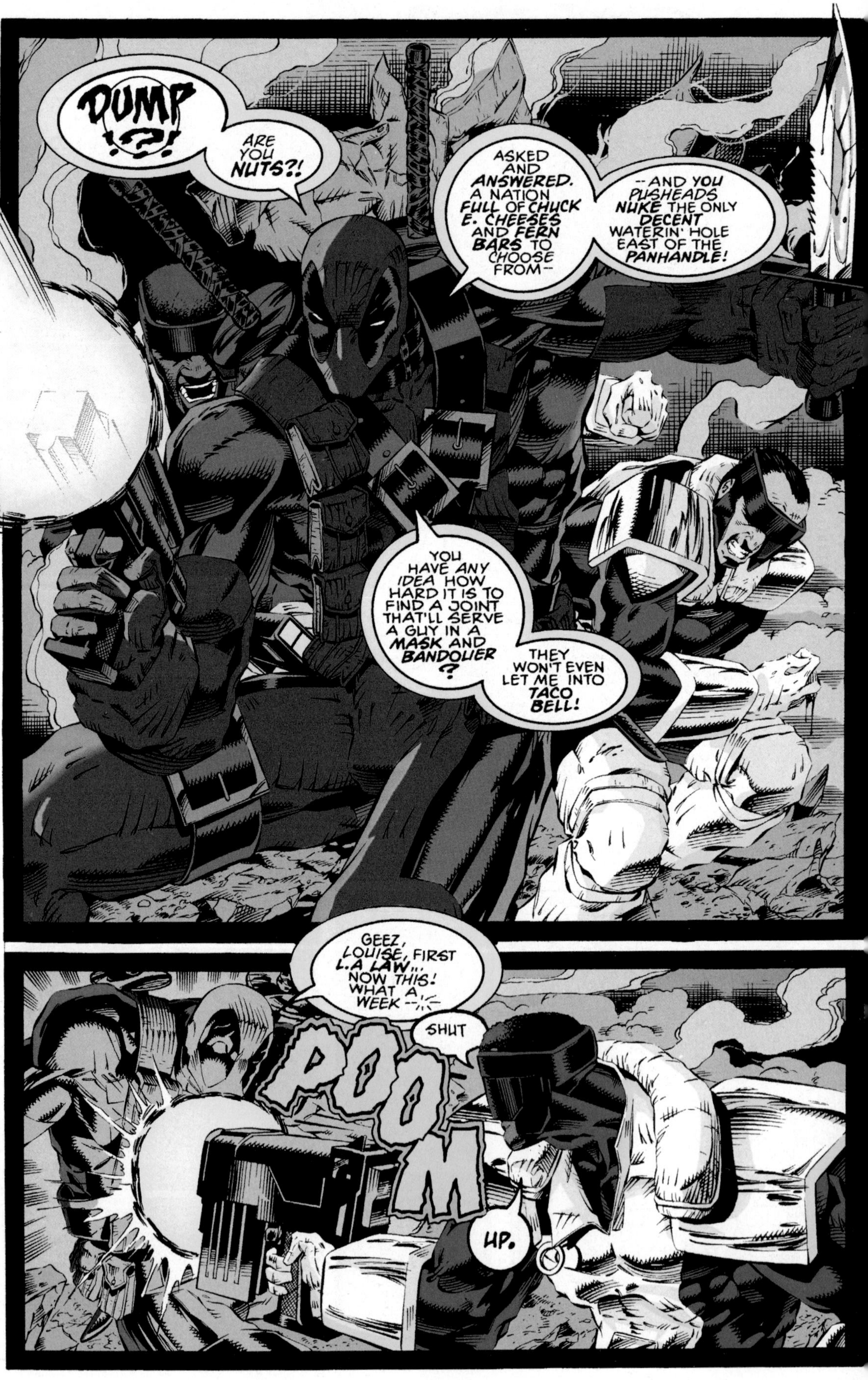
DUMP !?!
ARE YOU NUTS?!
ASKED AND ANSWERED. A NATION FULL OF CHUCK E. CHEESES AND FERN BARS TO CHOOSE FROM--
--AND YOU PUSHEADS NUKE THE ONLY DECENT WATERIN' HOLE EAST OF THE PANHANDLE!
YOU HAVE ANY IDEA HOW HARD IT IS TO FIND A JOINT THAT'LL SERVE A GUY IN A MASK AND BANDOLIER ?
THEY WON'T EVEN LET ME INTO TACO BELL!
GEEZ, LOUISE, FIRST L.A LAW... NOW THIS! WHAT A WEEK --
SHUT
POOM
UP.

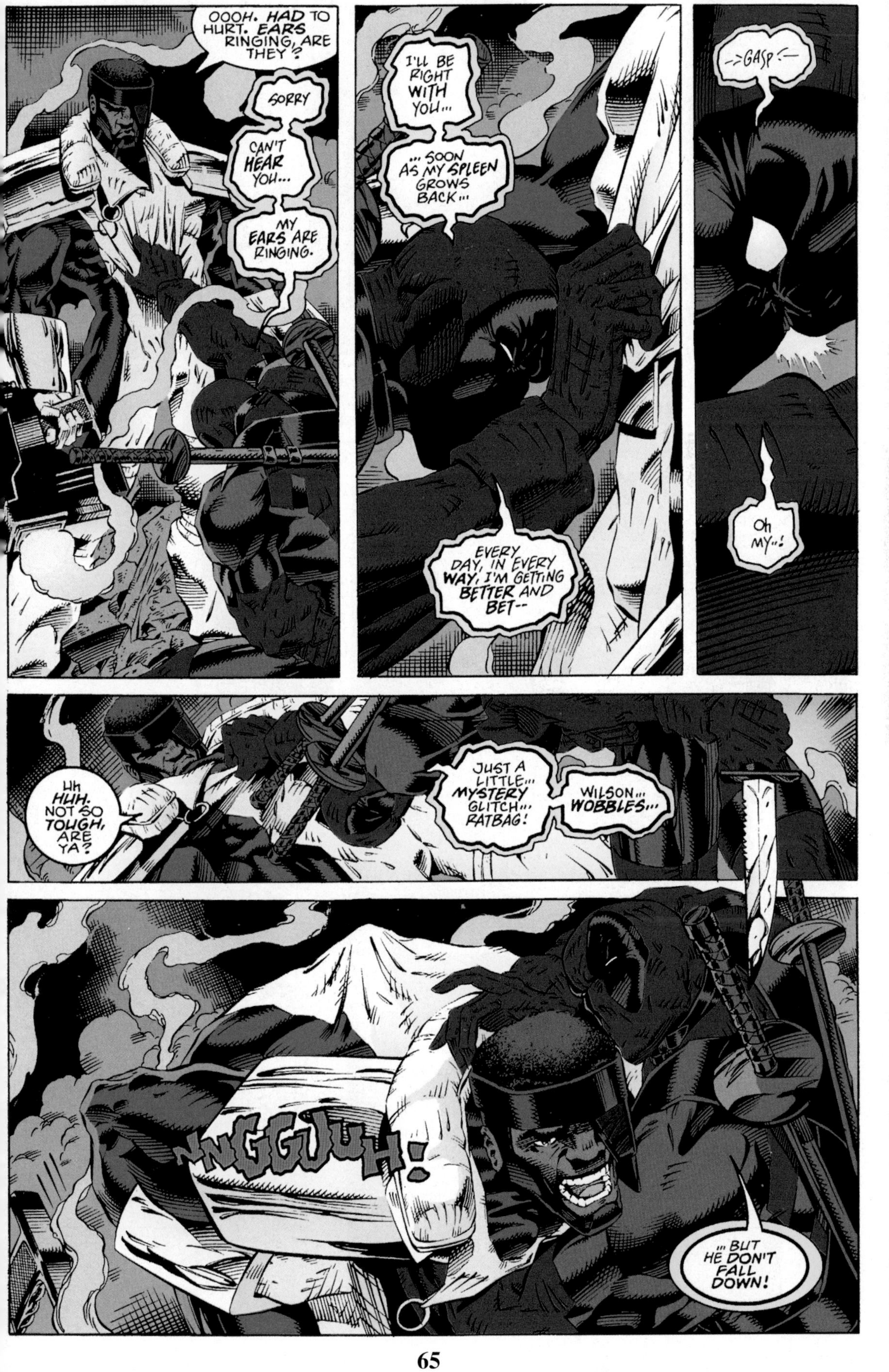
OOOH. HAD TO HURT. EARS RINGING, ARE THEY?
SORRY
CAN'T HEAR YOU...
MY EARS ARE RINGING.
I'LL BE RIGHT WITH YOU...
...SOON AS MY SPLEEN GROWS BACK...
EVERY DAY, IN EVERY WAY, I'M GETTING BETTER AND BET--
--GASP--
Oh MY..!
UH HUH. NOT SO TOUGH, ARE YA?
JUST A LITTLE... MYSTERY GLITCH... RATBAG!
WILSON... WOBBLES...
NNGGUUH!
...BUT HE DON'T FALL DOWN!

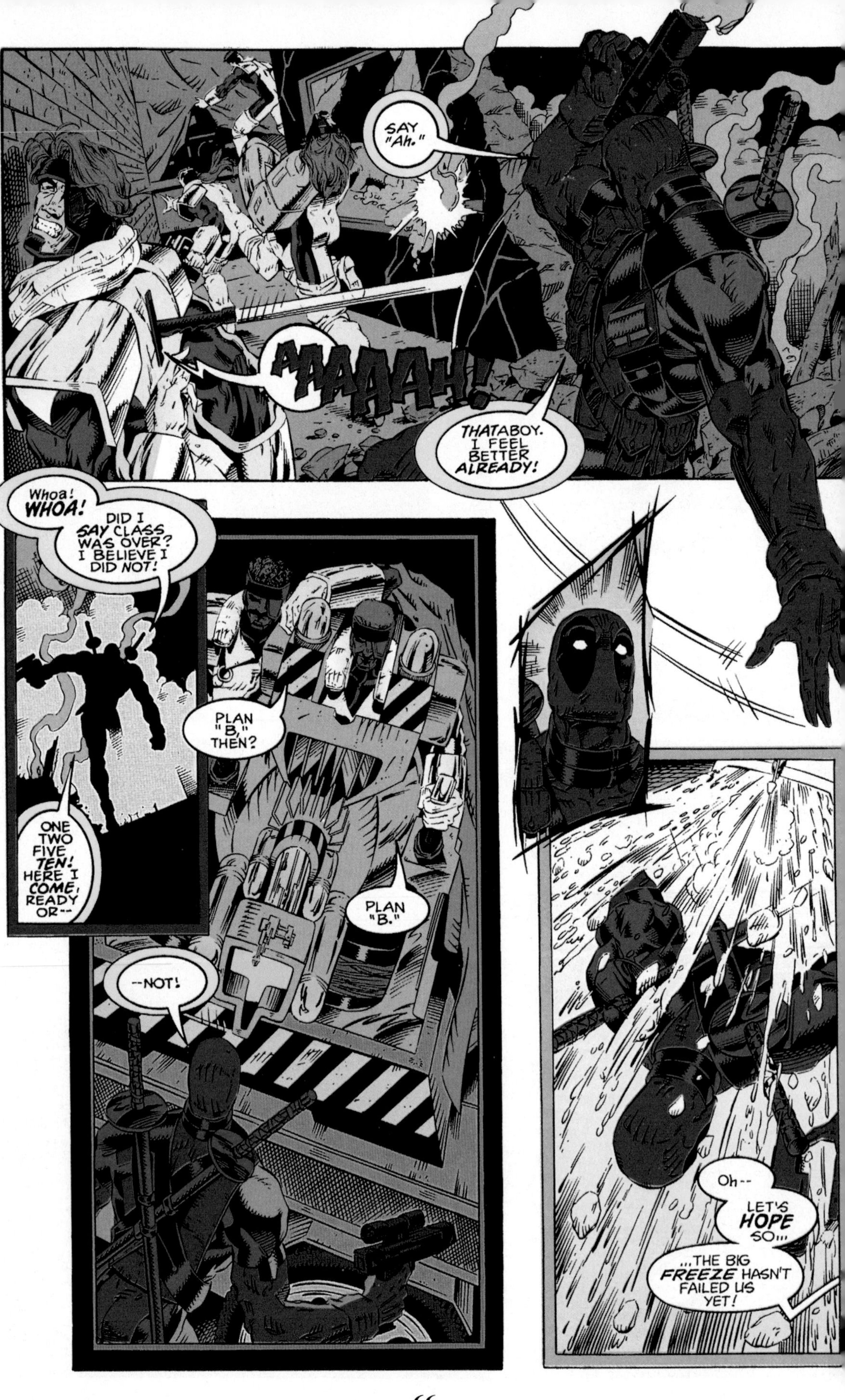
SAY "Ah."
AAAAAH!
THATABOY. I FEEL BETTER ALREADY!
Whoa! WHOA!
DID I SAY CLASS WAS OVER? I BELIEVE I DID NOT!
PLAN "B," THEN?
PLAN "B."
ONE TWO FIVE TEN! HERE I COME, READY OR--
--NOT!
Oh--
LET'S HOPE SO...
...THE BIG FREEZE HASN'T FAILED US YET!

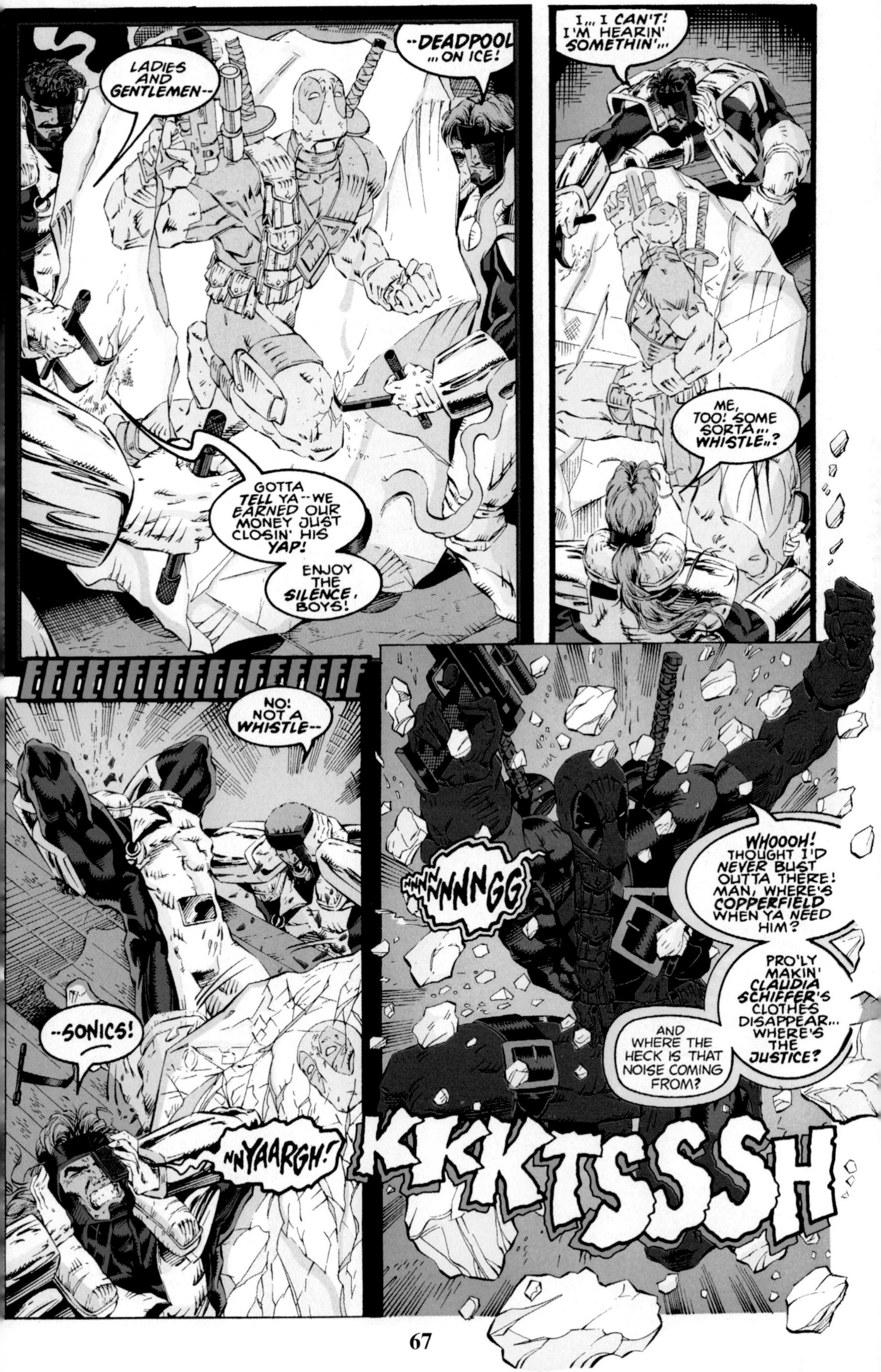
LADIES AND GENTLEMEN--
--DEADPOOL ...ON ICE!
GOTTA TELL YA--WE EARNED OUR MONEY JUST CLOSIN' HIS YAP!
ENJOY THE SILENCE, BOYS!
I... I CAN'T! I'M HEARIN' SOMETHIN'...
ME, TOO! SOME SORTA... WHISTLE..?
EEEEEEEEEEEEEEEEE
NO! NOT A WHISTLE--
--SONICS!
NNYAARGH!
NNNNNNNNGG
WHOOOH! THOUGHT I'D NEVER BUST OUTTA THERE! MAN, WHERE'S COPPERFIELD WHEN YA NEED HIM?
PRO'LY MAKIN' CLAUDIA SCHIFFER'S CLOTHES DISAPPEAR... WHERE'S THE JUSTICE?
AND WHERE THE HECK IS THAT NOISE COMING FROM?
KKKTSSSSH

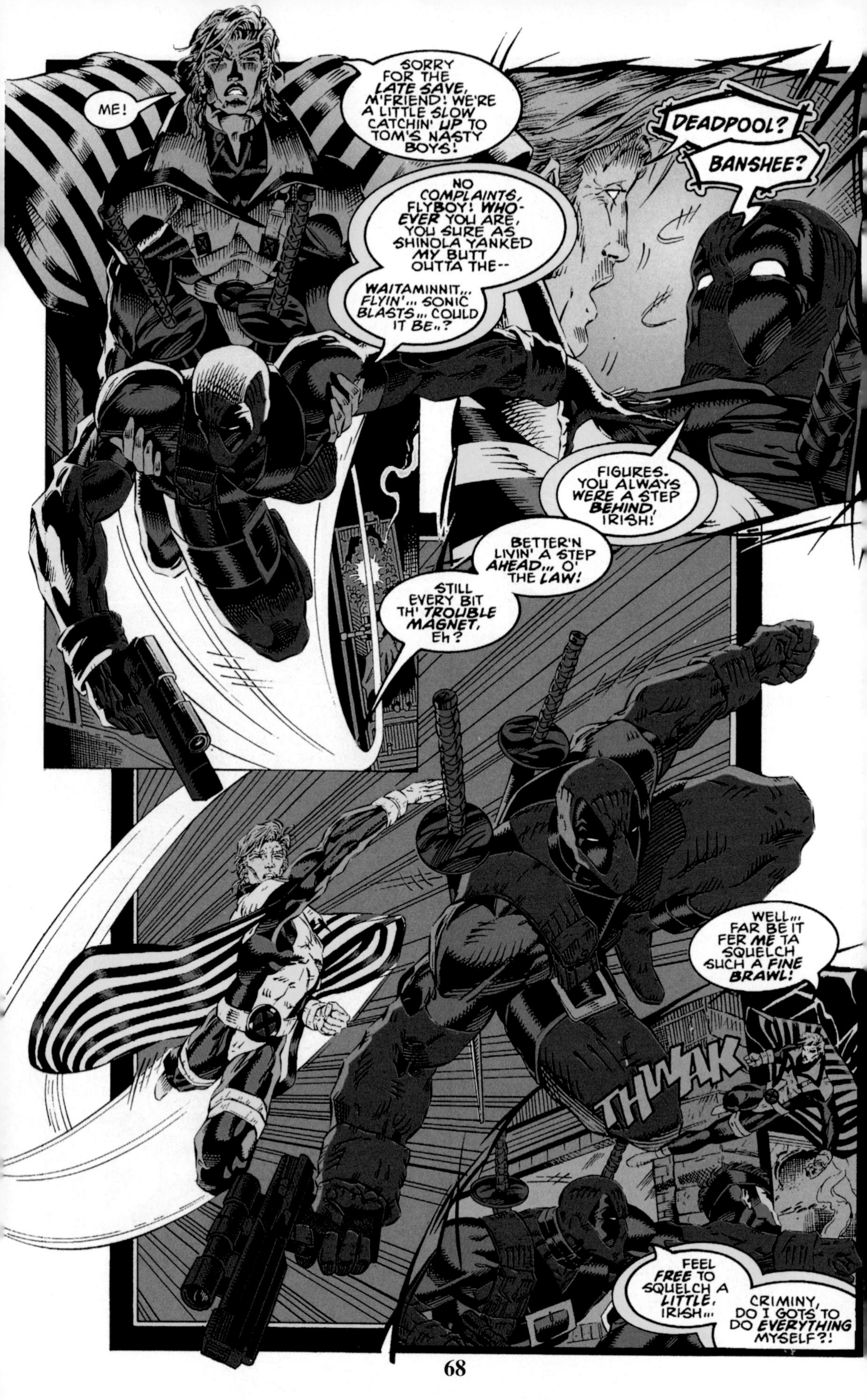
ME!
SORRY FOR THE LATE SAVE, M'FRIEND! WE'RE A LITTLE SLOW CATCHIN' UP TO TOM'S NASTY BOYS!
NO COMPLAINTS, FLYBOY! WHO-EVER YOU ARE, YOU SURE AS SHINOLA YANKED MY BUTT OUTTA THE--
WAITAMINNIT... FLYIN'... SONIC BLASTS... COULD IT BE..?
DEADPOOL?
BANSHEE?
FIGURES. YOU ALWAYS WERE A STEP BEHIND, IRISH!
BETTER'N LIVIN' A STEP AHEAD... O' THE LAW!
STILL EVERY BIT TH' TROUBLE MAGNET, EH?
WELL... FAR BE IT FER ME TA SQUELCH SUCH A FINE BRAWL!
THWAK
FEEL FREE TO SQUELCH A LITTLE, IRISH...
CRIMINY, DO I GOTS TO DO EVERYTHING MYSELF?!

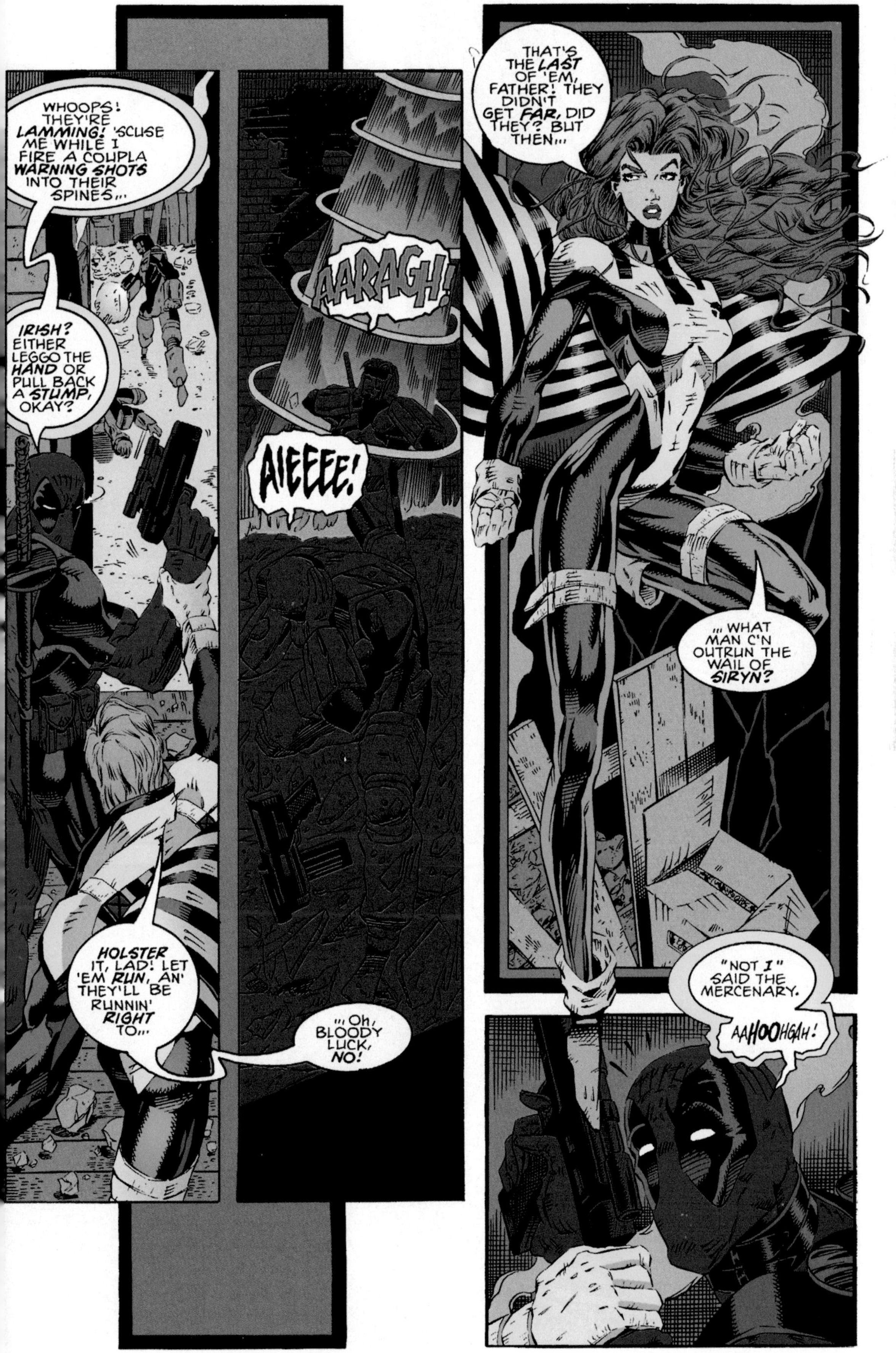
WHOOPS! THEY'RE LAMMING! 'SCUSE ME WHILE I FIRE A COUPLA WARNING SHOTS INTO THEIR SPINES...
IRISH? EITHER LEGGO THE HAND OR PULL BACK A STUMP, OKAY?
HOLSTER IT, LAD! LET 'EM RUN, AN' THEY'LL BE RUNNIN' RIGHT TO...
AARAGH!
AIEEEE!
...Oh, BLOODY LUCK, NO!
THAT'S THE LAST OF 'EM, FATHER! THEY DIDN'T GET FAR, DID THEY? BUT THEN...
...WHAT MAN C'N OUTRUN THE WAIL OF SIRYN?
"NOT I" SAID THE MERCENARY.
AAHOOHGAH!

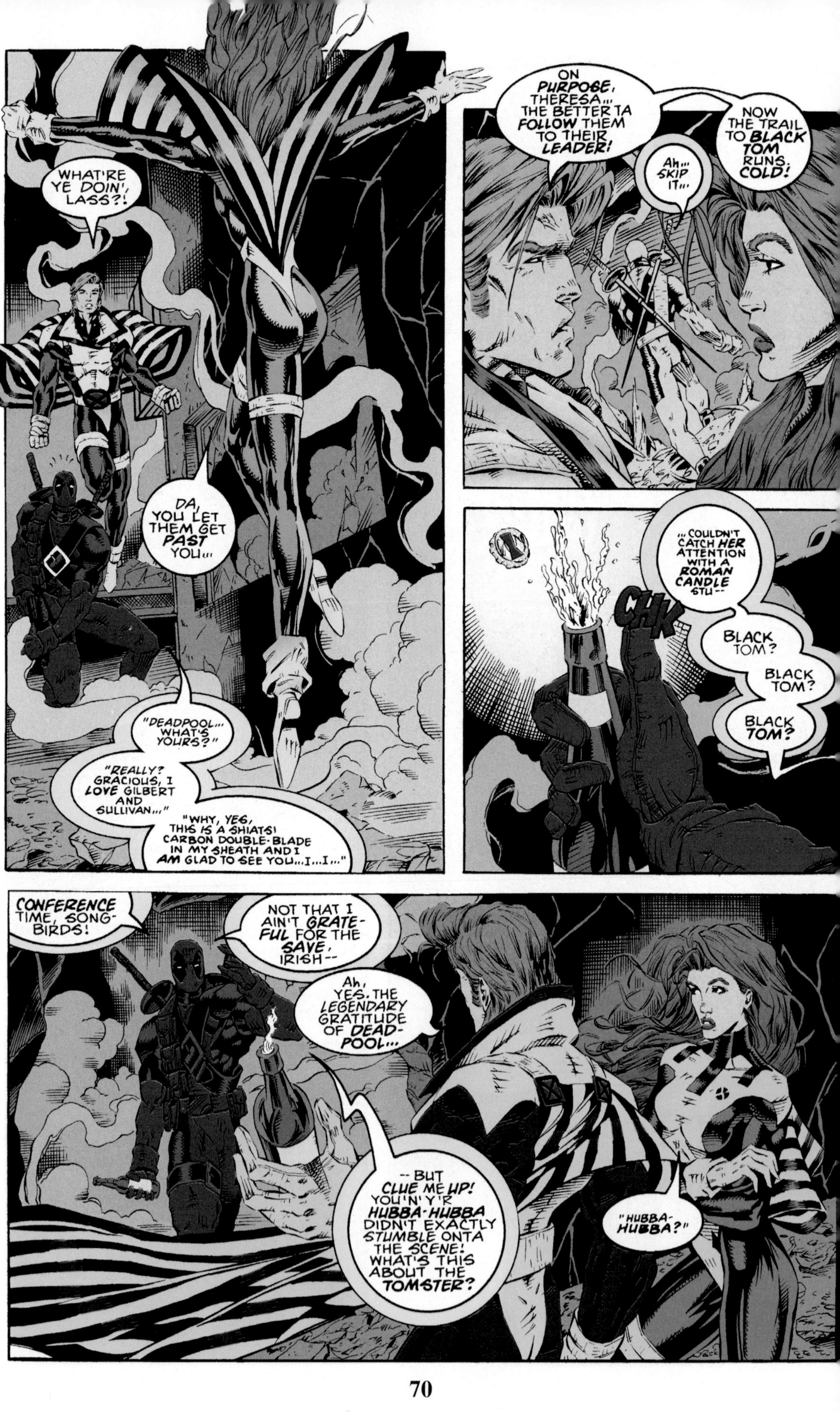
WHAT'RE YE DOIN', LASS?!
DA, YOU LET THEM GET PAST YOU...
"DEADPOOL... WHAT'S YOURS?"
"REALLY? GRACIOUS, I LOVE GILBERT AND SULLIVAN..."
"WHY, YES, THIS IS A SHIATSI CARBON DOUBLE-BLADE IN MY SHEATH AND I AM GLAD TO SEE YOU...I...I..."
ON PURPOSE, THERESA... THE BETTER TA FOLLOW THEM TO THEIR LEADER!
AH... SKIP IT...
NOW THE TRAIL TO BLACK TOM RUNS. COLD!
...COULDN'T CATCH HER ATTENTION WITH A ROMAN CANDLE STU--
CHK
BLACK TOM?
BLACK TOM?
BLACK TOM?
CONFERENCE TIME, SONG-BIRDS!
NOT THAT I AIN'T GRATE-FUL FOR THE SAVE, IRISH--
AH, YES. THE LEGENDARY GRATITUDE OF DEAD-POOL...
-- BUT CLUE ME UP! YOU'N'Y'R HUBBA-HUBBA DIDN'T EXACTLY STUMBLE ONTA THE SCENE! WHAT'S THIS ABOUT THE TOMSTER?
"HUBBA-HUBBA?"

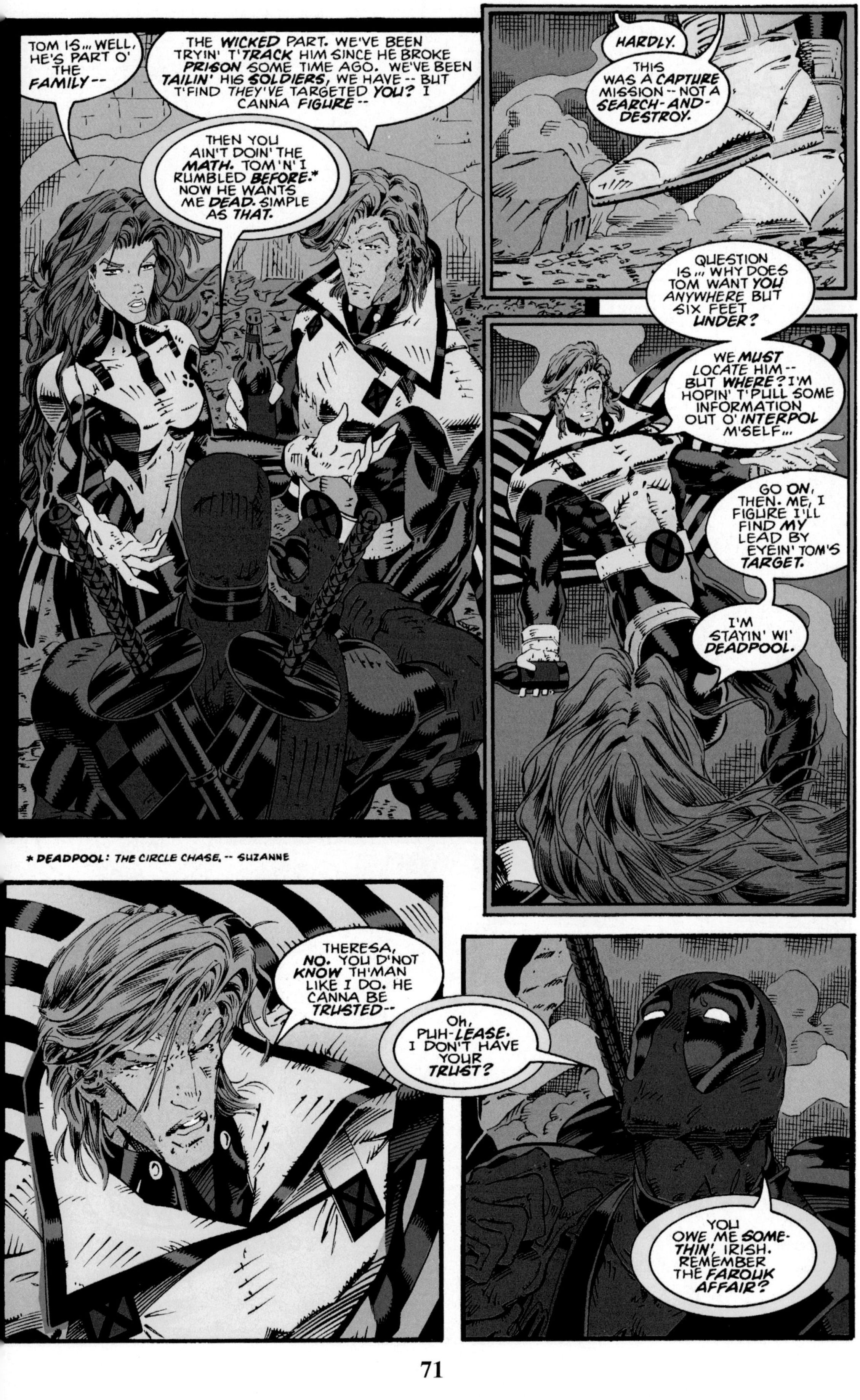
TOM IS... WELL, HE'S PART O' THE FAMILY--
THE WICKED PART. WE'VE BEEN TRYIN' T'TRACK HIM SINCE HE BROKE PRISON SOME TIME AGO. WE'VE BEEN TAILIN' HIS SOLDIERS, WE HAVE -- BUT T'FIND THEY'VE TARGETED YOU? I CANNA FIGURE --
THEN YOU AIN'T DOIN' THE MATH. TOM 'N' I RUMBLED BEFORE.* NOW HE WANTS ME DEAD. SIMPLE AS THAT.
HARDLY.
THIS WAS A CAPTURE MISSION -- NOT A SEARCH-AND-DESTROY.
QUESTION IS... WHY DOES TOM WANT YOU ANYWHERE BUT SIX FEET UNDER?
WE MUST LOCATE HIM -- BUT WHERE? I'M HOPIN' T'PULL SOME INFORMATION OUT O' INTERPOL M'SELF...
GO ON, THEN. ME, I FIGURE I'LL FIND MY LEAD BY EYEIN' TOM'S TARGET.
I'M STAYIN' WI' DEADPOOL.
THERESA, NO. YOU D'NOT KNOW TH'MAN LIKE I DO. HE CANNA BE TRUSTED--
Oh, PUH-LEASE. I DON'T HAVE YOUR TRUST?
YOU OWE ME SOME-THIN', IRISH. REMEMBER THE FAROUK AFFAIR?

* DEADPOOL: THE CIRCLE CHASE. -- SUZANNE

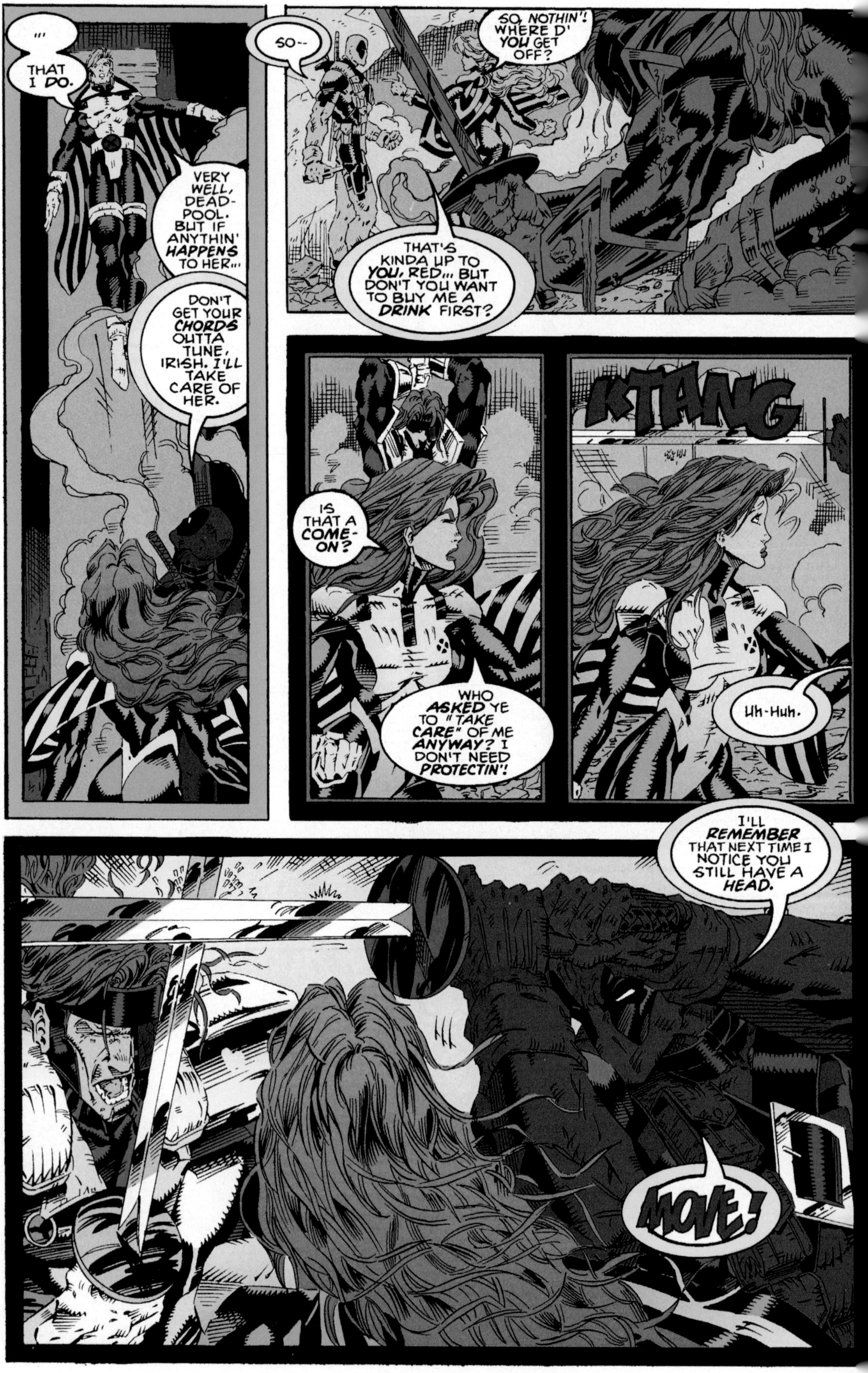
...
THAT I DO.
SO--
SO, NOTHIN'! WHERE D' YOU GET OFF?
VERY WELL, DEAD-POOL. BUT IF ANYTHIN' HAPPENS TO HER...
THAT'S KINDA UP TO YOU, RED... BUT DON'T YOU WANT TO BUY ME A DRINK FIRST?
DON'T GET YOUR CHORDS OUTTA TUNE, IRISH. I'LL TAKE CARE OF HER.
IS THAT A COME-ON?
KTANG
WHO ASKED YE TO "TAKE CARE" OF ME ANYWAY? I DON'T NEED PROTECTIN'!
Uh-Huh.
I'LL REMEMBER THAT NEXT TIME I NOTICE YOU STILL HAVE A HEAD.
MOVE!

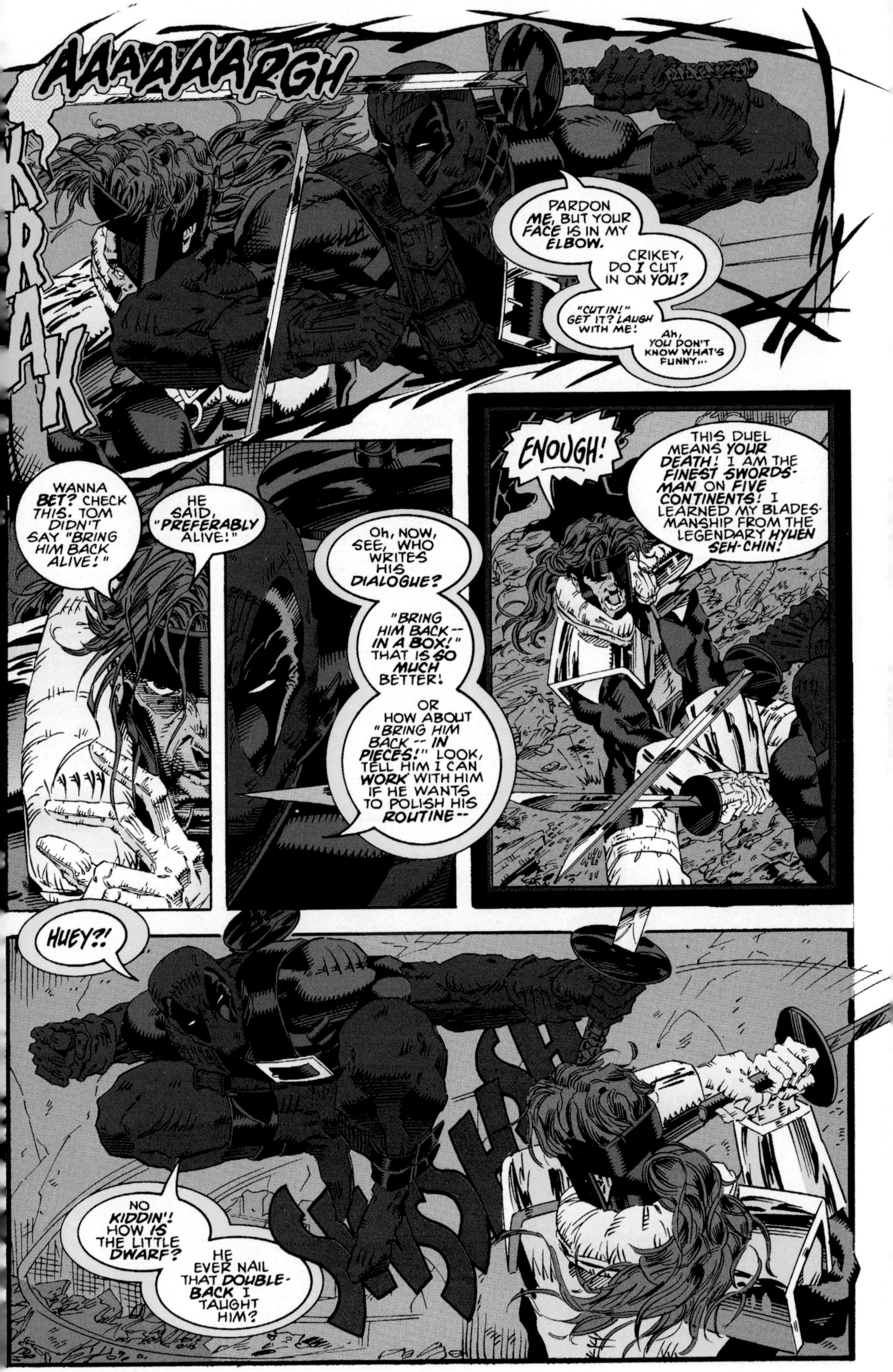
AAAAAARGH
KRAK
PARDON ME, BUT YOUR FACE IS IN MY ELBOW.
CRIKEY, DO I CUT IN ON YOU?
"CUT IN!" GET IT? LAUGH WITH ME!
Ah, YOU DON'T KNOW WHAT'S FUNNY...
WANNA BET? CHECK THIS. TOM DIDN'T SAY "BRING HIM BACK ALIVE!"
HE SAID, "PREFERABLY ALIVE!"
Oh, NOW, SEE, WHO WRITES HIS DIALOGUE?
"BRING HIM BACK -- IN A BOX!" THAT IS SO MUCH BETTER!
OR HOW ABOUT "BRING HIM BACK -- IN PIECES!" LOOK, TELL HIM I CAN WORK WITH HIM IF HE WANTS TO POLISH HIS ROUTINE --
ENOUGH!
THIS DUEL MEANS YOUR DEATH! I AM THE FINEST SWORDSMAN ON FIVE CONTINENTS! I LEARNED MY BLADESMANSHIP FROM THE LEGENDARY HYUEN SEH-CHIN!
HUEY?!
NO KIDDIN'! HOW IS THE LITTLE DWARF?
HE EVER NAIL THAT DOUBLE-BACK I TAUGHT HIM?
SHASH

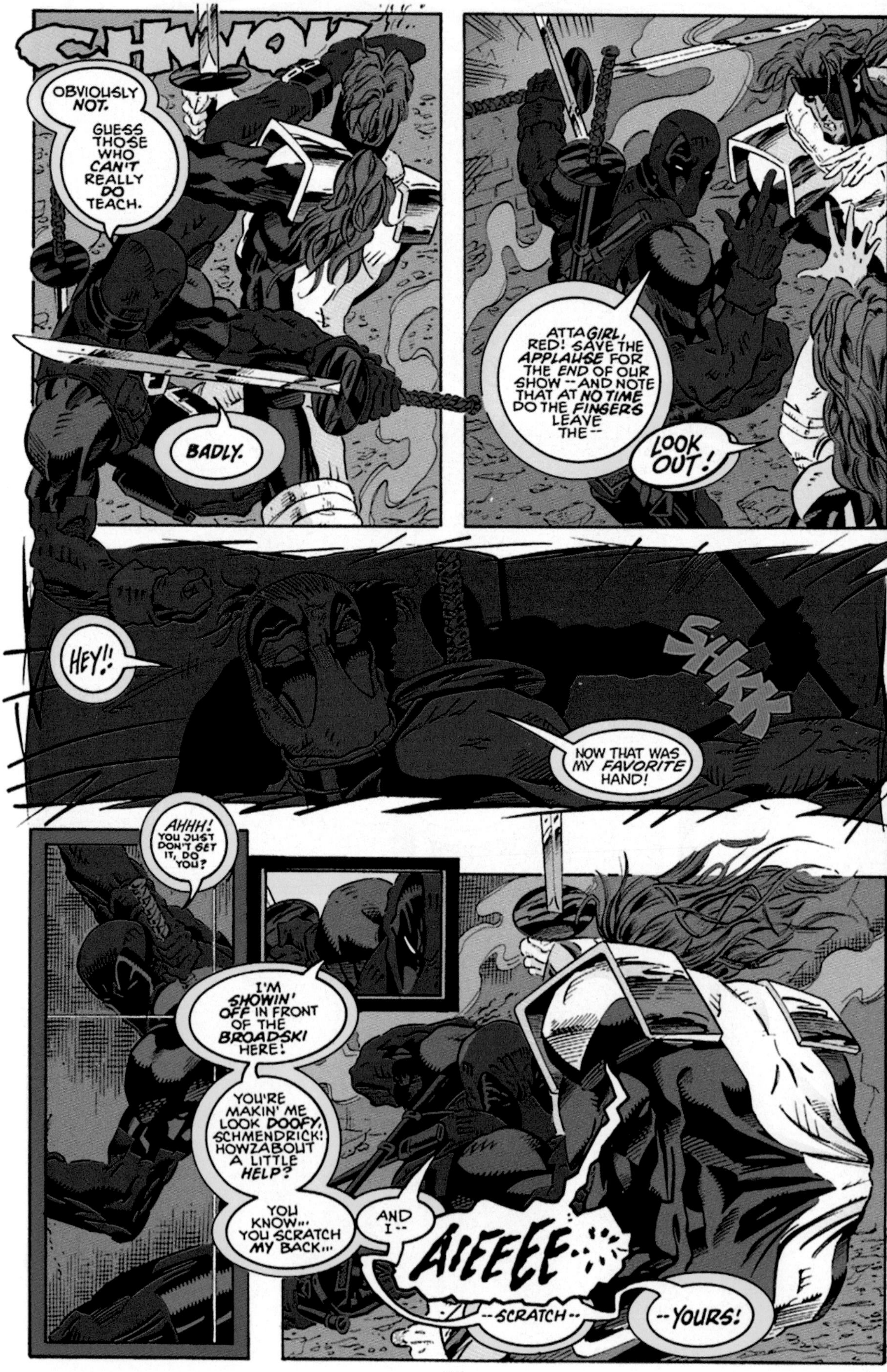
CHWOW
OBVIOUSLY NOT.
GUESS THOSE WHO CAN'T REALLY DO TEACH.
BADLY.
ATTAGIRL, RED! SAVE THE APPLAUSE FOR THE END OF OUR SHOW -- AND NOTE THAT AT NO TIME DO THE FINGERS LEAVE THE --
LOOK OUT!
HEY!!
SHKK
NOW THAT WAS MY FAVORITE HAND!
AHHH! YOU JUST DON'T GET IT, DO YOU?
I'M SHOWIN' OFF IN FRONT OF THE BROADSKI HERE!
YOU'RE MAKIN' ME LOOK DOOFY, SCHMENDRICK! HOWZABOUT A LITTLE HELP?
YOU KNOW... YOU SCRATCH MY BACK...
AND I --
AIEEEE
-- SCRATCH --
-- YOURS!

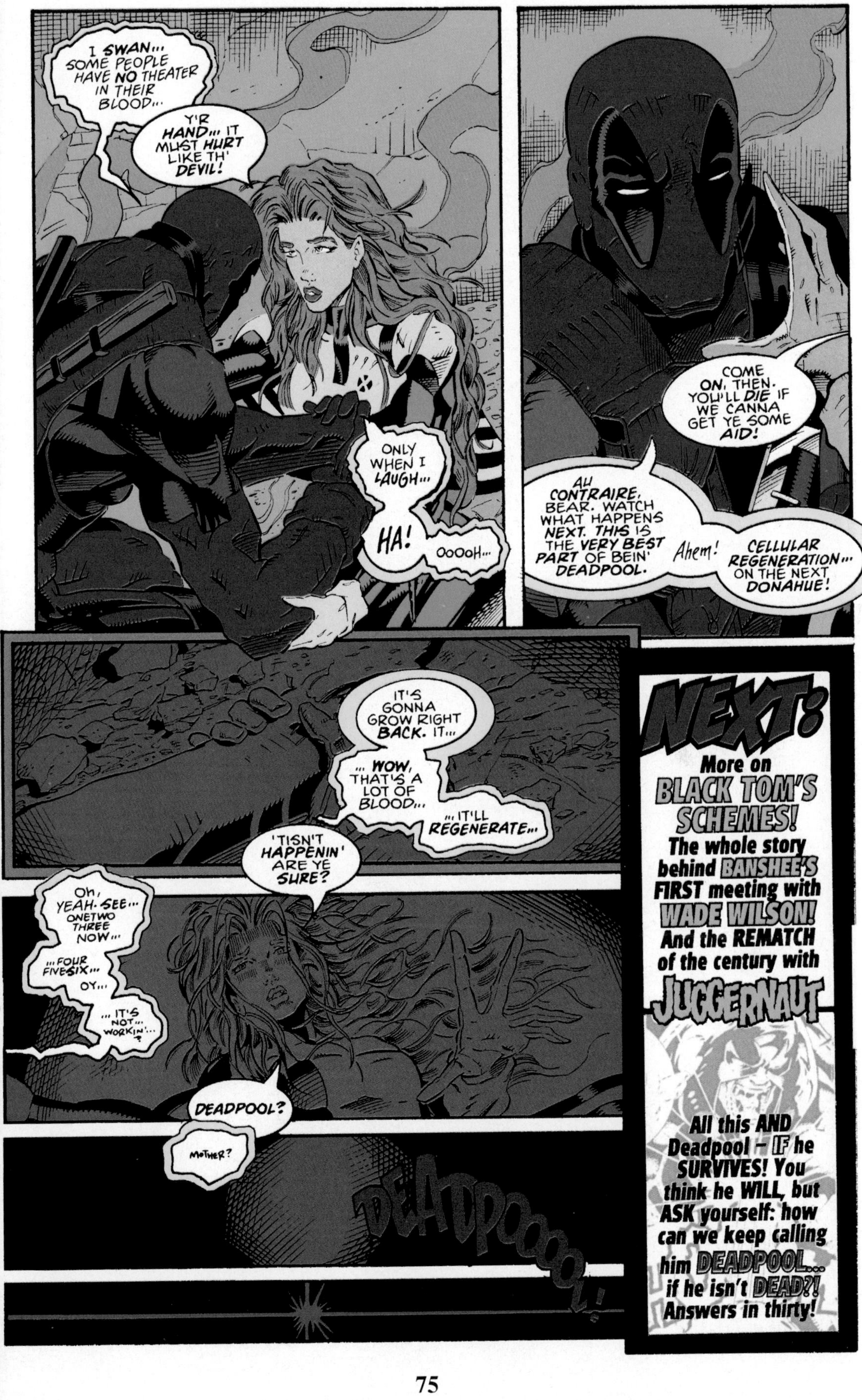

I SWAN... SOME PEOPLE HAVE NO THEATER IN THEIR BLOOD...
Y'R HAND... IT MUST HURT LIKE TH' DEVIL!
ONLY WHEN I LAUGH...
HA!
OOOOH...
COME ON, THEN. YOU'LL DIE IF WE CANNA GET YE SOME AID!
AU CONTRAIRE, BEAR. WATCH WHAT HAPPENS NEXT. THIS IS THE VERY BEST PART OF BEIN' DEADPOOL.
Ahem!
CELLULAR REGENERATION... ON THE NEXT DONAHUE!
IT'S GONNA GROW RIGHT BACK. IT...
... WOW, THAT'S A LOT OF BLOOD...
... IT'LL REGENERATE...
'TISN'T HAPPENIN' ARE YE SURE?
Oh, YEAH. SEE... ONETWO THREE NOW...
...FOUR FIVESIX... OY...
... IT'S NOT WORKIN'...?
DEADPOOL?
MOTHER?
DEADPOOOOOL!
NEXT:
More on BLACK TOM'S SCHEMES!
The whole story behind BANSHEE'S FIRST meeting with WADE WILSON!
And the REMATCH of the century with JUGGERNAUT
All this AND Deadpool – IF he SURVIVES! You think he WILL, but ASK yourself: how can we keep calling him DEADPOOL... if he isn't DEAD?!
Answers in thirty!

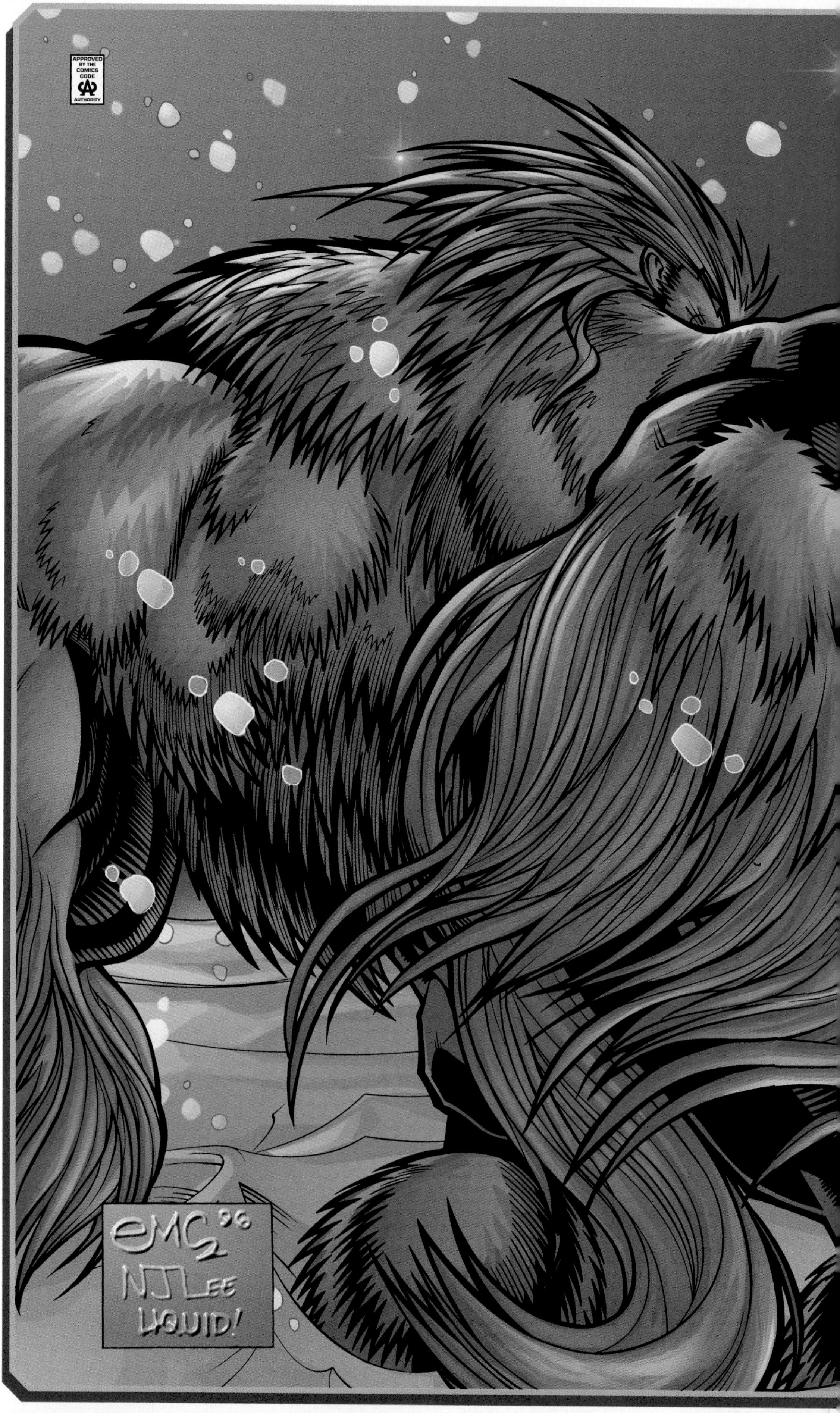
APPROVED BY THE COMICS CODE AUTHORITY
eMC2 96
NJLee
LIQUID!

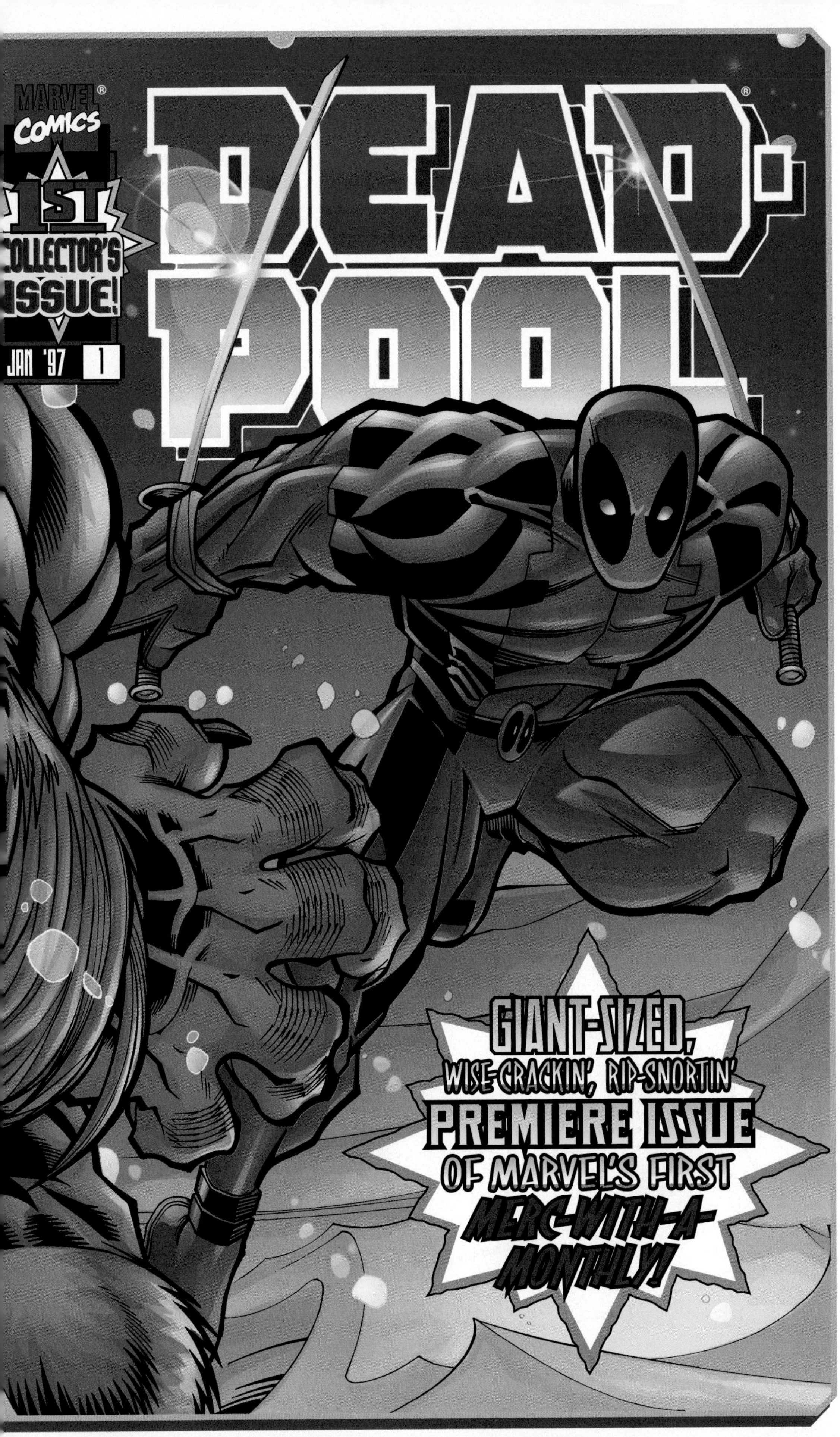
MARVEL® COMICS
1ST COLLECTOR'S ISSUE!
JAN '97 1
DEADPOOL®
GIANT-SIZED,
WISE-CRACKIN', RIP-SNORTIN'
PREMIERE ISSUE
OF MARVEL'S FIRST
MERC-WITH-A-MONTHLY!

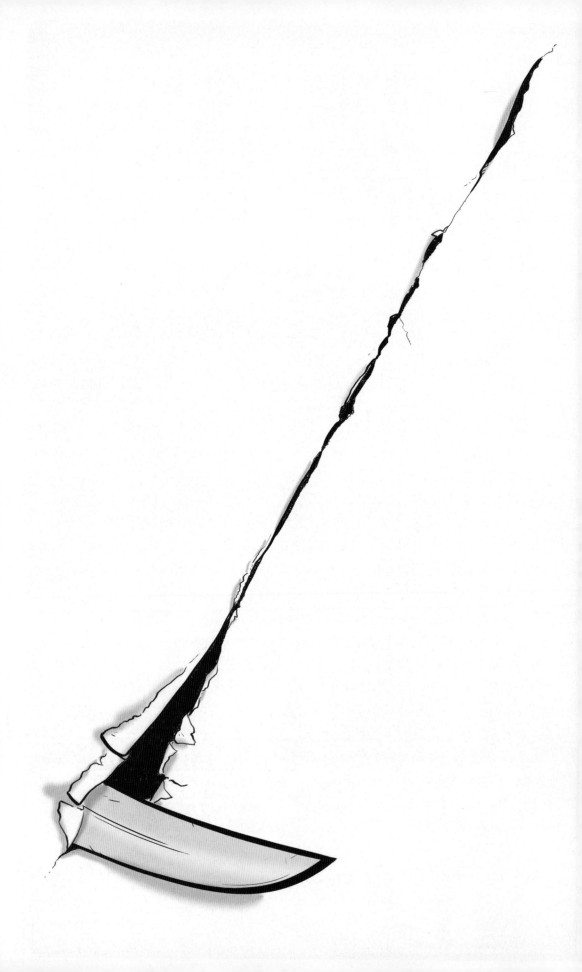

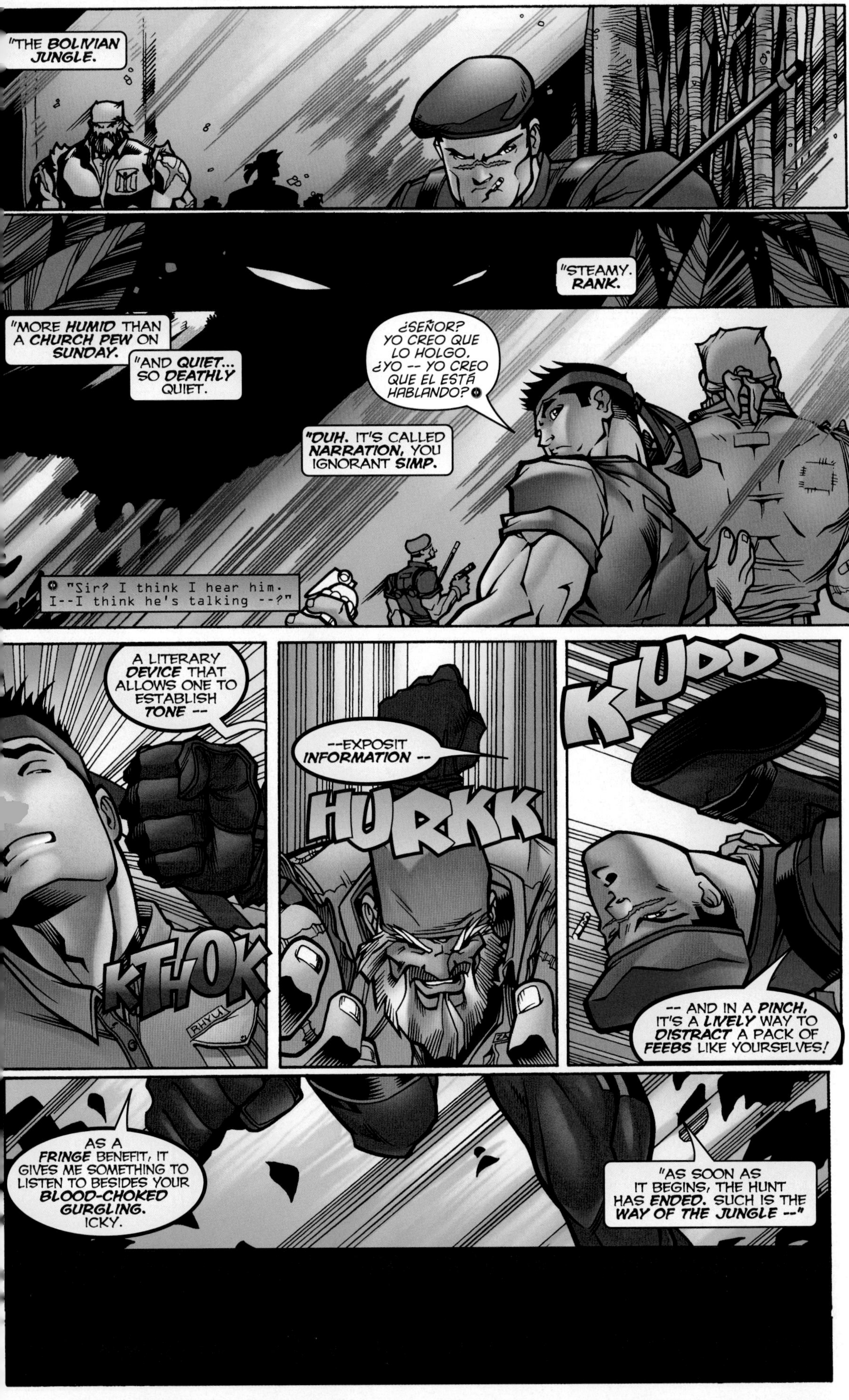
"THE BOLIVIAN JUNGLE.
"STEAMY. RANK.
"MORE HUMID THAN A CHURCH PEW ON SUNDAY.
"AND QUIET... SO DEATHLY QUIET.
¿SEÑOR? YO CREO QUE LO HOLGO. ¿YO -- YO CREO QUE EL ESTÁ HABLANDO?
"DUH. IT'S CALLED NARRATION, YOU IGNORANT SIMP.
"Sir? I think I hear him. I--I think he's talking --?"
A LITERARY DEVICE THAT ALLOWS ONE TO ESTABLISH TONE --
KTHOK
RHYU
--EXPOSIT INFORMATION --
HURKK
KLUDD
-- AND IN A PINCH, IT'S A LIVELY WAY TO DISTRACT A PACK OF FEEBS LIKE YOURSELVES!
AS A FRINGE BENEFIT, IT GIVES ME SOMETHING TO LISTEN TO BESIDES YOUR BLOOD-CHOKED GURGLING. ICKY.
"AS SOON AS IT BEGINS, THE HUNT HAS ENDED. SUCH IS THE WAY OF THE JUNGLE --"

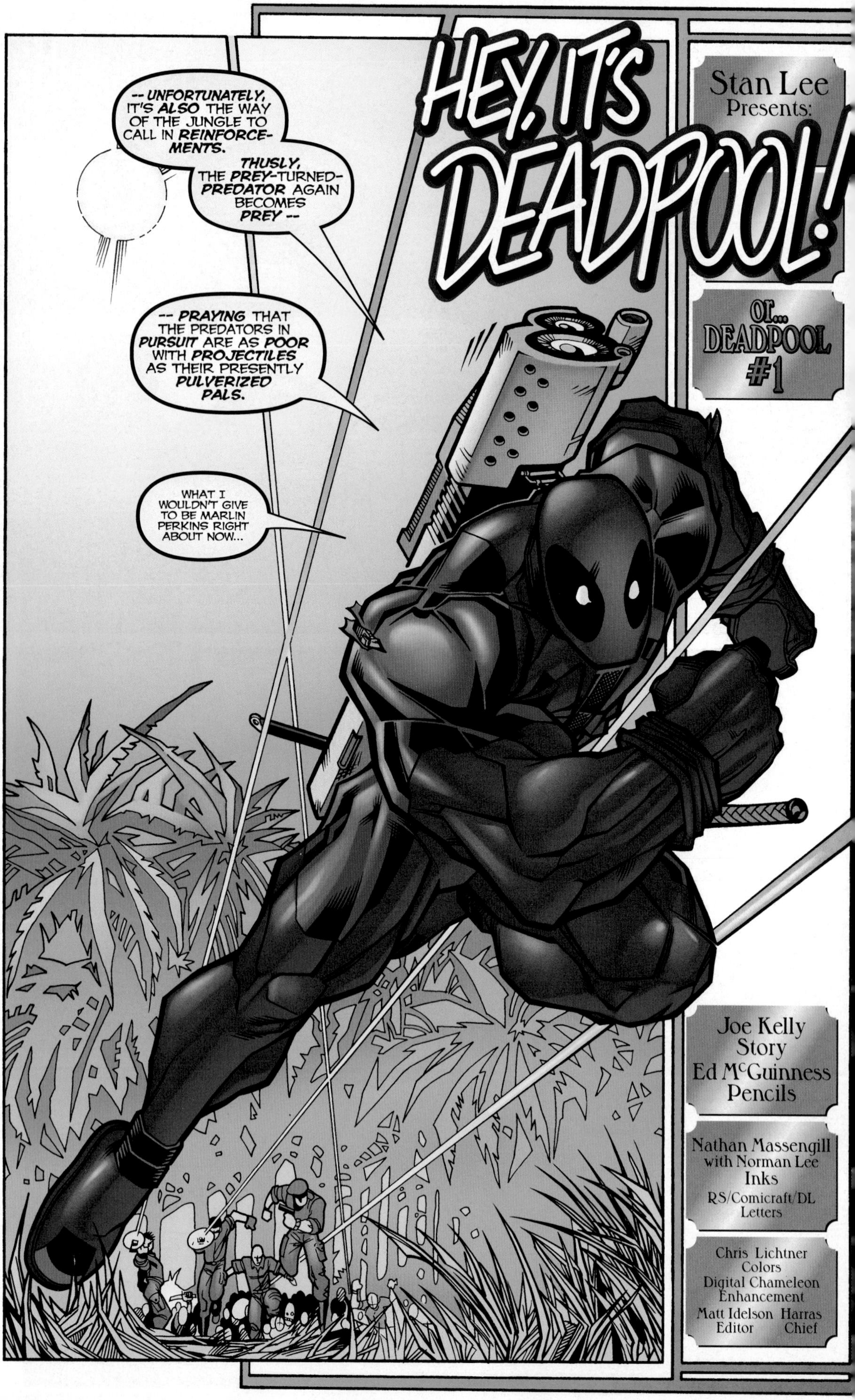
-- UNFORTUNATELY, IT'S ALSO THE WAY OF THE JUNGLE TO CALL IN REINFORCE- MENTS.
THUSLY, THE PREY-TURNED-PREDATOR AGAIN BECOMES PREY --
-- PRAYING THAT THE PREDATORS IN PURSUIT ARE AS POOR WITH PROJECTILES AS THEIR PRESENTLY PULVERIZED PALS.
WHAT I WOULDN'T GIVE TO BE MARLIN PERKINS RIGHT ABOUT NOW...
HEY, IT'S DEADPOOL!
Stan Lee Presents:
Or... DEADPOOL #1
Joe Kelly Story
Ed McGuinness Pencils
Nathan Massengill with Norman Lee Inks
RS/Comicraft/DL Letters
Chris Lichtner Colors
Digital Chameleon Enhancement
Matt Idelson Editor
Harras Chief

OR AT LEAST GET THE **POWER** IN MY FREAKIN' **FRAGGIN'** TELEPORTER BACK ON-LINE!

I SWEAR, IF **WEASEL** TOOK THE **BATTERIES** OUT OF MY SUIT TO RUN HIS **GAME-BOY** AGAIN --

TEK TEK TEK

-- I'M GONNA **SUPER-MARIO** HIS SORRY **BUTT** INTO A **BODY CAST!**

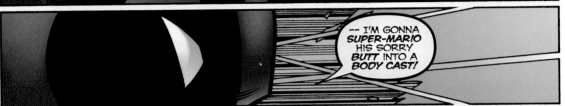

PWANGG

"PWANGG?"

TREES DON'T GO "PWANGG --"

LLAMAS DON'T GO "PWANGG--"

NOTHING FOUND IN **NATURE** GOES "PWANGG", WHICH MEANS --

-- WE'RE OFFICIALLY **HIP DEEP** IN THE **SMELLY STUFF.** LIKE, **POP QUIZ,** HOTSHOT.

YOU'RE **NOSE-TO-KNEE** WITH A **FIREBALL XLS THUNDERBIRD SUPER DUPER** SET OF **TITANIUM UNDER-ROOS!** WHAT DO YOU DO, DUDE?

WHAT DO YOU DO?!

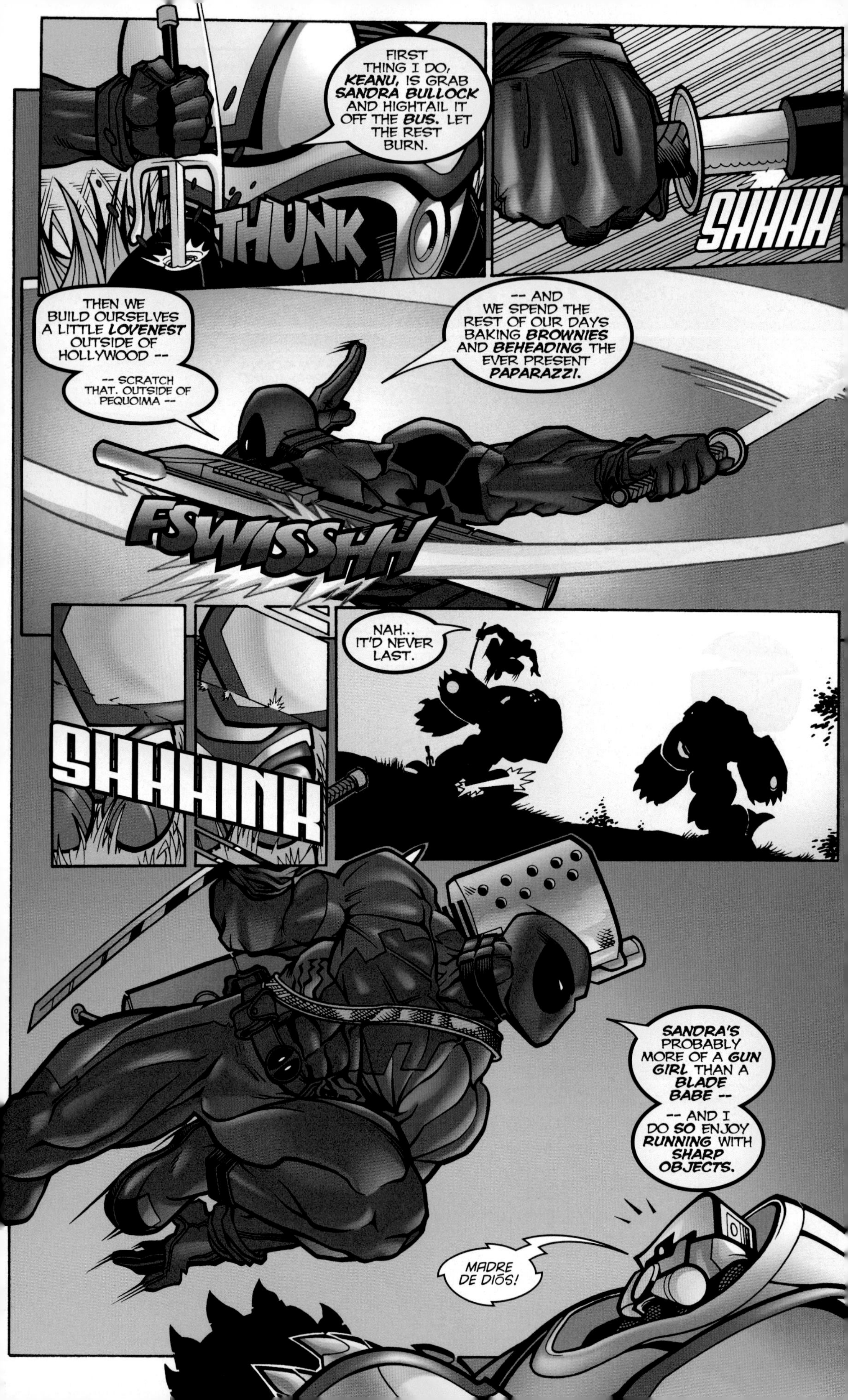
FIRST THING I DO, KEANU, IS GRAB SANDRA BULLOCK AND HIGHTAIL IT OFF THE BUS. LET THE REST BURN.
THUNK
SHHHH
THEN WE BUILD OURSELVES A LITTLE LOVENEST OUTSIDE OF HOLLYWOOD --
-- SCRATCH THAT. OUTSIDE OF PEQUOIMA --
-- AND WE SPEND THE REST OF OUR DAYS BAKING BROWNIES AND BEHEADING THE EVER PRESENT PAPARAZZI.
FSWISSHH
SHHINK
NAH... IT'D NEVER LAST.
SANDRA'S PROBABLY MORE OF A GUN GIRL THAN A BLADE BABE --
-- AND I DO SO ENJOY RUNNING WITH SHARP OBJECTS.
MADRE DE DIÓS!

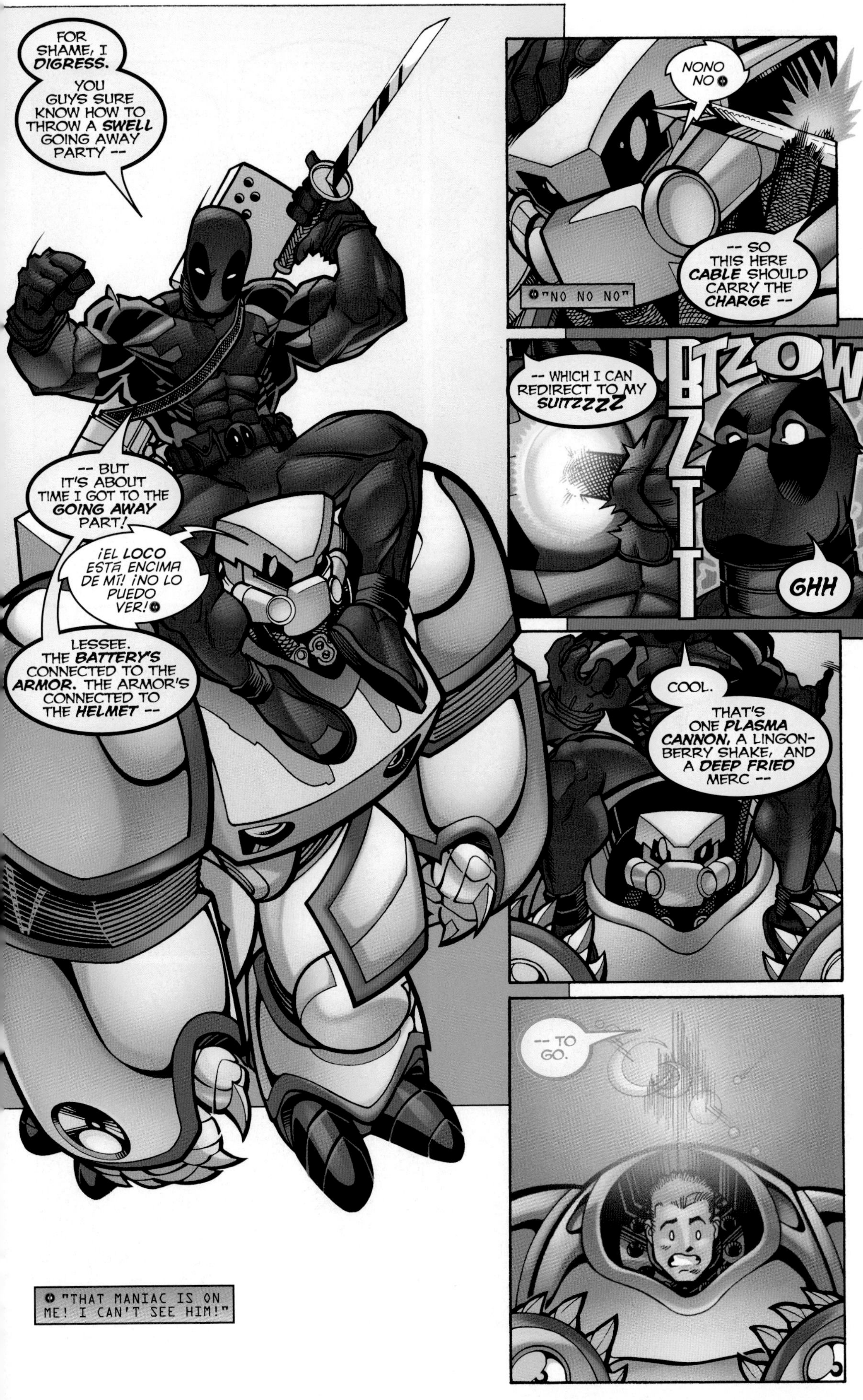

FOR SHAME, I DIGRESS.
YOU GUYS SURE KNOW HOW TO THROW A SWELL GOING AWAY PARTY --
-- BUT IT'S ABOUT TIME I GOT TO THE GOING AWAY PART!
¡EL LOCO ESTÁ ENCIMA DE MÍ! ¡NO LO PUEDO VER!
LESSEE. THE BATTERY'S CONNECTED TO THE ARMOR. THE ARMOR'S CONNECTED TO THE HELMET --
"THAT MANIAC IS ON ME! I CAN'T SEE HIM!"
NONO NO
"NO NO NO"
-- SO THIS HERE CABLE SHOULD CARRY THE CHARGE --
-- WHICH I CAN REDIRECT TO MY SUITZZZZ
BZZT
TZOW
GHH
COOL.
THAT'S ONE PLASMA CANNON, A LINGON-BERRY SHAKE, AND A DEEP FRIED MERC --
-- TO GO.

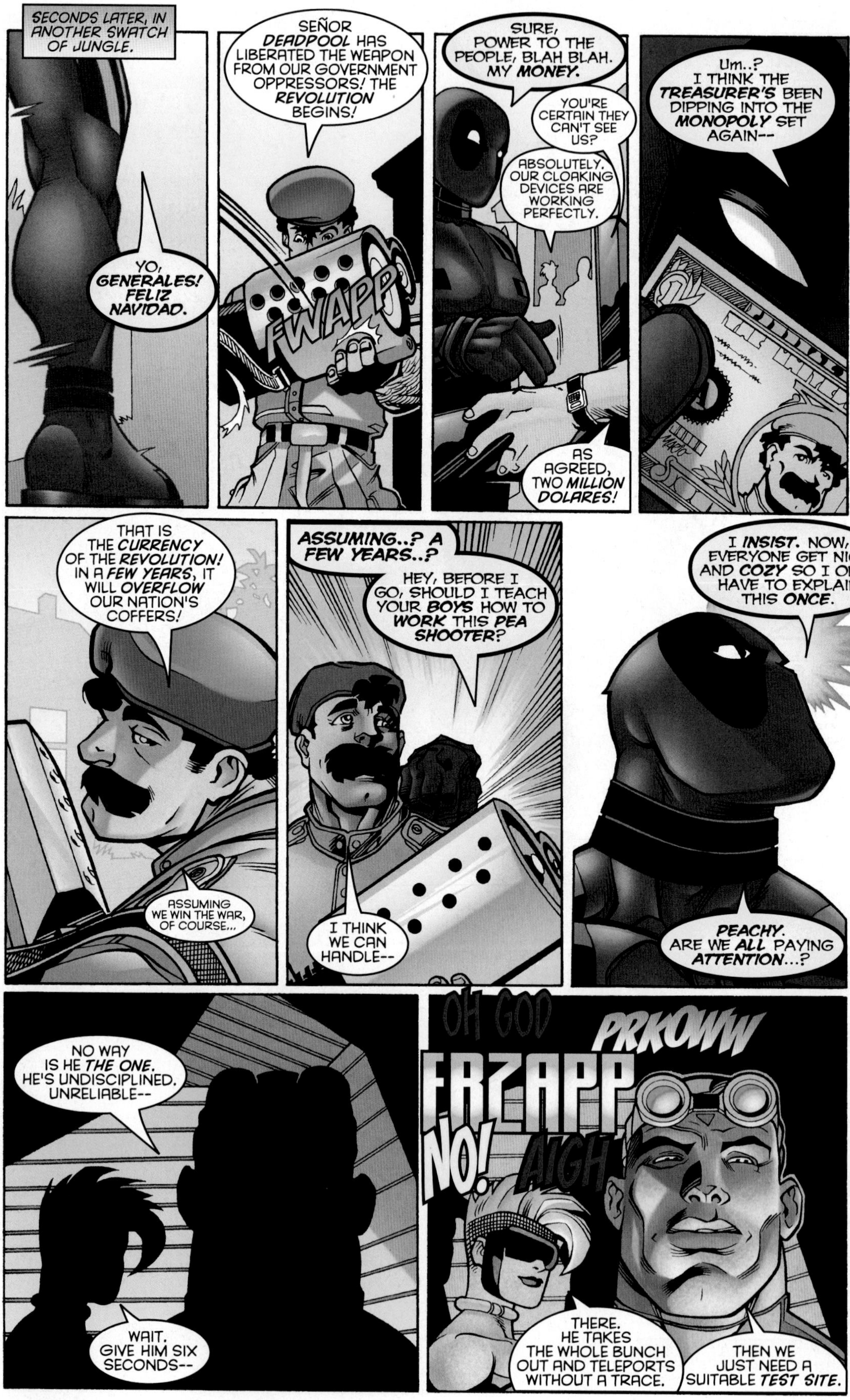
SECONDS LATER, IN ANOTHER SWATCH OF JUNGLE.
YO, GENERALES! FELIZ NAVIDAD.
SEÑOR DEADPOOL HAS LIBERATED THE WEAPON FROM OUR GOVERNMENT OPPRESSORS! THE REVOLUTION BEGINS!
FWAPP
SURE, POWER TO THE PEOPLE, BLAH BLAH. MY MONEY.
YOU'RE CERTAIN THEY CAN'T SEE US?
ABSOLUTELY. OUR CLOAKING DEVICES ARE WORKING PERFECTLY.
AS AGREED, TWO MILLION DOLARES!
Um..? I THINK THE TREASURER'S BEEN DIPPING INTO THE MONOPOLY SET AGAIN--
THAT IS THE CURRENCY OF THE REVOLUTION! IN A FEW YEARS, IT WILL OVERFLOW OUR NATION'S COFFERS!
ASSUMING WE WIN THE WAR, OF COURSE...
ASSUMING..? A FEW YEARS..?
HEY, BEFORE I GO, SHOULD I TEACH YOUR BOYS HOW TO WORK THIS PEA SHOOTER?
I THINK WE CAN HANDLE--
I INSIST. NOW, EVERYONE GET NICE AND COZY SO I ONLY HAVE TO EXPLAIN THIS ONCE.
PEACHY. ARE WE ALL PAYING ATTENTION...?
NO WAY IS HE THE ONE. HE'S UNDISCIPLINED. UNRELIABLE--
WAIT. GIVE HIM SIX SECONDS--
OH GOD
PRKOWW
FRZAPP
NO!
AIGH
THERE. HE TAKES THE WHOLE BUNCH OUT AND TELEPORTS WITHOUT A TRACE.
THEN WE JUST NEED A SUITABLE TEST SITE.

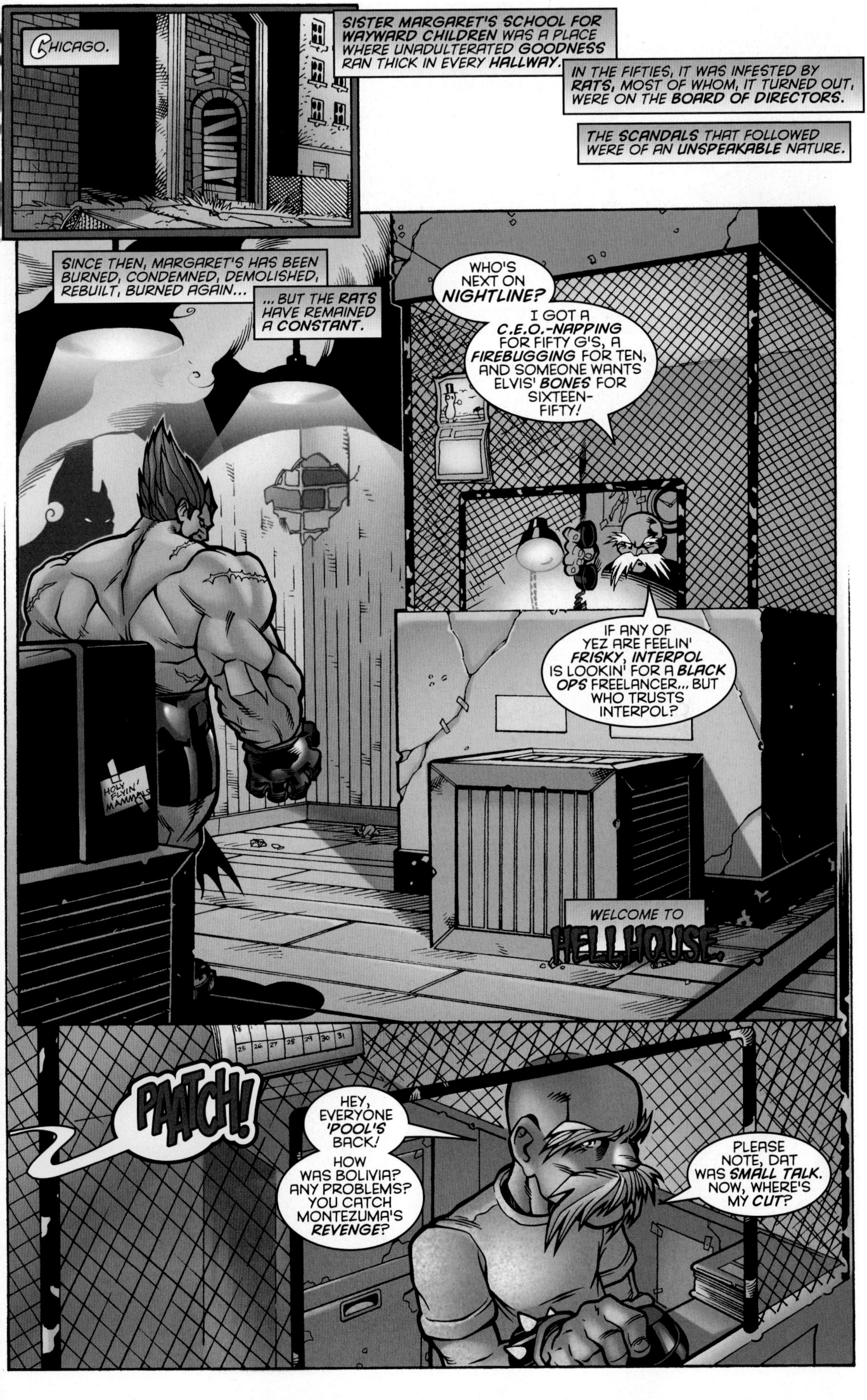
CHICAGO.
SISTER MARGARET'S SCHOOL FOR WAYWARD CHILDREN WAS A PLACE WHERE UNADULTERATED GOODNESS RAN THICK IN EVERY HALLWAY.
IN THE FIFTIES, IT WAS INFESTED BY RATS, MOST OF WHOM, IT TURNED OUT, WERE ON THE BOARD OF DIRECTORS.
THE SCANDALS THAT FOLLOWED WERE OF AN UNSPEAKABLE NATURE.
SINCE THEN, MARGARET'S HAS BEEN BURNED, CONDEMNED, DEMOLISHED, REBUILT, BURNED AGAIN...
...BUT THE RATS HAVE REMAINED A CONSTANT.
WHO'S NEXT ON NIGHTLINE?
I GOT A C.E.O.-NAPPING FOR FIFTY G'S, A FIREBUGGING FOR TEN, AND SOMEONE WANTS ELVIS' BONES FOR SIXTEEN-FIFTY!
IF ANY OF YEZ ARE FEELIN' FRISKY, INTERPOL IS LOOKIN' FOR A BLACK OPS FREELANCER... BUT WHO TRUSTS INTERPOL?
HOLY FLYIN' MAMMALS
WELCOME TO
HELLHOUSE.
PAATCH!
HEY, EVERYONE 'POOL'S BACK!
HOW WAS BOLIVIA? ANY PROBLEMS? YOU CATCH MONTEZUMA'S REVENGE?
PLEASE NOTE, DAT WAS SMALL TALK. NOW, WHERE'S MY CUT?

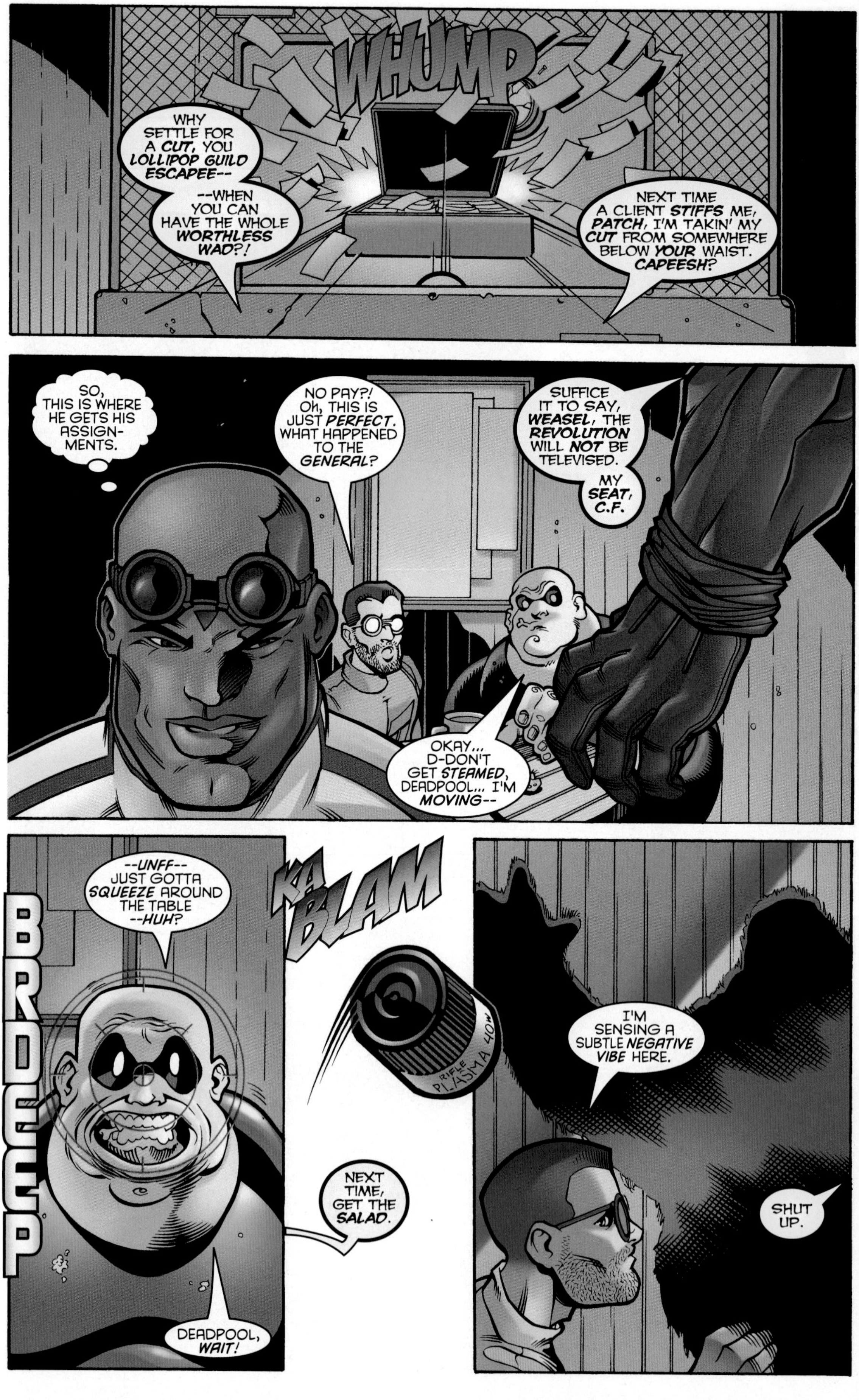
WHUMP
WHY SETTLE FOR A CUT, YOU LOLLIPOP GUILD ESCAPEE--
--WHEN YOU CAN HAVE THE WHOLE WORTHLESS WAD?!
NEXT TIME A CLIENT STIFFS ME, PATCH, I'M TAKIN' MY CUT FROM SOMEWHERE BELOW YOUR WAIST. CAPEESH?
SO, THIS IS WHERE HE GETS HIS ASSIGN-MENTS.
NO PAY?! Oh, THIS IS JUST PERFECT. WHAT HAPPENED TO THE GENERAL?
SUFFICE IT TO SAY, WEASEL, THE REVOLUTION WILL NOT BE TELEVISED.
MY SEAT, C.F.
OKAY... D-DON'T GET STEAMED, DEADPOOL... I'M MOVING--
--UNFF-- JUST GOTTA SQUEEZE AROUND THE TABLE --HUH?
BRDEEP
KA BLAM
RIFLE PLASMA 40W
NEXT TIME, GET THE SALAD.
DEADPOOL, WAIT!
I'M SENSING A SUBTLE NEGATIVE VIBE HERE.
SHUT UP.

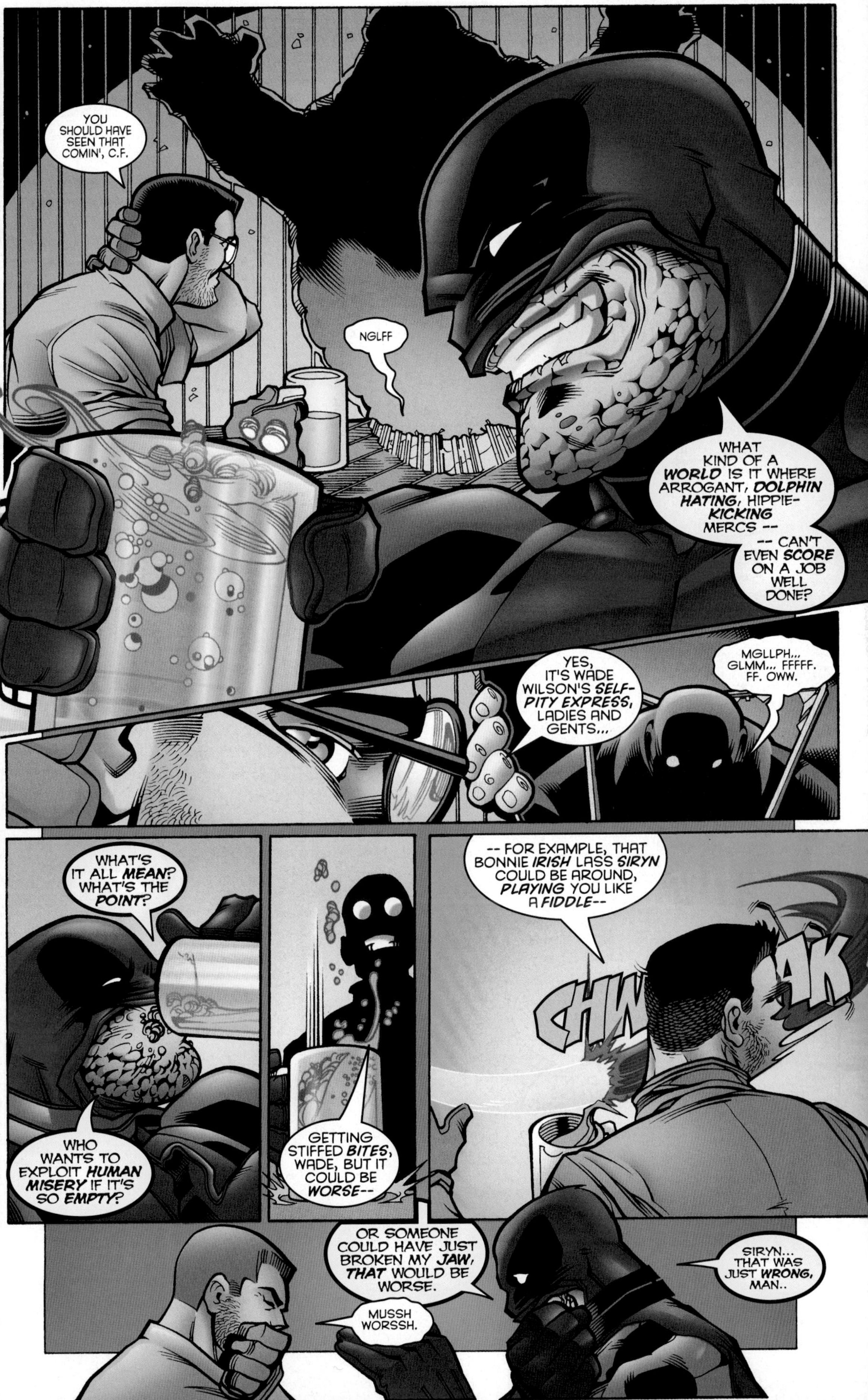
YOU SHOULD HAVE SEEN THAT COMIN', C.F.
NGLFF
WHAT KIND OF A WORLD IS IT WHERE ARROGANT, DOLPHIN HATING, HIPPIE-KICKING MERCS --
-- CAN'T EVEN SCORE ON A JOB WELL DONE?
YES, IT'S WADE WILSON'S SELF-PITY EXPRESS, LADIES AND GENTS...
MGLLPH... GLMM... FFFFF. FF. OWW.
WHAT'S IT ALL MEAN? WHAT'S THE POINT?
WHO WANTS TO EXPLOIT HUMAN MISERY IF IT'S SO EMPTY?
GETTING STIFFED BITES, WADE, BUT IT COULD BE WORSE--
-- FOR EXAMPLE, THAT BONNIE IRISH LASS SIRYN COULD BE AROUND, PLAYING YOU LIKE A FIDDLE--
CHW AK
OR SOMEONE COULD HAVE JUST BROKEN MY JAW, THAT WOULD BE WORSE.
MUSSH WORSSH.
SIRYN... THAT WAS JUST WRONG, MAN..

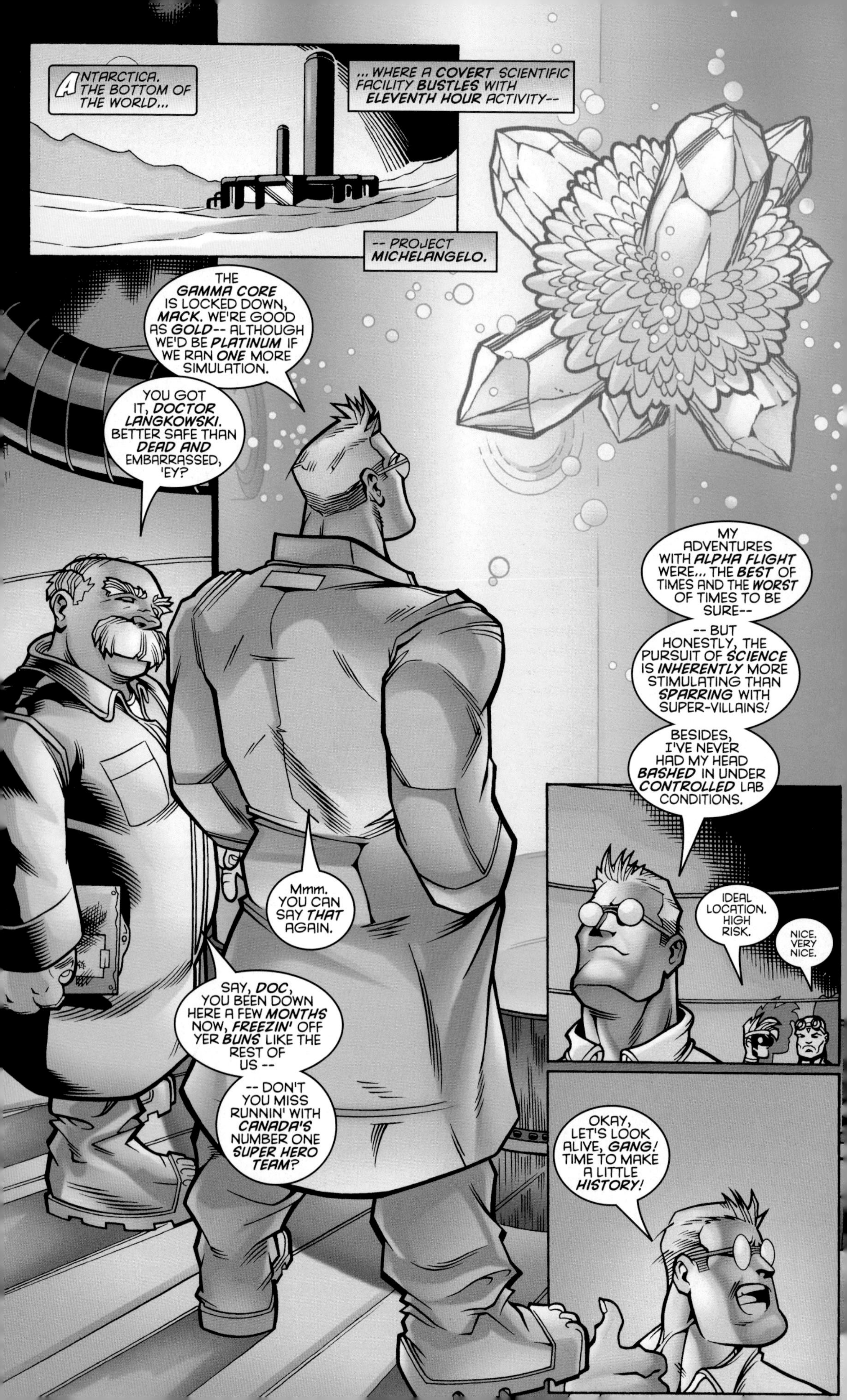

ANTARCTICA. THE BOTTOM OF THE WORLD...
...WHERE A COVERT SCIENTIFIC FACILITY BUSTLES WITH ELEVENTH HOUR ACTIVITY--
-- PROJECT MICHELANGELO.
THE GAMMA CORE IS LOCKED DOWN, MACK. WE'RE GOOD AS GOLD-- ALTHOUGH WE'D BE PLATINUM IF WE RAN ONE MORE SIMULATION.
YOU GOT IT, DOCTOR LANGKOWSKI. BETTER SAFE THAN DEAD AND EMBARRASSED, 'EY?
Mmm. YOU CAN SAY THAT AGAIN.
SAY, DOC, YOU BEEN DOWN HERE A FEW MONTHS NOW, FREEZIN' OFF YER BUNS LIKE THE REST OF US --
-- DON'T YOU MISS RUNNIN' WITH CANADA'S NUMBER ONE SUPER HERO TEAM?
MY ADVENTURES WITH ALPHA FLIGHT WERE... THE BEST OF TIMES AND THE WORST OF TIMES TO BE SURE--
-- BUT HONESTLY, THE PURSUIT OF SCIENCE IS INHERENTLY MORE STIMULATING THAN SPARRING WITH SUPER-VILLAINS!
BESIDES, I'VE NEVER HAD MY HEAD BASHED IN UNDER CONTROLLED LAB CONDITIONS.
IDEAL LOCATION. HIGH RISK.
NICE. VERY NICE.
OKAY, LET'S LOOK ALIVE, GANG! TIME TO MAKE A LITTLE HISTORY!

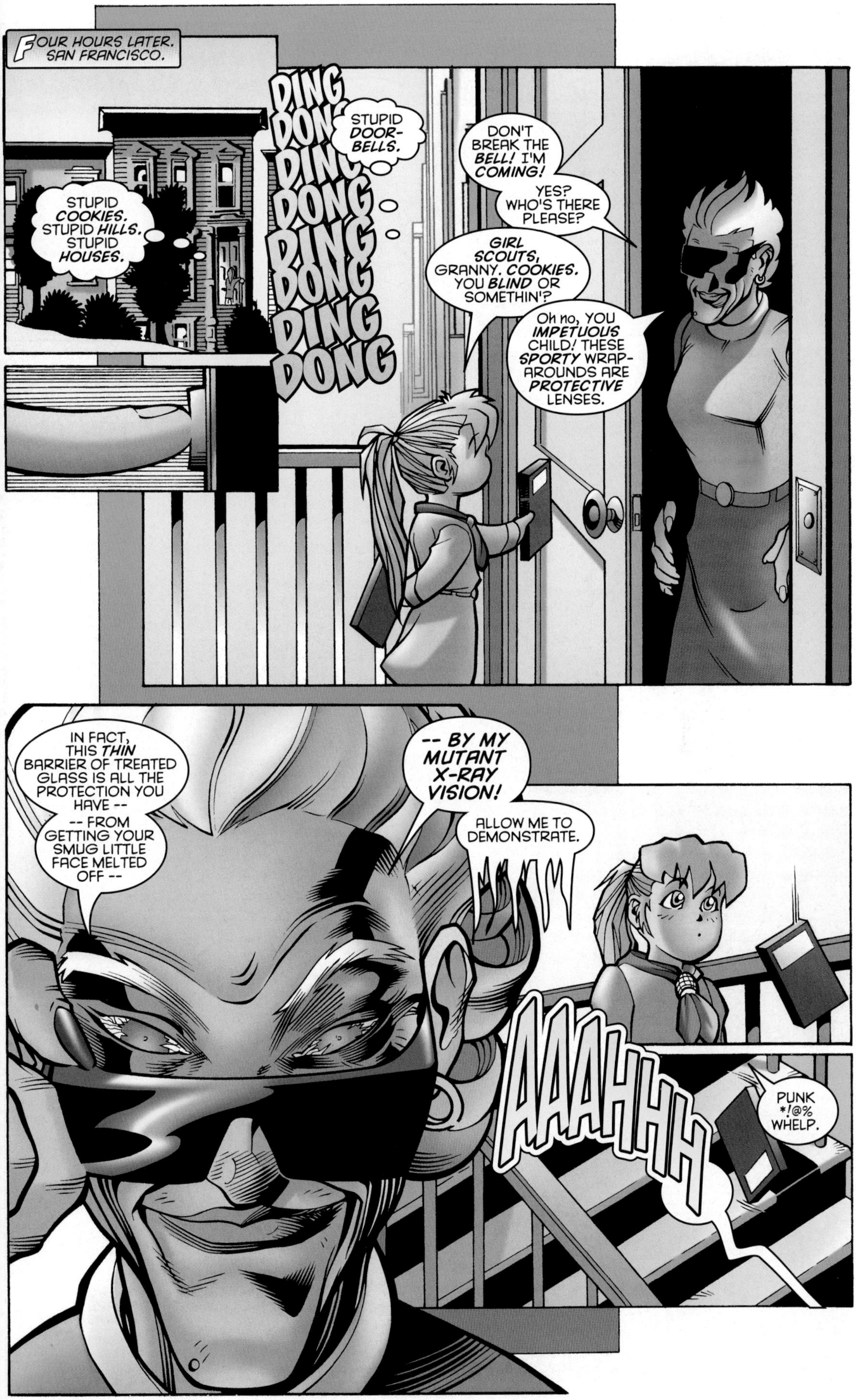

FOUR HOURS LATER. SAN FRANCISCO.
STUPID COOKIES. STUPID HILLS. STUPID HOUSES.
DING DONG DING DONG DING DONG DING DONG
STUPID DOORBELLS.
DON'T BREAK THE BELL! I'M COMING!
YES? WHO'S THERE PLEASE?
GIRL SCOUTS, GRANNY. COOKIES. YOU BLIND OR SOMETHIN'?
Oh no, YOU IMPETUOUS CHILD! THESE SPORTY WRAP-AROUNDS ARE PROTECTIVE LENSES.
IN FACT, THIS THIN BARRIER OF TREATED GLASS IS ALL THE PROTECTION YOU HAVE --
-- FROM GETTING YOUR SMUG LITTLE FACE MELTED OFF --
-- BY MY MUTANT X-RAY VISION!
ALLOW ME TO DEMONSTRATE.
AAAHHHH
PUNK *!@% WHELP.

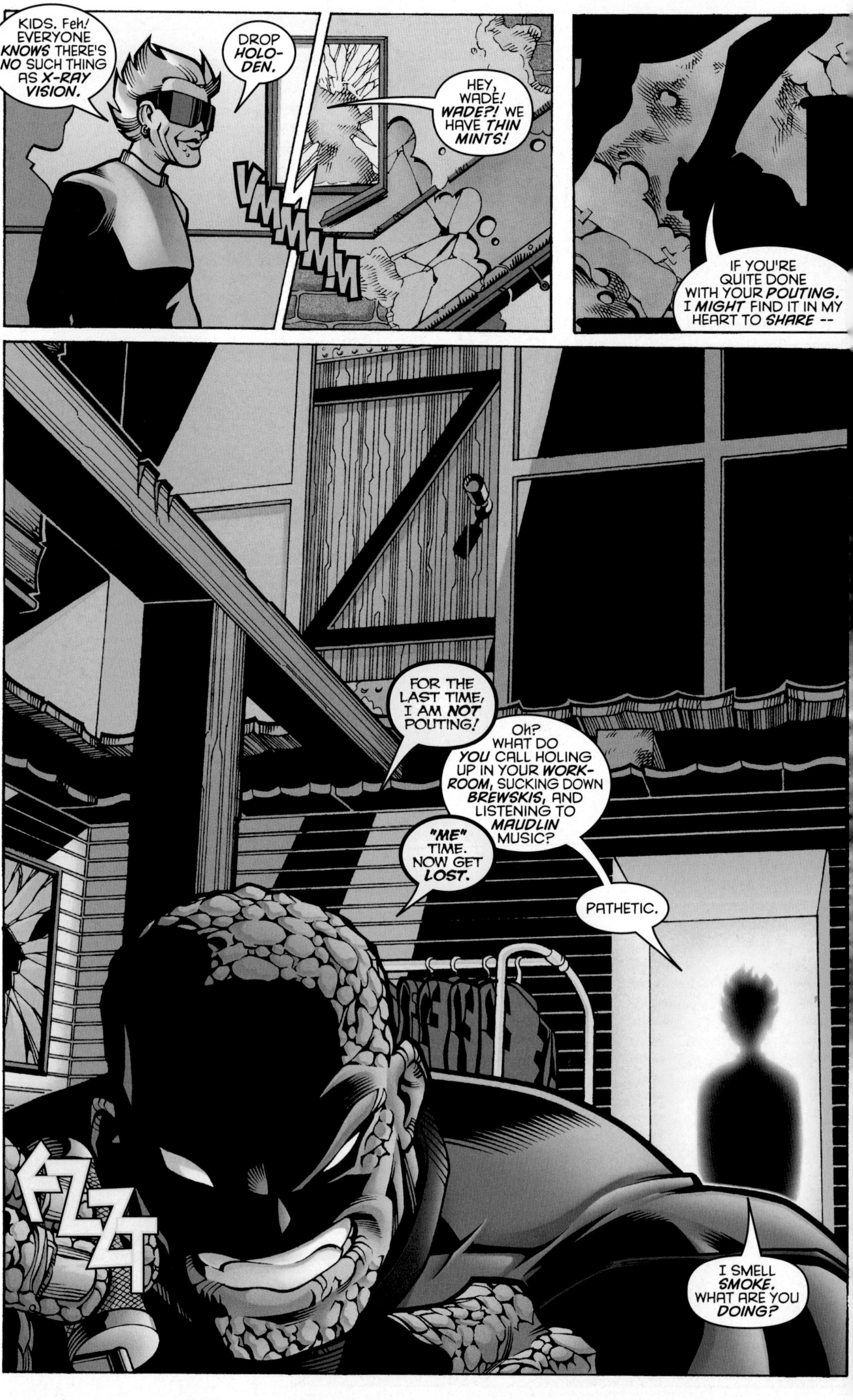
KIDS. Feh! EVERYONE KNOWS THERE'S NO SUCH THING AS X-RAY VISION.
DROP HOLO-DEN.
VMMMMMM
HEY, WADE! WADE?! WE HAVE THIN MINTS!
IF YOU'RE QUITE DONE WITH YOUR POUTING, I MIGHT FIND IT IN MY HEART TO SHARE --
FOR THE LAST TIME, I AM NOT POUTING!
Oh? WHAT DO YOU CALL HOLING UP IN YOUR WORK-ROOM, SUCKING DOWN BREWSKIS, AND LISTENING TO MAUDLIN MUSIC?
"ME" TIME. NOW GET LOST.
PATHETIC.
FZZZT
I SMELL SMOKE. WHAT ARE YOU DOING?

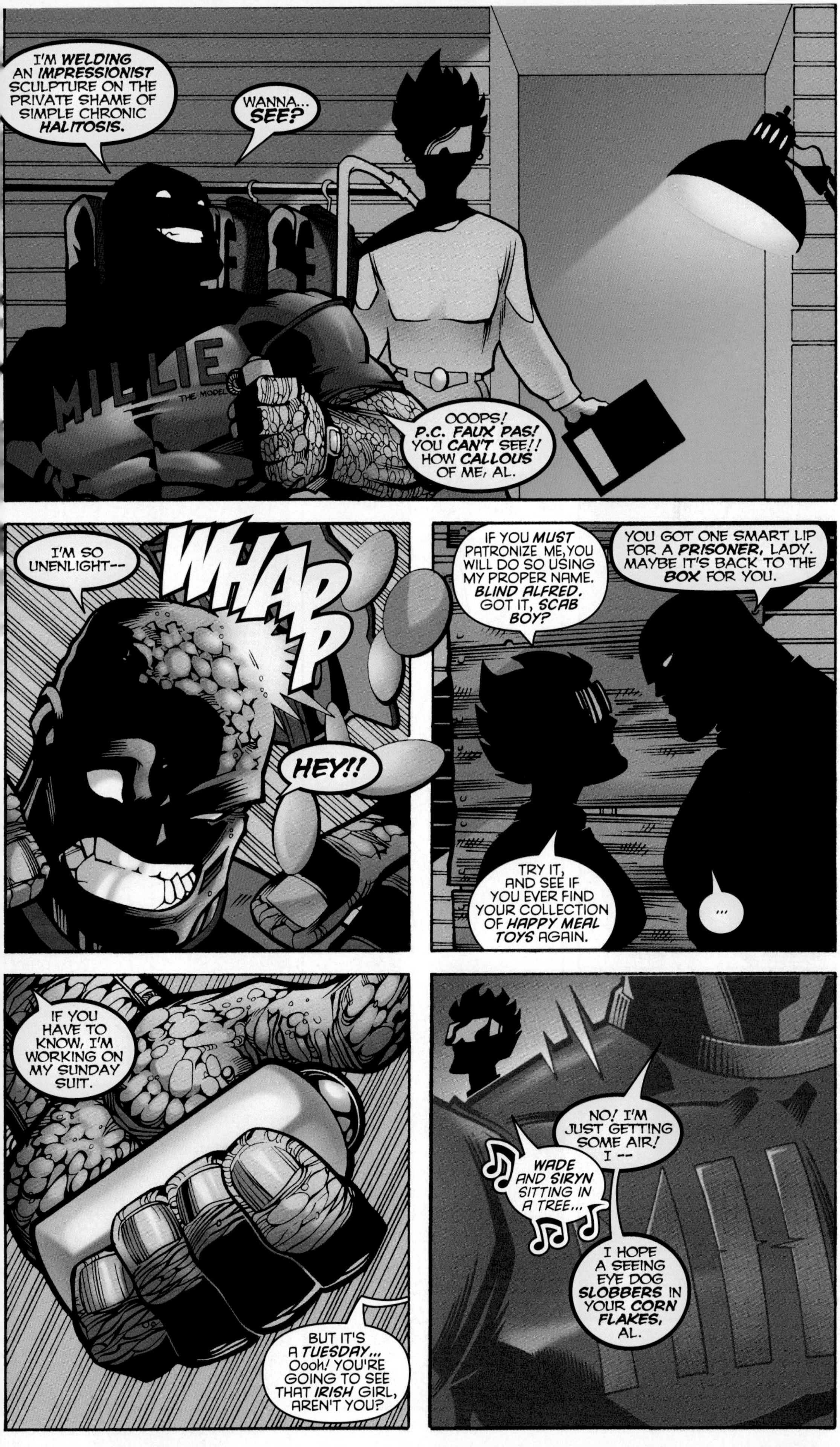

I'M WELDING AN IMPRESSIONIST SCULPTURE ON THE PRIVATE SHAME OF SIMPLE CHRONIC HALITOSIS.
WANNA... SEE?
MILLIE THE MODEL
OOOPS! P.C. FAUX PAS! YOU CAN'T SEE!! HOW CALLOUS OF ME, AL.
I'M SO UNENLIGHT--
WHAP
HEY!!
IF YOU MUST PATRONIZE ME, YOU WILL DO SO USING MY PROPER NAME. BLIND ALFRED. GOT IT, SCAB BOY?
YOU GOT ONE SMART LIP FOR A PRISONER, LADY. MAYBE IT'S BACK TO THE BOX FOR YOU.
TRY IT, AND SEE IF YOU EVER FIND YOUR COLLECTION OF HAPPY MEAL TOYS AGAIN.
...
IF YOU HAVE TO KNOW, I'M WORKING ON MY SUNDAY SUIT.
BUT IT'S A TUESDAY... Oooh! YOU'RE GOING TO SEE THAT IRISH GIRL, AREN'T YOU?
NO! I'M JUST GETTING SOME AIR! I --
WADE AND SIRYN SITTING IN A TREE...
I HOPE A SEEING EYE DOG SLOBBERS IN YOUR CORN FLAKES, AL.

ANTARCTICA.

CORE ON-LINE. PREPARING TO ENGAGE IN FIVE...

SHOW TIME.

...GAMMA LEVELS READ STRONG ON FOUR... THREE...

...REMOVING SAFETIES ON TWO...

...CROSSING FINGERS ON ONE.

CLIK

KZZZHK

KAZZKH

COME ON... ENGAGE... ENGAGE...

ENGAGE!

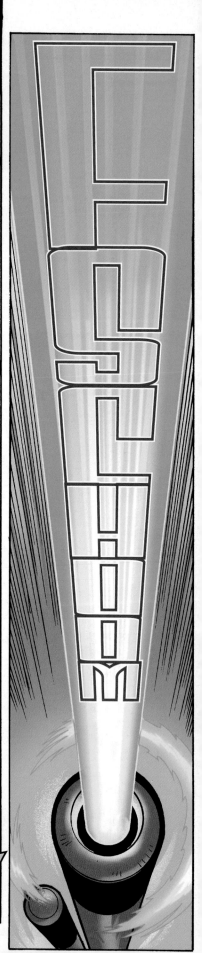

FFCHOOM

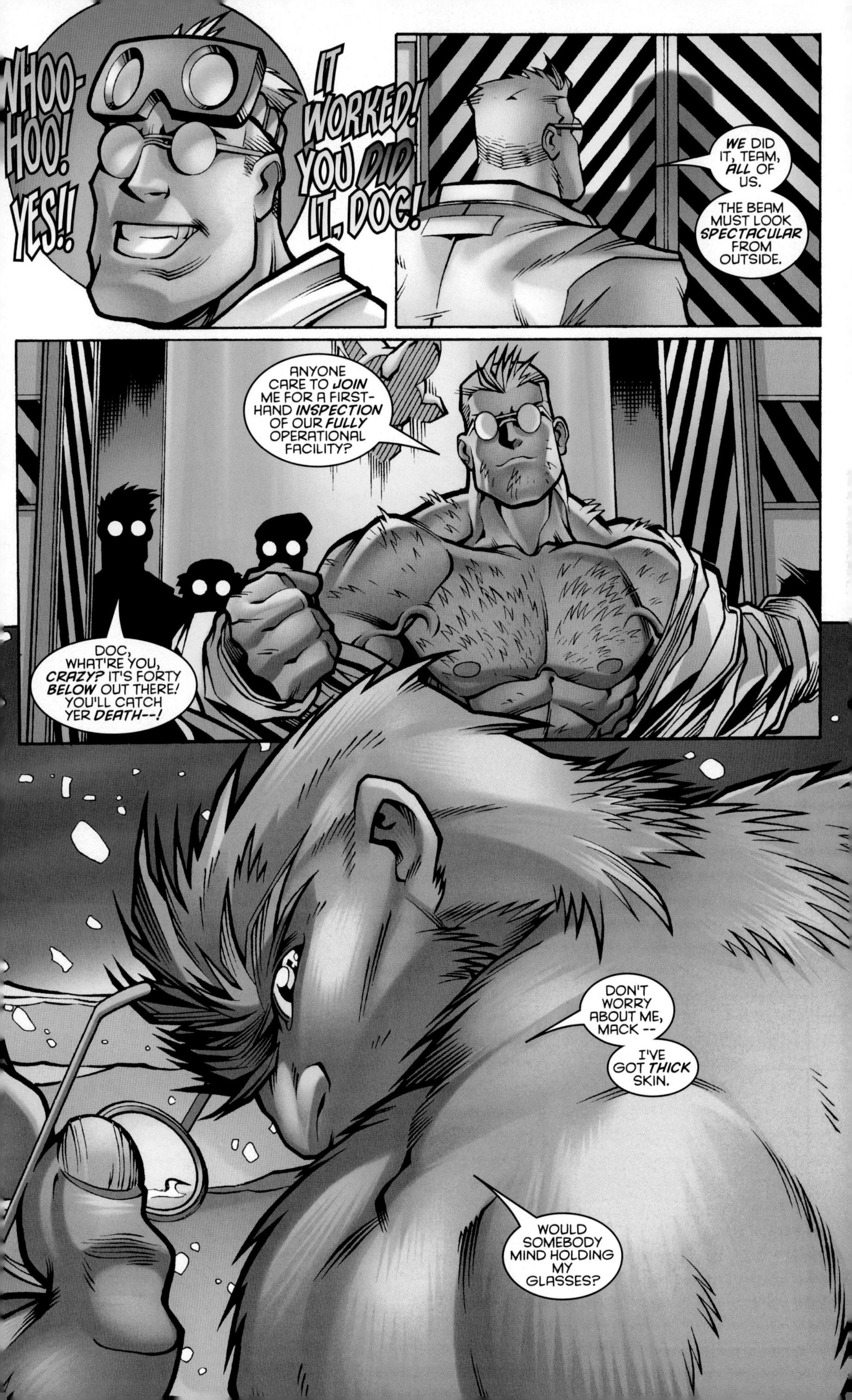
WHOO-HOO! YES!!
IT WORKED! YOU DID IT, DOC!
WE DID IT, TEAM, ALL OF US.
THE BEAM MUST LOOK SPECTACULAR FROM OUTSIDE.
ANYONE CARE TO JOIN ME FOR A FIRST-HAND INSPECTION OF OUR FULLY OPERATIONAL FACILITY?
DOC, WHAT'RE YOU, CRAZY? IT'S FORTY BELOW OUT THERE! YOU'LL CATCH YER DEATH--!
DON'T WORRY ABOUT ME, MACK --
I'VE GOT THICK SKIN.
WOULD SOMEBODY MIND HOLDING MY GLASSES?

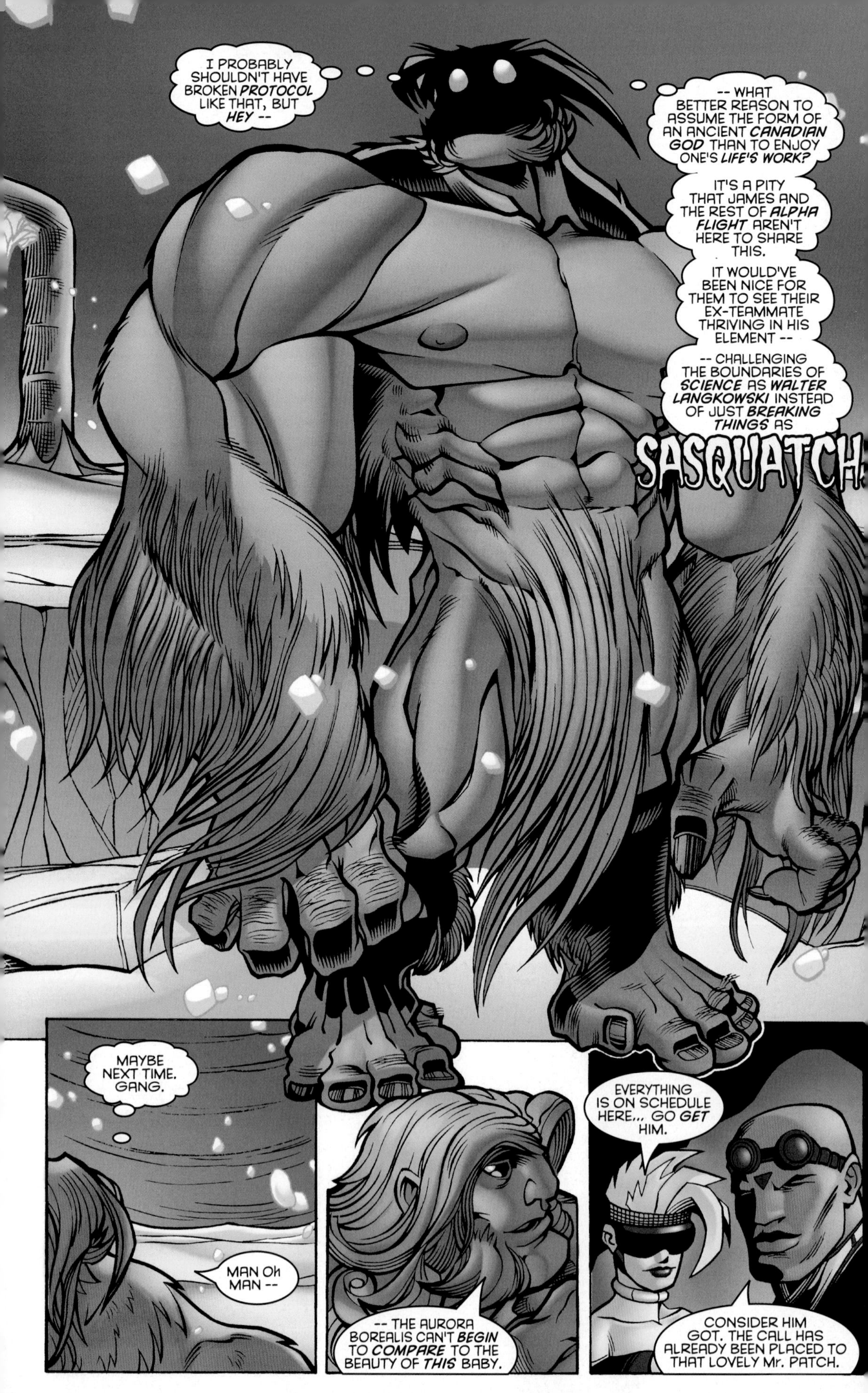
I PROBABLY SHOULDN'T HAVE BROKEN *PROTOCOL* LIKE THAT, BUT *HEY* --
-- WHAT BETTER REASON TO ASSUME THE FORM OF AN ANCIENT *CANADIAN GOD* THAN TO ENJOY ONE'S *LIFE'S WORK?*
IT'S A PITY THAT JAMES AND THE REST OF *ALPHA FLIGHT* AREN'T HERE TO SHARE THIS.
IT WOULD'VE BEEN NICE FOR THEM TO SEE THEIR EX-TEAMMATE THRIVING IN HIS ELEMENT --
-- CHALLENGING THE BOUNDARIES OF *SCIENCE* AS *WALTER LANGKOWSKI* INSTEAD OF JUST *BREAKING THINGS* AS
SASQUATCH
MAYBE NEXT TIME. GANG.
MAN OH MAN --
-- THE AURORA BOREALIS CAN'T *BEGIN* TO *COMPARE* TO THE BEAUTY OF *THIS* BABY.
EVERYTHING IS ON SCHEDULE HERE... GO *GET* HIM.
CONSIDER HIM GOT. THE CALL HAS ALREADY BEEN PLACED TO THAT LOVELY Mr. PATCH.

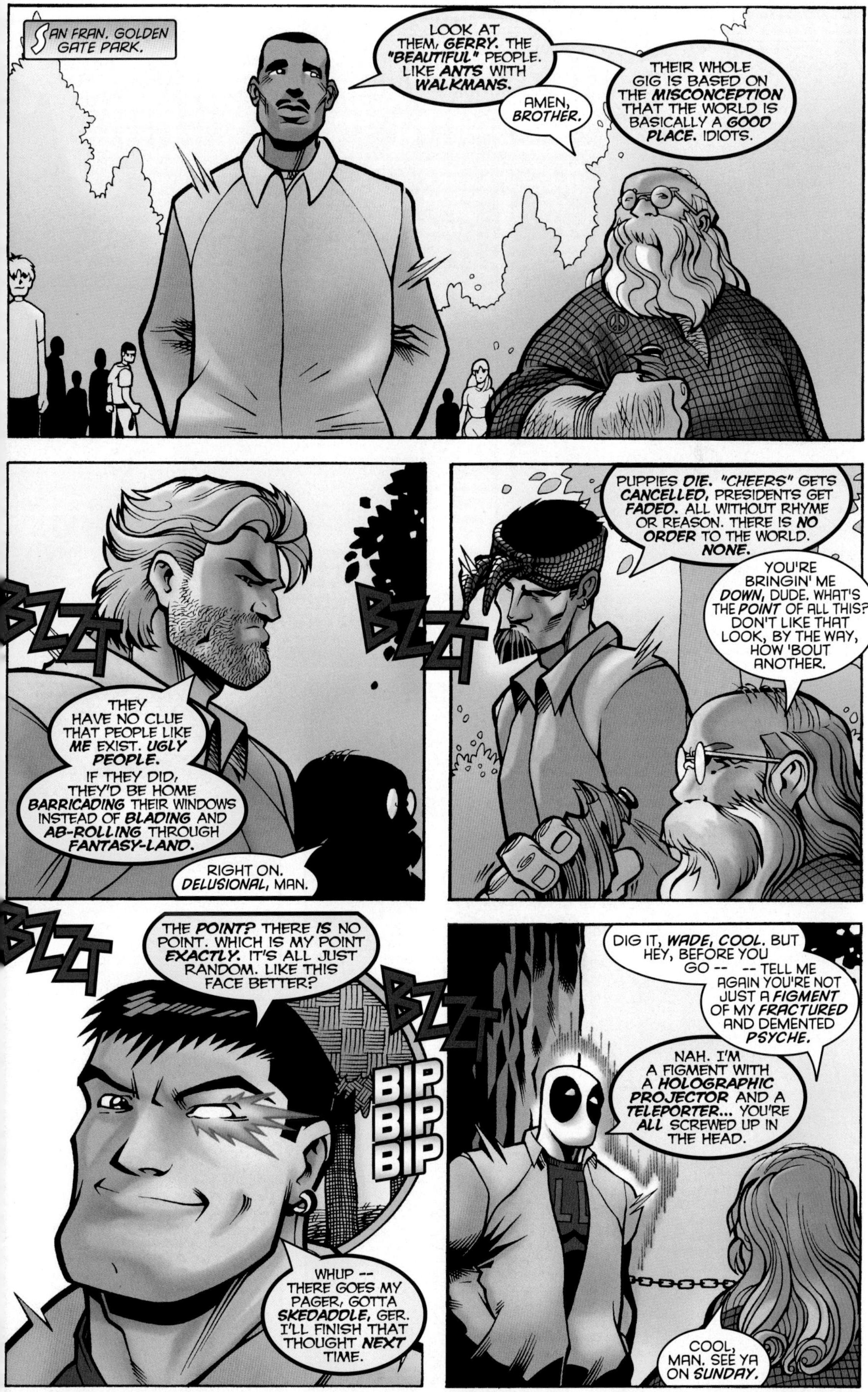
SAN FRAN. GOLDEN GATE PARK.
LOOK AT THEM, GERRY. THE "BEAUTIFUL" PEOPLE. LIKE ANTS WITH WALKMANS.
THEIR WHOLE GIG IS BASED ON THE MISCONCEPTION THAT THE WORLD IS BASICALLY A GOOD PLACE. IDIOTS.
AMEN, BROTHER.
BZZZT
THEY HAVE NO CLUE THAT PEOPLE LIKE ME EXIST. UGLY PEOPLE.
IF THEY DID, THEY'D BE HOME BARRICADING THEIR WINDOWS INSTEAD OF BLADING AND AB-ROLLING THROUGH FANTASY-LAND.
RIGHT ON. DELUSIONAL, MAN.
BZZZT
PUPPIES DIE. "CHEERS" GETS CANCELLED, PRESIDENTS GET FADED. ALL WITHOUT RHYME OR REASON. THERE IS NO ORDER TO THE WORLD. NONE.
YOU'RE BRINGIN' ME DOWN, DUDE. WHAT'S THE POINT OF ALL THIS? DON'T LIKE THAT LOOK, BY THE WAY, HOW 'BOUT ANOTHER.
BZZZT
THE POINT? THERE IS NO POINT. WHICH IS MY POINT EXACTLY. IT'S ALL JUST RANDOM. LIKE THIS FACE BETTER?
BZZZT
BIP BIP BIP
WHUP -- THERE GOES MY PAGER, GOTTA SKEDADDLE, GER. I'LL FINISH THAT THOUGHT NEXT TIME.
DIG IT, WADE, COOL. BUT HEY, BEFORE YOU GO -- -- TELL ME AGAIN YOU'RE NOT JUST A FIGMENT OF MY FRACTURED AND DEMENTED PSYCHE.
NAH. I'M A FIGMENT WITH A HOLOGRAPHIC PROJECTOR AND A TELEPORTER... YOU'RE ALL SCREWED UP IN THE HEAD.
COOL, MAN. SEE YA ON SUNDAY.

LATER, AT THE HELLHOUSE...

NICE OF YA TO ANSWER YER PAGE, 'POOL! YOU TAKE THE LOCAL OUT HERE OR WHAT?

SORRY MR. PATCH -- I OVERSLEPT -- THE DOG ATE MY AMMUNITION -- I'VE GOT A NOTE-

SHADDUP!

LONG TIME NO SEE, WADE.

NOT LONG ENOUGH, KILL ANY BABIES THIS WEEK, T-RAY?

ONLY UGLY ONES.

CUTE.

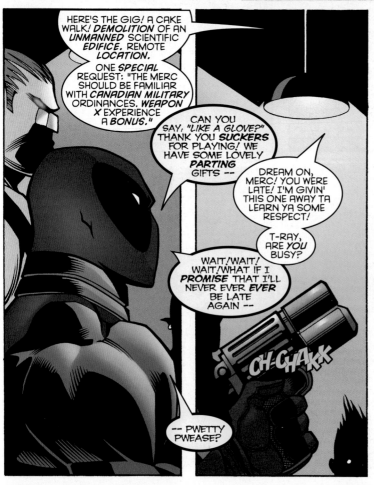

HERE'S THE GIG! A CAKE WALK! DEMOLITION OF AN UNMANNED SCIENTIFIC EDIFICE. REMOTE LOCATION.

ONE SPECIAL REQUEST: "THE MERC SHOULD BE FAMILIAR WITH CANADIAN MILITARY ORDINANCES. WEAPON X EXPERIENCE A BONUS."

CAN YOU SAY, "LIKE A GLOVE?" THANK YOU SUCKERS FOR PLAYING! WE HAVE SOME LOVELY PARTING GIFTS --

DREAM ON, MERC! YOU WERE LATE! I'M GIVIN' THIS ONE AWAY TA LEARN YA SOME RESPECT!

T-RAY, ARE YOU BUSY?

WAIT/WAIT! WAIT/WHAT IF I PROMISE THAT I'LL NEVER EVER EVER BE LATE AGAIN --

CH-CHAKK

-- PWETTY PWEASE?

ONE DAY I'M GONNA GET FED UP WITH YER CRAP, Y'KNOW THAT?

UH-HUH. GIMME.

I MEAN IT, 'POOL.

UH-HUH. GIMME.

YOU'RE A PRINCE AMONG GNOMES, PATCH. I MEAN IT. GIMME.

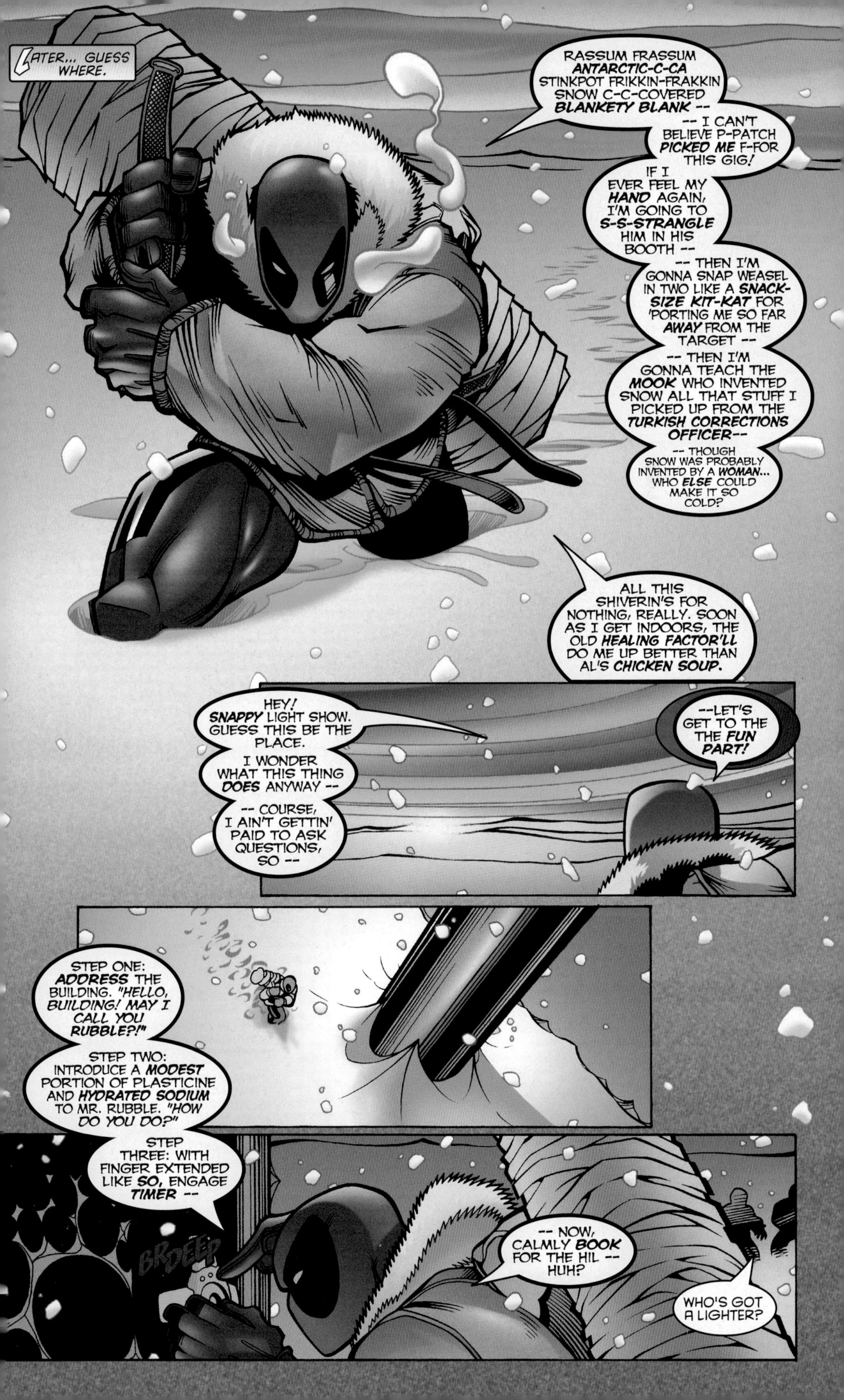
LATER... GUESS WHERE.
RASSUM FRASSUM ANTARCTIC-C-CA STINKPOT FRIKKIN-FRAKKIN SNOW C-C-COVERED BLANKETY BLANK --
-- I CAN'T BELIEVE P-PATCH PICKED ME F-FOR THIS GIG!
IF I EVER FEEL MY HAND AGAIN, I'M GOING TO S-S-STRANGLE HIM IN HIS BOOTH --
-- THEN I'M GONNA SNAP WEASEL IN TWO LIKE A SNACK-SIZE KIT-KAT FOR 'PORTING ME SO FAR AWAY FROM THE TARGET --
-- THEN I'M GONNA TEACH THE MOOK WHO INVENTED SNOW ALL THAT STUFF I PICKED UP FROM THE TURKISH CORRECTIONS OFFICER--
-- THOUGH SNOW WAS PROBABLY INVENTED BY A WOMAN... WHO ELSE COULD MAKE IT SO COLD?
ALL THIS SHIVERIN'S FOR NOTHING, REALLY. SOON AS I GET INDOORS, THE OLD HEALING FACTOR'LL DO ME UP BETTER THAN AL'S CHICKEN SOUP.
HEY! SNAPPY LIGHT SHOW. GUESS THIS BE THE PLACE.
I WONDER WHAT THIS THING DOES ANYWAY --
-- COURSE, I AIN'T GETTIN' PAID TO ASK QUESTIONS, SO --
--LET'S GET TO THE THE FUN PART!
STEP ONE: ADDRESS THE BUILDING. "HELLO, BUILDING! MAY I CALL YOU RUBBLE?!"
STEP TWO: INTRODUCE A MODEST PORTION OF PLASTICINE AND HYDRATED SODIUM TO MR. RUBBLE. "HOW DO YOU DO?"
STEP THREE: WITH FINGER EXTENDED LIKE SO, ENGAGE TIMER --
BRDEEP
-- NOW, CALMLY BOOK FOR THE HIL -- HUH?
WHO'S GOT A LIGHTER?

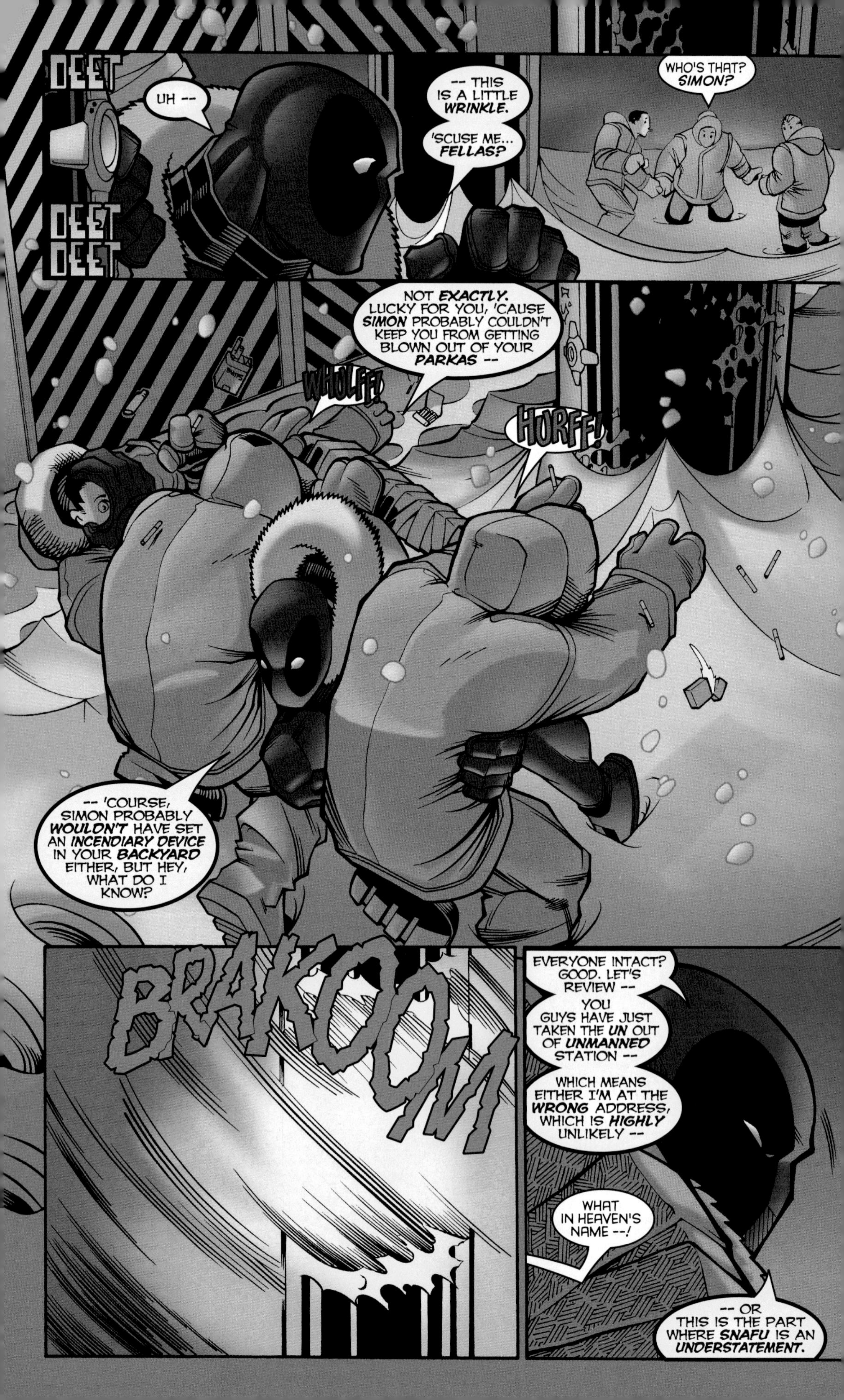
DEET
UH --
-- THIS IS A LITTLE WRINKLE.
'SCUSE ME... FELLAS?
DEET DEET
WHO'S THAT? SIMON?
NOT EXACTLY. LUCKY FOR YOU, 'CAUSE SIMON PROBABLY COULDN'T KEEP YOU FROM GETTING BLOWN OUT OF YOUR PARKAS --
WHOLFF!
HURFF!
-- 'COURSE, SIMON PROBABLY WOULDN'T HAVE SET AN INCENDIARY DEVICE IN YOUR BACKYARD EITHER, BUT HEY, WHAT DO I KNOW?
BRAKOOM
EVERYONE INTACT? GOOD. LET'S REVIEW --
YOU GUYS HAVE JUST TAKEN THE UN OUT OF UNMANNED STATION --
WHICH MEANS EITHER I'M AT THE WRONG ADDRESS, WHICH IS HIGHLY UNLIKELY --
WHAT IN HEAVEN'S NAME --!
-- OR THIS IS THE PART WHERE SNAFU IS AN UNDERSTATEMENT.

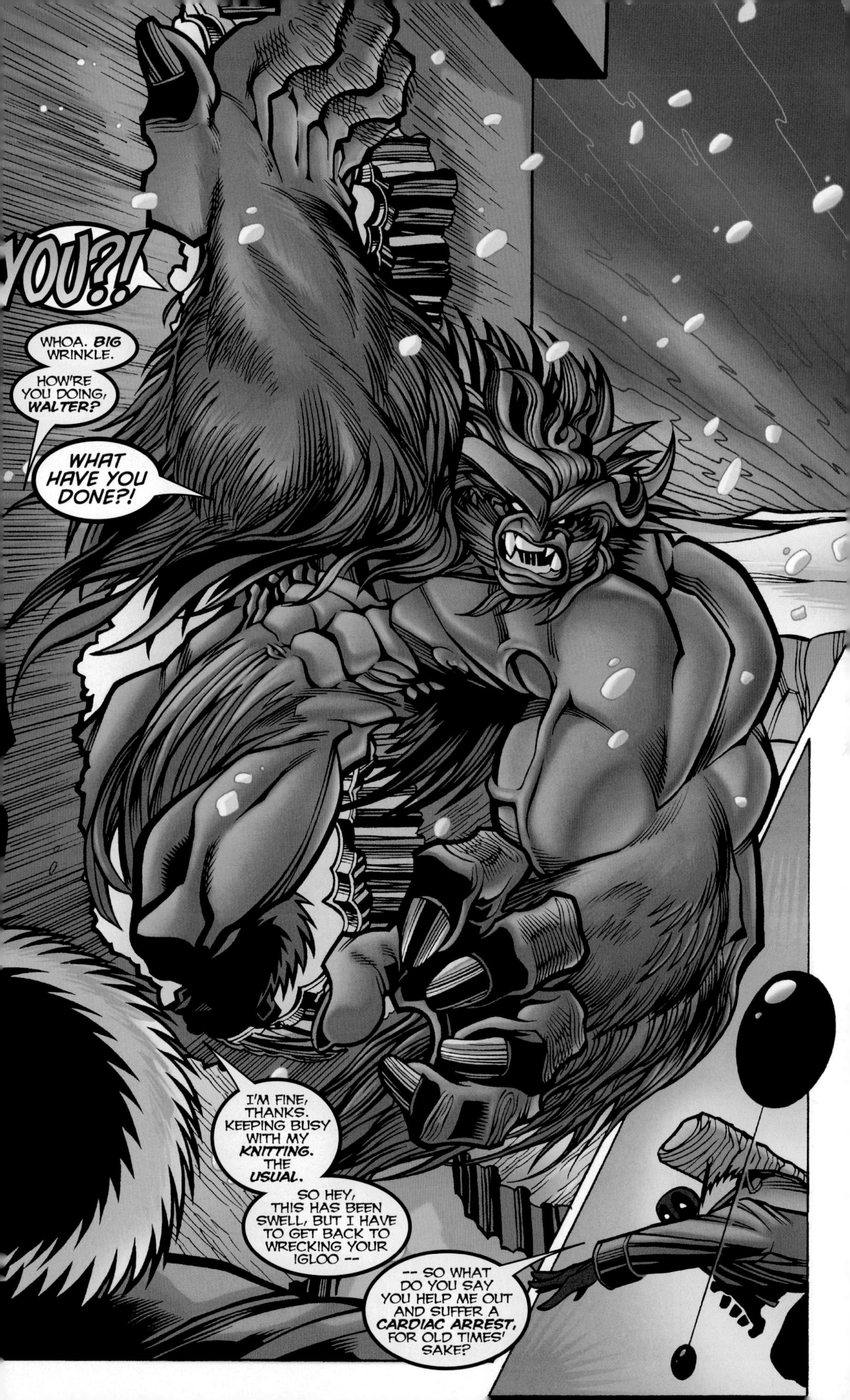
YOU?!
WHOA. BIG WRINKLE.
HOW'RE YOU DOING, WALTER?
WHAT HAVE YOU DONE?!
I'M FINE, THANKS. KEEPING BUSY WITH MY KNITTING. THE USUAL.
SO HEY, THIS HAS BEEN SWELL, BUT I HAVE TO GET BACK TO WRECKING YOUR IGLOO --
-- SO WHAT DO YOU SAY YOU HELP ME OUT AND SUFFER A CARDIAC ARREST, FOR OLD TIMES' SAKE?

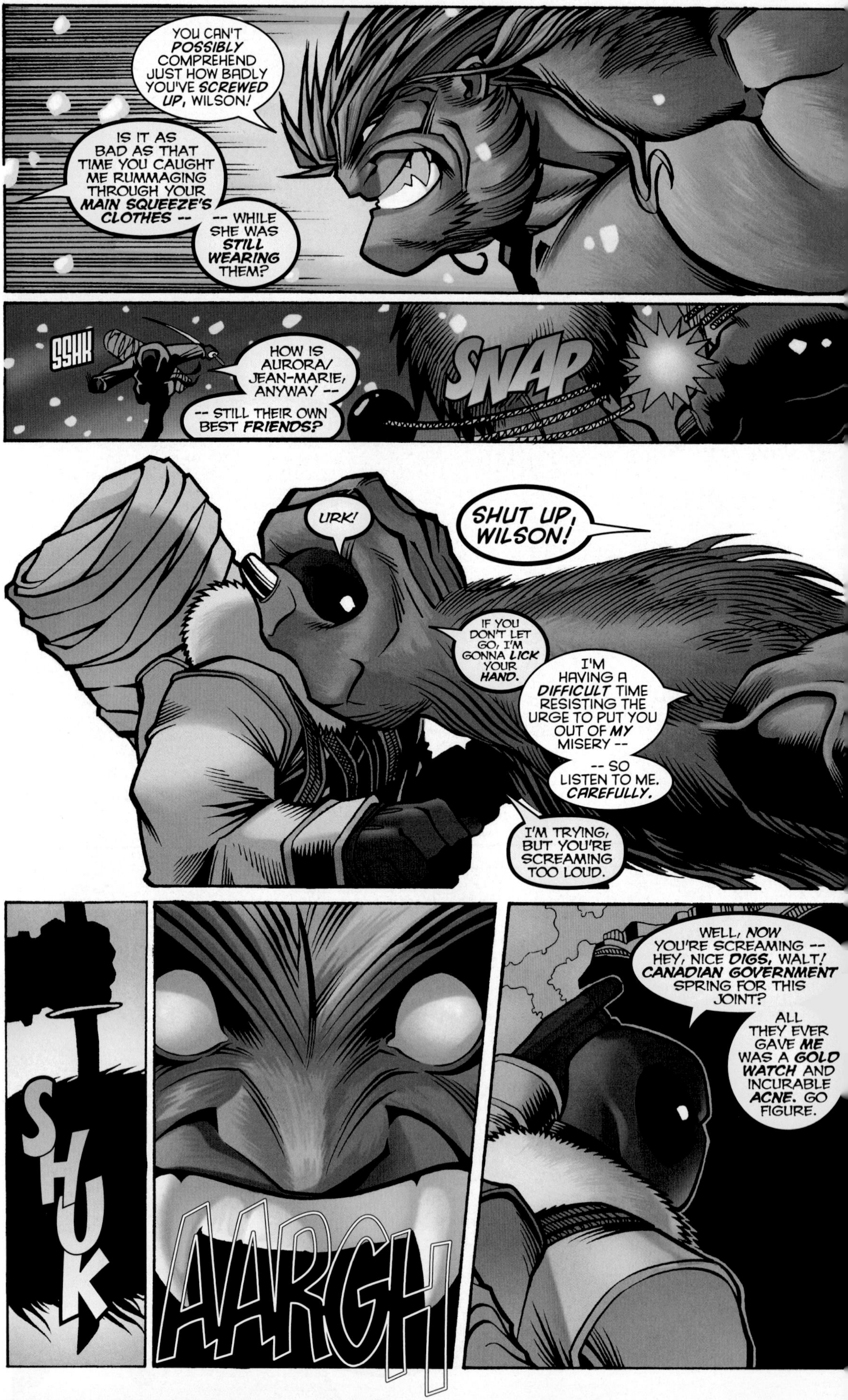
YOU CAN'T POSSIBLY COMPREHEND JUST HOW BADLY YOU'VE SCREWED UP, WILSON!
IS IT AS BAD AS THAT TIME YOU CAUGHT ME RUMMAGING THROUGH YOUR MAIN SQUEEZE'S CLOTHES --
-- WHILE SHE WAS STILL WEARING THEM?
SSHK
HOW IS AURORA/ JEAN-MARIE, ANYWAY --
-- STILL THEIR OWN BEST FRIENDS?
SNAP
URK!
SHUT UP, WILSON!
IF YOU DON'T LET GO, I'M GONNA LICK YOUR HAND.
I'M HAVING A DIFFICULT TIME RESISTING THE URGE TO PUT YOU OUT OF MY MISERY --
-- SO LISTEN TO ME. CAREFULLY.
I'M TRYING, BUT YOU'RE SCREAMING TOO LOUD.
SHUK
AARGH
WELL, NOW YOU'RE SCREAMING -- HEY, NICE DIGS, WALT! CANADIAN GOVERNMENT SPRING FOR THIS JOINT?
ALL THEY EVER GAVE ME WAS A GOLD WATCH AND INCURABLE ACNE. GO FIGURE.

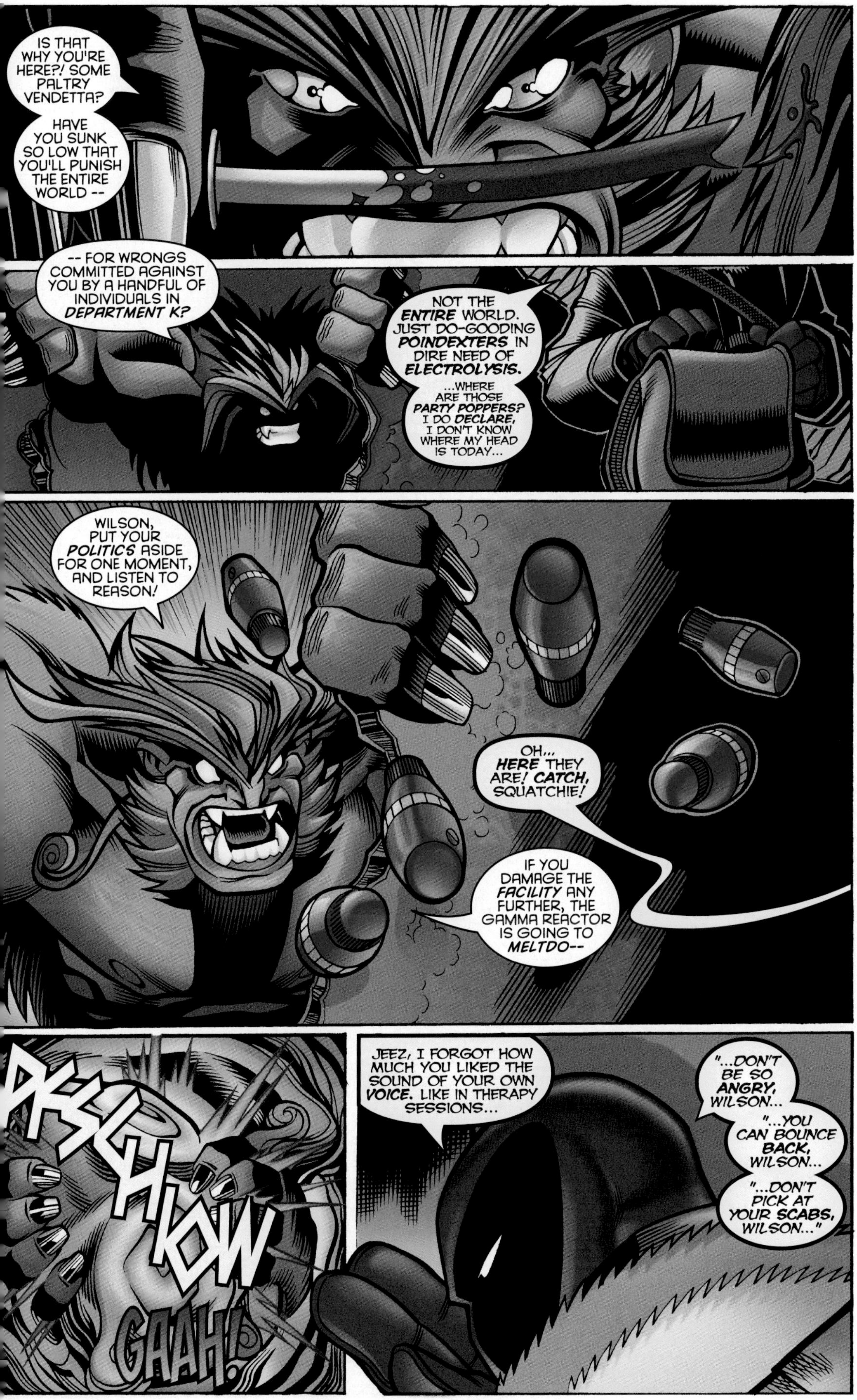

IS THAT WHY YOU'RE HERE?! SOME PALTRY VENDETTA?
HAVE YOU SUNK SO LOW THAT YOU'LL PUNISH THE ENTIRE WORLD --
-- FOR WRONGS COMMITTED AGAINST YOU BY A HANDFUL OF INDIVIDUALS IN DEPARTMENT K?
NOT THE ENTIRE WORLD. JUST DO-GOODING POINDEXTERS IN DIRE NEED OF ELECTROLYSIS.
...WHERE ARE THOSE PARTY POPPERS? I DO DECLARE, I DON'T KNOW WHERE MY HEAD IS TODAY...
WILSON, PUT YOUR POLITICS ASIDE FOR ONE MOMENT, AND LISTEN TO REASON!
OH... HERE THEY ARE! CATCH, SQUATCHIE!
IF YOU DAMAGE THE FACILITY ANY FURTHER, THE GAMMA REACTOR IS GOING TO MELTDO--
DASCHOW
GAAH!
JEEZ, I FORGOT HOW MUCH YOU LIKED THE SOUND OF YOUR OWN VOICE. LIKE IN THERAPY SESSIONS...
"...DON'T BE SO ANGRY, WILSON...
"...YOU CAN BOUNCE BACK, WILSON...
"...DON'T PICK AT YOUR SCABS, WILSON..."

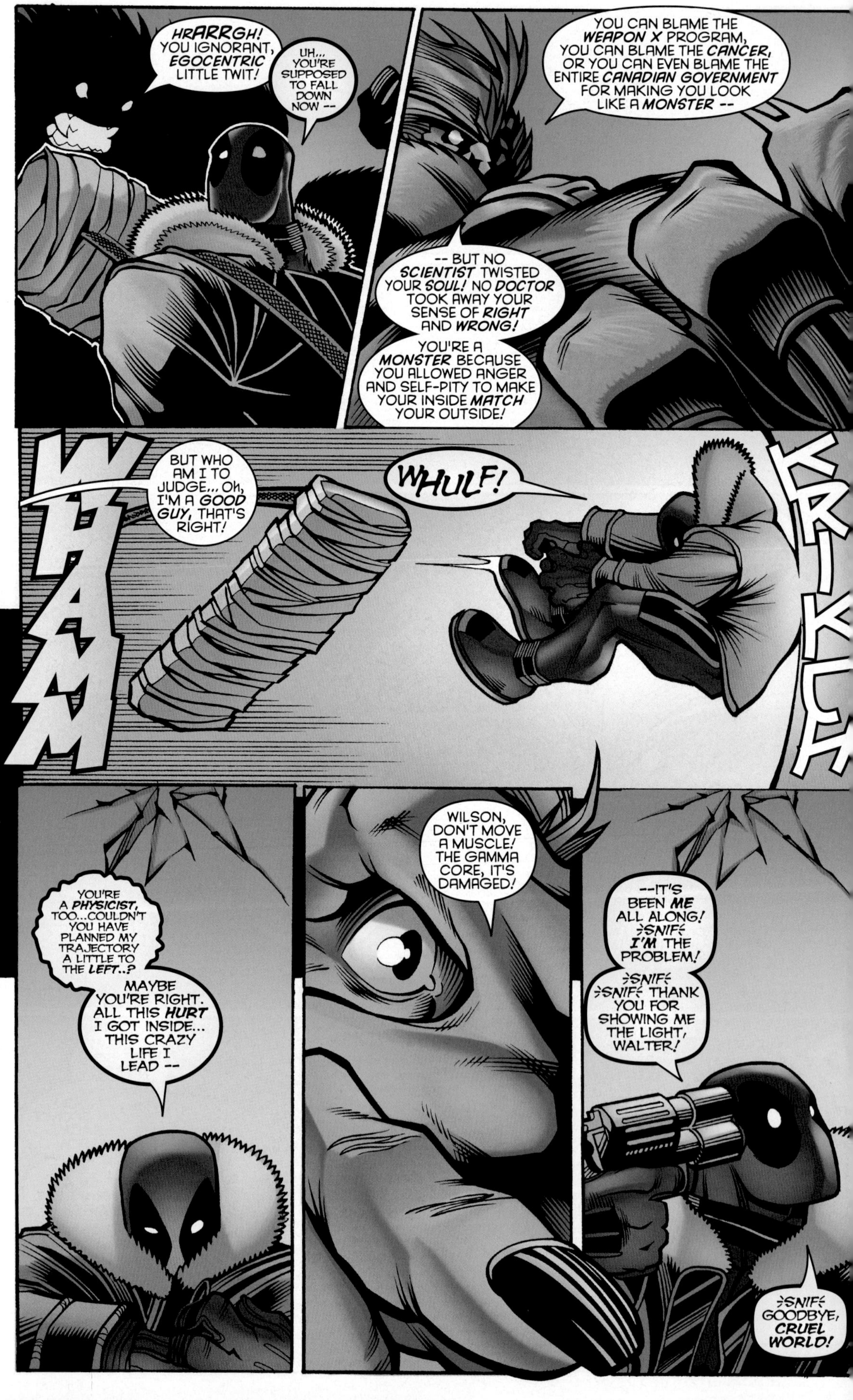

HRARRGH! YOU IGNORANT, EGOCENTRIC LITTLE TWIT!
UH... YOU'RE SUPPOSED TO FALL DOWN NOW --
YOU CAN BLAME THE WEAPON X PROGRAM, YOU CAN BLAME THE CANCER, OR YOU CAN EVEN BLAME THE ENTIRE CANADIAN GOVERNMENT FOR MAKING YOU LOOK LIKE A MONSTER --
-- BUT NO SCIENTIST TWISTED YOUR SOUL! NO DOCTOR TOOK AWAY YOUR SENSE OF RIGHT AND WRONG!
YOU'RE A MONSTER BECAUSE YOU ALLOWED ANGER AND SELF-PITY TO MAKE YOUR INSIDE MATCH YOUR OUTSIDE!
WHAM
BUT WHO AM I TO JUDGE... OH, I'M A GOOD GUY, THAT'S RIGHT!
WHULF!
KRIKUH
YOU'RE A PHYSICIST, TOO...COULDN'T YOU HAVE PLANNED MY TRAJECTORY A LITTLE TO THE LEFT..?
MAYBE YOU'RE RIGHT. ALL THIS HURT I GOT INSIDE... THIS CRAZY LIFE I LEAD --
WILSON, DON'T MOVE A MUSCLE! THE GAMMA CORE, IT'S DAMAGED!
--IT'S BEEN ME ALL ALONG! SNIF I'M THE PROBLEM!
SNIF SNIF THANK YOU FOR SHOWING ME THE LIGHT, WALTER!
SNIF GOODBYE, CRUEL WORLD!

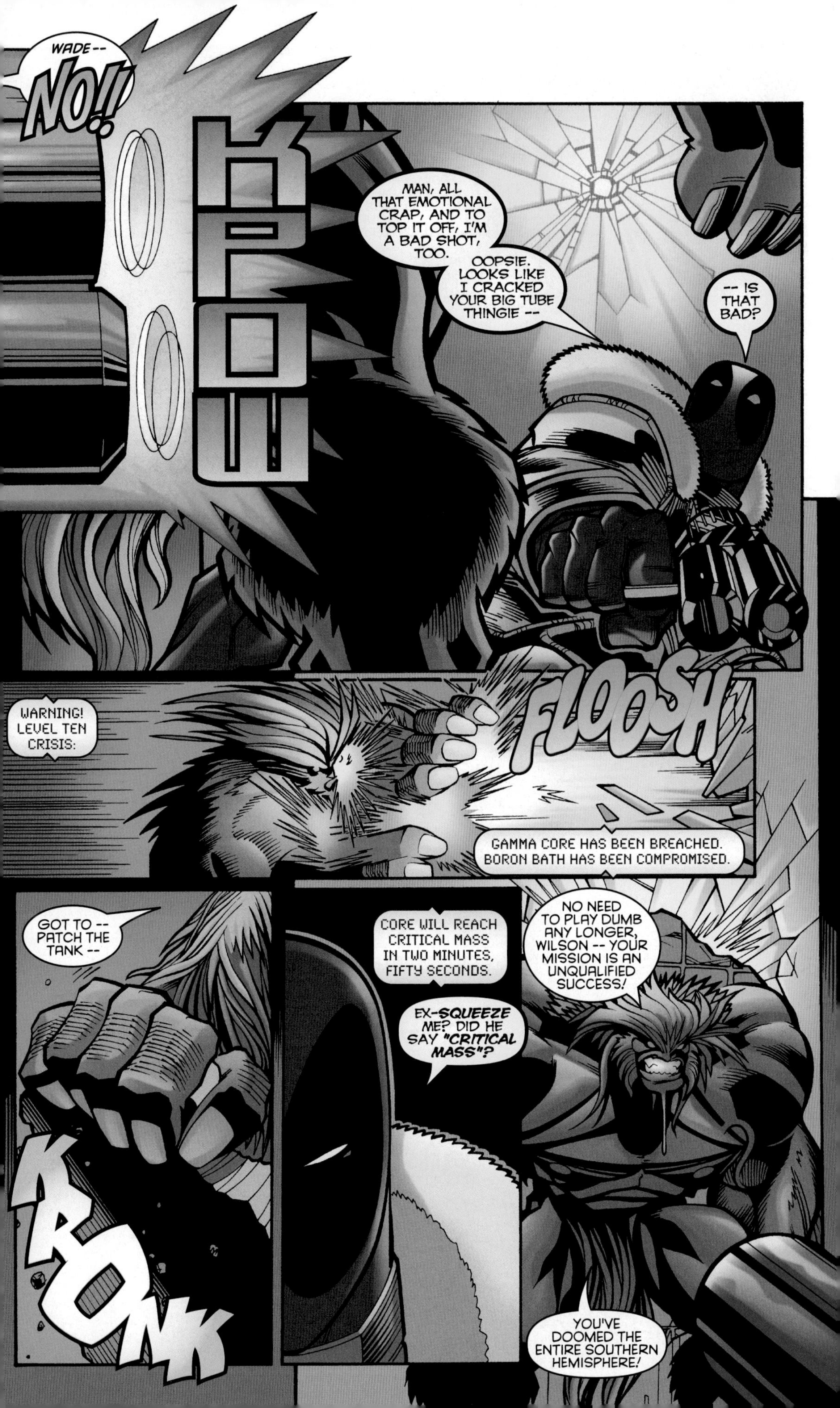
WADE --
NO!!
KPOW
MAN, ALL THAT EMOTIONAL CRAP, AND TO TOP IT OFF, I'M A BAD SHOT, TOO.
OOPSIE. LOOKS LIKE I CRACKED YOUR BIG TUBE THINGIE --
-- IS THAT BAD?
WARNING! LEVEL TEN CRISIS:
FLOOSH
GAMMA CORE HAS BEEN BREACHED. BORON BATH HAS BEEN COMPROMISED.
GOT TO -- PATCH THE TANK --
KRONK
CORE WILL REACH CRITICAL MASS IN TWO MINUTES, FIFTY SECONDS.
EX-SQUEEZE ME? DID HE SAY "CRITICAL MASS"?
NO NEED TO PLAY DUMB ANY LONGER, WILSON -- YOUR MISSION IS AN UNQUALIFIED SUCCESS!
YOU'VE DOOMED THE ENTIRE SOUTHERN HEMISPHERE!

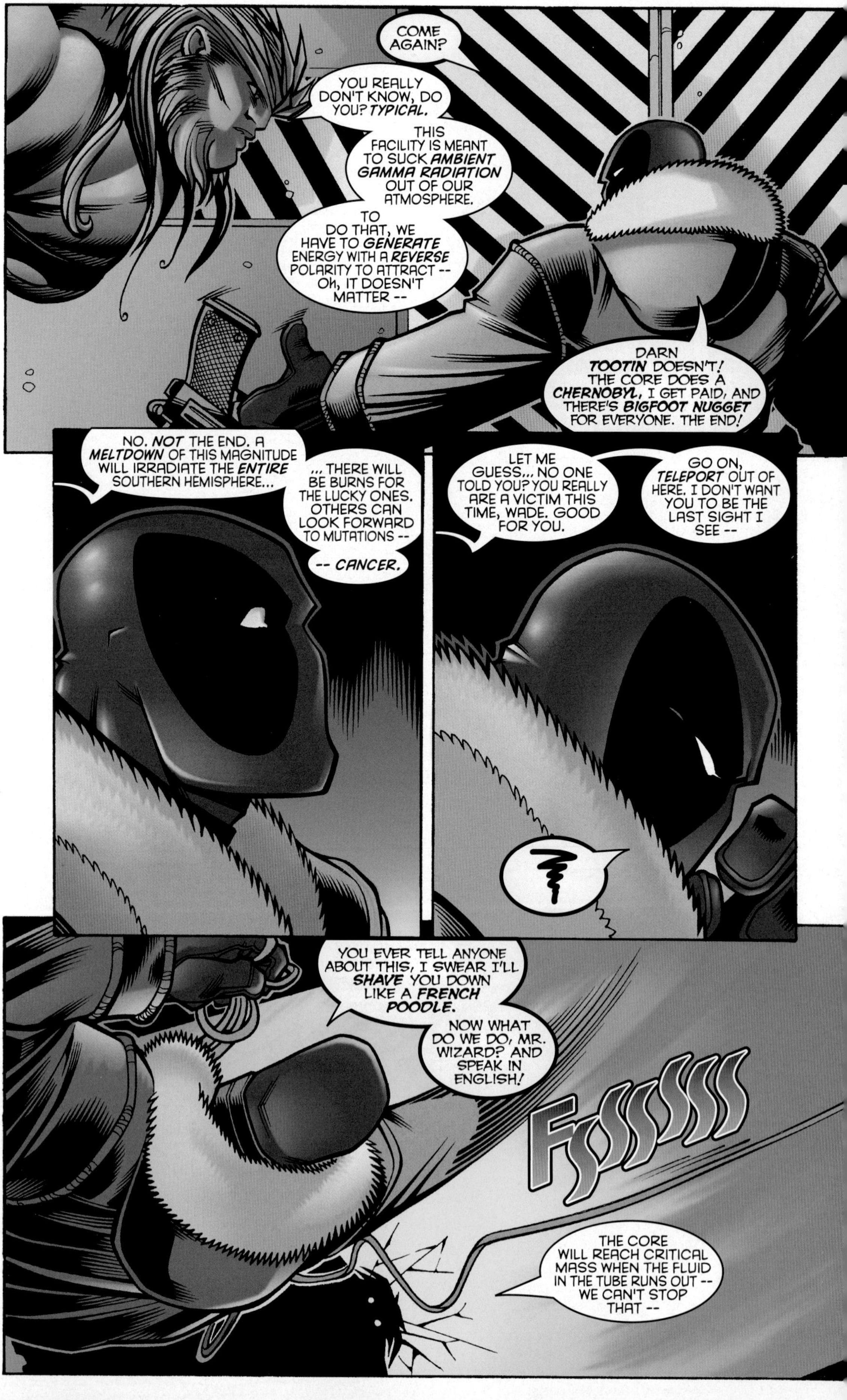
COME AGAIN?
YOU REALLY DON'T KNOW, DO YOU? TYPICAL.
THIS FACILITY IS MEANT TO SUCK AMBIENT GAMMA RADIATION OUT OF OUR ATMOSPHERE.
TO DO THAT, WE HAVE TO GENERATE ENERGY WITH A REVERSE POLARITY TO ATTRACT -- Oh, IT DOESN'T MATTER --
DARN TOOTIN DOESN'T! THE CORE DOES A CHERNOBYL, I GET PAID, AND THERE'S BIGFOOT NUGGET FOR EVERYONE. THE END!
NO. NOT THE END. A MELTDOWN OF THIS MAGNITUDE WILL IRRADIATE THE ENTIRE SOUTHERN HEMISPHERE...
... THERE WILL BE BURNS FOR THE LUCKY ONES. OTHERS CAN LOOK FORWARD TO MUTATIONS --
-- CANCER.
LET ME GUESS... NO ONE TOLD YOU? YOU REALLY ARE A VICTIM THIS TIME, WADE. GOOD FOR YOU.
GO ON, TELEPORT OUT OF HERE. I DON'T WANT YOU TO BE THE LAST SIGHT I SEE --
YOU EVER TELL ANYONE ABOUT THIS, I SWEAR I'LL SHAVE YOU DOWN LIKE A FRENCH POODLE.
NOW WHAT DO WE DO, MR. WIZARD? AND SPEAK IN ENGLISH!
FSSSSSS
THE CORE WILL REACH CRITICAL MASS WHEN THE FLUID IN THE TUBE RUNS OUT -- WE CAN'T STOP THAT --

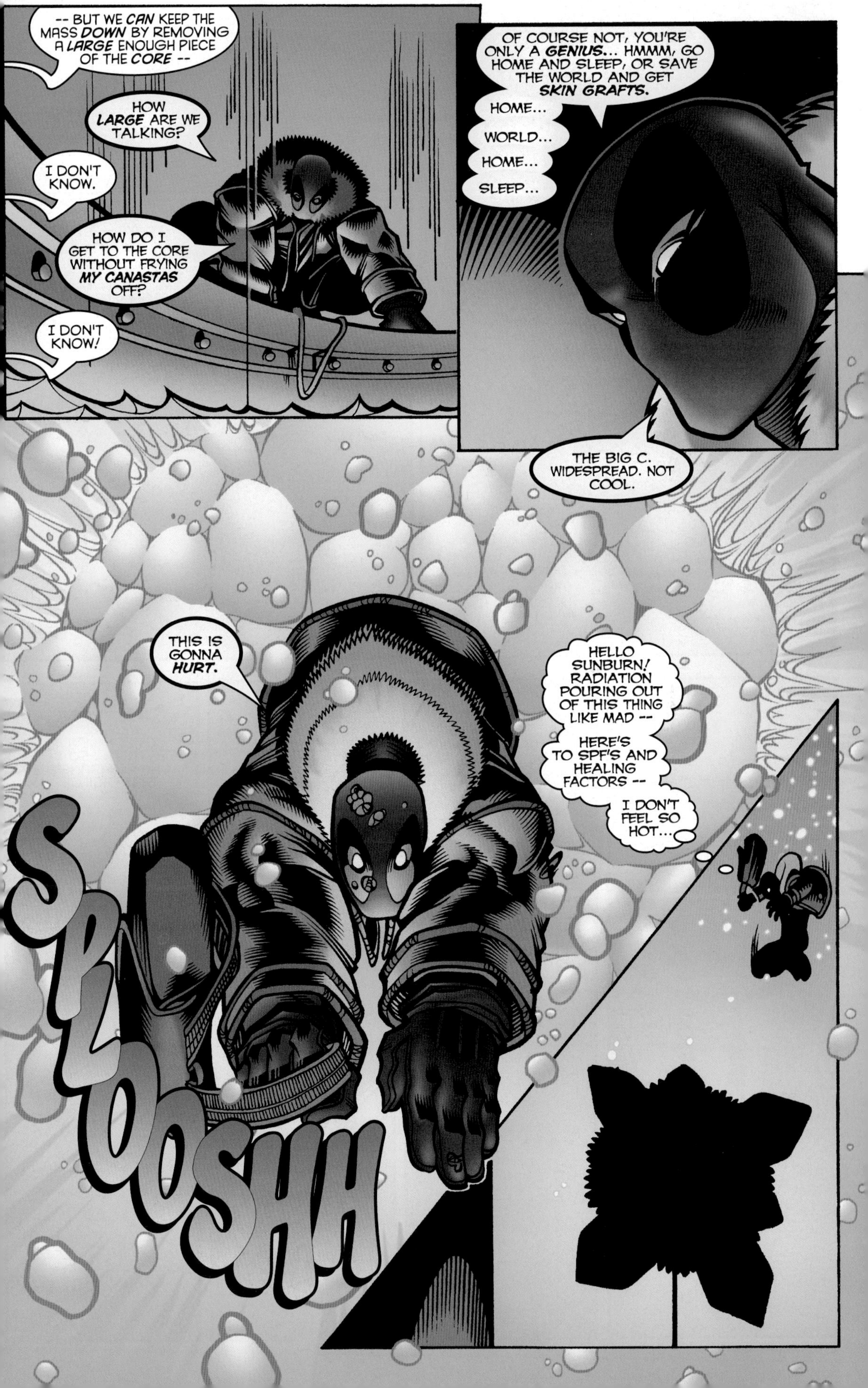
-- BUT WE CAN KEEP THE MASS DOWN BY REMOVING A LARGE ENOUGH PIECE OF THE CORE --
HOW LARGE ARE WE TALKING?
I DON'T KNOW.
HOW DO I GET TO THE CORE WITHOUT FRYING MY CANASTAS OFF?
I DON'T KNOW!
OF COURSE NOT, YOU'RE ONLY A GENIUS... HMMM, GO HOME AND SLEEP, OR SAVE THE WORLD AND GET SKIN GRAFTS.
HOME...
WORLD...
HOME...
SLEEP...
THE BIG C. WIDESPREAD. NOT COOL.
THIS IS GONNA HURT.
SPLOOSHH
HELLO SUNBURN! RADIATION POURING OUT OF THIS THING LIKE MAD --
HERE'S TO SPF'S AND HEALING FACTORS --
I DON'T FEEL SO HOT...

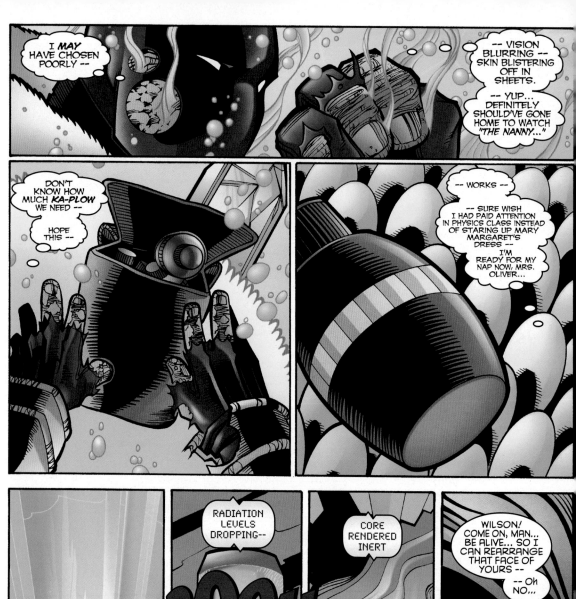

I MAY HAVE CHOSEN POORLY --

-- VISION BLURRING -- SKIN BLISTERING OFF IN SHEETS.

-- YUP... DEFINITELY SHOULD'VE GONE HOME TO WATCH *"THE NANNY..."*

DON'T KNOW HOW MUCH *KA-PLOW* WE NEED --

HOPE THIS --

-- WORKS --

-- SURE WISH I HAD PAID ATTENTION IN PHYSICS CLASS INSTEAD OF STARING UP MARY MARGARET'S DRESS --

I'M READY FOR MY NAP NOW, MRS. OLIVER...

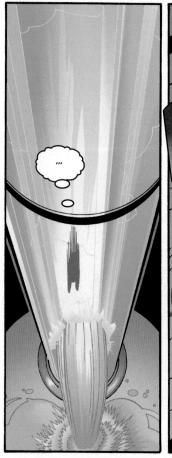

...

RADIATION LEVELS DROPPING--

BOOM

CORE RENDERED INERT

HE DID IT.

HE DID IT!

WILSON! COME ON, MAN... BE ALIVE... SO I CAN REARRANGE THAT FACE OF YOURS --

-- OH NO...

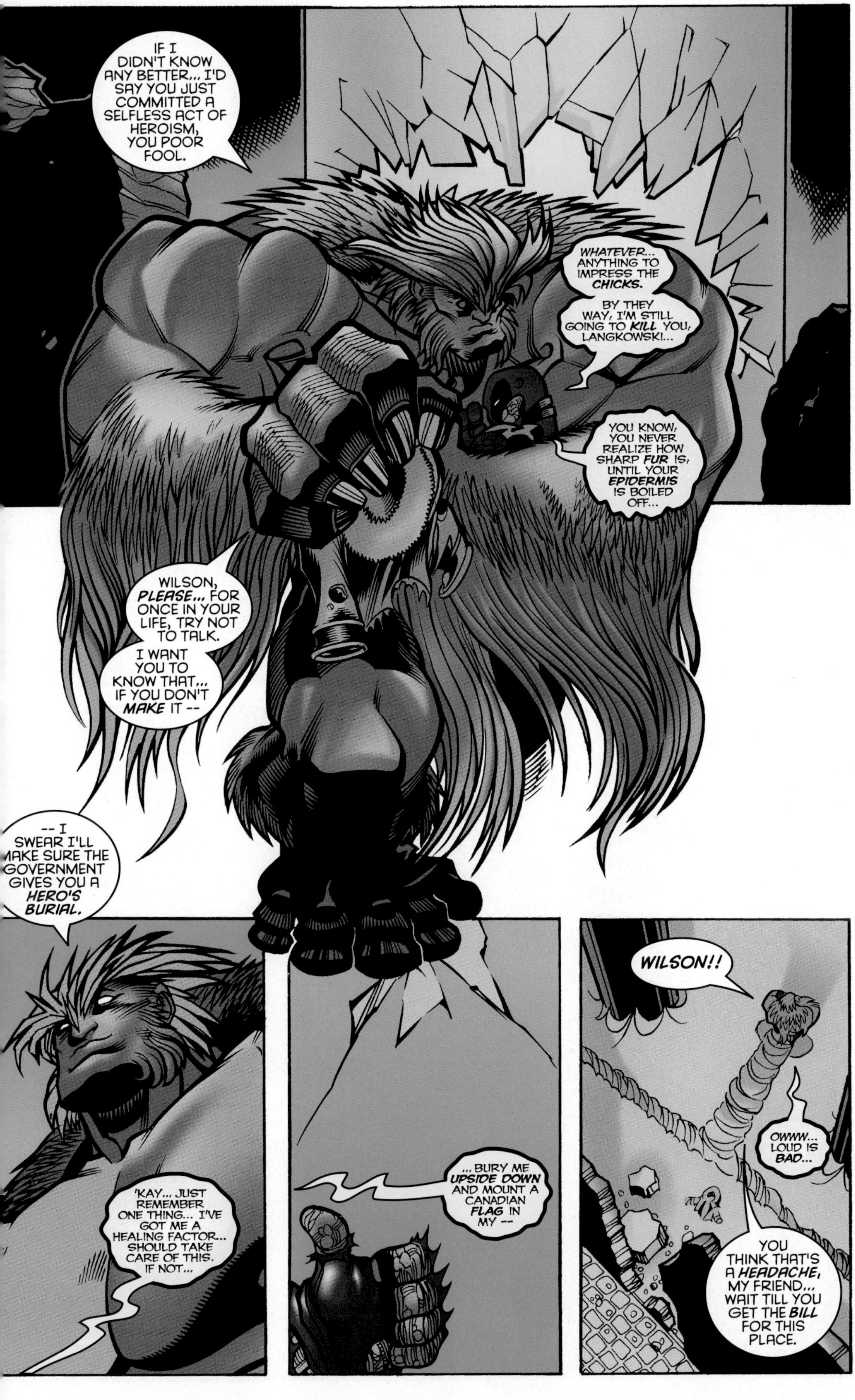
IF I DIDN'T KNOW ANY BETTER... I'D SAY YOU JUST COMMITTED A SELFLESS ACT OF HEROISM, YOU POOR FOOL.
WHATEVER... ANYTHING TO IMPRESS THE CHICKS.
BY THEY WAY, I'M STILL GOING TO KILL YOU, LANGKOWSKI...
YOU KNOW, YOU NEVER REALIZE HOW SHARP FUR IS, UNTIL YOUR EPIDERMIS IS BOILED OFF...
WILSON, PLEASE... FOR ONCE IN YOUR LIFE, TRY NOT TO TALK.
I WANT YOU TO KNOW THAT... IF YOU DON'T MAKE IT --
-- I SWEAR I'LL MAKE SURE THE GOVERNMENT GIVES YOU A HERO'S BURIAL.
'KAY... JUST REMEMBER ONE THING... I'VE GOT ME A HEALING FACTOR... SHOULD TAKE CARE OF THIS. IF NOT...
...BURY ME UPSIDE DOWN AND MOUNT A CANADIAN FLAG IN MY --
WILSON!!
OWWW... LOUD IS BAD...
YOU THINK THAT'S A HEADACHE, MY FRIEND... WAIT TILL YOU GET THE BILL FOR THIS PLACE.

NEW YORK. A FEW DAYS LATER.

"THIRTY-FIVE MINUTES *LATE*-- OBVIOUSLY, *PATCH* DIDN'T GIVE HIM THE *MESSAGE* -- HE'S A *NO-SHOW*."

"HE'LL COME. HAVE *FAITH*, *NOAH*."

"FAITH IS FOR *CHILDREN*, ZOE. IT'S *OVER*. I'M CALLING IN FOR TRANSPORT."

ALPHA TEAM TO CENTRAL, THIS IS A *WASHOUT*. PREPARE TO *SLIDE* US HOME--

PING

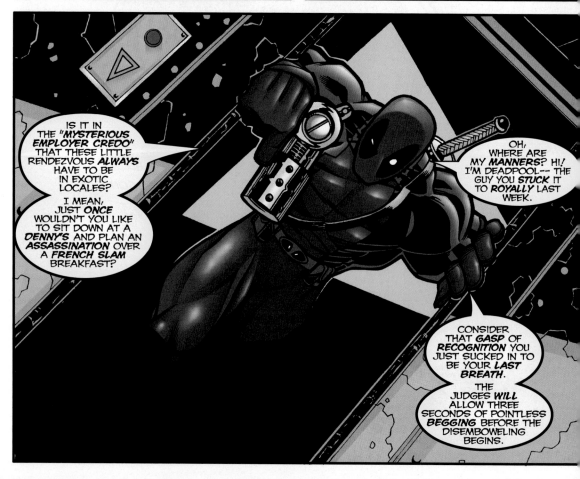

IS IT IN THE *"MYSTERIOUS EMPLOYER CREDO"* THAT THESE LITTLE RENDEZVOUS *ALWAYS* HAVE TO BE IN EXOTIC LOCALES?

I MEAN, JUST *ONCE* WOULDN'T YOU LIKE TO SIT DOWN AT A *DENNY'S* AND PLAN AN *ASSASSINATION* OVER A *FRENCH SLAM* BREAKFAST?

OH, WHERE ARE MY *MANNERS*? HI! I'M DEADPOOL-- THE GUY YOU *STUCK* IT TO *ROYALLY* LAST WEEK.

CONSIDER THAT *GASP* OF *RECOGNITION* YOU JUST SUCKED IN TO BE YOUR *LAST BREATH*.

THE JUDGES *WILL* ALLOW THREE SECONDS OF POINTLESS *BEGGING* BEFORE THE DISEMBOWELING BEGINS.

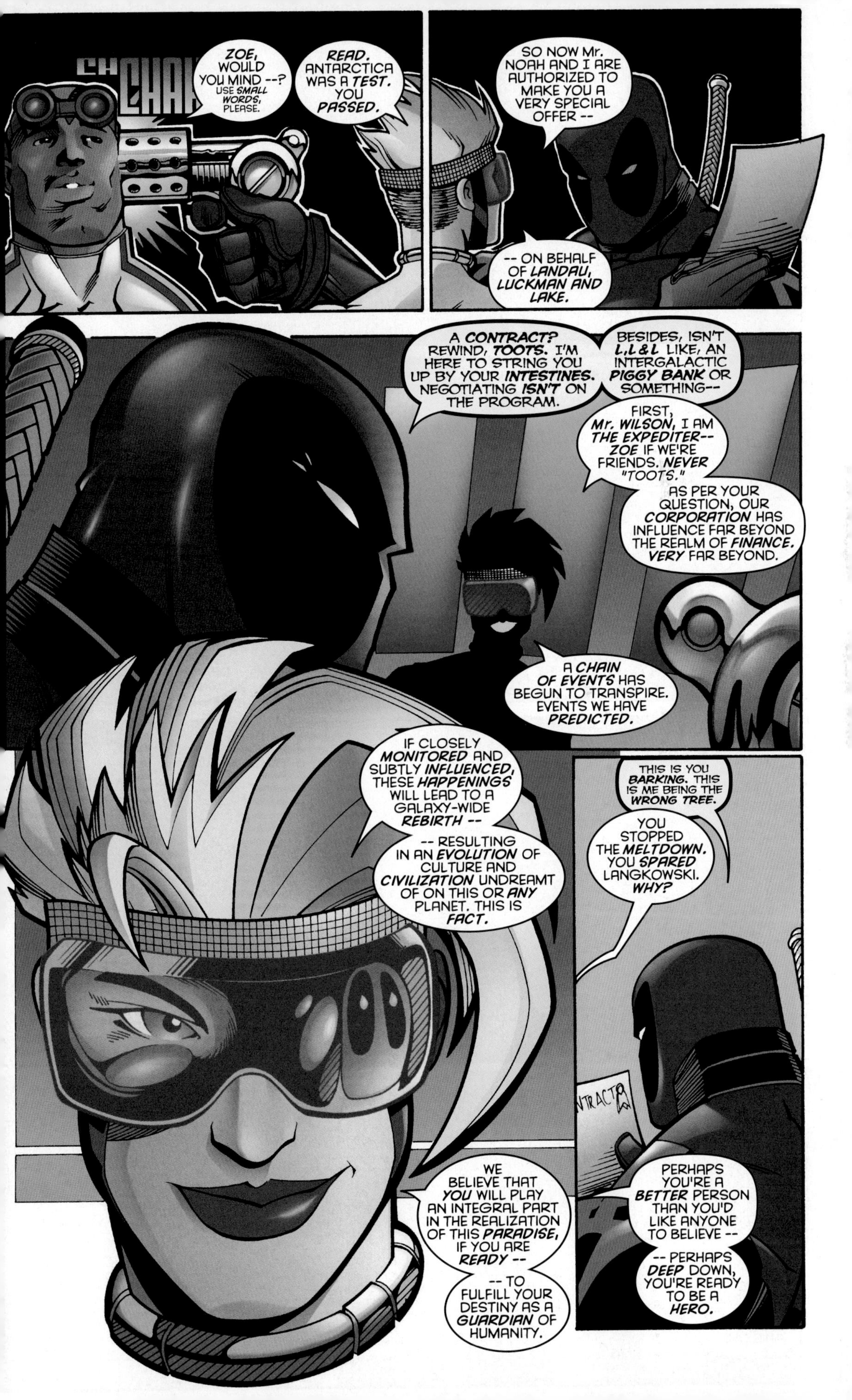

CHCHAK
ZOE, WOULD YOU MIND --? USE SMALL WORDS, PLEASE.
READ. ANTARCTICA WAS A TEST. YOU PASSED.
SO NOW Mr. NOAH AND I ARE AUTHORIZED TO MAKE YOU A VERY SPECIAL OFFER --
-- ON BEHALF OF LANDAU, LUCKMAN AND LAKE.
A CONTRACT? REWIND, TOOTS. I'M HERE TO STRING YOU UP BY YOUR INTESTINES. NEGOTIATING ISN'T ON THE PROGRAM.
BESIDES, ISN'T L,L&L LIKE, AN INTERGALACTIC PIGGY BANK OR SOMETHING--
FIRST, Mr. WILSON, I AM THE EXPEDITER-- ZOE IF WE'RE FRIENDS. NEVER "TOOTS."
AS PER YOUR QUESTION, OUR CORPORATION HAS INFLUENCE FAR BEYOND THE REALM OF FINANCE. VERY FAR BEYOND.
A CHAIN OF EVENTS HAS BEGUN TO TRANSPIRE. EVENTS WE HAVE PREDICTED.
IF CLOSELY MONITORED AND SUBTLY INFLUENCED, THESE HAPPENINGS WILL LEAD TO A GALAXY-WIDE REBIRTH --
-- RESULTING IN AN EVOLUTION OF CULTURE AND CIVILIZATION UNDREAMT OF ON THIS OR ANY PLANET. THIS IS FACT.
WE BELIEVE THAT YOU WILL PLAY AN INTEGRAL PART IN THE REALIZATION OF THIS PARADISE, IF YOU ARE READY --
-- TO FULFILL YOUR DESTINY AS A GUARDIAN OF HUMANITY.
THIS IS YOU BARKING. THIS IS ME BEING THE WRONG TREE.
YOU STOPPED THE MELTDOWN. YOU SPARED LANGKOWSKI. WHY?
NTRACT
PERHAPS YOU'RE A BETTER PERSON THAN YOU'D LIKE ANYONE TO BELIEVE --
-- PERHAPS DEEP DOWN, YOU'RE READY TO BE A HERO.

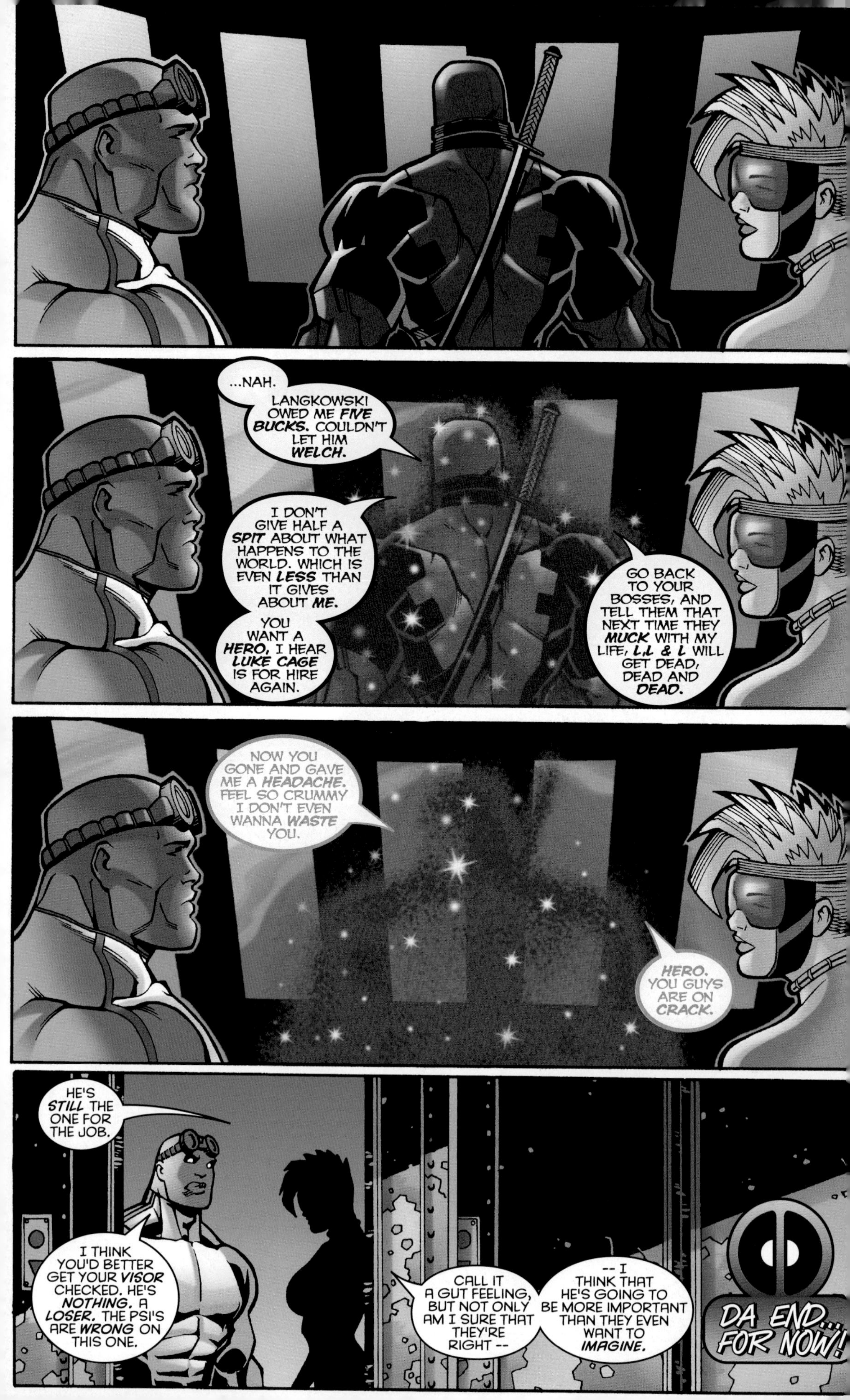
...NAH.
LANGKOWSKI OWED ME FIVE BUCKS. COULDN'T LET HIM WELCH.
I DON'T GIVE HALF A SPIT ABOUT WHAT HAPPENS TO THE WORLD. WHICH IS EVEN LESS THAN IT GIVES ABOUT ME.
YOU WANT A HERO, I HEAR LUKE CAGE IS FOR HIRE AGAIN.
GO BACK TO YOUR BOSSES, AND TELL THEM THAT NEXT TIME THEY MUCK WITH MY LIFE, L,L & L WILL GET DEAD, DEAD AND DEAD.
NOW YOU GONE AND GAVE ME A HEADACHE. FEEL SO CRUMMY I DON'T EVEN WANNA WASTE YOU.
HERO. YOU GUYS ARE ON CRACK.
HE'S STILL THE ONE FOR THE JOB.
I THINK YOU'D BETTER GET YOUR VISOR CHECKED. HE'S NOTHING. A LOSER. THE PSI'S ARE WRONG ON THIS ONE.
CALL IT A GUT FEELING, BUT NOT ONLY AM I SURE THAT THEY'RE RIGHT --
-- I THINK THAT HE'S GOING TO BE MORE IMPORTANT THAN THEY EVEN WANT TO IMAGINE.
DA END... FOR NOW!

BEHIND THE SCENES

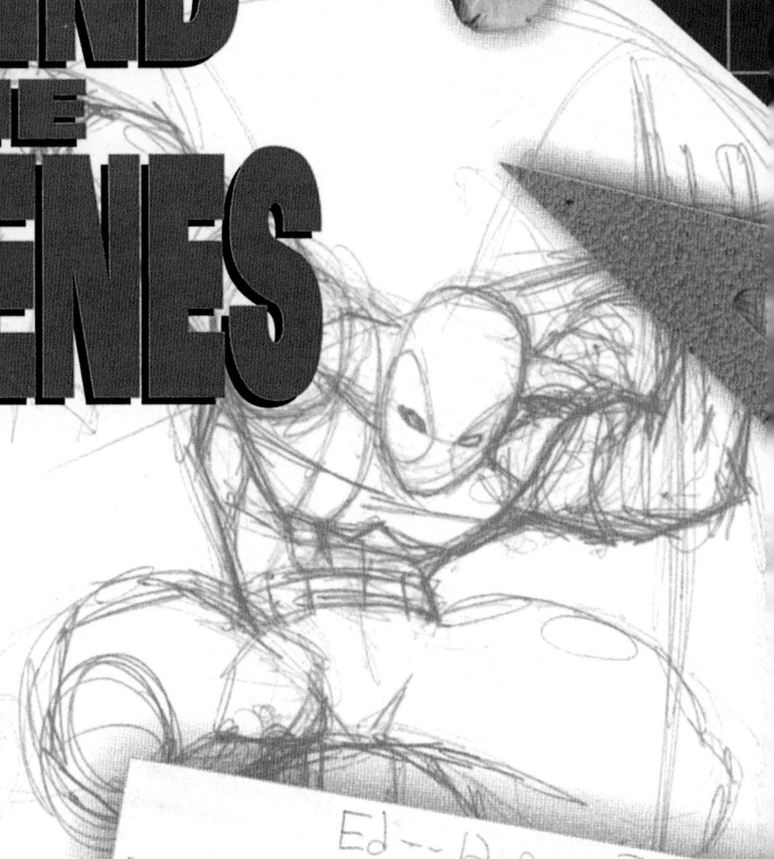

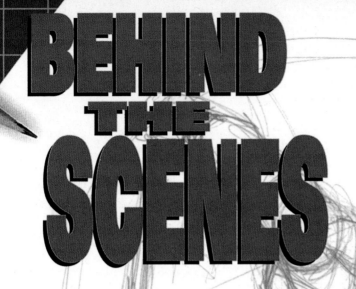

Behind every finished comic there is a story, and the story behind the premiere issue of any series is especially interesting. The assembled creative team must build the framework for what will hopefully be a long series almost from scratch, creating a world inside the Marvel Universe within which the book can grow and thrive. In the case of DEADPOOL, this was especially difficult, since so very little about the character is really known.

Over the next few pages, we're going to take you behind the scenes, showing you a small part of the massive creative and subsequent evolutionary processes that resulted in the book you now hold in your hands.

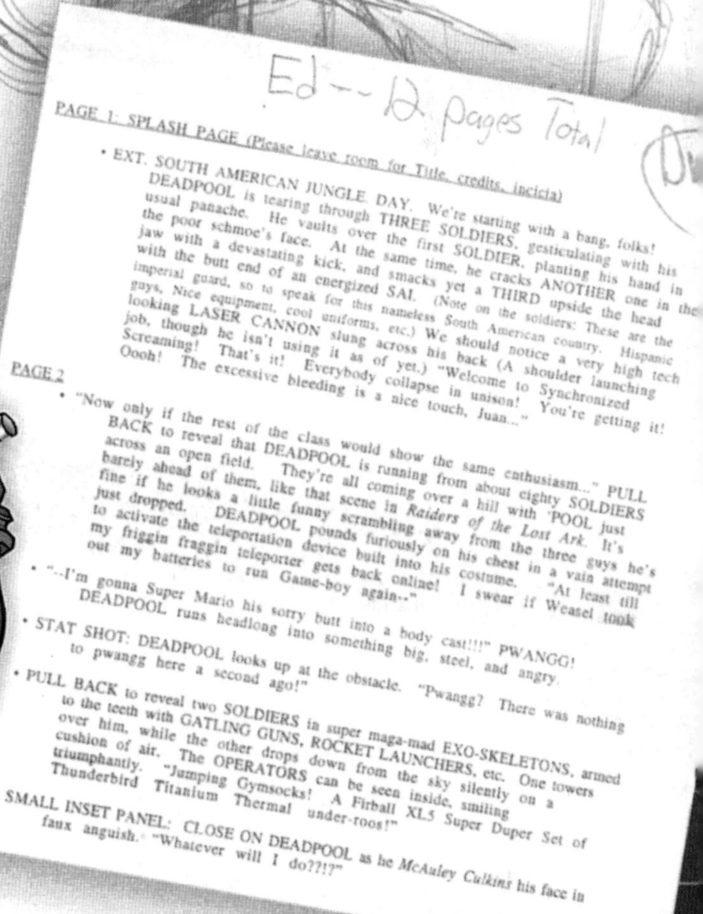

Ed -- 12 pages Total

PAGE 1: SPLASH PAGE (Please leave room for Title, credits, incicia)

• EXT. SOUTH AMERICAN JUNGLE. DAY. We're starting with a bang, folks! DEADPOOL is tearing through THREE SOLDIERS, gesticulating with his usual panache. He vaults over the first SOLDIER, planting his hand in the poor schmoe's face. At the same time, he cracks ANOTHER one in the jaw with a devastating kick, and smacks yet a THIRD upside the head with the butt end of an energized SAI. (Note on the soldiers: These are the imperial guard, so to speak for this nameless South American country. Hispanic guys, Nice equipment, cool uniforms, etc.) We should notice a very high tech looking LASER CANNON slung across his back (A shoulder launching job, though he isn't using it as of yet.) "Welcome to Synchronized Screaming! That's it! Everybody collapse in unison! You're getting it! Oooh! The excessive bleeding is a nice touch, Juan..."

PAGE 2

• "Now only if the rest of the class would show the same enthusiasm..." PULL BACK to reveal that DEADPOOL is running from about eighty SOLDIERS across an open field. They're all coming over a hill with 'POOL just barely ahead of them, like that scene in *Raiders of the Lost Ark*. It's fine if he looks a little funny scrambling away from the three guys he's just dropped. DEADPOOL pounds furiously on his chest in a vain attempt to activate the teleportation device built into his costume. "At least till my friggin fraggin teleporter gets back online! I swear if Weasel took out my batteries to run Game-boy again--"

• "--I'm gonna Super Mario his sorry butt into a body cast!!!" PWANGG! DEADPOOL runs headlong into something big, steel, and angry.

• STAT SHOT: DEADPOOL looks up at the obstacle. "Pwangg? There was nothing to pwangg here a second ago!"

• PULL BACK to reveal two SOLDIERS in super maga-mad EXO-SKELETONS, armed to the teeth with GATLING GUNS, ROCKET LAUNCHERS, etc. One towers over him, while the other drops down from the sky silently on a cushion of air. The OPERATORS can be seen inside, smiling triumphantly. "Jumping Gymsocks! A Firball XL5 Super Duper Set of Thunderbird Titanium Thermal under-roos!"

• SMALL INSET PANEL: CLOSE ON DEADPOOL as he *McAuley Culkins* his face in faux anguish. "Whatever will I do??!?"

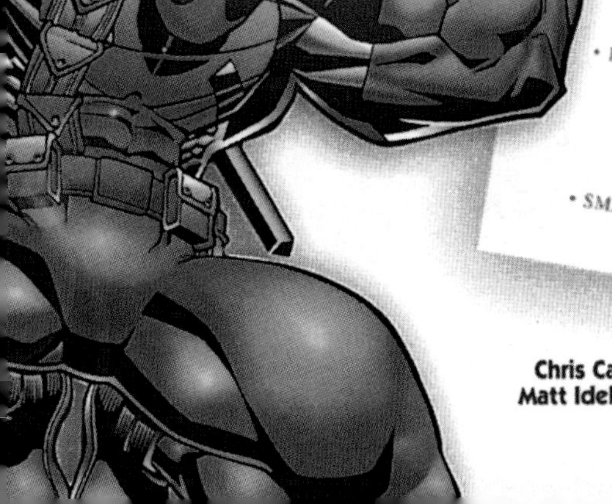

Chris Carroll: Designer
Matt Idelson: Tour Guide

THE STORY

Almost from the outset, it was clear that Landau, Luckman & Lake would be hiring Deadpool to do something bad as a test to see if he was the man for their plans. Originally, writer Joe Kelly envisioned Deadpool being hired to take out the mysterious heads of LL&L themselves. It would be Deadpool's brains that prevented him from pulling the trigger, and Wade Wilson would find himself with a new employer. Editor in chief Bob Harras felt that this was perhaps too cosmic a story for such a down-to-Earth character, and instead suggested using Sasquatch as Deadpool's assigned target. He also thought that Sasquatch and Deadpool doing battle would be an interesting visual. With all that orange and red, it might be a little difficult to make out what's going on, or at least make for a potentially really boring looking page, color-wise. It was quickly decided that having them face off in the snow would make these garish fellows pop out on the page. After that, the revised story quickly fell into place.

In Joe's revised plot, there was a scene that was later cut out in which Langkowski's Gamma Reactor overloads, forcing Langkowski to transform into Sasquatch and save the day. (A) This scene was later cut for dramatic reasons; the story would be better served if it was Deadpool who set off the reactor overload and then had to set things right.

(A)

- REFLECTED IN WALTER'S GLASSES we see the POWER CORE glow with energy. "Gamma levels rising... approaching critical level..." "Steady... Steady..." "Gamma levels at 99% capacity... Doctor--"

- CLOSE ON the controller as WALTER presses a button. The part of the screen we can see reads, "-- DISPERSAL OF GAMMA RADIAT--" "Engage the core NOW!!"

- EXT. THE LAB. POOOOMMM!!! A shaft of energy erupts from the lab into the sky, taking half of the roof with it in a very unexpected explosion!!! (Ed, this is the roof around the tower I'm talking about. The tower itself is still intact.)

PAGE 11
- INT. THE CORE. Even though the core still pumps out energy, the rest of this massive chamber is in ruins. The roof has caved in, FLAMES are everywhere caused by ENERGY DISCHARGES that fire randomly from the core. SNOW trickles in through the missing roof section. TECHNICIANS and SCIENTISTS run around the room, trying their best to put out the blaze. OTHERS are trapped under debris, hurt, etc. "Someone get to the source!" "Are you crazy!?" "Where are Marsten and Hopper?!?"

- THROUGH THICK SMOKE, a man appears, carrying two unconscious TECHIES, one under each arm. "He's got them!!!" "Everyone! Clear out of here! The core is unstable!"

- WALTER LANGKOWSKI, just a tad cooked by the blast, emerges from the smoke with his men. "Dr. Langkowski has them!!!" "Come on, don't stand there gawking! Get them to med-center!"

(MORE)

PAGE 11 (CONTD.)
- FRANCIS grabs WALTER by the arm as the two men are carried off by other TECHIES. He points upwards towards the explosion. "What are we going to do, Walter?" "You and the rest are going to get to a safe distance while I take care of business here..."

- CLOSE ON WALTER, as he looks upwards towards the hole in the ceiling. He is clearly stunned by what he sees. "While I make sure that there's still a safe distance left to go to!"

In another early plot twist, Deadpool was originally hired for his mission by Noah while atop the Statue of Liberty (B). The scene was cut and replaced with the second Hellhouse scene on page 18. We figured that Deadpool was supposed to get his assignments via the Hellhouse, and it wouldn't make a whole lot of sense for him to be hired by Noah directly. Since this scene served the dual purpose of revealing much of Deadpool's backstory, that function had to be worked into the new scene, and was, in a cleverly constructed moment which also features the first appearance of T-Ray, a fellow merc at the Hellhouse who's going to be causing more than a little trouble in later issues.

(B)

PAGE 18

- EXT. STATUE OF LIBERTY. NIGHT. ATOP THE CROWN. A MAN (NOAH) in shadow, leans on one of the windows, looking out at the water. "Fifteen minutes late... I think he's a no-show."
- CLOSE ON THE WINDOW. The man continues speaking out loud, prepares to light a cigarette. "Central, Prepare to slide me home--"
- KTHINK! A KATANA slices the air right in front of NOAH'S face as he ignites the lighter. The sword splits the Cig perfectly in half. Noah's eyes go wide with surprise. "Why do you high-rollers always choose to meet in such inaccessible locales? Just once I'd like to sit down in Denny's with the rest of the Schmoes and talk shop over a French Slam breakfast.""Deadpool I presume?"
- COOL SHOT of DEADPOOL as he hangs upside down in front of the WINDOW attatched to a RAPELLING LINE, casually picking at his "fingernails" with the tip of his sword. "Figured I'd sweat you out till I knew who else was nearby. SOP, you understand." NOAH holds out a thin DOSSIER for DEADPOOL to peruse. "I knew you were there. I was just testing..." "Ch'yahh, right! As IF!"
- DEADPOOL studies the file intently, though it is clearly upside down. "In this file you will find the location and layout of a secret research facility in the Antarctic. There's been an accident there.""Love what you did here! Extra points for neatness! Snazzy dress for the cover... where's the bubble gum?"

PAGE 19

- DEADPOOL lowers himself onto the ledge, dangling his feet boyishly as NOAH tries to brief him. "Gamma Radiation is spreading at an alarming rate." "Not for nothing, sir. But I fell asleep during nuclear physics... or I was looking up suzi James skirt... either way, I can't stop a three-mile-popsicle."
- REACTION SHOT: DEADPOOL almost drops the file when NOAH sternly explains. "We don't want you to stop it. We want you to help it along." "Ex-squeeze me?" "I represent employers with intrests in the southern hemisphere that are failing miserably--"
- NOAH indicates the DOSSIER, turning it rightside up for DEADPOOL, who sits up suddenly, paying close attention. "--A disaster of this magnitude could ease their pain with an insurance winfall. Loss of life will be restricted to the personnel at the plant, who're dead men anyway. They are willing to pay twenty million dollars to ensure that the Gamma spill runs its course." "Patch said that you requested me personally. Aside from my dashing smile and well defined buttocks, why the special attention?"
- CLOSE ON NOAH, almost smiling. "You have a reputation as a wild card. Whenyou're around, things get broke. That's number one. Number two, your vaunted healing factor makes you resistant to any radiation you'll encounter before the job is done." "Who does your homework? Encyclopedia brown? So much for private medical history... And number three?
- CLOSE ON the DOSSIER, where we see a CANADIAN GOVT. PIC of WALTER LANGKOWSKI. "The man who you'll have to kill to complete the job is an office mate from your Canadian Days."

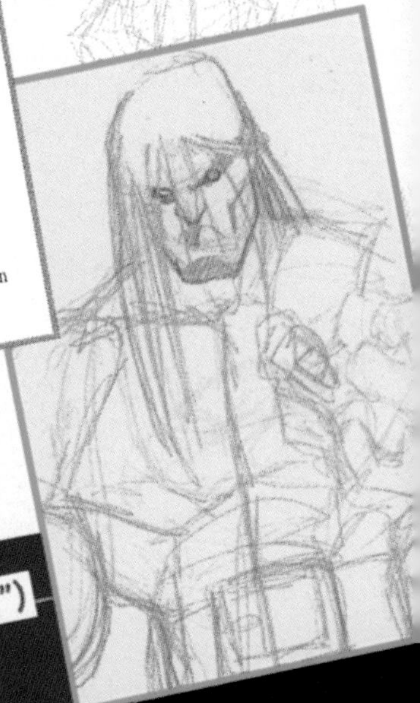

(The Villianous "T-Ray")

THE COVER

ART PAPER FOR BLEED PAGES (BOOKSHELF FORMAT OR SADDLE STITCH)
ALL BLEED ART MUST EXTEND TO SOLID LINE
PRINTS AT 67%
ILLUSTRATION QUALITY
KEEP ALL LETTERING INSIDE BROKEN-LINE BOX
Book Issue Story Page # Line Up Page #

The cover of any comic book goes through generations of sketches and revisions before a final design is approved. In this case, the cover was particularly important since this was the first issue of the series. The character had to be well spotlighted, and the logo had to be clear and as unobstructed as possible. To complicate matters further, this was to be a wrap-around cover. The inherent problem with wrap-arounds is that since we're not contending with the logo or tradedress on the backside, the back cover tends to look cooler than the front half.

(1)

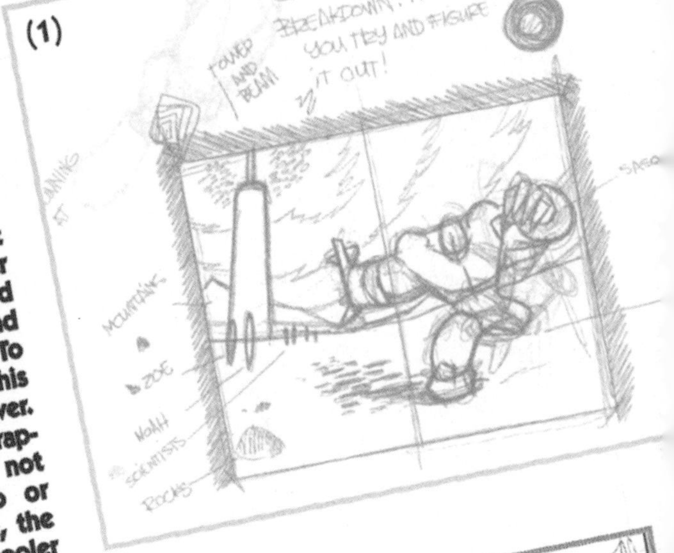
SORRY ABOUT THE POOR BREAKDOWN... YOU TRY AND FIGURE IT OUT!
TOWER AND BEAM
MOUNTAINS
ZOE
NOAH
SCIENTISTS
ROCKS

(1A)

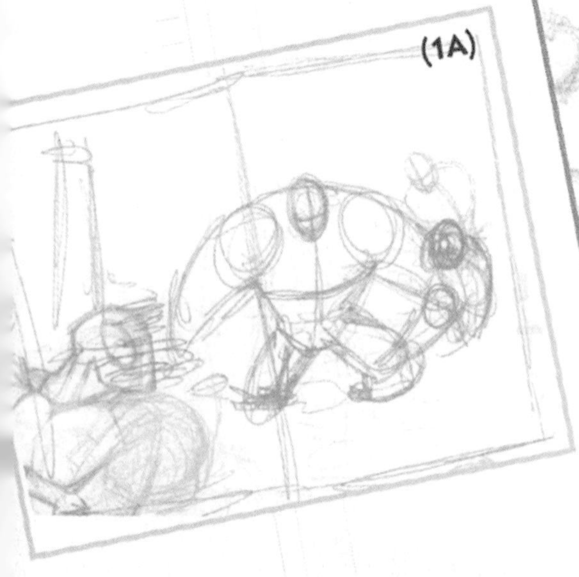

(2)

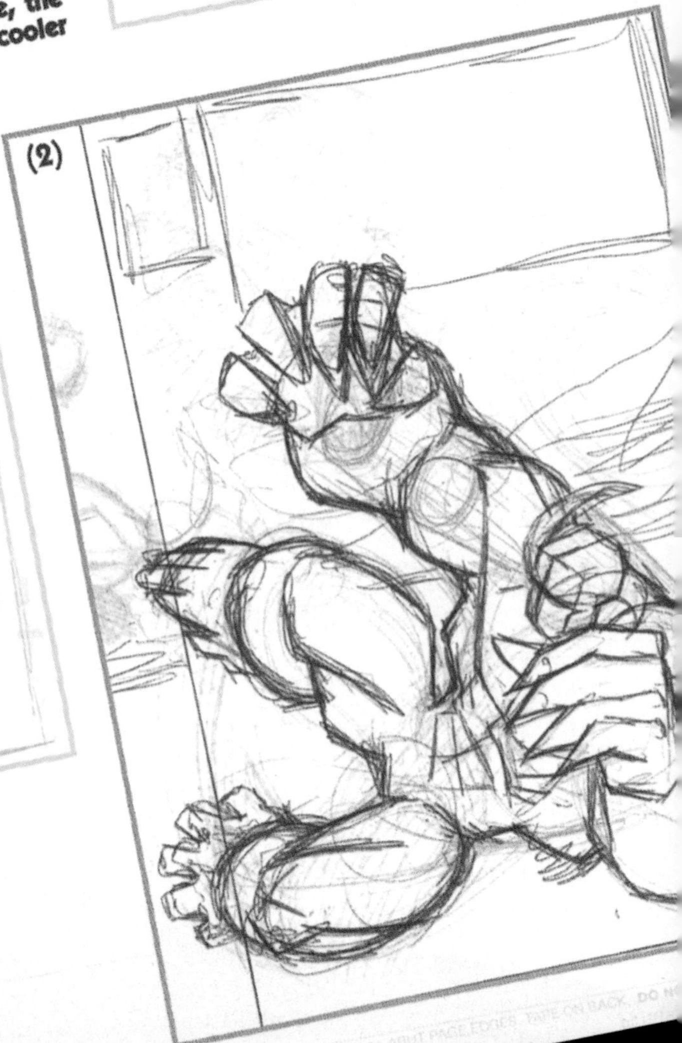

ART PAPER FOR BLEED PAGES (BOOKSHELF FORMAT
ALL BLEED ART MUST EXTEND TO
Issue
Book
Story
Page #
Line
Page #

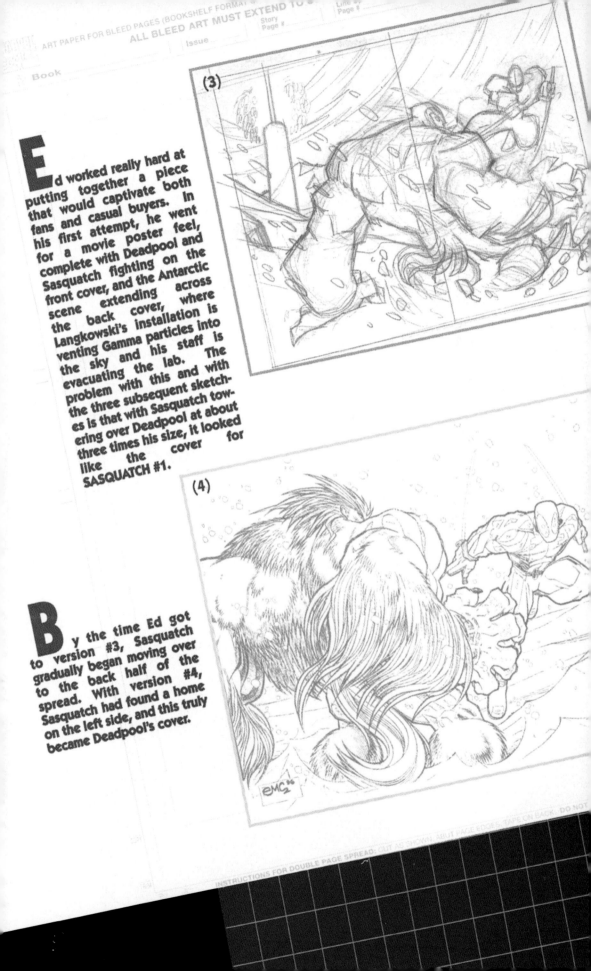

(3)

Ed worked really hard at putting together a piece that would captivate both fans and casual buyers. In his first attempt, he went for a movie poster feel, complete with Deadpool and Sasquatch fighting on the front cover, and the Antarctic scene extending across the back cover, where Langkowski's installation is venting Gamma particles into the sky and his staff is evacuating the lab. The problem with this and with the three subsequent sketches is that with Sasquatch towering over Deadpool at about three times his size, it looked like the cover for SASQUATCH #1.

(4)

By the time Ed got to version #3, Sasquatch gradually began moving over to the back half of the spread. With version #4, Sasquatch had found a home on the left side, and this truly became Deadpool's cover.

PRINTS AT 67% · ILLUSTRATION QUALITY

GES (BOOKSHELF FORMAT OR SADDLE STITCH)
ALL BLEED ART MUST EXTEND TO SOLID LINE

KEEP ALL
LETTERING INSIDE
BROKEN-LINE BOX

Story
Page #

Line Up
Page #

IF AT FIRST YOU DON T SUCCEED...

Variations, both large and small, are not confined to just the plotting stage. Change is often the name of the game, particularly when a new series is starting up. With the relentless and unforgiving nature of The Schedule, many are the moments when the inker is called upon to bail out... uh, sorry, *correct* a problem in the pencils.

In this scene, Walter Langkowski has decided to take a trip outdoors to admire his fabulous gamma experiment. Now Walter was *supposed* to transform into Sasquatch as he was undressing. Instead, Ed depicted Walt heading outdoors (panel two), undressing like some kind of streaker (panel three), and finally as Sasquatch in panel four. To fans unfamiliar with the character and his powers, this could be a problem (besides which, watching him transform is kind of cool). No sweat!

Our inker-extraordinaire, Nathan rolled up his sleeves and went to work, give our boy Langkowski some fluffy patches of fur on his face and body in panel three.

Then Chris Lichtner colored the piece, taking into account not just the fur color but changes in Walter's skin color as well, and the problem was solved and none were the wiser (well, until now, anyway).

ART PAPER FOR BLEED PAGES (BOOKSHELF FORMAT OR SADDLE STITCH)

ALL BLEED ART MUST EXTEND TO SOLID LINE

Story Page # | Line Up Page #

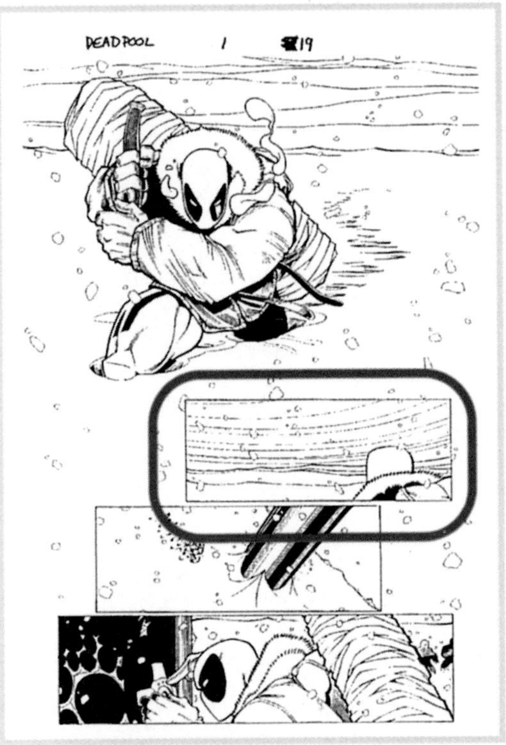

DEADPOOL 1 19

Oftentimes, the colorist alone must carry the burden of saving the day. In this next example, Chris did his subtle best to right a grave injustice perpetrated upon the innocent.

In this familiar shot, Deadpool is trudging through the frozen wasteland of Antarctica, mile after mile. His target: Langkowski's Antarctic lab. Problem is, the lab wasn't drawn in the second panel. We considered asking Nathan to ink in the lab. Photostatting the establishing shot of the lab from an earlier page and dropping it into the panel was another option, but Chris had the best suggestion of all: "Leave it to me!"

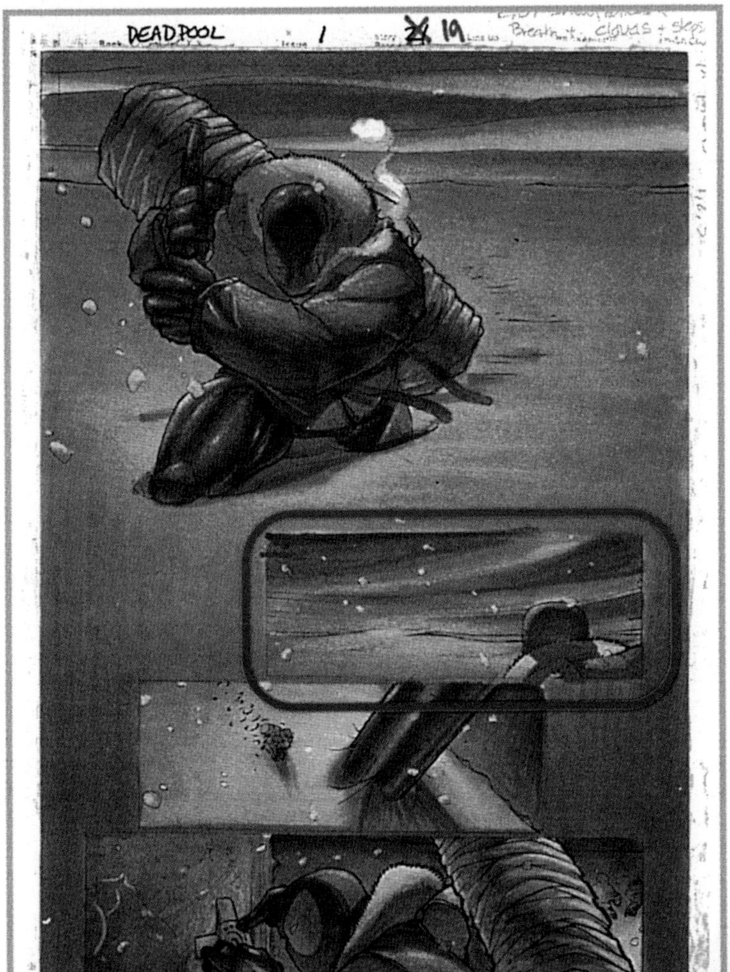

DEADPOOL 1 19

Chris added an eerie, surreal green glow to the second panel, indicating the location of the lab. This not only showed what it was Deadpool was heading for, but also gave the reader a sense of distance and isolation as Deadpool trudged through the snow.

CHARACTER DESIGN

Before an artist can begin a project, he has to define how he or she is going to interpret the characters to their own style while also keeping them recognizable. Here, taken from Ed's sketchbook, are some of his early stabs at Sasquatch, Blind Alfred and of course, our main character, Deadpool.

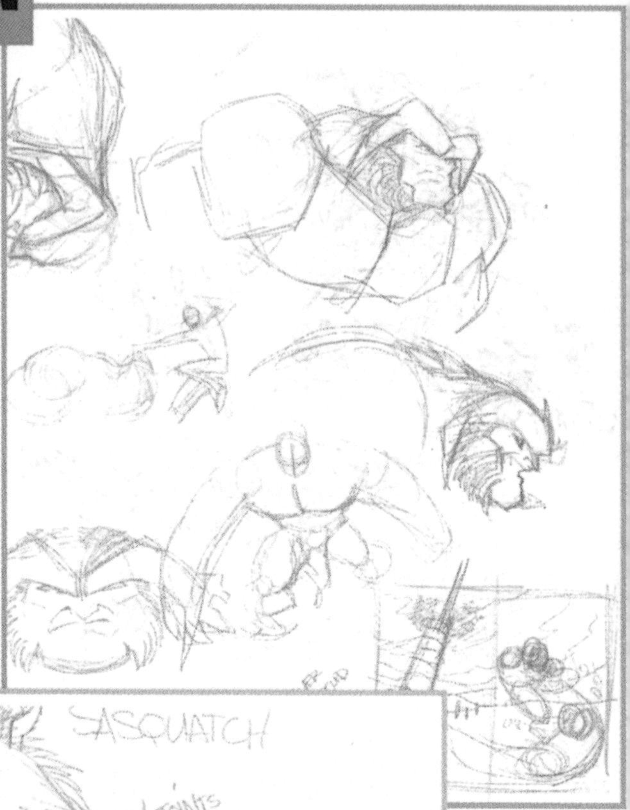

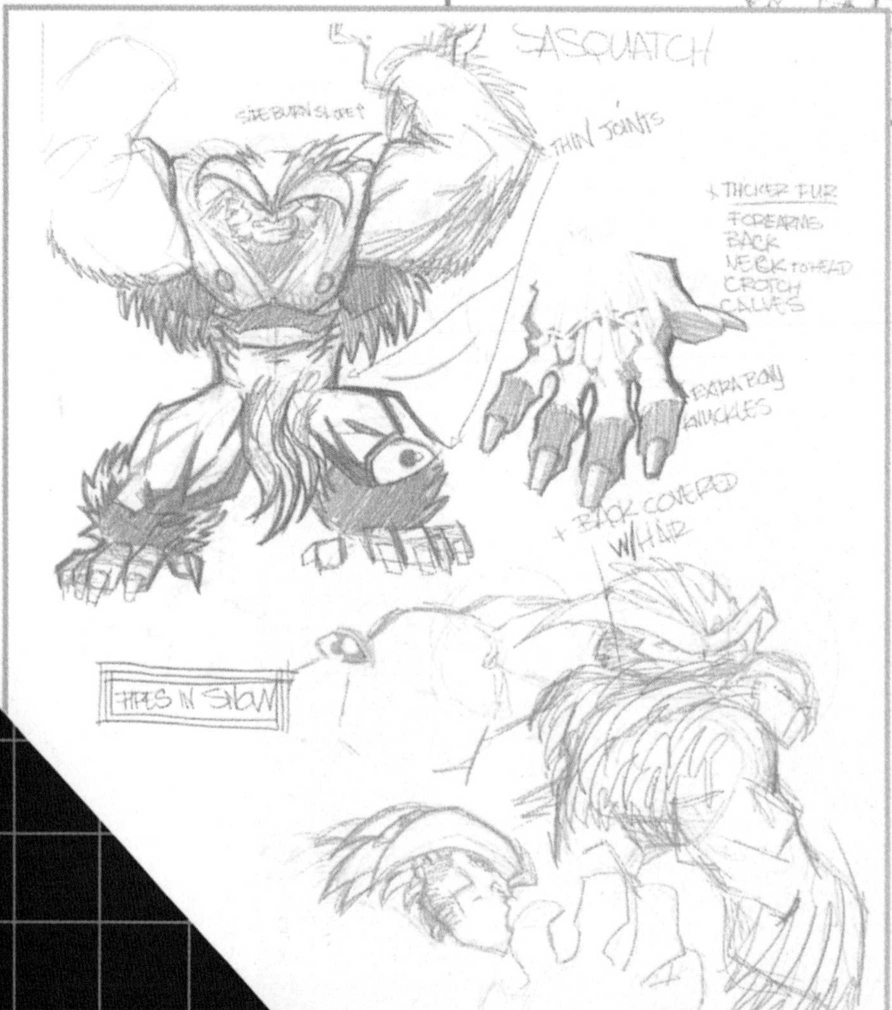
SASQUATCH
SIDEBURN SHORT
THIN JOINTS
+ THICKER FUR
FOREARMS
BACK
NECK TO HEAD
CROTCH
CALVES
EXTRA BONY KNUCKLES
+ BACK COVERED W/HAIR
PIPES IN SNOW

ART PAPER FOR BLEED PAGES (BOOKSHELF FORMAT OR SADDLE STITCH)

ALL BLEED ART MUST EXTEND TO SOLID LINE

Book Issue Story Page # Line Up Page #

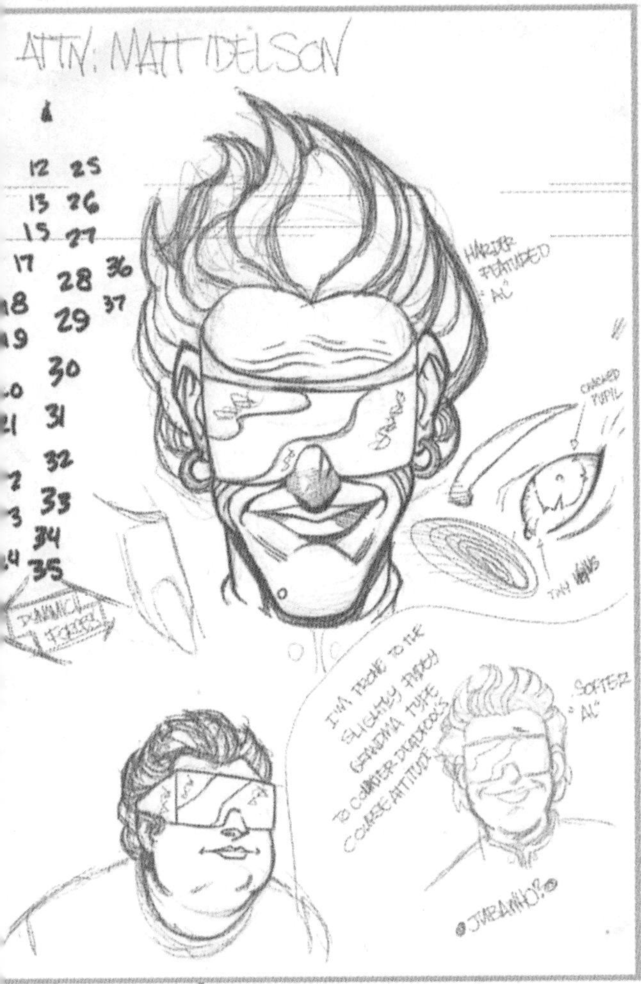

ATTN: MATT IDELSON
HARDER FEATURED "AL"
CHANGED PUPIL
SOFTER "AL"

Notice the two alternate versions of Blind Al. Ed favored the shot at the lower left, the "kinder, pudgier" Blind Alfred, but we shot him down, since we have some special plans for Al which require her to look the way she does in this issue. The shot on the lower right was also dropped for that reason, plus the fear that she looked like Jubilee: 2099. The narrow-faced, hair-in-a-bun Blind Al led to some humorous speculation that she might really be Aunt May reincarnated.

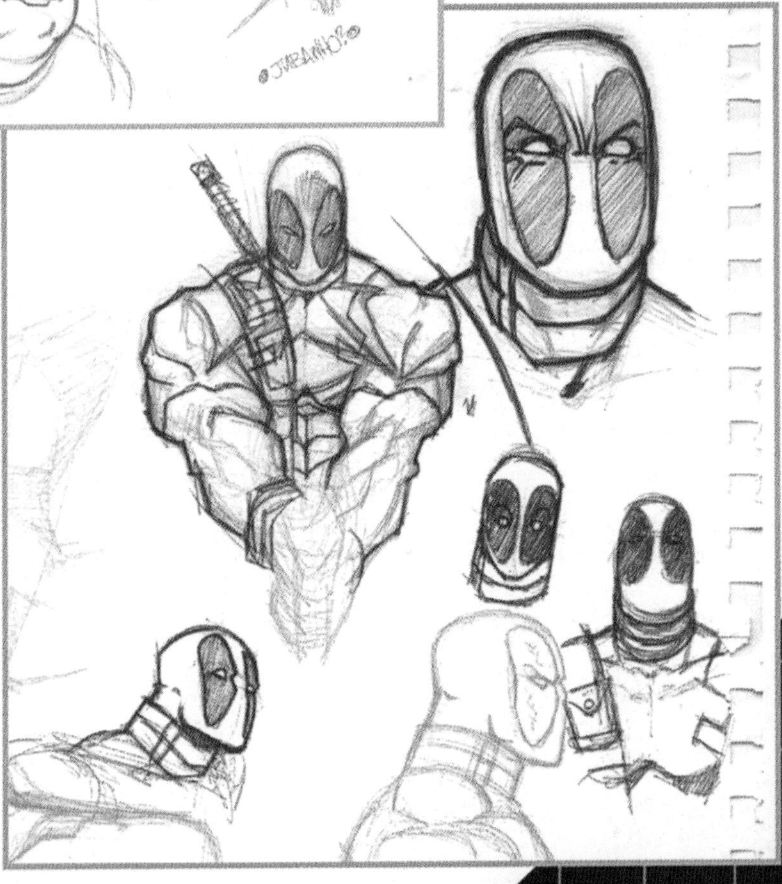

INSTRUCTIONS FOR DOUBLE PAGE SPREAD: CUT AS SHOWN. ABUT PAGE

DEADPOOL - DEADLINES

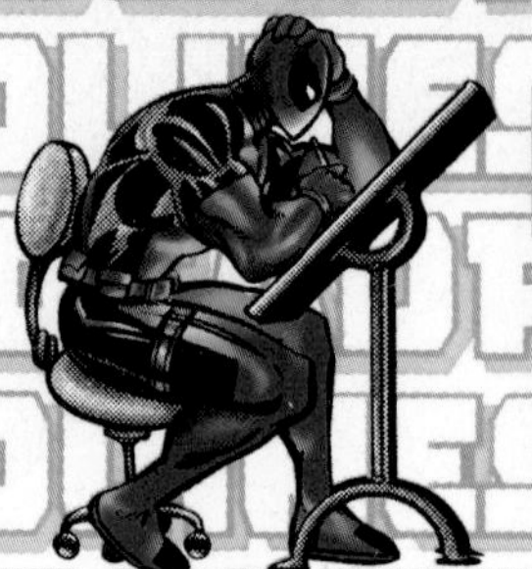

DEADLINES

DESIGN BY COMICRA

Hola, and welcome to the first, most terrific, bestest... well, you've heard the "welcome aboard" speech a billion times, so I'll keep that part short. If you've made it this far into the issue, you know that this is but the first of what will be a *monthly* DEADPOOL comic. Pretty neat, huh? I can't tell you the honest-to-god excitement this project has and will continue to give me! My initial trepidation about doing a series featuring a guy who's not a hero, but can't be an out-and-out villain either left me kind of wondering how the heck we were going to pull this off, but pull it off I think we have.

A large load of the credit really has to go to Joe Kelly (who's going to babble on about this project himself in just a few moments), who really had this character pretty well nailed down from day one. Fully realizing Deadpool's personality is fundamental to making this thing work, and I think Joe got it with his first swing of the bat (well, maybe the *second* swing). And Ed... Ed, Ed, Ed. This guy is special, folks. He's just got that knack for this book. Working with Ed has already been one of the most unique and exciting experiences of my young and questionable career, and I truly expect that Ed's work will be twice as good in issue two, and triply good in issue three (and so forth). As for Nathan... what can I say, Mr. M? Nathan really looks *good* over our young Mr. Ed, and while he will probably become the unsung hero of this book, we here in the office are definitely singing his praises (right after "I Left My Heart In San Francisco," but that's a different story). And then there's Chris. I knew we were going to need a really, really talented colorist to fill out all that open space in Ed's art, and when Chris came aboard, I knew he was either going to make us or break us. Well, I think he made us. Simply put, Chris is one of the best colorists in the industry, and I'm lucky to be working with him. 'Nuff said! As always, the typical and professional tip of the cap to our old pal, Richard Starkings and his staff at Comicraft, for lettering this book properly and with great care. Richard, you are a friend to the editor. And finally, I would be remiss in not putting the spotlight on my able-bodied, wee-pal assistant, Paul, who can speak any alien tongue from *Star Wars* but still struggles with English. "Artoodetowha bo Seethreepiowha ey toota odd mischka Jabba du Hutt" to you too, pal!

Why have a letters page without letters, you ask? Good question. We figured many of you might be reluctant to send a letter if you didn't know exactly where to send it. After seeing a big piece of eye-candy like this... well, now you know. If you happen to own a modem and are the sort of comics reader who likes to check out the MARVEL: ONLINE web page on America Online (and who isn't?), then check this out: you can send your letters to this page via the DEADPOOL message boards! That's right: just post your letter to this book within the DEADPOOL folder inside either the adult or children's message boards. If your letter reads like a letter, and most importantly, has something to say, pipe it through, and we'll toss it in here.

Which brings me to my next point: please be constructive and specific about what you like and don't like. We want to do more than just a rah-rah page for DEADPOOL here; producing a monthly title around a character who's closer to being a villain than a hero is bound to elicit some measure of positive and negative response. We definitely want to know what you do and don't like about what we're doing each month. Don't hold back!

And now, we've come the point which all read probably fear—the "Spec Thanks/Gush" section. Not make this sound like t Academy Awards, but there a a few people to whom either "thanks" or a "curse on yo first-born" are due. In n particular order, they are.. Mark Powers, who was suppose to edit this series when it was just a wee limited series-in-development. Mark hired Ed for DEADPOOL before making the fatal mistake of devoting his time to the main X-books with Bob Harras. When he gave up DEADPOOL, Mark was kind enough to give up Ed, as well.

I'd also like to thank The Professor, James Felder, who gave immeasurable and invaluable input to this series, with suggestions and tips that really kept this thing on course, and Ben Raab, who was a sturdy sounding board for myself and Joe Kelly, and had more than a couple terrific suggestions. Also, thanks to Alison Gill and Melisa Danon of our Manufacturing Department, and to the Bullpen (particularly Dawn Guzzo and Dan Carr) whose individual and collective efforts resulted in the high production values you have seen here. Thanks also to Scott Koblish, who illustrated those cute li'l, hard-working Deadpool's up at the top of the page, and John Marasigan, who put this puppy together. Finally, in the great tradition of brown-nosing that has come before me, I'd really like to thank The Boss, Bob Harras, for taking a chance on an editorial and creative team who's great grandparents were still in diapers when he first started editing the X-Men. Goo-goo to you!

Now I hate the sound of my own voice, and this thing has gone on longer than anything I'll ever write for the rest of my life, but no first issue

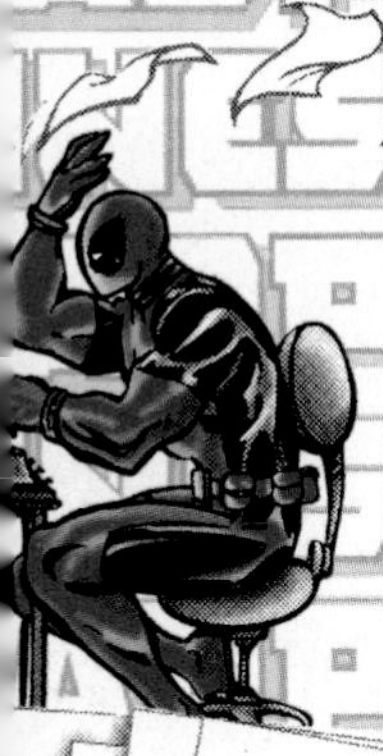

SEND LETTERS TO:
DEADLINES
c/o MARVEL COMICS GROUP
387 PARK AVE. SOUTH
NEW YORK, NY
10016

EDITOR:
MATT IDELSON

ASSISTANT EDITOR:
PAUL TUTRONE

EDITOR-IN-CHIEF:
BOB HARRAS

NEXT TIME: A MURDEROUS ADVERSARY STRIKES AND A MEMBER OF OUR CAST FALLS VICTIM (WELL, SORT OF)! PLUS: BREAKFAST WITH DEADPOOL!

letters page is complete without some hints and clues as to what lies ahead, so I'm just going to throw some stuff out there. Next issue reintroduces a Marvel villain we've seen before, who's going to be playing a role in this series as time progresses. It's also a Weasel-intensive tale. Issue three kicks off a two-part story that picks up on a couple of threads from the second DEADPOOL limited series, and will lead our poor Wade Wilson straight into some very large and angry hands in issue four. And then issue five... man, issue five's going to throw *all* you readers for a real loop!

Enjoy!

—Matt Idelson

Dear Everyone,

I've been sitting at the computer for over an hour now trying to come up with a witty way to introduce myself to you folks... And I'm stuck. I'm stuck on one phrase that's zipping through my brainpan over and again. It's not very clever, or all that funny, but it seems to hit the nail on the head:

I love Deadpool.

Plain, simple, to the point. That means that writing him is more than just a job. It means that the integrity of the Merc-with-a-Mouth's basic character is as important to me as it is to you. Most importantly, it means that from month to month I'm gonna bust my hump to make his life as manic, miserable, exciting, bloody, twisted, perverse, angst-ridden and hysterical as semi-good taste and the Comics Code will allow. That's a promise, folks... You can call me on it if you ever feel the need. That said, if you've made it this far in the book, then I have to assume that to some degree, you love Deadpool too. Good. We've got something in common. If you also happen to like sitting in a tub of banana-strawberry gelatin while reciting lines from *Pulp Fiction*, then we have *a lot* in common...

Writing Deadpool has been one of those rare experiences where the character takes on a life of his own almost from second one. This is due in no small part to the hard work of fellas like Fabian Nicieza, Rob Liefeld, Mark Waid and many others who worked Frankesteinian magic and gave this monster his spirit in the first place. I can tell you first-hand that this is not a simple task, and I tip my hat to the maniacs who came before me and made it look so easy.

This is my first solo crack at an ongoing book, and I couldn't have asked for a better place to start. The creative team is the tops. Matt Idelson is a gentleman and a scholar, a man who knows when to reign Deadpool in and when to keep his yap shut and let the psycho run amok. Matt has a keen sense of storytelling and a thirst for quality that I expect to come through in every issue.

Before Ed McGuinness even put pencil to paper, I knew that he'd be an excellent collaborator. Not only was his work clean and exciting, but his enthusiasm for Deadpool was a tangible force. Ed has managed to capture both the comedic and the demented elements of Deadpool's character, and I look forward to watching them both grow together as the series goes on. Ed is also from Boston, which makes him an easy target of ridicule. If anyone ever writes Ed a letter, please pick on Boston, the Celtics, that weird accent... anything. It's fun, I swear...

The rest of the team, Nathan, Chris, and Richard have done a bang-up job on this book, the quality of which goes without saying. (In case you missed it, just go back to any page and take a sec to look at the inking, the colors and the letters. If you still missed it, then get to a hospital cause you're freakin' blind!!!) As of this writing, most of the team have returned from the Marvel House for Overworked Artists and should all be ready to dive into issue two with a clean bill of health... and a healthy prescription or two!

On a brown-nosing note, thanks to Bob Harras for taking a chance on me for this unique series, and for not firing me the second I said, "So, like at the end of the first issue, we find out that Deadpool is actually the third Summers brother!" (I WAS KIDDING!!!) The fact that I wasn't canned on the spot shows that the man has a sense of humor, one that I hope to have satisfied with this issue...

This is the beginning of a long and bizarre ride my friends, and if you just sit back and relax, I promise that you won't be disappointed. To tell you the truth, I really don't have any choice but to make it good, because I've got one whacked out Merc with an itchy trigger finger sitting on the edge of my desk at all times, telling me in his worst Brando cotton-chewing voice, "Either your brains or some cool stories'll be on the computer by morning... you decide. Now, what about that Larry King? Good kisser, don't you agree? How about my scenes in *The Freshman*? Did I look heavy to you?"

Did I mention that I love this guy?

See you next month,

-Joe Kelly

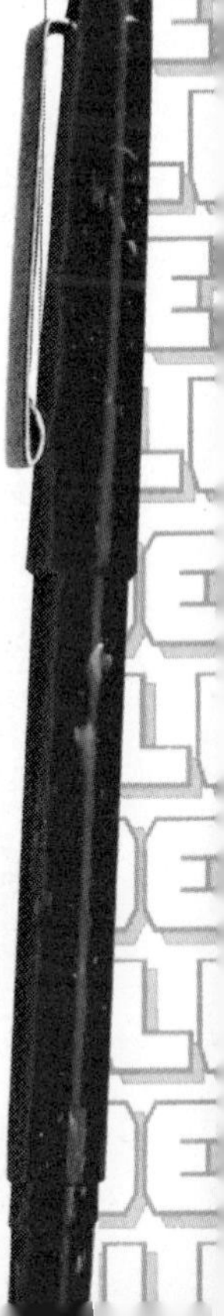

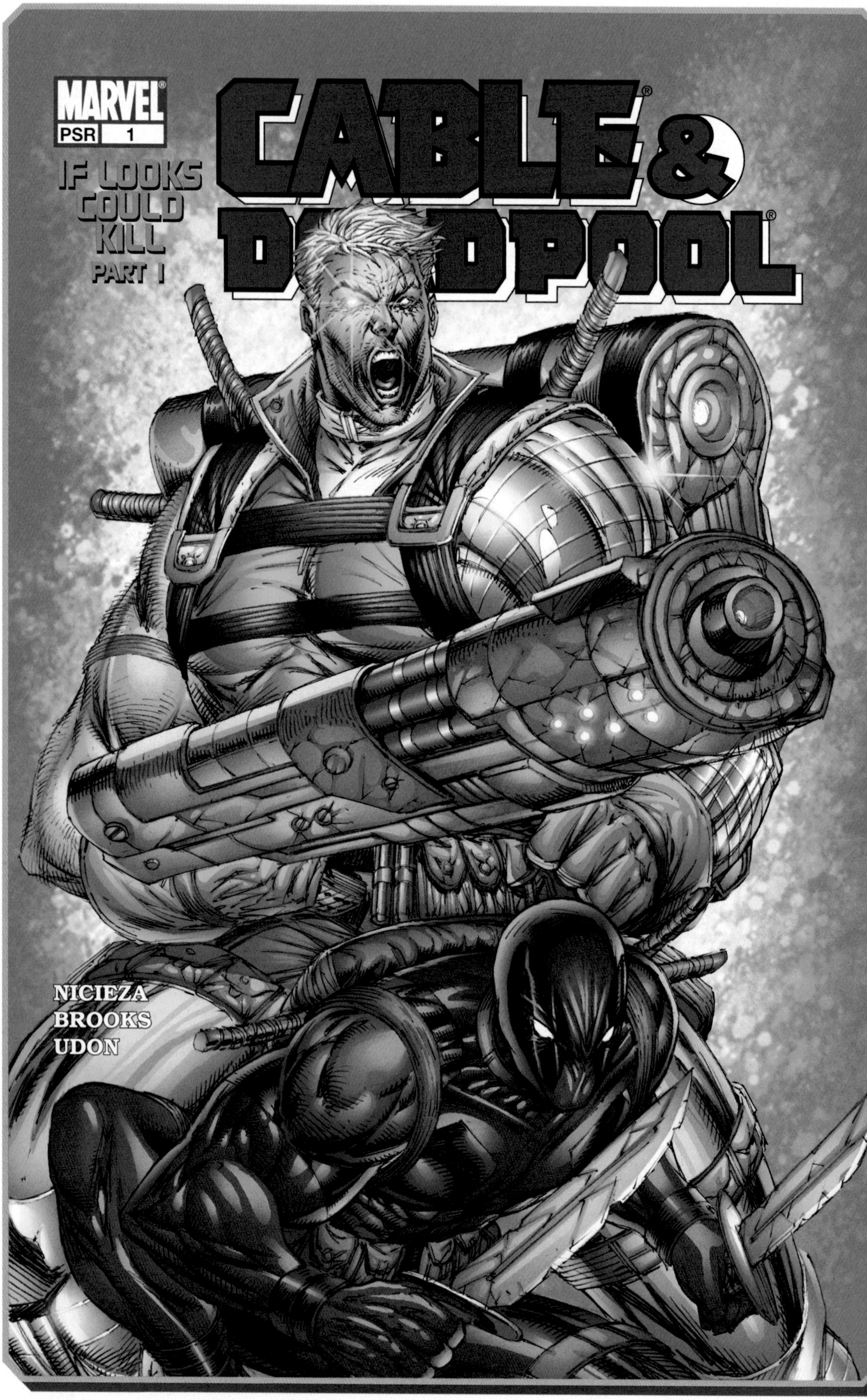
MARVEL
PSR 1
CABLE & DEADPOOL
IF LOOKS COULD KILL PART 1
NICIEZA
BROOKS
UDON

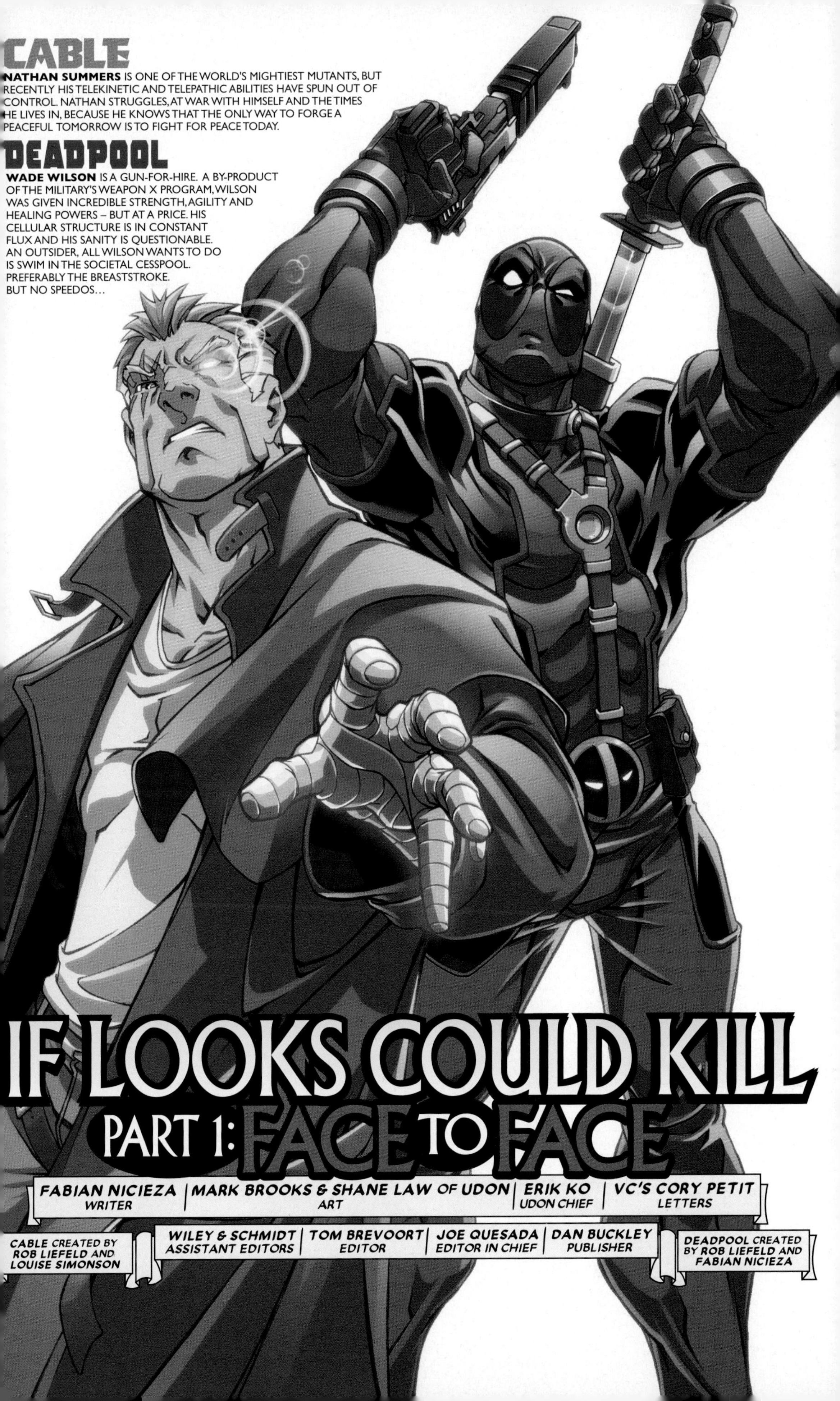
CABLE
NATHAN SUMMERS IS ONE OF THE WORLD'S MIGHTIEST MUTANTS, BUT RECENTLY HIS TELEKINETIC AND TELEPATHIC ABILITIES HAVE SPUN OUT OF CONTROL. NATHAN STRUGGLES, AT WAR WITH HIMSELF AND THE TIMES HE LIVES IN, BECAUSE HE KNOWS THAT THE ONLY WAY TO FORGE A PEACEFUL TOMORROW IS TO FIGHT FOR PEACE TODAY.
DEADPOOL
WADE WILSON IS A GUN-FOR-HIRE. A BY-PRODUCT OF THE MILITARY'S WEAPON X PROGRAM, WILSON WAS GIVEN INCREDIBLE STRENGTH, AGILITY AND HEALING POWERS – BUT AT A PRICE. HIS CELLULAR STRUCTURE IS IN CONSTANT FLUX AND HIS SANITY IS QUESTIONABLE. AN OUTSIDER, ALL WILSON WANTS TO DO IS SWIM IN THE SOCIETAL CESSPOOL. PREFERABLY THE BREASTSTROKE. BUT NO SPEEDOS…
IF LOOKS COULD KILL
PART 1: FACE TO FACE
FABIAN NICIEZA WRITER
MARK BROOKS & SHANE LAW OF UDON ART
ERIK KO UDON CHIEF
VC'S CORY PETIT LETTERS
CABLE CREATED BY ROB LIEFELD AND LOUISE SIMONSON
WILEY & SCHMIDT ASSISTANT EDITORS
TOM BREVOORT EDITOR
JOE QUESADA EDITOR IN CHIEF
DAN BUCKLEY PUBLISHER
DEADPOOL CREATED BY ROB LIEFELD AND FABIAN NICIEZA

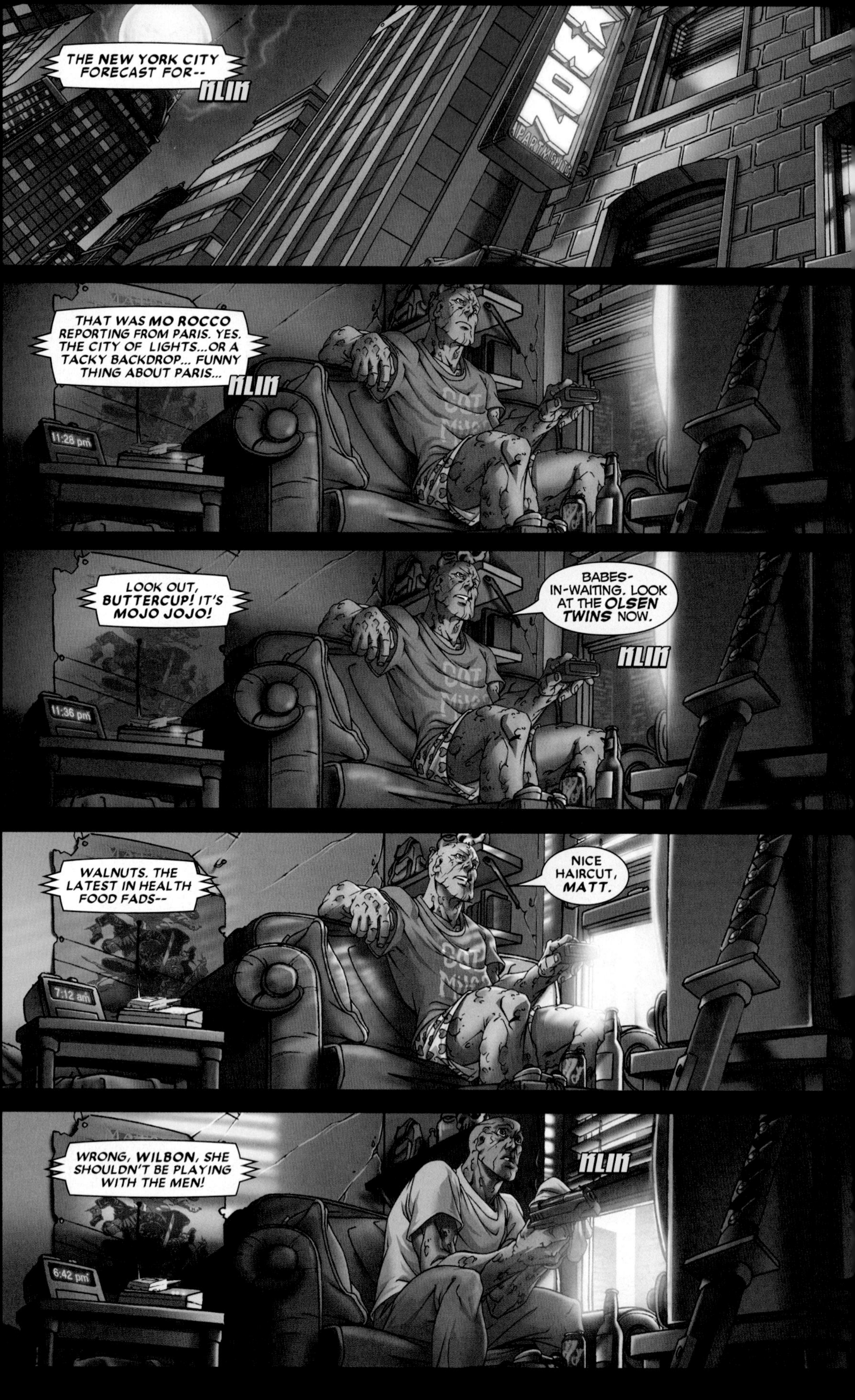
THE NEW YORK CITY FORECAST FOR--
KLIK
APARTMENTS
THAT WAS MO ROCCO REPORTING FROM PARIS. YES. THE CITY OF LIGHTS...OR A TACKY BACKDROP... FUNNY THING ABOUT PARIS...
KLIK
11:28 pm
LOOK OUT, BUTTERCUP! IT'S MOJO JOJO!
BABES-IN-WAITING. LOOK AT THE OLSEN TWINS NOW.
KLIK
11:36 pm
WALNUTS. THE LATEST IN HEALTH FOOD FADS--
NICE HAIRCUT, MATT.
7:12 am
WRONG, WILBON, SHE SHOULDN'T BE PLAYING WITH THE MEN!
KLIK
6:42 pm

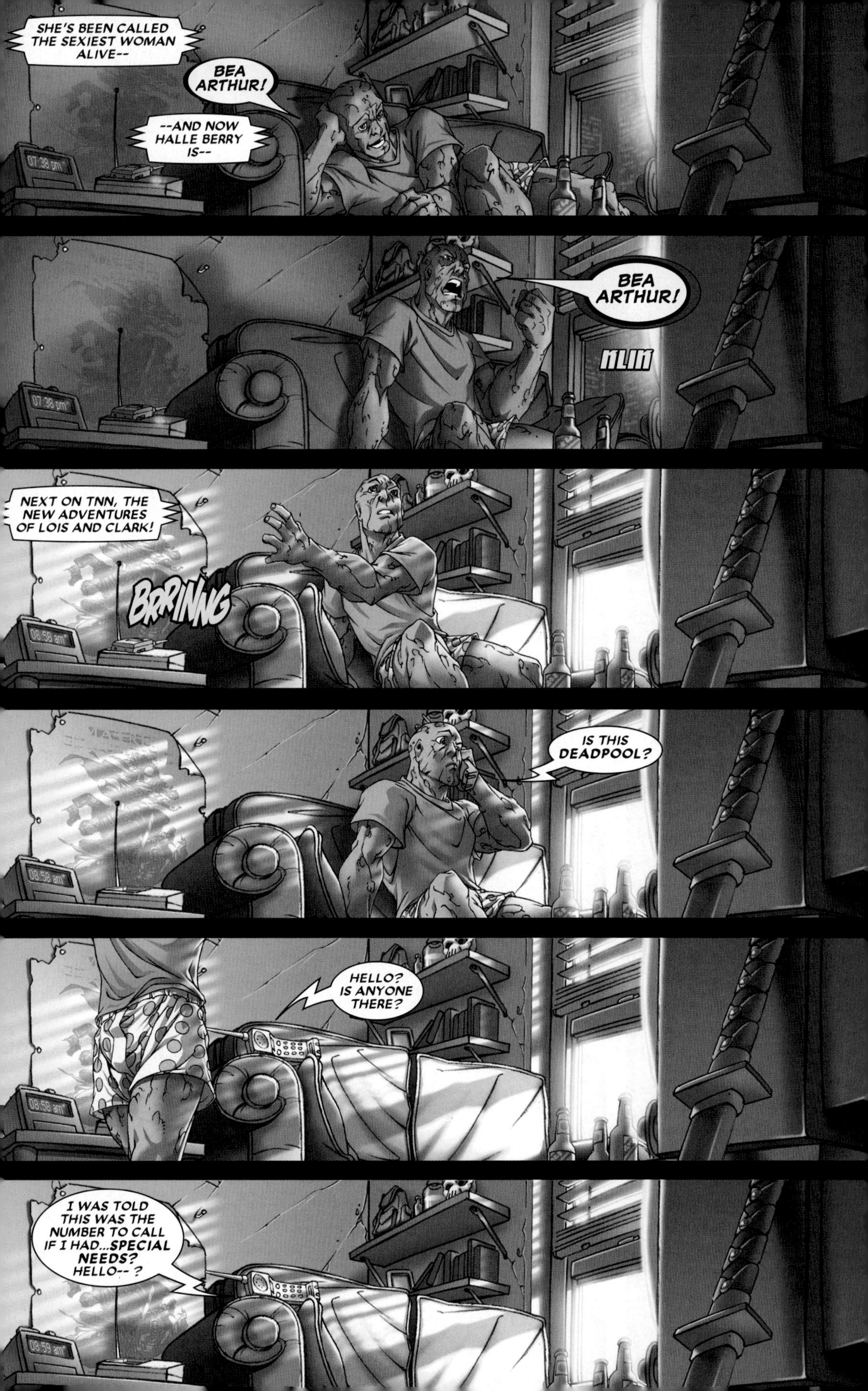
SHE'S BEEN CALLED THE SEXIEST WOMAN ALIVE--
BEA ARTHUR!
--AND NOW HALLE BERRY IS--
07:38 pm
BEA ARTHUR!
KLIK
NEXT ON TNN, THE NEW ADVENTURES OF LOIS AND CLARK!
BRRINNG
08:58 am
IS THIS DEADPOOL?
HELLO? IS ANYONE THERE?
I WAS TOLD THIS WAS THE NUMBER TO CALL IF I HAD...SPECIAL NEEDS? HELLO-- ?
08:59 am

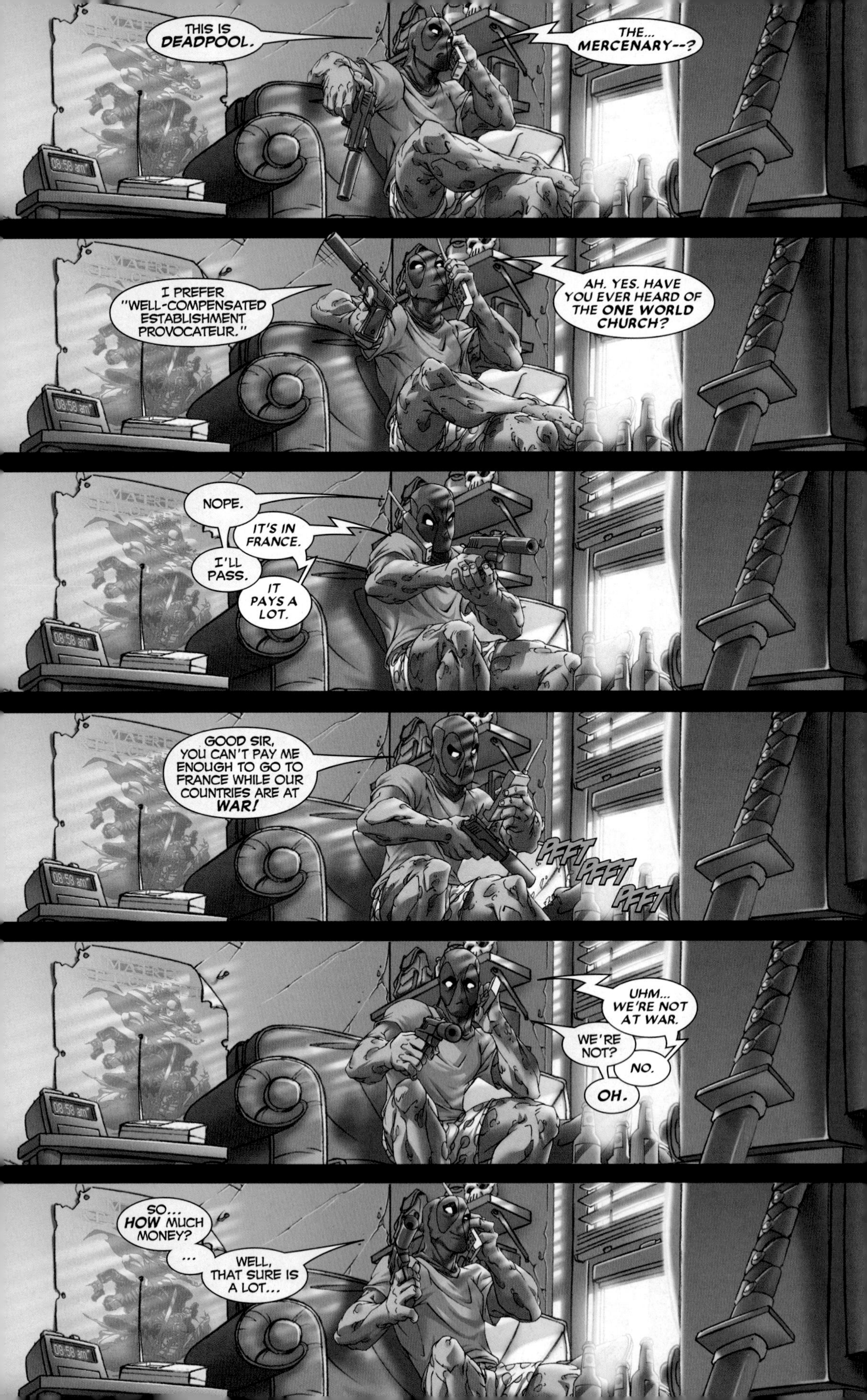
THIS IS DEADPOOL.
THE... MERCENARY--?
I PREFER "WELL-COMPENSATED ESTABLISHMENT PROVOCATEUR."
AH. YES. HAVE YOU EVER HEARD OF THE ONE WORLD CHURCH?
NOPE.
IT'S IN FRANCE.
I'LL PASS.
IT PAYS A LOT.
GOOD SIR, YOU CAN'T PAY ME ENOUGH TO GO TO FRANCE WHILE OUR COUNTRIES ARE AT WAR!
PFFT PFFT PFFT
UHM... WE'RE NOT AT WAR.
WE'RE NOT?
NO.
OH.
SO... HOW MUCH MONEY?
...
WELL, THAT SURE IS A LOT...

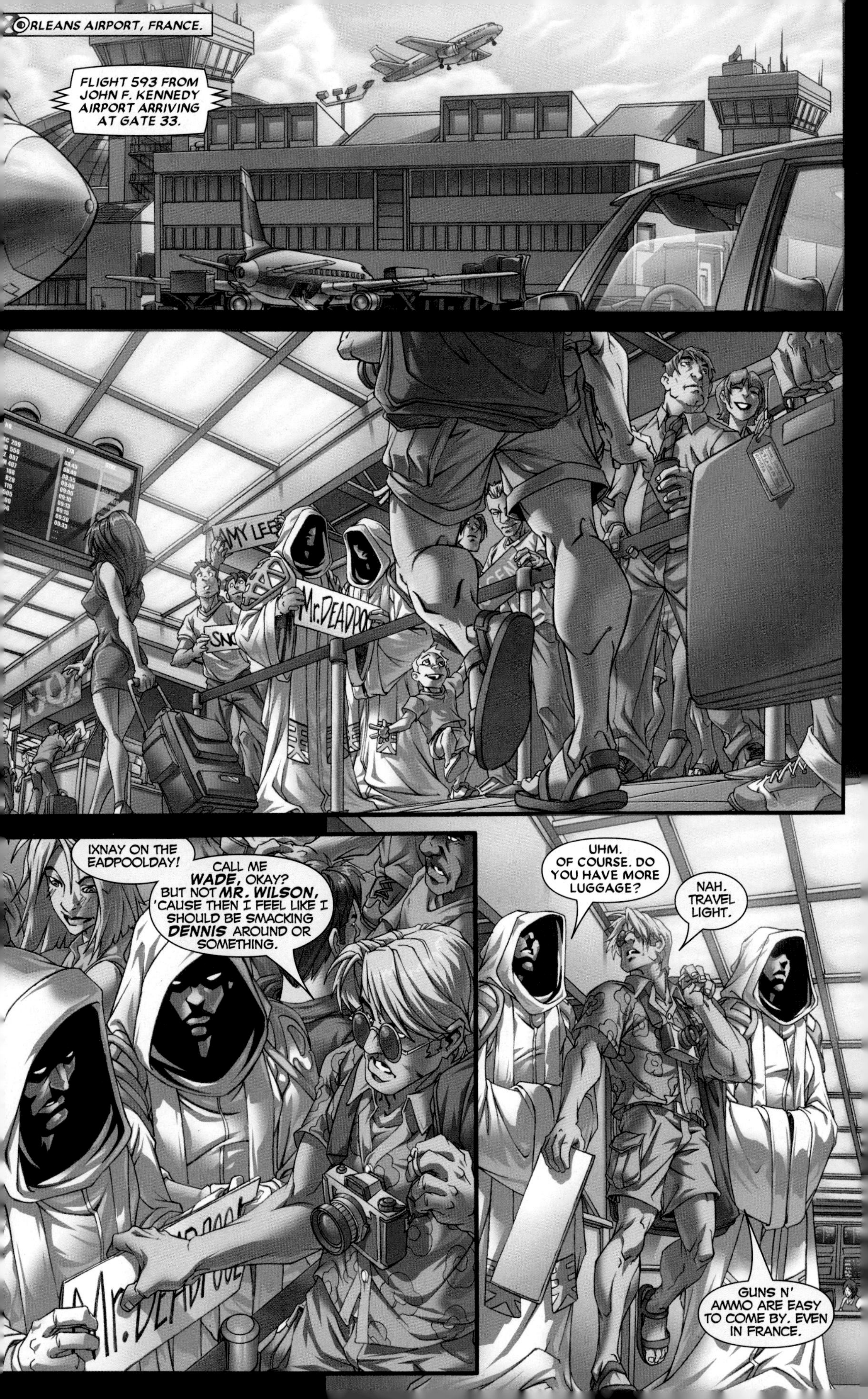
ORLEANS AIRPORT, FRANCE.
FLIGHT 593 FROM JOHN F. KENNEDY AIRPORT ARRIVING AT GATE 33.
AMY LEE
Mr. DEADPO
IXNAY ON THE EADPOOLDAY!
CALL ME WADE, OKAY? BUT NOT MR. WILSON, 'CAUSE THEN I FEEL LIKE I SHOULD BE SMACKING DENNIS AROUND OR SOMETHING.
UHM. OF COURSE. DO YOU HAVE MORE LUGGAGE?
NAH. TRAVEL LIGHT.
GUNS N' AMMO ARE EASY TO COME BY. EVEN IN FRANCE.

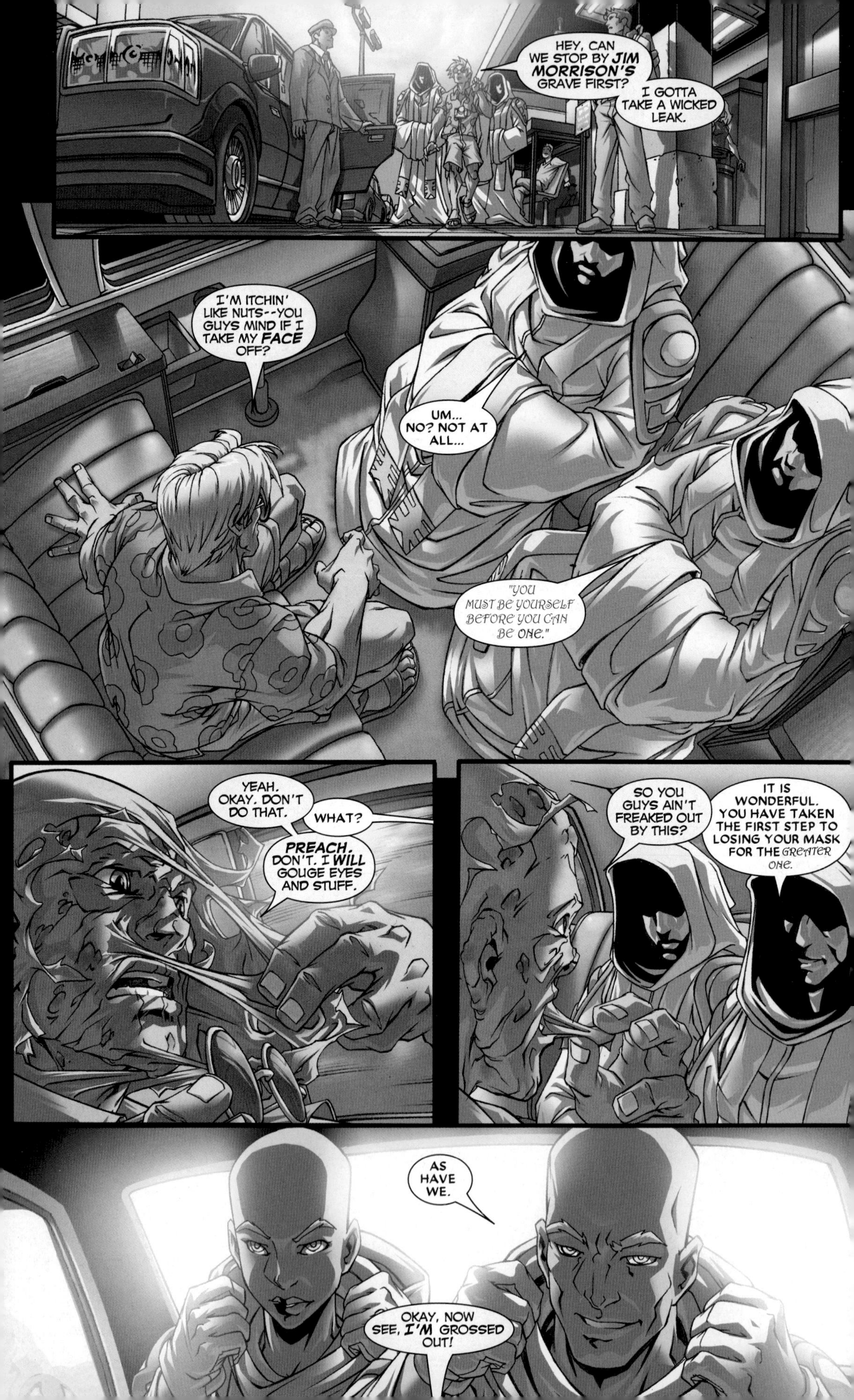
HEY, CAN WE STOP BY JIM MORRISON'S GRAVE FIRST?
I GOTTA TAKE A WICKED LEAK.
I'M ITCHIN' LIKE NUTS--YOU GUYS MIND IF I TAKE MY FACE OFF?
UM... NO? NOT AT ALL...
"YOU MUST BE YOURSELF BEFORE YOU CAN BE ONE."
YEAH. OKAY. DON'T DO THAT.
WHAT?
PREACH. DON'T. I WILL GOUGE EYES AND STUFF.
SO YOU GUYS AIN'T FREAKED OUT BY THIS?
IT IS WONDERFUL. YOU HAVE TAKEN THE FIRST STEP TO LOSING YOUR MASK FOR THE GREATER ONE.
AS HAVE WE.
OKAY, NOW SEE, I'M GROSSED OUT!

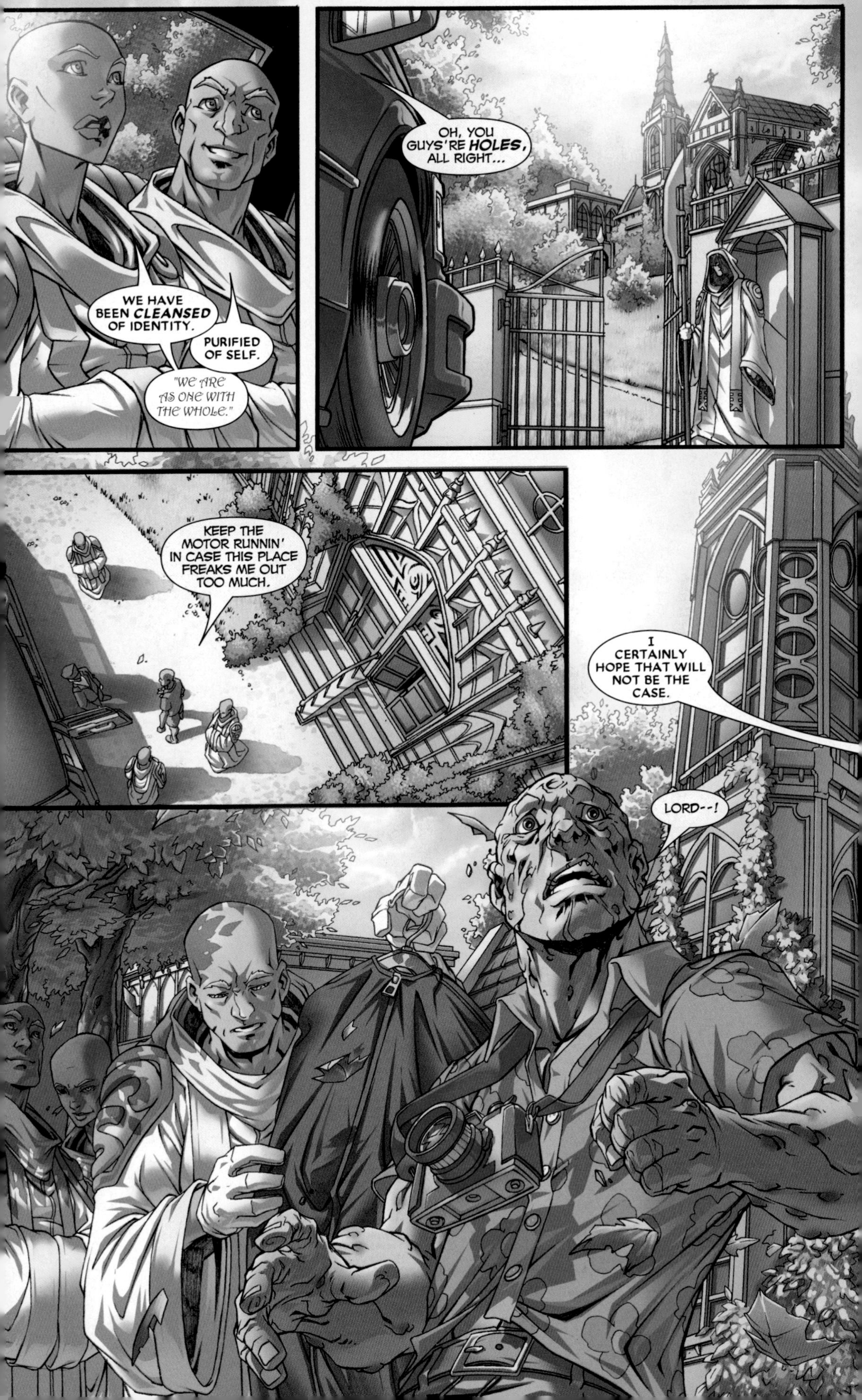
WE HAVE BEEN CLEANSED OF IDENTITY.
PURIFIED OF SELF.
"WE ARE AS ONE WITH THE WHOLE."
OH, YOU GUYS'RE HOLES, ALL RIGHT...
KEEP THE MOTOR RUNNIN' IN CASE THIS PLACE FREAKS ME OUT TOO MUCH.
I CERTAINLY HOPE THAT WILL NOT BE THE CASE.
LORD--!

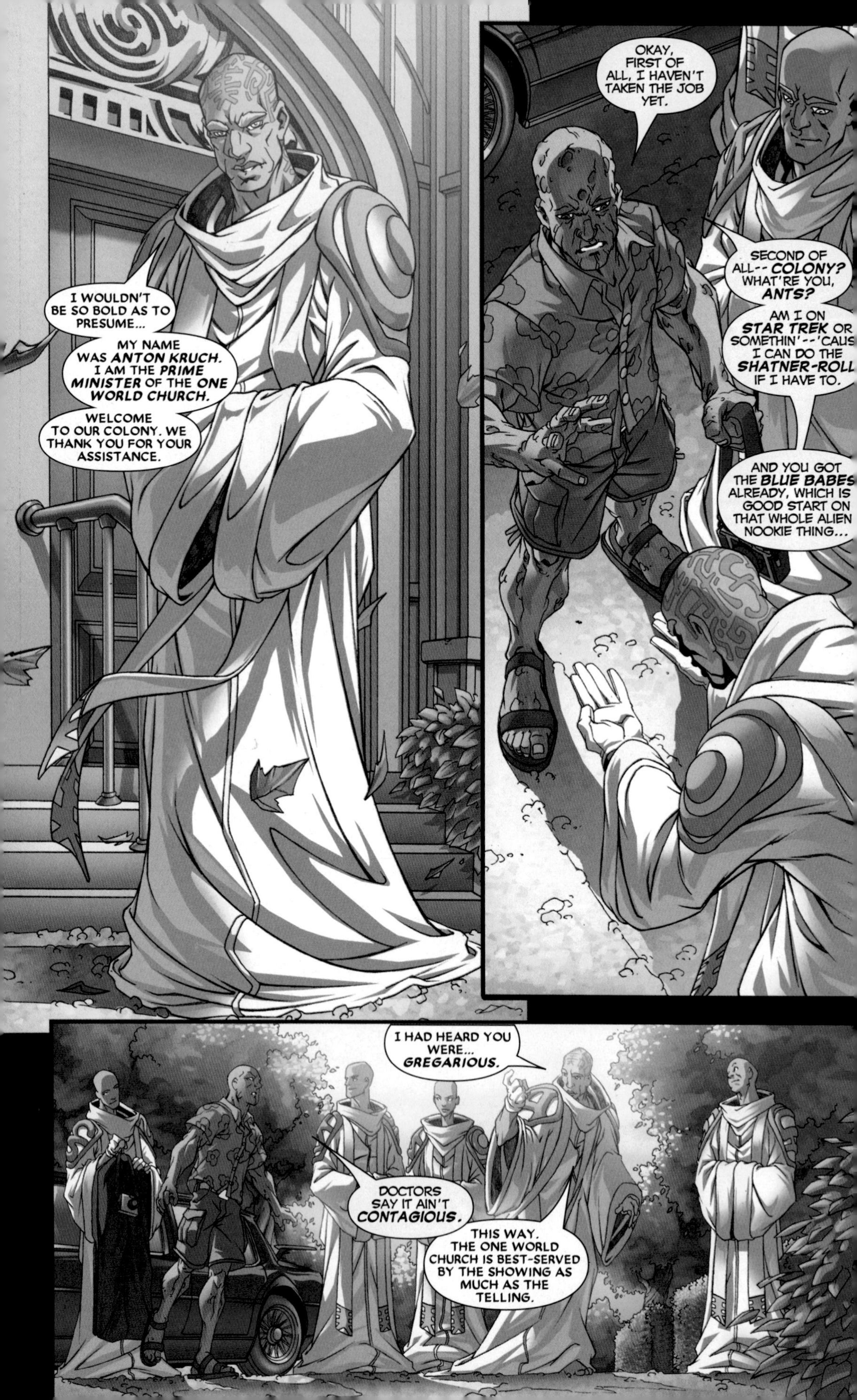
I WOULDN'T BE SO BOLD AS TO PRESUME...
MY NAME WAS ANTON KRUCH. I AM THE PRIME MINISTER OF THE ONE WORLD CHURCH.
WELCOME TO OUR COLONY. WE THANK YOU FOR YOUR ASSISTANCE.
OKAY, FIRST OF ALL, I HAVEN'T TAKEN THE JOB YET.
SECOND OF ALL-- COLONY? WHAT'RE YOU, ANTS?
AM I ON STAR TREK OR SOMETHIN'--'CAUS I CAN DO THE SHATNER-ROLL IF I HAVE TO.
AND YOU GOT THE BLUE BABES ALREADY, WHICH IS GOOD START ON THAT WHOLE ALIEN NOOKIE THING...
I HAD HEARD YOU WERE... GREGARIOUS.
DOCTORS SAY IT AIN'T CONTAGIOUS.
THIS WAY. THE ONE WORLD CHURCH IS BEST-SERVED BY THE SHOWING AS MUCH AS THE TELLING.

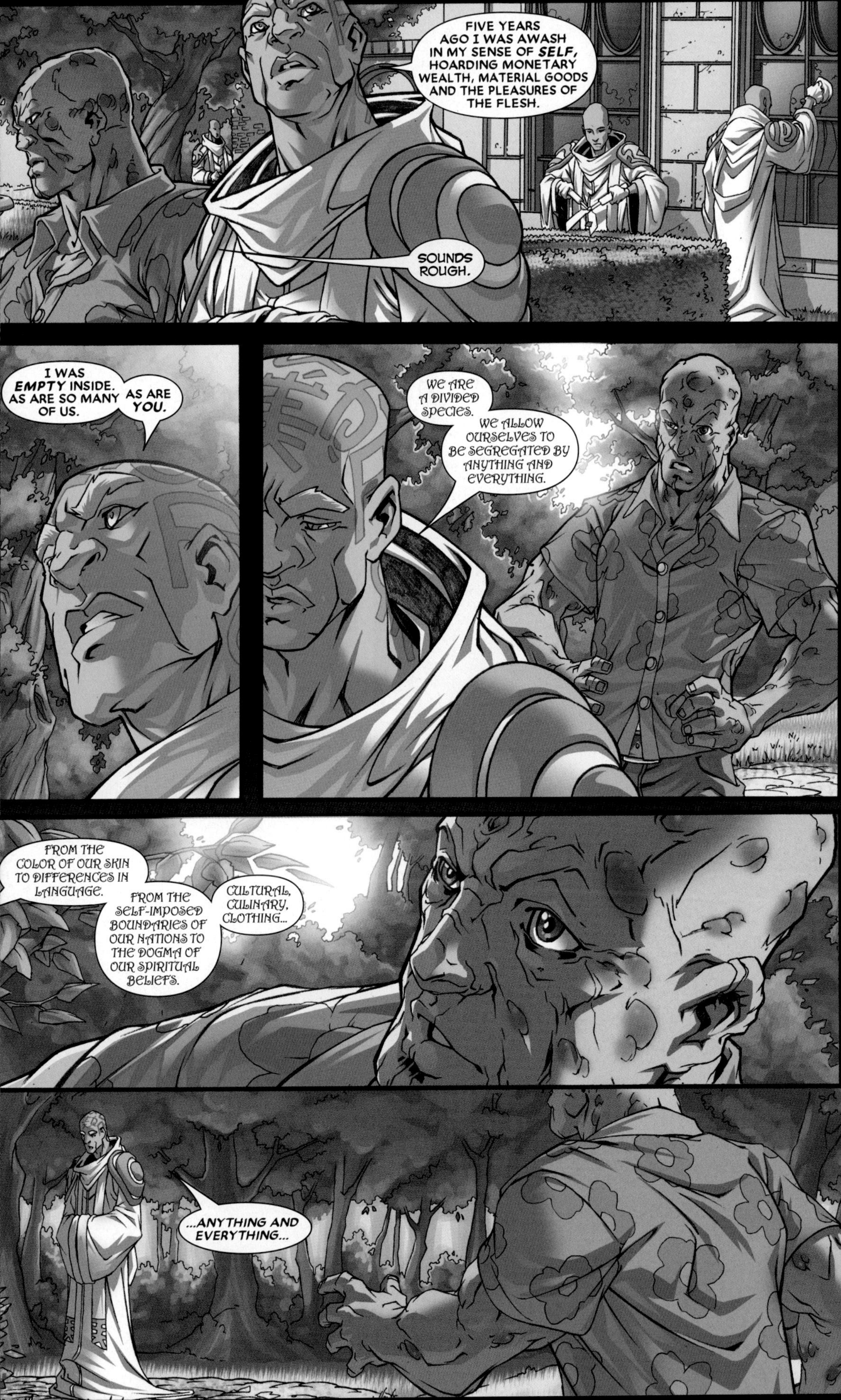
FIVE YEARS AGO I WAS AWASH IN MY SENSE OF SELF, HOARDING MONETARY WEALTH, MATERIAL GOODS AND THE PLEASURES OF THE FLESH.
SOUNDS ROUGH.
I WAS EMPTY INSIDE. AS ARE SO MANY OF US.
AS ARE YOU.
WE ARE A DIVIDED SPECIES.
WE ALLOW OURSELVES TO BE SEGREGATED BY ANYTHING AND EVERYTHING.
FROM THE COLOR OF OUR SKIN TO DIFFERENCES IN LANGUAGE.
FROM THE SELF-IMPOSED BOUNDARIES OF OUR NATIONS TO THE DOGMA OF OUR SPIRITUAL BELIEFS.
CULTURAL, CULINARY, CLOTHING...
...ANYTHING AND EVERYTHING...

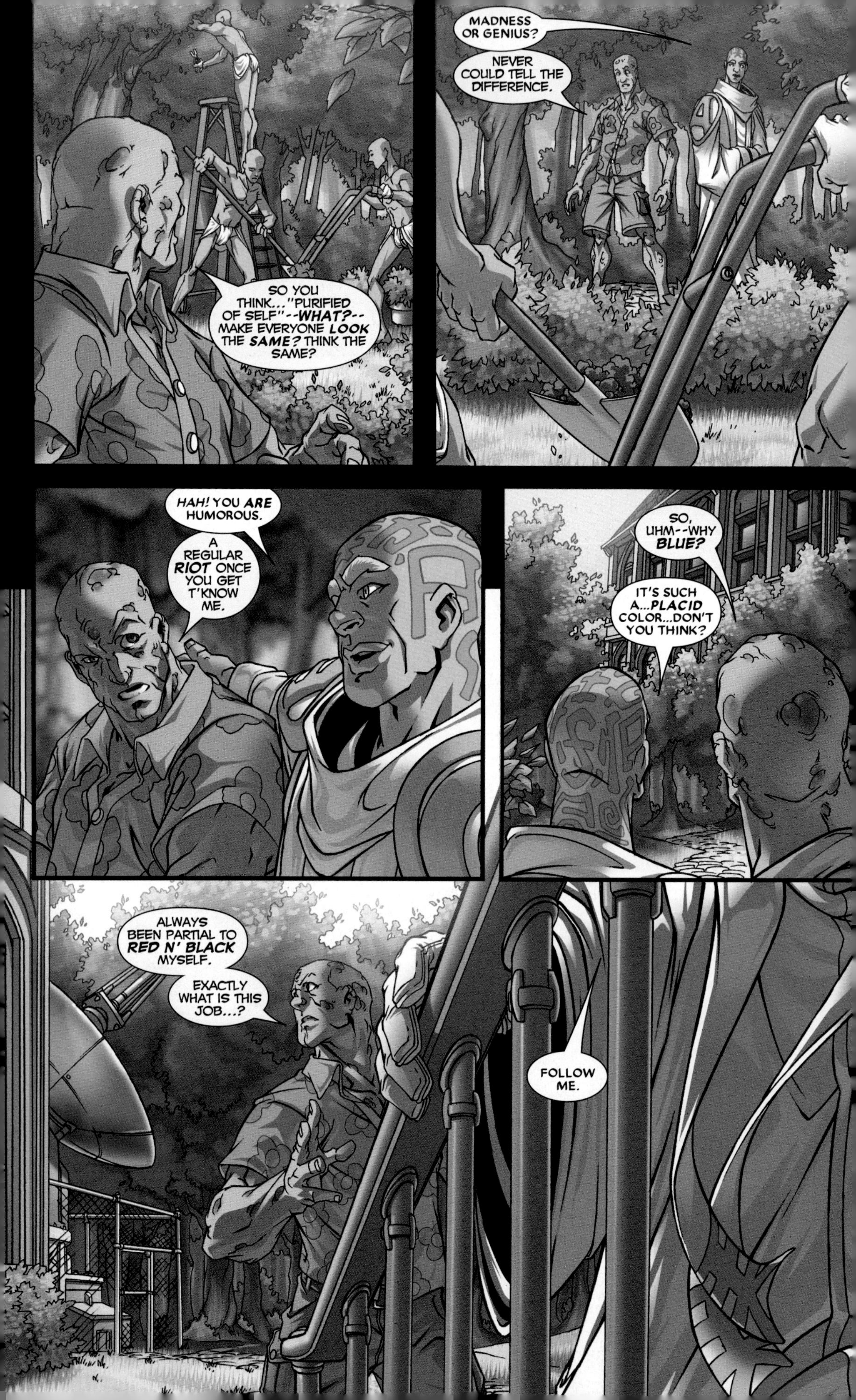
SO YOU THINK... "PURIFIED OF SELF"--WHAT?-- MAKE EVERYONE LOOK THE SAME? THINK THE SAME?
MADNESS OR GENIUS?
NEVER COULD TELL THE DIFFERENCE.
HAH! YOU ARE HUMOROUS.
A REGULAR RIOT ONCE YOU GET T'KNOW ME.
SO, UHM--WHY BLUE?
IT'S SUCH A...PLACID COLOR...DON'T YOU THINK?
ALWAYS BEEN PARTIAL TO RED N' BLACK MYSELF.
EXACTLY WHAT IS THIS JOB...?
FOLLOW ME.

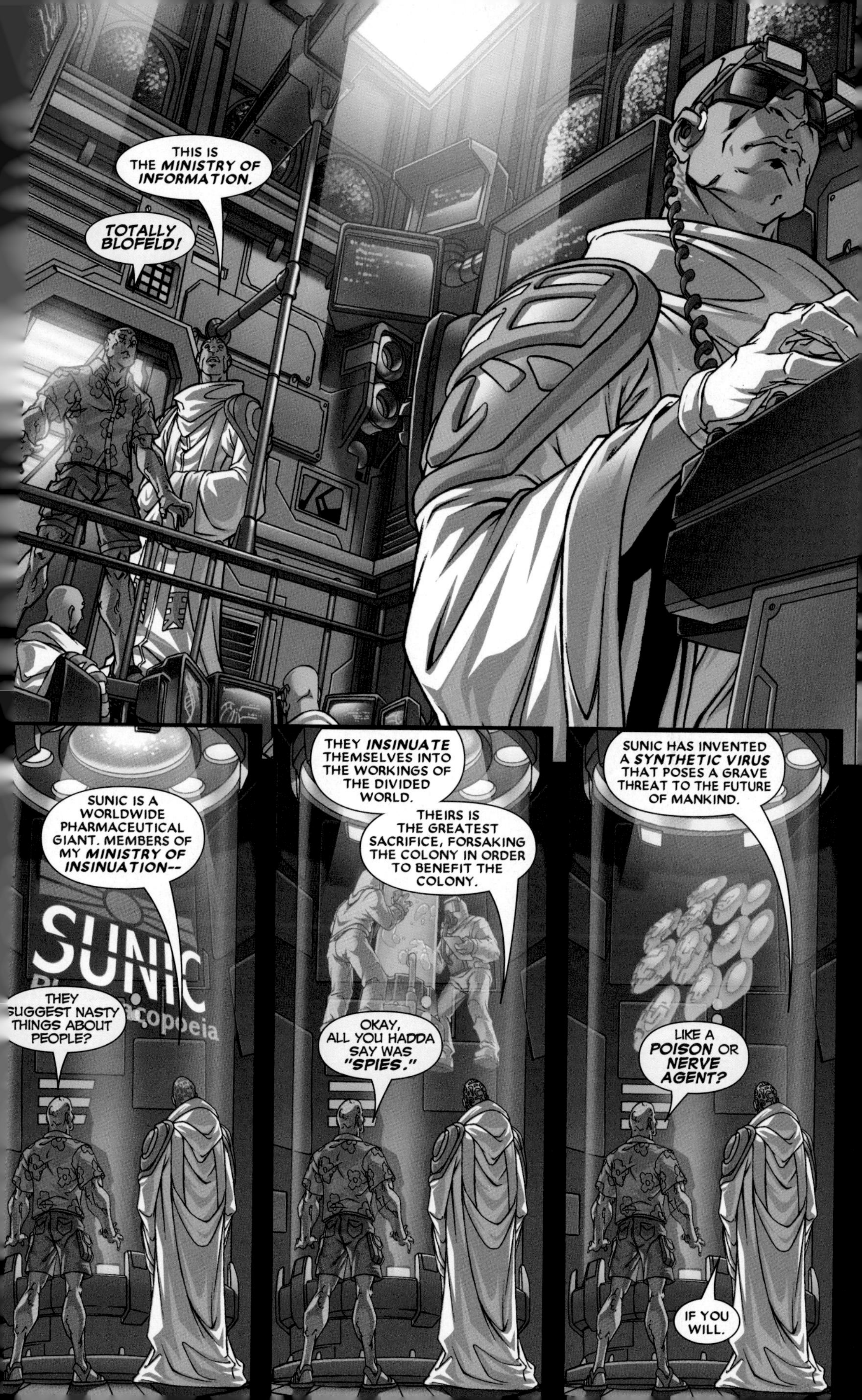
THIS IS THE MINISTRY OF INFORMATION.
TOTALLY BLOFELD!
SUNIC IS A WORLDWIDE PHARMACEUTICAL GIANT. MEMBERS OF MY MINISTRY OF INSINUATION--
SUNIC
THEY SUGGEST NASTY THINGS ABOUT PEOPLE?
THEY INSINUATE THEMSELVES INTO THE WORKINGS OF THE DIVIDED WORLD.
THEIRS IS THE GREATEST SACRIFICE, FORSAKING THE COLONY IN ORDER TO BENEFIT THE COLONY.
OKAY, ALL YOU HADDA SAY WAS "SPIES."
SUNIC HAS INVENTED A SYNTHETIC VIRUS THAT POSES A GRAVE THREAT TO THE FUTURE OF MANKIND.
LIKE A POISON OR NERVE AGENT?
IF YOU WILL.

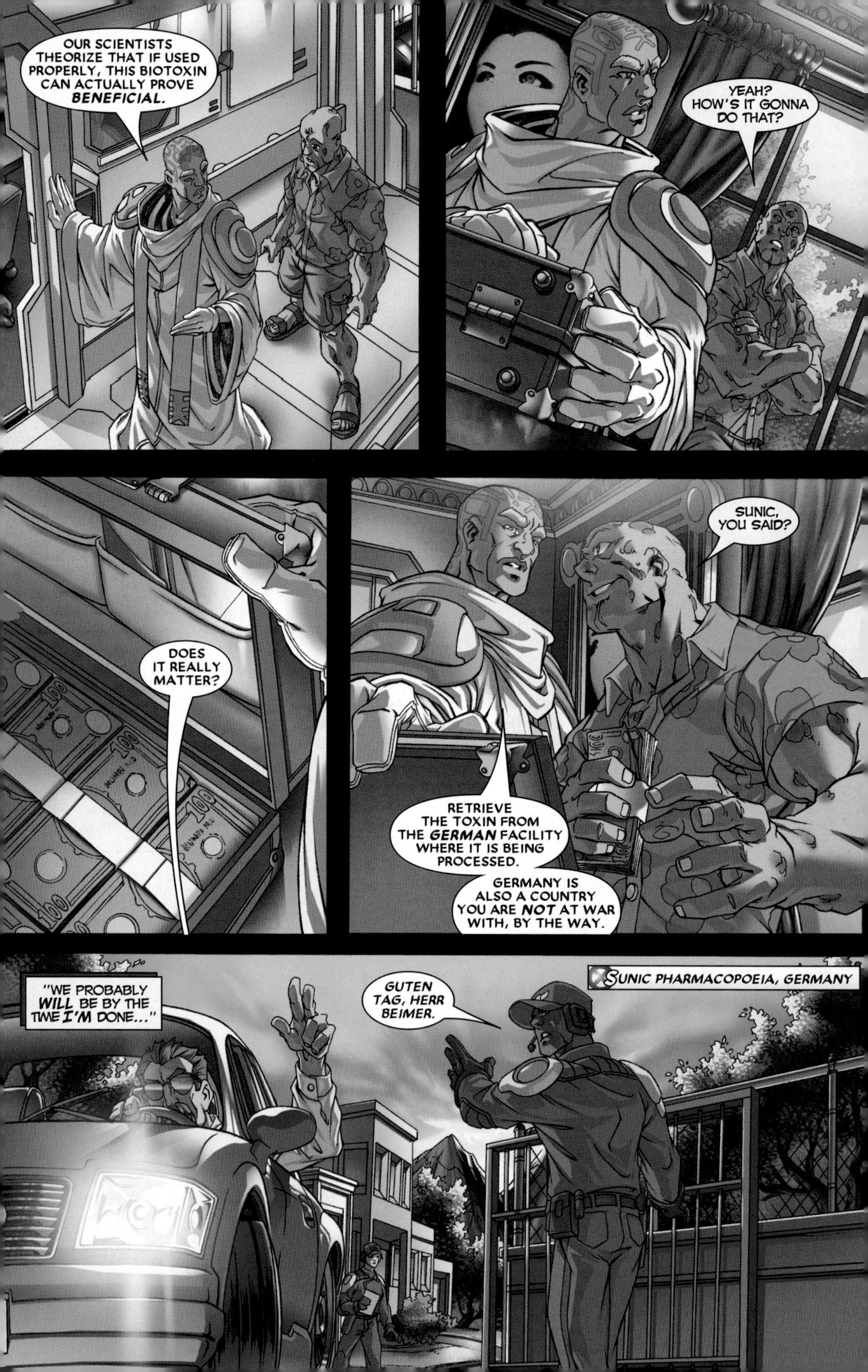
OUR SCIENTISTS THEORIZE THAT IF USED PROPERLY, THIS BIOTOXIN CAN ACTUALLY PROVE BENEFICIAL.
YEAH? HOW'S IT GONNA DO THAT?
DOES IT REALLY MATTER?
SUNIC, YOU SAID?
RETRIEVE THE TOXIN FROM THE GERMAN FACILITY WHERE IT IS BEING PROCESSED.
GERMANY IS ALSO A COUNTRY YOU ARE NOT AT WAR WITH, BY THE WAY.
"WE PROBABLY WILL BE BY THE TIME I'M DONE..."
SUNIC PHARMACOPOEIA, GERMANY
GUTEN TAG, HERR BEIMER.

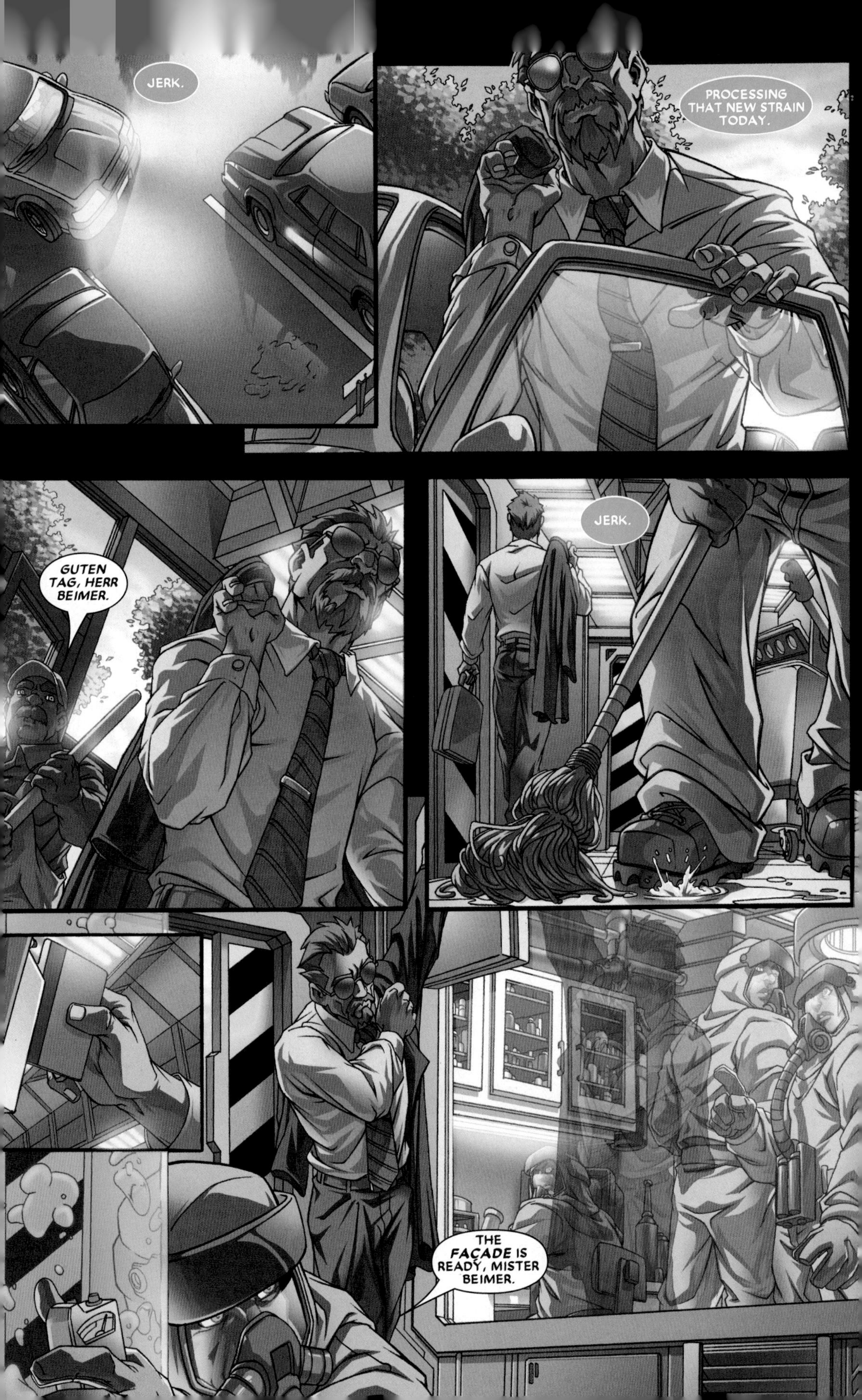
JERK.
PROCESSING THAT NEW STRAIN TODAY.
GUTEN TAG, HERR BEIMER.
JERK.
THE FAÇADE IS READY, MISTER BEIMER.

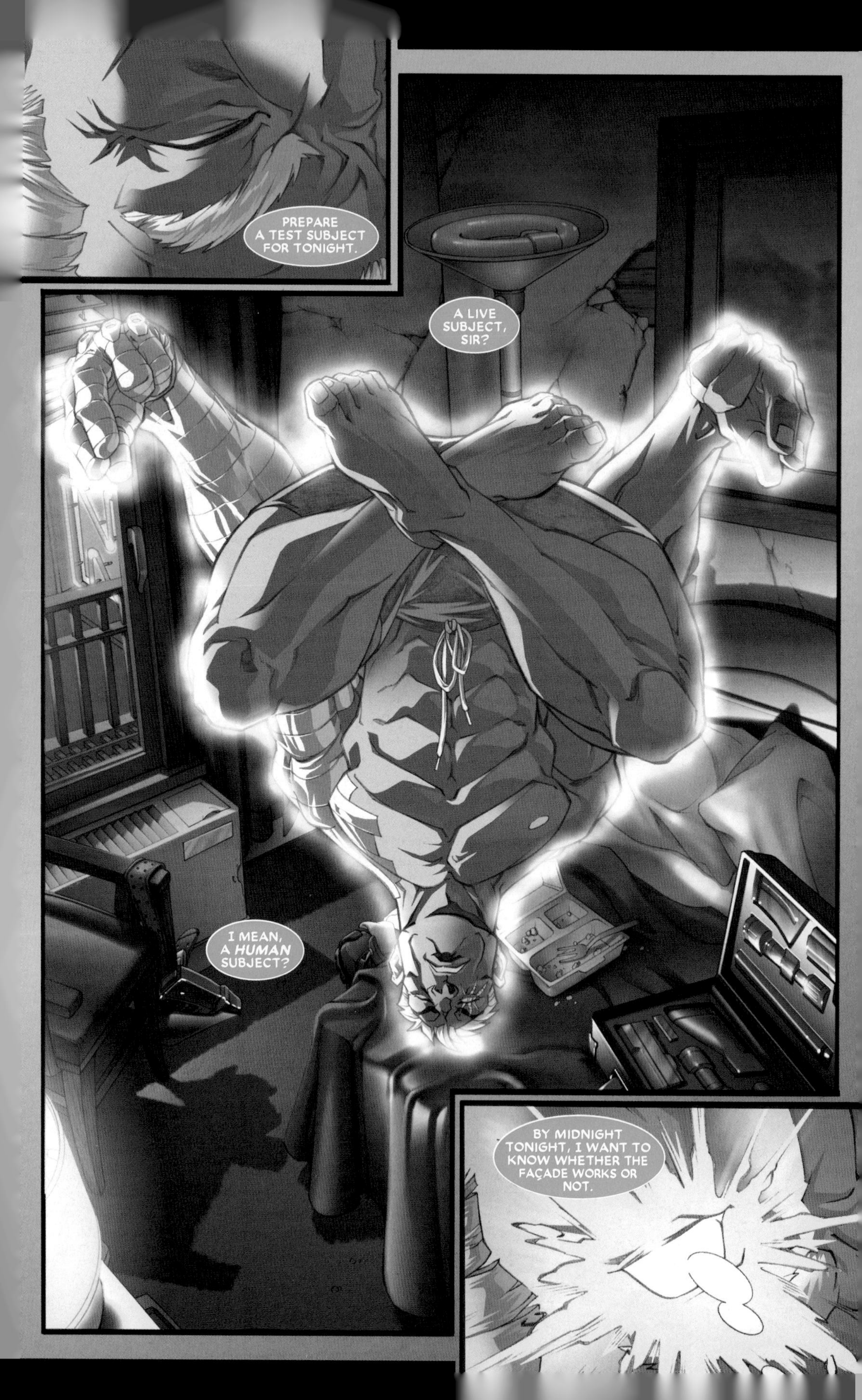
PREPARE A TEST SUBJECT FOR TONIGHT.
A LIVE SUBJECT, SIR?
I MEAN, A *HUMAN* SUBJECT?
BY MIDNIGHT TONIGHT, I WANT TO KNOW WHETHER THE FAÇADE WORKS OR NOT.

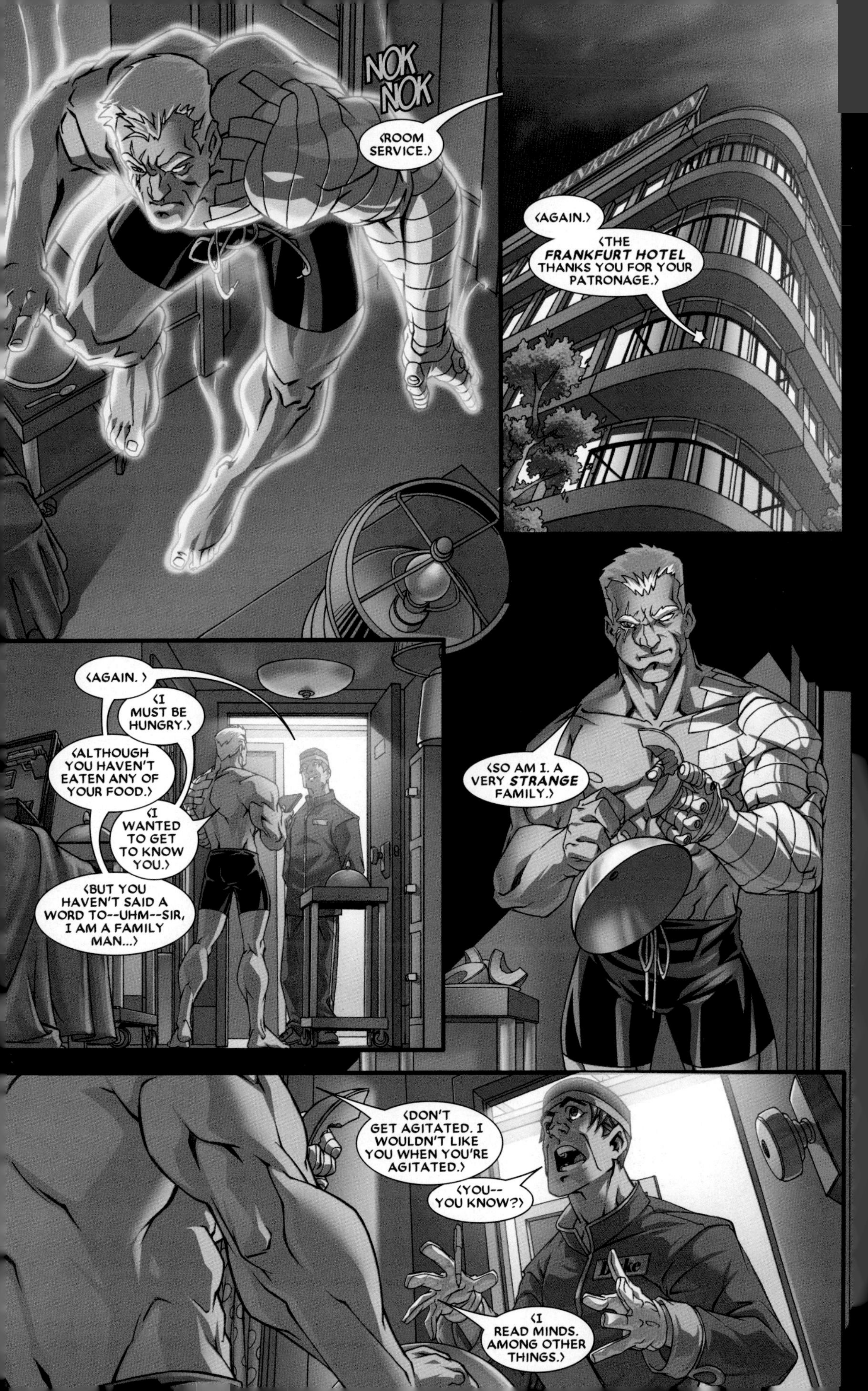
NOK NOK
‹ROOM SERVICE.›
‹AGAIN.›
‹THE FRANKFURT HOTEL THANKS YOU FOR YOUR PATRONAGE.›
FRANKFURT INN
‹AGAIN. ›
‹I MUST BE HUNGRY.›
‹ALTHOUGH YOU HAVEN'T EATEN ANY OF YOUR FOOD.›
‹I WANTED TO GET TO KNOW YOU.›
‹BUT YOU HAVEN'T SAID A WORD TO--UHM--SIR, I AM A FAMILY MAN...›
‹SO AM I. A VERY STRANGE FAMILY.›
‹DON'T GET AGITATED. I WOULDN'T LIKE YOU WHEN YOU'RE AGITATED.›
‹YOU-- YOU KNOW?›
‹I READ MINDS. AMONG OTHER THINGS.›

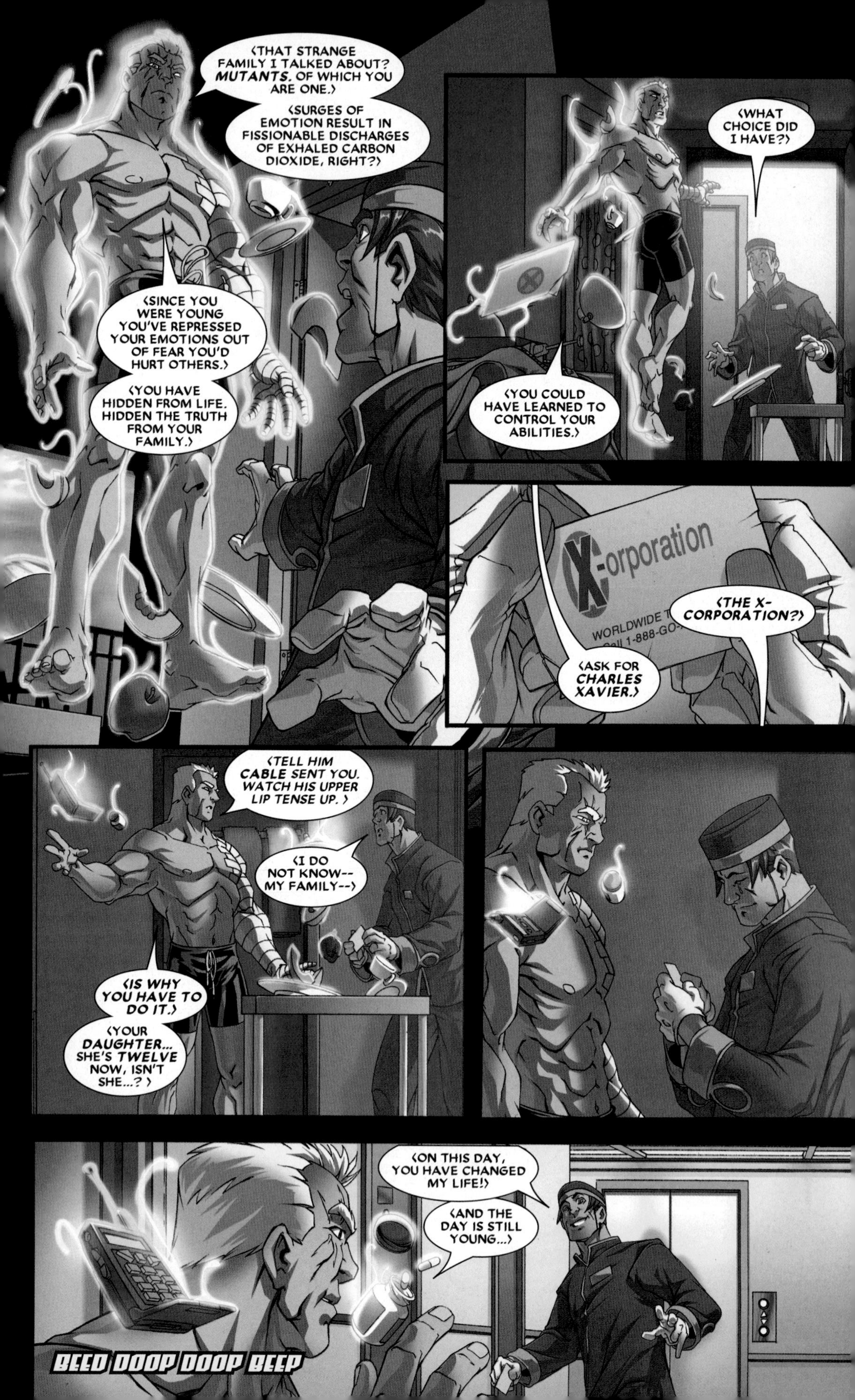

‹THAT STRANGE FAMILY I TALKED ABOUT? MUTANTS, OF WHICH YOU ARE ONE.›
‹SURGES OF EMOTION RESULT IN FISSIONABLE DISCHARGES OF EXHALED CARBON DIOXIDE, RIGHT?›
‹SINCE YOU WERE YOUNG YOU'VE REPRESSED YOUR EMOTIONS OUT OF FEAR YOU'D HURT OTHERS.›
‹YOU HAVE HIDDEN FROM LIFE. HIDDEN THE TRUTH FROM YOUR FAMILY.›
‹WHAT CHOICE DID I HAVE?›
‹YOU COULD HAVE LEARNED TO CONTROL YOUR ABILITIES.›
X-orporation
WORLDWIDE T
Call 1-888-GO-
‹THE X-CORPORATION?›
‹ASK FOR CHARLES XAVIER.›
‹TELL HIM CABLE SENT YOU. WATCH HIS UPPER LIP TENSE UP.›
‹I DO NOT KNOW-- MY FAMILY--›
‹IS WHY YOU HAVE TO DO IT.›
‹YOUR DAUGHTER... SHE'S TWELVE NOW, ISN'T SHE...?›
‹ON THIS DAY, YOU HAVE CHANGED MY LIFE!›
‹AND THE DAY IS STILL YOUNG...›
BEEP DOOP DOOP BEEP

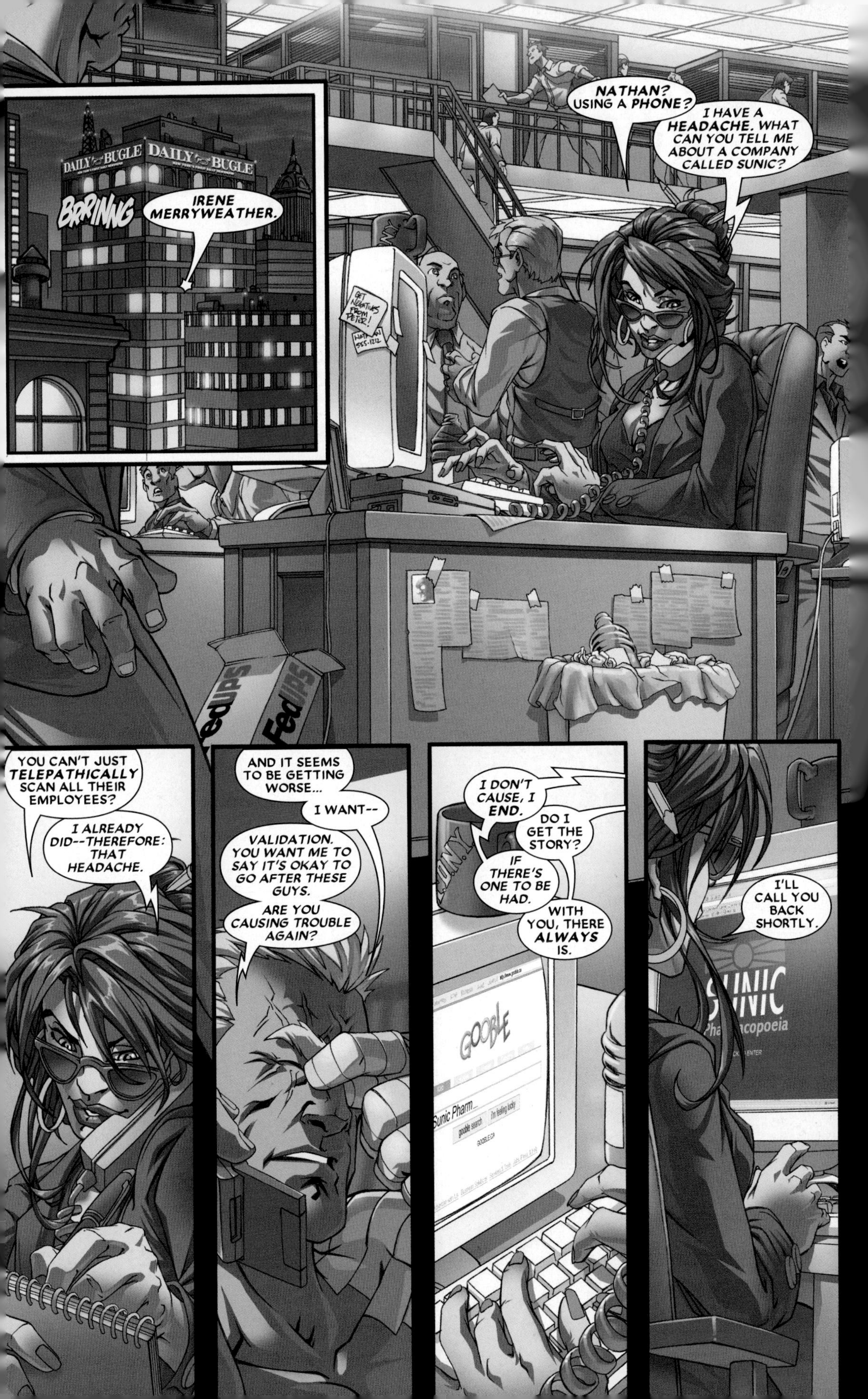

DAILY BUGLE
DAILY BUGLE
BRRINNG
IRENE MERRYWEATHER.
NATHAN? USING A PHONE?
I HAVE A HEADACHE. WHAT CAN YOU TELL ME ABOUT A COMPANY CALLED SUNIC?
GET NEGATIVES FROM PETER!
555-1212
FedUPS
YOU CAN'T JUST TELEPATHICALLY SCAN ALL THEIR EMPLOYEES?
I ALREADY DID--THEREFORE: THAT HEADACHE.
AND IT SEEMS TO BE GETTING WORSE...
I WANT--
VALIDATION. YOU WANT ME TO SAY IT'S OKAY TO GO AFTER THESE GUYS.
ARE YOU CAUSING TROUBLE AGAIN?
I DON'T CAUSE, I END.
DO I GET THE STORY?
IF THERE'S ONE TO BE HAD.
WITH YOU, THERE ALWAYS IS.
GOOBLE
Sunic Pharm_
gooble search
I'm feeling lucky
I'LL CALL YOU BACK SHORTLY.
SUNIC

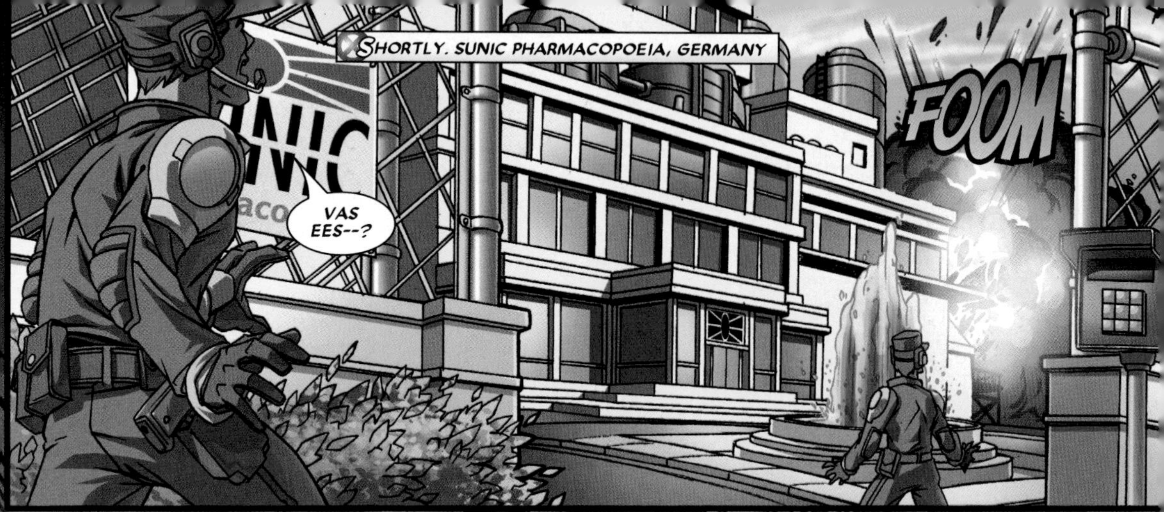
SHORTLY. SUNIC PHARMACOPOEIA, GERMANY
VAS EES--?
FOOM

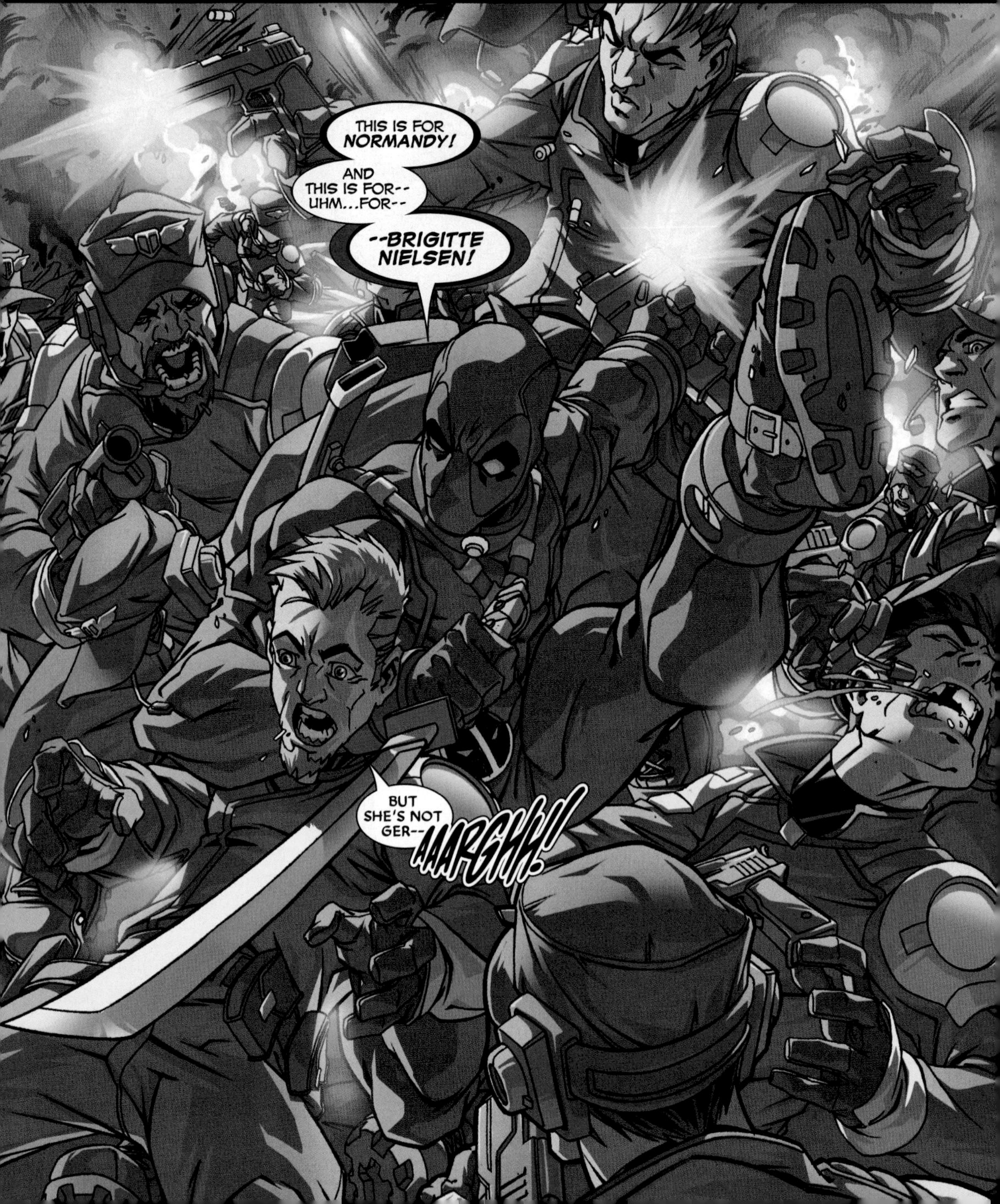
THIS IS FOR NORMANDY!
AND THIS IS FOR-- UHM...FOR--
--BRIGITTE NIELSEN!
BUT SHE'S NOT GER--
AAARGHH!

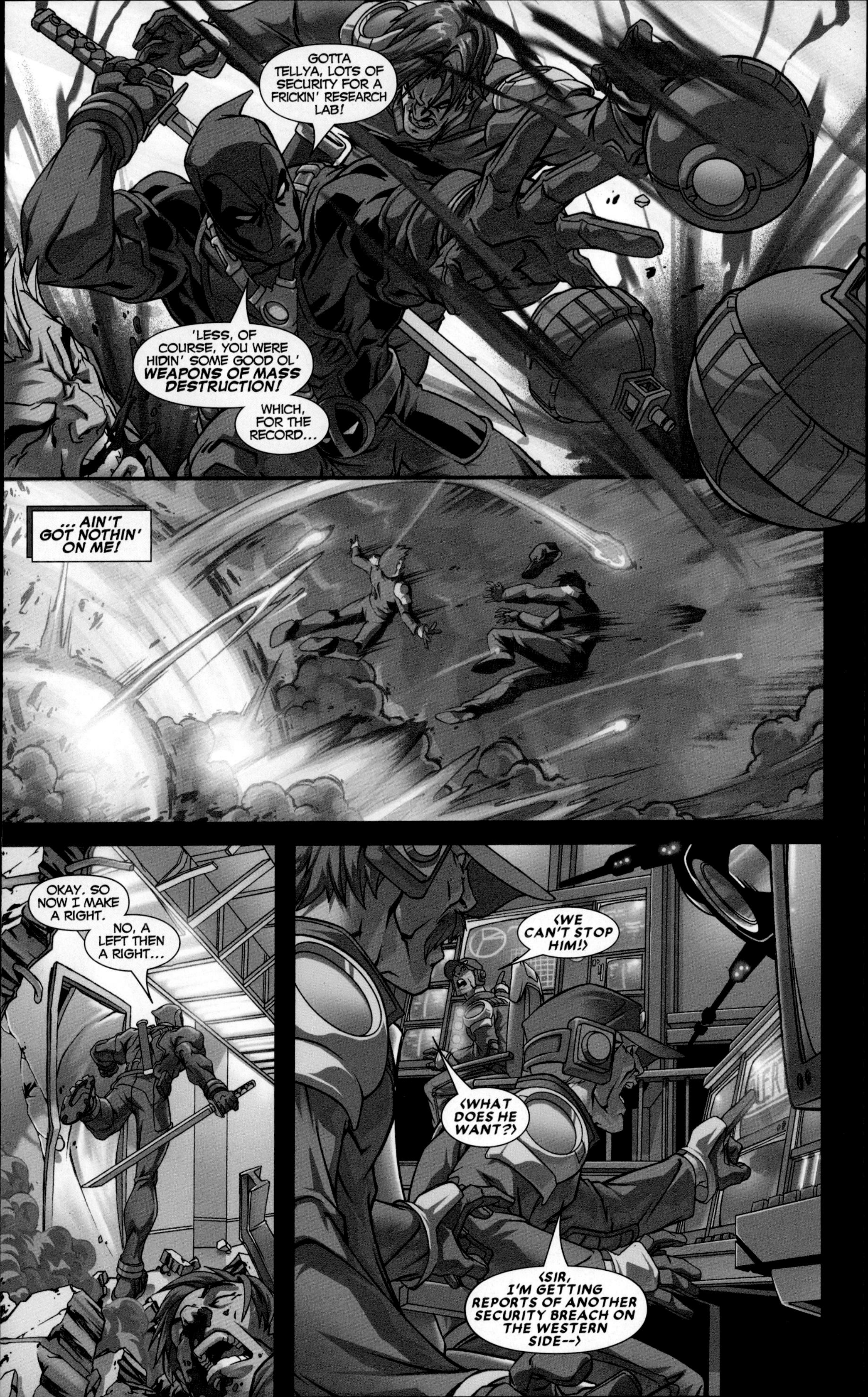
GOTTA TELLYA, LOTS OF SECURITY FOR A FRICKIN' RESEARCH LAB!
'LESS, OF COURSE, YOU WERE HIDIN' SOME GOOD OL' WEAPONS OF MASS DESTRUCTION!
WHICH, FOR THE RECORD...
...AIN'T GOT NOTHIN' ON ME!
OKAY. SO NOW I MAKE A RIGHT.
NO, A LEFT THEN A RIGHT...
‹WE CAN'T STOP HIM!›
‹WHAT DOES HE WANT?›
‹SIR, I'M GETTING REPORTS OF ANOTHER SECURITY BREACH ON THE WESTERN SIDE--›

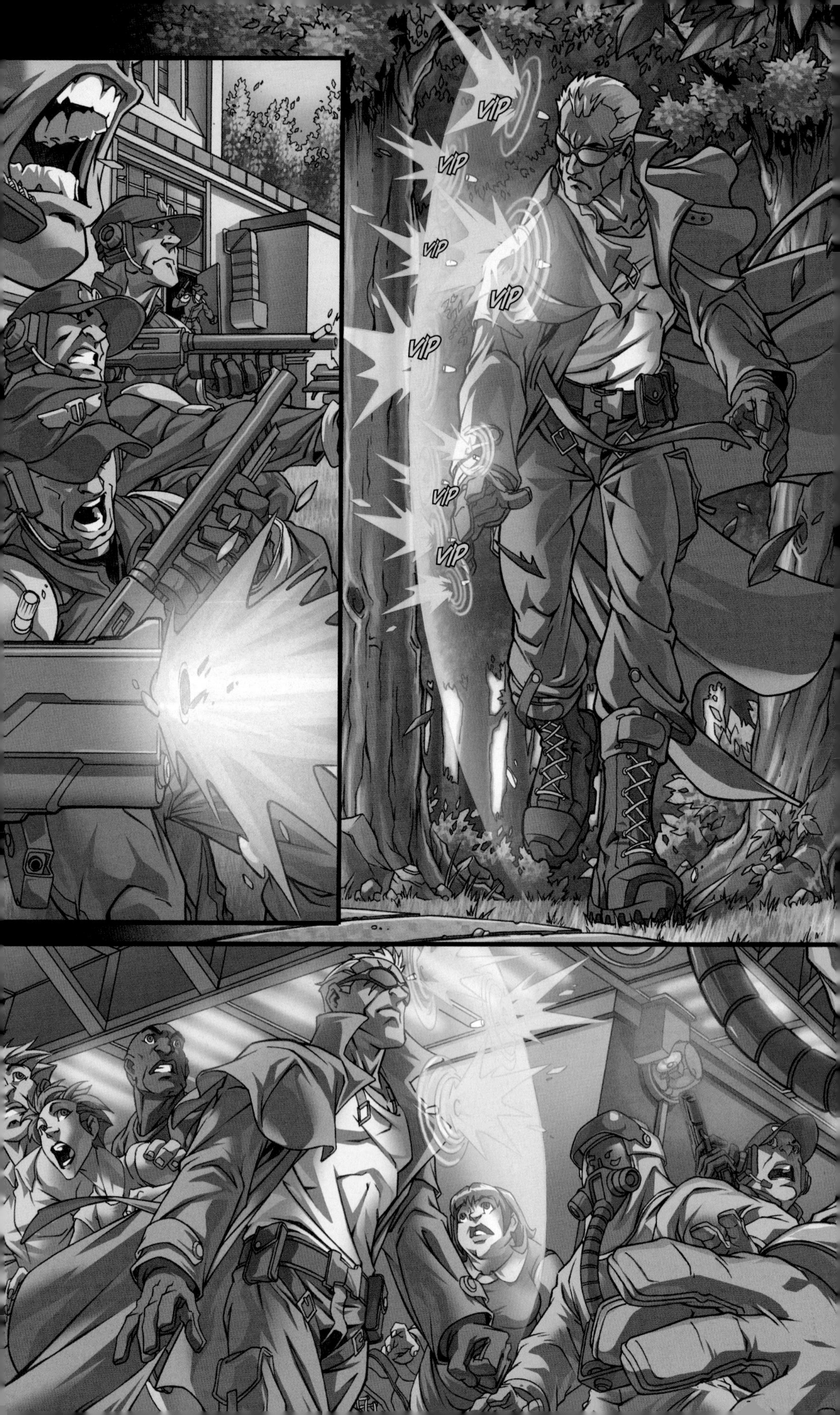
VIP
VIP
VIP
VIP
VIP
VIP
VIP

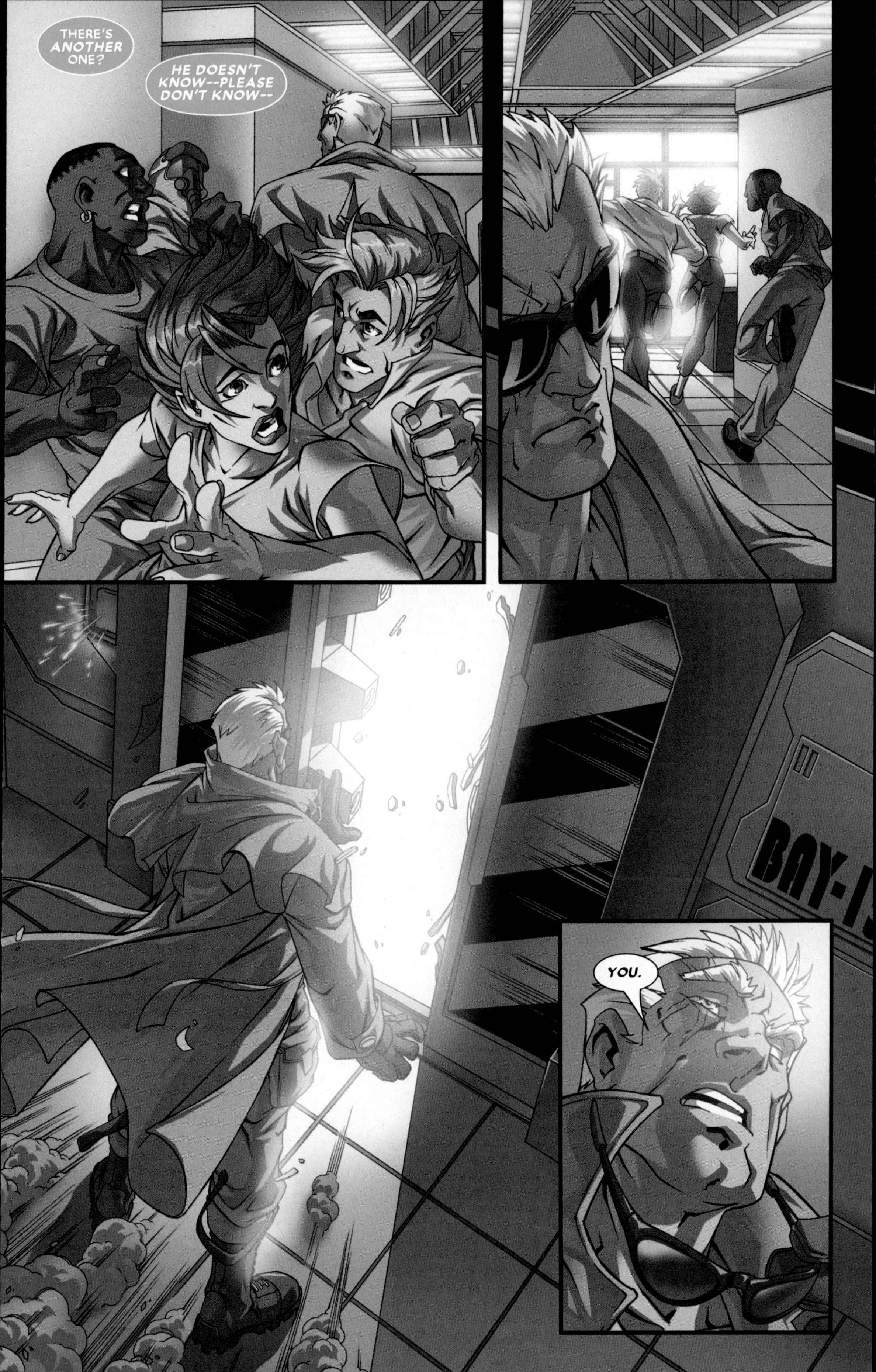
THERE'S ANOTHER ONE?
HE DOESN'T KNOW--PLEASE DON'T KNOW--
BAY-1
YOU.

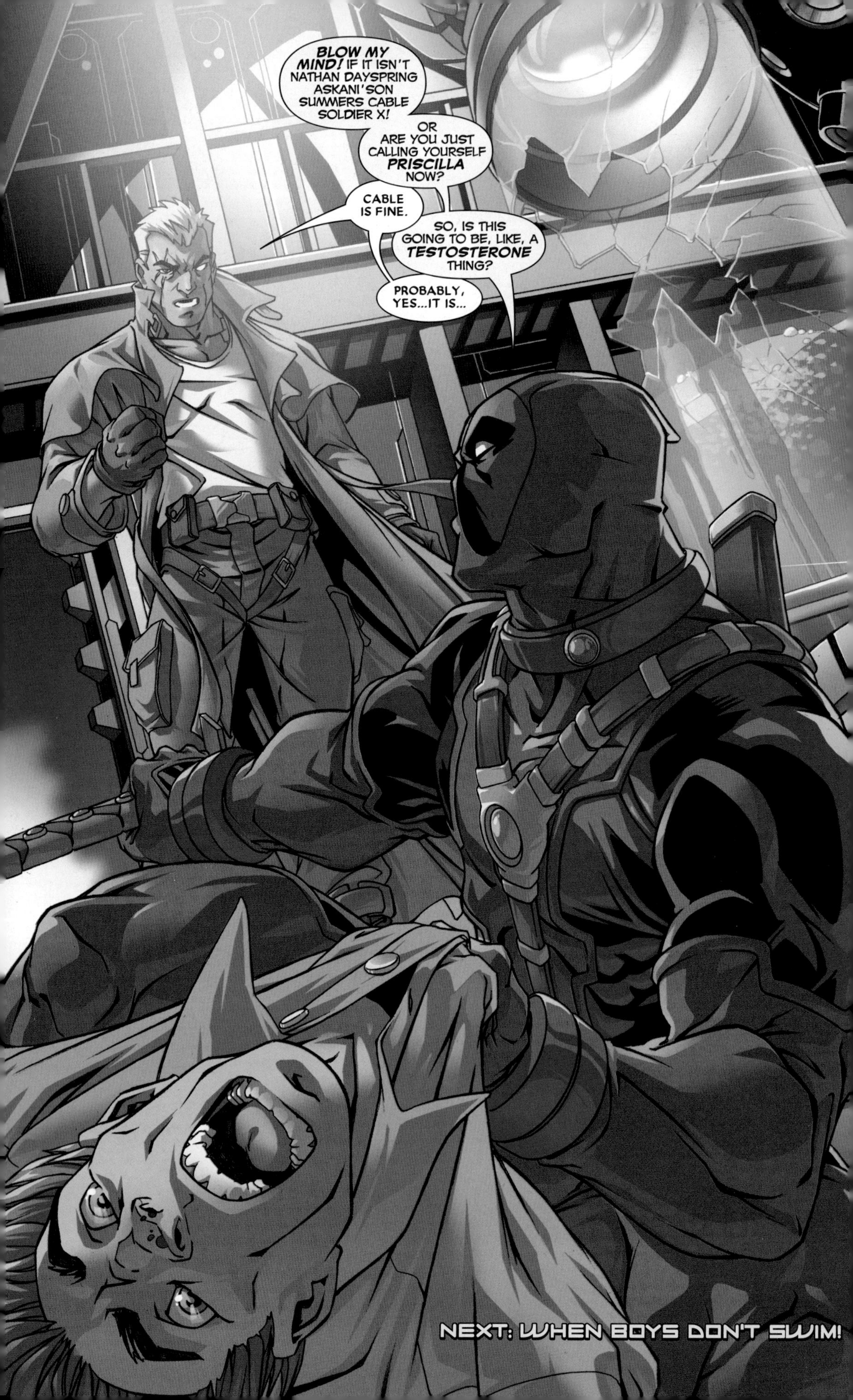
BLOW MY MIND! IF IT ISN'T NATHAN DAYSPRING ASKANI'SON SUMMERS CABLE SOLDIER X!
OR ARE YOU JUST CALLING YOURSELF PRISCILLA NOW?
CABLE IS FINE.
SO, IS THIS GOING TO BE, LIKE, A TESTOSTERONE THING?
PROBABLY, YES...IT IS...
NEXT: WHEN BOYS DON'T SWIM!

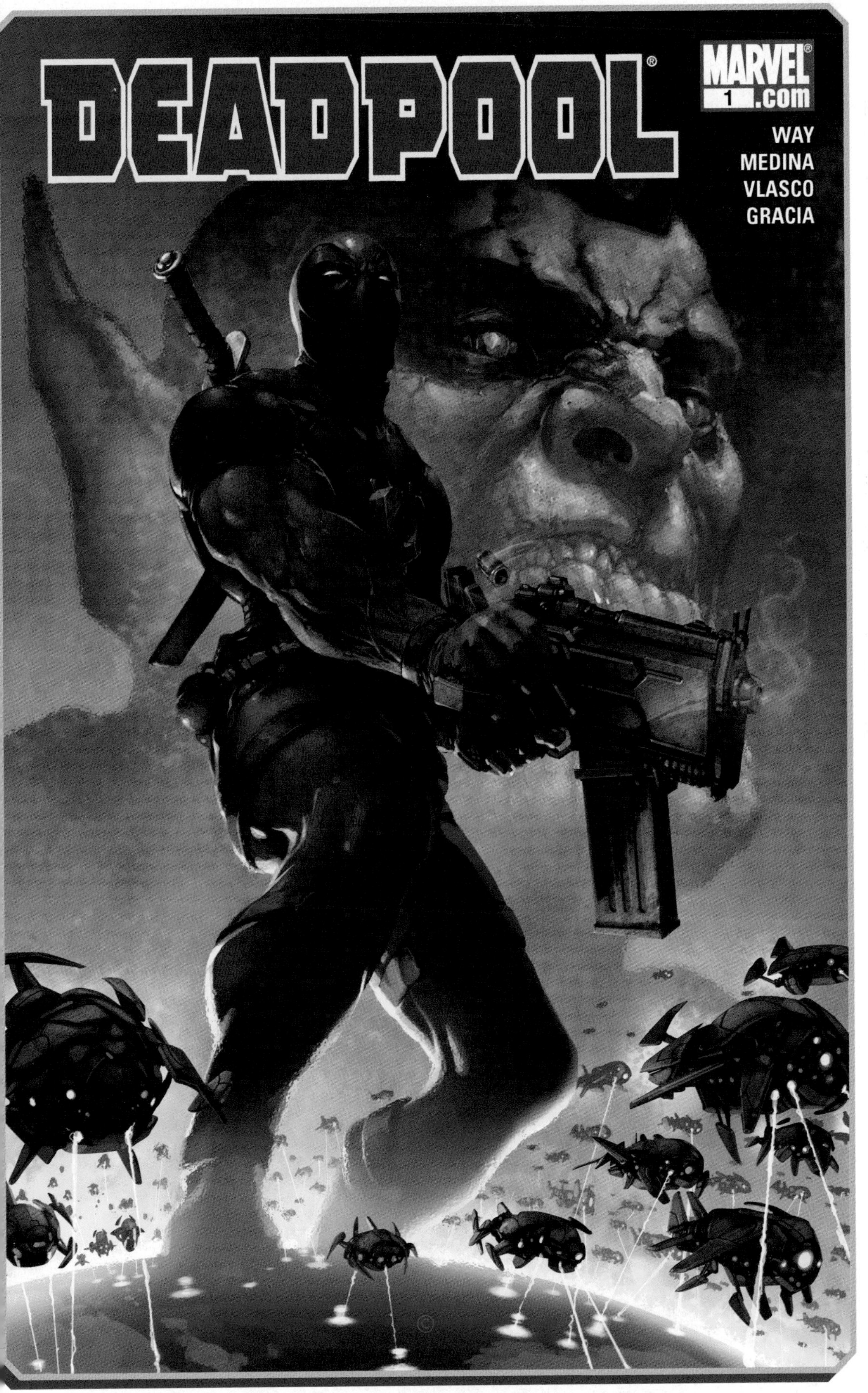

DEADPOOL®
MARVEL®
1 .com
WAY
MEDINA
VLASCO
GRACIA

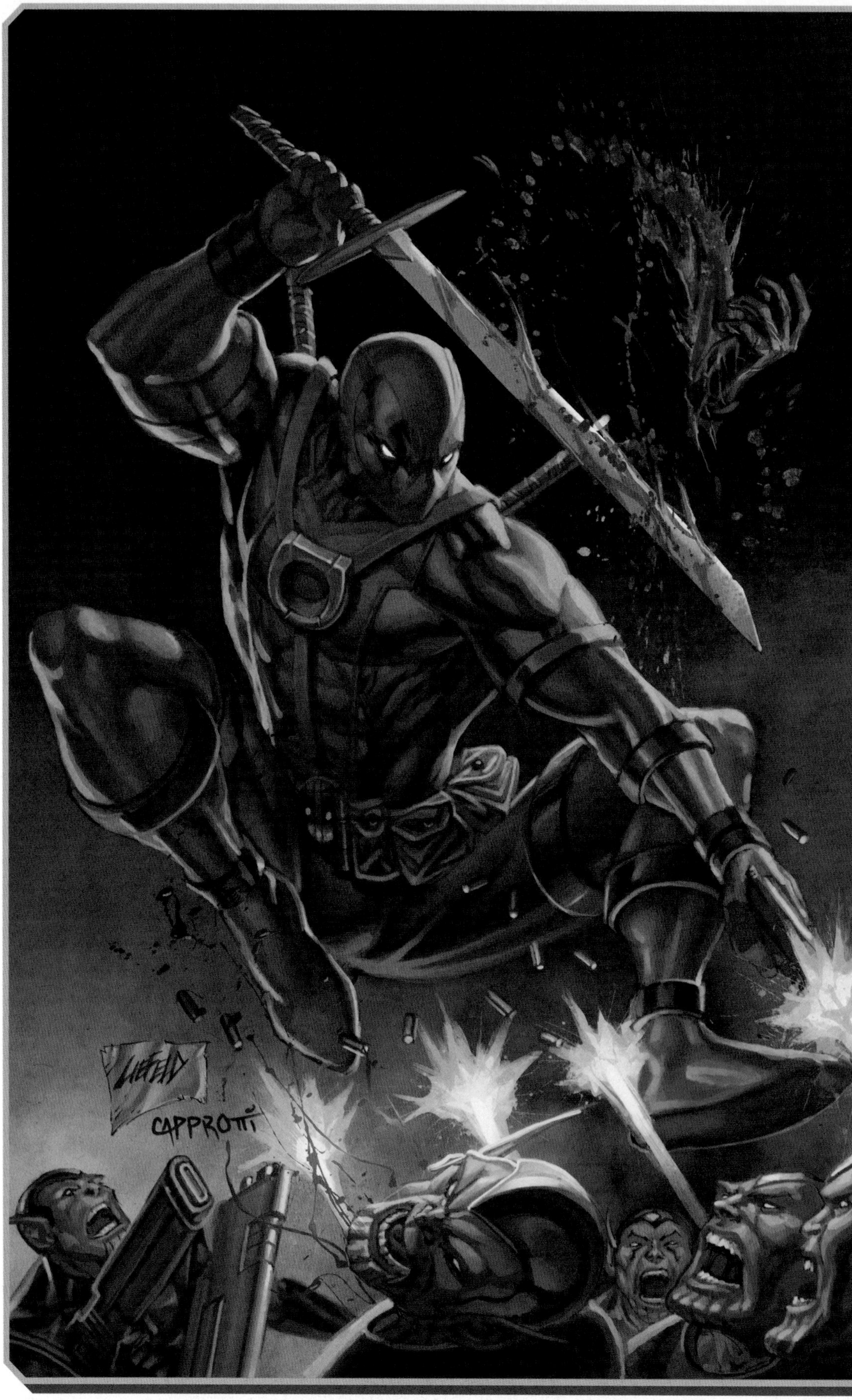
LIEFELD
CAPPROTTI

DEADPOOL (2008) #1 Variant by ROB LIEFELD & MIKE CAPPROTTI

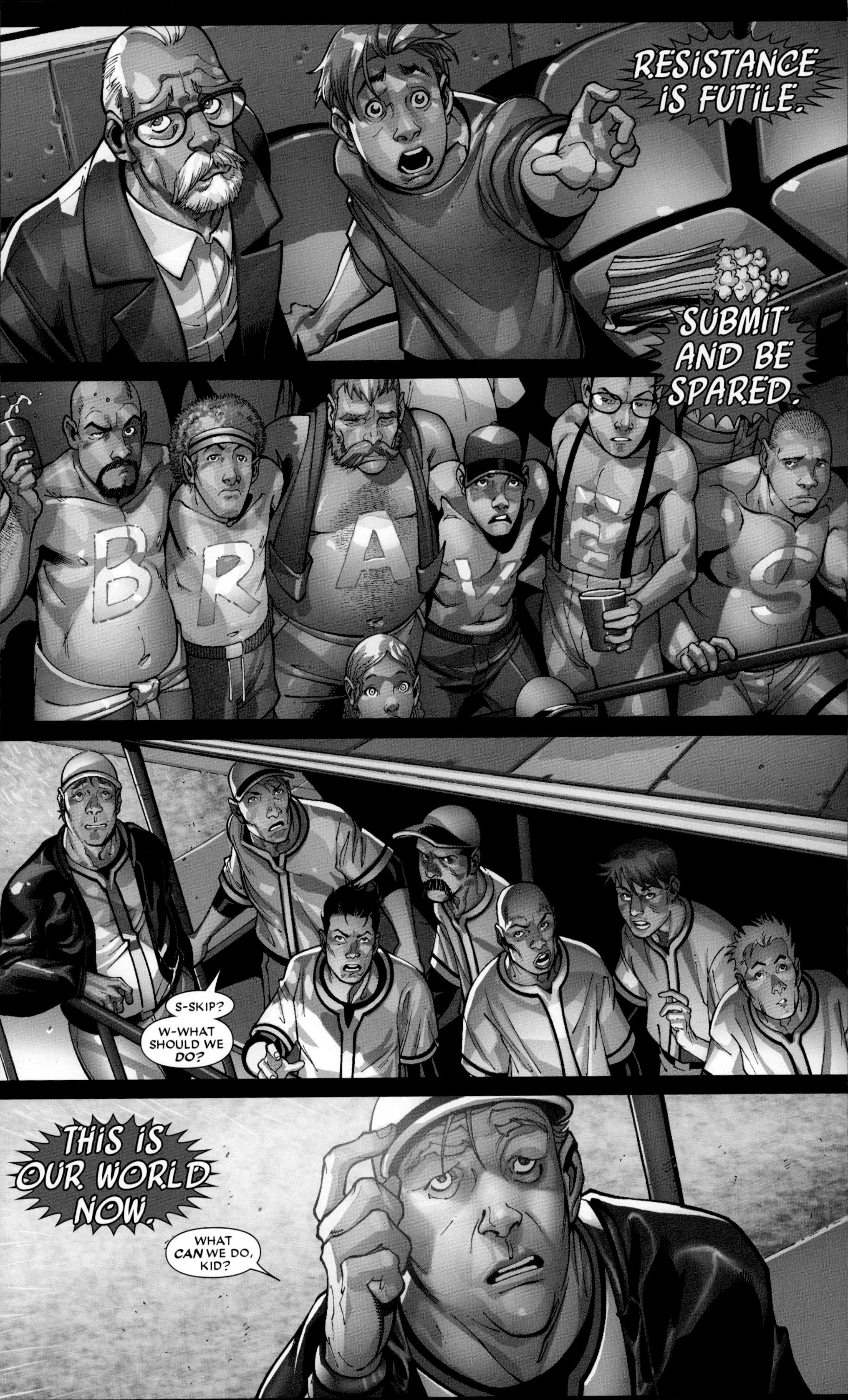
RESISTANCE IS FUTILE.
SUBMIT AND BE SPARED.
B R A V E S
S-SKIP?
W-WHAT SHOULD WE DO?
THIS IS OUR WORLD NOW.
WHAT CAN WE DO, KID?

THE INVASION HAS BEGUN! SHAPESHIFTING ALIEN SKRULLS HAVE INFILTRATED EARTH. COMPLETELY UNDETECTABLE, THEY HAVE ASSUMED POSITIONS IN GOVERNMENT, THE MILITARY, AND EVEN THE SUPER-HERO COMMUNITY. THEY POSSESS HIGHLY ADVANCED TECHNOLOGY, A MASSIVE ARMADA OF WARSHIPS, ENOUGH SOLDIERS TO OCCUPY THE PLANET AND A SECRET WEAPON – SUPER SKRULLS, WHICH CAN IMITATE THE POWERS OF MULTIPLE SUPER-HEROES.

ONE OF US: PART 1

| DANIEL WAY WRITER | PACO MEDINA PENCILS | JUAN VLASCO INKS | MARTE GRACIA COLORS | CHRIS ELIOPOULOS LETTERS | CLAYTON CRAIN COVER | ROB LIEFELD VARIANT COVER | PAUL ACERIOS PRODUCTION | DANIEL KETCHUM & JODY LEHEUP ASSISTANT EDITORS |

AXEL ALONSO EDITOR   JOE QUESADA EDITOR IN CHIEF   DAN BUCKLEY PUBLISHER

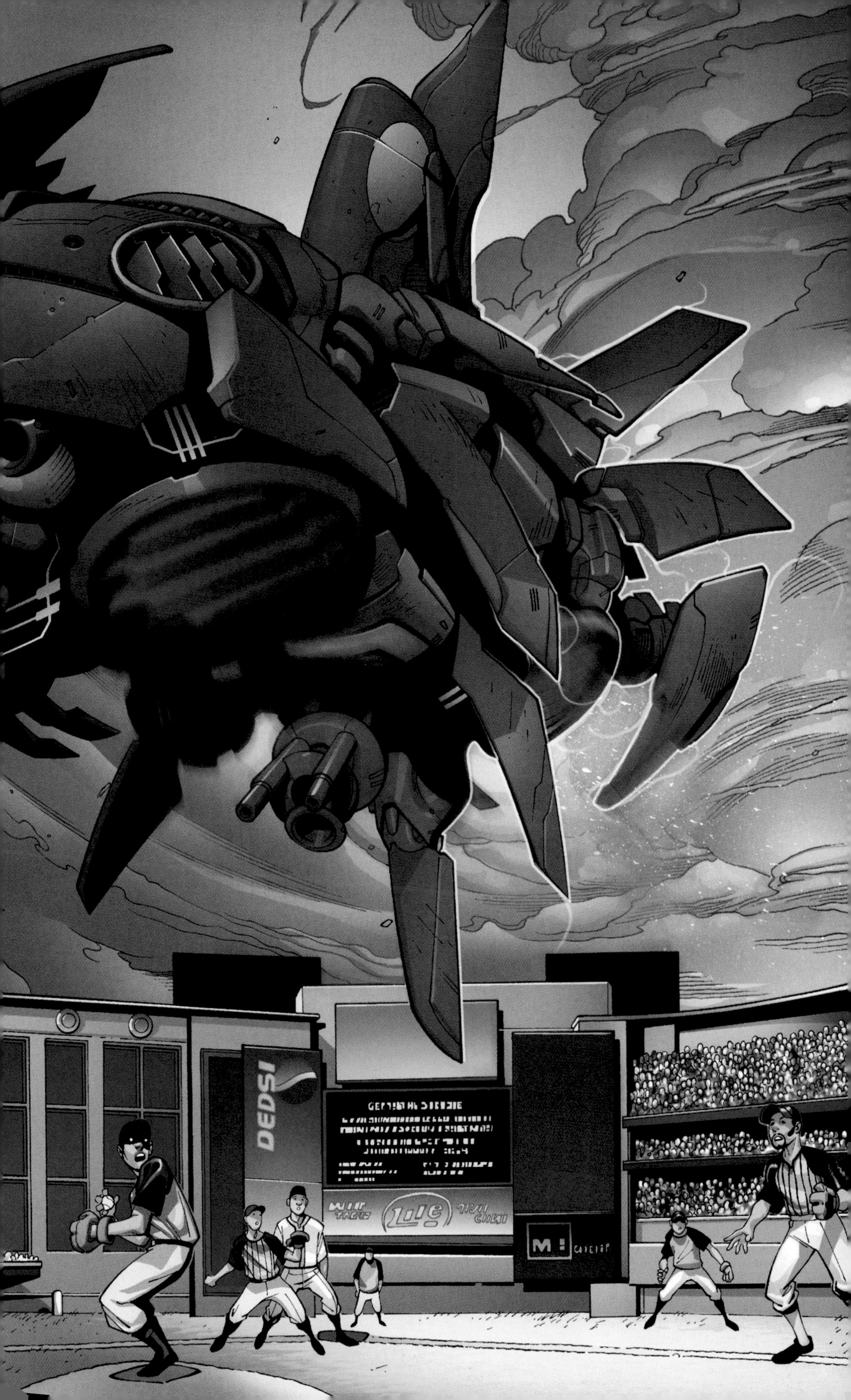
DEDSI

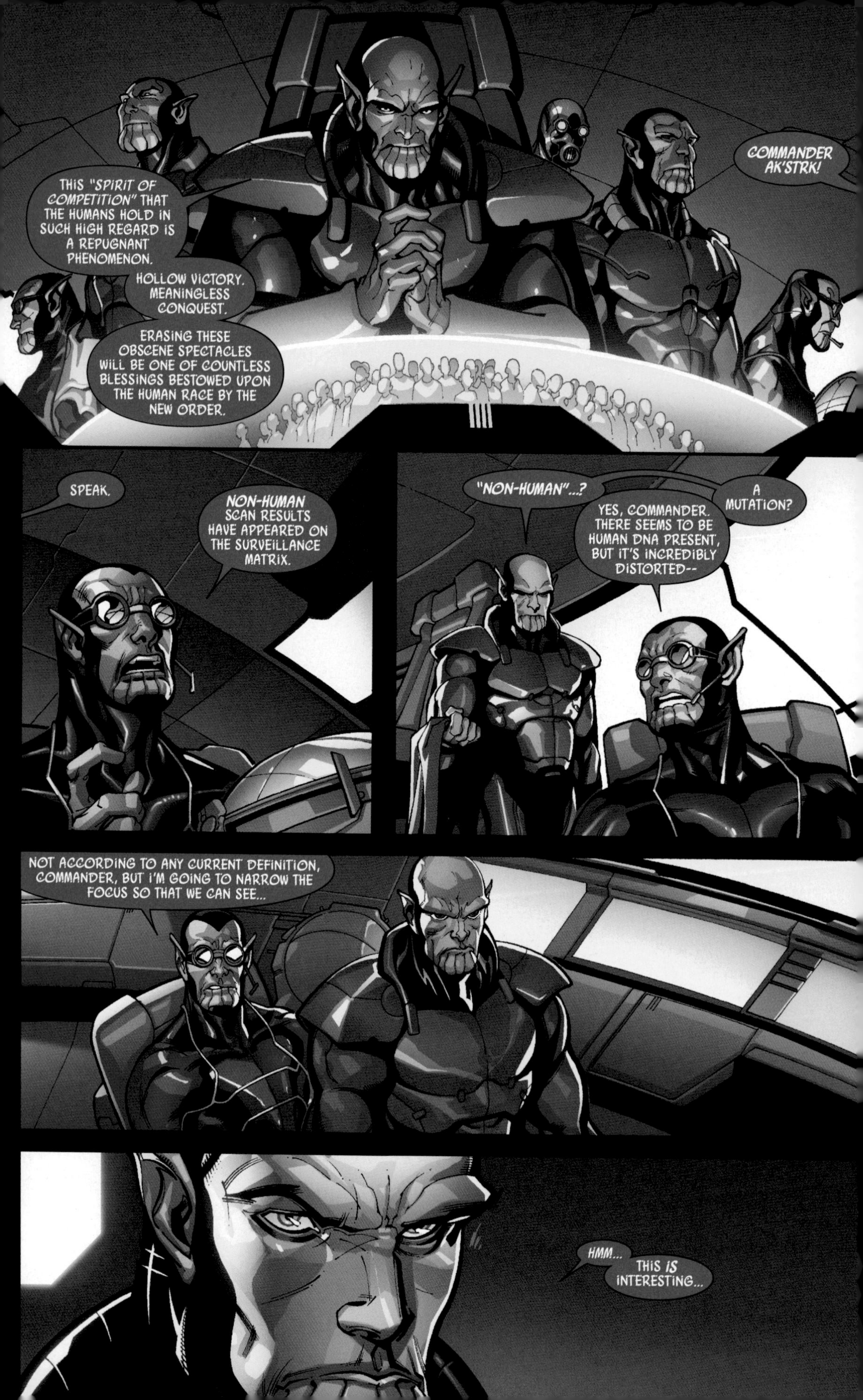
THIS "SPIRIT OF COMPETITION" THAT THE HUMANS HOLD IN SUCH HIGH REGARD IS A REPUGNANT PHENOMENON.
HOLLOW VICTORY. MEANINGLESS CONQUEST.
ERASING THESE OBSCENE SPECTACLES WILL BE ONE OF COUNTLESS BLESSINGS BESTOWED UPON THE HUMAN RACE BY THE NEW ORDER.
COMMANDER AK'STRK!
SPEAK.
NON-HUMAN SCAN RESULTS HAVE APPEARED ON THE SURVEILLANCE MATRIX.
"NON-HUMAN"...?
A MUTATION?
YES, COMMANDER. THERE SEEMS TO BE HUMAN DNA PRESENT, BUT IT'S INCREDIBLY DISTORTED--
NOT ACCORDING TO ANY CURRENT DEFINITION, COMMANDER, BUT I'M GOING TO NARROW THE FOCUS SO THAT WE CAN SEE...
HMM... THIS IS INTERESTING...

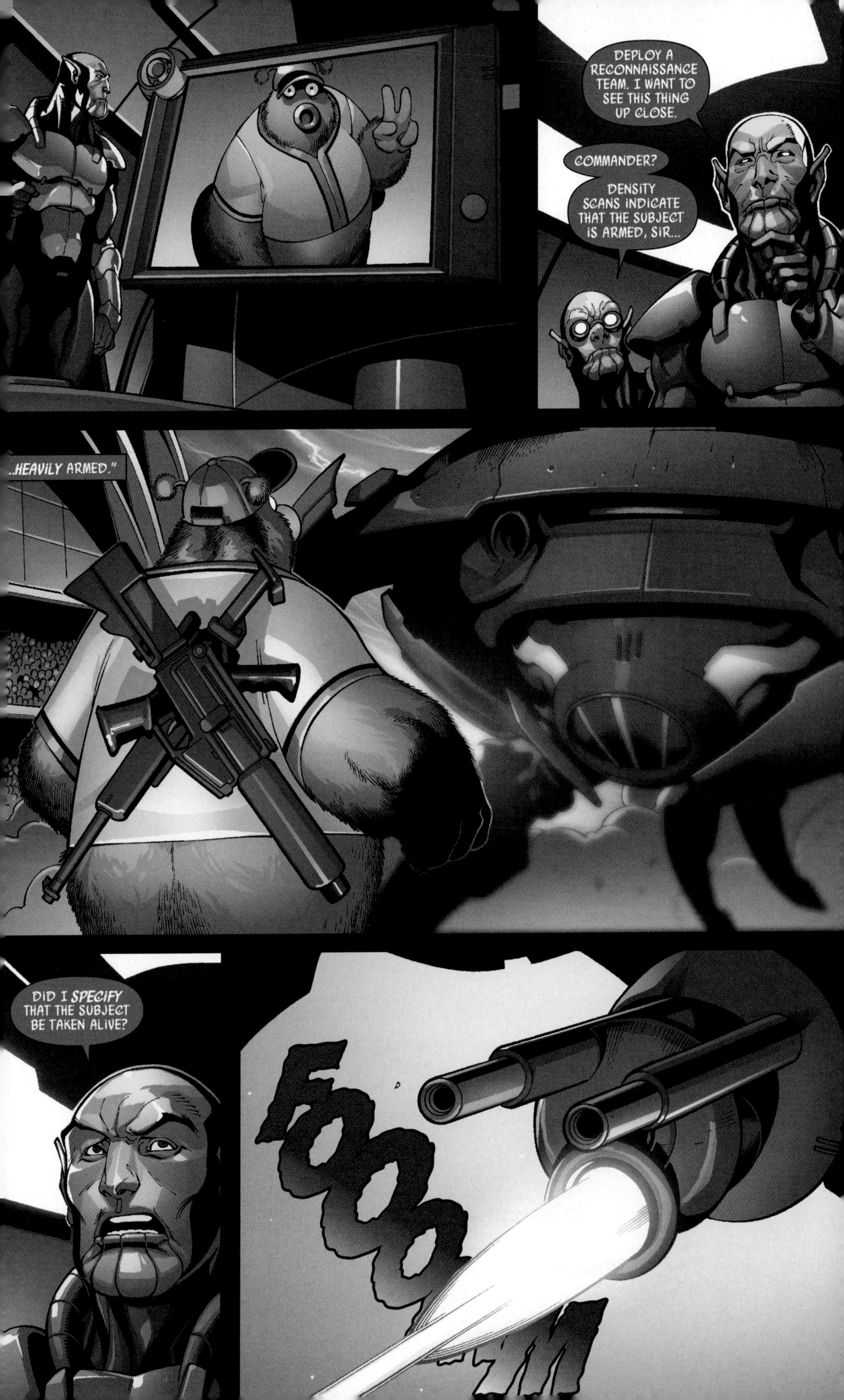
DEPLOY A RECONNAISSANCE TEAM. I WANT TO SEE THIS THING UP CLOSE.
COMMANDER?
DENSITY SCANS INDICATE THAT THE SUBJECT IS ARMED, SIR...
..HEAVILY ARMED."
DID I SPECIFY THAT THE SUBJECT BE TAKEN ALIVE?
FOOOOM

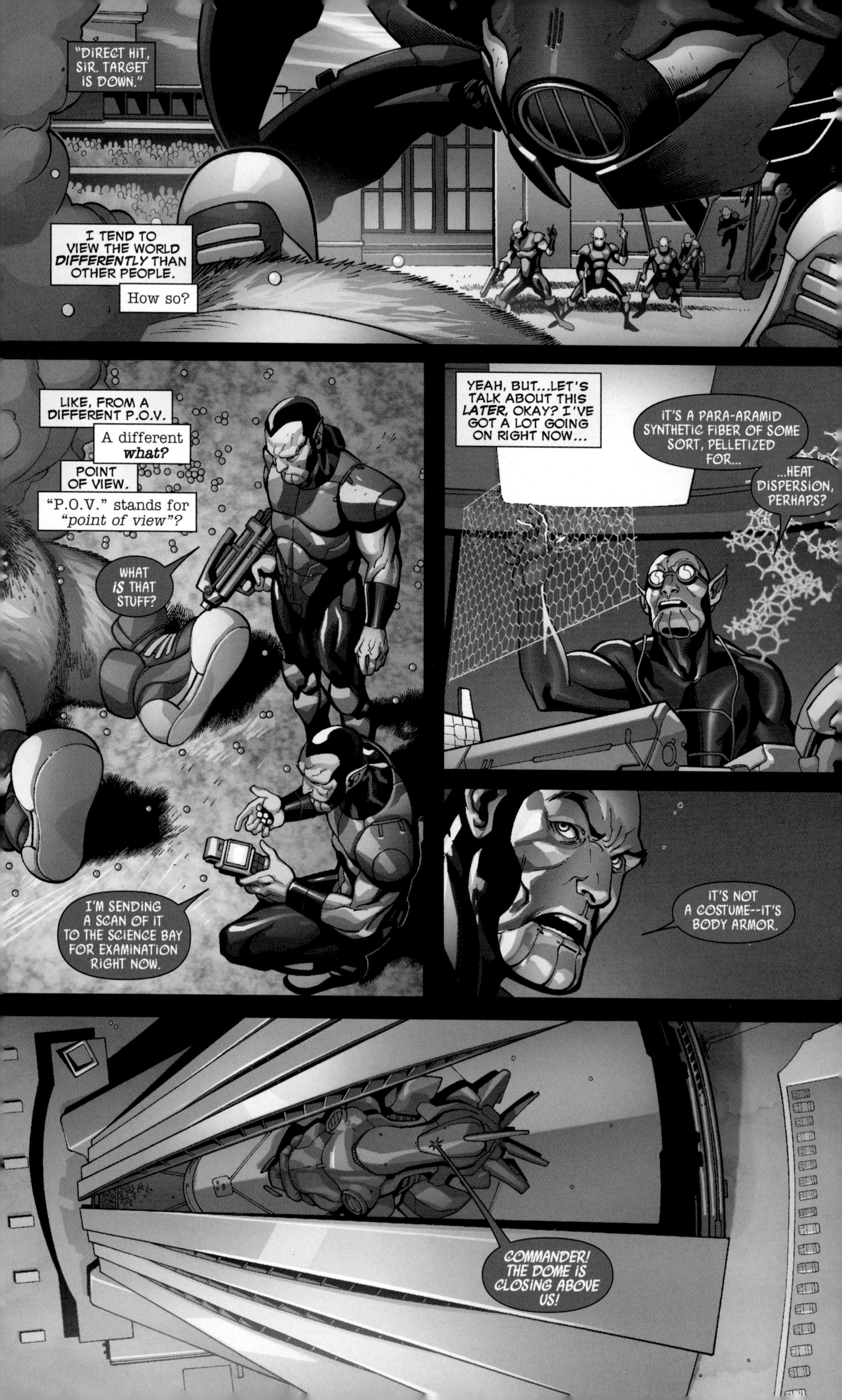

"DIRECT HIT, SIR. TARGET IS DOWN."
I TEND TO VIEW THE WORLD DIFFERENTLY THAN OTHER PEOPLE.
How so?
LIKE, FROM A DIFFERENT P.O.V.
A different what?
POINT OF VIEW.
"P.O.V." stands for "point of view"?
WHAT IS THAT STUFF?
I'M SENDING A SCAN OF IT TO THE SCIENCE BAY FOR EXAMINATION RIGHT NOW.
YEAH, BUT...LET'S TALK ABOUT THIS LATER, OKAY? I'VE GOT A LOT GOING ON RIGHT NOW...
IT'S A PARA-ARAMID SYNTHETIC FIBER OF SOME SORT, PELLETIZED FOR...
...HEAT DISPERSION, PERHAPS?
IT'S NOT A COSTUME--IT'S BODY ARMOR.
COMMANDER! THE DOME IS CLOSING ABOVE US!

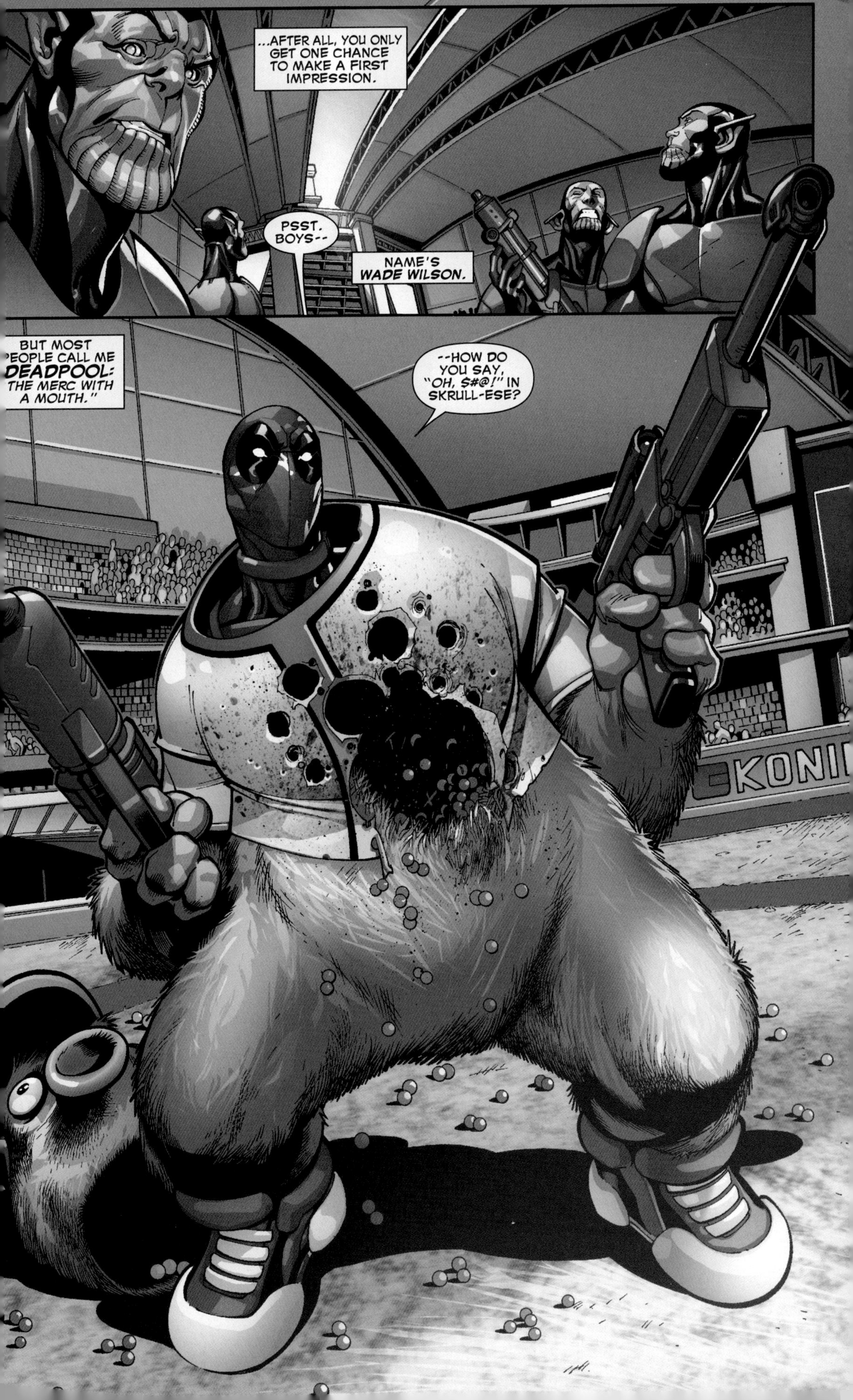
...AFTER ALL, YOU ONLY GET ONE CHANCE TO MAKE A FIRST IMPRESSION.
PSST. BOYS--
NAME'S *WADE WILSON.*
BUT MOST PEOPLE CALL ME **DEADPOOL:** "THE MERC WITH A MOUTH."
--HOW DO YOU SAY, "OH, $#@!" IN SKRULL-ESE?
KONI

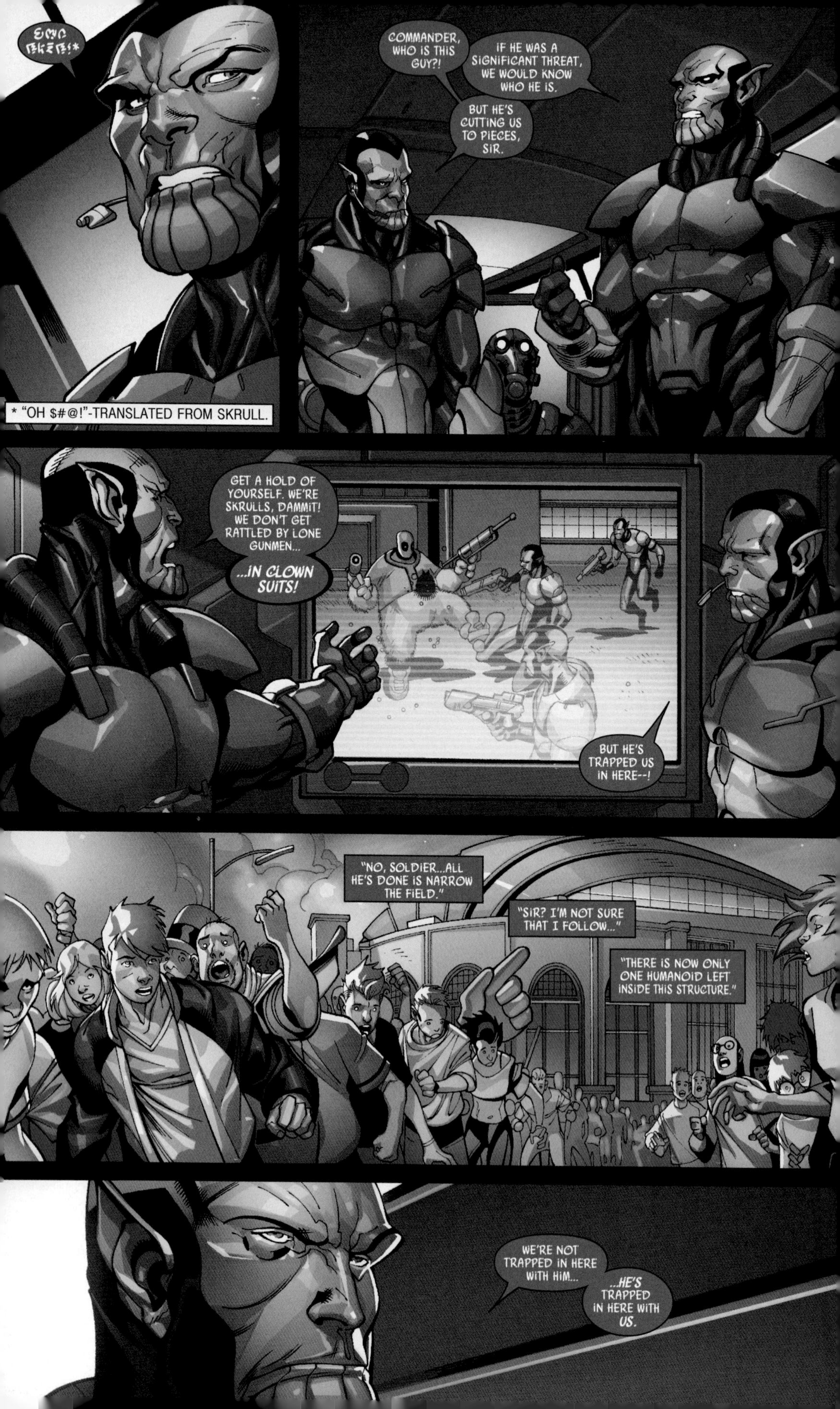
* "OH $#@!"-TRANSLATED FROM SKRULL.
COMMANDER, WHO IS THIS GUY?!
IF HE WAS A SIGNIFICANT THREAT, WE WOULD KNOW WHO HE IS.
BUT HE'S CUTTING US TO PIECES, SIR.
GET A HOLD OF YOURSELF. WE'RE SKRULLS, DAMMIT! WE DON'T GET RATTLED BY LONE GUNMEN...
...IN CLOWN SUITS!
BUT HE'S TRAPPED US IN HERE--!
"NO, SOLDIER...ALL HE'S DONE IS NARROW THE FIELD."
"SIR? I'M NOT SURE THAT I FOLLOW..."
"THERE IS NOW ONLY ONE HUMANOID LEFT INSIDE THIS STRUCTURE."
WE'RE NOT TRAPPED IN HERE WITH HIM...
...HE'S TRAPPED IN HERE WITH US.

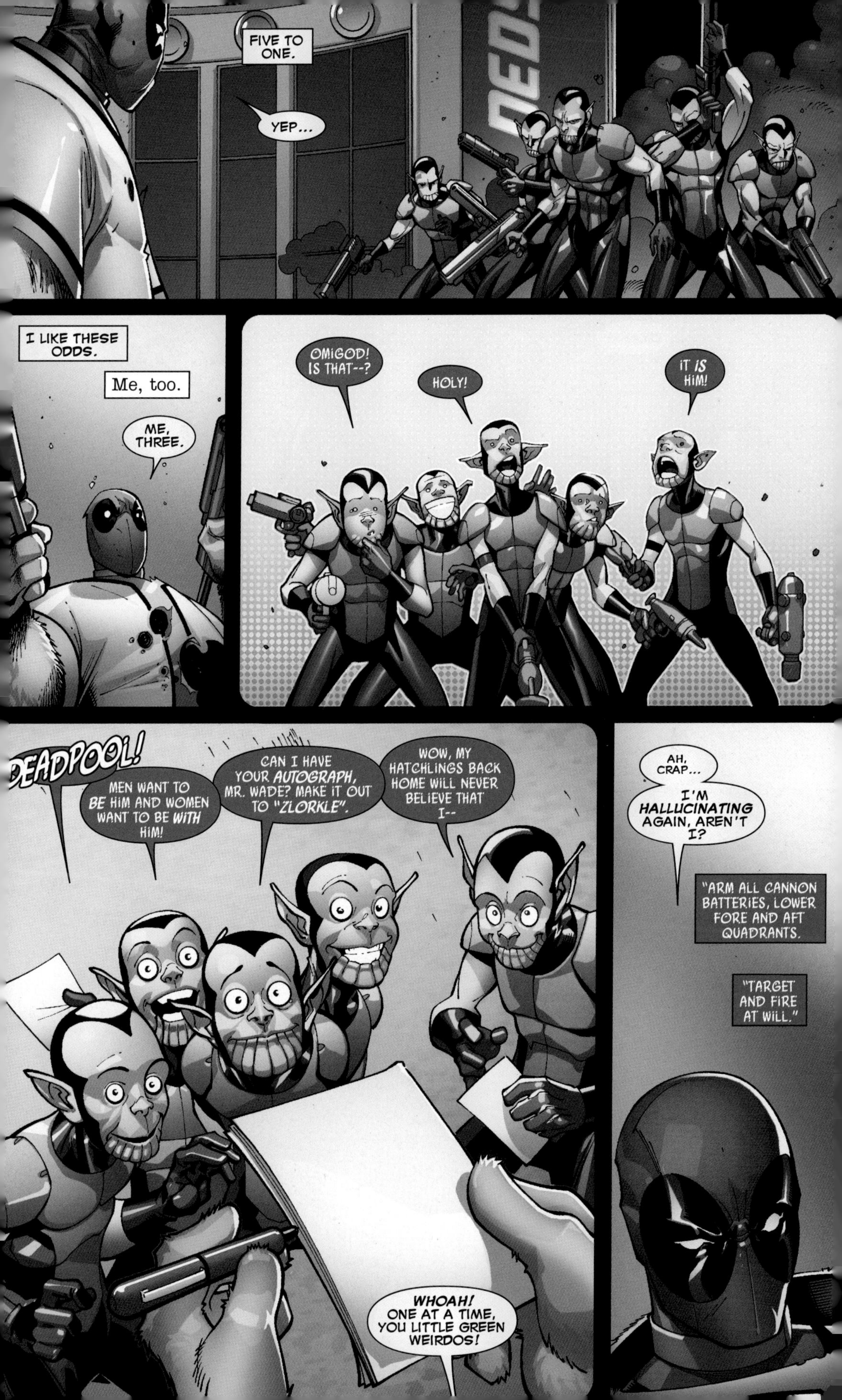
FIVE TO ONE.
YEP...
I LIKE THESE ODDS.
Me, too.
ME, THREE.
OMIGOD! IS THAT--?
HOLY!
IT IS HIM!
DEADPOOL!
MEN WANT TO BE HIM AND WOMEN WANT TO BE WITH HIM!
CAN I HAVE YOUR AUTOGRAPH, MR. WADE? MAKE IT OUT TO "ZLORKLE".
WOW, MY HATCHLINGS BACK HOME WILL NEVER BELIEVE THAT I--
WHOAH! ONE AT A TIME, YOU LITTLE GREEN WEIRDOS!
AH, CRAP...
I'M HALLUCINATING AGAIN, AREN'T I?
"ARM ALL CANNON BATTERIES, LOWER FORE AND AFT QUADRANTS.
"TARGET AND FIRE AT WILL."

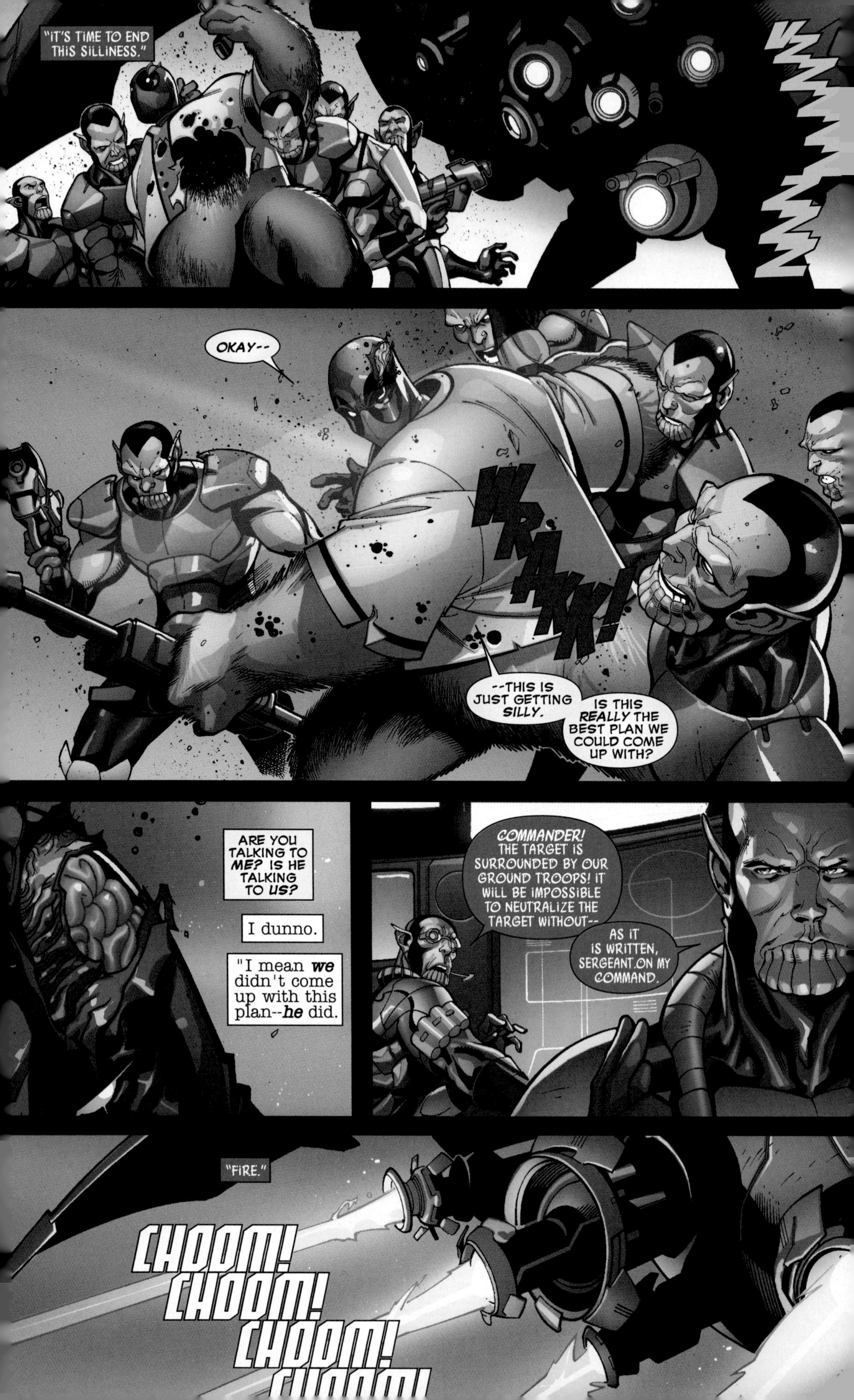
"IT'S TIME TO END THIS SILLINESS."
VWMMMM
OKAY--
WRAKK!
--THIS IS JUST GETTING SILLY.
IS THIS REALLY THE BEST PLAN WE COULD COME UP WITH?
ARE YOU TALKING TO ME? IS HE TALKING TO US?
I dunno.
"I mean we didn't come up with this plan--he did.
COMMANDER! THE TARGET IS SURROUNDED BY OUR GROUND TROOPS! IT WILL BE IMPOSSIBLE TO NEUTRALIZE THE TARGET WITHOUT--
AS IT IS WRITTEN, SERGEANT. ON MY COMMAND.
"FIRE."
CHOOM!
CHOOM!
CHOOM!

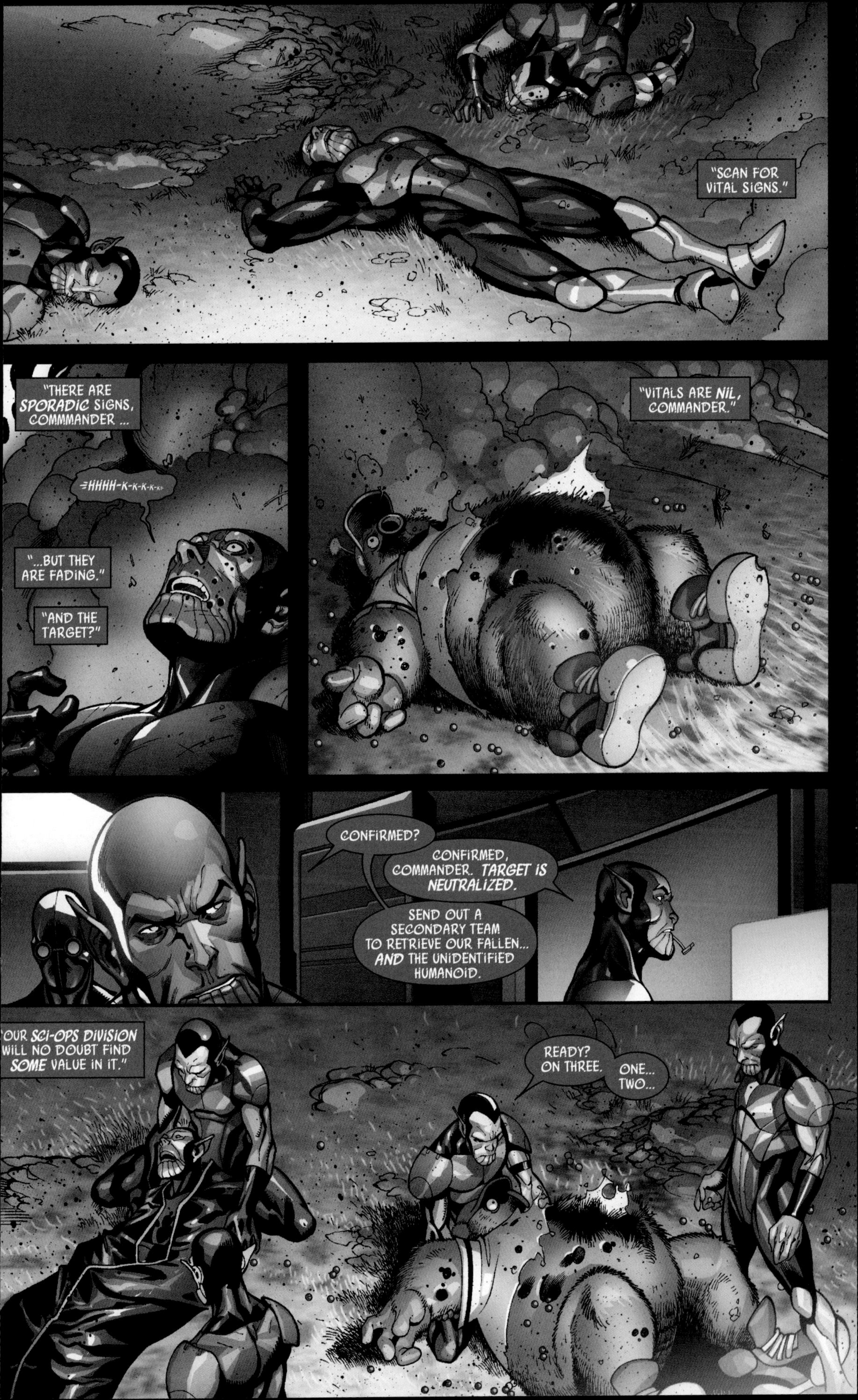
"SCAN FOR VITAL SIGNS."
"THERE ARE SPORADIC SIGNS, COMMMANDER ...
=HHHH-K-K-K-K-K
"...BUT THEY ARE FADING."
"AND THE TARGET?"
"VITALS ARE NIL, COMMANDER."
CONFIRMED?
CONFIRMED, COMMANDER. TARGET IS NEUTRALIZED.
SEND OUT A SECONDARY TEAM TO RETRIEVE OUR FALLEN... AND THE UNIDENTIFIED HUMANOID.
"OUR SCI-OPS DIVISION WILL NO DOUBT FIND SOME VALUE IN IT."
READY? ON THREE.
ONE... TWO...

THREE!

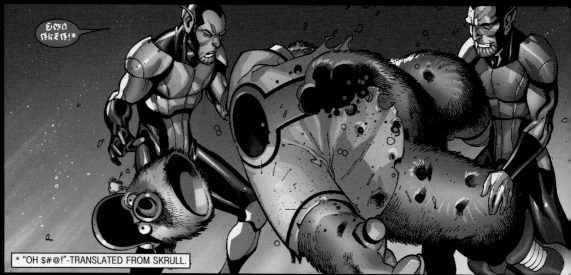

ϵϲϥ⸱ ᵬᵏᵉᵬ!*

* "OH $#@!"-TRANSLATED FROM SKRULL.

THAT... IS...IT!

COMMANDER?

EVERY SINGLE ONE OF YOU HAS FAILED! DUE TO IGNORANCE, INCOMPETENCE...

...AND COWARDICE.

I THINK IT'S TIME TO SHOW BOTH YOU AND THIS HUMANOID HOW A REAL SKRULL HANDLES THEIR BUSINESS.

DEPLOY THE SUPER-SKRULL.

KLIK

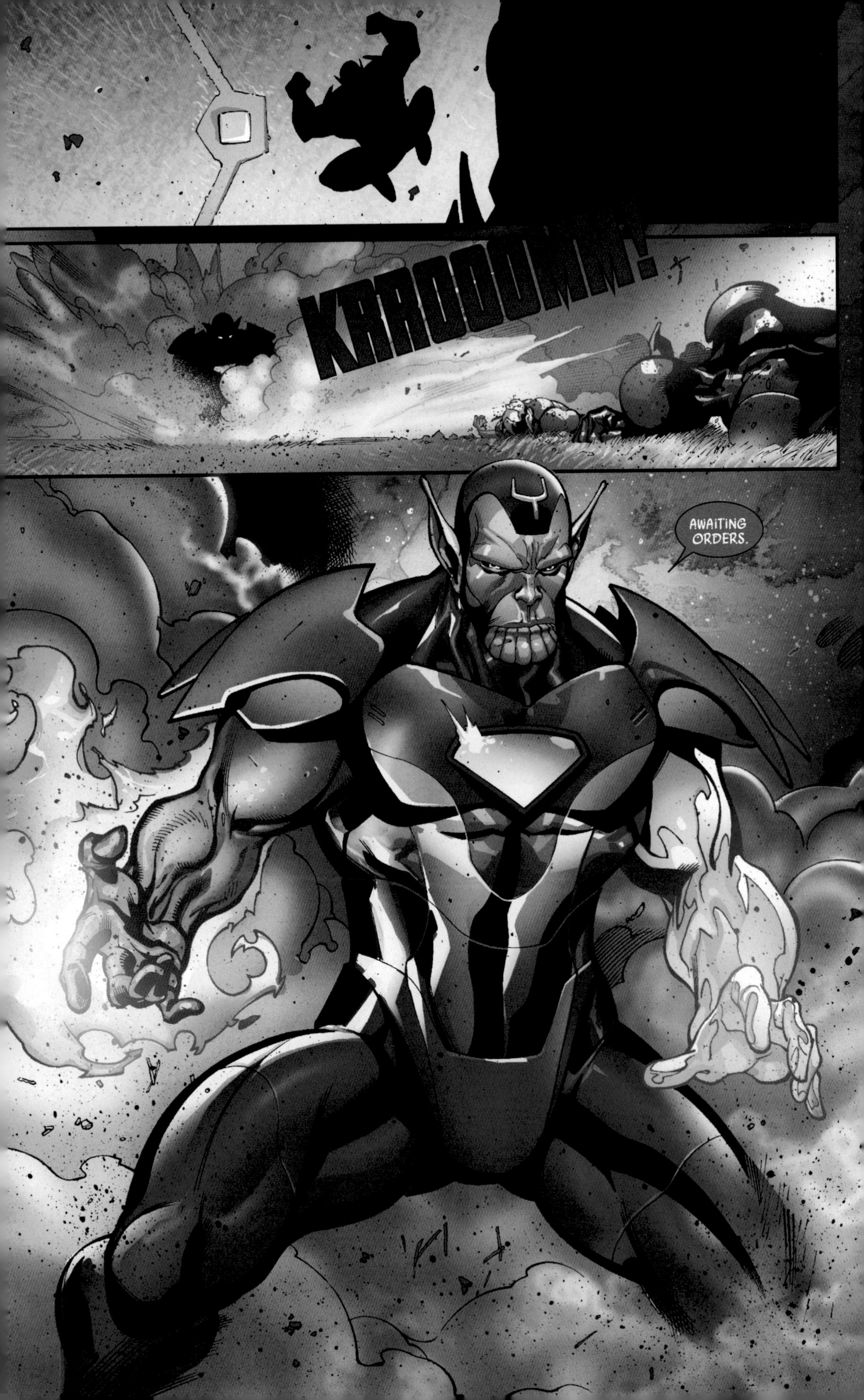
KRROOOMM!
AWAITING ORDERS.

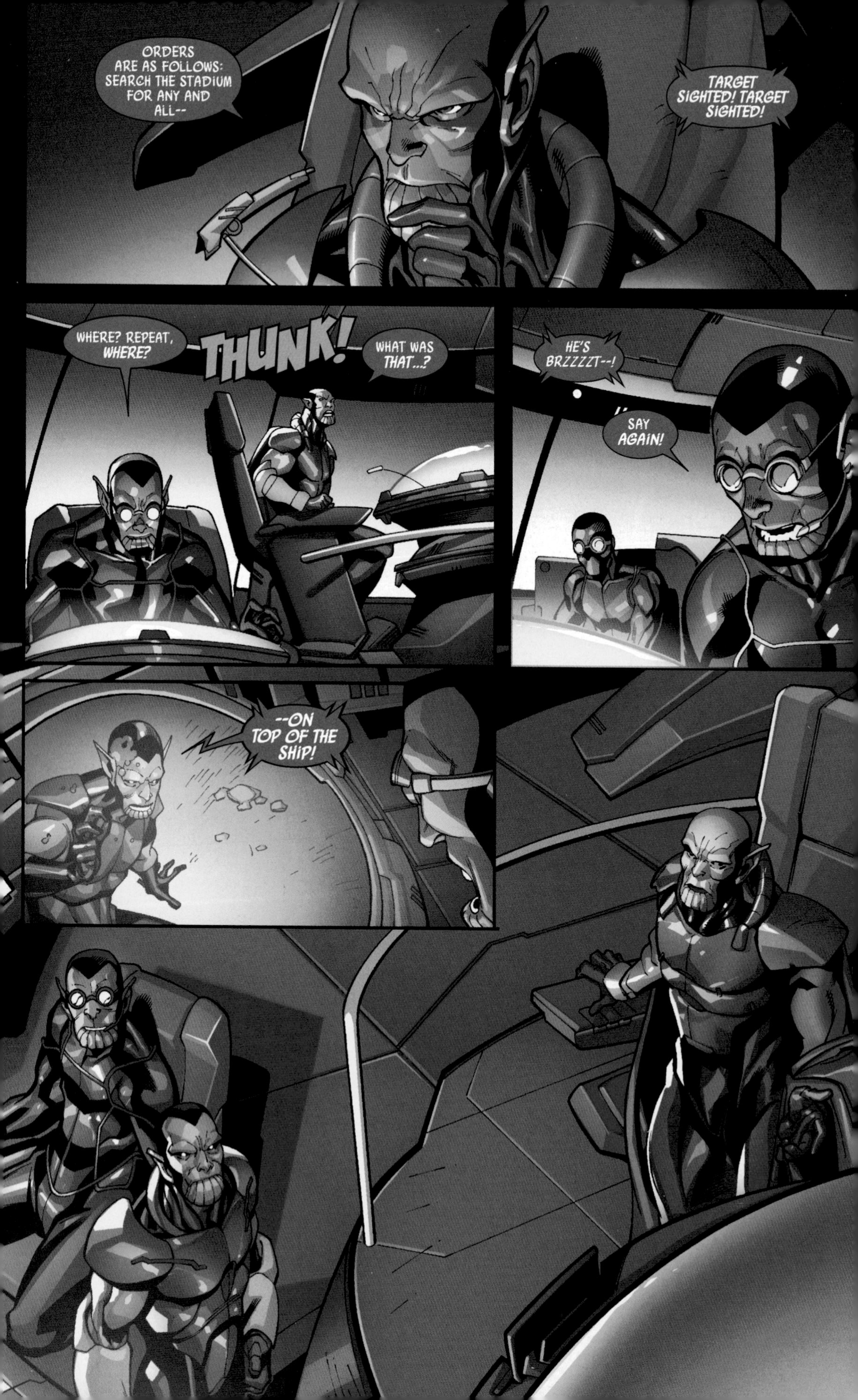

ORDERS ARE AS FOLLOWS: SEARCH THE STADIUM FOR ANY AND ALL--
TARGET SIGHTED! TARGET SIGHTED!
WHERE? REPEAT, WHERE?
THUNK!
WHAT WAS THAT...?
HE'S BRZZZZT--!
SAY AGAIN!
--ON TOP OF THE SHIP!

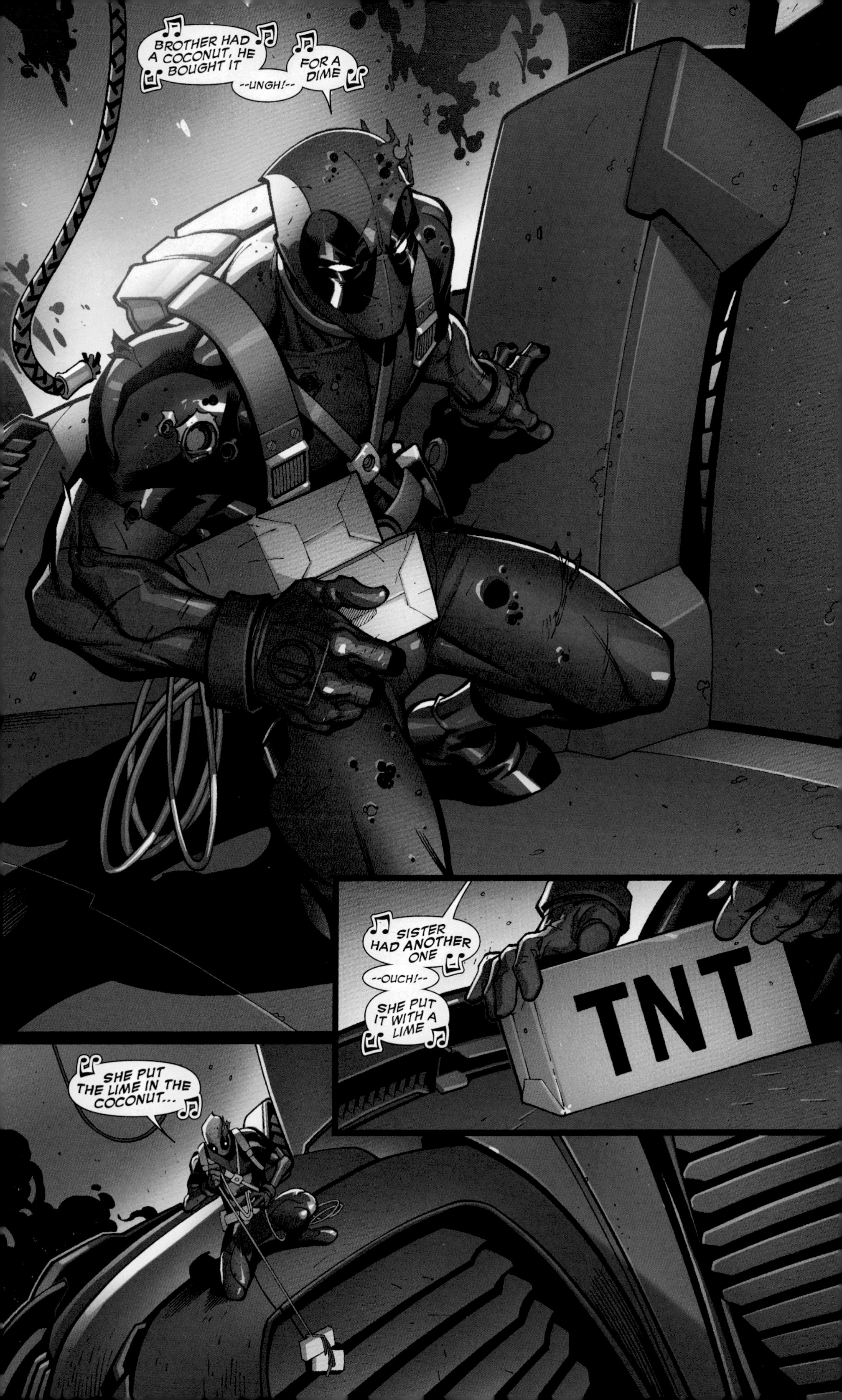
BROTHER HAD A COCONUT, HE BOUGHT IT
--UNGH!--
FOR A DIME
SISTER HAD ANOTHER ONE
--OUCH!--
SHE PUT IT WITH A LIME
TNT
SHE PUT THE LIME IN THE COCONUT...

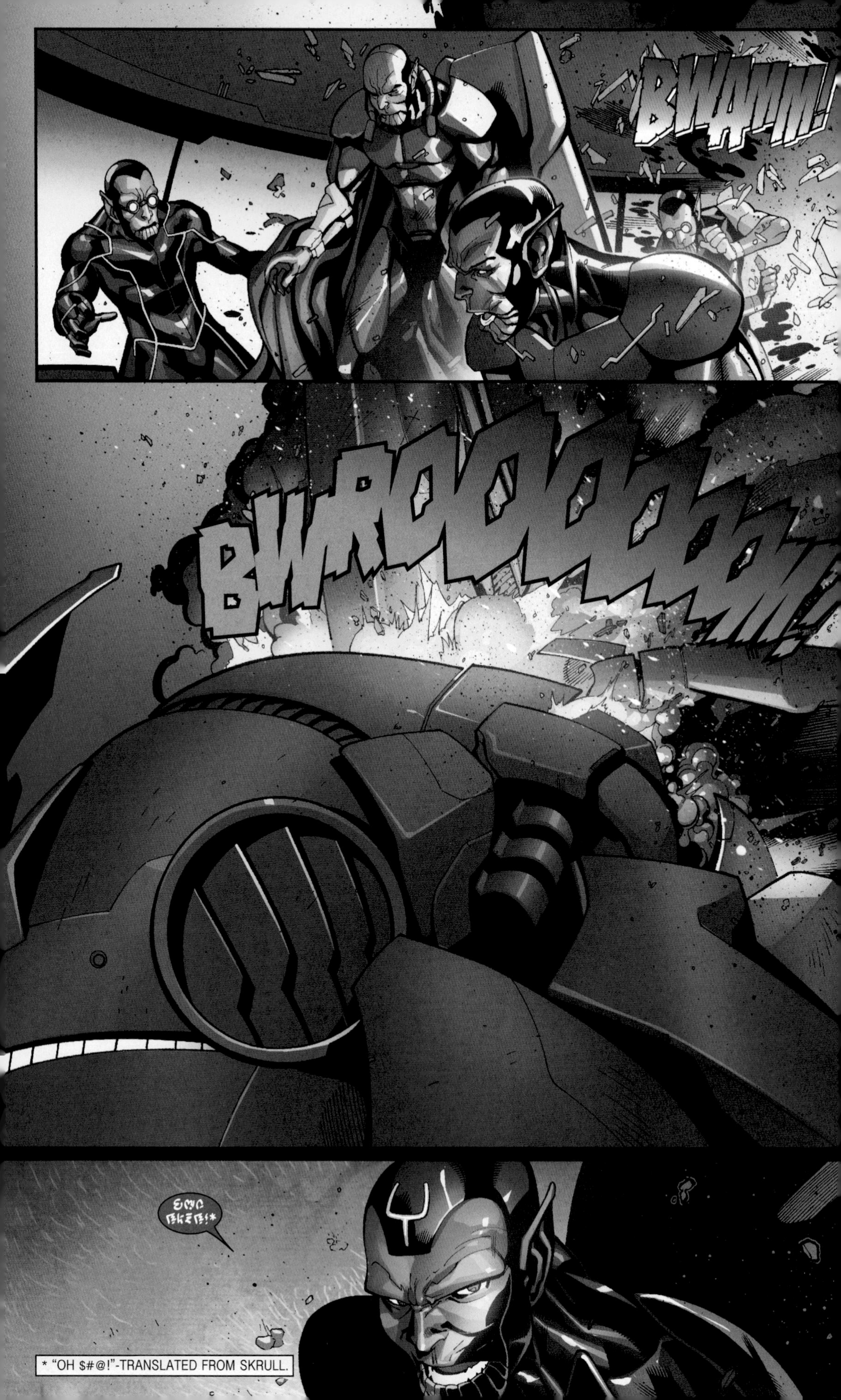
BWAMM!
BWROOOOOM!
* "OH $#@!"-TRANSLATED FROM SKRULL.

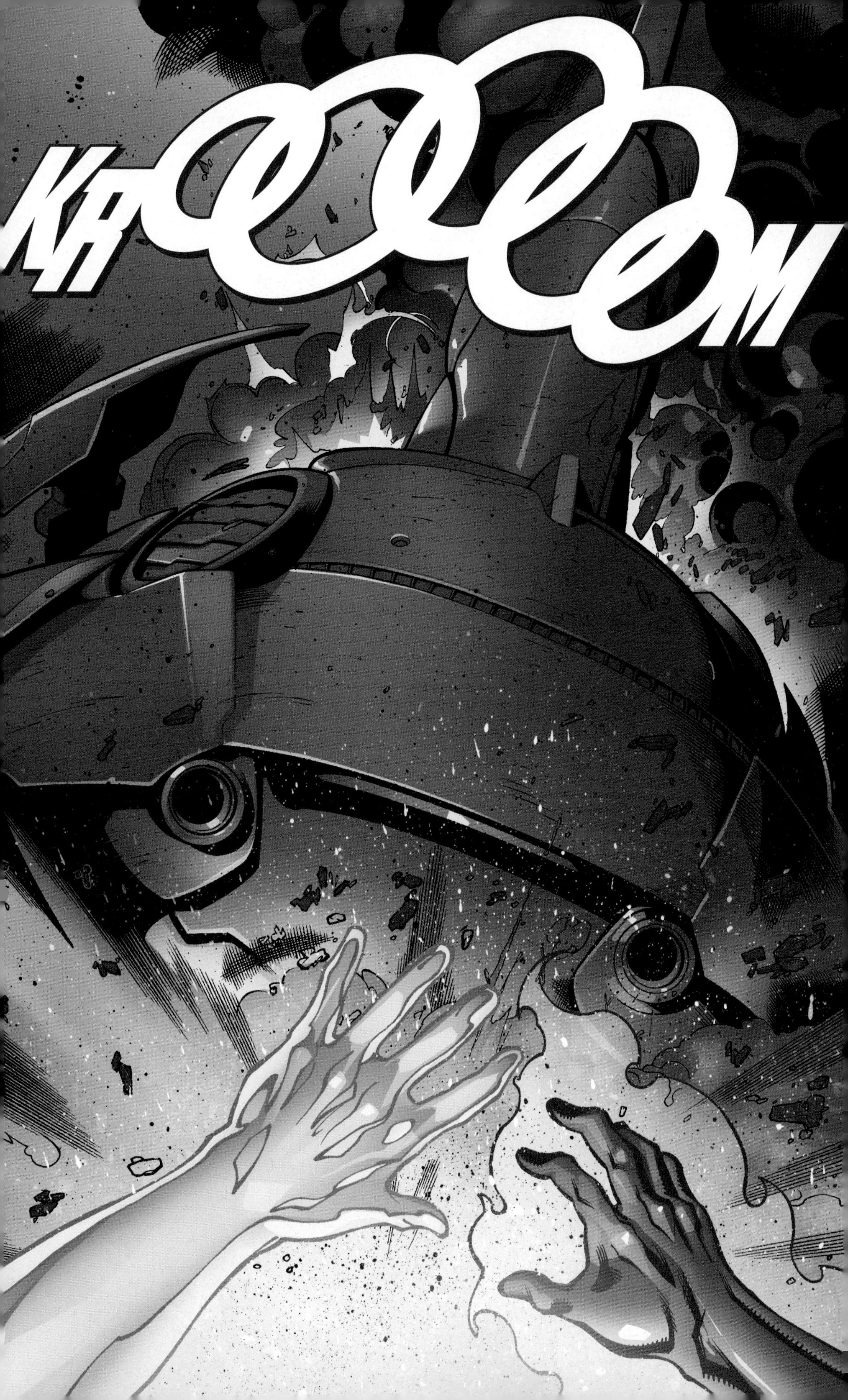
KAOOOOM

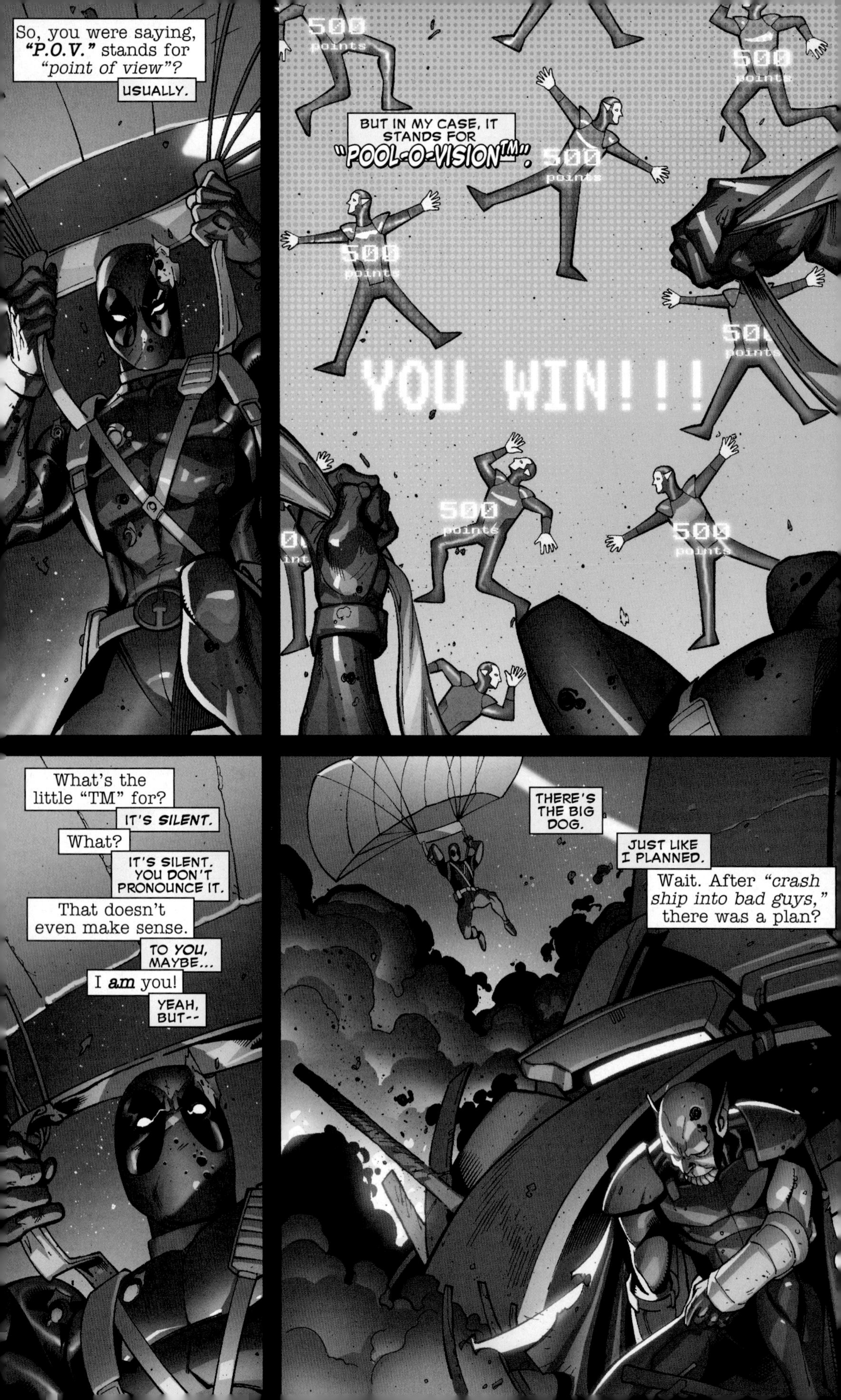
So, you were saying, ***"P.O.V."*** stands for *"point of view"*?
USUALLY.
BUT IN MY CASE, IT STANDS FOR "POOL-O-VISION™".
500 points
YOU WIN!!!
What's the little "TM" for?
IT'S *SILENT*.
What?
IT'S SILENT. YOU DON'T PRONOUNCE IT.
That doesn't even make sense.
TO *YOU*, MAYBE...
I ***am*** you!
YEAH, BUT--
THERE'S THE BIG DOG.
JUST LIKE I PLANNED.
Wait. After *"crash ship into bad guys,"* there was a plan?

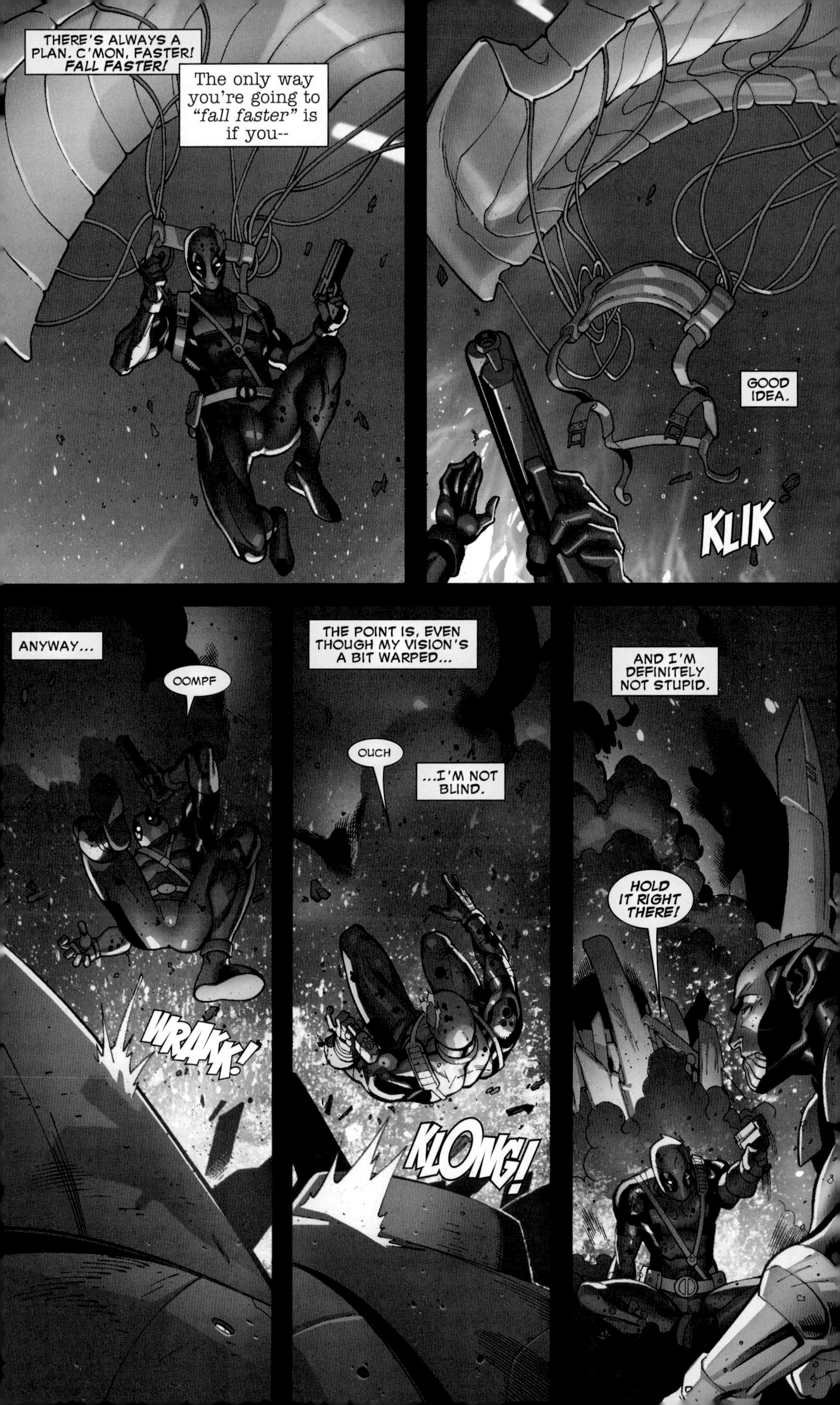
THERE'S ALWAYS A PLAN. C'MON, FASTER! FALL FASTER!
The only way you're going to "fall faster" is if you--
GOOD IDEA.
KLIK
ANYWAY...
OOMPF
WRAKK!
THE POINT IS, EVEN THOUGH MY VISION'S A BIT WARPED...
OUCH
...I'M NOT BLIND.
KLONG!
AND I'M DEFINITELY NOT STUPID.
HOLD IT RIGHT THERE!

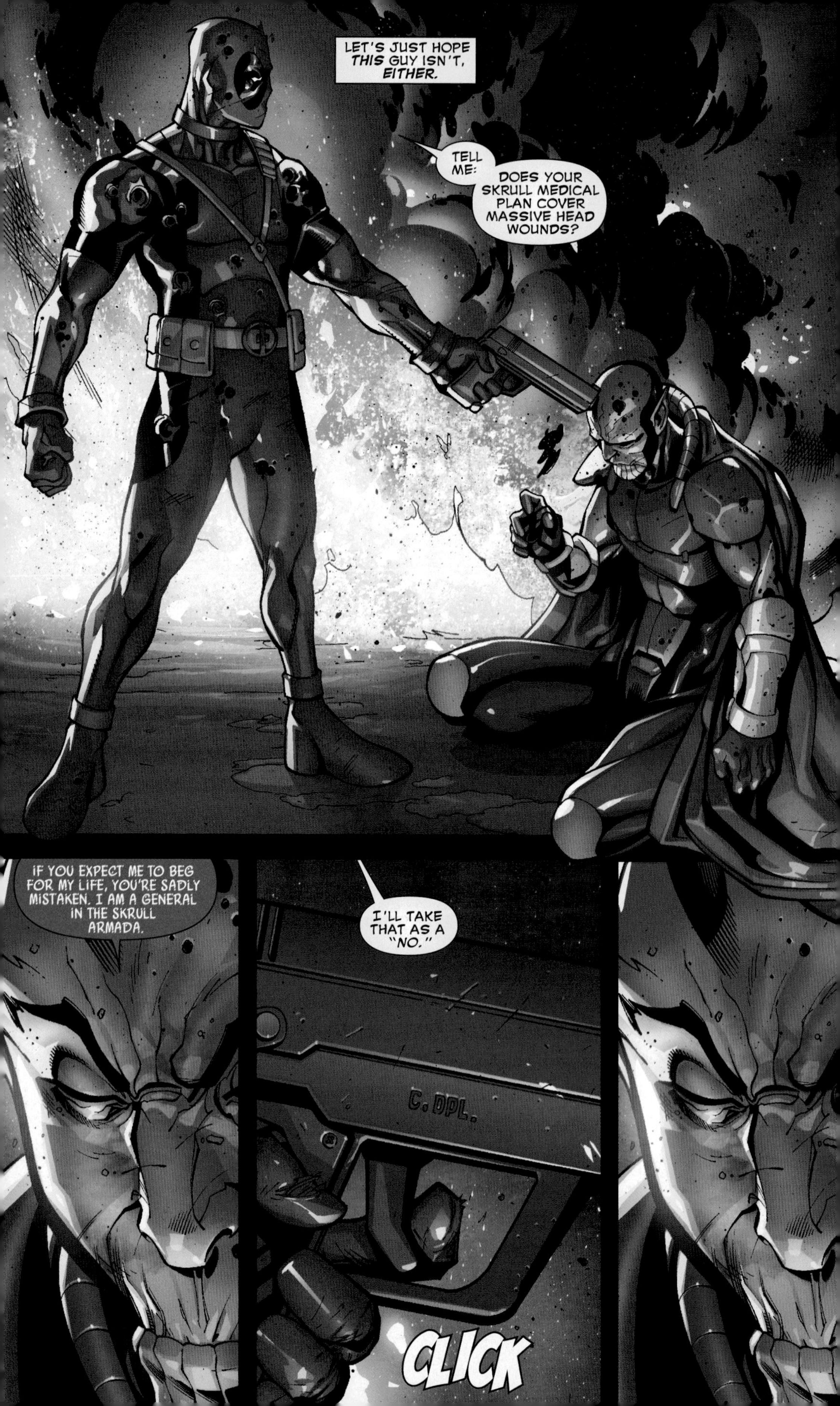
LET'S JUST HOPE THIS GUY ISN'T, EITHER.
TELL ME:
DOES YOUR SKRULL MEDICAL PLAN COVER MASSIVE HEAD WOUNDS?
IF YOU EXPECT ME TO BEG FOR MY LIFE, YOU'RE SADLY MISTAKEN. I AM A GENERAL IN THE SKRULL ARMADA.
I'LL TAKE THAT AS A "NO."
C. DPL.
CLICK

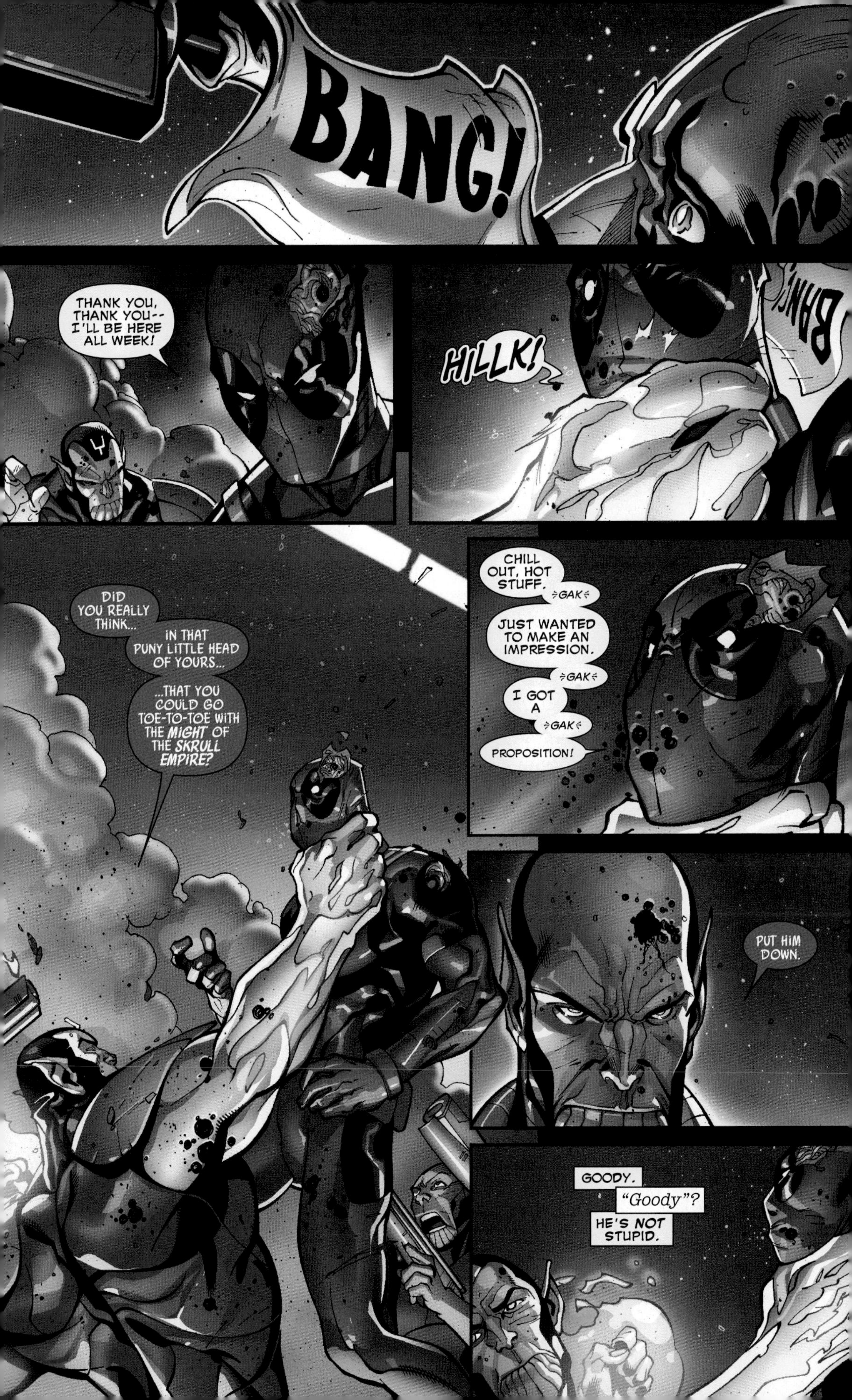
BANG!
THANK YOU, THANK YOU-- I'LL BE HERE ALL WEEK!
BANG!
HILLK!
DID YOU REALLY THINK...
IN THAT PUNY LITTLE HEAD OF YOURS...
...THAT YOU COULD GO TOE-TO-TOE WITH THE MIGHT OF THE SKRULL EMPIRE?
CHILL OUT, HOT STUFF.
GAK
JUST WANTED TO MAKE AN IMPRESSION.
GAK
I GOT A
GAK
PROPOSITION!
PUT HIM DOWN.
GOODY.
"Goody"?
HE'S NOT STUPID.

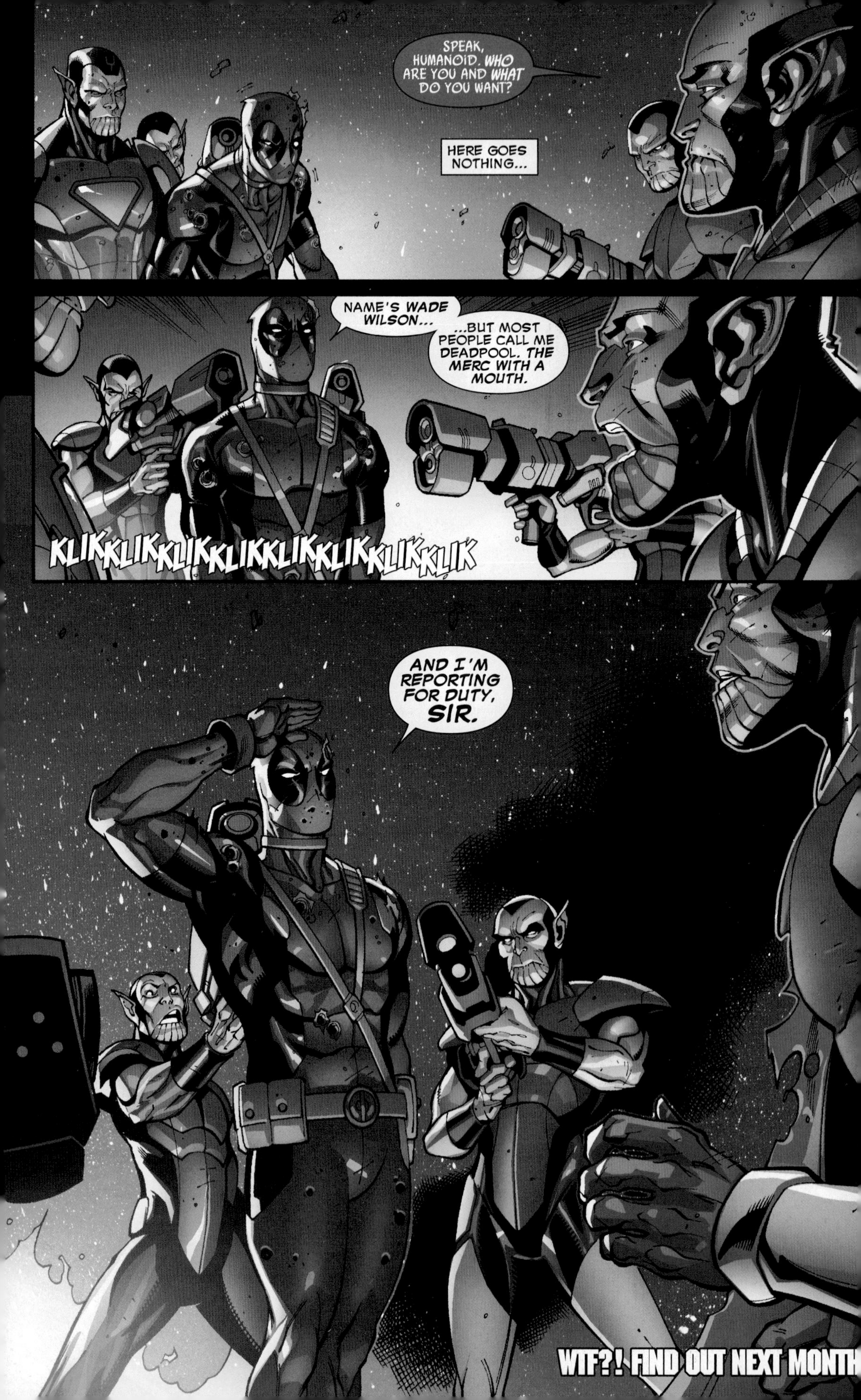
SPEAK, HUMANOID. WHO ARE YOU AND WHAT DO YOU WANT?
HERE GOES NOTHING...
NAME'S WADE WILSON...
...BUT MOST PEOPLE CALL ME DEADPOOL. THE MERC WITH A MOUTH.
KLIKKLIKKLIKKLIKKLIKKLIKKLIKKLIK
AND I'M REPORTING FOR DUTY, SIR.
WTF?! FIND OUT NEXT MONTH

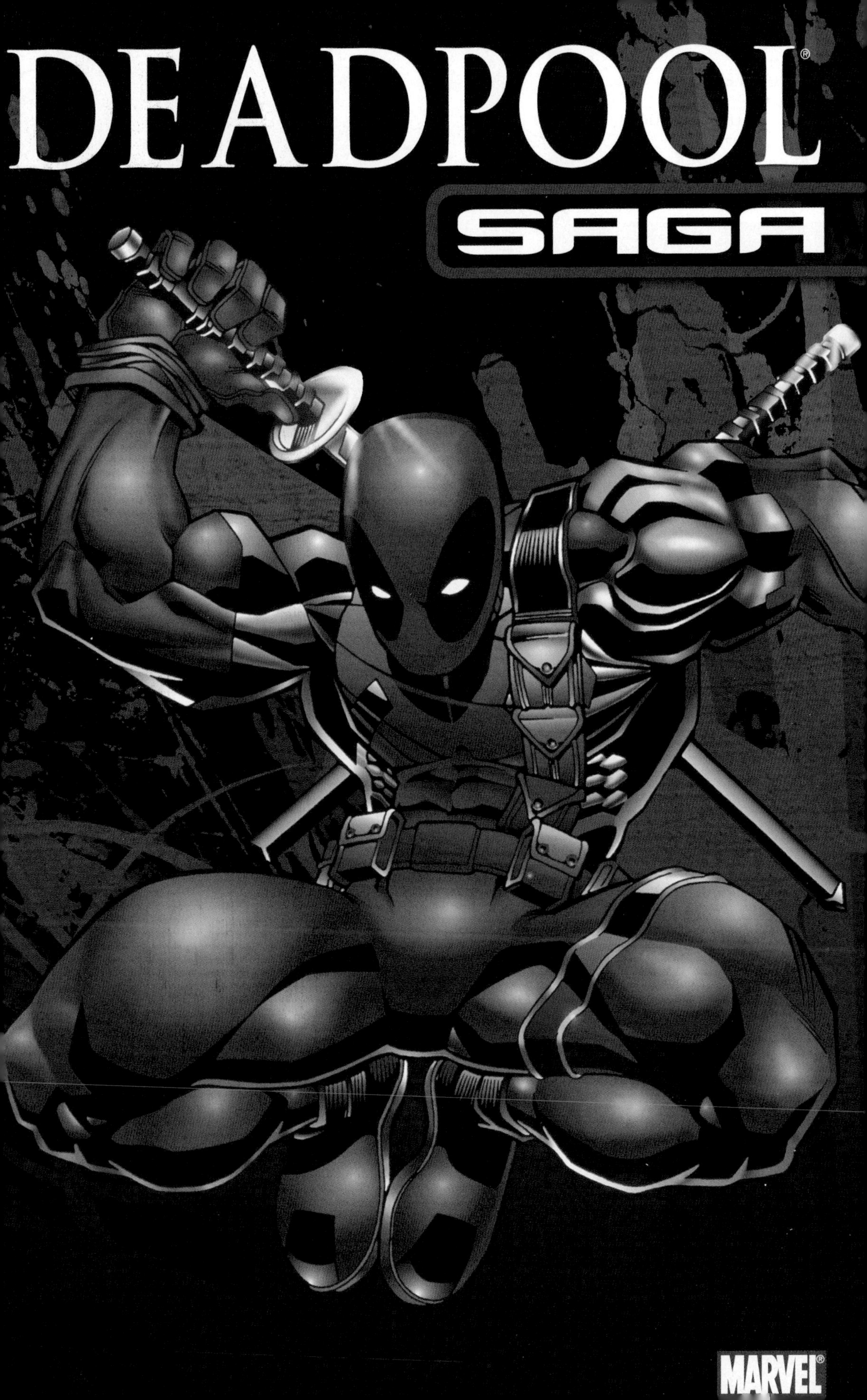
DEADPOOL®
SAGA
MARVEL®

Writer:
RONALD BYRD
Design:
RODOLFO MURAGUCHI
Assistant Editor:
ALEX STARBUCK
Editor:
JEFF YOUNGQUIST

Almost nothing is known for certain about the youth of the man called "Wade Wilson," not even if he was born with that name. He remembers a mother who died when he was five and a mother who beat him during his teen years, a father he hasn't seen since childhood and a father who was shot in a barroom altercation when his son was 17. Whatever his past, the youth who became Deadpool grew up to be a violent, conflicted man.

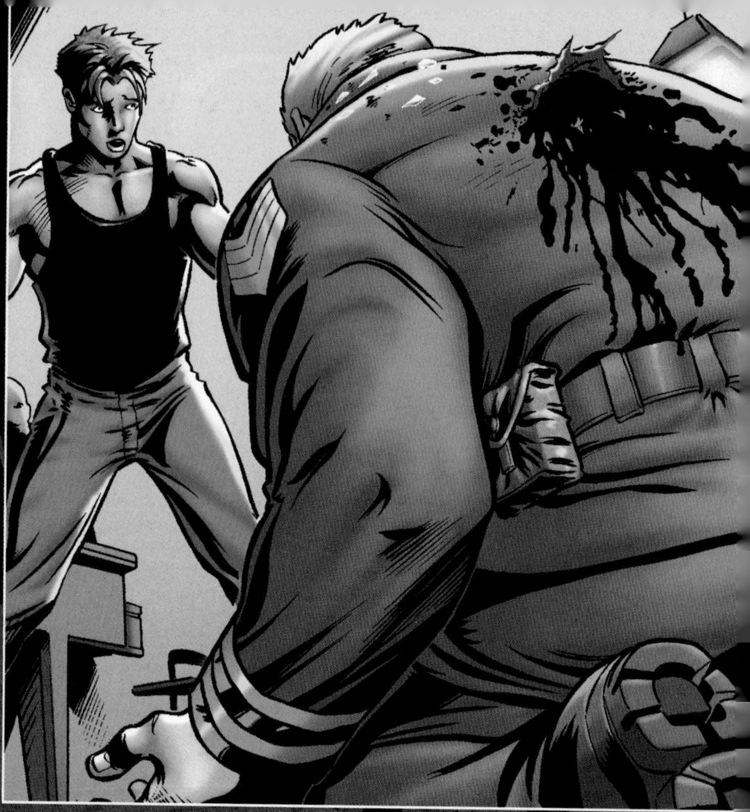

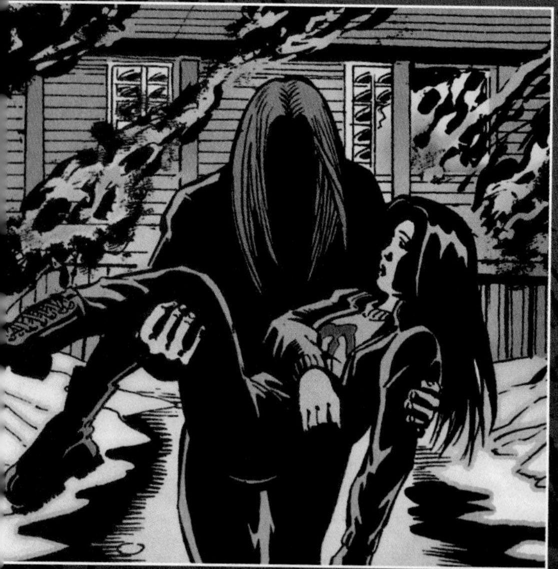

After serving in the military, that violent man became a teenage mercenary, taking assignments against those he felt warranted death. After failed assignments, he took new identities, and his true self, whoever that was, may have been lost in the process. A turning point came when, while on the run, he was nursed back to health by a husband and wife. Supposedly the husband's name was "Wade Wilson," and the mercenary craved that identity for himself. While trying to kill his benefactor, however, he inadvertently killed his wife Mercedes. Having broken his self-imposed rule against harming the innocent, the unhinged mercenary decided that **he** was Mercedes' husband, "Wade Wilson," and he mourned her before moving on.

Still a mercenary, Wilson traveled the world in the course of his assignments but never again abandoned the identity he believed was his. Eventually turning up in the USA, he fell in love with young Vanessa Carlysle, and although the couple lived their lives on the outskirts of society, they shared hopes for a better life. Unfortunately, Wilson contracted cancer, and he left Vanessa rather than force upon her what he perceived as the burden of a stricken man.

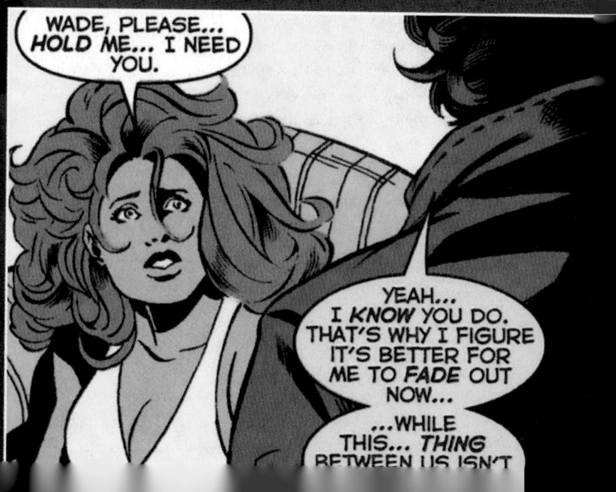
WADE, PLEASE... *HOLD* ME... I NEED YOU.
YEAH... I *KNOW* YOU DO. THAT'S WHY I FIGURE IT'S BETTER FOR ME TO *FADE* OUT NOW...
...WHILE THIS... *THING*

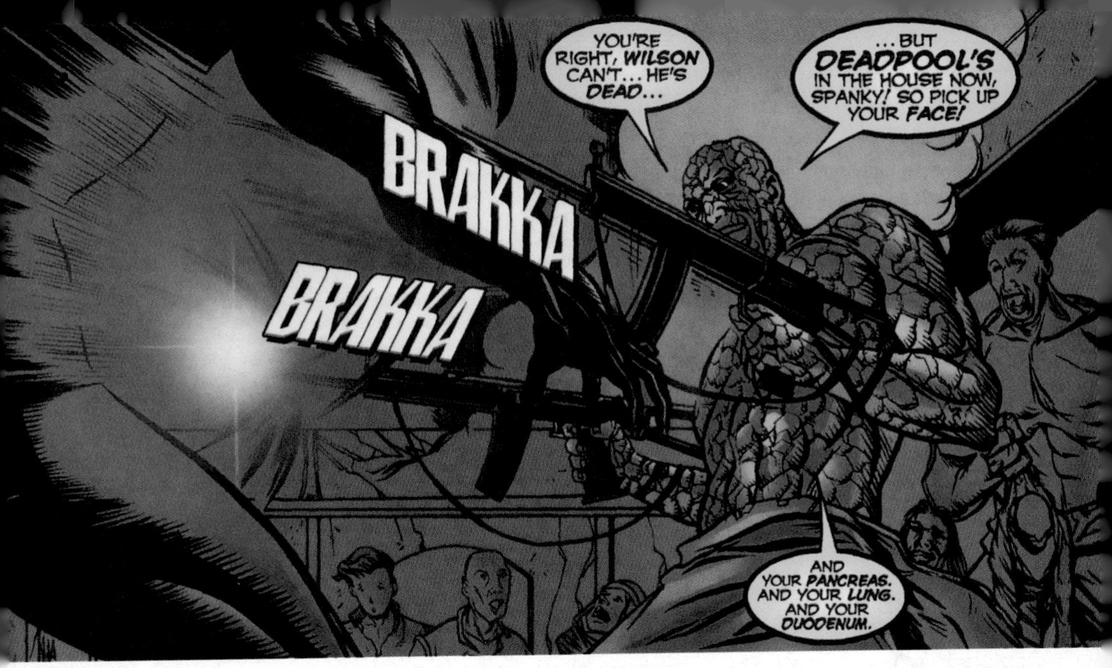
YOU'RE RIGHT, WILSON CAN'T... HE'S DEAD...
...BUT DEADPOOL'S IN THE HOUSE NOW, SPANKY! SO PICK UP YOUR FACE!
BRAKKA
BRAKKA
AND YOUR PANCREAS. AND YOUR LUNG. AND YOUR DUODENUM.

Wilson joined Canada's Department K and was mutated with a healing factor intended to cure his cancer. He worked with other operatives like Kane and Sluggo, but something went wrong. Whether due to a breakdown from his treatments or some other factor, Wilson apparently killed teammate Slayback. The government sent him to the Hospice for treatment, unaware of the sadistic experiments conducted by Dr. Emrys Killebrew. Killed for his rebellious streak, Wilson was revived by his healing factor, severely disfigured but no longer terminal. He tore the Hospice apart, freed his fellow test subjects, and proclaimed a new name for himself.

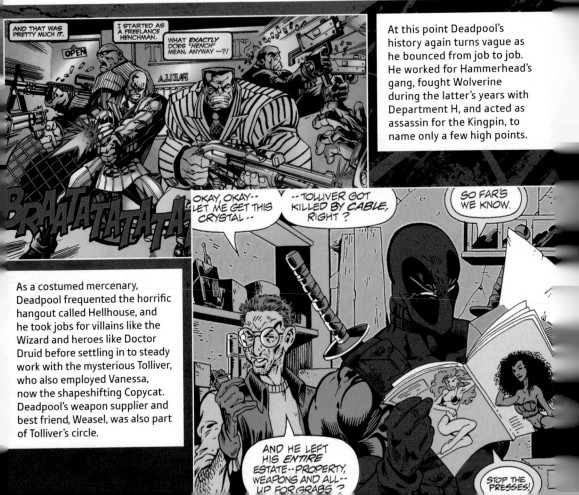

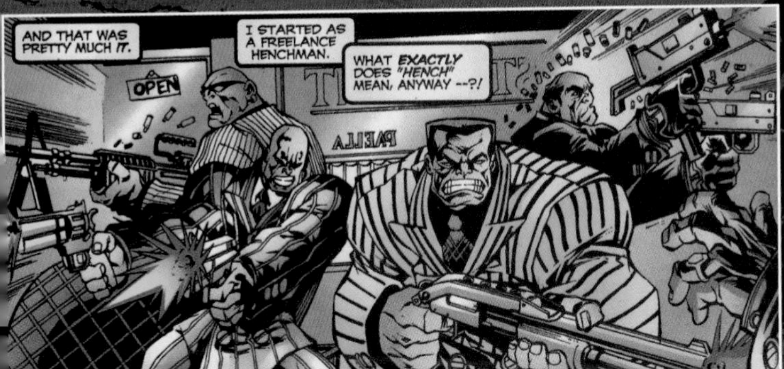
AND THAT WAS PRETTY MUCH IT.
I STARTED AS A FREELANCE HENCHMAN.
WHAT EXACTLY DOES "HENCH" MEAN, ANYWAY --?!
OPEN
BRAATATATATA

At this point Deadpool's history again turns vague as he bounced from job to job. He worked for Hammerhead's gang, fought Wolverine during the latter's years with Department H, and acted as assassin for the Kingpin, to name only a few high points.

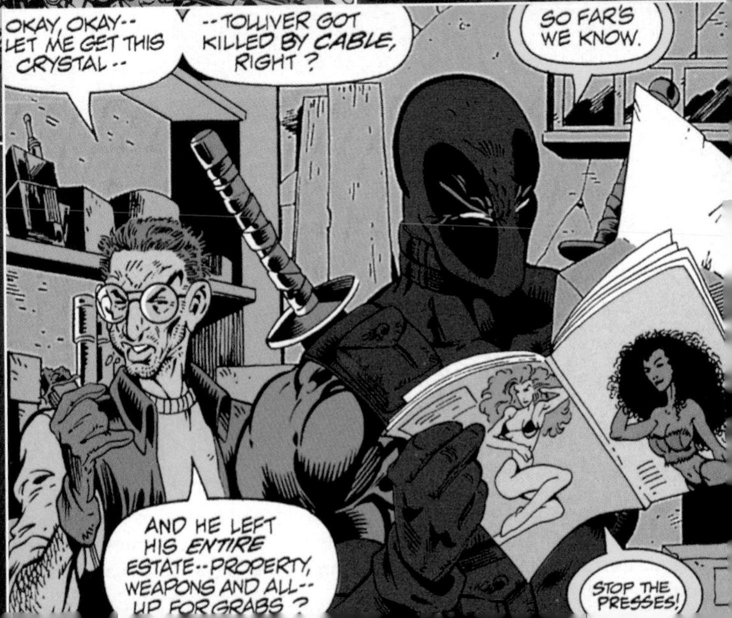
OKAY, OKAY-- LET ME GET THIS CRYSTAL--
--TOLLIVER GOT KILLED BY CABLE, RIGHT?
SO FAR'S WE KNOW.
AND HE LEFT HIS ENTIRE ESTATE--PROPERTY, WEAPONS AND ALL-- UP FOR GRABS?
STOP THE PRESSES!

As a costumed mercenary, Deadpool frequented the horrific hangout called Hellhouse, and he took jobs for villains like the Wizard and heroes like Doctor Druid before settling in to steady work with the mysterious Tolliver, who also employed Vanessa, now the shapeshifting Copycat. Deadpool's weapon supplier and best friend, Weasel, was also part of Tolliver's circle.

entually Tolliver sent Deadpool kill Cable, another super-wered mercenary and, cretly, Tolliver's father. At e time, Cable was acting as entor to the New Mutants, so adpool burst into the Xavier stitute, ready to rumble, but ble defeated him and mailed n back to Tolliver. Deadpool uld little imagine how portant Cable and his cohorts ould become in his later life.

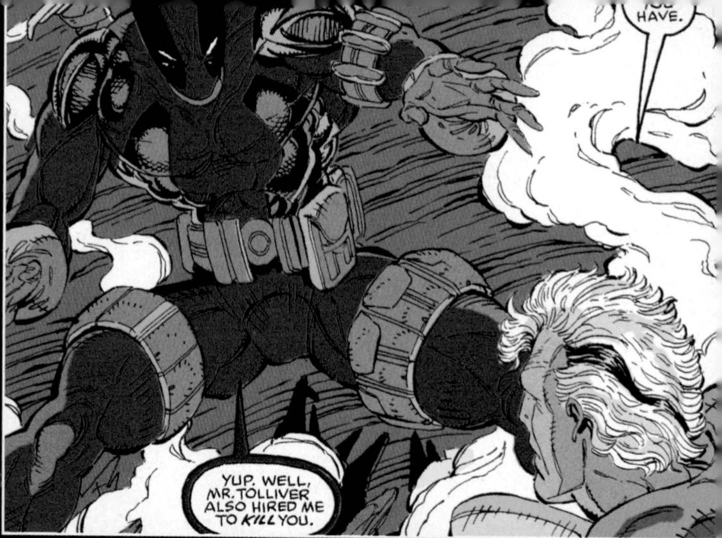
HAVE.
YUP. WELL, MR. TOLLIVER ALSO HIRED ME TO *KILL* YOU.

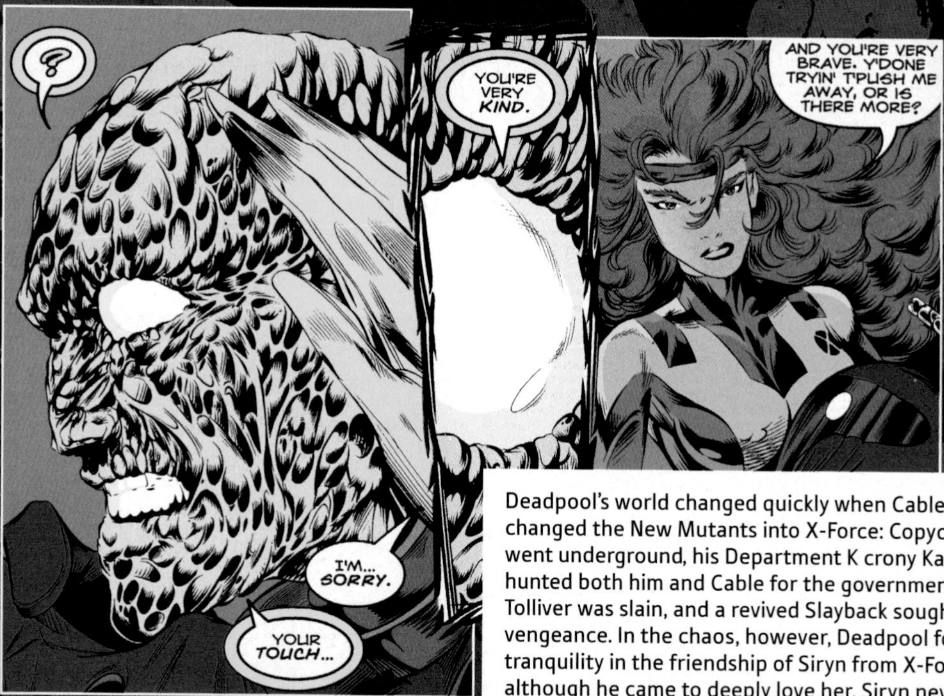
?
YOU'RE VERY *KIND*.
AND YOU'RE VERY BRAVE. Y'DONE TRYIN' T'PUSH ME AWAY, OR IS THERE MORE?
I'M... *SORRY*.
YOUR *TOUCH*...

Deadpool's world changed quickly when Cable changed the New Mutants into X-Force: Copycat went underground, his Department K crony Kane hunted both him and Cable for the government, Tolliver was slain, and a revived Slayback sought vengeance. In the chaos, however, Deadpool found tranquility in the friendship of Siryn from X-Force; although he came to deeply love her, Siryn never fully reciprocated his feelings.

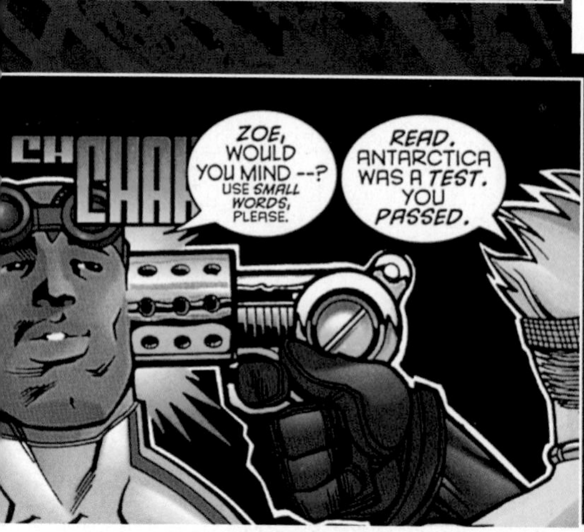
ZOE, WOULD YOU MIND --? USE *SMALL WORDS*, PLEASE.
READ. ANTARCTICA WAS A *TEST*. YOU *PASSED*.

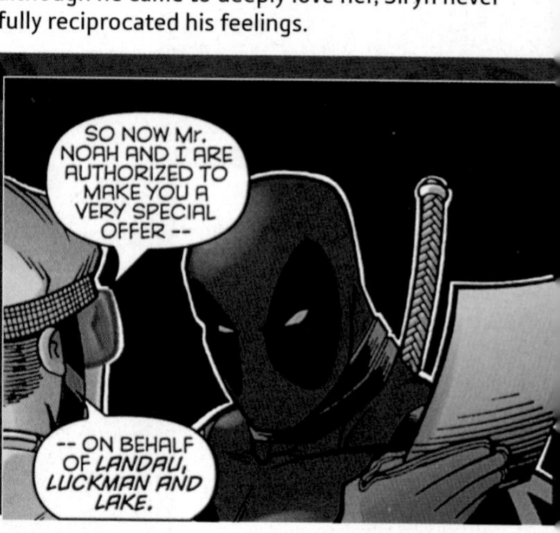
SO NOW MR. NOAH AND I ARE AUTHORIZED TO MAKE YOU A VERY SPECIAL OFFER --
-- ON BEHALF OF *LANDAU, LUCKMAN AND LAKE*.

eadpool's life settled back to normal, or as close to normal as he wanted it, but Zoe Culloden of the mystery m Landau, Luckman, and Lake felt Deadpool was meant for more than mercenary misadventures. Zoe claimed eroic destiny awaited the dubious Deadpool, who was sure that, although he had worn many names, "hero" ould never be one of them.

Deadpool continued moving from assignment to assignment, battle to battle, confronting Taskmaster, the Hulk, Typhoid Mary, Daredevil, and others. He grew less and less sure of what Zoe's offer might mean, but he discussed his doubts with no one save Blind Al, an elderly woman whom he inexplicably held hostage and against whom he sharpened his wits in repeat matches of pranks and sardonic barbs.

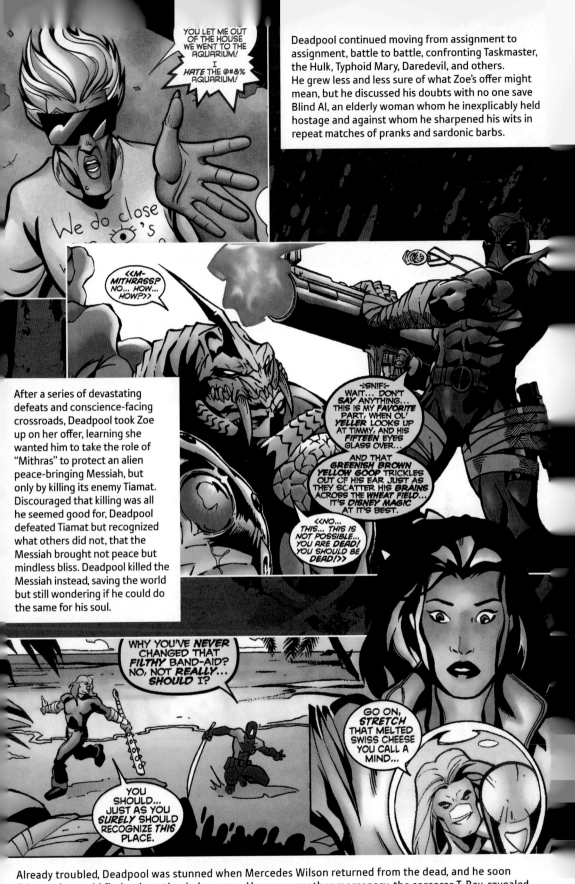

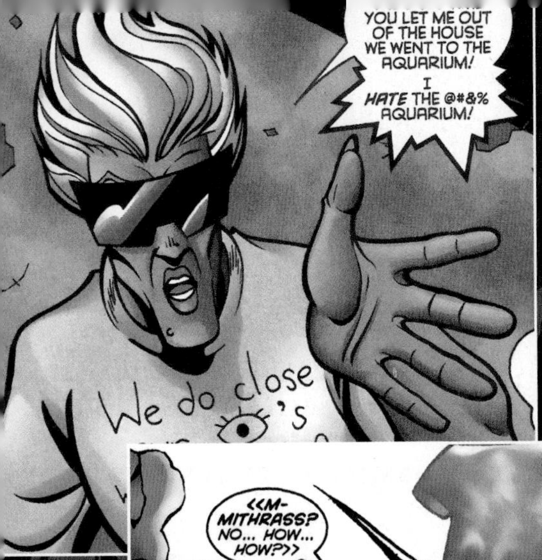
YOU LET ME OUT OF THE HOUSE WE WENT TO THE AQUARIUM!
I HATE THE @#&% AQUARIUM!
We do close

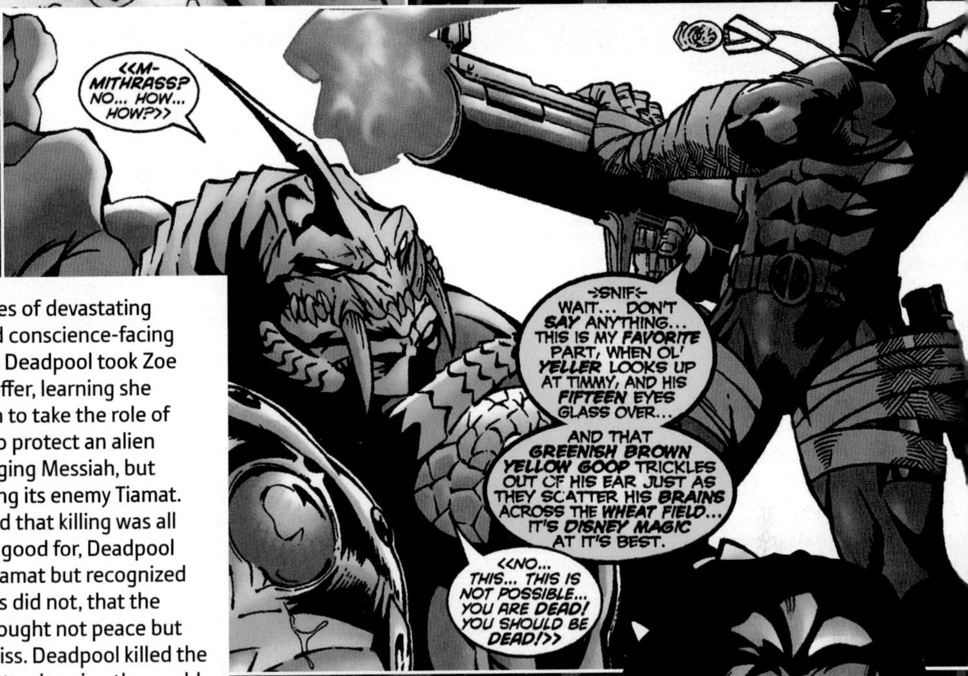
<<M- MITHRAS? NO... HOW... HOW?>>
-SNIF- WAIT... DON'T SAY ANYTHING... THIS IS MY FAVORITE PART, WHEN OL' YELLER LOOKS UP AT TIMMY, AND HIS FIFTEEN EYES GLASS OVER...
AND THAT GREENISH BROWN YELLOW GOOP TRICKLES OUT OF HIS EAR JUST AS THEY SCATTER HIS BRAINS ACROSS THE WHEAT FIELD... IT'S DISNEY MAGIC AT IT'S BEST.
<<NO... THIS... THIS IS NOT POSSIBLE... YOU ARE DEAD! YOU SHOULD BE DEAD!>>

After a series of devastating defeats and conscience-facing crossroads, Deadpool took Zoe up on her offer, learning she wanted him to take the role of "Mithras" to protect an alien peace-bringing Messiah, but only by killing its enemy Tiamat. Discouraged that killing was all he seemed good for, Deadpool defeated Tiamat but recognized what others did not, that the Messiah brought not peace but mindless bliss. Deadpool killed the Messiah instead, saving the world but still wondering if he could do the same for his soul.

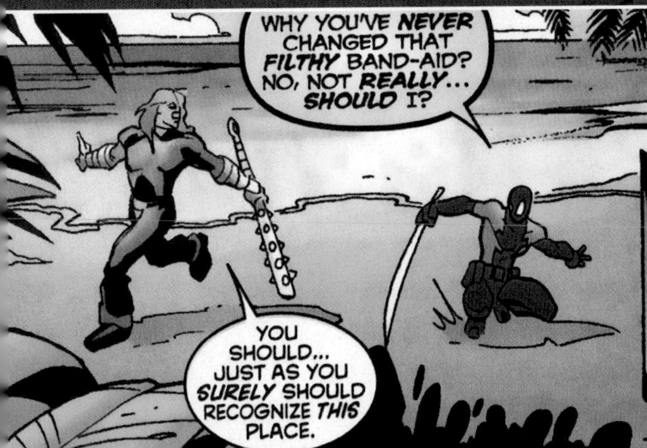
WHY YOU'VE NEVER CHANGED THAT FILTHY BAND-AID? NO, NOT REALLY... SHOULD I?
YOU SHOULD... JUST AS YOU SURELY SHOULD RECOGNIZE THIS PLACE.

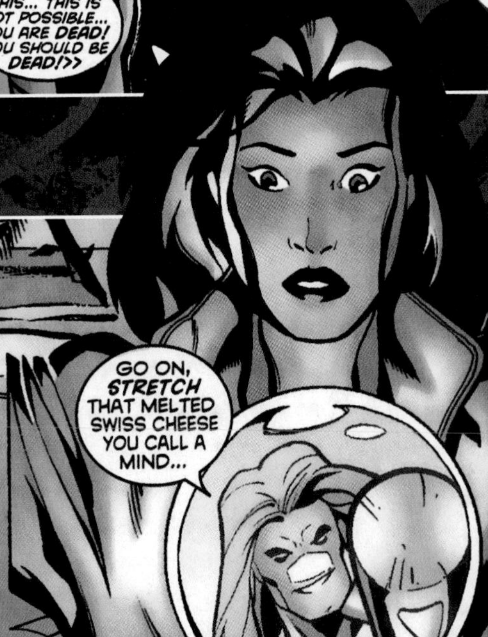
GO ON, STRETCH THAT MELTED SWISS CHEESE YOU CALL A MIND...

Already troubled, Deadpool was stunned when Mercedes Wilson returned from the dead, and he soon felt sure he could find redemption in her arms. However, another mercenary, the sorcerer T-Ray, revealed that Deadpool could never find peace as Mercedes' husband...because **T-Ray** was her husband, the man Deadpool had left for dead long ago. Overwhelmed by the revelation, Deadpool nevertheless refused to break down in defeat the way T-Ray wanted.

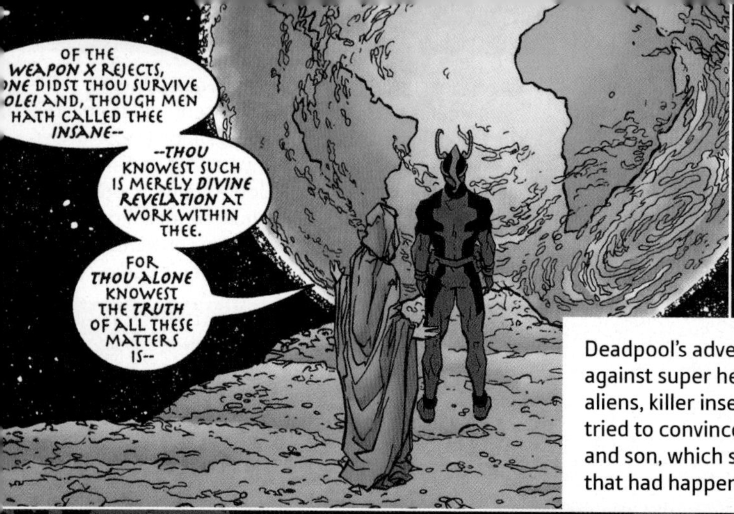
OF THE WEAPON X REJECTS, NE DIDST THOU SURVIVE OLE! AND, THOUGH MEN HATH CALLED THEE INSANE--
--THOU KNOWEST SUCH IS MERELY DIVINE REVELATION AT WORK WITHIN THEE.
FOR THOU ALONE KNOWEST THE TRUTH OF ALL THESE MATTERS IS--

Deadpool's adventures continued, setting him against super heroes, super-villains, werewolves, aliens, killer insects, and more. The god Loki even tried to convince Deadpool that they were father and son, which seemed as believable as anything else that had happened in Deadpool's life.

Deadpool then received an upgrade to his healing factor from Malcolm "Director" Colcord's Weapon X Program, which recruited him to oppose "the mutant menace." Joining Kane, who had turned callous while Deadpool had become more sympathetic to others, Deadpool was appalled when Kane murdered a mutant child. When Sabretooth, also in Weapon X, killed Copycat, a furious Deadpool was all but incinerated when he confronted her murderers.

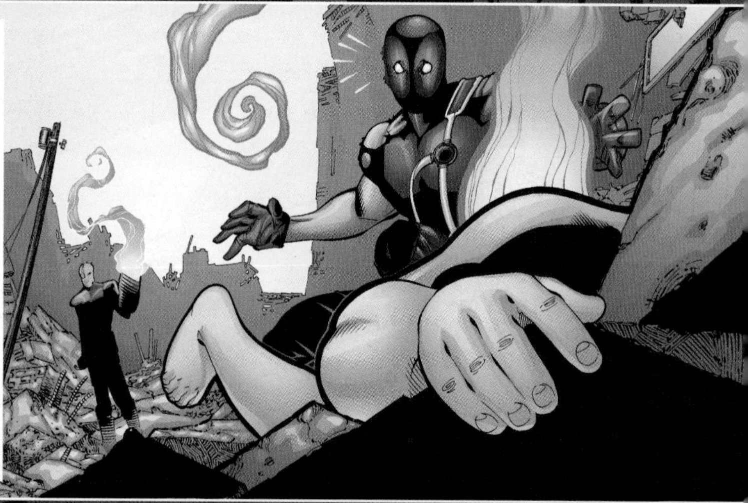

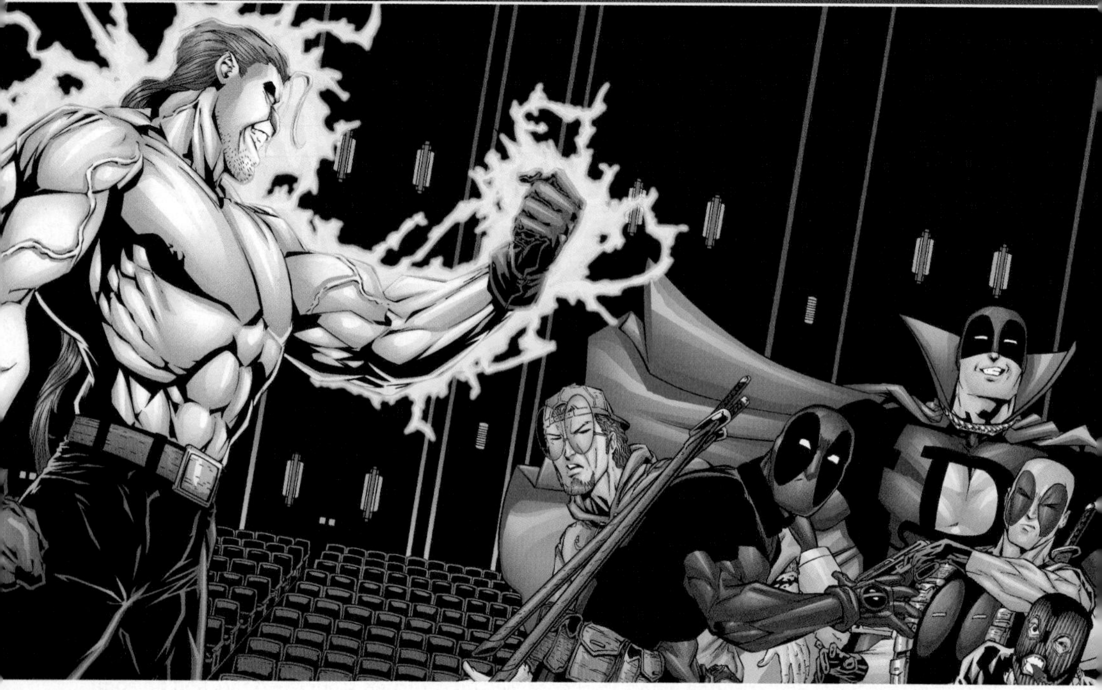

To everyone's surprise, including his own, Deadpool regenerated and revived, alive but amnesiac. While he struggled to regain his memories, four mysterious men, also calling themselves "Deadpool," burst on the scene in various venues. Deadpool learned they were aspects of his own personality, created by T-Ray in a scheme that ultimately failed.

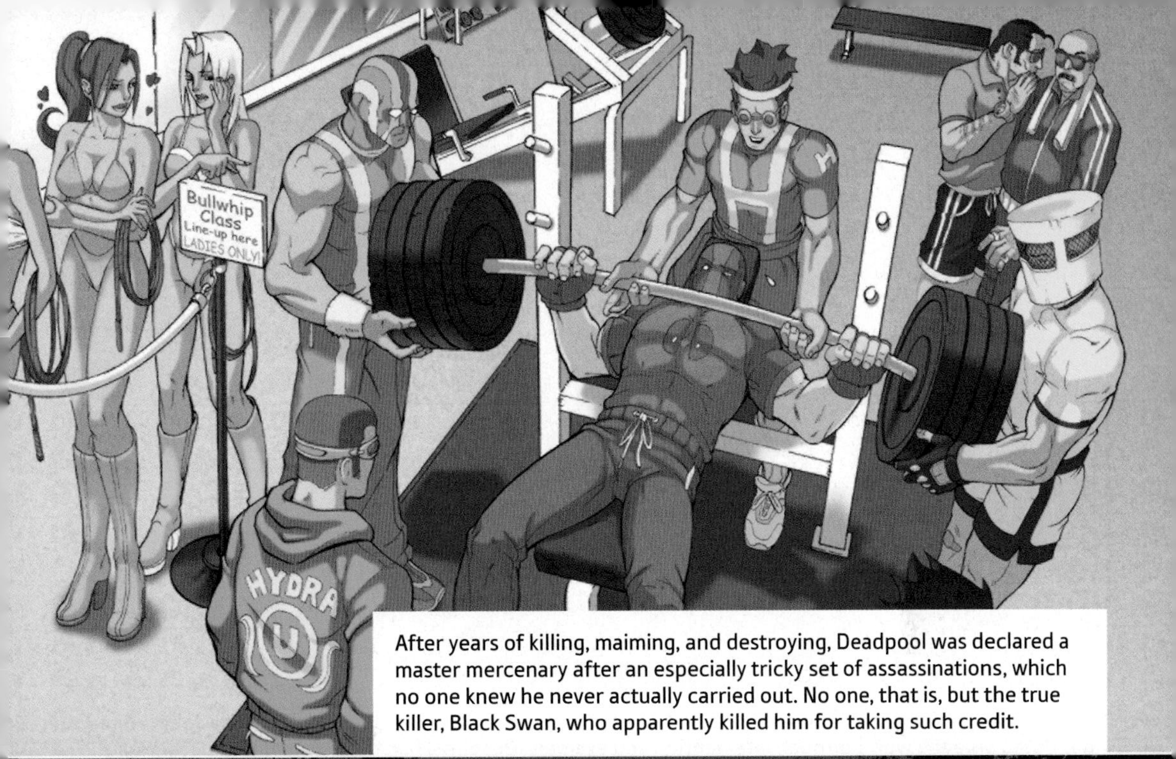
Bullwhip Class Line-up here LADIES ONLY!
HYDRA
After years of killing, maiming, and destroying, Deadpool was declared a master mercenary after an especially tricky set of assassinations, which no one knew he never actually carried out. No one, that is, but the true killer, Black Swan, who apparently killed him for taking such credit.

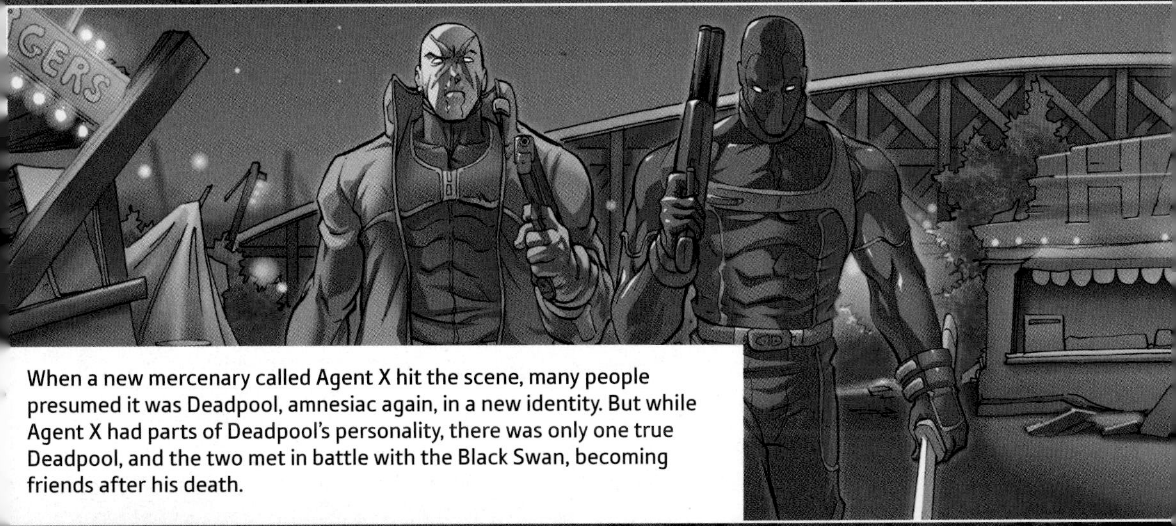
GERS
When a new mercenary called Agent X hit the scene, many people presumed it was Deadpool, amnesiac again, in a new identity. But while Agent X had parts of Deadpool's personality, there was only one true Deadpool, and the two met in battle with the Black Swan, becoming friends after his death.

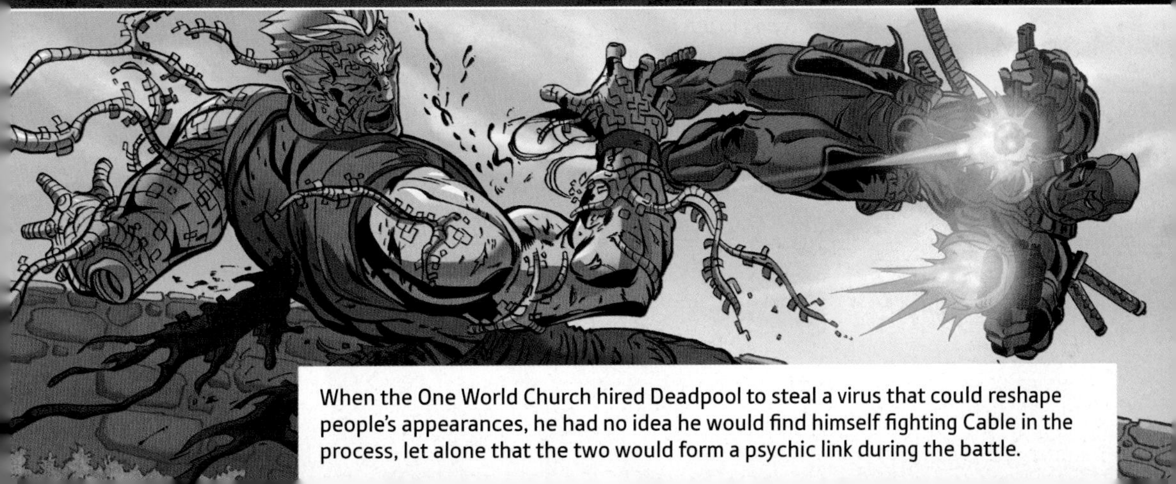
When the One World Church hired Deadpool to steal a virus that could reshape people's appearances, he had no idea he would find himself fighting Cable in the process, let alone that the two would form a psychic link during the battle.

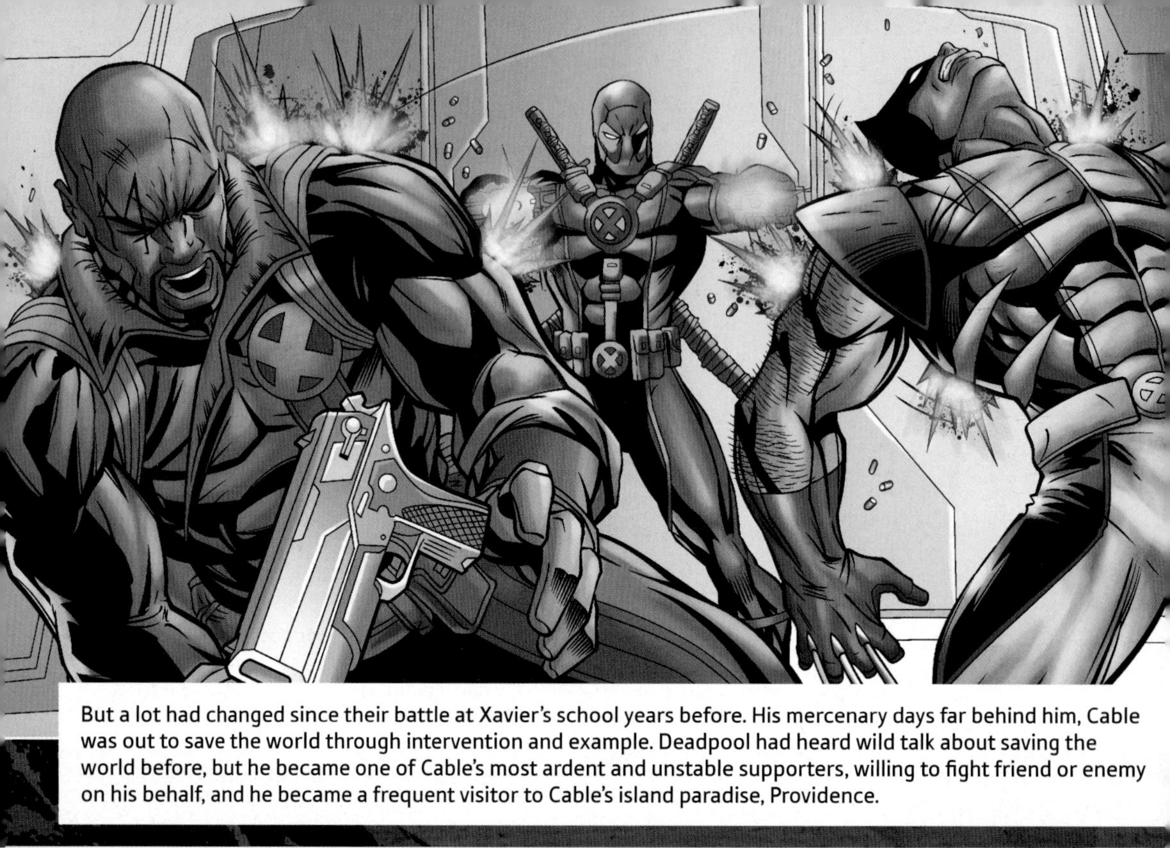

But a lot had changed since their battle at Xavier's school years before. His mercenary days far behind him, Cable was out to save the world through intervention and example. Deadpool had heard wild talk about saving the world before, but he became one of Cable's most ardent and unstable supporters, willing to fight friend or enemy on his behalf, and he became a frequent visitor to Cable's island paradise, Providence.

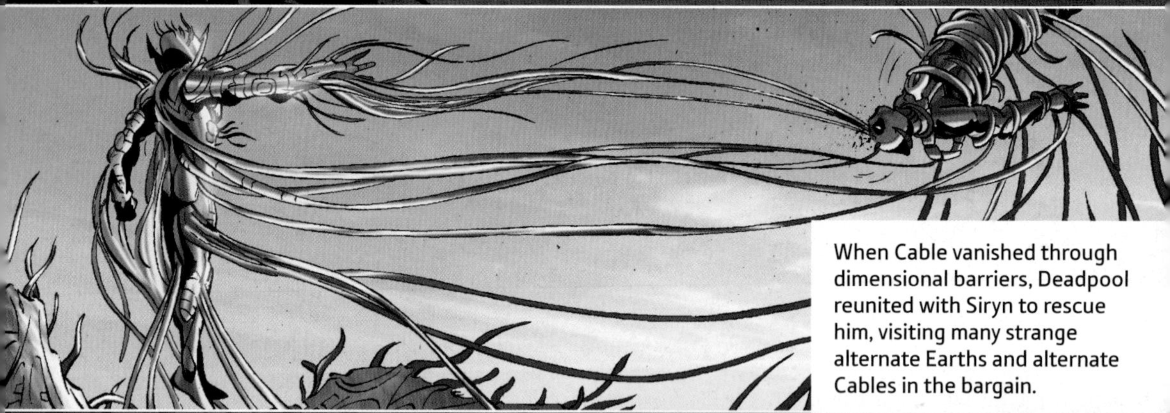

When Cable vanished through dimensional barriers, Deadpool reunited with Siryn to rescue him, visiting many strange alternate Earths and alternate Cables in the bargain.

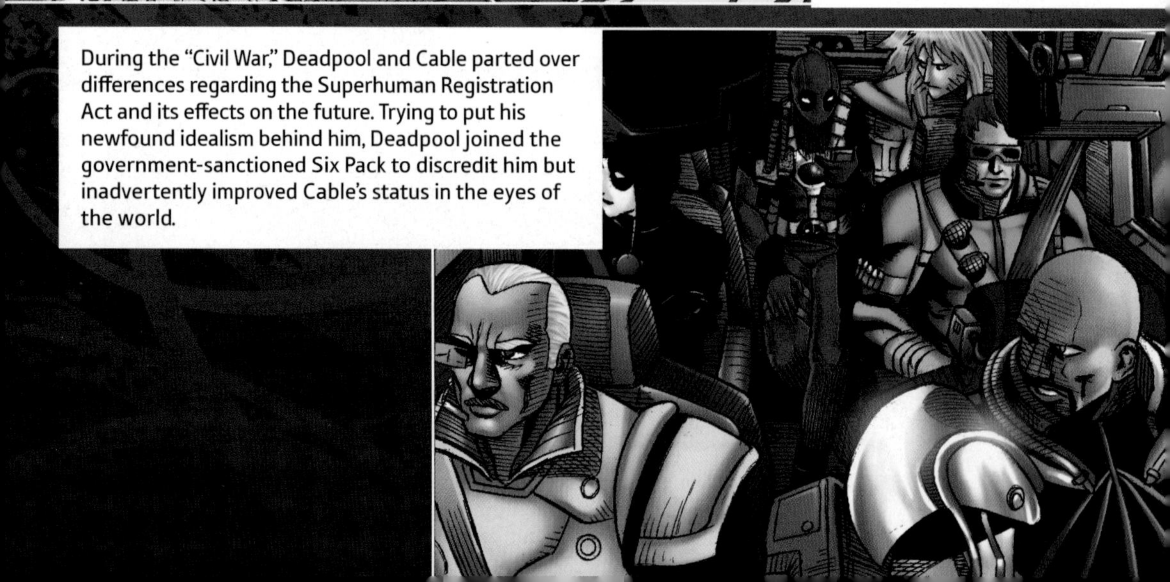

During the "Civil War," Deadpool and Cable parted over differences regarding the Superhuman Registration Act and its effects on the future. Trying to put his newfound idealism behind him, Deadpool joined the government-sanctioned Six Pack to discredit him but inadvertently improved Cable's status in the eyes of the world.

Unfortunately, Cable's dream reached an apparent end when Providence sank. Regardless of regrets over what might have been, Deadpool is now back in the mercenary game full-time, joining Weasel and other friends in Agency X. Cable may have disappeared into the future, but what future is waiting for Deadpool now?

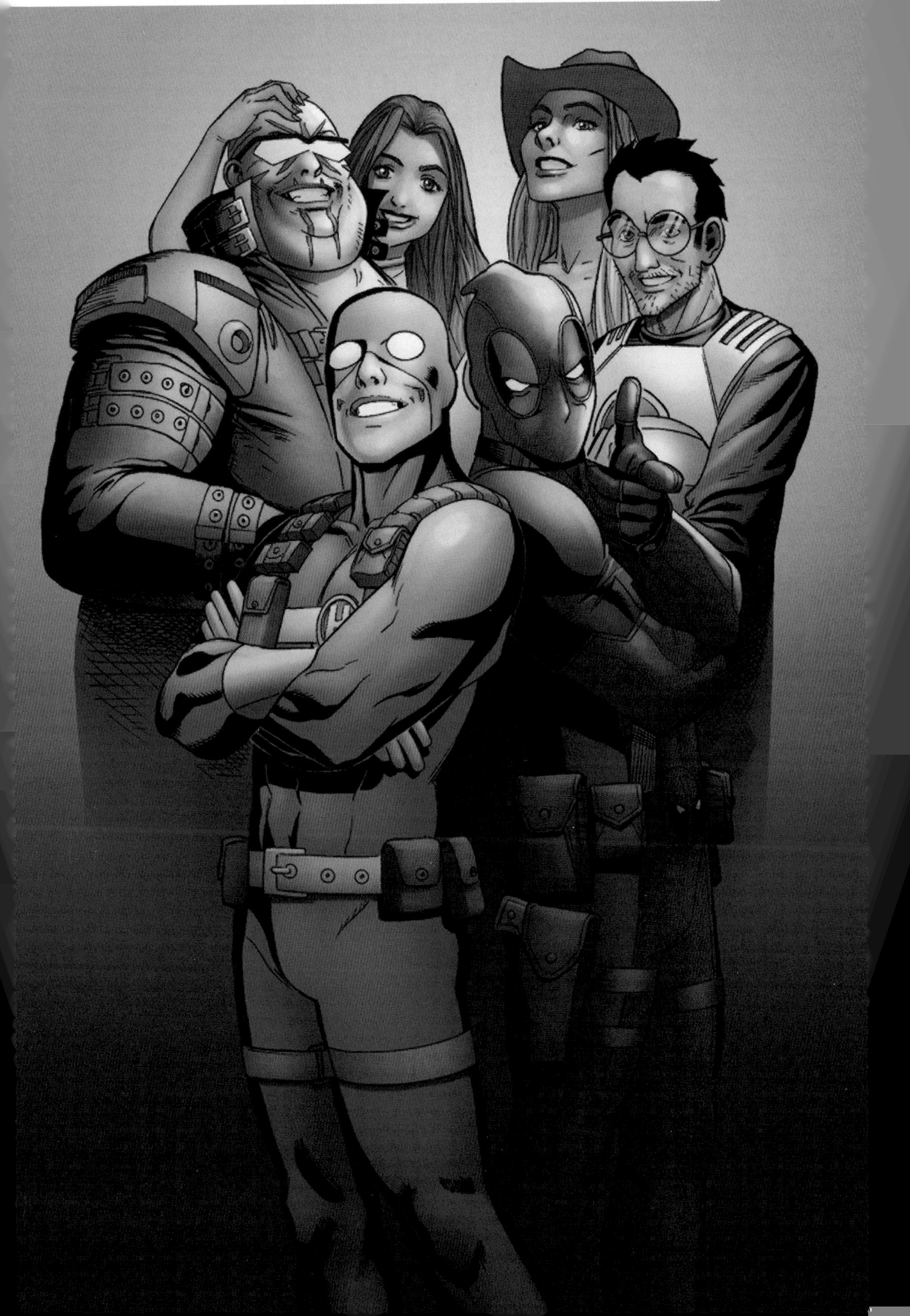

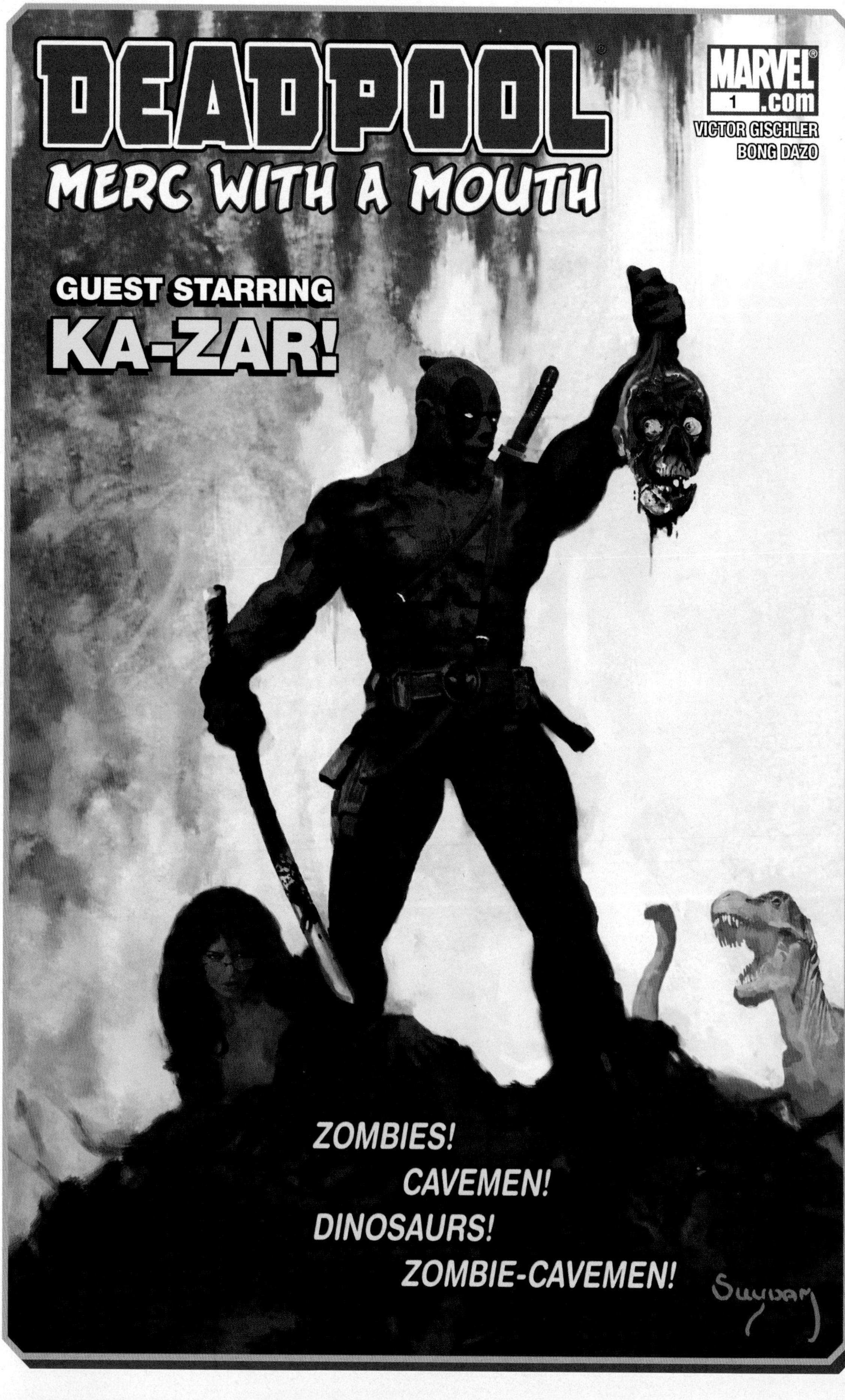
DEADPOOL
MERC WITH A MOUTH
MARVEL
1 .com
VICTOR GISCHLER
BONG DAZO
GUEST STARRING
KA-ZAR!
ZOMBIES!
CAVEMEN!
DINOSAURS!
ZOMBIE-CAVEMEN!

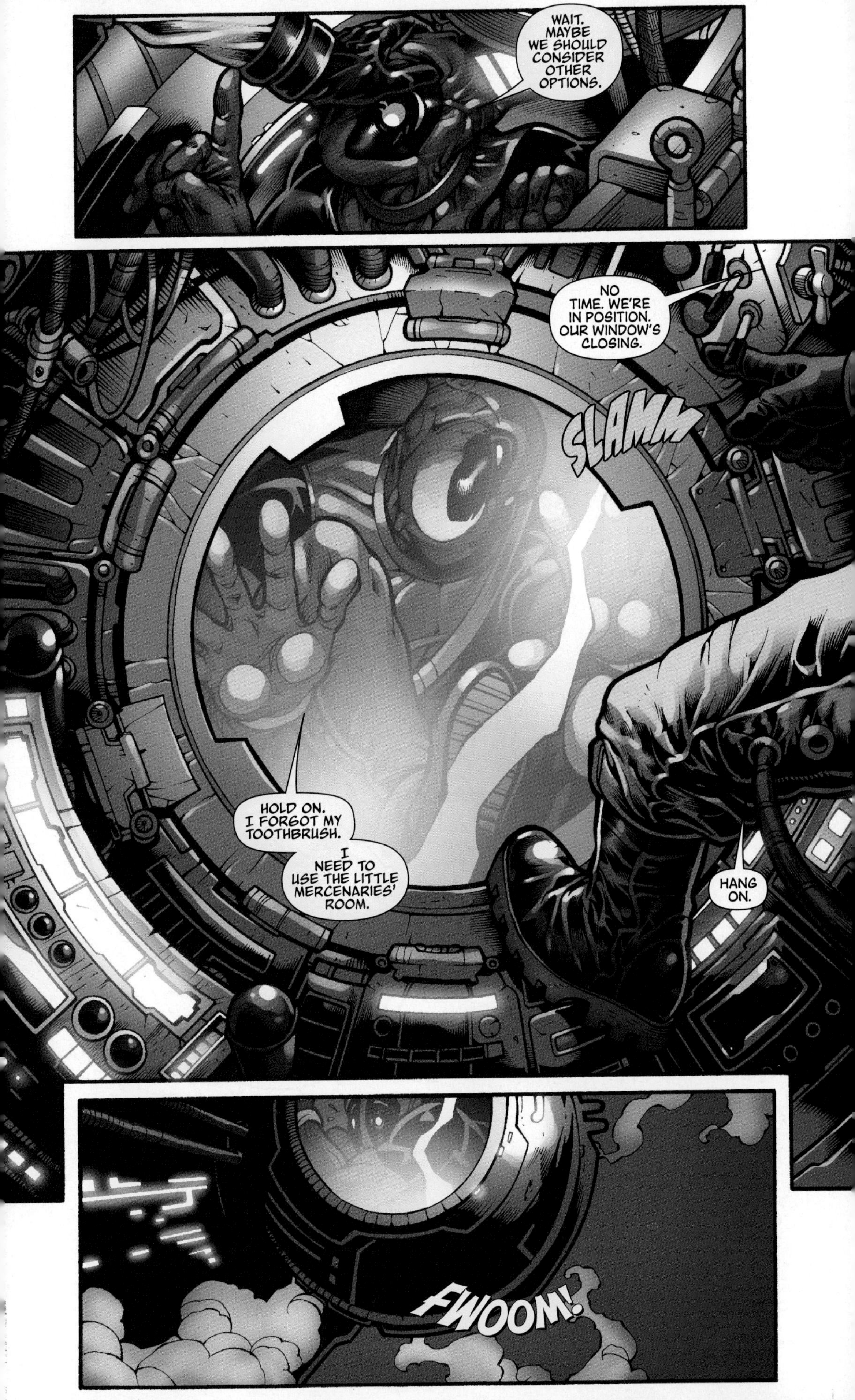

WAIT. MAYBE WE SHOULD CONSIDER OTHER OPTIONS.
NO TIME. WE'RE IN POSITION. OUR WINDOW'S CLOSING.
SLAMM
HOLD ON. I FORGOT MY TOOTHBRUSH.
I NEED TO USE THE LITTLE MERCENARIES' ROOM.
HANG ON.
FWOOM!

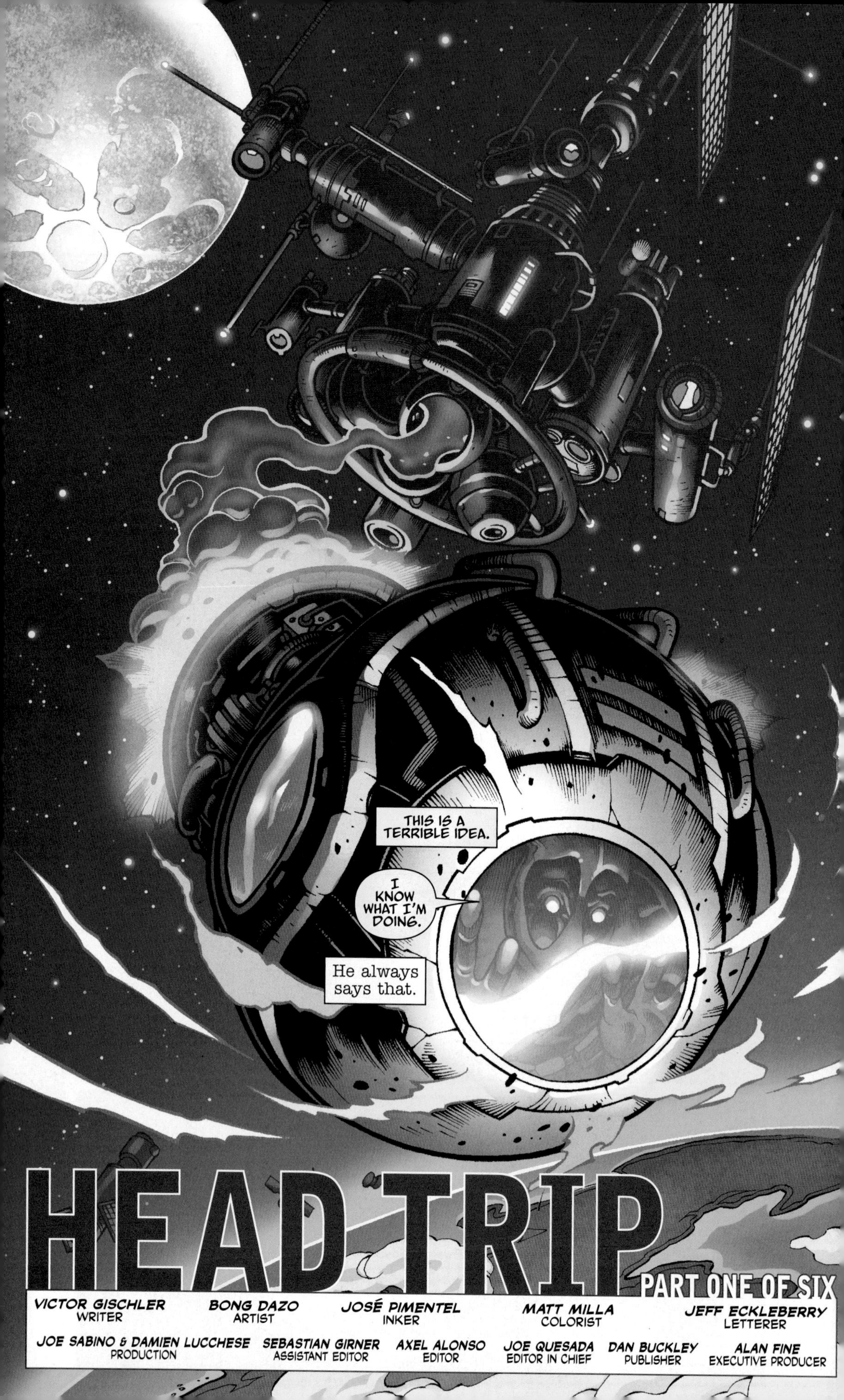
THIS IS A TERRIBLE IDEA.
I KNOW WHAT I'M DOING.
He always says that.
HEAD TRIP
PART ONE OF SIX
VICTOR GISCHLER WRITER
BONG DAZO ARTIST
JOSÉ PIMENTEL INKER
MATT MILLA COLORIST
JEFF ECKLEBERRY LETTERER
JOE SABINO & DAMIEN LUCCHESE PRODUCTION
SEBASTIAN GIRNER ASSISTANT EDITOR
AXEL ALONSO EDITOR
JOE QUESADA EDITOR IN CHIEF
DAN BUCKLEY PUBLISHER
ALAN FINE EXECUTIVE PRODUCER

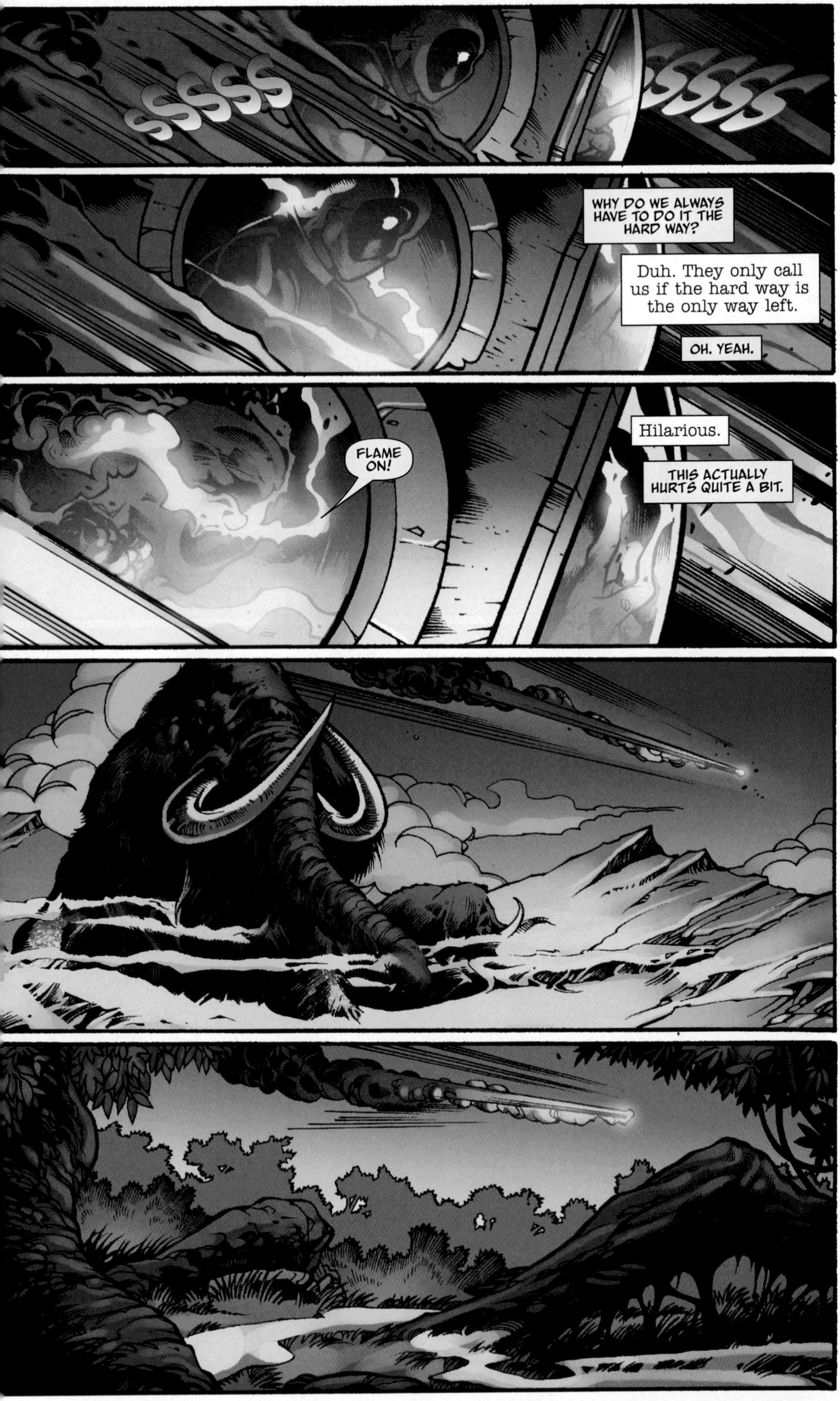
SSSSS
SSSSS
WHY DO WE ALWAYS HAVE TO DO IT THE HARD WAY?
Duh. They only call us if the hard way is the only way left.
OH. YEAH.
FLAME ON!
Hilarious.
THIS ACTUALLY HURTS QUITE A BIT.

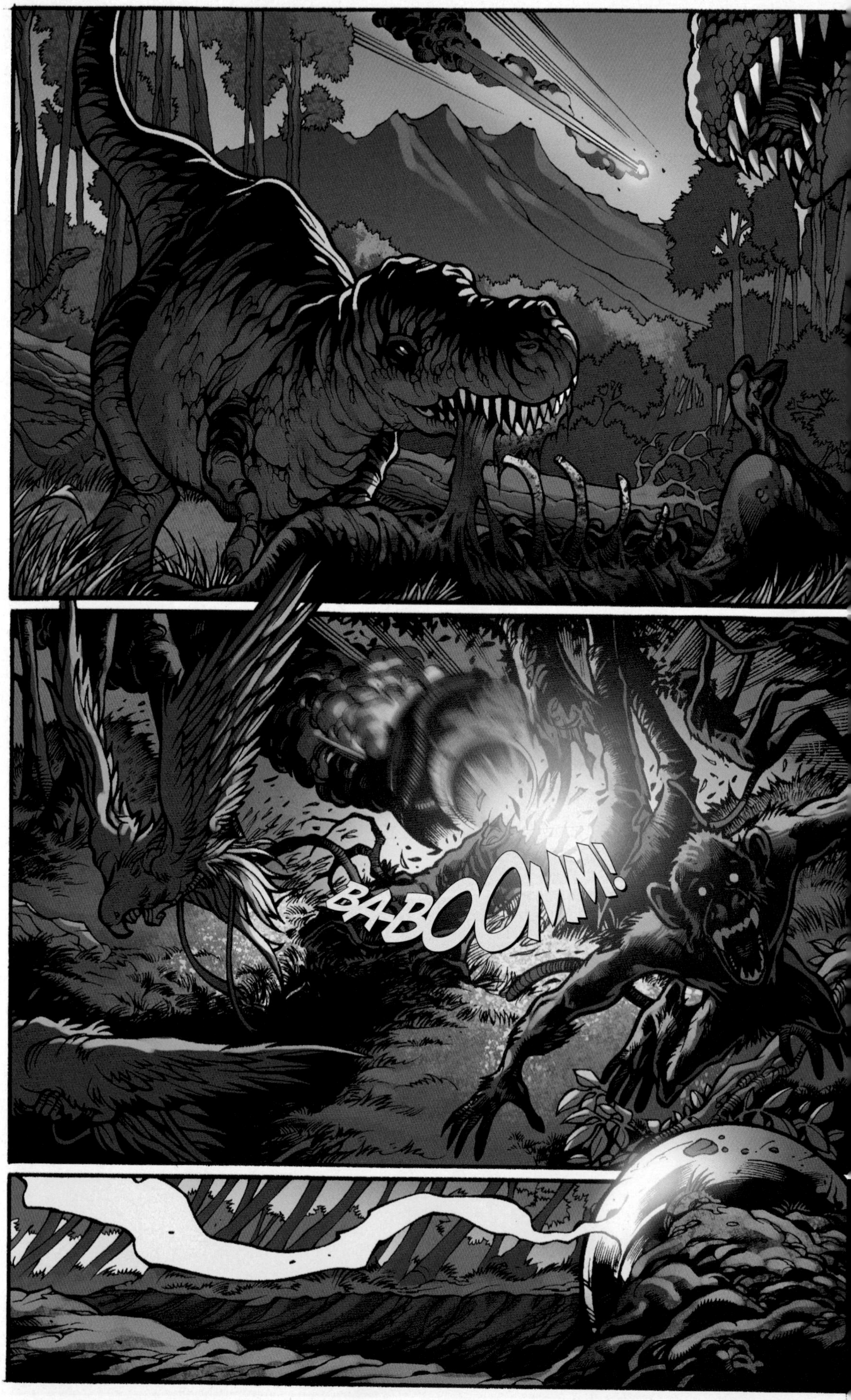
BA-BOOMM!

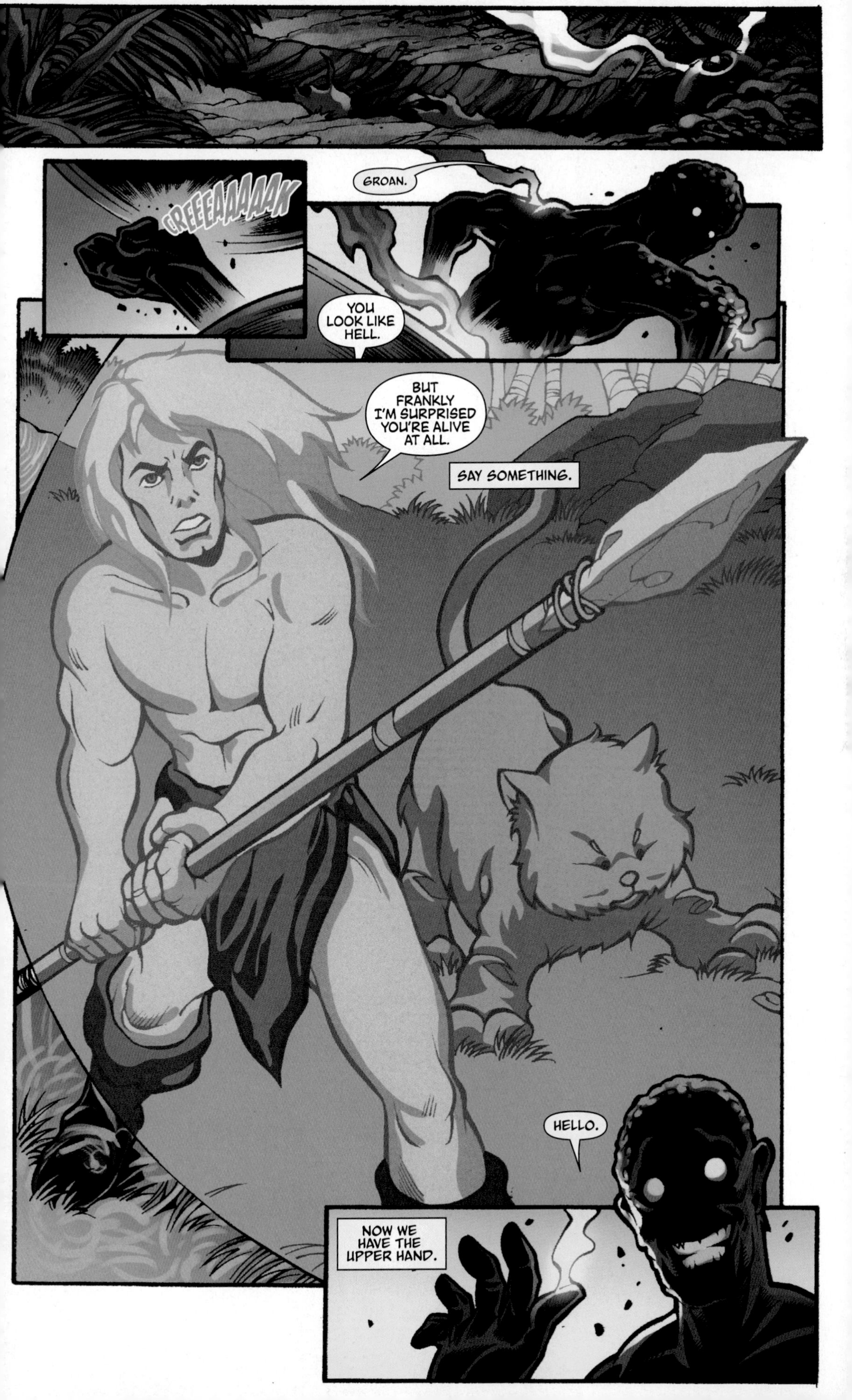
CREEEAAAAAK
GROAN.
YOU LOOK LIKE HELL.
BUT FRANKLY I'M SURPRISED YOU'RE ALIVE AT ALL.
SAY SOMETHING.
HELLO.
NOW WE HAVE THE UPPER HAND.

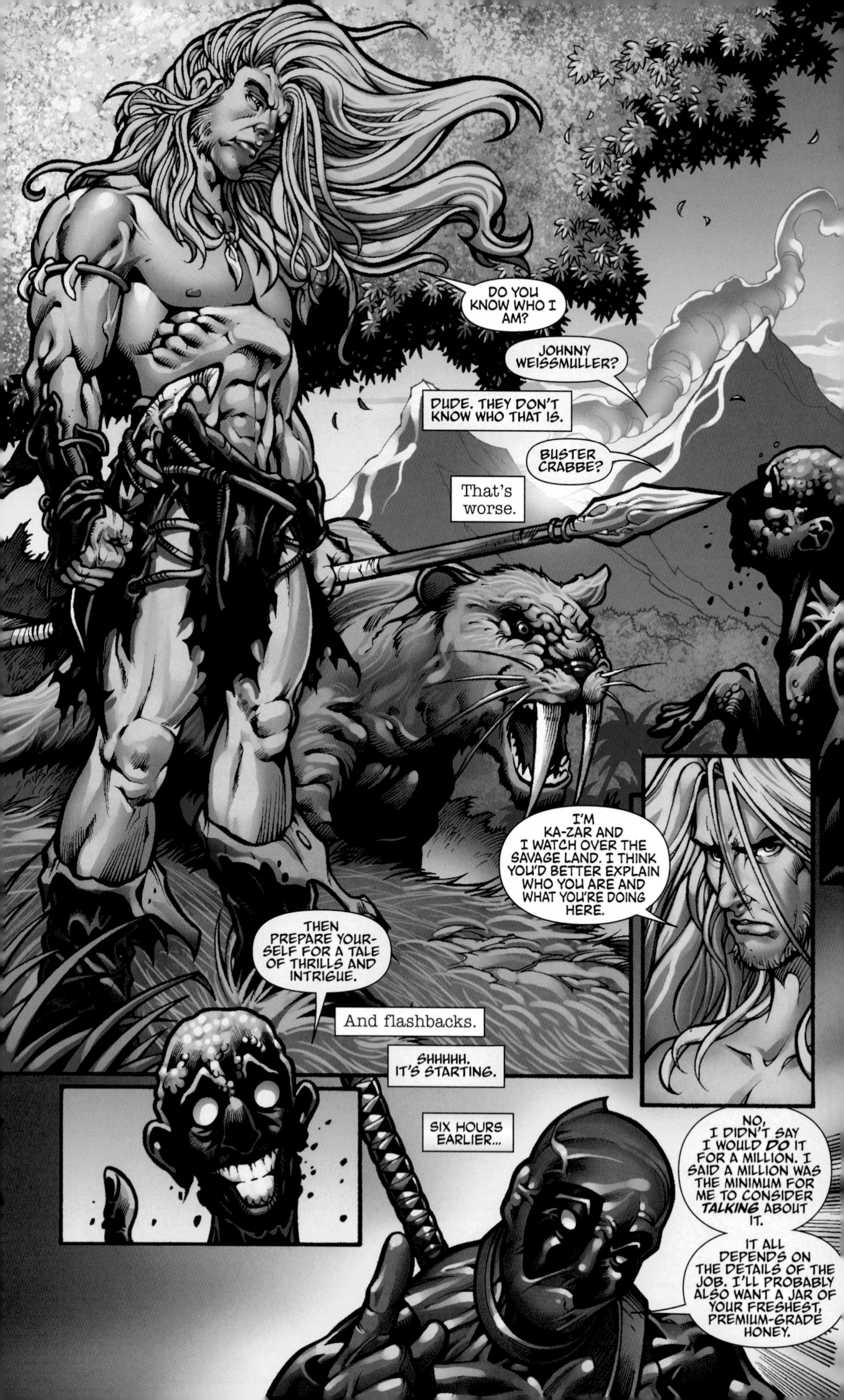
DO YOU KNOW WHO I AM?
JOHNNY WEISSMULLER?
DUDE. THEY DON'T KNOW WHO THAT IS.
BUSTER CRABBE?
That's worse.
I'M KA-ZAR AND I WATCH OVER THE SAVAGE LAND. I THINK YOU'D BETTER EXPLAIN WHO YOU ARE AND WHAT YOU'RE DOING HERE.
THEN PREPARE YOUR-SELF FOR A TALE OF THRILLS AND INTRIGUE.
And flashbacks.
SHHHHH. IT'S STARTING.
SIX HOURS EARLIER...
NO, I DIDN'T SAY I WOULD *DO* IT FOR A MILLION. I SAID A MILLION WAS THE MINIMUM FOR ME TO CONSIDER *TALKING* ABOUT IT.
IT ALL DEPENDS ON THE DETAILS OF THE JOB. I'LL PROBABLY ALSO WANT A JAR OF YOUR FRESHEST, PREMIUM-GRADE HONEY.

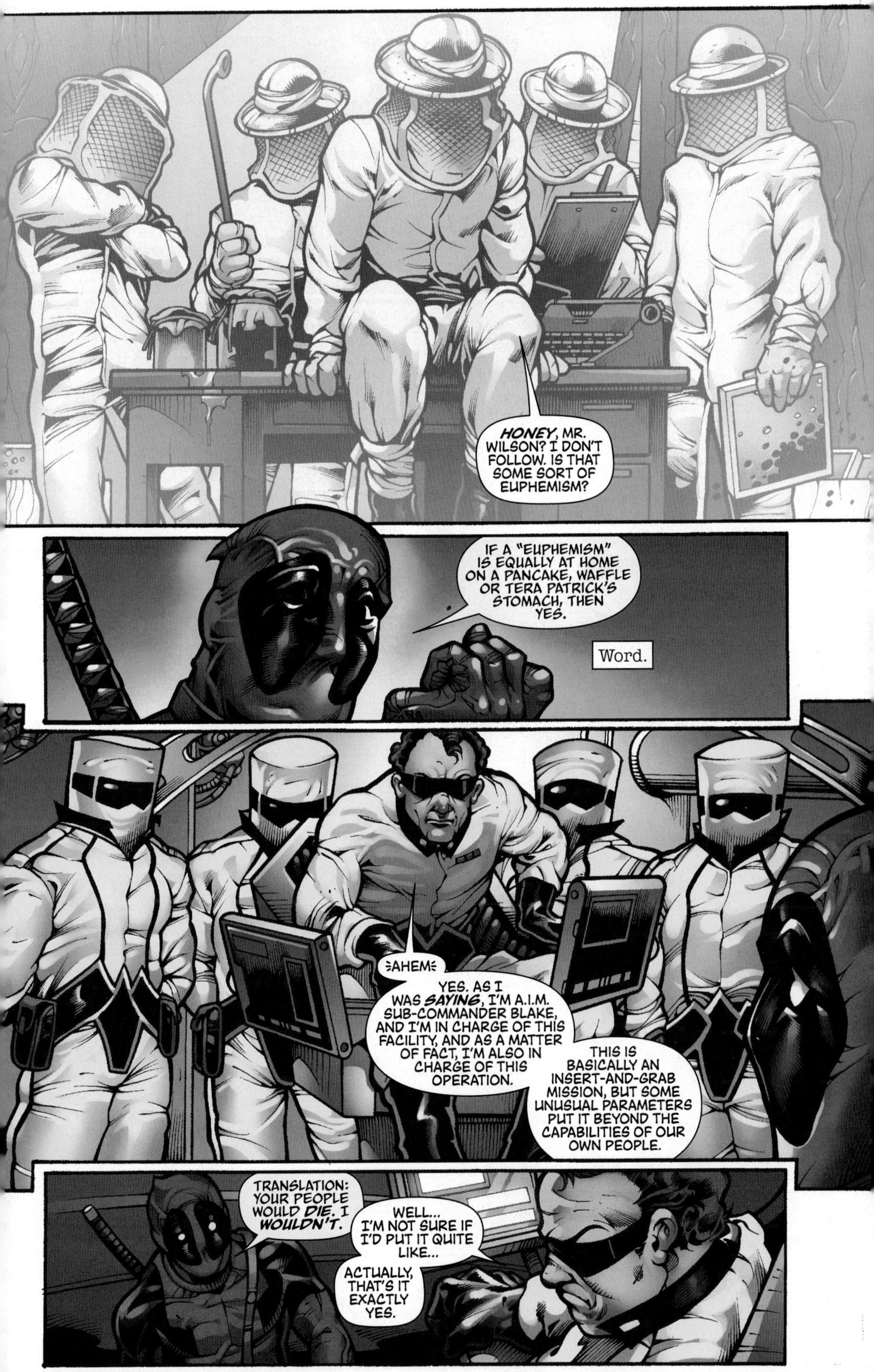
HONEY, MR. WILSON? I DON'T FOLLOW. IS THAT SOME SORT OF EUPHEMISM?
IF A "EUPHEMISM" IS EQUALLY AT HOME ON A PANCAKE, WAFFLE OR TERA PATRICK'S STOMACH, THEN YES.
Word.
AHEM
YES. AS I WAS SAYING, I'M A.I.M. SUB-COMMANDER BLAKE, AND I'M IN CHARGE OF THIS FACILITY, AND AS A MATTER OF FACT, I'M ALSO IN CHARGE OF THIS OPERATION.
THIS IS BASICALLY AN INSERT-AND-GRAB MISSION, BUT SOME UNUSUAL PARAMETERS PUT IT BEYOND THE CAPABILITIES OF OUR OWN PEOPLE.
TRANSLATION: YOUR PEOPLE WOULD DIE. I WOULDN'T.
WELL... I'M NOT SURE IF I'D PUT IT QUITE LIKE...
ACTUALLY, THAT'S IT EXACTLY YES.

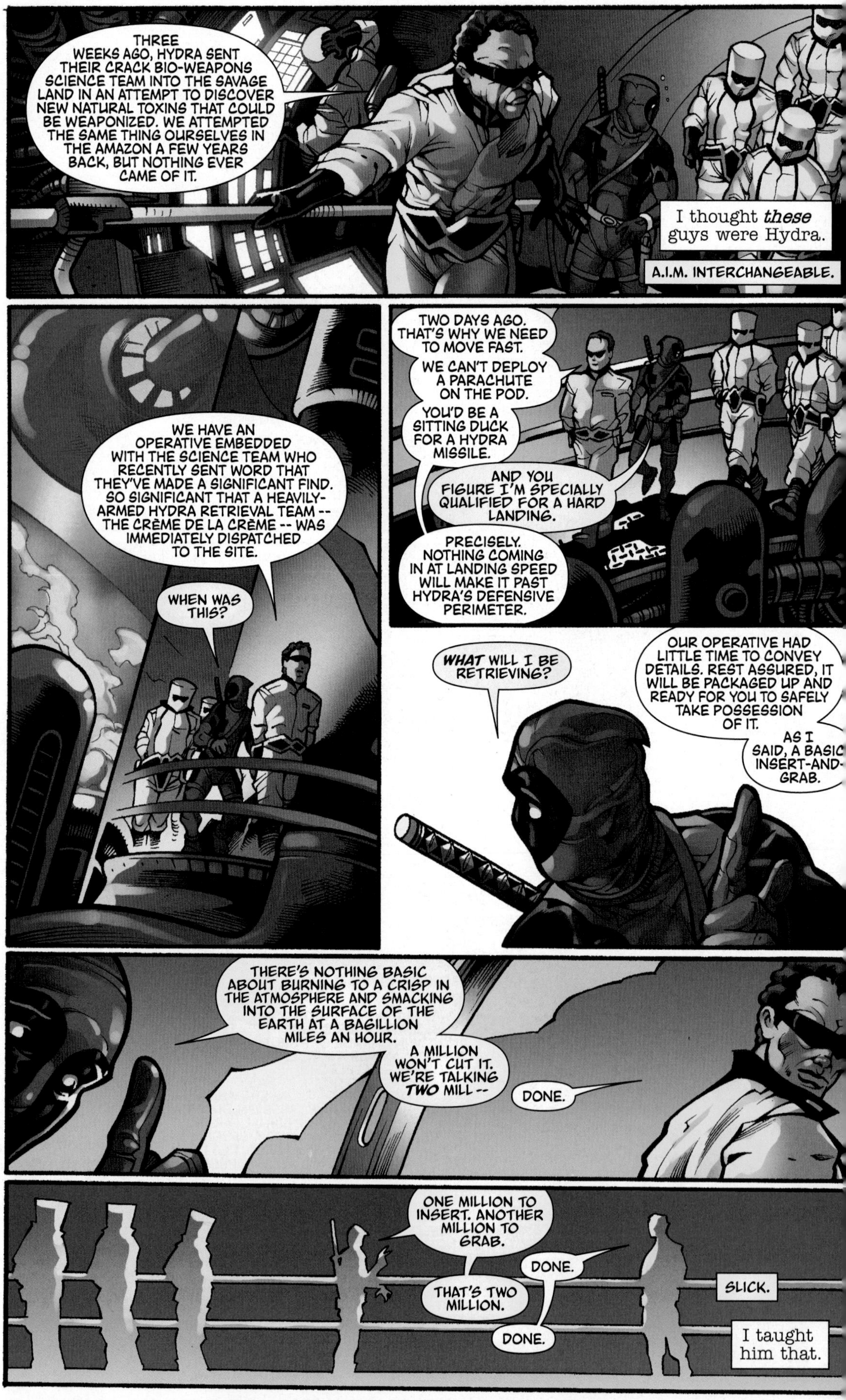
THREE WEEKS AGO, HYDRA SENT THEIR CRACK BIO-WEAPONS SCIENCE TEAM INTO THE SAVAGE LAND IN AN ATTEMPT TO DISCOVER NEW NATURAL TOXINS THAT COULD BE WEAPONIZED. WE ATTEMPTED THE SAME THING OURSELVES IN THE AMAZON A FEW YEARS BACK, BUT NOTHING EVER CAME OF IT.
I thought *these* guys were Hydra.
A.I.M. INTERCHANGEABLE.
WE HAVE AN OPERATIVE EMBEDDED WITH THE SCIENCE TEAM WHO RECENTLY SENT WORD THAT THEY'VE MADE A SIGNIFICANT FIND. SO SIGNIFICANT THAT A HEAVILY-ARMED HYDRA RETRIEVAL TEAM -- THE CRÈME DE LA CRÈME -- WAS IMMEDIATELY DISPATCHED TO THE SITE.
WHEN WAS THIS?
TWO DAYS AGO. THAT'S WHY WE NEED TO MOVE FAST.
WE CAN'T DEPLOY A PARACHUTE ON THE POD.
YOU'D BE A SITTING DUCK FOR A HYDRA MISSILE.
AND YOU FIGURE I'M SPECIALLY QUALIFIED FOR A HARD LANDING.
PRECISELY. NOTHING COMING IN AT LANDING SPEED WILL MAKE IT PAST HYDRA'S DEFENSIVE PERIMETER.
WHAT WILL I BE RETRIEVING?
OUR OPERATIVE HAD LITTLE TIME TO CONVEY DETAILS. REST ASSURED, IT WILL BE PACKAGED UP AND READY FOR YOU TO SAFELY TAKE POSSESSION OF IT.
AS I SAID, A BASIC INSERT-AND-GRAB.
THERE'S NOTHING BASIC ABOUT BURNING TO A CRISP IN THE ATMOSPHERE AND SMACKING INTO THE SURFACE OF THE EARTH AT A BAGILLION MILES AN HOUR.
A MILLION WON'T CUT IT. WE'RE TALKING *TWO* MILL --
DONE.
ONE MILLION TO INSERT. ANOTHER MILLION TO GRAB.
DONE.
THAT'S TWO MILLION.
DONE.
SLICK.
I taught him that.

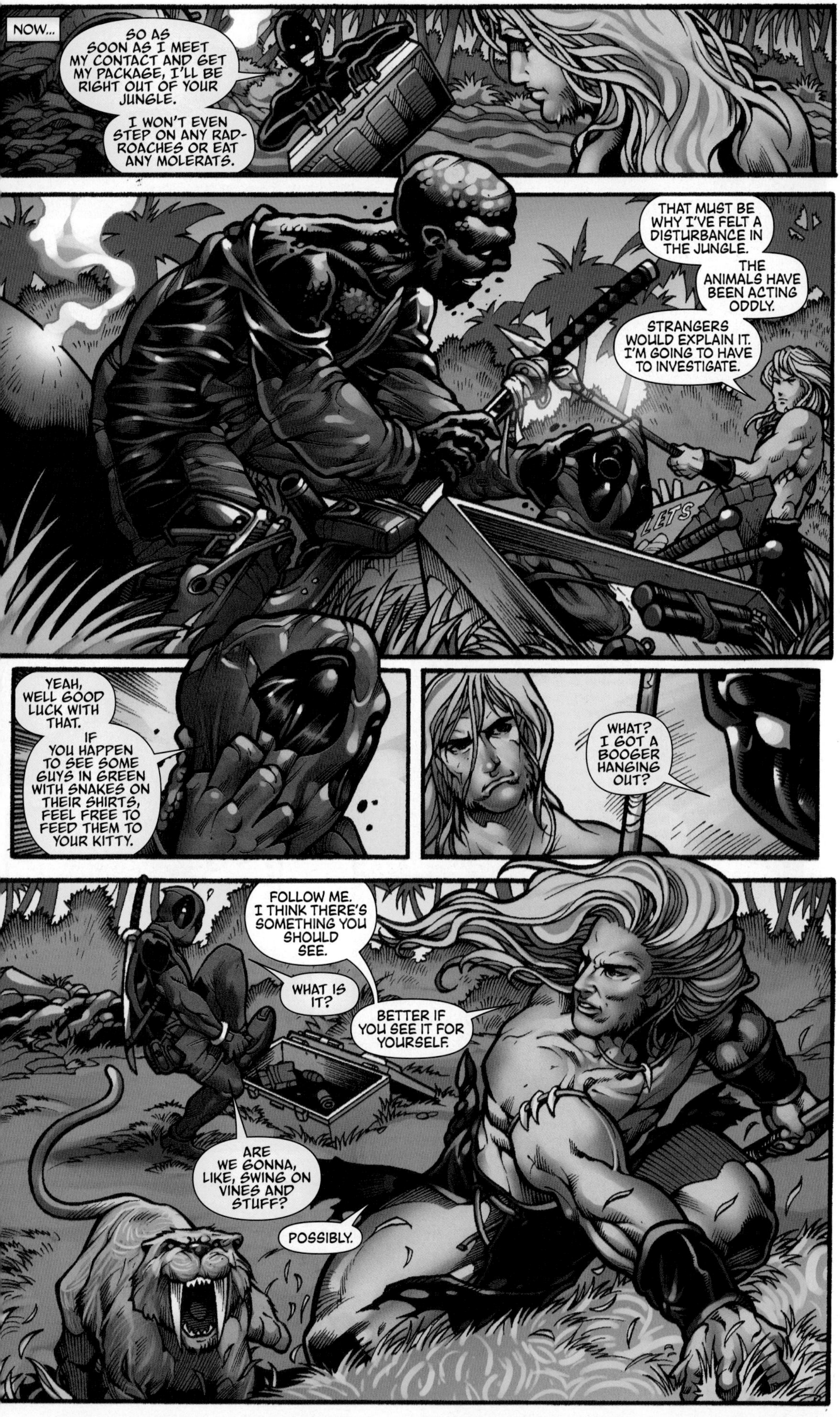
NOW...
SO AS SOON AS I MEET MY CONTACT AND GET MY PACKAGE, I'LL BE RIGHT OUT OF YOUR JUNGLE.
I WON'T EVEN STEP ON ANY RAD-ROACHES OR EAT ANY MOLERATS.
THAT MUST BE WHY I'VE FELT A DISTURBANCE IN THE JUNGLE.
THE ANIMALS HAVE BEEN ACTING ODDLY.
STRANGERS WOULD EXPLAIN IT. I'M GOING TO HAVE TO INVESTIGATE.
LETS
YEAH, WELL GOOD LUCK WITH THAT.
IF YOU HAPPEN TO SEE SOME GUYS IN GREEN WITH SNAKES ON THEIR SHIRTS, FEEL FREE TO FEED THEM TO YOUR KITTY.
WHAT? I GOT A BOOGER HANGING OUT?
FOLLOW ME. I THINK THERE'S SOMETHING YOU SHOULD SEE.
WHAT IS IT?
BETTER IF YOU SEE IT FOR YOURSELF.
ARE WE GONNA, LIKE, SWING ON VINES AND STUFF?
POSSIBLY.

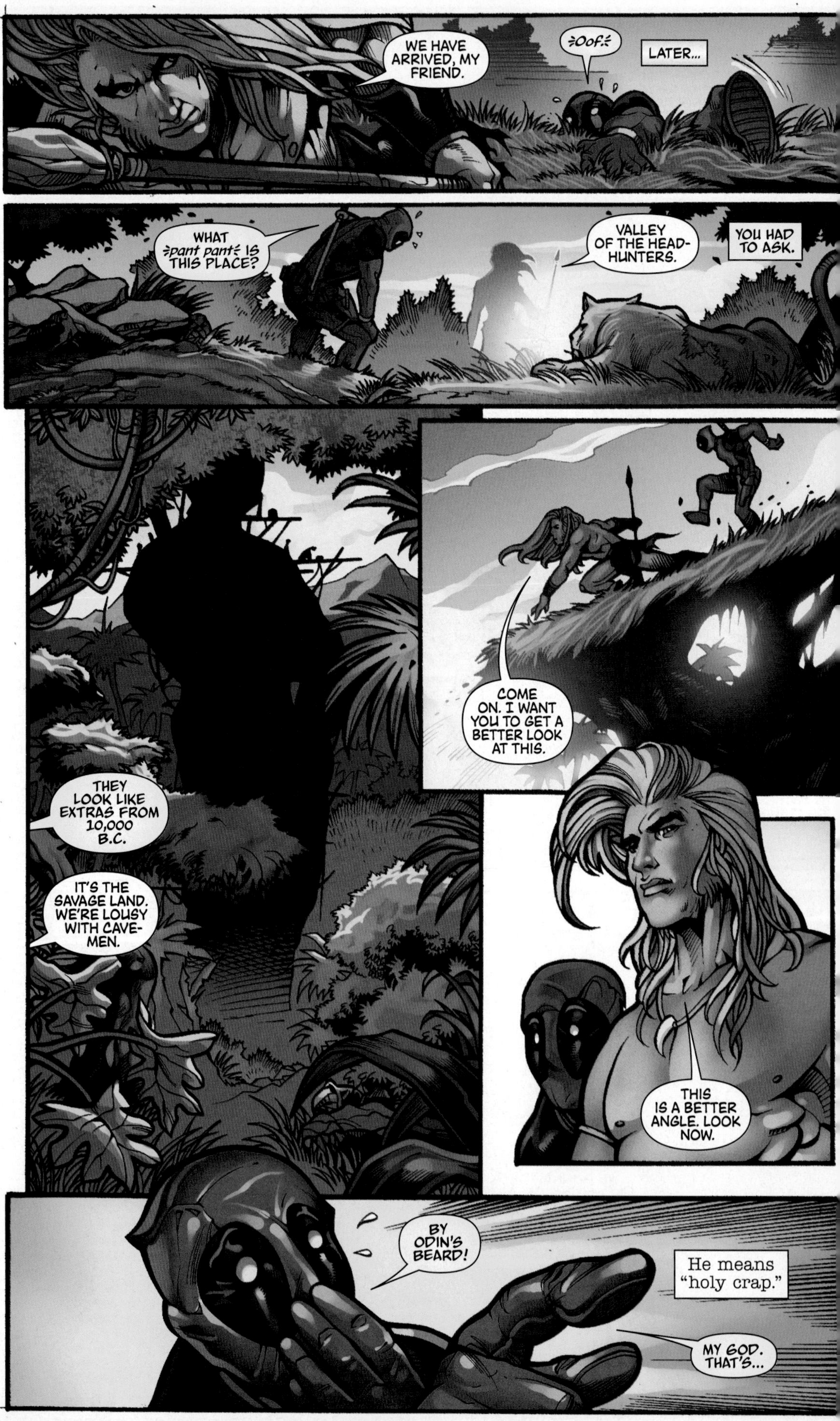
WE HAVE ARRIVED, MY FRIEND.
OOF
LATER...
WHAT pant pant IS THIS PLACE?
VALLEY OF THE HEAD-HUNTERS.
YOU HAD TO ASK.
THEY LOOK LIKE EXTRAS FROM 10,000 B.C.
IT'S THE SAVAGE LAND. WE'RE LOUSY WITH CAVE-MEN.
COME ON. I WANT YOU TO GET A BETTER LOOK AT THIS.
THIS IS A BETTER ANGLE. LOOK NOW.
BY ODIN'S BEARD!
He means "holy crap."
MY GOD. THAT'S...

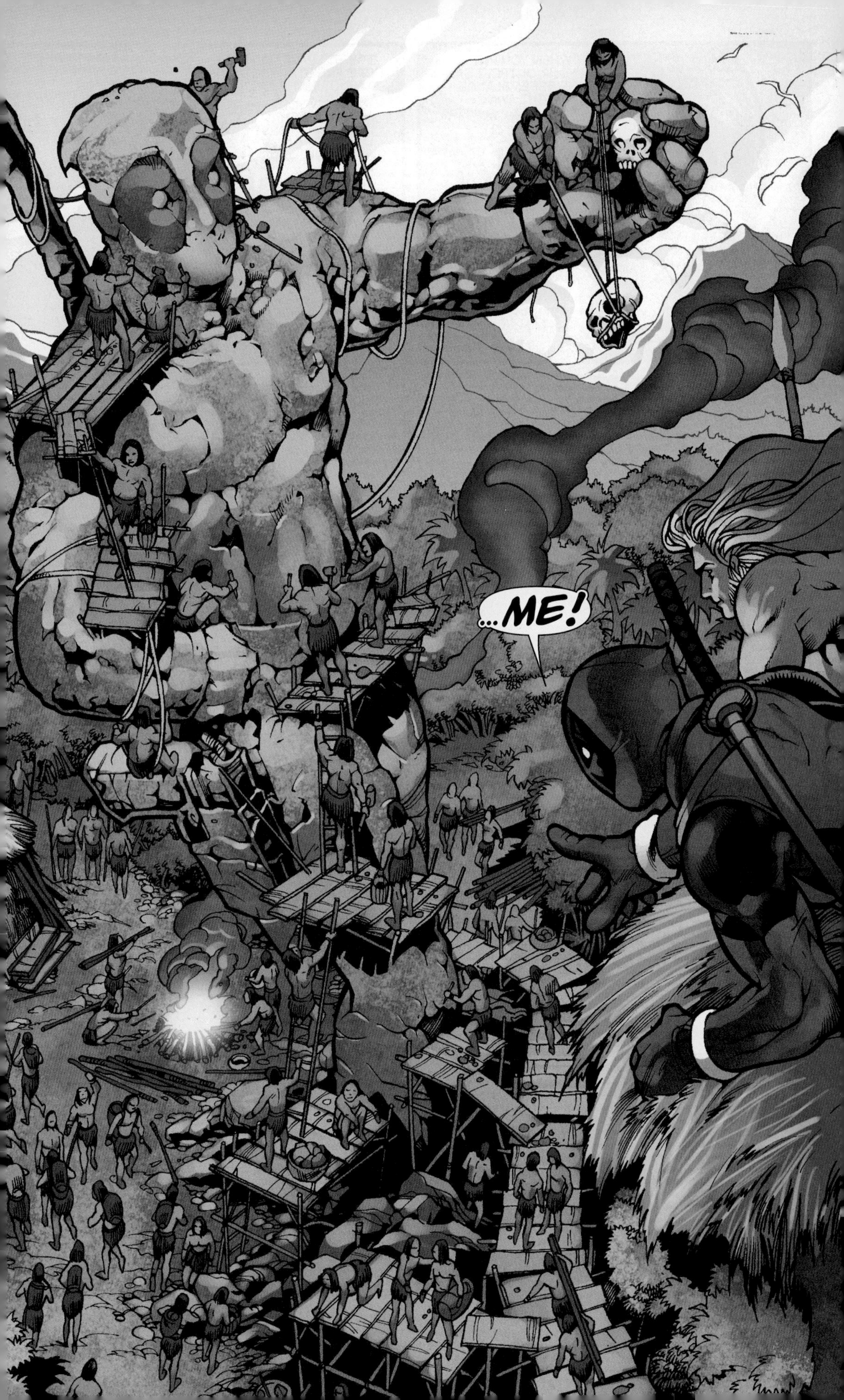
...ME!

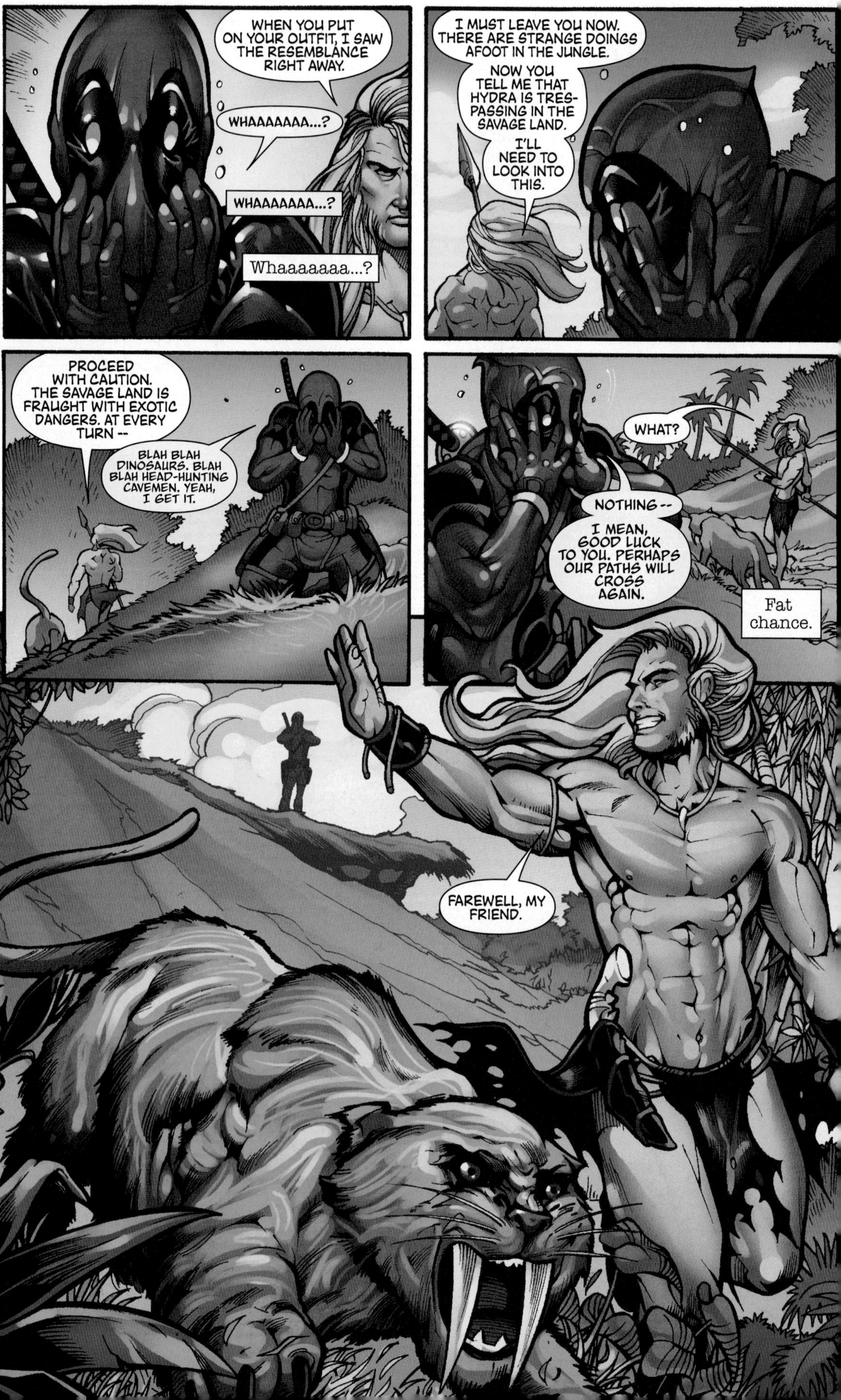

WHEN YOU PUT ON YOUR OUTFIT, I SAW THE RESEMBLANCE RIGHT AWAY.
WHAAAAAAA...?
WHAAAAAAA...?
Whaaaaaaa...?
I MUST LEAVE YOU NOW. THERE ARE STRANGE DOINGS AFOOT IN THE JUNGLE.
NOW YOU TELL ME THAT HYDRA IS TRES-PASSING IN THE SAVAGE LAND.
I'LL NEED TO LOOK INTO THIS.
PROCEED WITH CAUTION. THE SAVAGE LAND IS FRAUGHT WITH EXOTIC DANGERS. AT EVERY TURN --
BLAH BLAH DINOSAURS. BLAH BLAH HEAD-HUNTING CAVEMEN. YEAH, I GET IT.
WHAT?
NOTHING --
I MEAN, GOOD LUCK TO YOU. PERHAPS OUR PATHS WILL CROSS AGAIN.
Fat chance.
FAREWELL, MY FRIEND.

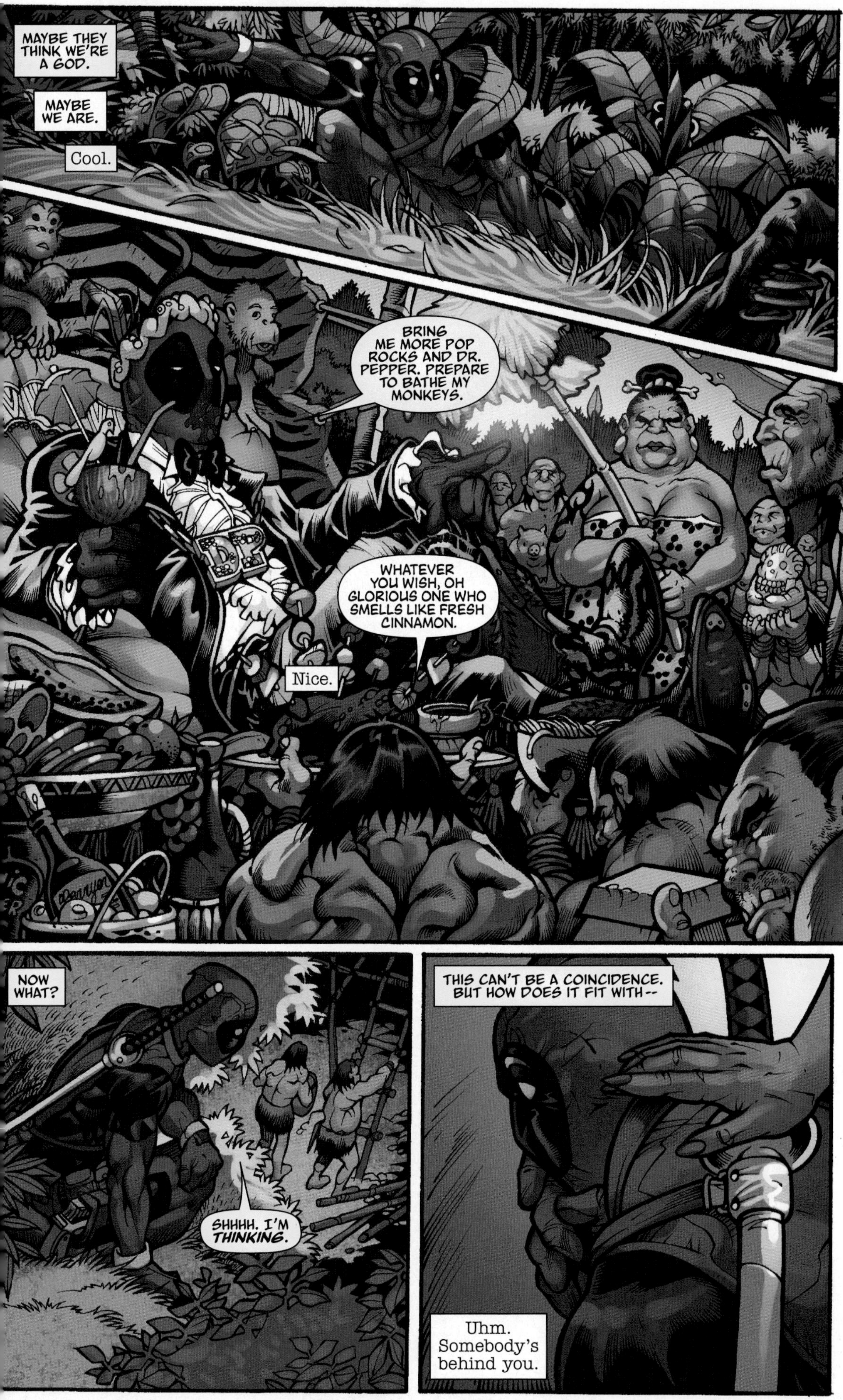
MAYBE THEY THINK WE'RE A GOD.
MAYBE WE ARE.
Cool.
BRING ME MORE POP ROCKS AND DR. PEPPER. PREPARE TO BATHE MY MONKEYS.
WHATEVER YOU WISH, OH GLORIOUS ONE WHO SMELLS LIKE FRESH CINNAMON.
Nice.
NOW WHAT?
SHHHH. I'M THINKING.
THIS CAN'T BE A COINCIDENCE. BUT HOW DOES IT FIT WITH --
Uhm. Somebody's behind you.

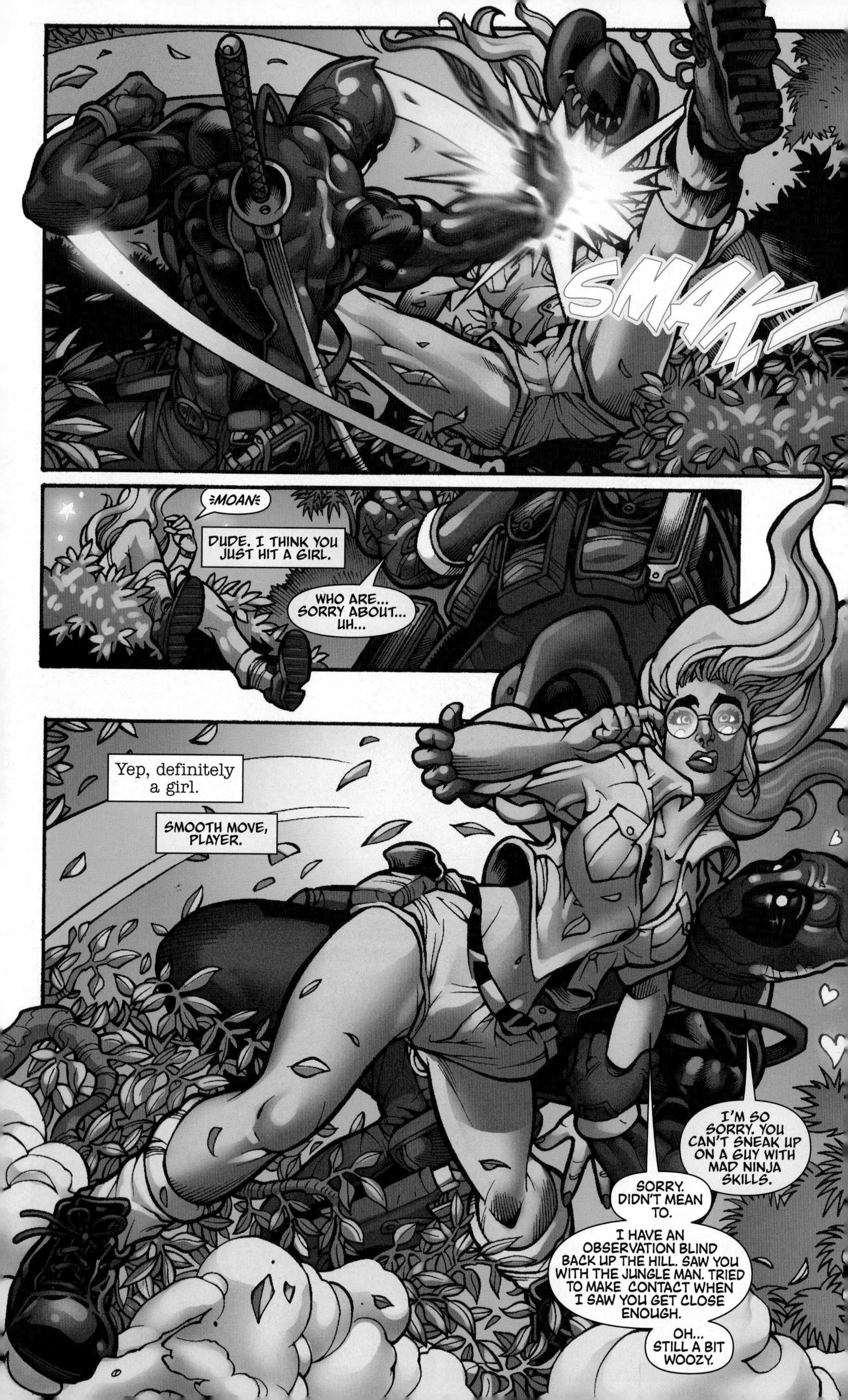
SMAK!
MOAN
DUDE. I THINK YOU JUST HIT A GIRL.
WHO ARE... SORRY ABOUT... UH...
Yep, definitely a girl.
SMOOTH MOVE, PLAYER.
I'M SO SORRY. YOU CAN'T SNEAK UP ON A GUY WITH MAD NINJA SKILLS.
SORRY. DIDN'T MEAN TO.
I HAVE AN OBSERVATION BLIND BACK UP THE HILL. SAW YOU WITH THE JUNGLE MAN. TRIED TO MAKE CONTACT WHEN I SAW YOU GET CLOSE ENOUGH.
OH... STILL A BIT WOOZY.

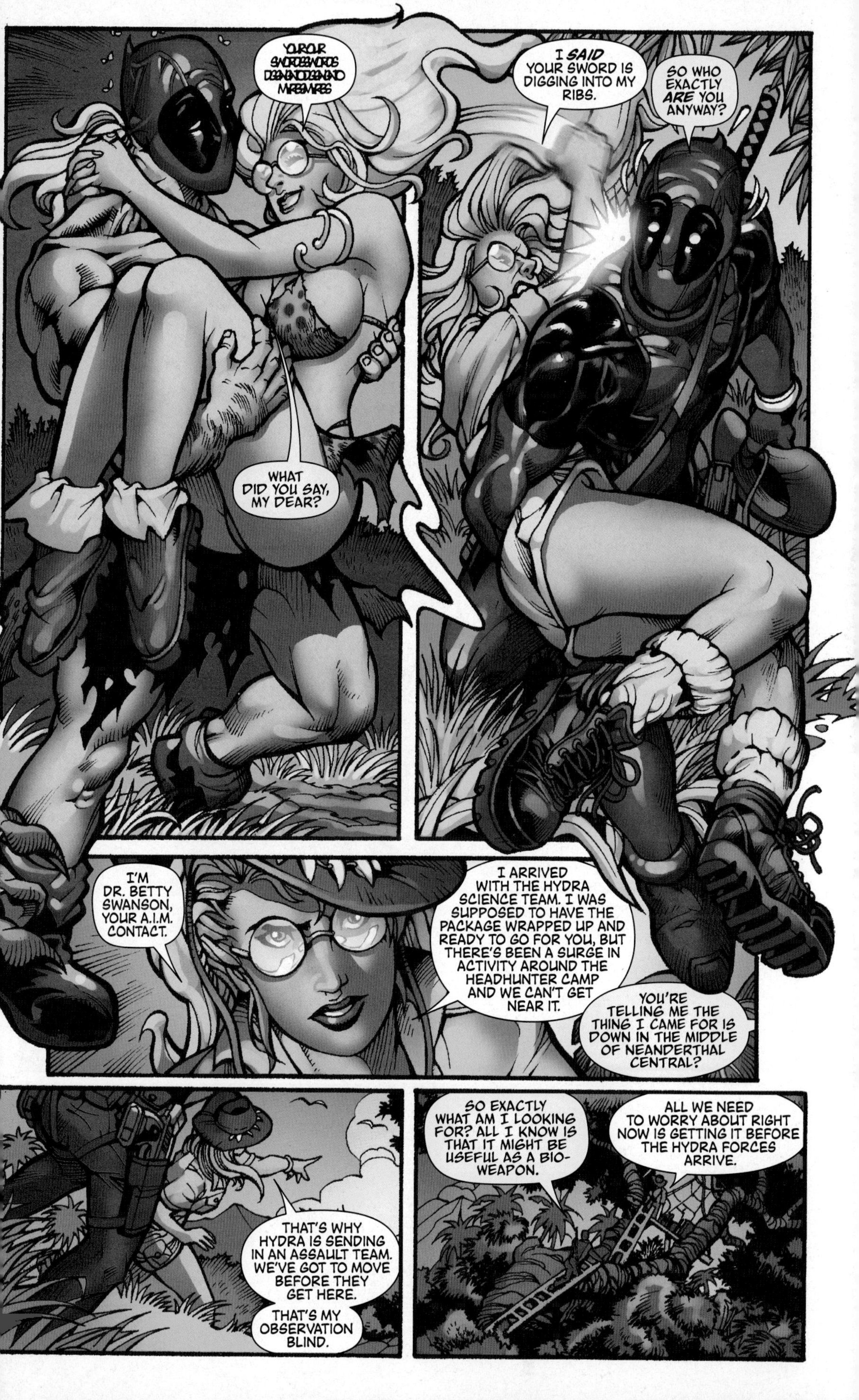

WHAT DID YOU SAY, MY DEAR?
I *SAID* YOUR SWORD IS DIGGING INTO MY RIBS.
SO WHO EXACTLY *ARE* YOU ANYWAY?
I'M DR. BETTY SWANSON, YOUR A.I.M. CONTACT.
I ARRIVED WITH THE HYDRA SCIENCE TEAM. I WAS SUPPOSED TO HAVE THE PACKAGE WRAPPED UP AND READY TO GO FOR YOU, BUT THERE'S BEEN A SURGE IN ACTIVITY AROUND THE HEADHUNTER CAMP AND WE CAN'T GET NEAR IT.
YOU'RE TELLING ME THE THING I CAME FOR IS DOWN IN THE MIDDLE OF NEANDERTHAL CENTRAL?
THAT'S WHY HYDRA IS SENDING IN AN ASSAULT TEAM. WE'VE GOT TO MOVE BEFORE THEY GET HERE.
THAT'S MY OBSERVATION BLIND.
SO EXACTLY WHAT AM I LOOKING FOR? ALL I KNOW IS THAT IT MIGHT BE USEFUL AS A BIO-WEAPON.
ALL WE NEED TO WORRY ABOUT RIGHT NOW IS GETTING IT BEFORE THE HYDRA FORCES ARRIVE.

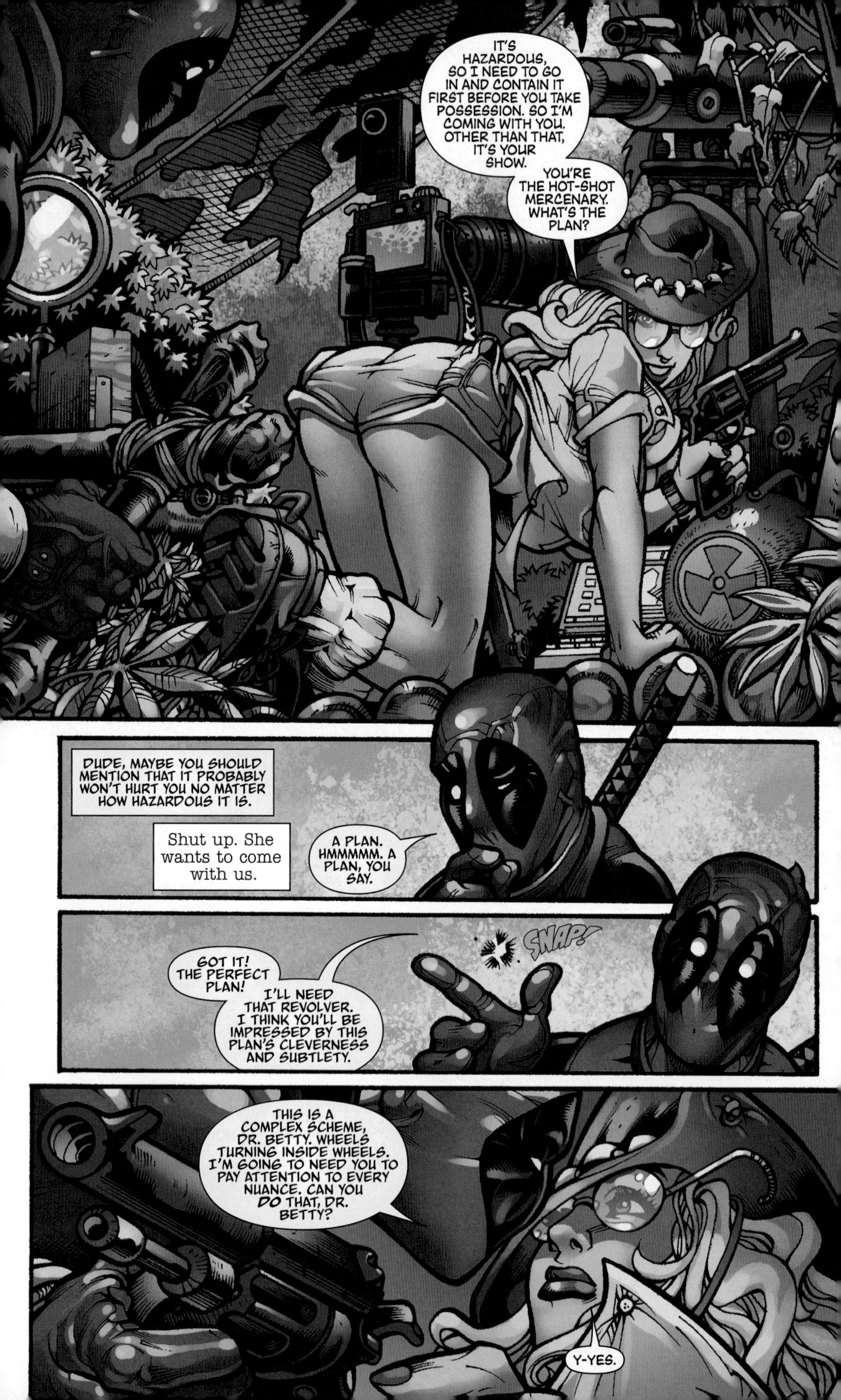
IT'S HAZARDOUS, SO I NEED TO GO IN AND CONTAIN IT FIRST BEFORE YOU TAKE POSSESSION. SO I'M COMING WITH YOU. OTHER THAN THAT, IT'S YOUR SHOW.
YOU'RE THE HOT-SHOT MERCENARY. WHAT'S THE PLAN?
DUDE, MAYBE YOU SHOULD MENTION THAT IT PROBABLY WON'T HURT YOU NO MATTER HOW HAZARDOUS IT IS.
Shut up. She wants to come with us.
A PLAN. HMMMMM. A PLAN, YOU SAY.
SNAP!
GOT IT! THE PERFECT PLAN!
I'LL NEED THAT REVOLVER. I THINK YOU'LL BE IMPRESSED BY THIS PLAN'S CLEVERNESS AND SUBTLETY.
THIS IS A COMPLEX SCHEME, DR. BETTY. WHEELS TURNING INSIDE WHEELS. I'M GOING TO NEED YOU TO PAY ATTENTION TO EVERY NUANCE. CAN YOU DO THAT, DR. BETTY?
Y-YES.

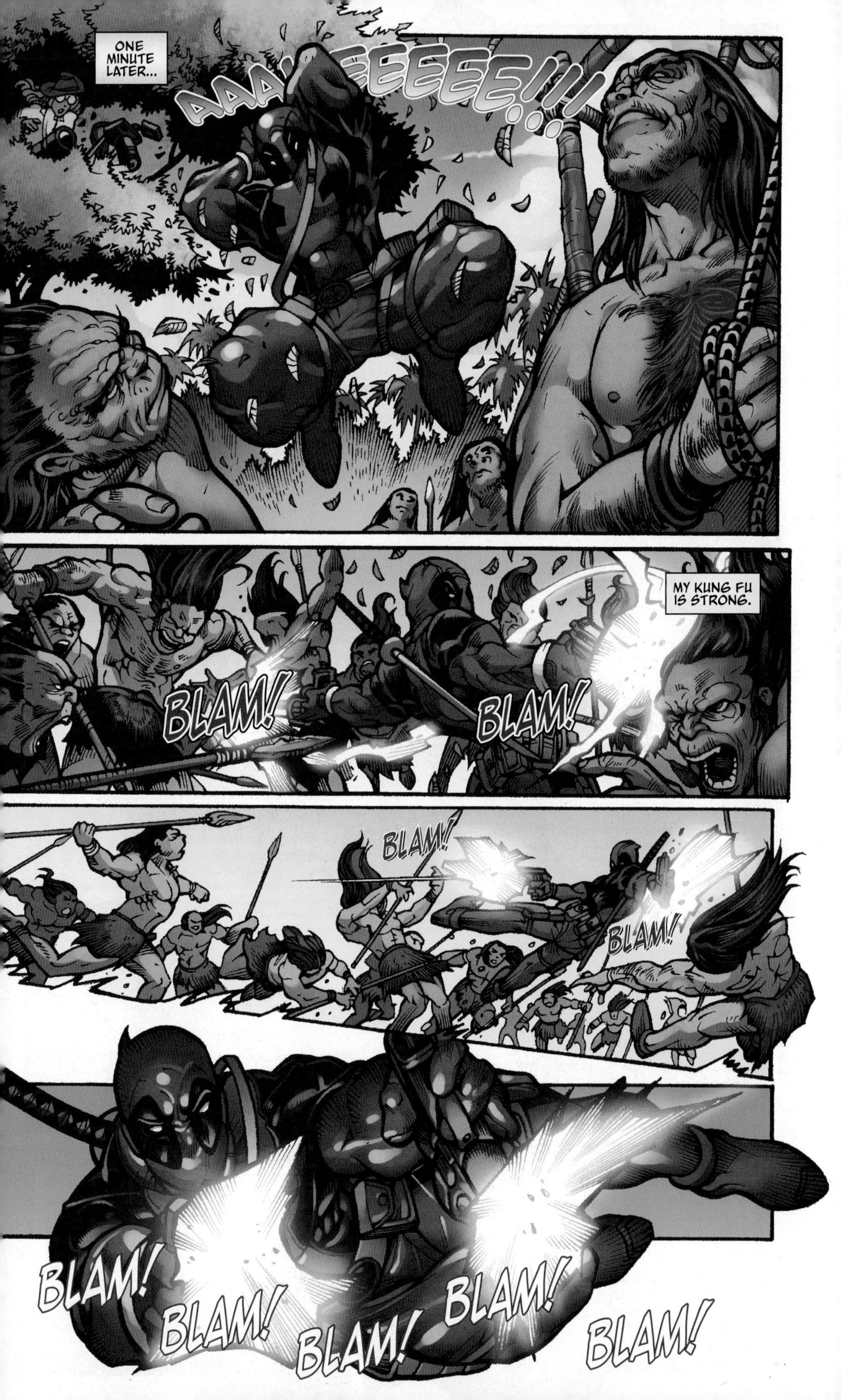
ONE MINUTE LATER...
AAAYEEEEEE!!!...
MY KUNG FU IS STRONG.
BLAM!
BLAM!
BLAM!
BLAM!
BLAM!
BLAM!
BLAM!
BLAM!

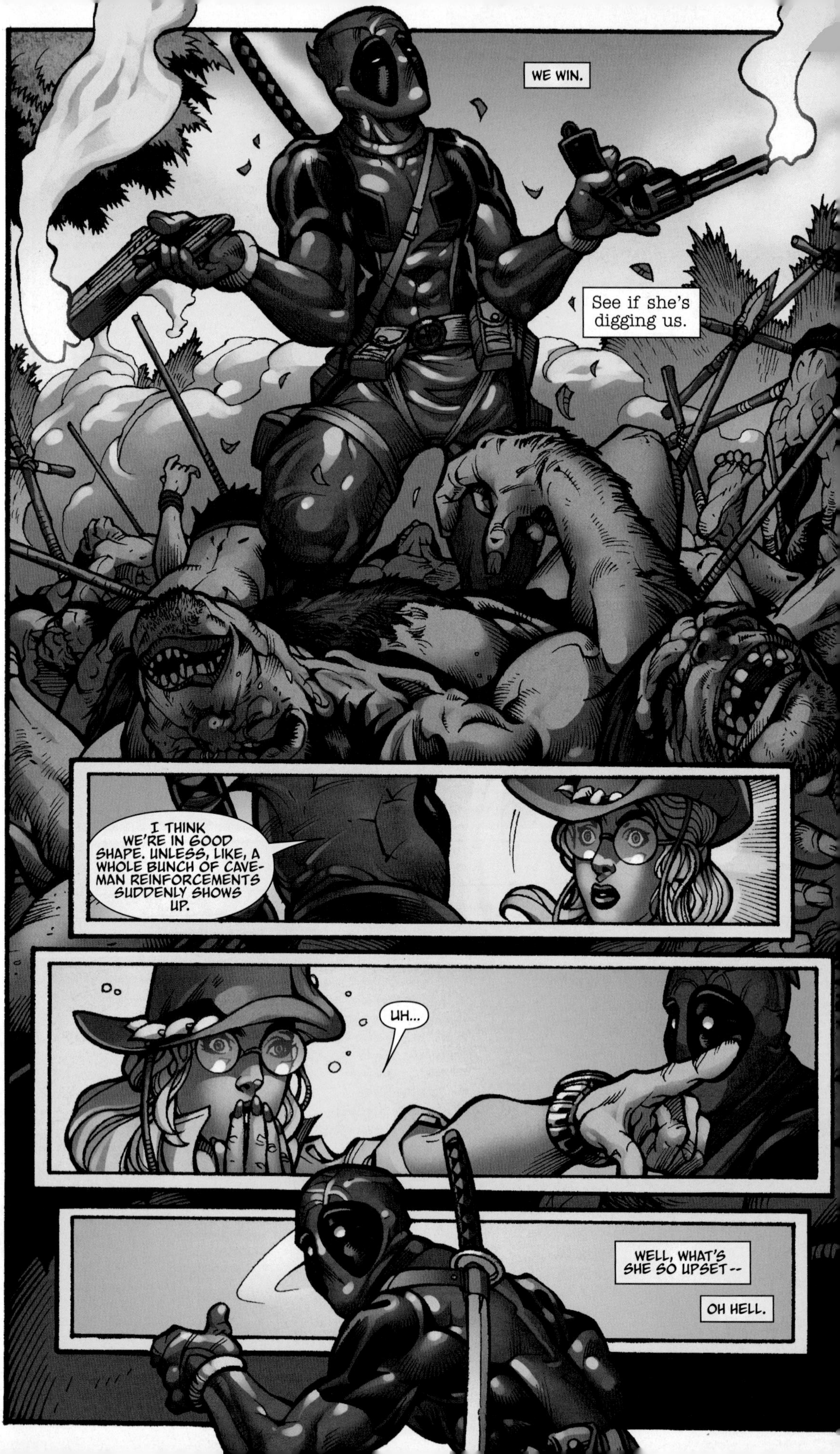
WE WIN.
See if she's digging us.
I THINK WE'RE IN GOOD SHAPE. UNLESS, LIKE, A WHOLE BUNCH OF CAVE-MAN REINFORCEMENTS SUDDENLY SHOWS UP.
UH...
WELL, WHAT'S SHE SO UPSET --
OH HELL.

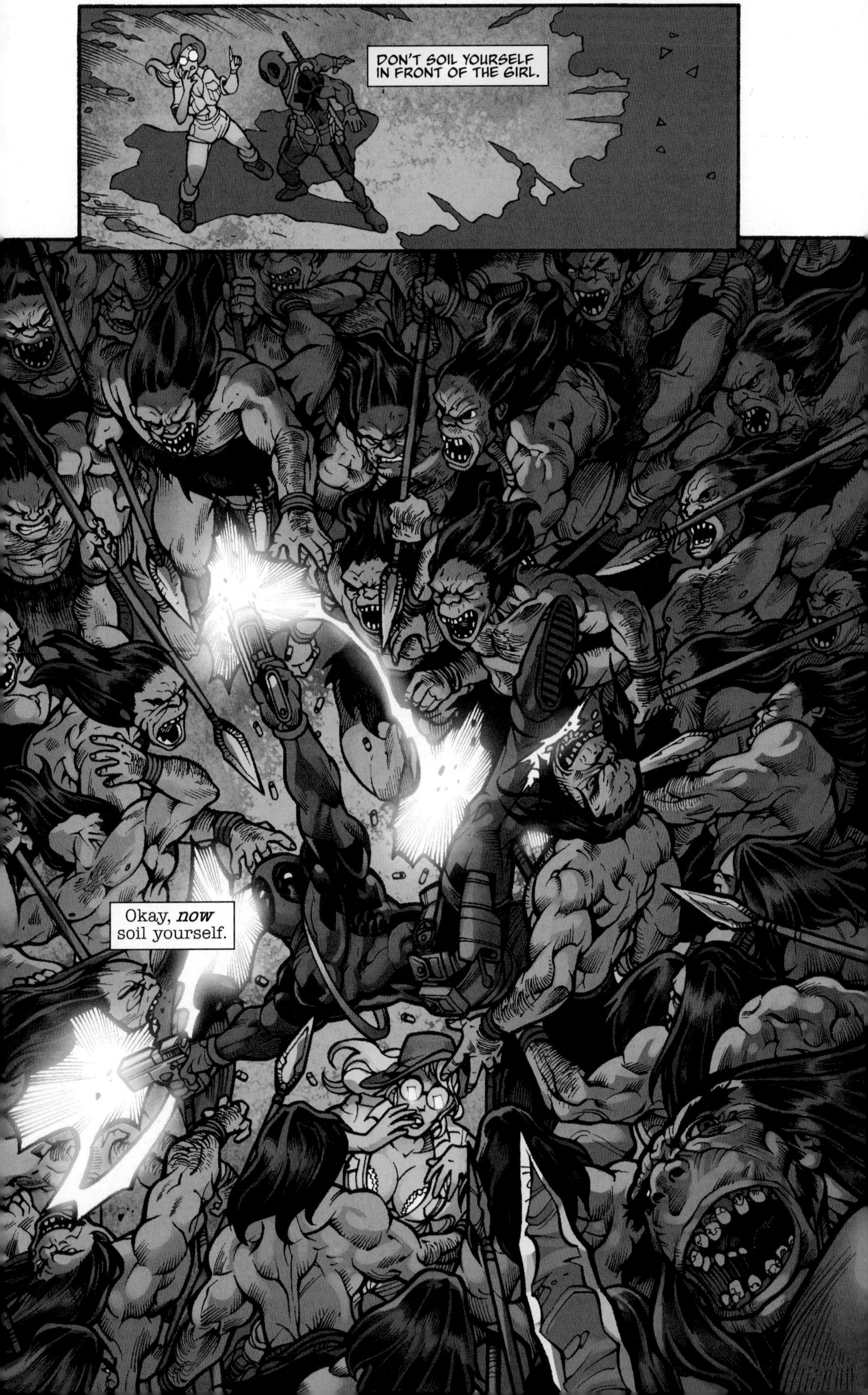
DON'T SOIL YOURSELF IN FRONT OF THE GIRL.
Okay, *now* soil yourself.

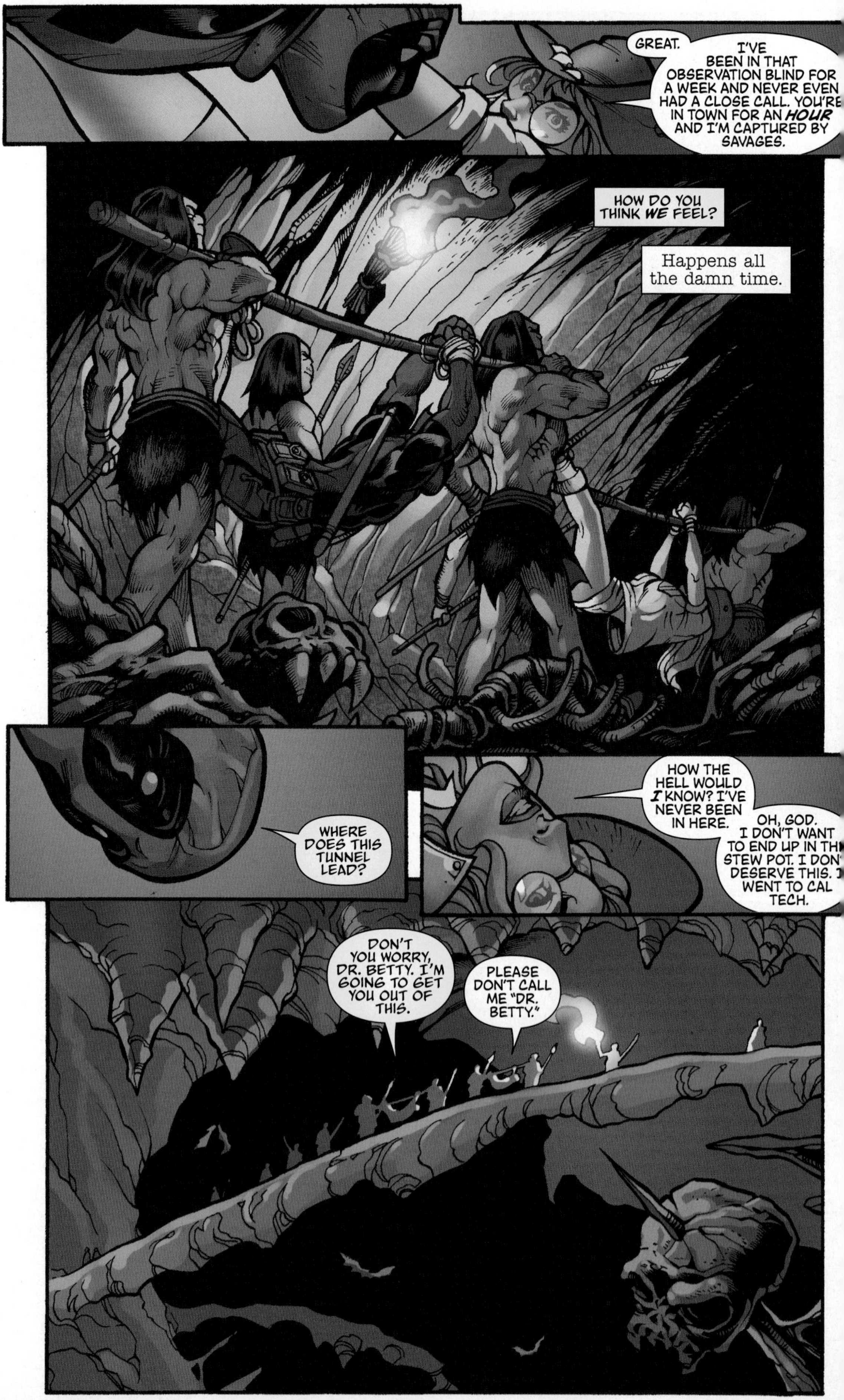
GREAT.
I'VE BEEN IN THAT OBSERVATION BLIND FOR A WEEK AND NEVER EVEN HAD A CLOSE CALL. YOU'RE IN TOWN FOR AN *HOUR* AND I'M CAPTURED BY SAVAGES.
HOW DO YOU THINK *WE* FEEL?
Happens all the damn time.
WHERE DOES THIS TUNNEL LEAD?
HOW THE HELL WOULD *I* KNOW? I'VE NEVER BEEN IN HERE.
OH, GOD. I DON'T WANT TO END UP IN TH STEW POT. I DON DESERVE THIS. I WENT TO CAL TECH.
DON'T YOU WORRY, DR. BETTY. I'M GOING TO GET YOU OUT OF THIS.
PLEASE DON'T CALL ME "DR. BETTY."

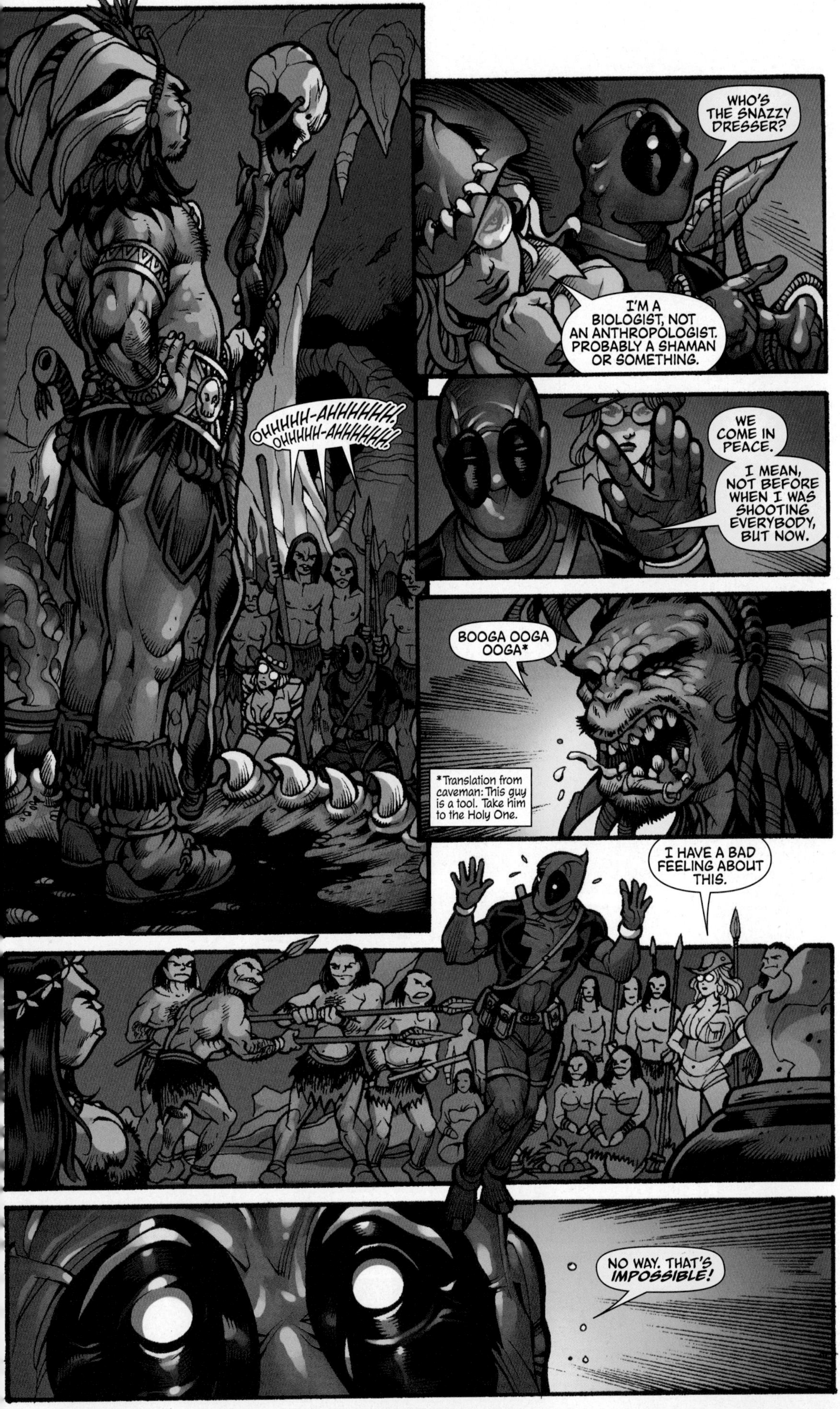

OHHHHH-AHHHHHH!
OHHHHH-AHHHHHH!
WHO'S THE SNAZZY DRESSER?
I'M A BIOLOGIST, NOT AN ANTHROPOLOGIST. PROBABLY A SHAMAN OR SOMETHING.
WE COME IN PEACE.
I MEAN, NOT BEFORE WHEN I WAS SHOOTING EVERYBODY, BUT NOW.
BOOGA OOGA OOGA*
*Translation from caveman: This guy is a tool. Take him to the Holy One.
I HAVE A BAD FEELING ABOUT THIS.
NO WAY. THAT'S *IMPOSSIBLE!*

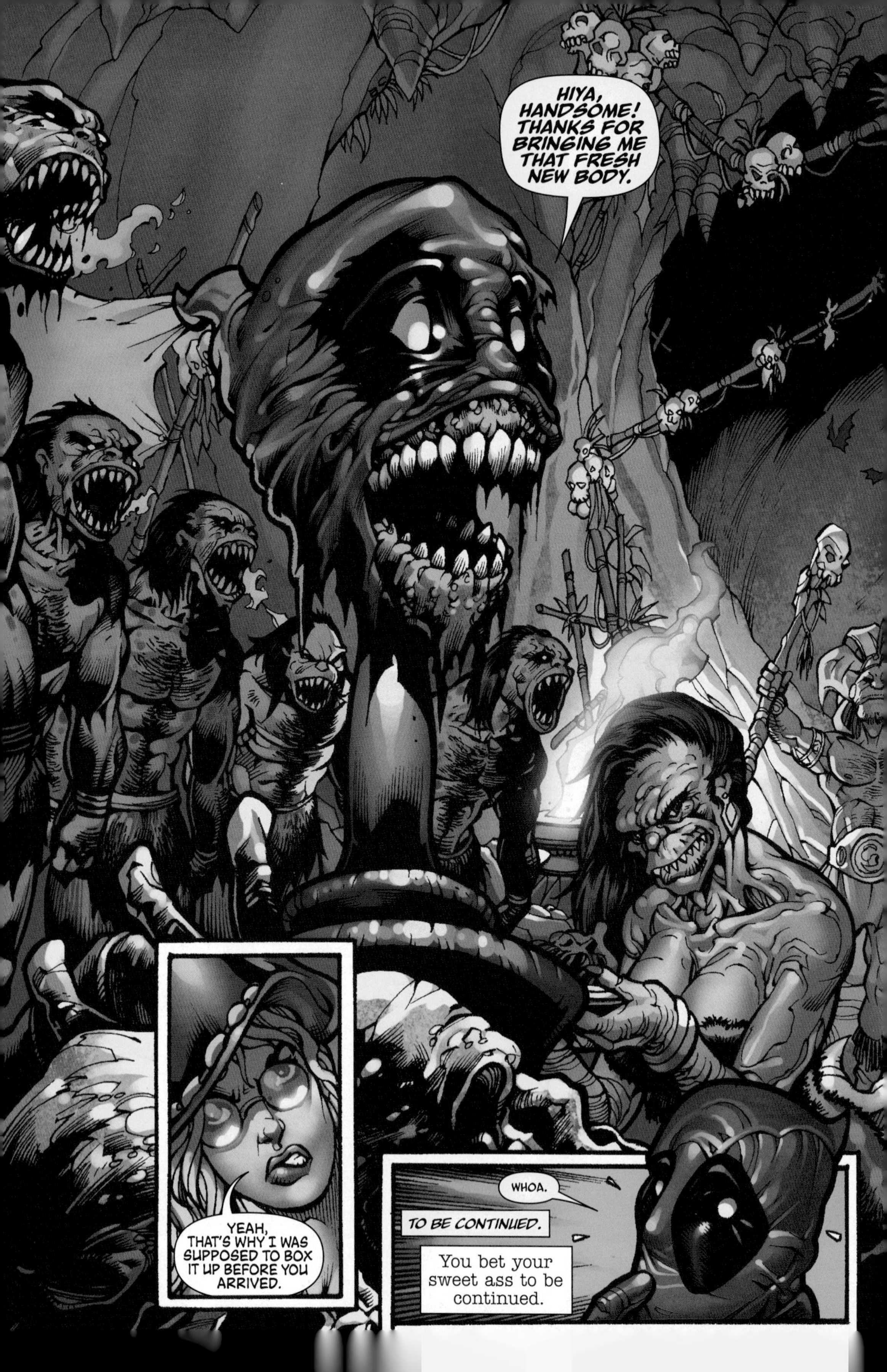
HIYA, HANDSOME! THANKS FOR BRINGING ME THAT FRESH NEW BODY.
YEAH, THAT'S WHY I WAS SUPPOSED TO BOX IT UP BEFORE YOU ARRIVED.
WHOA.
TO BE CONTINUED.
You bet your sweet ass to be continued.

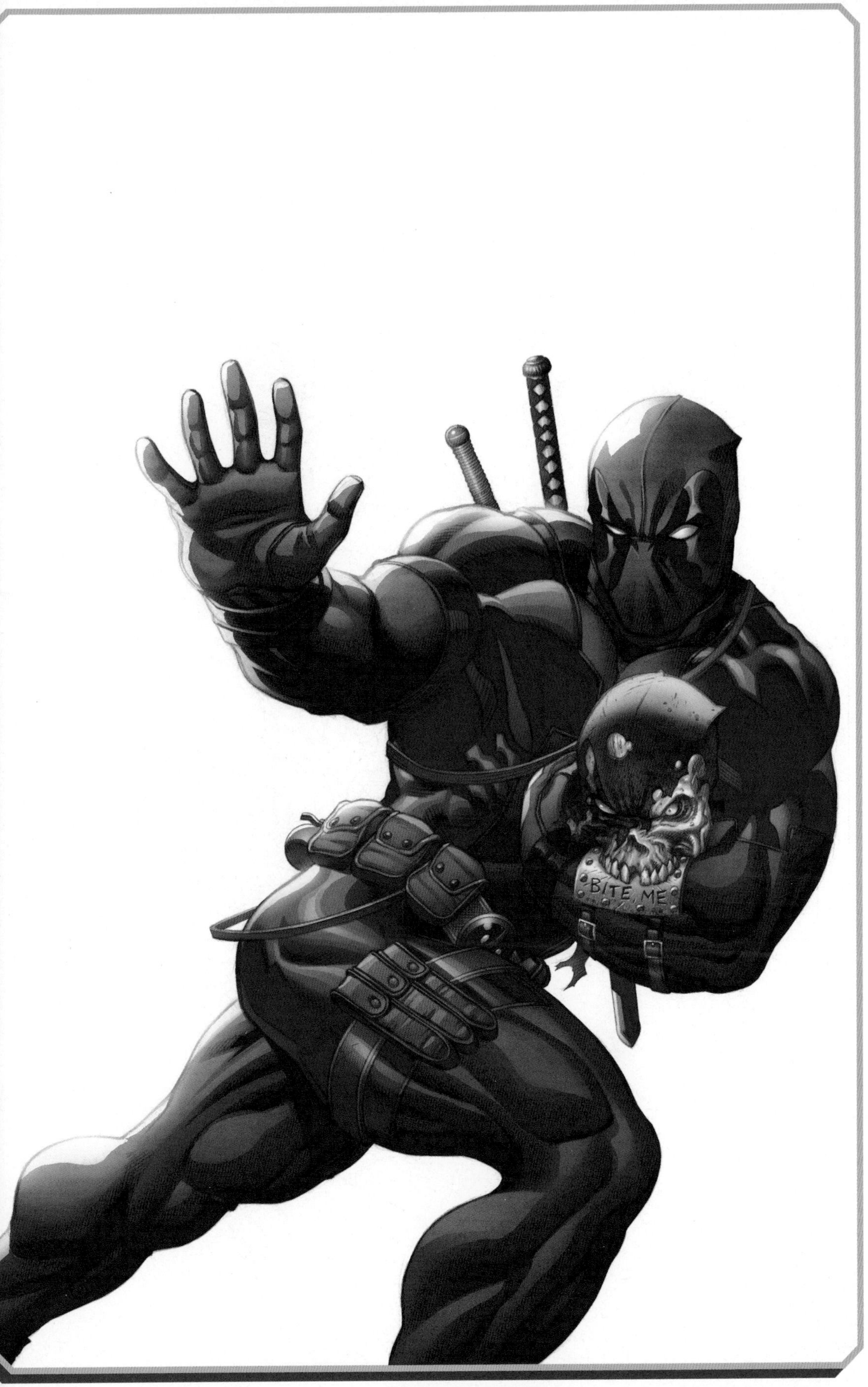
BITE ME

DEADPOOL: MERC WITH A MOUTH #1 Variant by ED MCGUINNESS

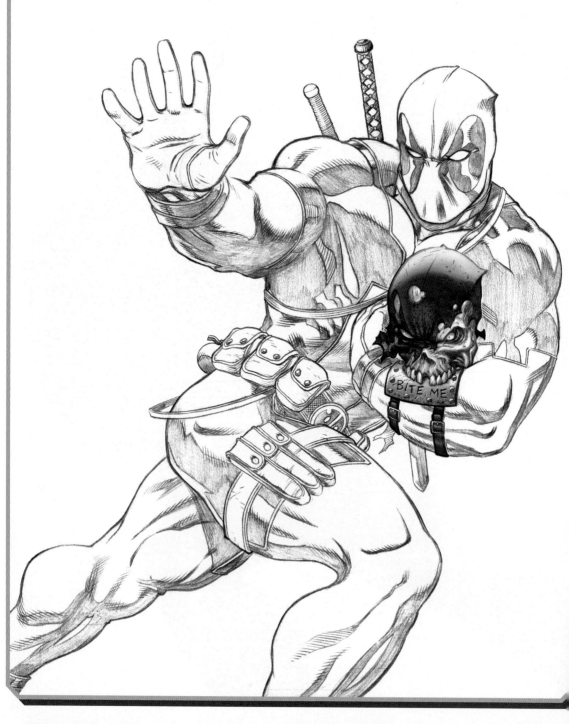

DEADPOOL: MERC WITH A MOUTH #1 Sketch Variant by ED MCGUINNESS

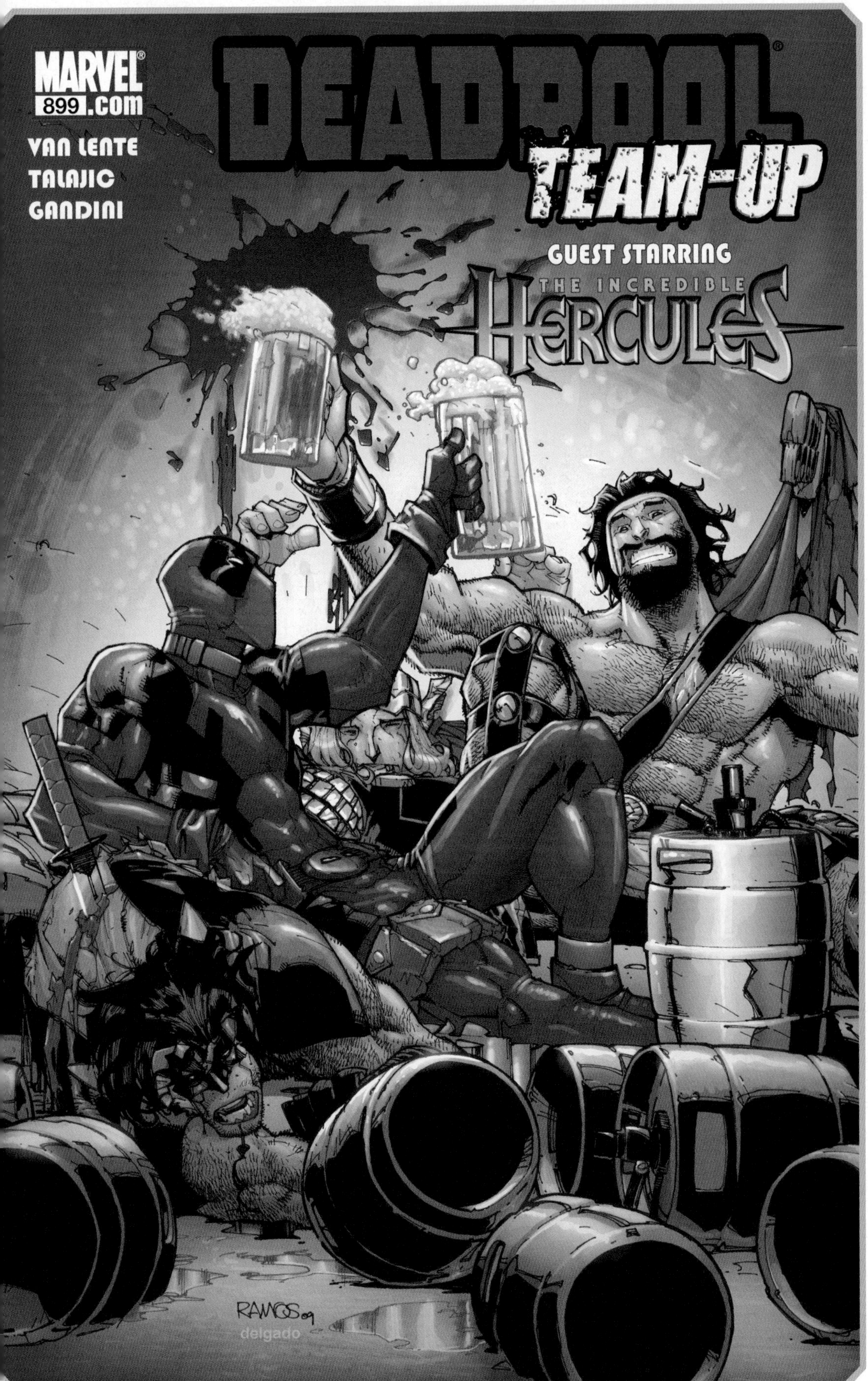

MARVEL
899 .com
DEADPOOL
TEAM-UP
VAN LENTE
TALAJIC
GANDINI
GUEST STARRING
THE INCREDIBLE
HERCULES
RAMOS 09
delgado

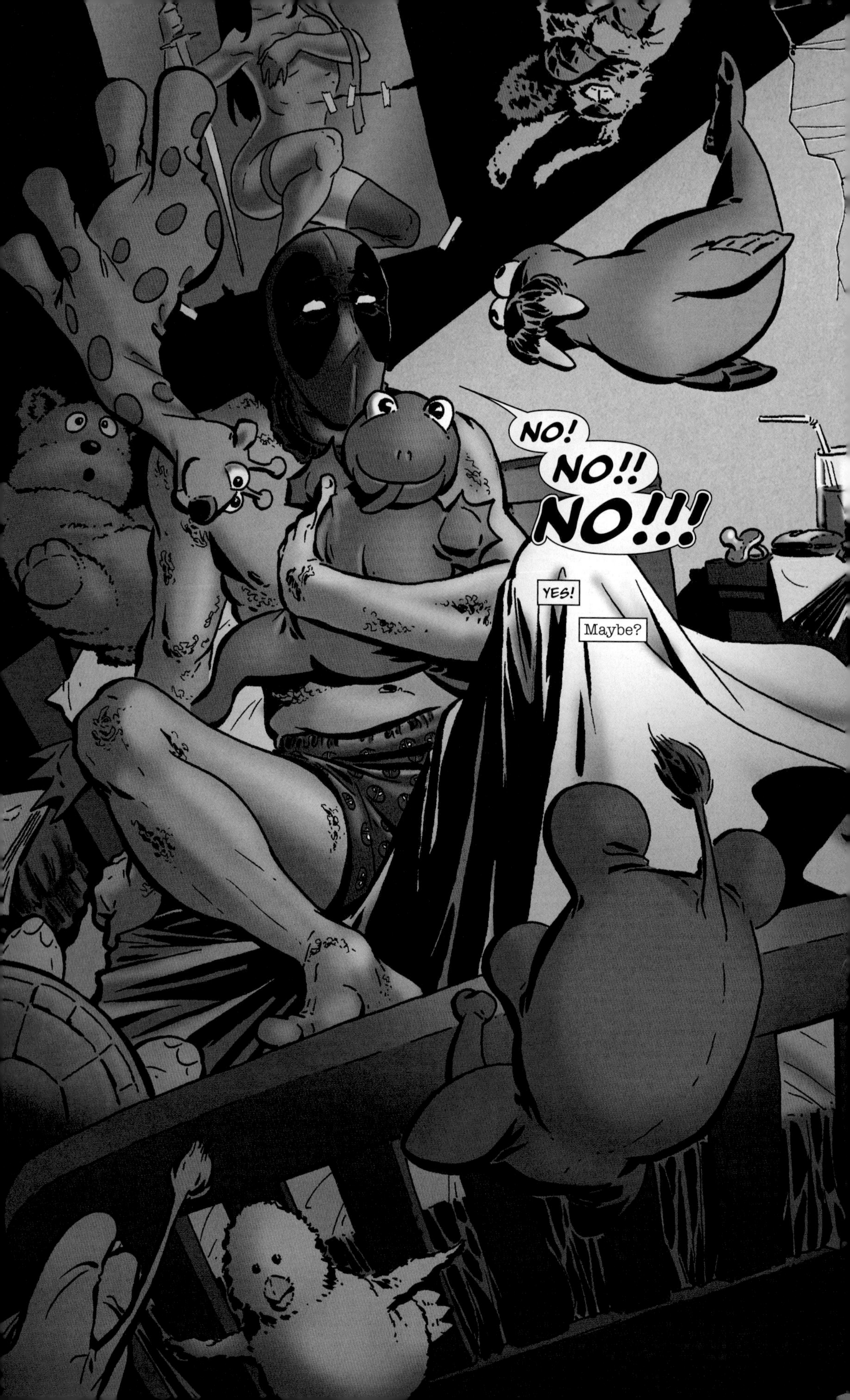
NO!
NO!!
NO!!!
YES!
Maybe?

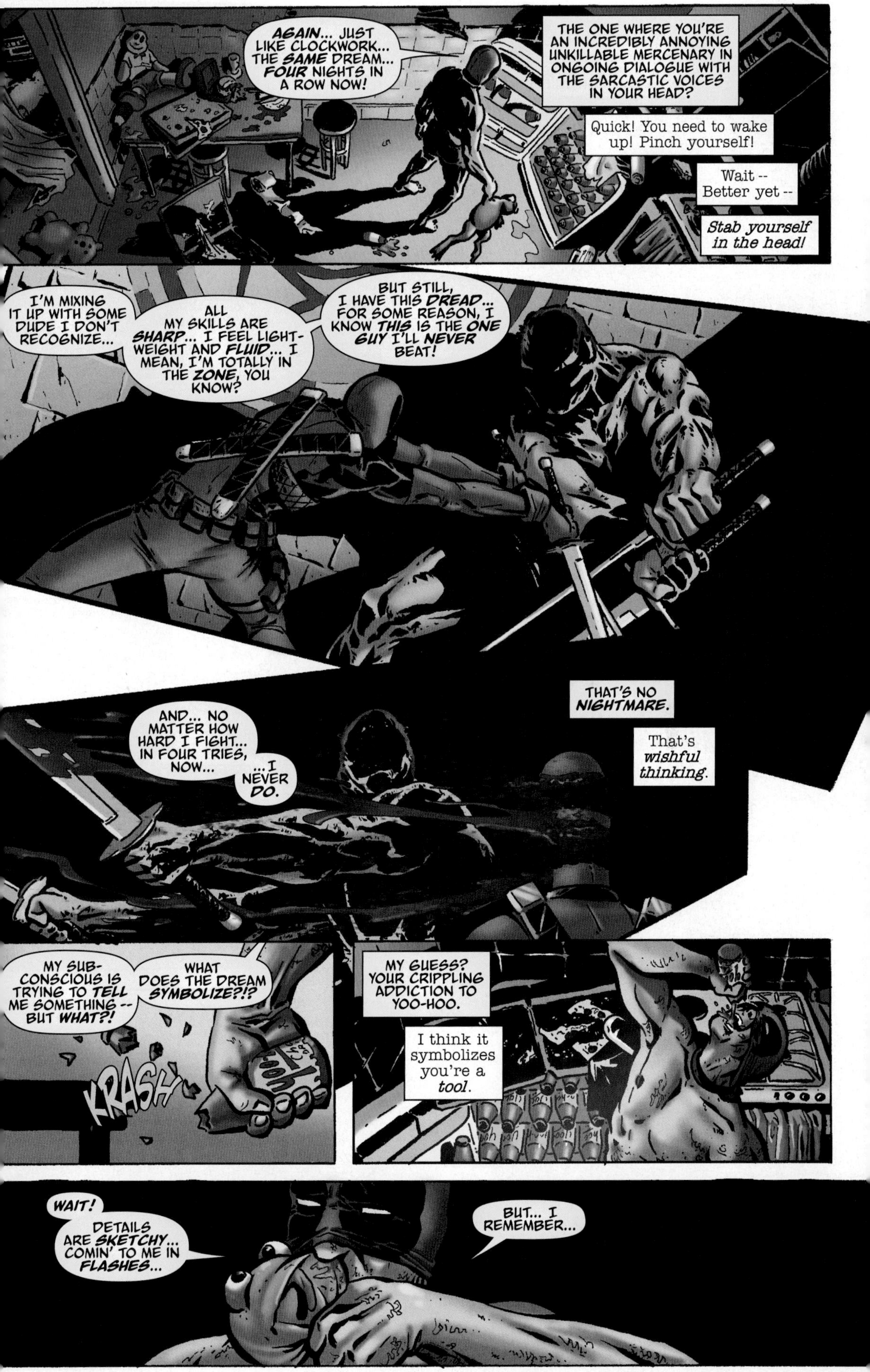
AGAIN... JUST LIKE CLOCKWORK... THE SAME DREAM... FOUR NIGHTS IN A ROW NOW!
THE ONE WHERE YOU'RE AN INCREDIBLY ANNOYING UNKILLABLE MERCENARY IN ONGOING DIALOGUE WITH THE SARCASTIC VOICES IN YOUR HEAD?
Quick! You need to wake up! Pinch yourself!
Wait -- Better yet --
Stab yourself in the head!
I'M MIXING IT UP WITH SOME DUDE I DON'T RECOGNIZE...
ALL MY SKILLS ARE SHARP... I FEEL LIGHT-WEIGHT AND FLUID... I MEAN, I'M TOTALLY IN THE ZONE, YOU KNOW?
BUT STILL, I HAVE THIS DREAD... FOR SOME REASON, I KNOW THIS IS THE ONE GUY I'LL NEVER BEAT!
AND... NO MATTER HOW HARD I FIGHT... IN FOUR TRIES, NOW...
...I NEVER DO.
THAT'S NO NIGHTMARE.
That's wishful thinking.
MY SUB-CONSCIOUS IS TRYING TO TELL ME SOMETHING -- BUT WHAT?!
WHAT DOES THE DREAM SYMBOLIZE?!?
KRASH
MY GUESS? YOUR CRIPPLING ADDICTION TO YOO-HOO.
I think it symbolizes you're a tool.
WAIT! DETAILS ARE SKETCHY... COMIN' TO ME IN FLASHES...
BUT... I REMEMBER...

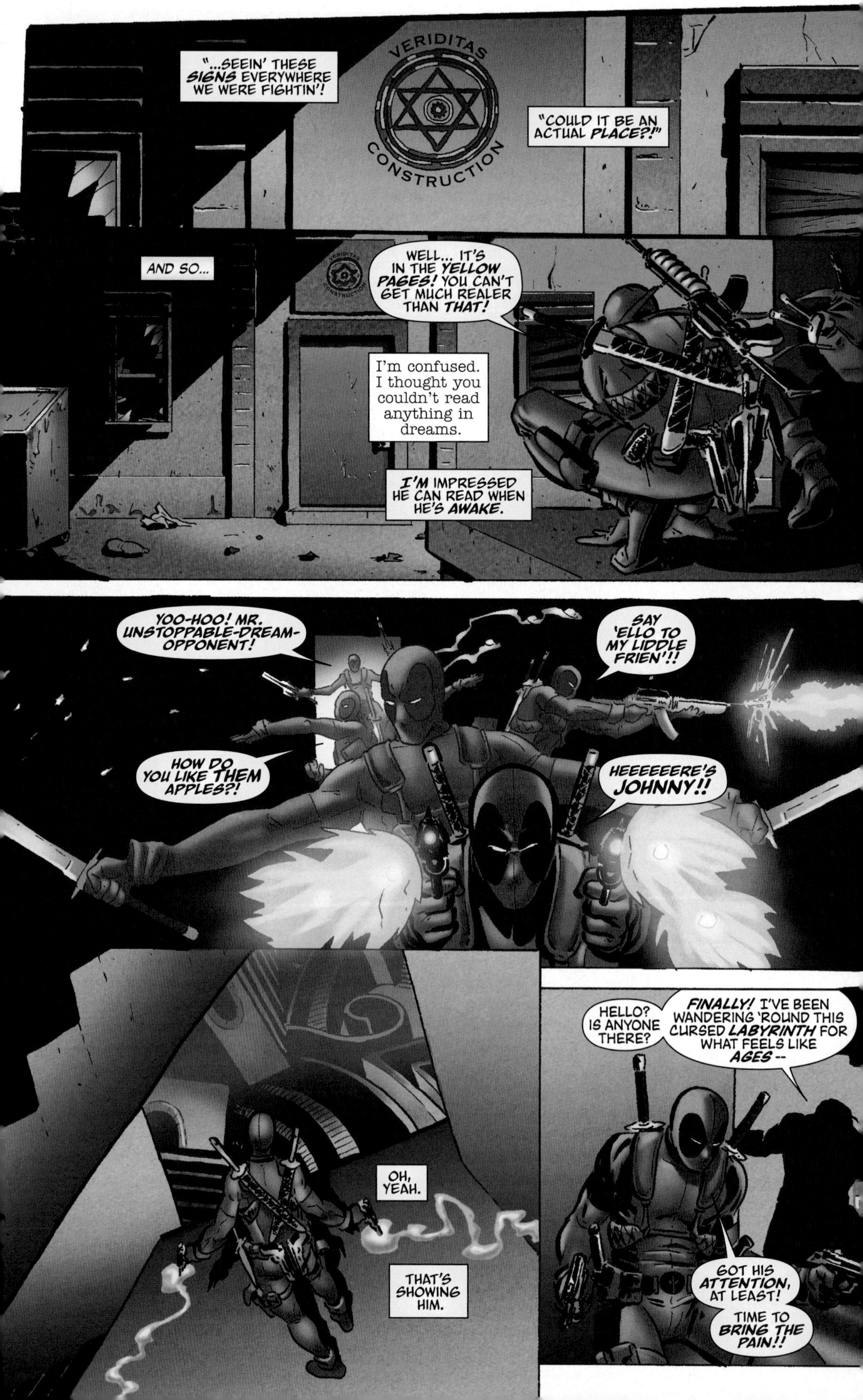
"...SEEIN' THESE SIGNS EVERYWHERE WE WERE FIGHTIN'!
VERIDITAS CONSTRUCTION
"COULD IT BE AN ACTUAL PLACE?!"
AND SO...
WELL... IT'S IN THE YELLOW PAGES! YOU CAN'T GET MUCH REALER THAN THAT!
I'm confused. I thought you couldn't read anything in dreams.
I'M IMPRESSED HE CAN READ WHEN HE'S AWAKE.
YOO-HOO! MR. UNSTOPPABLE-DREAM-OPPONENT!
SAY 'ELLO TO MY LIDDLE FRIEN'!!
HOW DO YOU LIKE THEM APPLES?!
HEEEEEERE'S JOHNNY!!
HELLO? IS ANYONE THERE?
FINALLY! I'VE BEEN WANDERING 'ROUND THIS CURSED LABYRINTH FOR WHAT FEELS LIKE AGES --
OH, YEAH.
THAT'S SHOWING HIM.
GOT HIS ATTENTION, AT LEAST!
TIME TO BRING THE PAIN!!

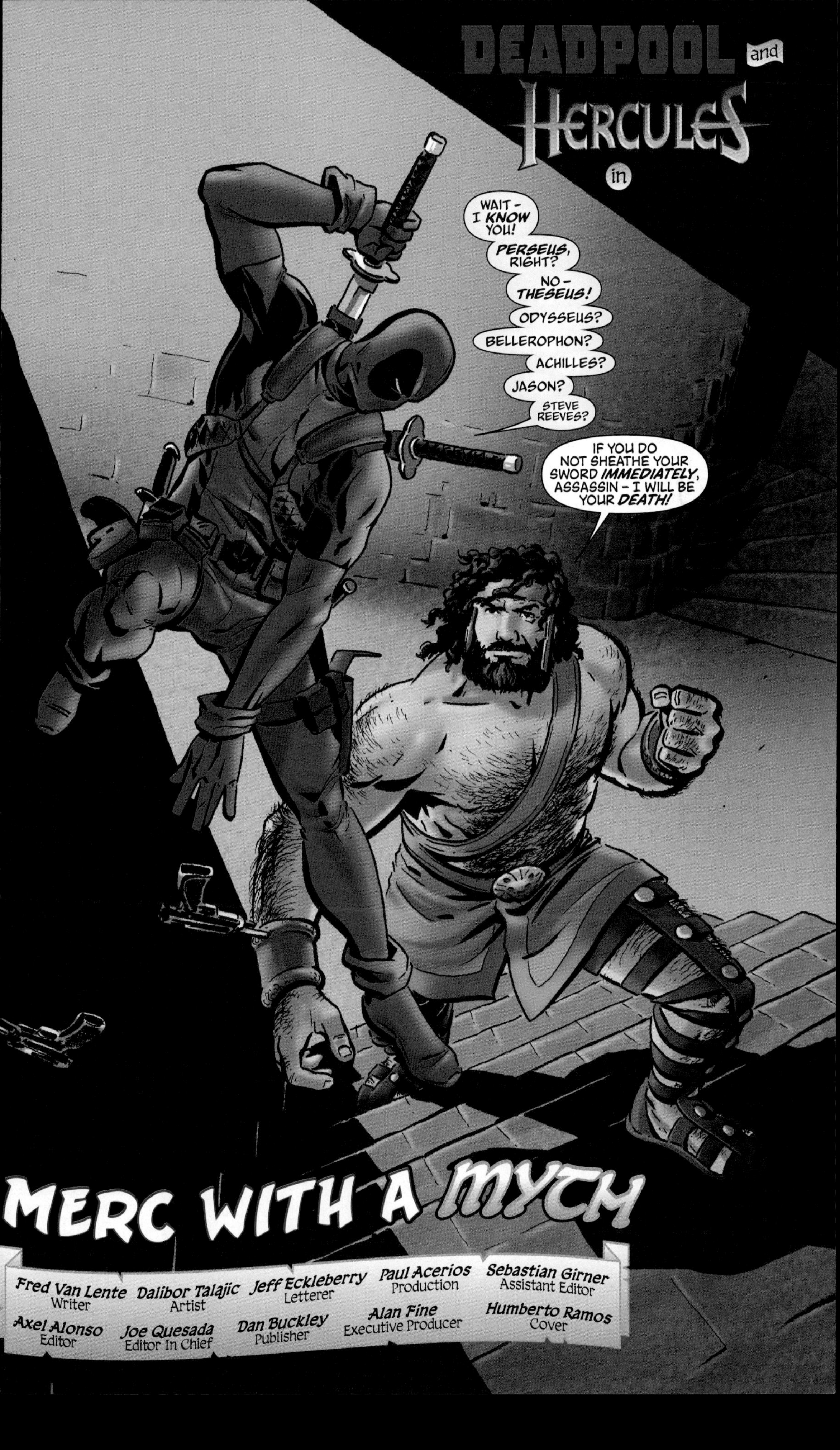

DEADPOOL and HERCULES in
WAIT - I KNOW YOU!
PERSEUS, RIGHT?
NO - THESEUS!
ODYSSEUS?
BELLEROPHON?
ACHILLES?
JASON?
STEVE REEVES?
IF YOU DO NOT SHEATHE YOUR SWORD IMMEDIATELY, ASSASSIN - I WILL BE YOUR DEATH!
MERC WITH A MYTH
Fred Van Lente Writer
Dalibor Talajic Artist
Jeff Eckleberry Letterer
Paul Acerios Production
Sebastian Girner Assistant Editor
Axel Alonso Editor
Joe Quesada Editor In Chief
Dan Buckley Publisher
Alan Fine Executive Producer
Humberto Ramos Cover

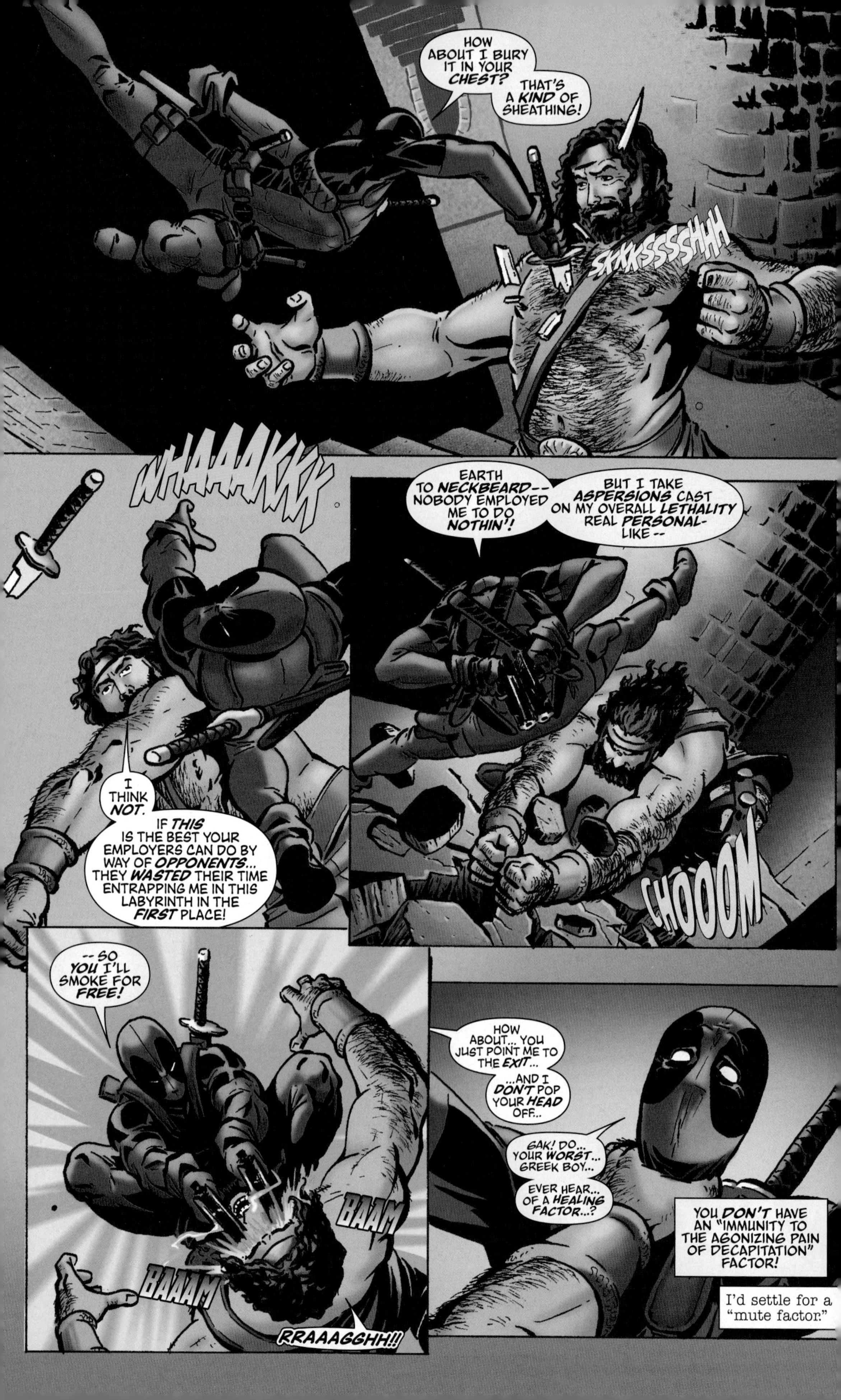
HOW ABOUT I BURY IT IN YOUR CHEST?
THAT'S A KIND OF SHEATHING!
SKKKSSSSHHH
WHAAAKKK
I THINK NOT.
IF THIS IS THE BEST YOUR EMPLOYERS CAN DO BY WAY OF OPPONENTS... THEY WASTED THEIR TIME ENTRAPPING ME IN THIS LABYRINTH IN THE FIRST PLACE!
EARTH TO NECKBEARD-- NOBODY EMPLOYED ME TO DO NOTHIN'!
BUT I TAKE ASPERSIONS CAST ON MY OVERALL LETHALITY REAL PERSONAL-LIKE --
CHOOOM
-- SO YOU I'LL SMOKE FOR FREE!
BAAM
BAAAM
RRAAAGGHH!!
HOW ABOUT... YOU JUST POINT ME TO THE EXIT...
...AND I DON'T POP YOUR HEAD OFF...
GAK! DO... YOUR WORST... GREEK BOY...
EVER HEAR... OF A HEALING FACTOR...?
YOU DON'T HAVE AN "IMMUNITY TO THE AGONIZING PAIN OF DECAPITATION" FACTOR!
I'd settle for a "mute factor."

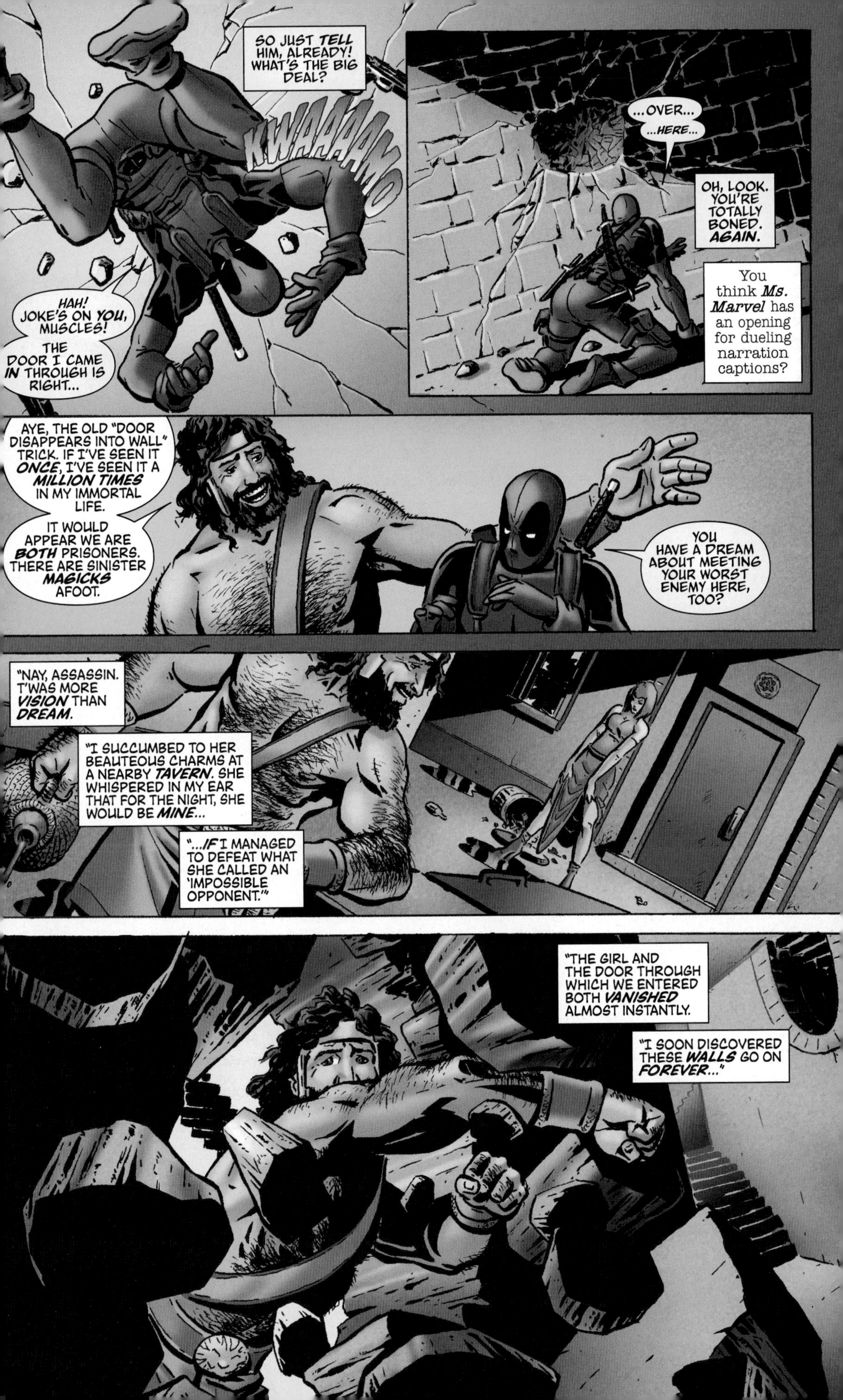
SO JUST TELL HIM, ALREADY! WHAT'S THE BIG DEAL?
KWAAAAAMO
HAH! JOKE'S ON YOU, MUSCLES!
THE DOOR I CAME IN THROUGH IS RIGHT...
...OVER...
...HERE...
OH, LOOK. YOU'RE TOTALLY BONED. AGAIN.
You think Ms. Marvel has an opening for dueling narration captions?
AYE, THE OLD "DOOR DISAPPEARS INTO WALL" TRICK. IF I'VE SEEN IT ONCE, I'VE SEEN IT A MILLION TIMES IN MY IMMORTAL LIFE.
IT WOULD APPEAR WE ARE BOTH PRISONERS. THERE ARE SINISTER MAGICKS AFOOT.
YOU HAVE A DREAM ABOUT MEETING YOUR WORST ENEMY HERE, TOO?
"NAY, ASSASSIN. T'WAS MORE VISION THAN DREAM.
"I SUCCUMBED TO HER BEAUTEOUS CHARMS AT A NEARBY TAVERN. SHE WHISPERED IN MY EAR THAT FOR THE NIGHT, SHE WOULD BE MINE...
"...IF I MANAGED TO DEFEAT WHAT SHE CALLED AN 'IMPOSSIBLE OPPONENT.'"
"THE GIRL AND THE DOOR THROUGH WHICH WE ENTERED BOTH VANISHED ALMOST INSTANTLY.
"I SOON DISCOVERED THESE WALLS GO ON FOREVER..."

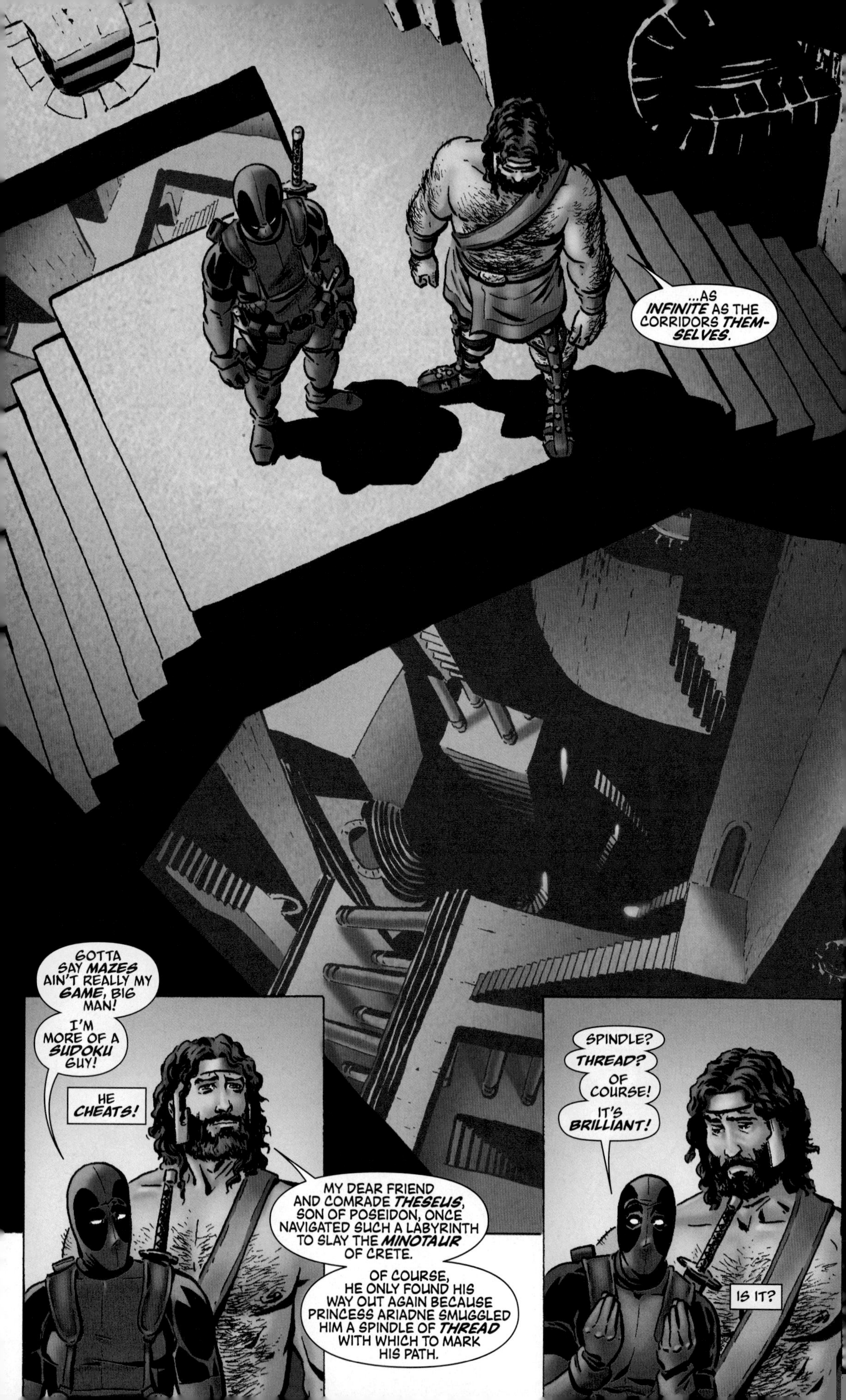
...AS INFINITE AS THE CORRIDORS THEM-SELVES.
GOTTA SAY MAZES AIN'T REALLY MY GAME, BIG MAN!
I'M MORE OF A SUDOKU GUY!
HE CHEATS!
MY DEAR FRIEND AND COMRADE THESEUS, SON OF POSEIDON, ONCE NAVIGATED SUCH A LABYRINTH TO SLAY THE MINOTAUR OF CRETE.
OF COURSE, HE ONLY FOUND HIS WAY OUT AGAIN BECAUSE PRINCESS ARIADNE SMUGGLED HIM A SPINDLE OF THREAD WITH WHICH TO MARK HIS PATH.
SPINDLE?
THREAD?
OF COURSE!
IT'S BRILLIANT!
IS IT?

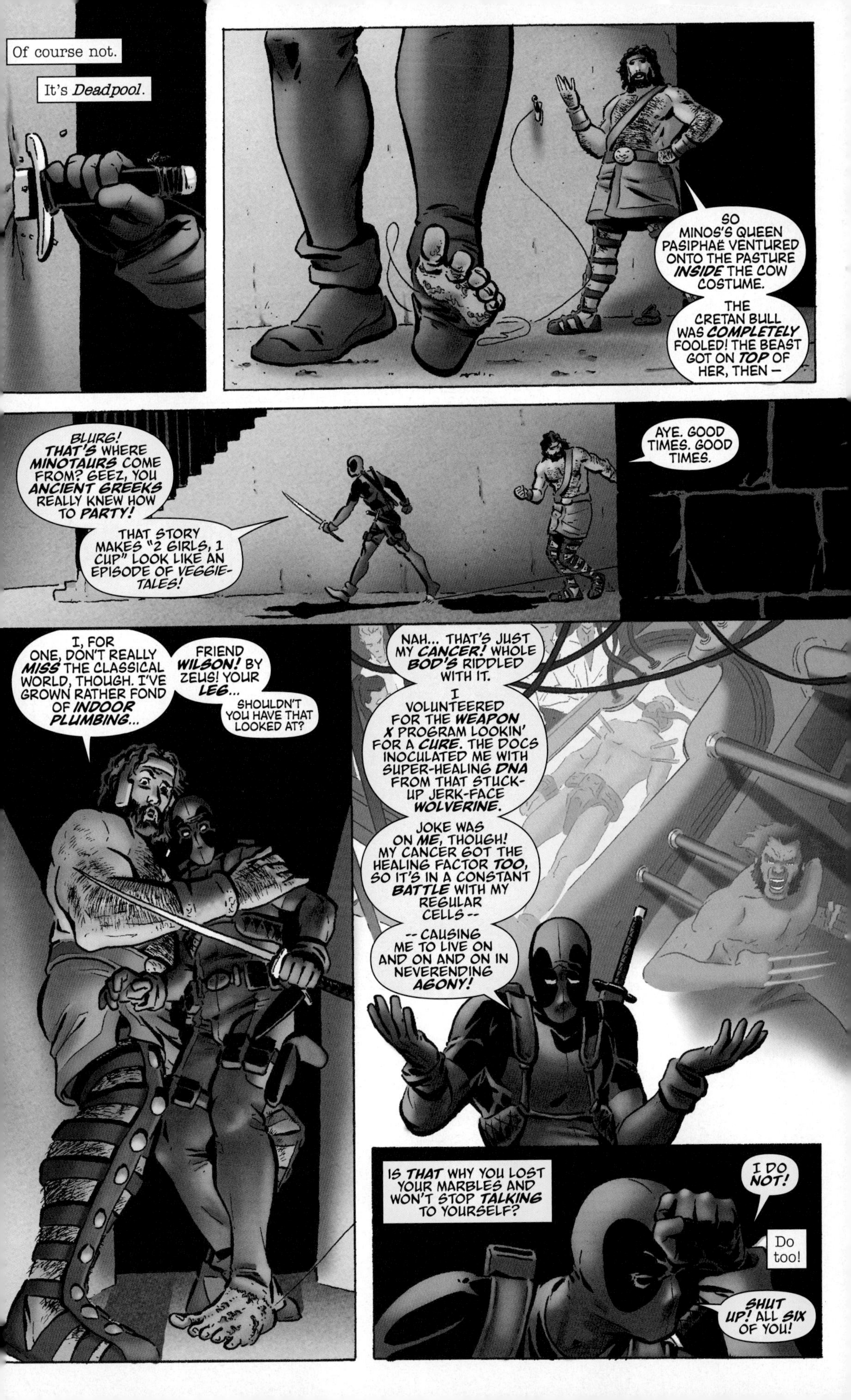
Of course not.
It's *Deadpool*.
SO MINOS'S QUEEN PASIPHAË VENTURED ONTO THE PASTURE *INSIDE* THE COW COSTUME.
THE CRETAN BULL WAS *COMPLETELY* FOOLED! THE BEAST GOT ON *TOP* OF HER, THEN —
BLURG! *THAT'S* WHERE *MINOTAURS* COME FROM? GEEZ, YOU *ANCIENT GREEKS* REALLY KNEW HOW TO *PARTY!*
THAT STORY MAKES "2 GIRLS, 1 CUP" LOOK LIKE AN EPISODE OF *VEGGIE-TALES!*
AYE. GOOD TIMES. GOOD TIMES.
I, FOR ONE, DON'T REALLY *MISS* THE CLASSICAL WORLD, THOUGH. I'VE GROWN RATHER FOND OF *INDOOR PLUMBING*...
FRIEND *WILSON!* BY ZEUS! YOUR *LEG*...
SHOULDN'T YOU HAVE THAT LOOKED AT?
NAH... THAT'S JUST MY *CANCER!* WHOLE *BOD'S* RIDDLED WITH IT.
I VOLUNTEERED FOR THE *WEAPON X* PROGRAM LOOKIN' FOR A *CURE*. THE DOCS INOCULATED ME WITH SUPER-HEALING *DNA* FROM THAT STUCK-UP JERK-FACE *WOLVERINE*.
JOKE WAS ON *ME*, THOUGH! MY CANCER GOT THE HEALING FACTOR *TOO*, SO IT'S IN A CONSTANT *BATTLE* WITH MY REGULAR CELLS --
-- CAUSING ME TO LIVE ON AND ON AND ON IN NEVERENDING *AGONY!*
IS *THAT* WHY YOU LOST YOUR MARBLES AND WON'T STOP *TALKING* TO YOURSELF?
I DO *NOT!*
Do too!
SHUT UP! ALL *SIX* OF YOU!

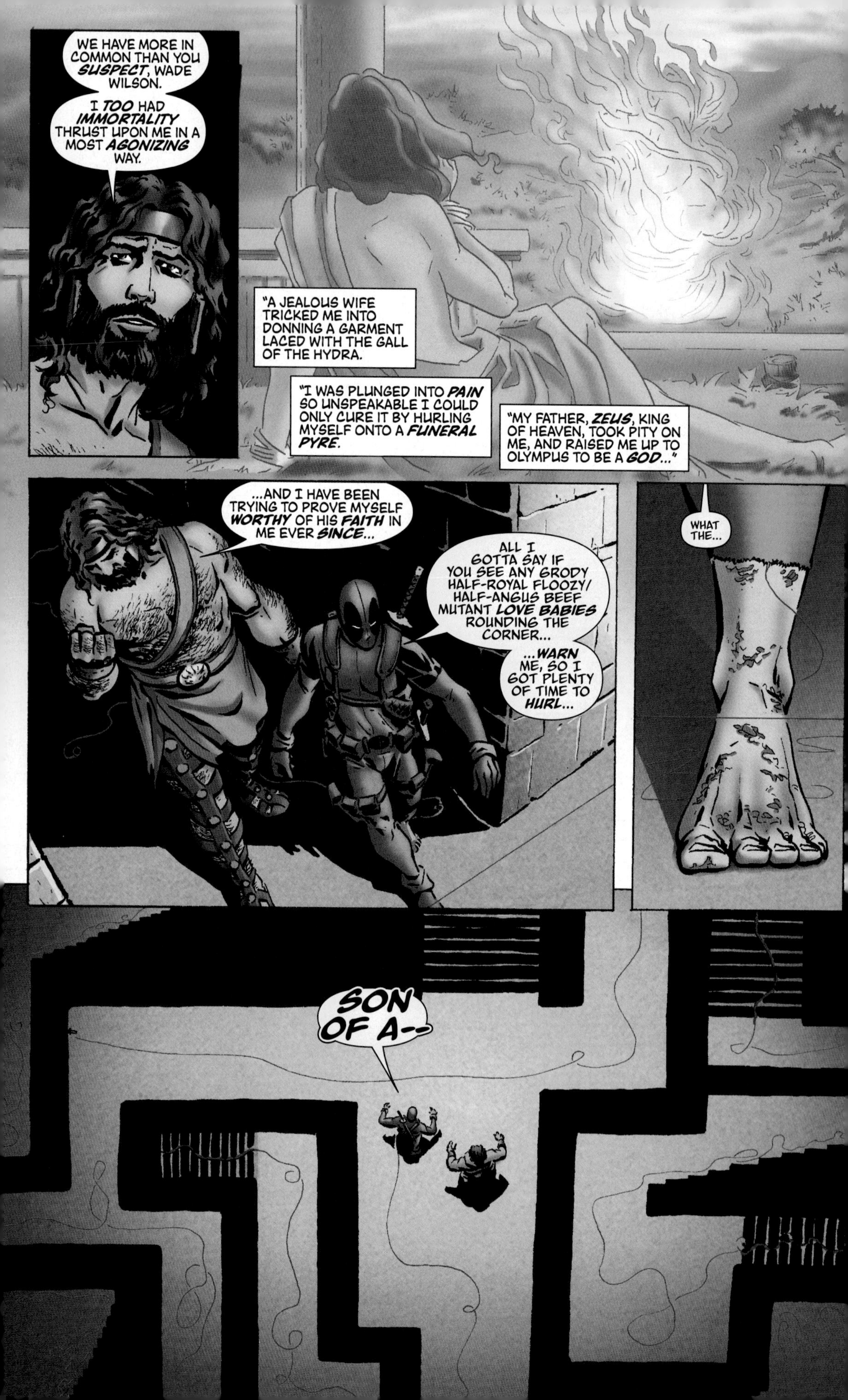

WE HAVE MORE IN COMMON THAN YOU SUSPECT, WADE WILSON.
I TOO HAD IMMORTALITY THRUST UPON ME IN A MOST AGONIZING WAY.
"A JEALOUS WIFE TRICKED ME INTO DONNING A GARMENT LACED WITH THE GALL OF THE HYDRA.
"I WAS PLUNGED INTO PAIN SO UNSPEAKABLE I COULD ONLY CURE IT BY HURLING MYSELF ONTO A FUNERAL PYRE.
"MY FATHER, ZEUS, KING OF HEAVEN, TOOK PITY ON ME, AND RAISED ME UP TO OLYMPUS TO BE A GOD..."
...AND I HAVE BEEN TRYING TO PROVE MYSELF WORTHY OF HIS FAITH IN ME EVER SINCE...
ALL I GOTTA SAY IF YOU SEE ANY GRODY HALF-ROYAL FLOOZY/ HALF-ANGUS BEEF MUTANT LOVE BABIES ROUNDING THE CORNER...
...WARN ME, SO I GOT PLENTY OF TIME TO HURL...
WHAT THE...
SON OF A--

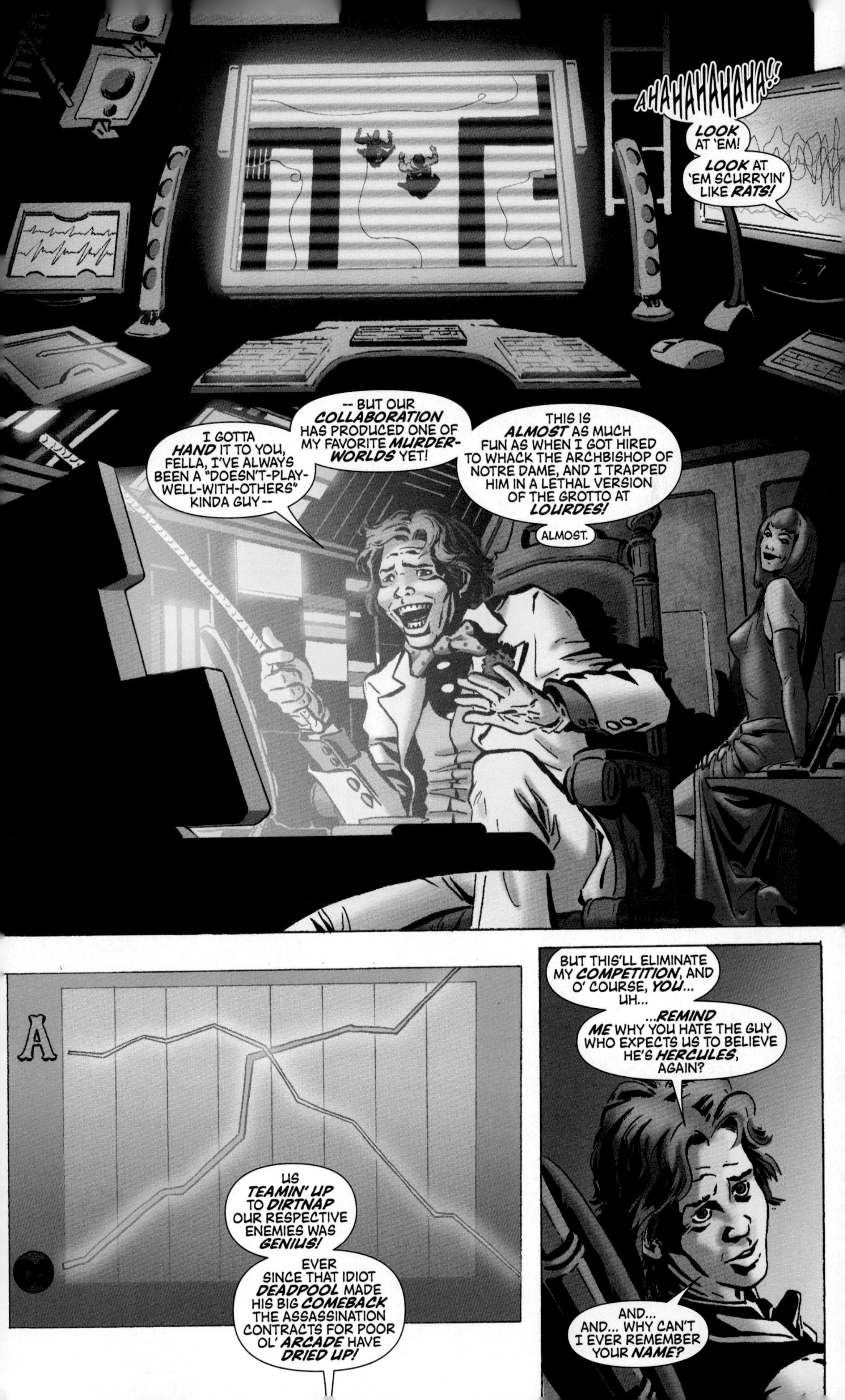
AHAHAHAHAHAHA!!
LOOK AT 'EM!
LOOK AT 'EM SCURRYIN' LIKE RATS!
I GOTTA HAND IT TO YOU, FELLA, I'VE ALWAYS BEEN A "DOESN'T-PLAY-WELL-WITH-OTHERS" KINDA GUY --
-- BUT OUR COLLABORATION HAS PRODUCED ONE OF MY FAVORITE MURDER-WORLDS YET!
THIS IS ALMOST AS MUCH FUN AS WHEN I GOT HIRED TO WHACK THE ARCHBISHOP OF NOTRE DAME, AND I TRAPPED HIM IN A LETHAL VERSION OF THE GROTTO AT LOURDES!
ALMOST.
A
US TEAMIN' UP TO DIRTNAP OUR RESPECTIVE ENEMIES WAS GENIUS!
EVER SINCE THAT IDIOT DEADPOOL MADE HIS BIG COMEBACK THE ASSASSINATION CONTRACTS FOR POOR OL' ARCADE HAVE DRIED UP!
BUT THIS'LL ELIMINATE MY COMPETITION, AND O' COURSE, YOU... UH...
...REMIND ME WHY YOU HATE THE GUY WHO EXPECTS US TO BELIEVE HE'S HERCULES, AGAIN?
AND... AND... WHY CAN'T I EVER REMEMBER YOUR NAME?

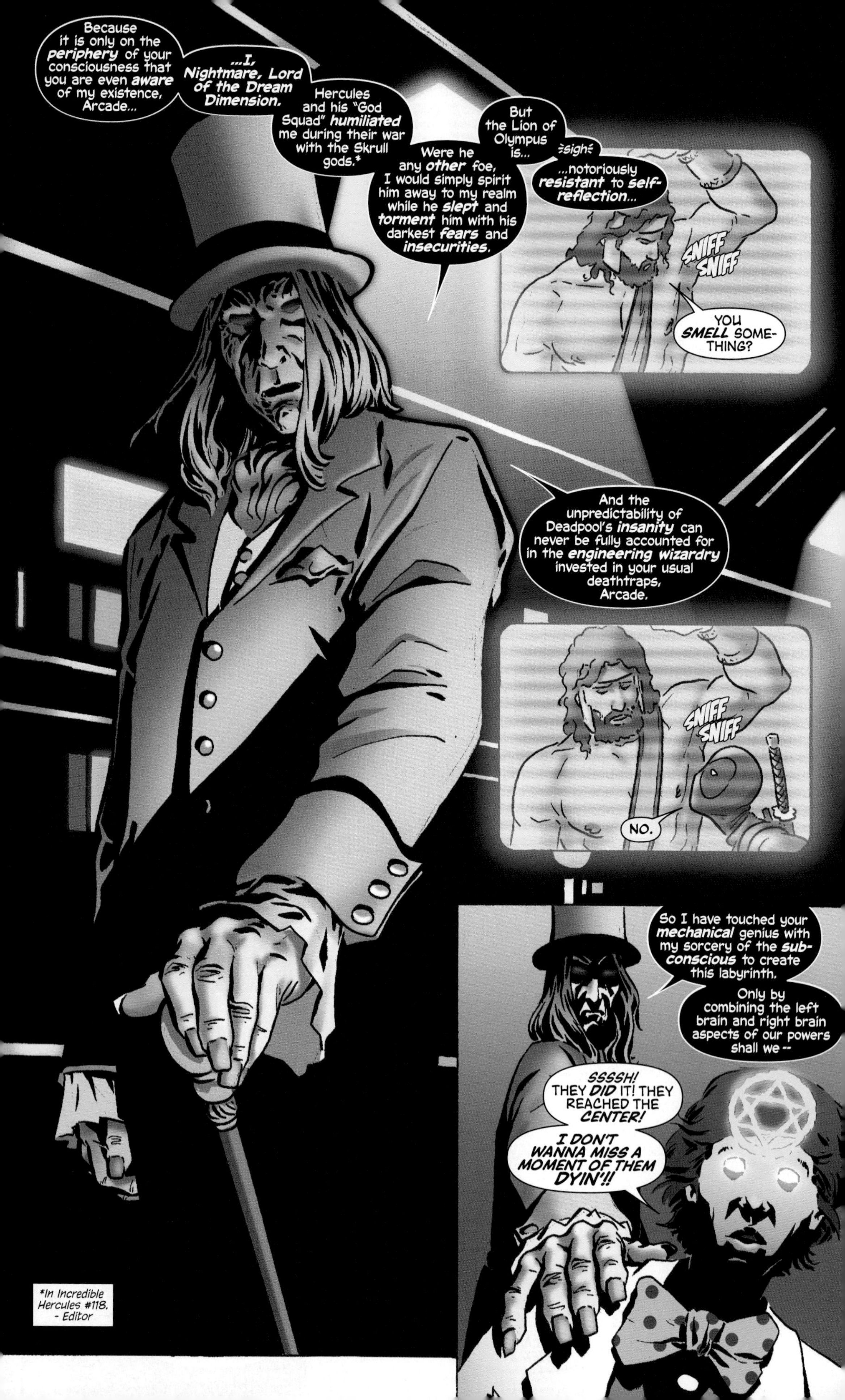

Because it is only on the periphery of your consciousness that you are even aware of my existence, Arcade...
...I, Nightmare, Lord of the Dream Dimension.
Hercules and his "God Squad" humiliated me during their war with the Skrull gods.*
Were he any other foe, I would simply spirit him away to my realm while he slept and torment him with his darkest fears and insecurities.
But the Lion of Olympus is...
<sigh>
...notoriously resistant to self-reflection...
SNIFF SNIFF
YOU SMELL SOME-THING?
And the unpredictability of Deadpool's insanity can never be fully accounted for in the engineering wizardry invested in your usual deathtraps, Arcade.
SNIFF SNIFF
NO.
So I have touched your mechanical genius with my sorcery of the sub-conscious to create this labyrinth.
Only by combining the left brain and right brain aspects of our powers shall we --
SSSSH! THEY DID IT! THEY REACHED THE CENTER!
I DON'T WANNA MISS A MOMENT OF THEM DYIN'!!
*In Incredible Hercules #118. - Editor

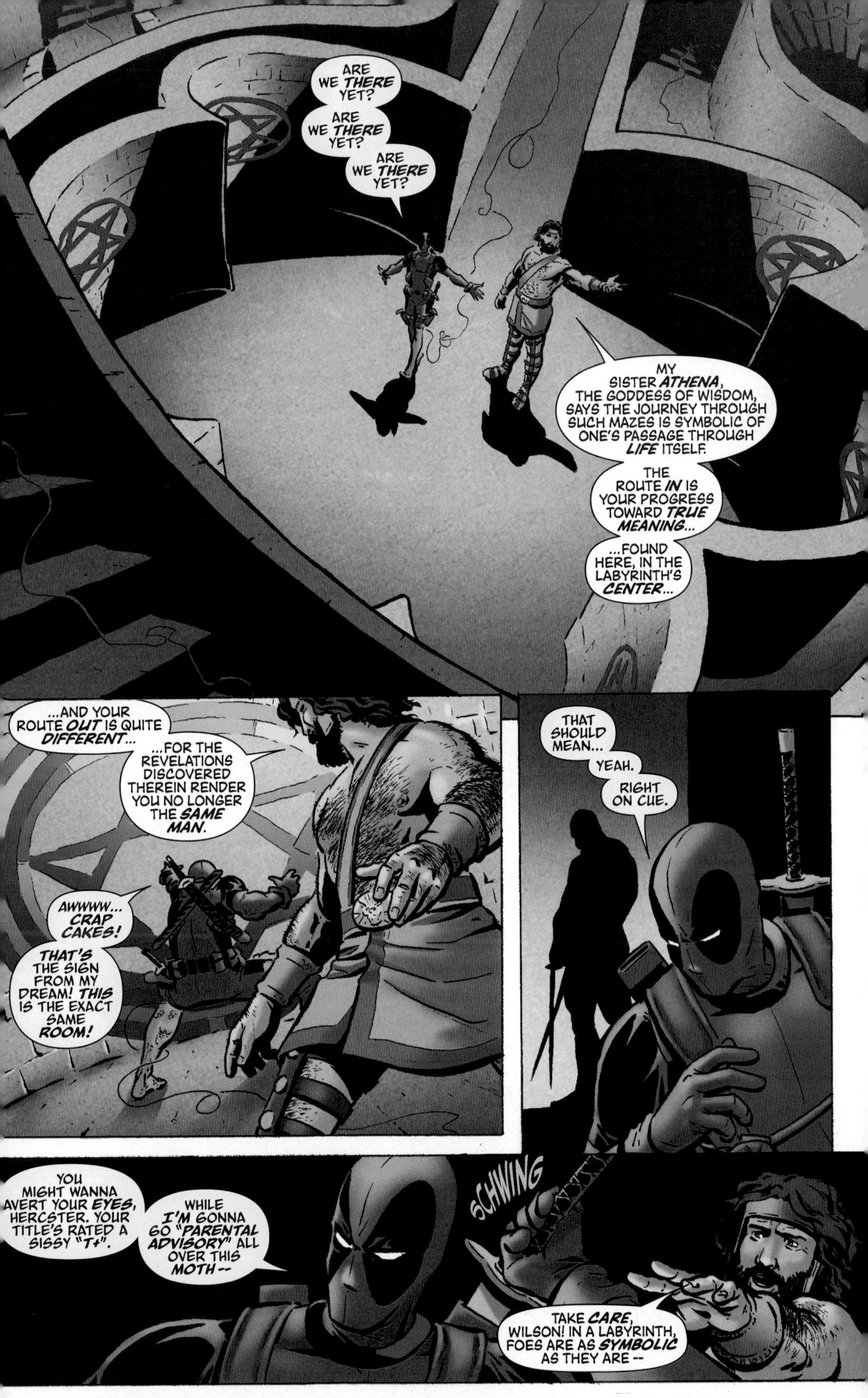
ARE WE THERE YET?
ARE WE THERE YET?
ARE WE THERE YET?
MY SISTER ATHENA, THE GODDESS OF WISDOM, SAYS THE JOURNEY THROUGH SUCH MAZES IS SYMBOLIC OF ONE'S PASSAGE THROUGH LIFE ITSELF.
THE ROUTE IN IS YOUR PROGRESS TOWARD TRUE MEANING...
...FOUND HERE, IN THE LABYRINTH'S CENTER...
...AND YOUR ROUTE OUT IS QUITE DIFFERENT...
...FOR THE REVELATIONS DISCOVERED THEREIN RENDER YOU NO LONGER THE SAME MAN.
AWWWW... CRAP CAKES!
THAT'S THE SIGN FROM MY DREAM! THIS IS THE EXACT SAME ROOM!
THAT SHOULD MEAN...
YEAH.
RIGHT ON CUE.
YOU MIGHT WANNA AVERT YOUR EYES, HERCSTER. YOUR TITLE'S RATED A SISSY "T+".
WHILE I'M GONNA GO "PARENTAL ADVISORY" ALL OVER THIS MOTH --
SCHWING
TAKE CARE, WILSON! IN A LABYRINTH, FOES ARE AS SYMBOLIC AS THEY ARE --

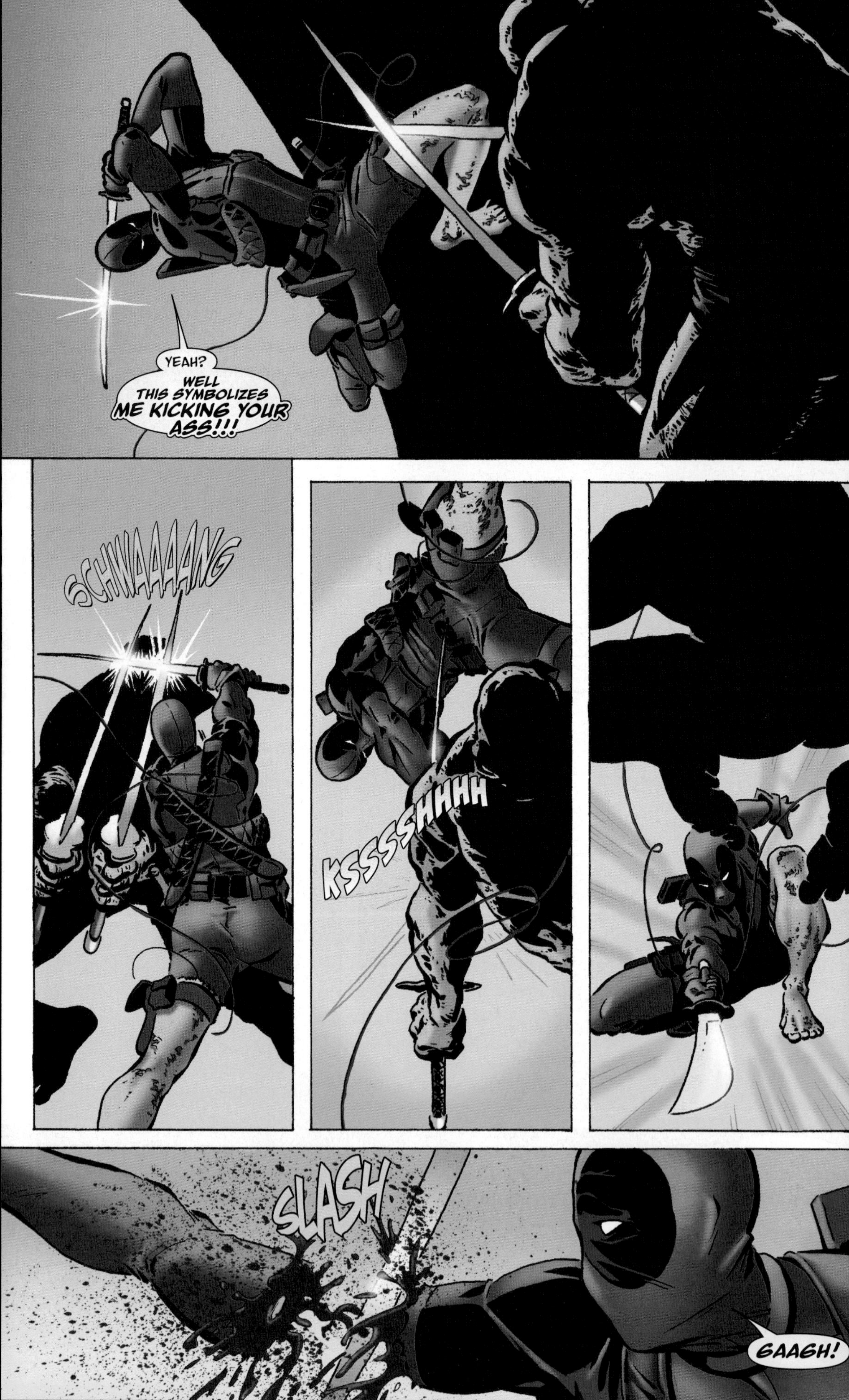
YEAH? WELL THIS SYMBOLIZES ME KICKING YOUR ASS!!!
SCHWAAAAANG
KSSSSSHHHH
SLASH
GAAGH!

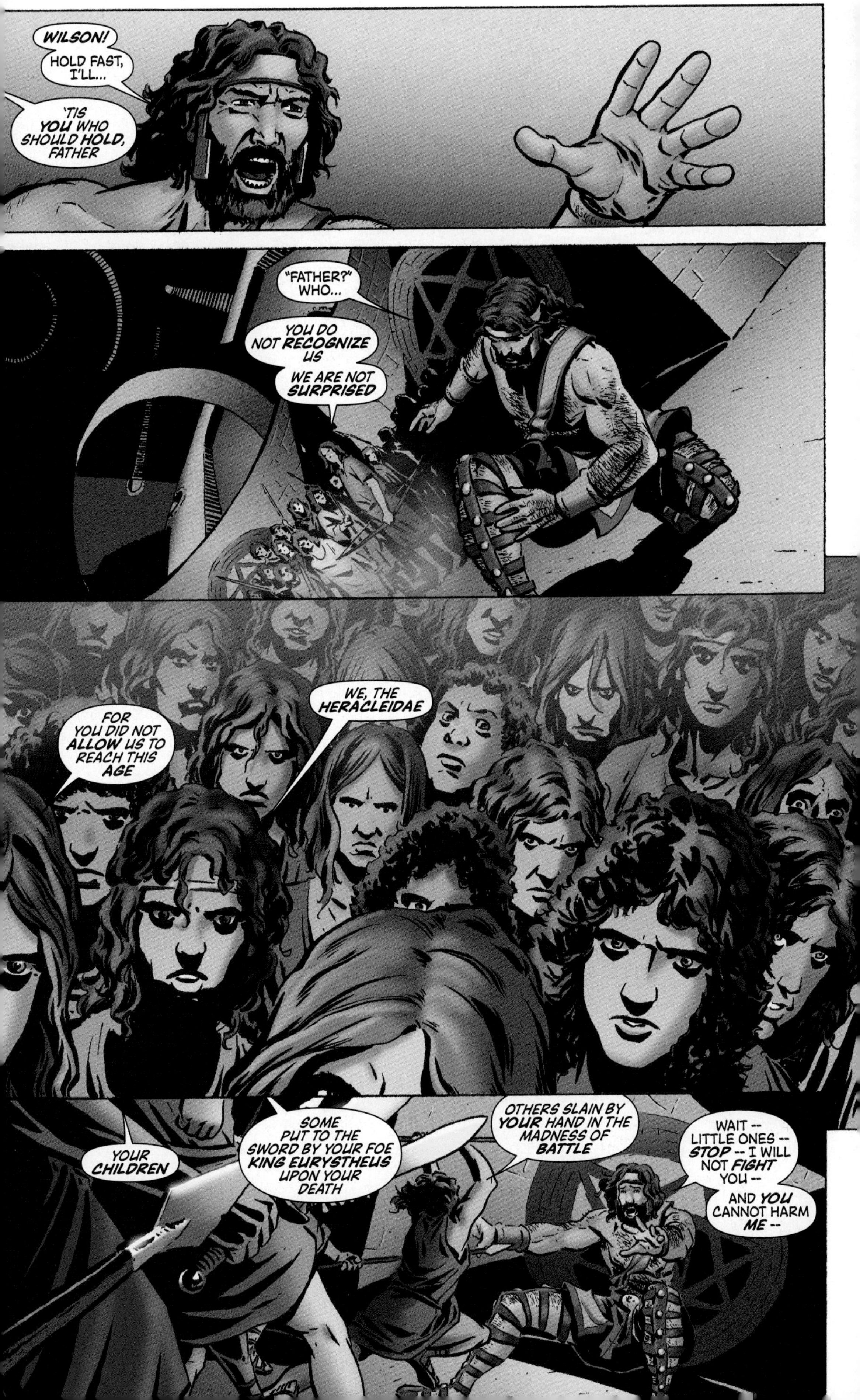
WILSON!
HOLD FAST, I'LL...
'TIS YOU WHO SHOULD HOLD, FATHER
"FATHER?" WHO...
YOU DO NOT RECOGNIZE US
WE ARE NOT SURPRISED
WE, THE HERACLEIDAE
FOR YOU DID NOT ALLOW US TO REACH THIS AGE
YOUR CHILDREN
SOME PUT TO THE SWORD BY YOUR FOE KING EURYSTHEUS UPON YOUR DEATH
OTHERS SLAIN BY YOUR HAND IN THE MADNESS OF BATTLE
WAIT -- LITTLE ONES -- STOP -- I WILL NOT FIGHT YOU --
AND YOU CANNOT HARM ME --

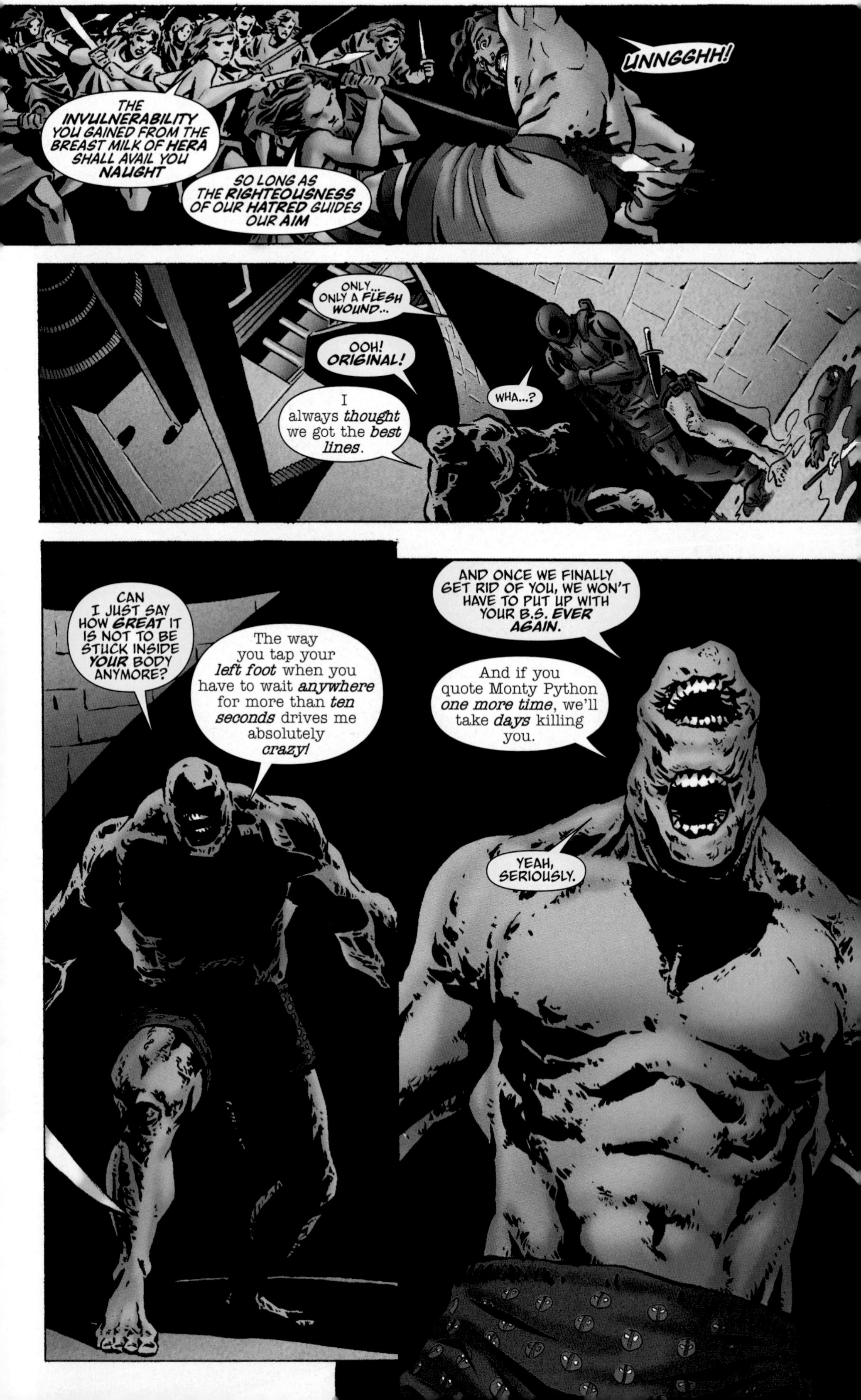

UNNGGHH!
THE INVULNERABILITY YOU GAINED FROM THE BREAST MILK OF HERA SHALL AVAIL YOU NAUGHT
SO LONG AS THE RIGHTEOUSNESS OF OUR HATRED GUIDES OUR AIM
ONLY... ONLY A FLESH WOUND...
OOH! ORIGINAL!
I always thought we got the best lines.
WHA...?
CAN I JUST SAY HOW GREAT IT IS NOT TO BE STUCK INSIDE YOUR BODY ANYMORE?
The way you tap your left foot when you have to wait anywhere for more than ten seconds drives me absolutely crazy!
AND ONCE WE FINALLY GET RID OF YOU, WE WON'T HAVE TO PUT UP WITH YOUR B.S. EVER AGAIN.
And if you quote Monty Python one more time, we'll take days killing you.
YEAH, SERIOUSLY.

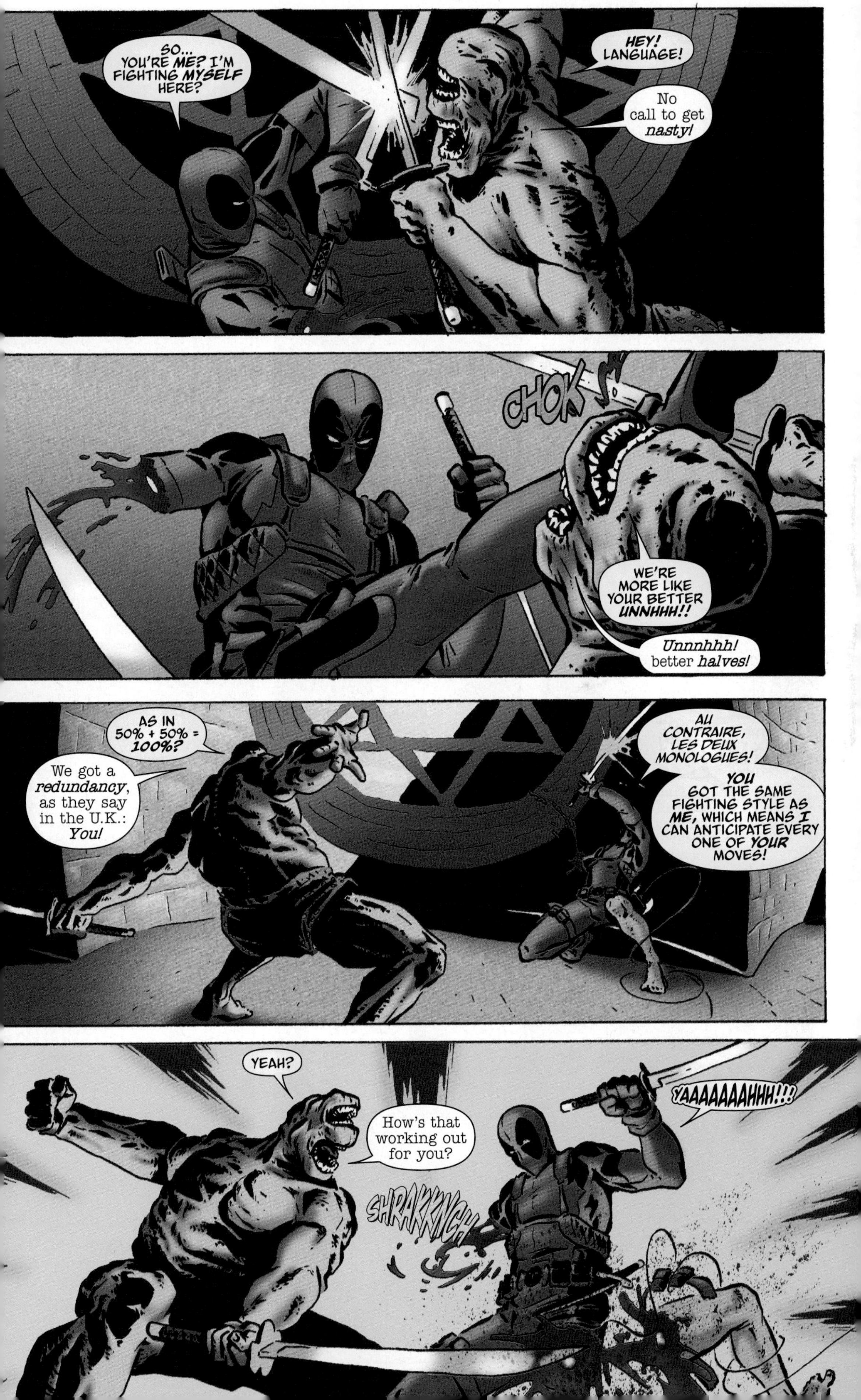
SO... YOU'RE ME? I'M FIGHTING MYSELF HERE?
HEY! LANGUAGE!
No call to get nasty!
CHOK
WE'RE MORE LIKE YOUR BETTER UNNHHH!!
Unnnhhh! better halves!
AS IN 50% + 50% = 100%?
We got a redundancy, as they say in the U.K.: You!
AU CONTRAIRE, LES DEUX MONOLOGUES!
YOU GOT THE SAME FIGHTING STYLE AS ME, WHICH MEANS I CAN ANTICIPATE EVERY ONE OF YOUR MOVES!
YEAH?
How's that working out for you?
YAAAAAAAHHH!!!
SHRAKKNCH

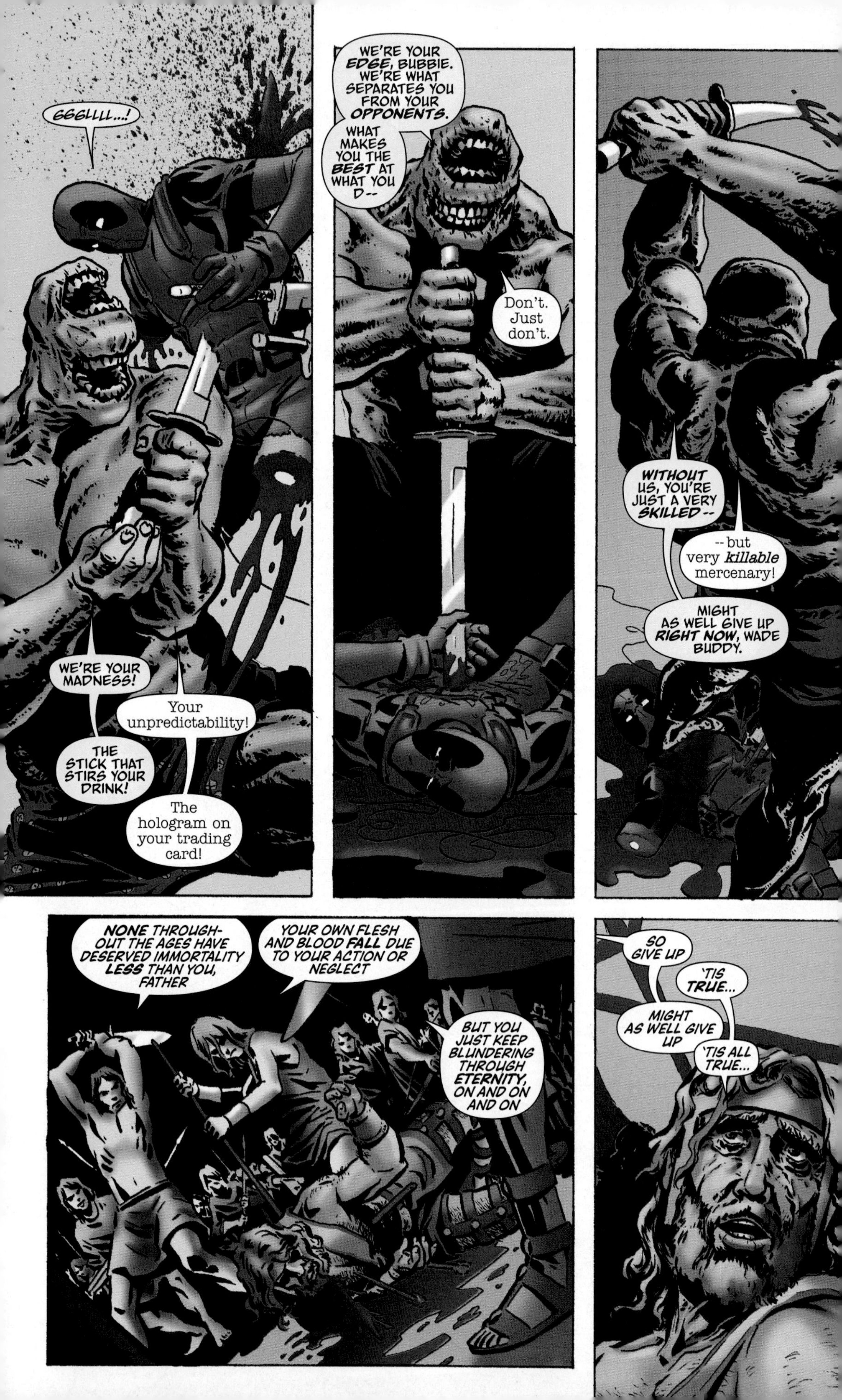
GGGLLLL...!
WE'RE YOUR MADNESS!
Your unpredictability!
THE STICK THAT STIRS YOUR DRINK!
The hologram on your trading card!
WE'RE YOUR EDGE, BUBBIE. WE'RE WHAT SEPARATES YOU FROM YOUR OPPONENTS.
WHAT MAKES YOU THE BEST AT WHAT YOU D--
Don't. Just don't.
WITHOUT US, YOU'RE JUST A VERY SKILLED --
--but very killable mercenary!
MIGHT AS WELL GIVE UP RIGHT NOW, WADE BUDDY.
NONE THROUGH-OUT THE AGES HAVE DESERVED IMMORTALITY LESS THAN YOU, FATHER
YOUR OWN FLESH AND BLOOD FALL DUE TO YOUR ACTION OR NEGLECT
BUT YOU JUST KEEP BLUNDERING THROUGH ETERNITY, ON AND ON AND ON
SO GIVE UP
'TIS TRUE...
MIGHT AS WELL GIVE UP
'TIS ALL TRUE...

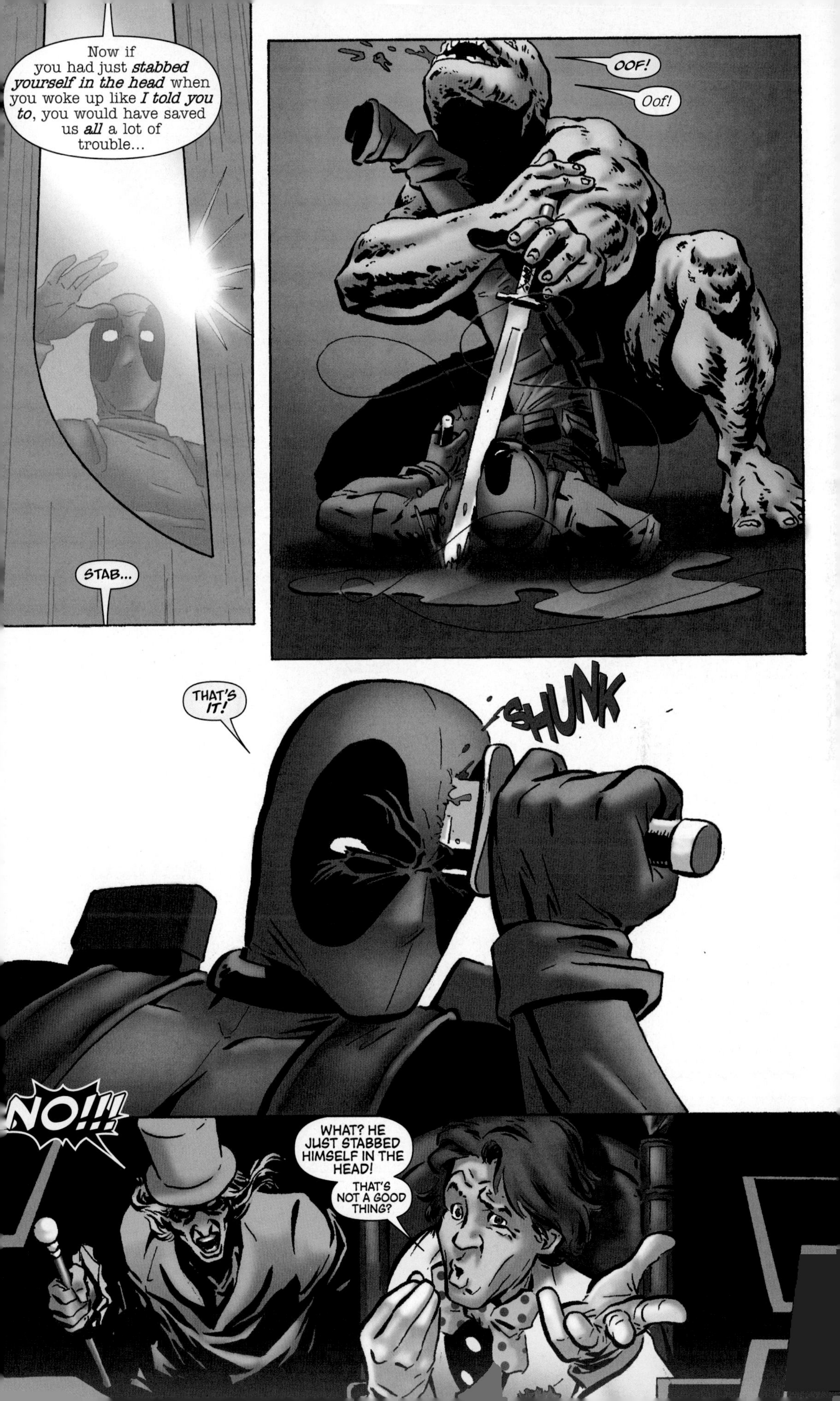

Now if you had just stabbed yourself in the head when you woke up like I told you to, you would have saved us all a lot of trouble...
STAB...
OOF!
Oof!
THAT'S IT!
SHUNK
NO!!!
WHAT? HE JUST STABBED HIMSELF IN THE HEAD!
THAT'S NOT A GOOD THING?

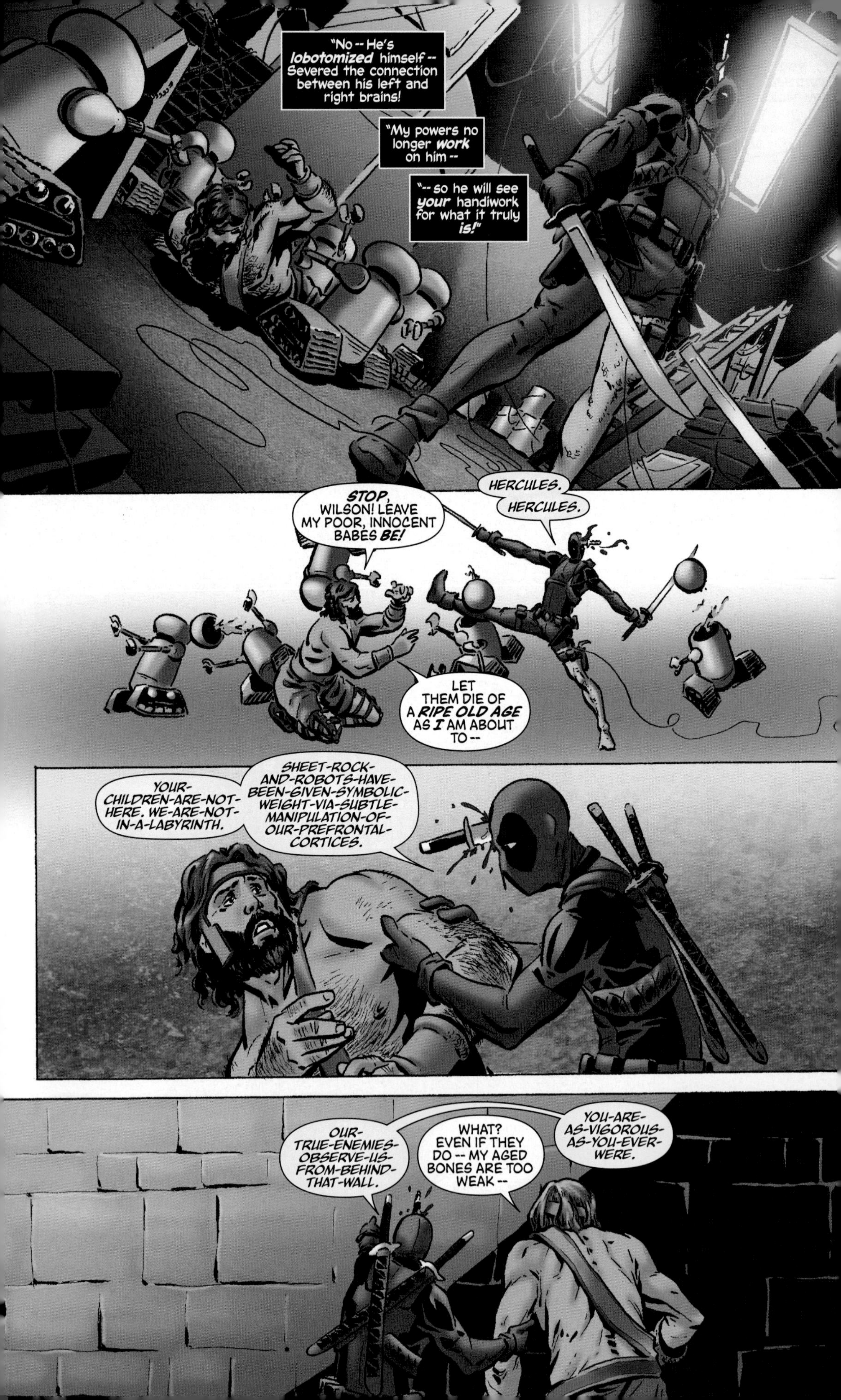
"No -- He's lobotomized himself -- Severed the connection between his left and right brains!
"My powers no longer work on him --
"-- so he will see your handiwork for what it truly is!"
STOP, WILSON! LEAVE MY POOR, INNOCENT BABES BE!
HERCULES. HERCULES.
LET THEM DIE OF A RIPE OLD AGE AS I AM ABOUT TO --
YOUR-CHILDREN-ARE-NOT-HERE. WE-ARE-NOT-IN-A-LABYRINTH.
SHEET-ROCK-AND-ROBOTS-HAVE-BEEN-GIVEN-SYMBOLIC-WEIGHT-VIA-SUBTLE-MANIPULATION-OF-OUR-PREFRONTAL-CORTICES.
OUR-TRUE-ENEMIES-OBSERVE-US-FROM-BEHIND-THAT-WALL.
WHAT? EVEN IF THEY DO -- MY AGED BONES ARE TOO WEAK --
YOU-ARE-AS-VIGOROUS-AS-YOU-EVER-WERE.

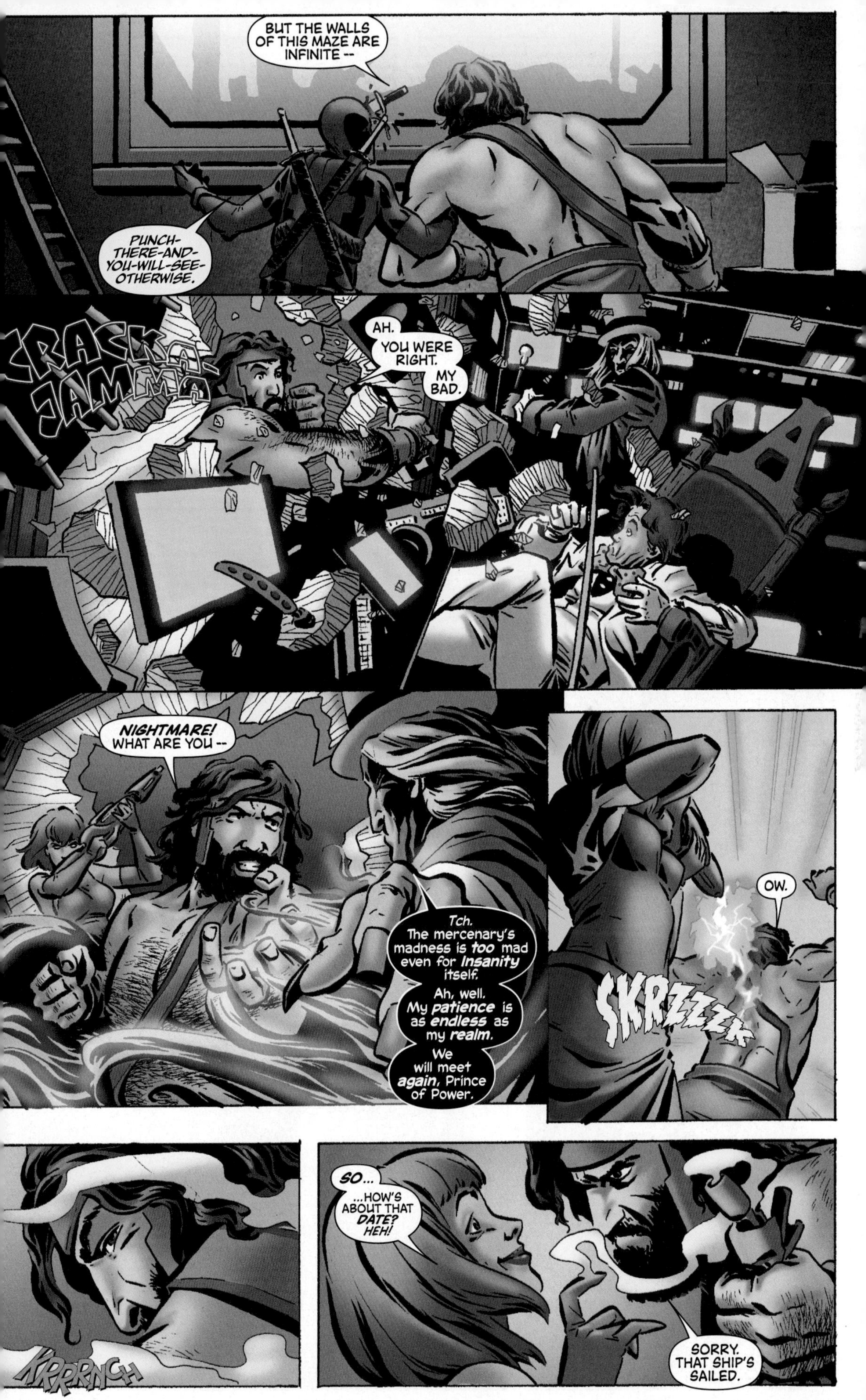
BUT THE WALLS OF THIS MAZE ARE INFINITE --
PUNCH-THERE-AND-YOU-WILL-SEE-OTHERWISE.
CRACKA-JAMMA
AH.
YOU WERE RIGHT.
MY BAD.
NIGHTMARE! WHAT ARE YOU --
Tch. The mercenary's madness is too mad even for Insanity itself.
Ah, well. My patience is as endless as my realm.
We will meet again, Prince of Power.
OW.
SKRZZZZK
KRRRNCH
SO...
...HOW'S ABOUT THAT DATE? HEH!
SORRY. THAT SHIP'S SAILED.

YOU KNOW THIS WEREN'T NOTHIN' *PERSONAL*, D.P. -- JUST ABOUT UPPIN' MY *MARKET SHARE!*

MY GUESS IS YOUR CRAZY VOICES WERE *ON* TO SOMETHING --

BANG

[INSERT WITTY NON SEQUITUR HERE]

-- SANS *PSYCHOSIS*, YOU AIN'T SO *TOUGH!*

PROING

[BREAKING 4TH WALL WITH AMUSING COMICS REFERENCE]

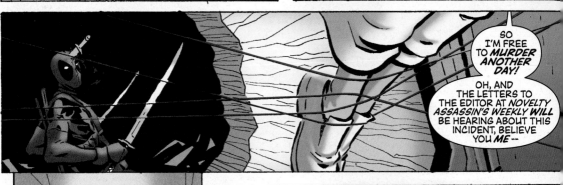

SO I'M FREE TO *MURDER ANOTHER DAY!*

OH, AND THE LETTERS TO THE EDITOR AT *NOVELTY ASSASSIN'S WEEKLY* WILL BE HEARING ABOUT THIS INCIDENT, BELIEVE YOU *ME* --

KZOOONG

THANKS TO YOUR *QUICK THINKING* WE HAVE *CARRIED THE DAY,* FRIEND WILSON!

TELL ME...THE *KNIFE* IN YOUR HEAD...DOES IT *HURT?*

I-THINK-THAT-RUSH-LIMBAUGH-AND-SEAN-HANNITY-ACTUALLY-MAKE-A-LOT-OF-VALID-POINTS.

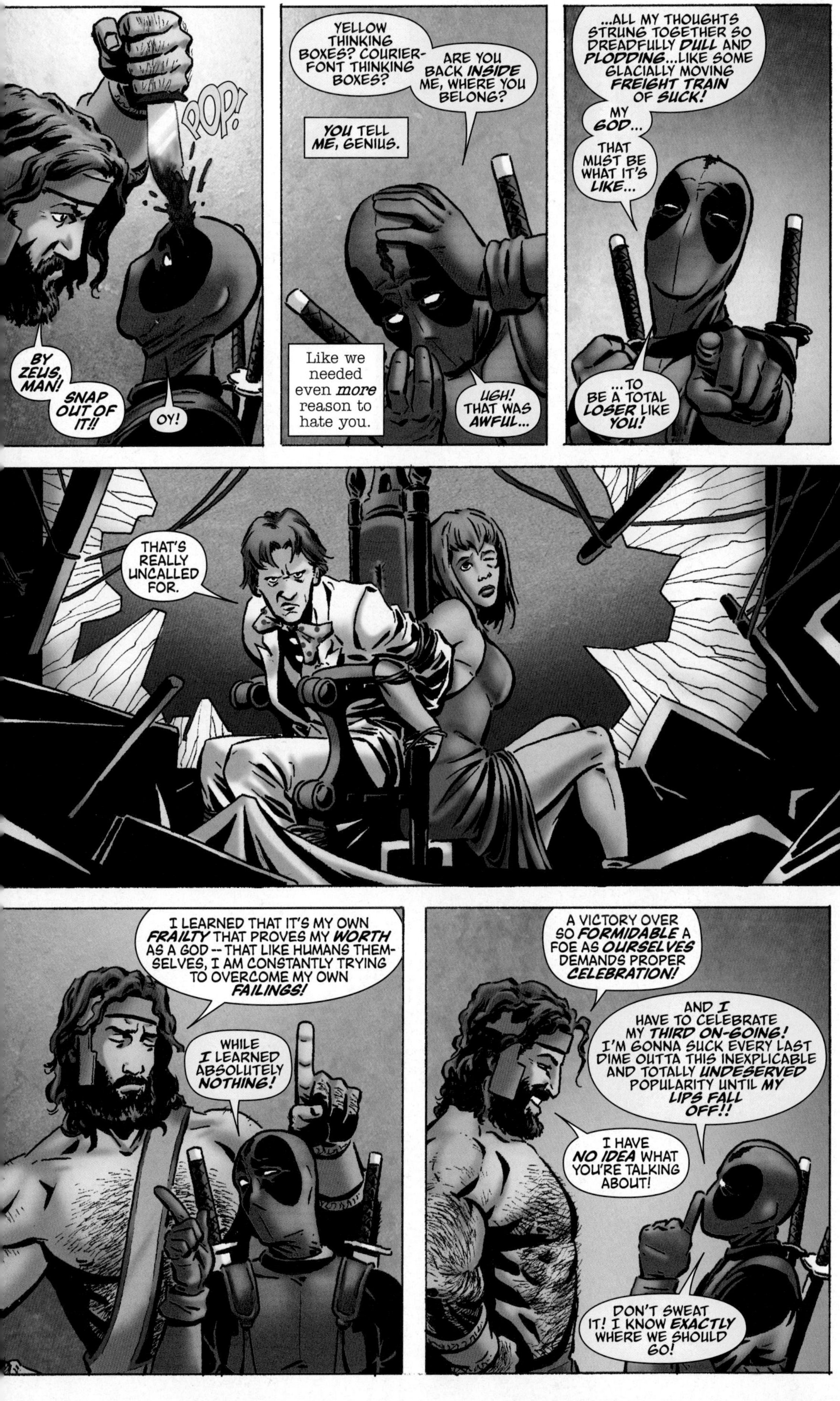
POP!
BY ZEUS, MAN! SNAP OUT OF IT!!
OY!
YELLOW THINKING BOXES? COURIER-FONT THINKING BOXES?
ARE YOU BACK INSIDE ME, WHERE YOU BELONG?
YOU TELL ME, GENIUS.
Like we needed even more reason to hate you.
UGH! THAT WAS AWFUL...
...ALL MY THOUGHTS STRUNG TOGETHER SO DREADFULLY DULL AND PLODDING...LIKE SOME GLACIALLY MOVING FREIGHT TRAIN OF SUCK!
MY GOD...
THAT MUST BE WHAT IT'S LIKE...
...TO BE A TOTAL LOSER LIKE YOU!
THAT'S REALLY UNCALLED FOR.
I LEARNED THAT IT'S MY OWN FRAILTY THAT PROVES MY WORTH AS A GOD -- THAT LIKE HUMANS THEMSELVES, I AM CONSTANTLY TRYING TO OVERCOME MY OWN FAILINGS!
WHILE I LEARNED ABSOLUTELY NOTHING!
A VICTORY OVER SO FORMIDABLE A FOE AS OURSELVES DEMANDS PROPER CELEBRATION!
AND I HAVE TO CELEBRATE MY THIRD ON-GOING! I'M GONNA SUCK EVERY LAST DIME OUTTA THIS INEXPLICABLE AND TOTALLY UNDESERVED POPULARITY UNTIL MY LIPS FALL OFF!!
I HAVE NO IDEA WHAT YOU'RE TALKING ABOUT!
DON'T SWEAT IT! I KNOW EXACTLY WHERE WE SHOULD GO!

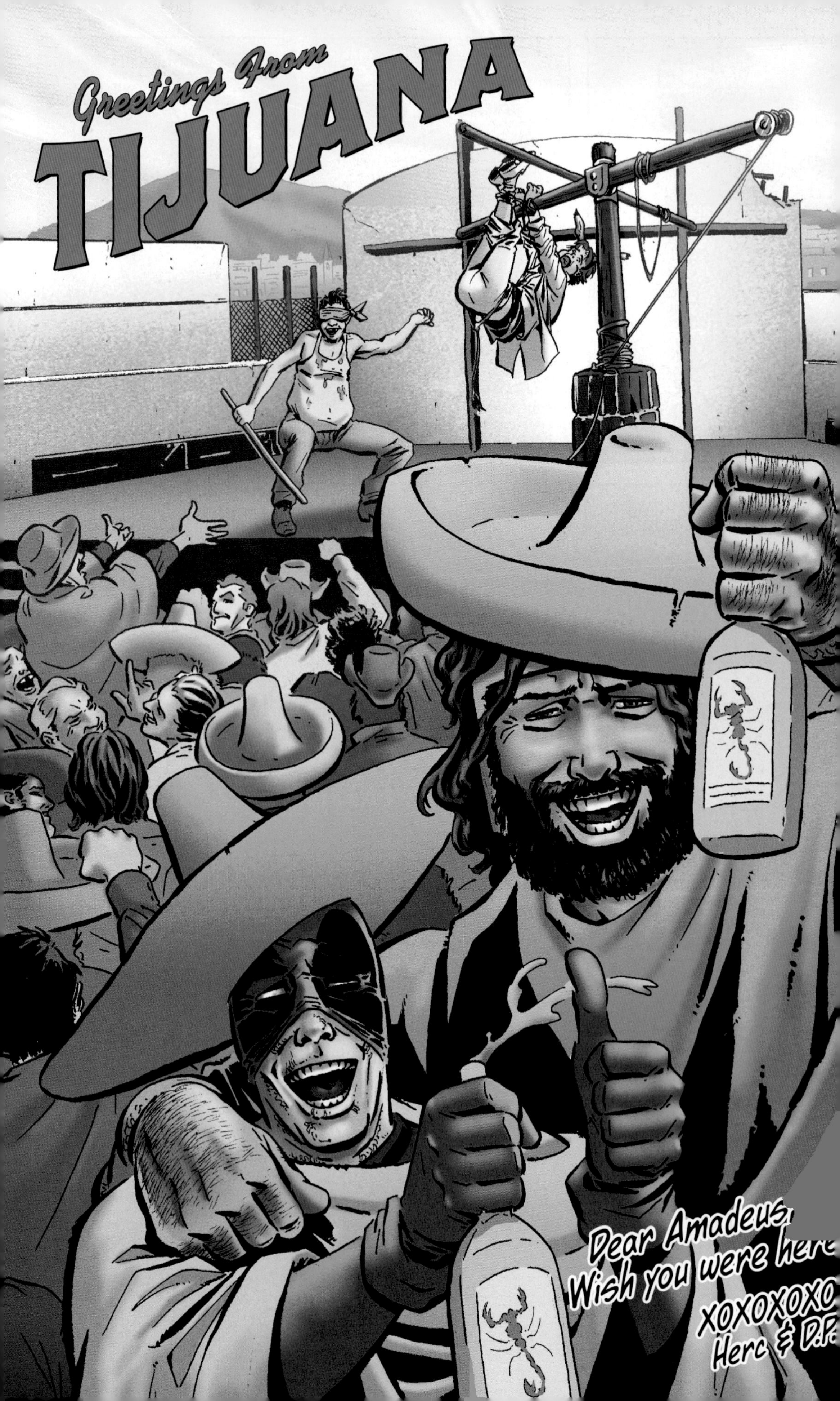
Greetings From
TIJUANA
Dear Amadeus,
Wish you were here
XOXOXOXO
Herc & D.P.

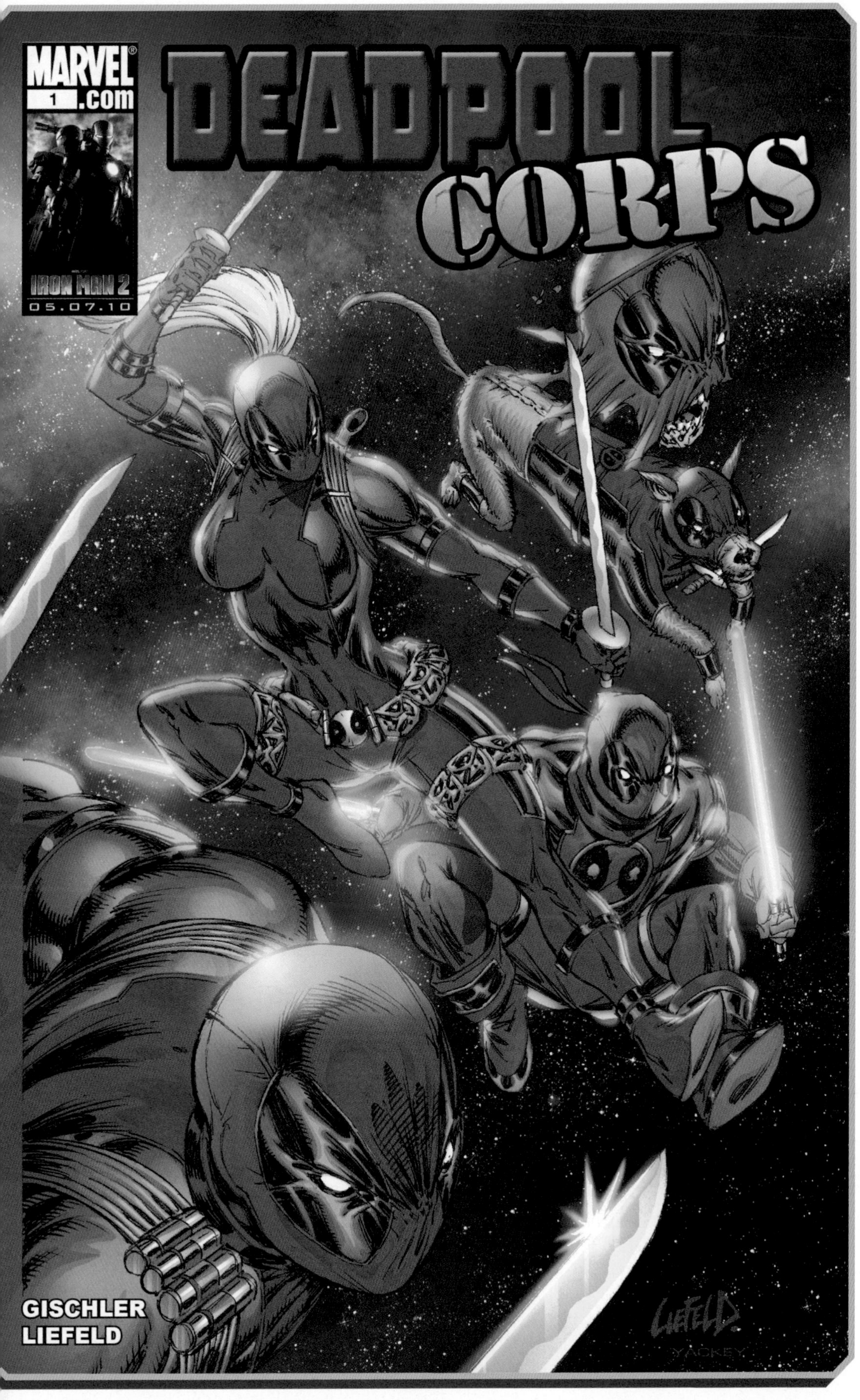

MARVEL
1 .com
IRON MAN 2
05.07.10
DEADPOOL
CORPS
GISCHLER
LIEFELD
LIEFELD

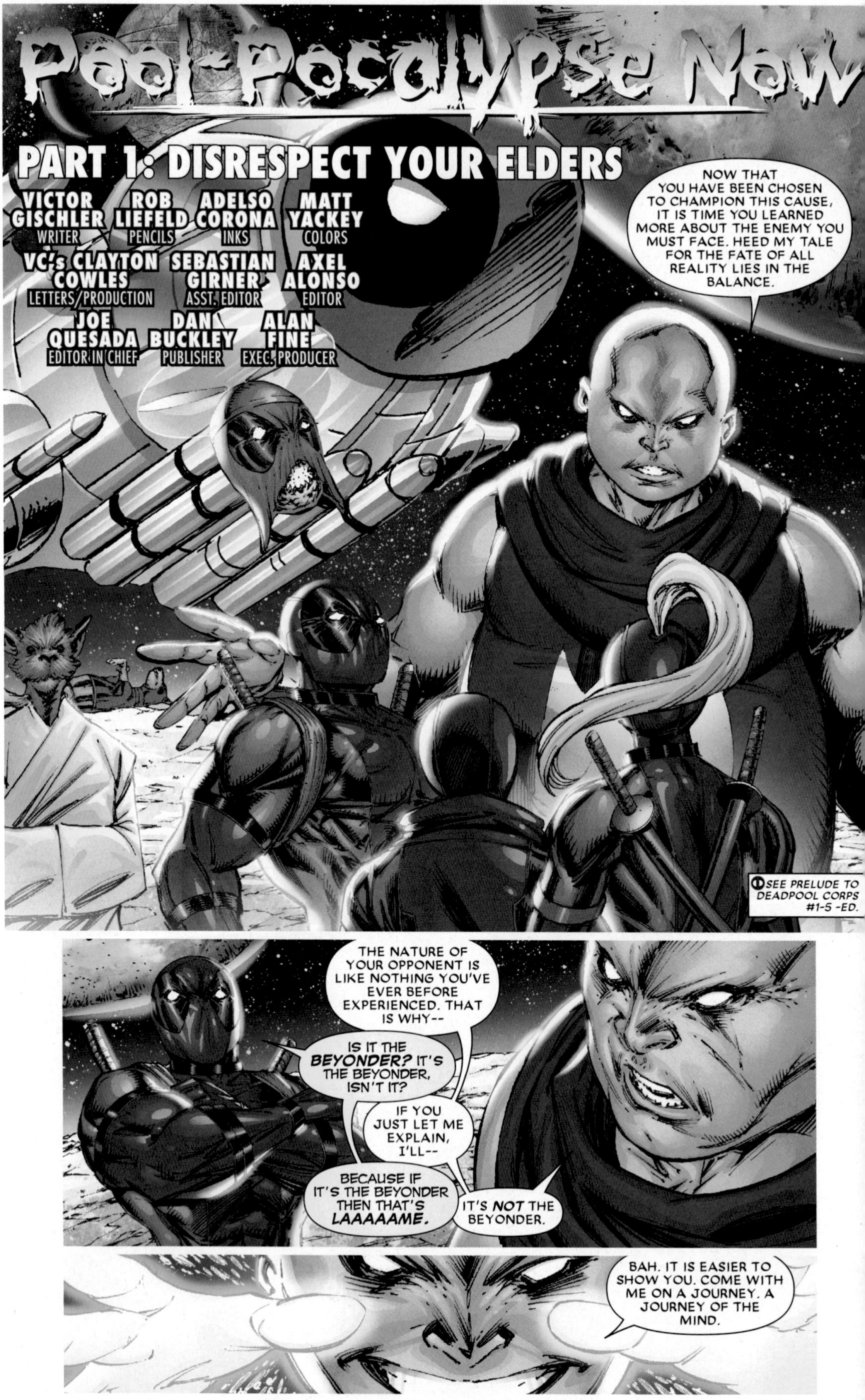
Pool-Pocalypse Now
PART 1: DISRESPECT YOUR ELDERS
VICTOR GISCHLER WRITER
ROB LIEFELD PENCILS
ADELSO CORONA INKS
MATT YACKEY COLORS
VC's CLAYTON COWLES LETTERS/PRODUCTION
SEBASTIAN GIRNER ASST. EDITOR
AXEL ALONSO EDITOR
JOE QUESADA EDITOR IN CHIEF
DAN BUCKLEY PUBLISHER
ALAN FINE EXEC. PRODUCER
NOW THAT YOU HAVE BEEN CHOSEN TO CHAMPION THIS CAUSE, IT IS TIME YOU LEARNED MORE ABOUT THE ENEMY YOU MUST FACE. HEED MY TALE FOR THE FATE OF ALL REALITY LIES IN THE BALANCE.
SEE PRELUDE TO DEADPOOL CORPS #1-5 -ED.
THE NATURE OF YOUR OPPONENT IS LIKE NOTHING YOU'VE EVER BEFORE EXPERIENCED. THAT IS WHY--
IS IT THE BEYONDER? IT'S THE BEYONDER, ISN'T IT?
IF YOU JUST LET ME EXPLAIN, I'LL--
BECAUSE IF IT'S THE BEYONDER THEN THAT'S LAAAAAME.
IT'S NOT THE BEYONDER.
BAH. IT IS EASIER TO SHOW YOU. COME WITH ME ON A JOURNEY. A JOURNEY OF THE MIND.

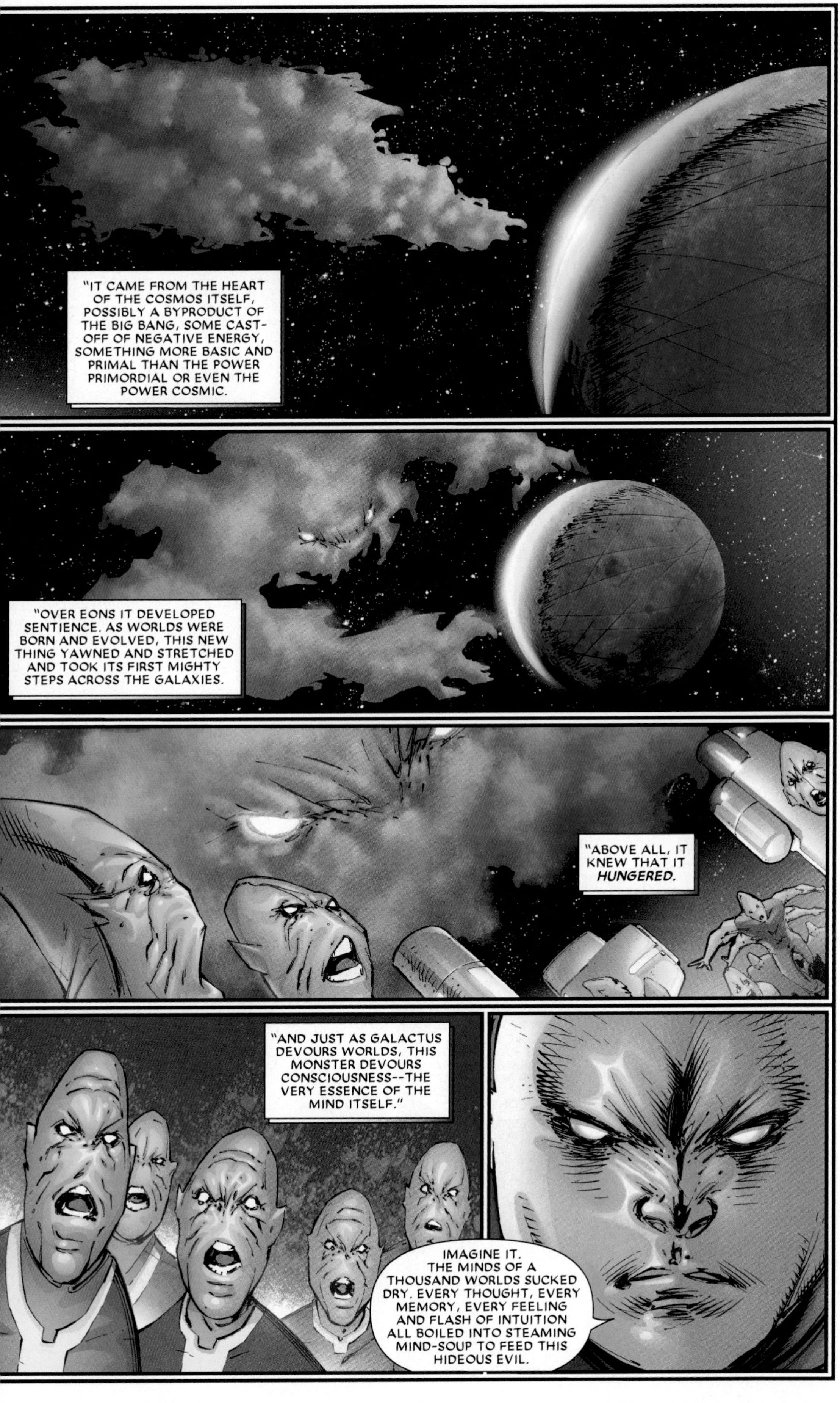
"IT CAME FROM THE HEART OF THE COSMOS ITSELF, POSSIBLY A BYPRODUCT OF THE BIG BANG, SOME CAST-OFF OF NEGATIVE ENERGY, SOMETHING MORE BASIC AND PRIMAL THAN THE POWER PRIMORDIAL OR EVEN THE POWER COSMIC.
"OVER EONS IT DEVELOPED SENTIENCE. AS WORLDS WERE BORN AND EVOLVED, THIS NEW THING YAWNED AND STRETCHED AND TOOK ITS FIRST MIGHTY STEPS ACROSS THE GALAXIES.
"ABOVE ALL, IT KNEW THAT IT *HUNGERED.*
"AND JUST AS GALACTUS DEVOURS WORLDS, THIS MONSTER DEVOURS CONSCIOUSNESS--THE VERY ESSENCE OF THE MIND ITSELF."
IMAGINE IT. THE MINDS OF A THOUSAND WORLDS SUCKED DRY. EVERY THOUGHT, EVERY MEMORY, EVERY FEELING AND FLASH OF INTUITION ALL BOILED INTO STEAMING MIND-SOUP TO FEED THIS HIDEOUS EVIL.

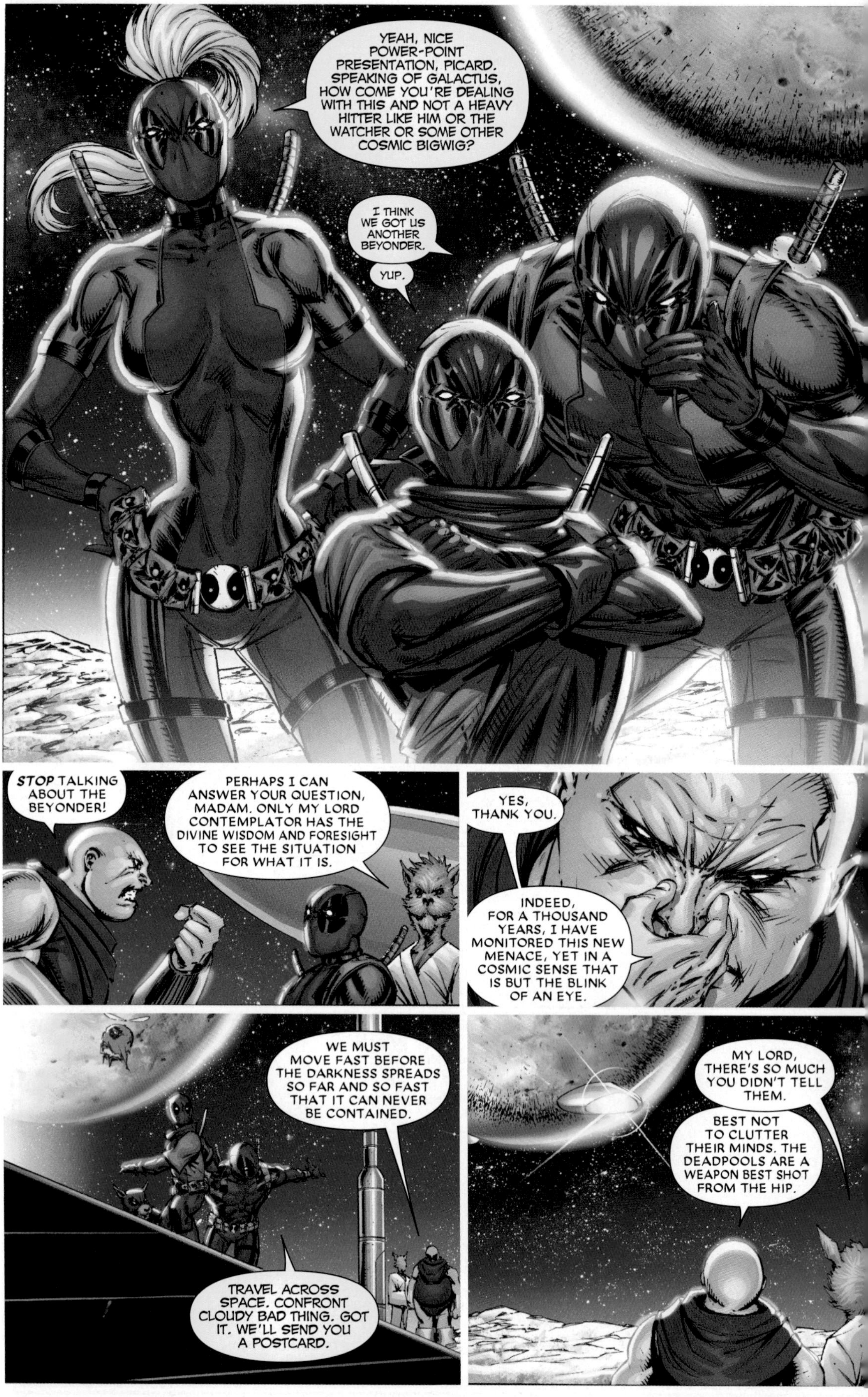
YEAH, NICE POWER-POINT PRESENTATION, PICARD. SPEAKING OF GALACTUS, HOW COME YOU'RE DEALING WITH THIS AND NOT A HEAVY HITTER LIKE HIM OR THE WATCHER OR SOME OTHER COSMIC BIGWIG?
I THINK WE GOT US ANOTHER BEYONDER.
YUP.
STOP TALKING ABOUT THE BEYONDER!
PERHAPS I CAN ANSWER YOUR QUESTION, MADAM. ONLY MY LORD CONTEMPLATOR HAS THE DIVINE WISDOM AND FORESIGHT TO SEE THE SITUATION FOR WHAT IT IS.
YES, THANK YOU.
INDEED, FOR A THOUSAND YEARS, I HAVE MONITORED THIS NEW MENACE, YET IN A COSMIC SENSE THAT IS BUT THE BLINK OF AN EYE.
WE MUST MOVE FAST BEFORE THE DARKNESS SPREADS SO FAR AND SO FAST THAT IT CAN NEVER BE CONTAINED.
TRAVEL ACROSS SPACE. CONFRONT CLOUDY BAD THING. GOT IT. WE'LL SEND YOU A POSTCARD.
MY LORD, THERE'S SO MUCH YOU DIDN'T TELL THEM.
BEST NOT TO CLUTTER THEIR MINDS. THE DEADPOOLS ARE A WEAPON BEST SHOT FROM THE HIP.

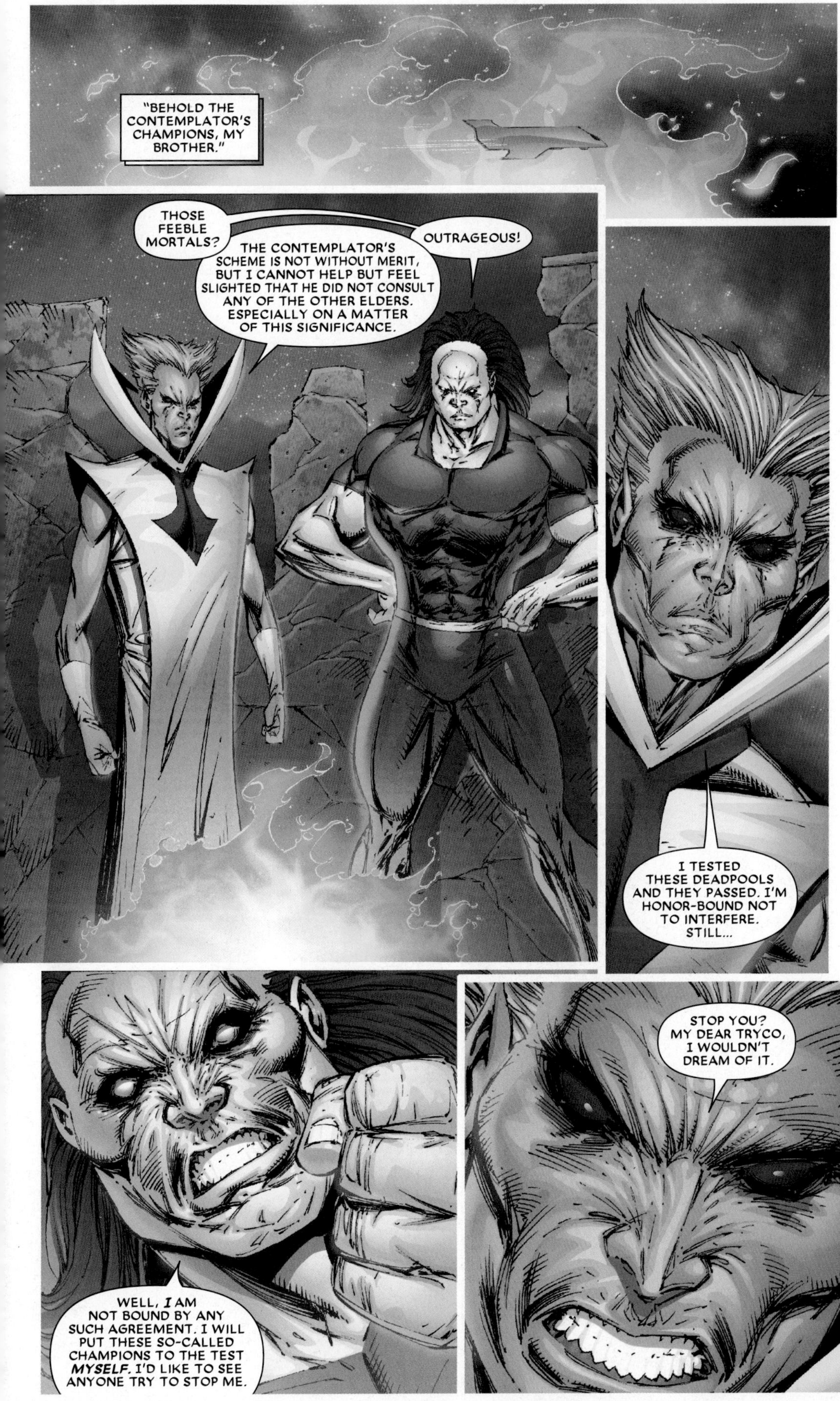
"BEHOLD THE CONTEMPLATOR'S CHAMPIONS, MY BROTHER."
THOSE FEEBLE MORTALS?
OUTRAGEOUS!
THE CONTEMPLATOR'S SCHEME IS NOT WITHOUT MERIT, BUT I CANNOT HELP BUT FEEL SLIGHTED THAT HE DID NOT CONSULT ANY OF THE OTHER ELDERS. ESPECIALLY ON A MATTER OF THIS SIGNIFICANCE.
I TESTED THESE DEADPOOLS AND THEY PASSED. I'M HONOR-BOUND NOT TO INTERFERE. STILL...
WELL, *I* AM NOT BOUND BY ANY SUCH AGREEMENT. I WILL PUT THESE SO-CALLED CHAMPIONS TO THE TEST ***MYSELF***. I'D LIKE TO SEE ANYONE TRY TO STOP ME.
STOP YOU? MY DEAR TRYCO, I WOULDN'T DREAM OF IT.

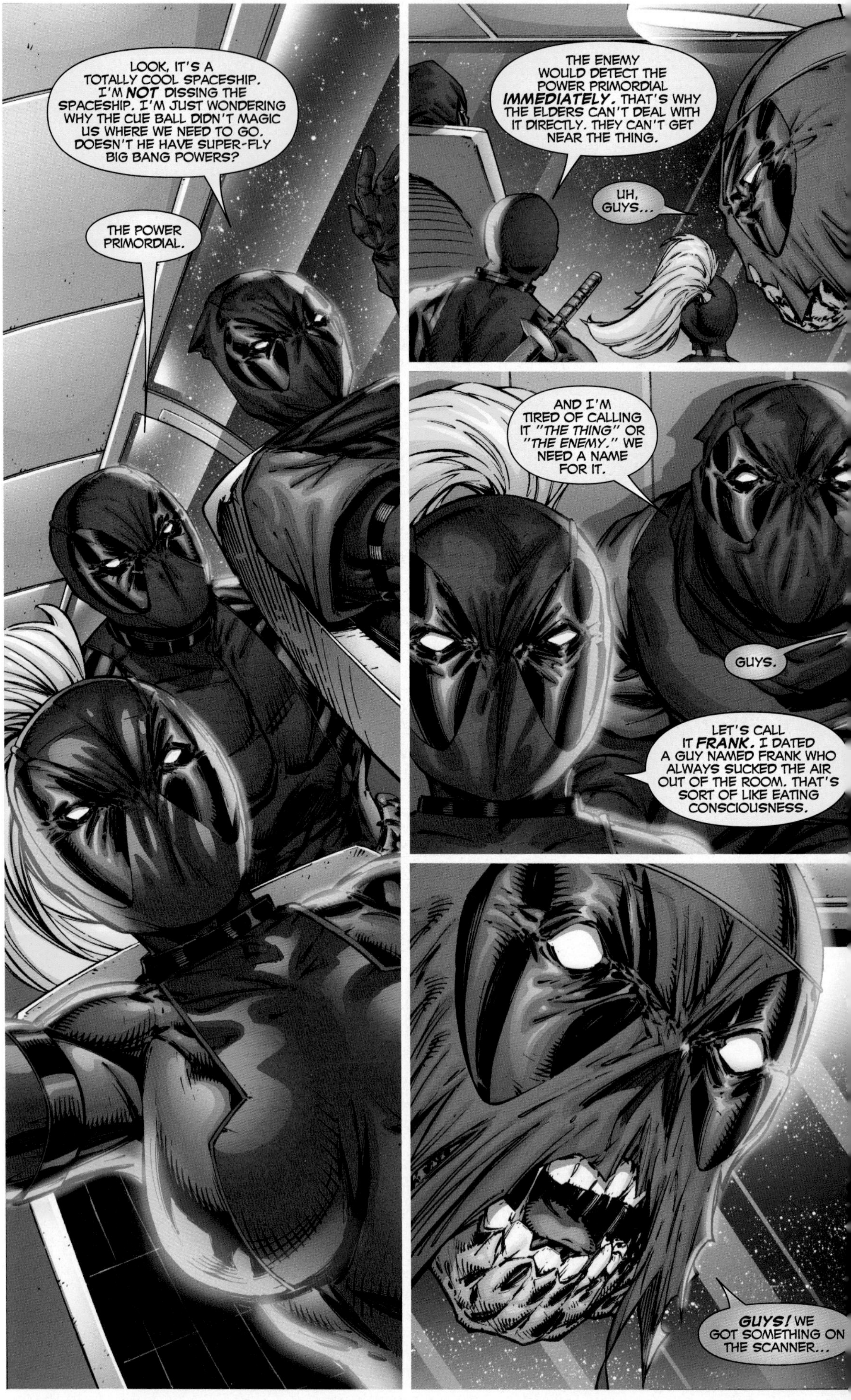
LOOK, IT'S A TOTALLY COOL SPACESHIP. I'M **NOT** DISSING THE SPACESHIP. I'M JUST WONDERING WHY THE CUE BALL DIDN'T MAGIC US WHERE WE NEED TO GO. DOESN'T HE HAVE SUPER-FLY BIG BANG POWERS?
THE POWER PRIMORDIAL.
THE ENEMY WOULD DETECT THE POWER PRIMORDIAL ***IMMEDIATELY.*** THAT'S WHY THE ELDERS CAN'T DEAL WITH IT DIRECTLY. THEY CAN'T GET NEAR THE THING.
UH, GUYS...
AND I'M TIRED OF CALLING IT *"THE THING"* OR *"THE ENEMY."* WE NEED A NAME FOR IT.
GUYS.
LET'S CALL IT **FRANK.** I DATED A GUY NAMED FRANK WHO ALWAYS SUCKED THE AIR OUT OF THE ROOM. THAT'S SORT OF LIKE EATING CONSCIOUSNESS.
GUYS! WE GOT SOMETHING ON THE SCANNER...

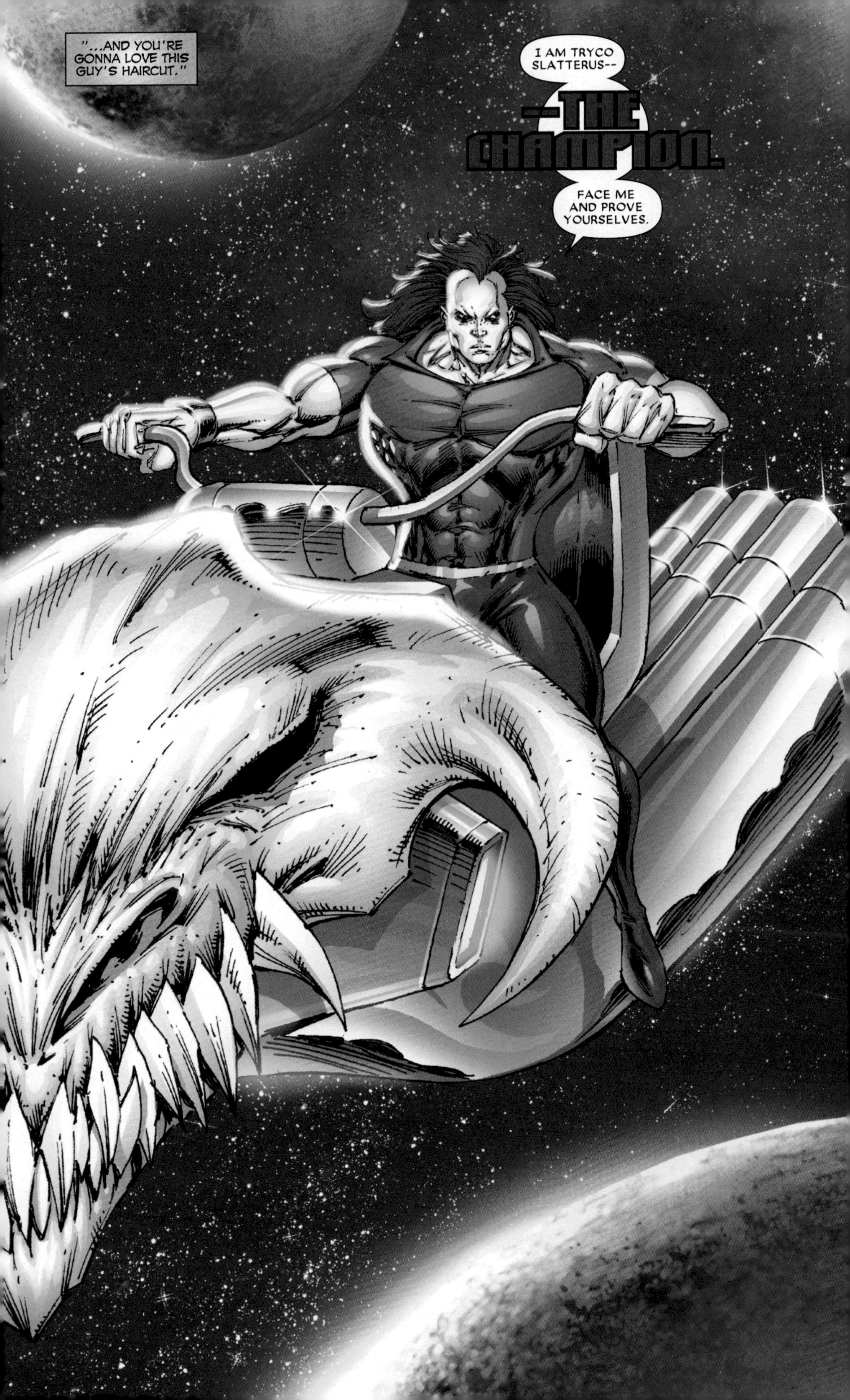
"...AND YOU'RE GONNA LOVE THIS GUY'S HAIRCUT."
I AM TRYCO SLATTERUS--
--THE CHAMPION.
FACE ME AND PROVE YOURSELVES.

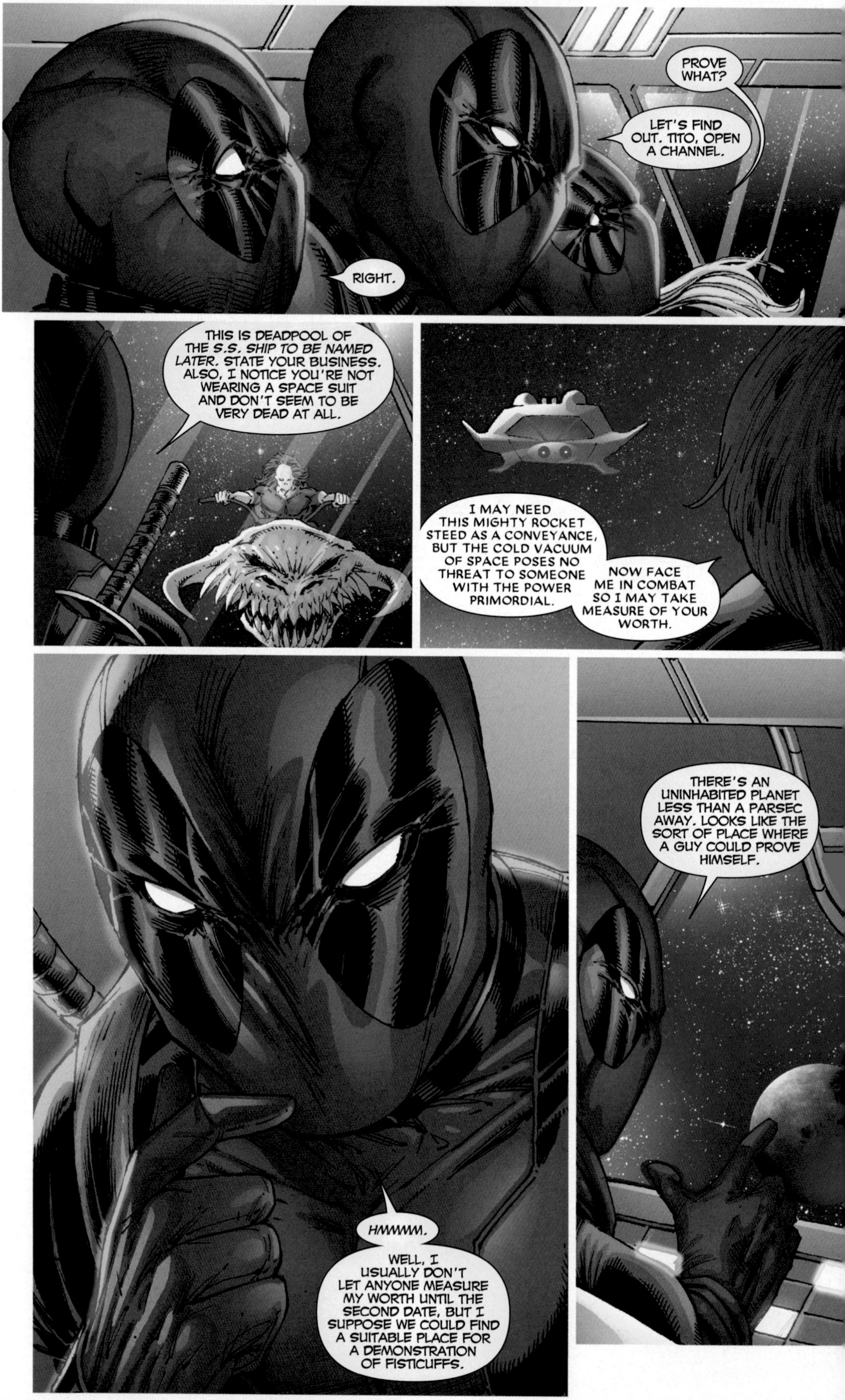
PROVE WHAT?
LET'S FIND OUT. TITO, OPEN A CHANNEL.
RIGHT.
THIS IS DEADPOOL OF THE S.S. SHIP TO BE NAMED LATER. STATE YOUR BUSINESS. ALSO, I NOTICE YOU'RE NOT WEARING A SPACE SUIT AND DON'T SEEM TO BE VERY DEAD AT ALL.
I MAY NEED THIS MIGHTY ROCKET STEED AS A CONVEYANCE, BUT THE COLD VACUUM OF SPACE POSES NO THREAT TO SOMEONE WITH THE POWER PRIMORDIAL.
NOW FACE ME IN COMBAT SO I MAY TAKE MEASURE OF YOUR WORTH.
HMMMM.
WELL, I USUALLY DON'T LET ANYONE MEASURE MY WORTH UNTIL THE SECOND DATE, BUT I SUPPOSE WE COULD FIND A SUITABLE PLACE FOR A DEMONSTRATION OF FISTICUFFS.
THERE'S AN UNINHABITED PLANET LESS THAN A PARSEC AWAY. LOOKS LIKE THE SORT OF PLACE WHERE A GUY COULD PROVE HIMSELF.

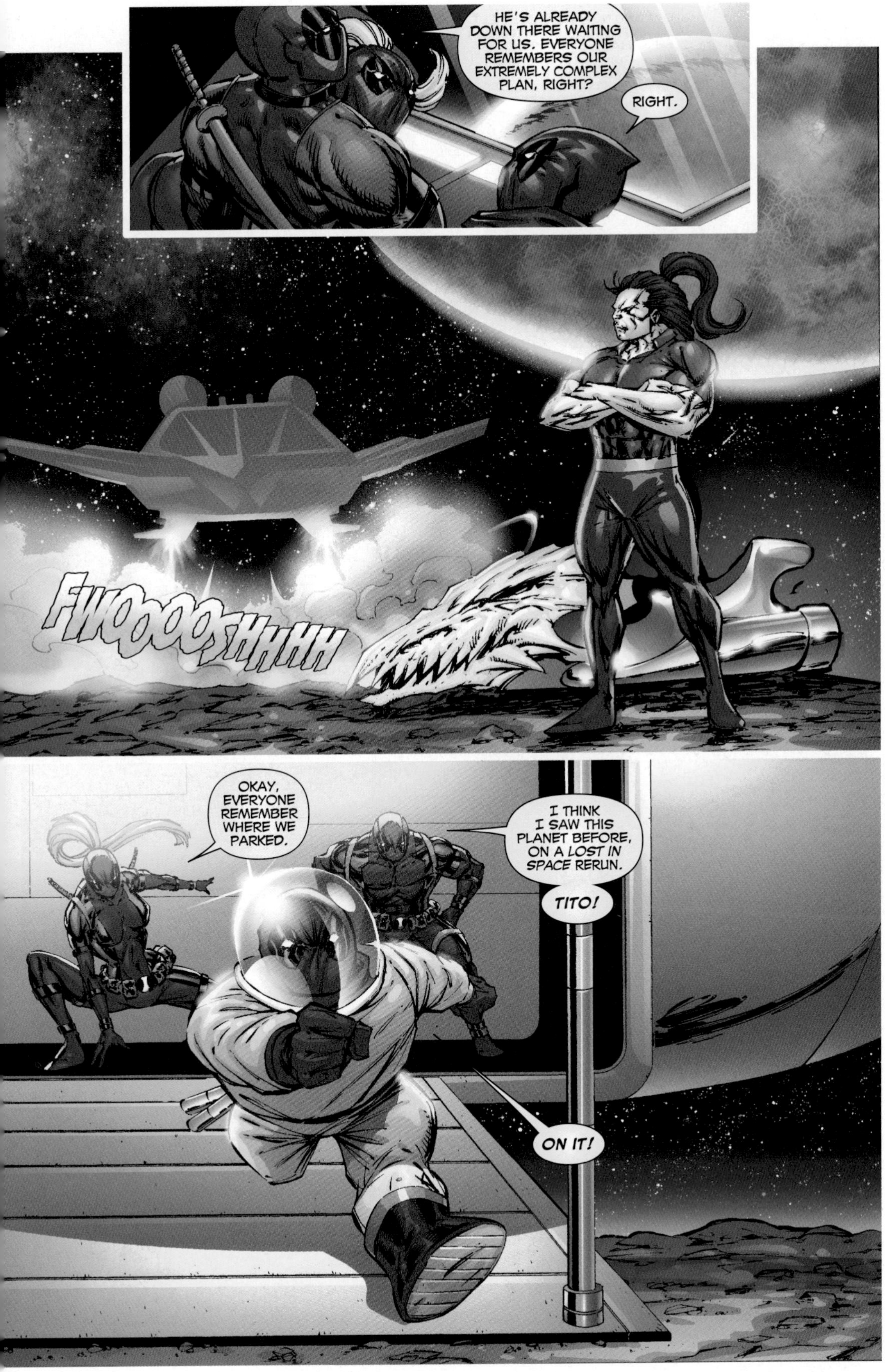
HE'S ALREADY DOWN THERE WAITING FOR US. EVERYONE REMEMBERS OUR EXTREMELY COMPLEX PLAN, RIGHT?
RIGHT.
FWOOOOOSHHHHH
OKAY, EVERYONE REMEMBER WHERE WE PARKED.
I THINK I SAW THIS PLANET BEFORE, ON A *LOST IN SPACE* RERUN.
TITO!
ON IT!

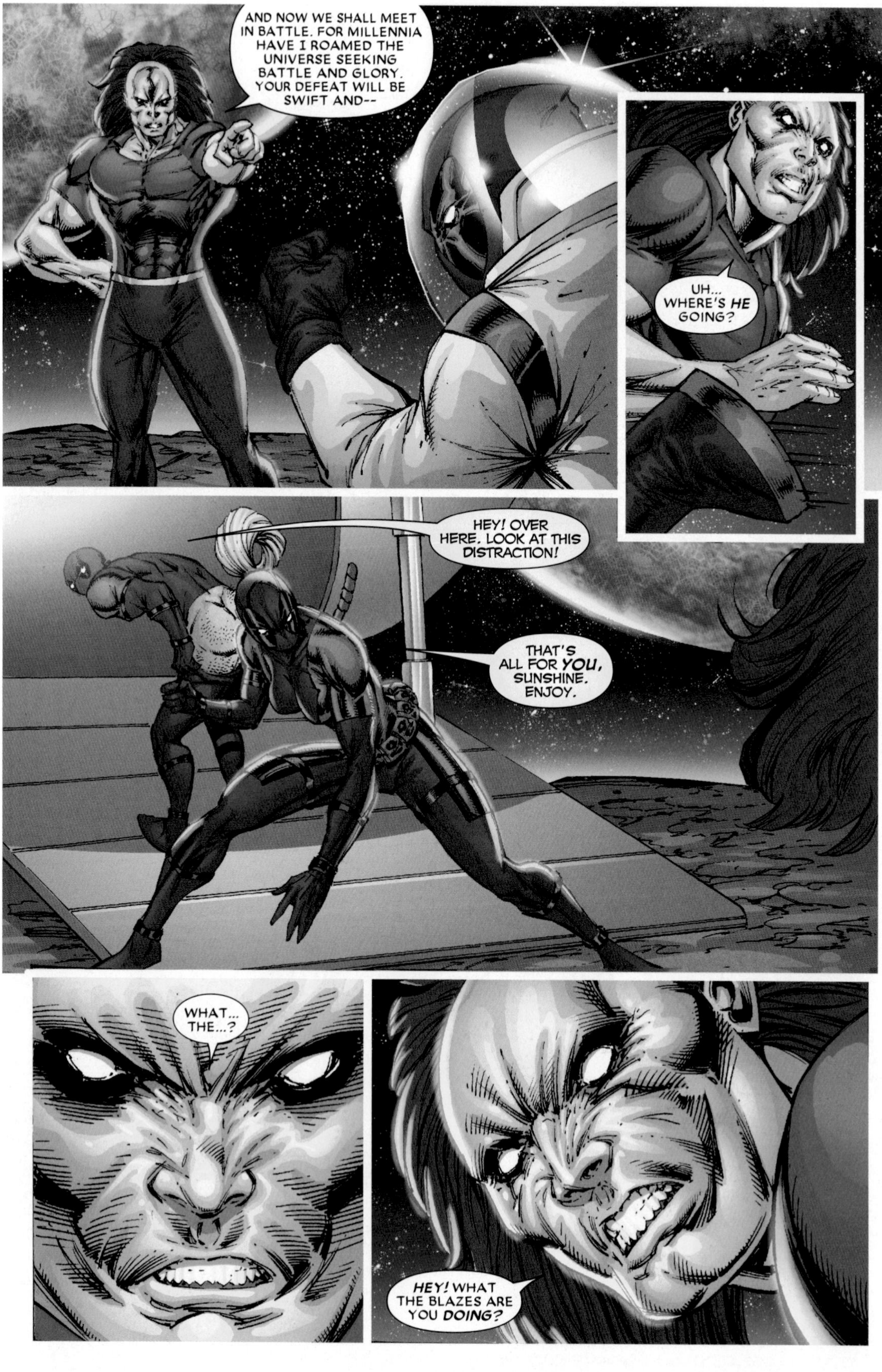
AND NOW WE SHALL MEET IN BATTLE. FOR MILLENNIA HAVE I ROAMED THE UNIVERSE SEEKING BATTLE AND GLORY. YOUR DEFEAT WILL BE SWIFT AND--
UH... WHERE'S HE GOING?
HEY! OVER HERE. LOOK AT THIS DISTRACTION!
THAT'S ALL FOR YOU, SUNSHINE. ENJOY.
WHAT... THE...?
HEY! WHAT THE BLAZES ARE YOU DOING?

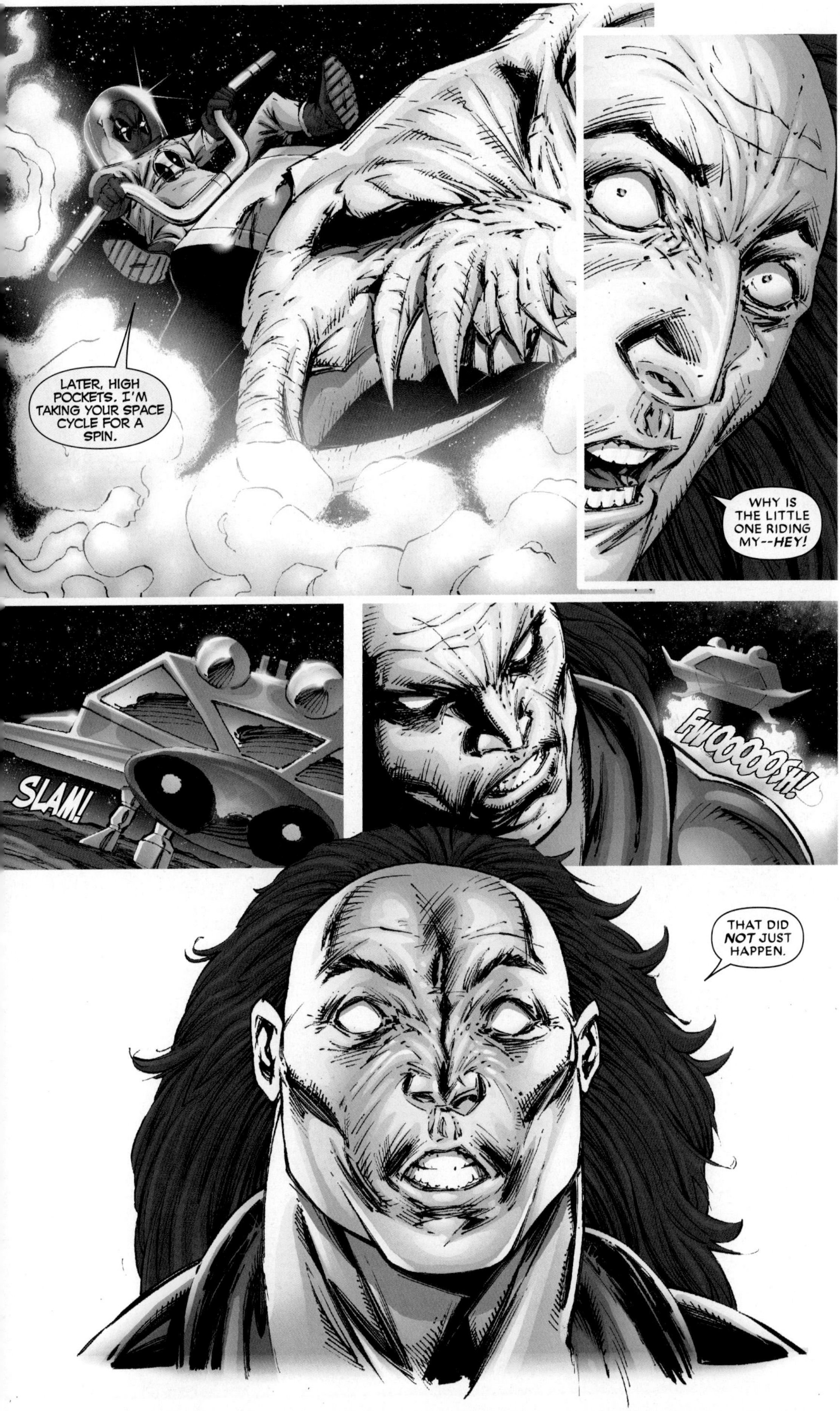
LATER, HIGH POCKETS. I'M TAKING YOUR SPACE CYCLE FOR A SPIN.
WHY IS THE LITTLE ONE RIDING MY--*HEY!*
SLAM!
FWOOOOOSH!
THAT DID *NOT* JUST HAPPEN.

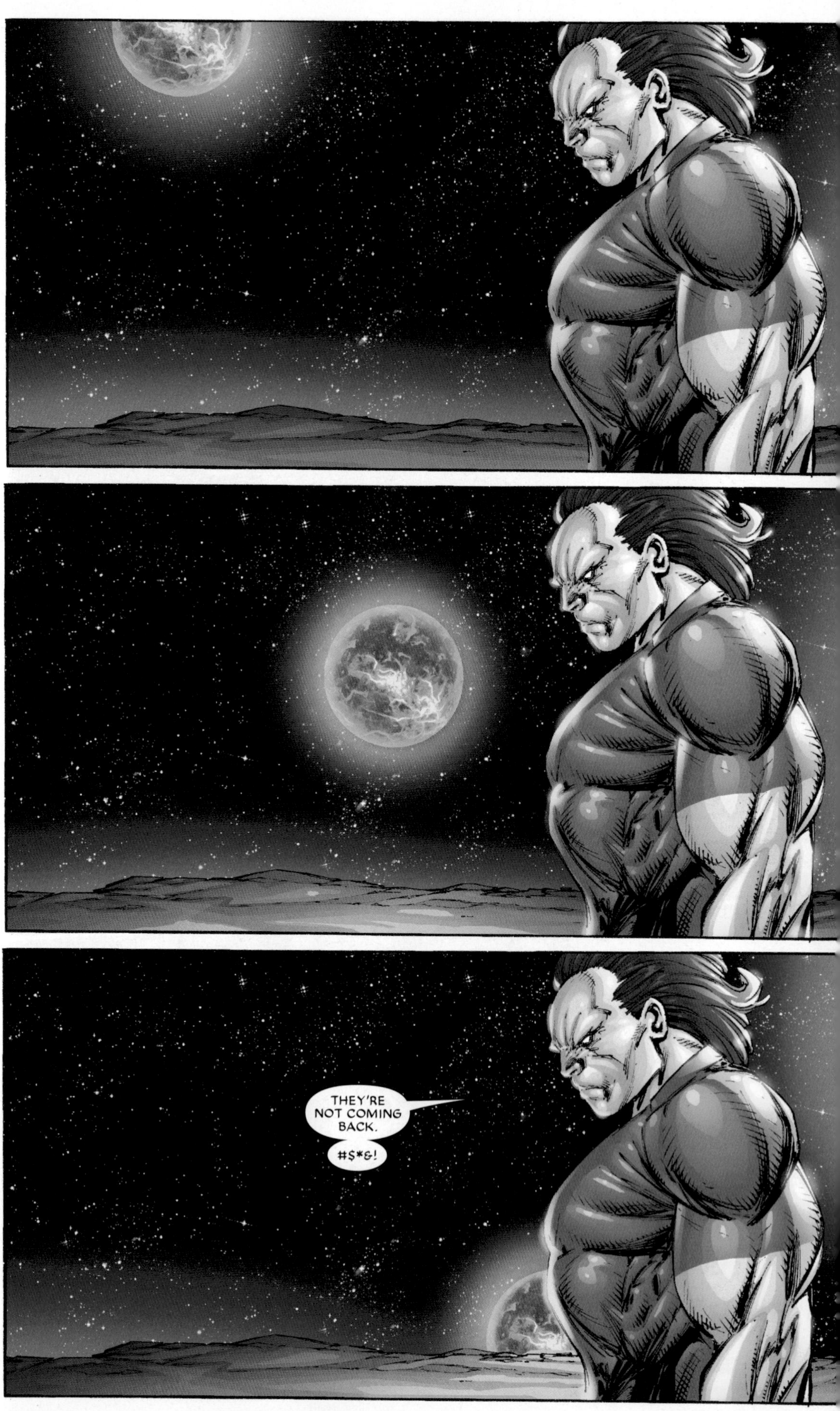
THEY'RE NOT COMING BACK.
#$*&!

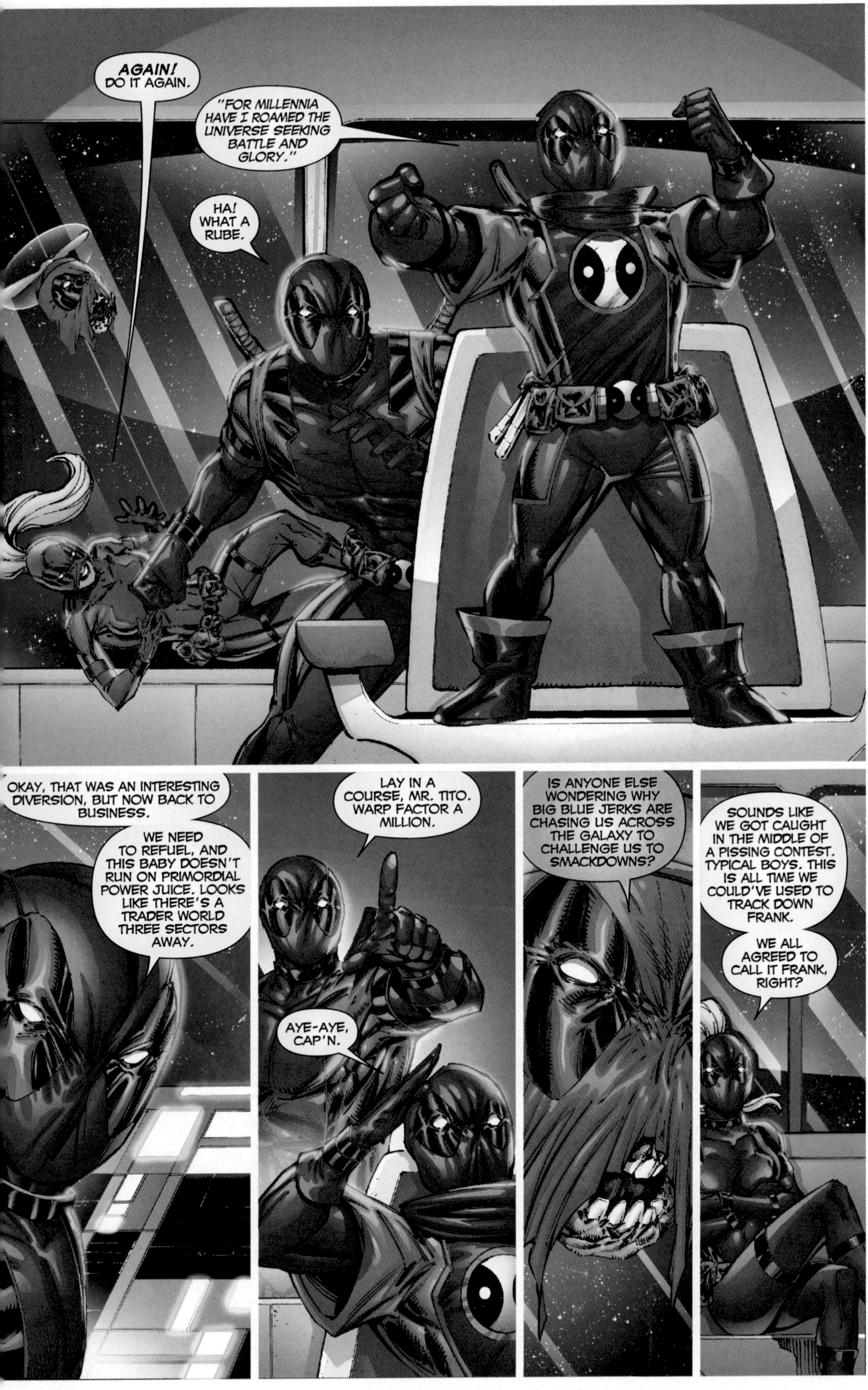

AGAIN! DO IT AGAIN.
"FOR MILLENNIA HAVE I ROAMED THE UNIVERSE SEEKING BATTLE AND GLORY."
HA! WHAT A RUBE.
OKAY, THAT WAS AN INTERESTING DIVERSION, BUT NOW BACK TO BUSINESS.
WE NEED TO REFUEL, AND THIS BABY DOESN'T RUN ON PRIMORDIAL POWER JUICE. LOOKS LIKE THERE'S A TRADER WORLD THREE SECTORS AWAY.
LAY IN A COURSE, MR. TITO. WARP FACTOR A MILLION.
AYE-AYE, CAP'N.
IS ANYONE ELSE WONDERING WHY BIG BLUE JERKS ARE CHASING US ACROSS THE GALAXY TO CHALLENGE US TO SMACKDOWNS?
SOUNDS LIKE WE GOT CAUGHT IN THE MIDDLE OF A PISSING CONTEST. TYPICAL BOYS. THIS IS ALL TIME WE COULD'VE USED TO TRACK DOWN FRANK.
WE ALL AGREED TO CALL IT FRANK, RIGHT?

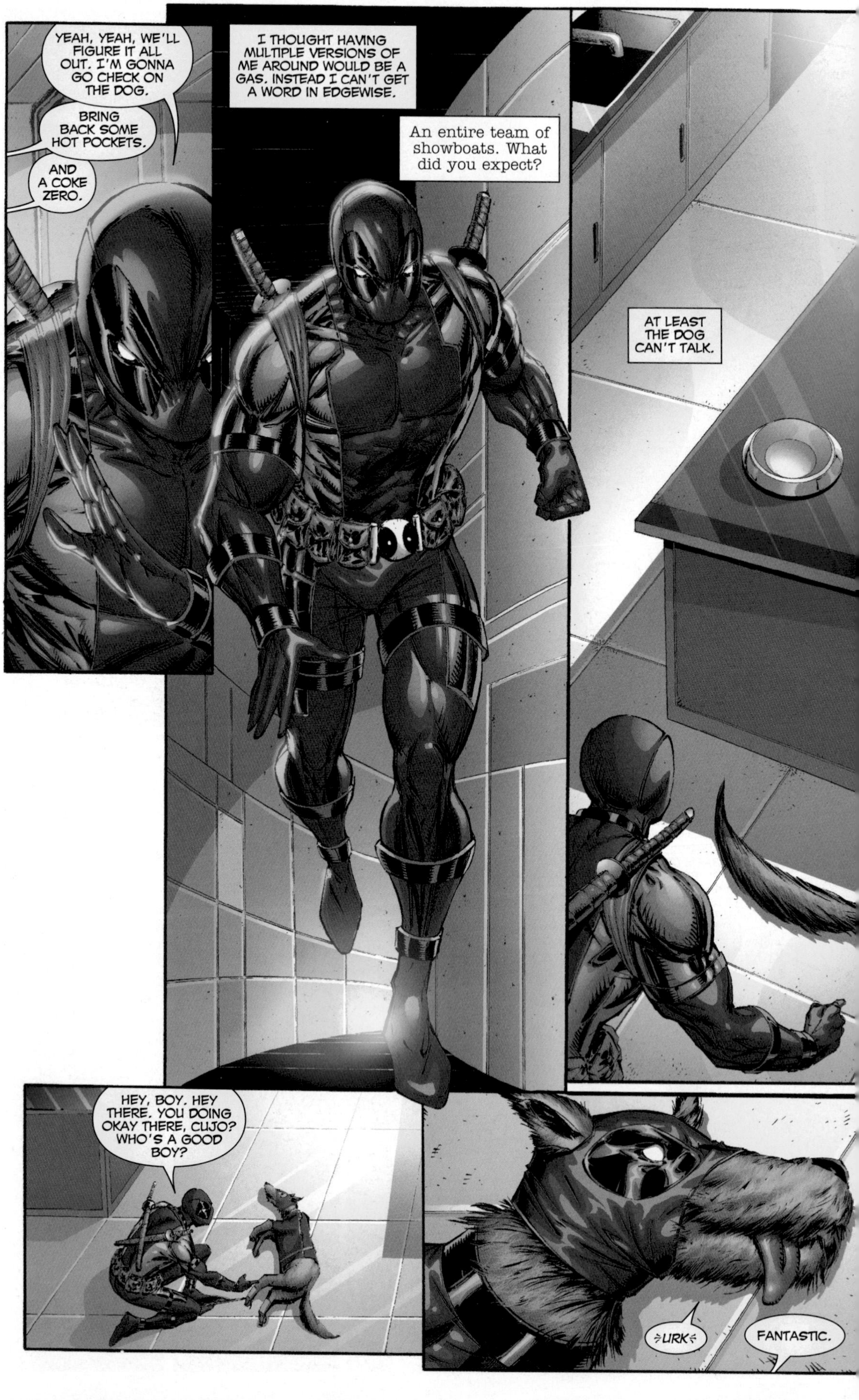
YEAH, YEAH, WE'LL FIGURE IT ALL OUT. I'M GONNA GO CHECK ON THE DOG.
BRING BACK SOME HOT POCKETS.
AND A COKE ZERO.
I THOUGHT HAVING MULTIPLE VERSIONS OF ME AROUND WOULD BE A GAS. INSTEAD I CAN'T GET A WORD IN EDGEWISE.
An entire team of showboats. What did you expect?
AT LEAST THE DOG CAN'T TALK.
HEY, BOY. HEY THERE. YOU DOING OKAY THERE, CUJO? WHO'S A GOOD BOY?
URK
FANTASTIC.

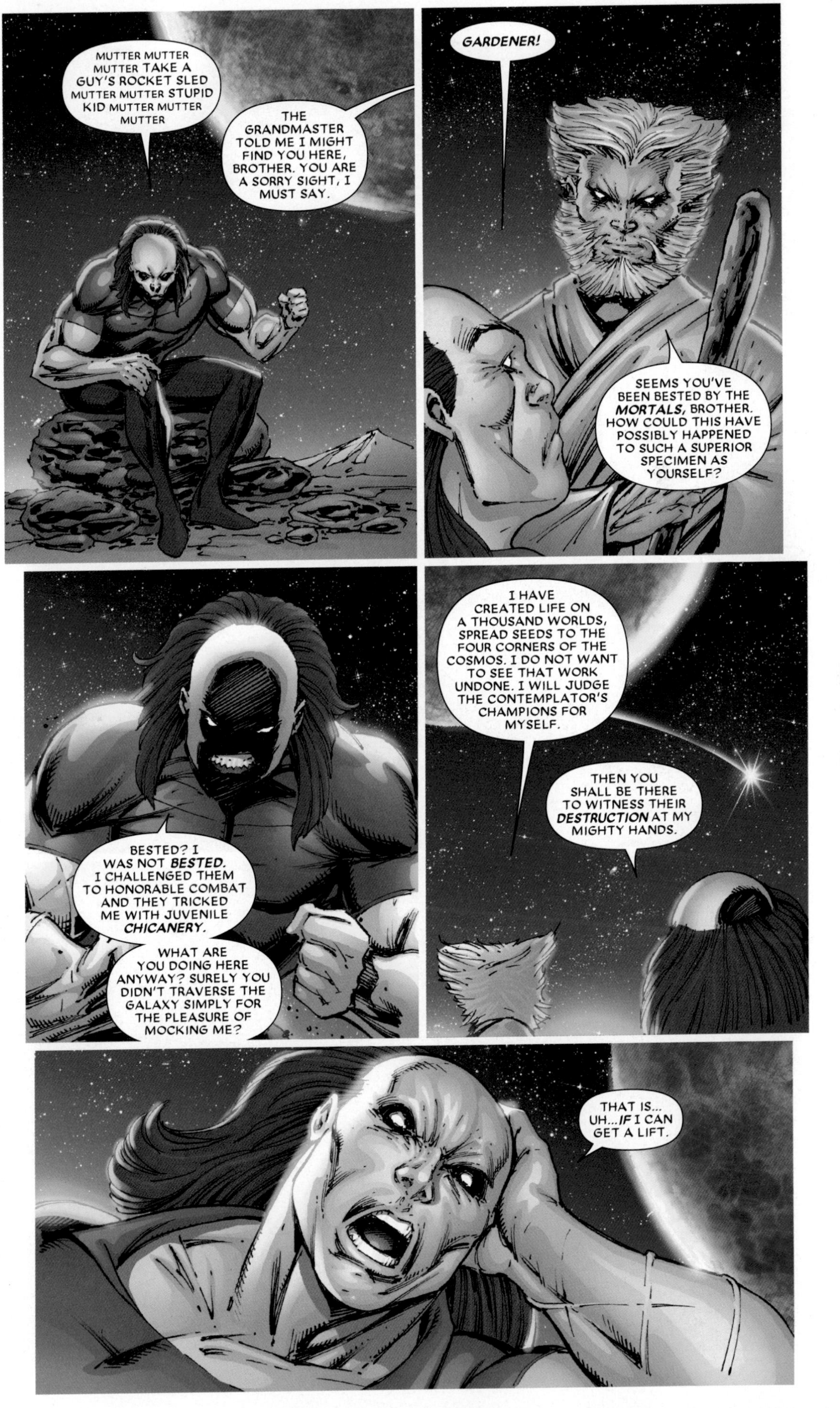
MUTTER MUTTER MUTTER TAKE A GUY'S ROCKET SLED MUTTER MUTTER STUPID KID MUTTER MUTTER MUTTER
THE GRANDMASTER TOLD ME I MIGHT FIND YOU HERE, BROTHER. YOU ARE A SORRY SIGHT, I MUST SAY.
GARDENER!
SEEMS YOU'VE BEEN BESTED BY THE MORTALS, BROTHER. HOW COULD THIS HAVE POSSIBLY HAPPENED TO SUCH A SUPERIOR SPECIMEN AS YOURSELF?
BESTED? I WAS NOT BESTED. I CHALLENGED THEM TO HONORABLE COMBAT AND THEY TRICKED ME WITH JUVENILE CHICANERY.
WHAT ARE YOU DOING HERE ANYWAY? SURELY YOU DIDN'T TRAVERSE THE GALAXY SIMPLY FOR THE PLEASURE OF MOCKING ME?
I HAVE CREATED LIFE ON A THOUSAND WORLDS, SPREAD SEEDS TO THE FOUR CORNERS OF THE COSMOS. I DO NOT WANT TO SEE THAT WORK UNDONE. I WILL JUDGE THE CONTEMPLATOR'S CHAMPIONS FOR MYSELF.
THEN YOU SHALL BE THERE TO WITNESS THEIR DESTRUCTION AT MY MIGHTY HANDS.
THAT IS... UH...IF I CAN GET A LIFT.

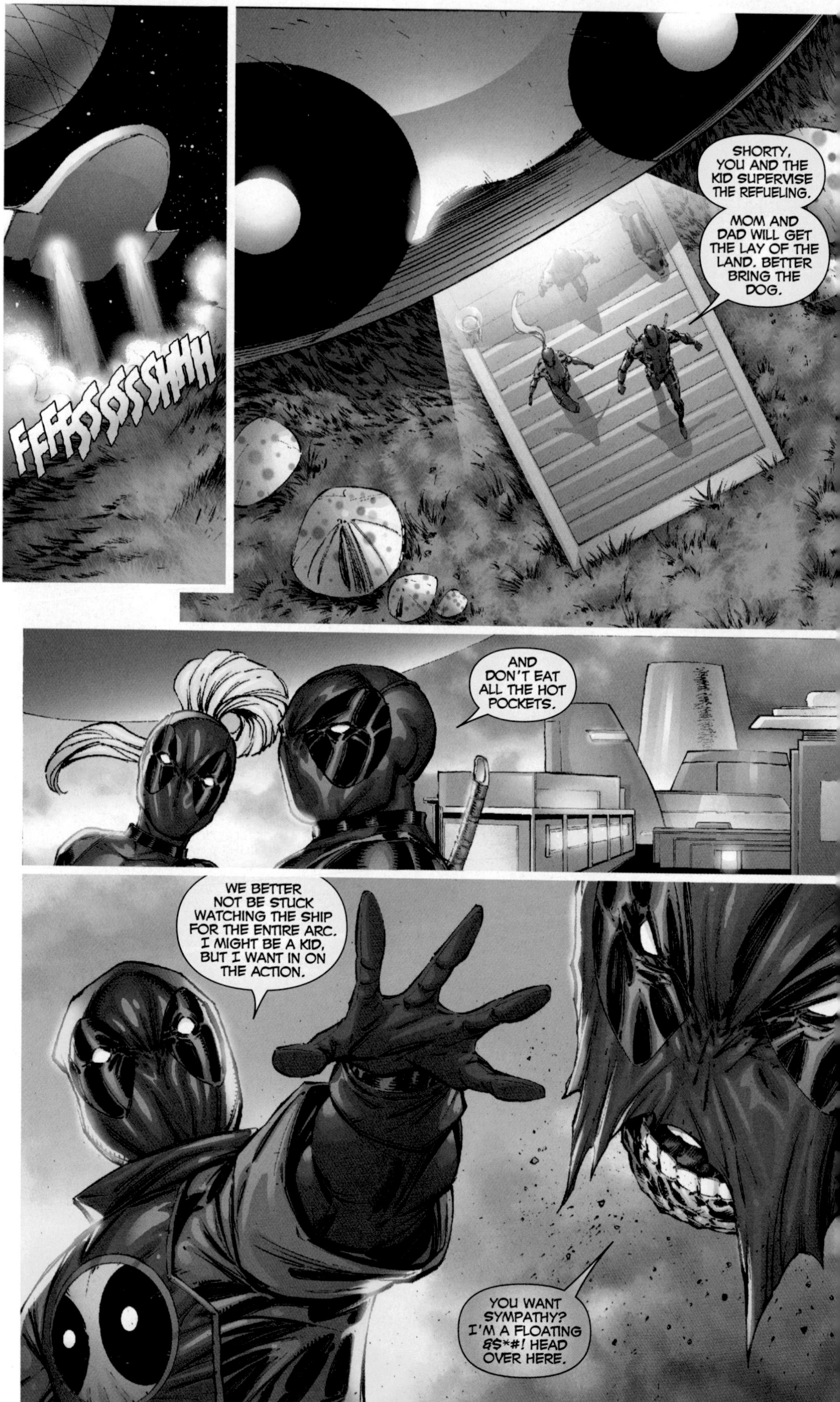
FFRSSSSSHHH
SHORTY, YOU AND THE KID SUPERVISE THE REFUELING.
MOM AND DAD WILL GET THE LAY OF THE LAND. BETTER BRING THE DOG.
AND DON'T EAT ALL THE HOT POCKETS.
WE BETTER NOT BE STUCK WATCHING THE SHIP FOR THE ENTIRE ARC. I MIGHT BE A KID, BUT I WANT IN ON THE ACTION.
YOU WANT SYMPATHY? I'M A FLOATING &$*#! HEAD OVER HERE.

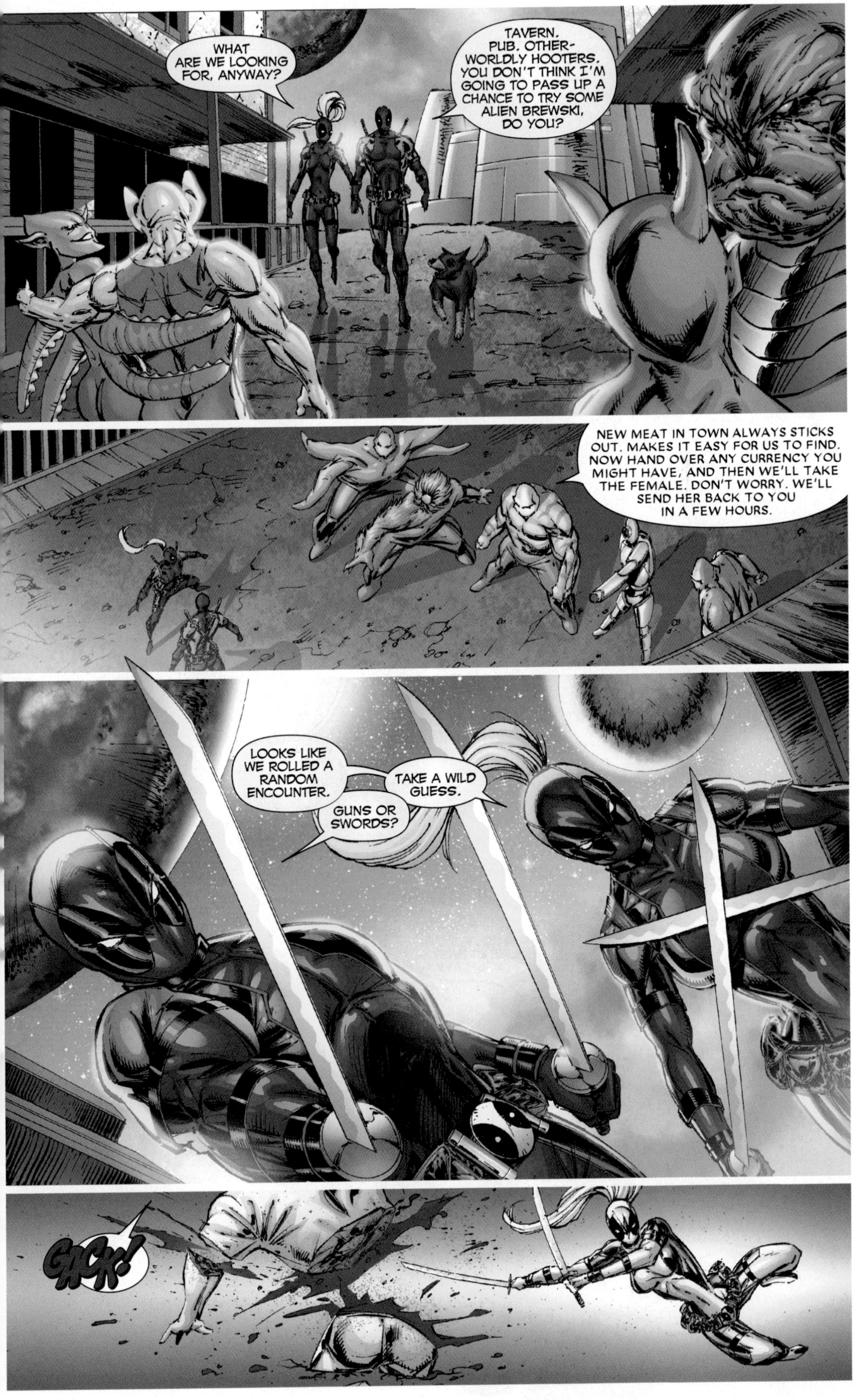
WHAT ARE WE LOOKING FOR, ANYWAY?
TAVERN. PUB. OTHER-WORLDLY HOOTERS. YOU DON'T THINK I'M GOING TO PASS UP A CHANCE TO TRY SOME ALIEN BREWSKI, DO YOU?
NEW MEAT IN TOWN ALWAYS STICKS OUT. MAKES IT EASY FOR US TO FIND. NOW HAND OVER ANY CURRENCY YOU MIGHT HAVE, AND THEN WE'LL TAKE THE FEMALE. DON'T WORRY. WE'LL SEND HER BACK TO YOU IN A FEW HOURS.
LOOKS LIKE WE ROLLED A RANDOM ENCOUNTER.
TAKE A WILD GUESS.
GUNS OR SWORDS?
GACK!

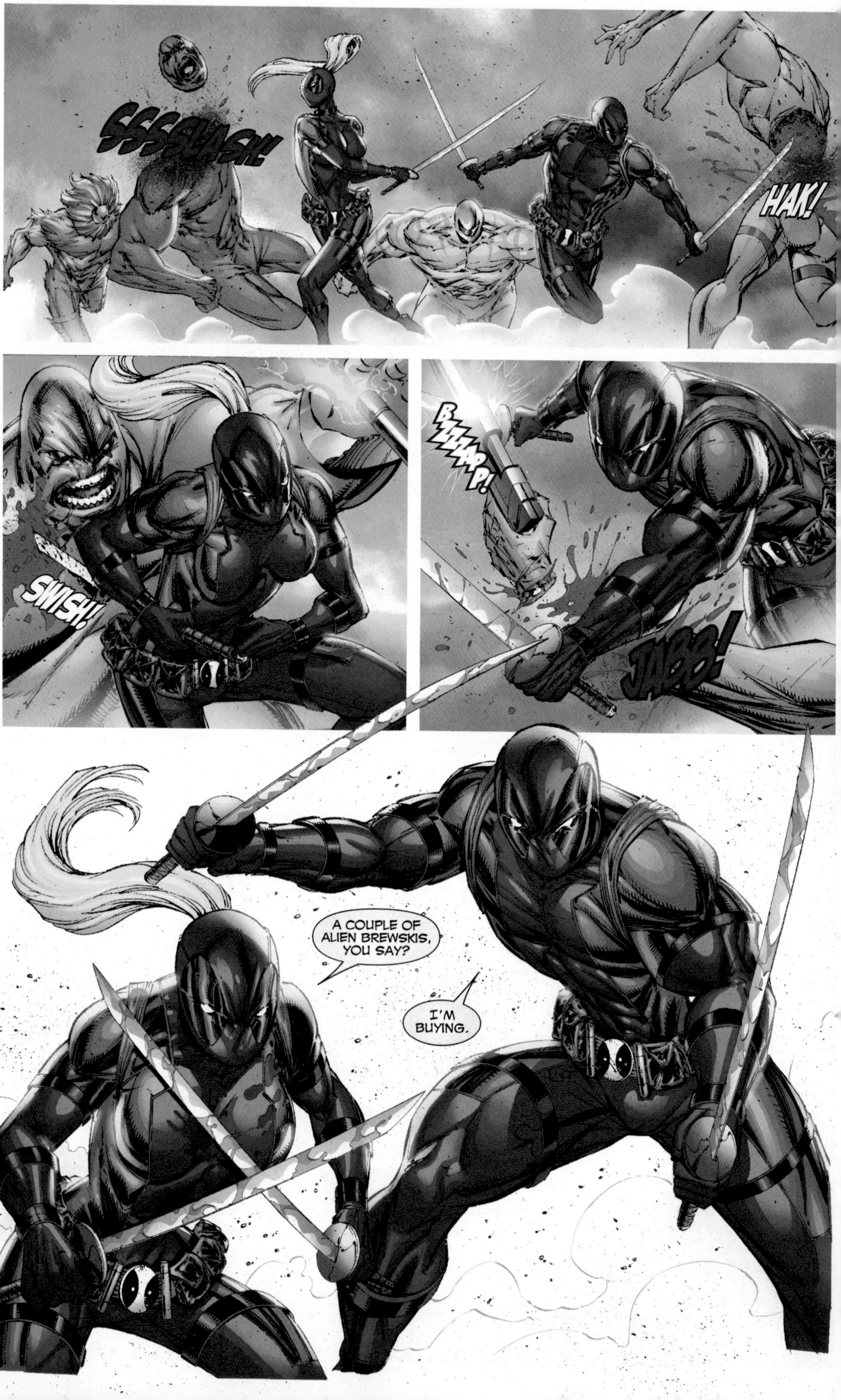
SSSSLASH!
HAK!
SWISH!
BZZZZAP!
JABB!
A COUPLE OF ALIEN BREWSKIS, YOU SAY?
I'M BUYING.

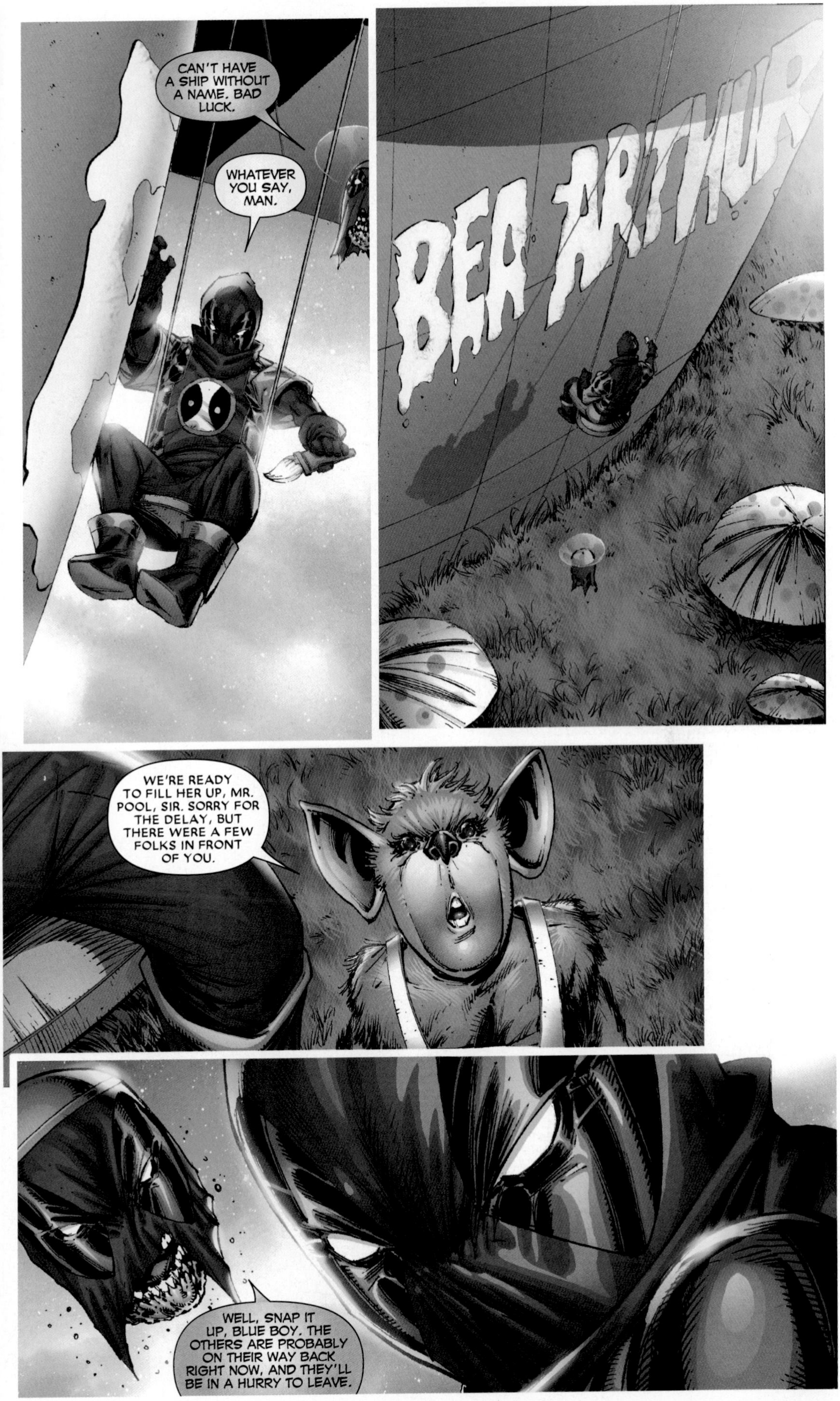
CAN'T HAVE A SHIP WITHOUT A NAME. BAD LUCK.
WHATEVER YOU SAY, MAN.
BEA ARTHUR
WE'RE READY TO FILL HER UP, MR. POOL, SIR. SORRY FOR THE DELAY, BUT THERE WERE A FEW FOLKS IN FRONT OF YOU.
WELL, SNAP IT UP, BLUE BOY. THE OTHERS ARE PROBABLY ON THEIR WAY BACK RIGHT NOW, AND THEY'LL BE IN A HURRY TO LEAVE.

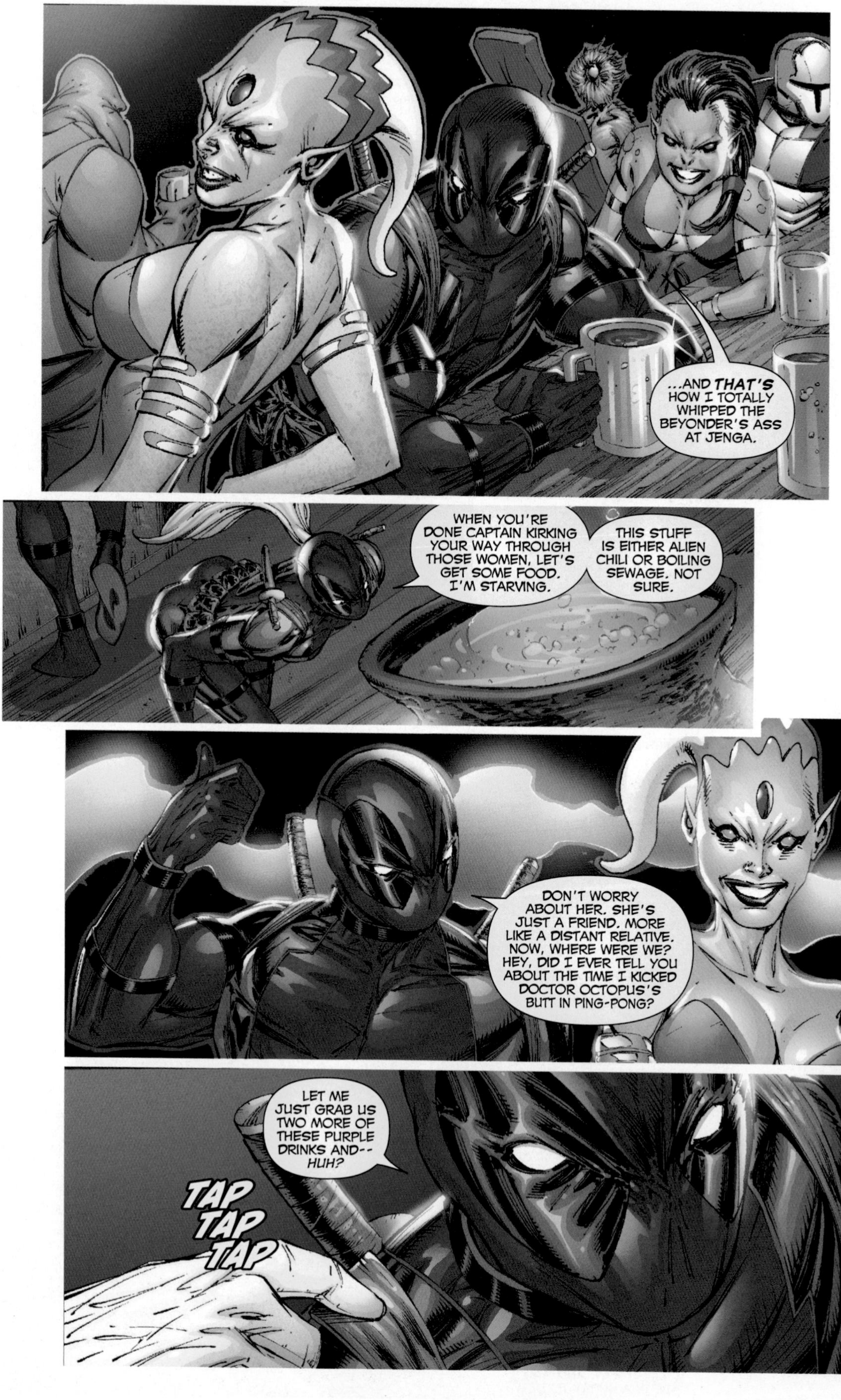
...AND THAT'S HOW I TOTALLY WHIPPED THE BEYONDER'S ASS AT JENGA.
WHEN YOU'RE DONE CAPTAIN KIRKING YOUR WAY THROUGH THOSE WOMEN, LET'S GET SOME FOOD. I'M STARVING.
THIS STUFF IS EITHER ALIEN CHILI OR BOILING SEWAGE. NOT SURE.
DON'T WORRY ABOUT HER. SHE'S JUST A FRIEND. MORE LIKE A DISTANT RELATIVE. NOW, WHERE WERE WE? HEY, DID I EVER TELL YOU ABOUT THE TIME I KICKED DOCTOR OCTOPUS'S BUTT IN PING-PONG?
LET ME JUST GRAB US TWO MORE OF THESE PURPLE DRINKS AND-- HUH?
TAP TAP TAP

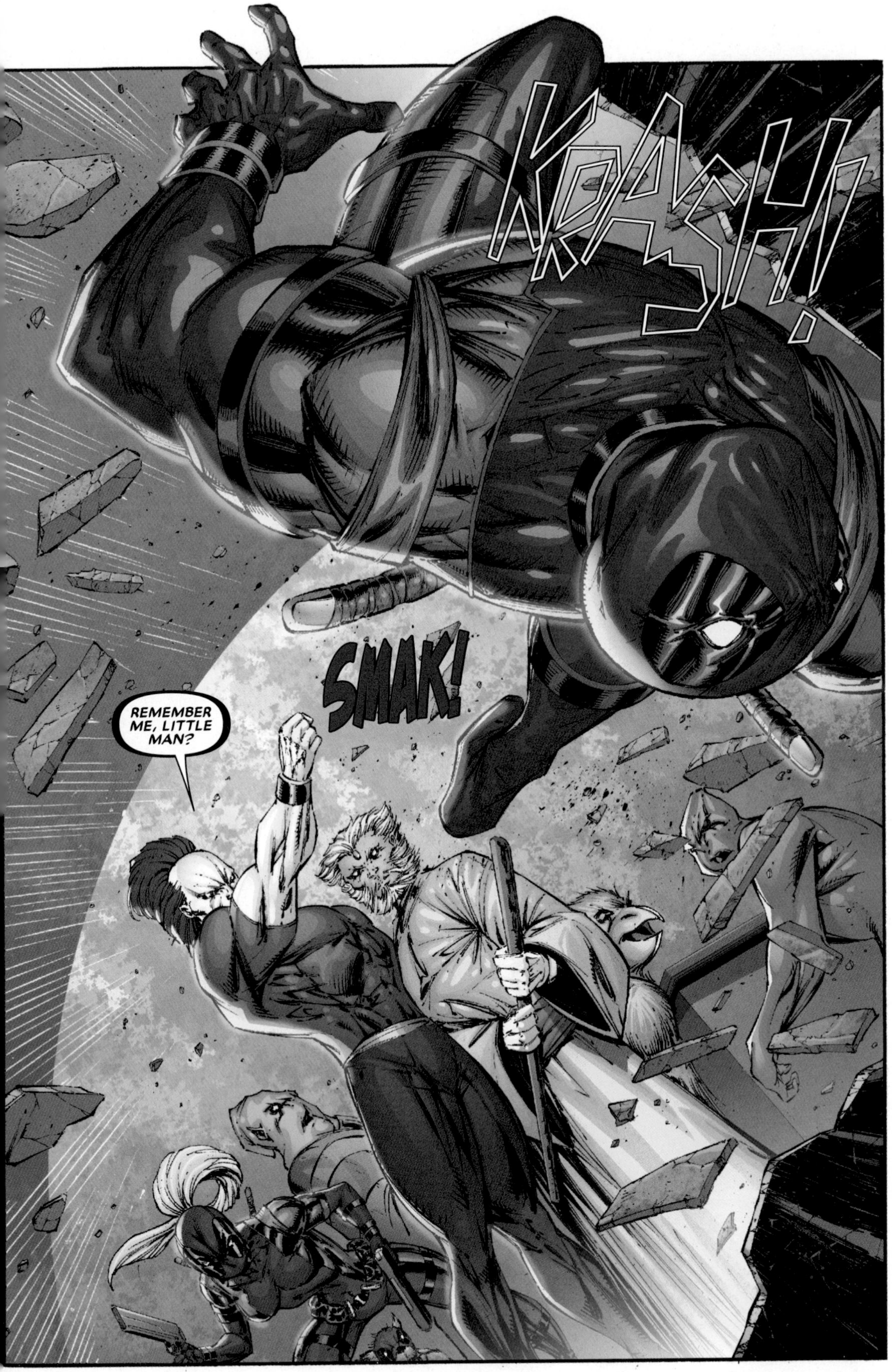
KRAASH!
SMAK!
REMEMBER ME, LITTLE MAN?

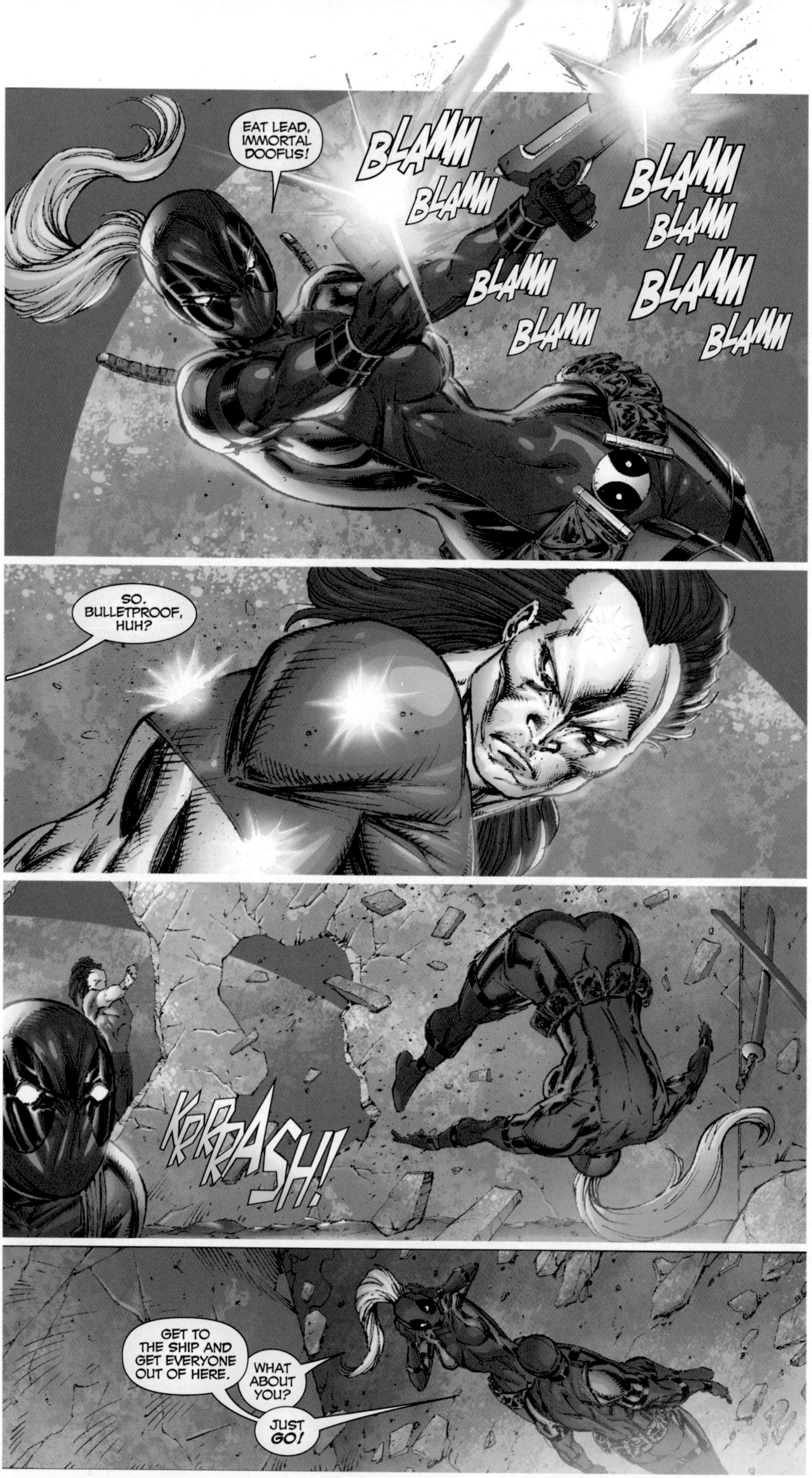
EAT LEAD, IMMORTAL DOOFUS!
BLAMM BLAMM
BLAMM BLAMM
BLAMM BLAMM
BLAMM BLAMM
BLAMM
SO, BULLETPROOF, HUH?
KRRRRASH!
GET TO THE SHIP AND GET EVERYONE OUT OF HERE.
WHAT ABOUT YOU?
JUST GO!

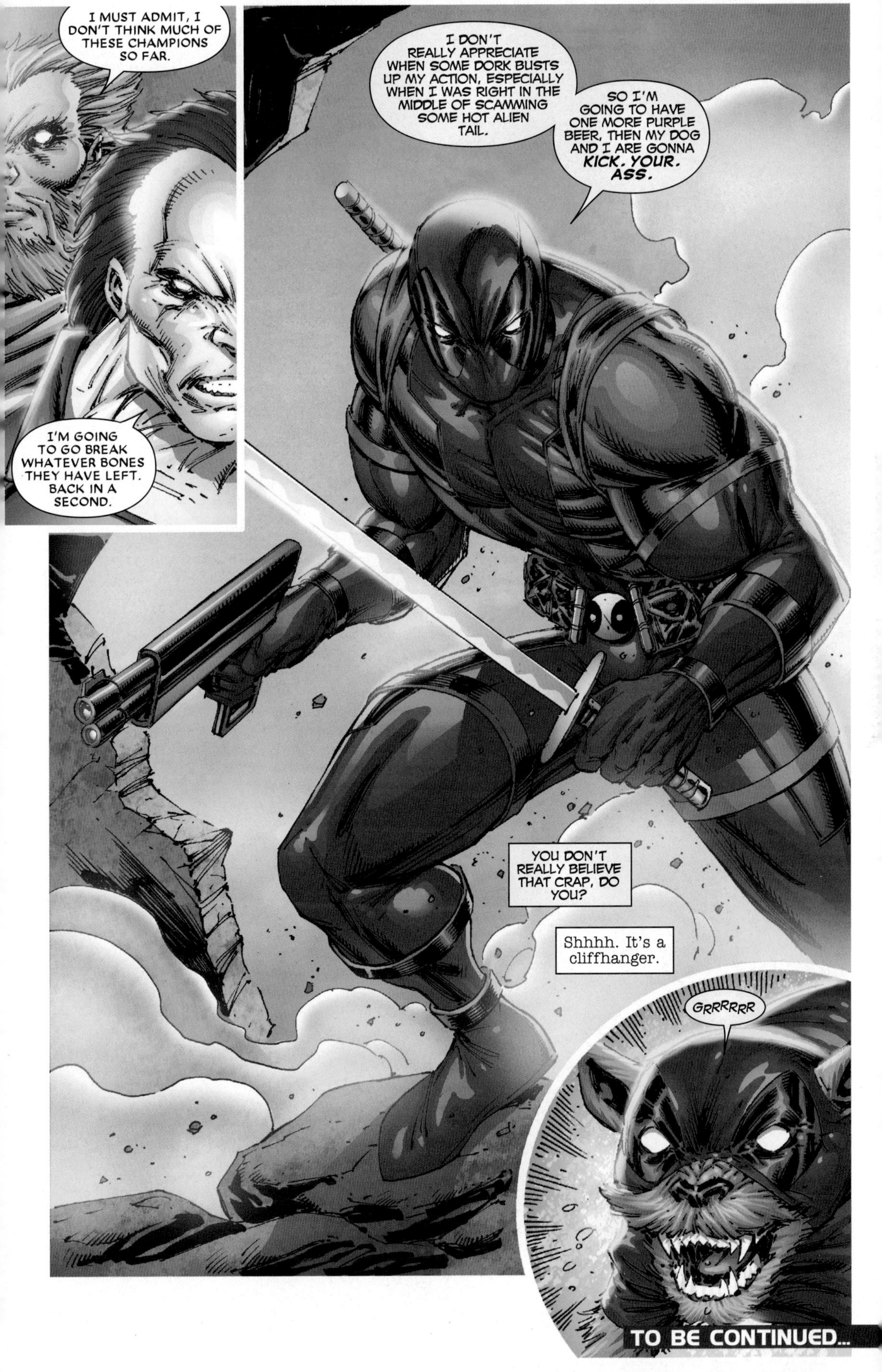
I MUST ADMIT, I DON'T THINK MUCH OF THESE CHAMPIONS SO FAR.
I'M GOING TO GO BREAK WHATEVER BONES THEY HAVE LEFT. BACK IN A SECOND.
I DON'T REALLY APPRECIATE WHEN SOME DORK BUSTS UP MY ACTION, ESPECIALLY WHEN I WAS RIGHT IN THE MIDDLE OF SCAMMING SOME HOT ALIEN TAIL.
SO I'M GOING TO HAVE ONE MORE PURPLE BEER, THEN MY DOG AND I ARE GONNA ***KICK. YOUR. ASS.***
YOU DON'T REALLY BELIEVE THAT CRAP, DO YOU?
Shhhh. It's a cliffhanger.
GRRRRRR
TO BE CONTINUED...

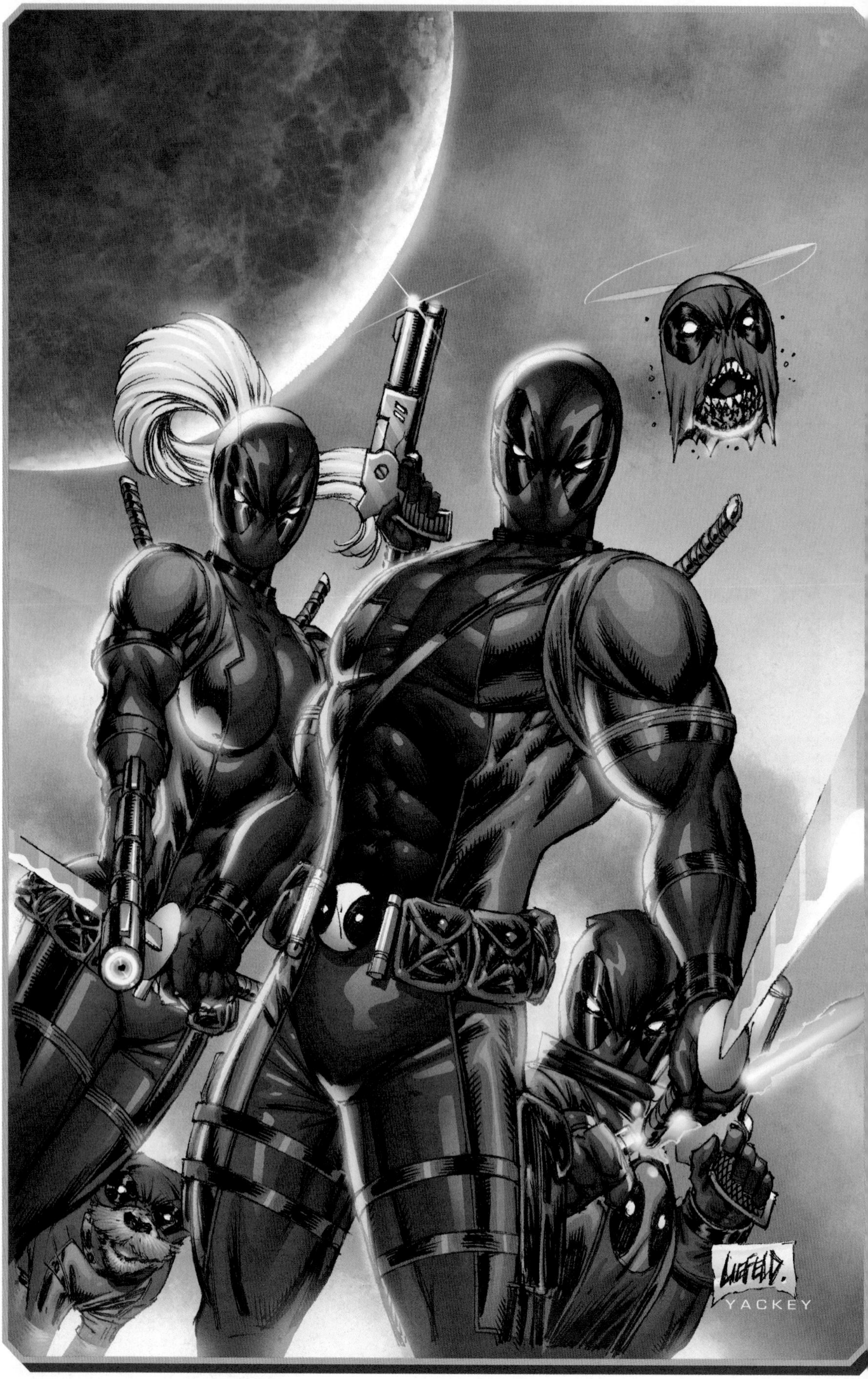
LIEFELD.
YACKEY

DEADPOOL CORPS #1 Variant by ROB LIEFELD & MATT YACKEY

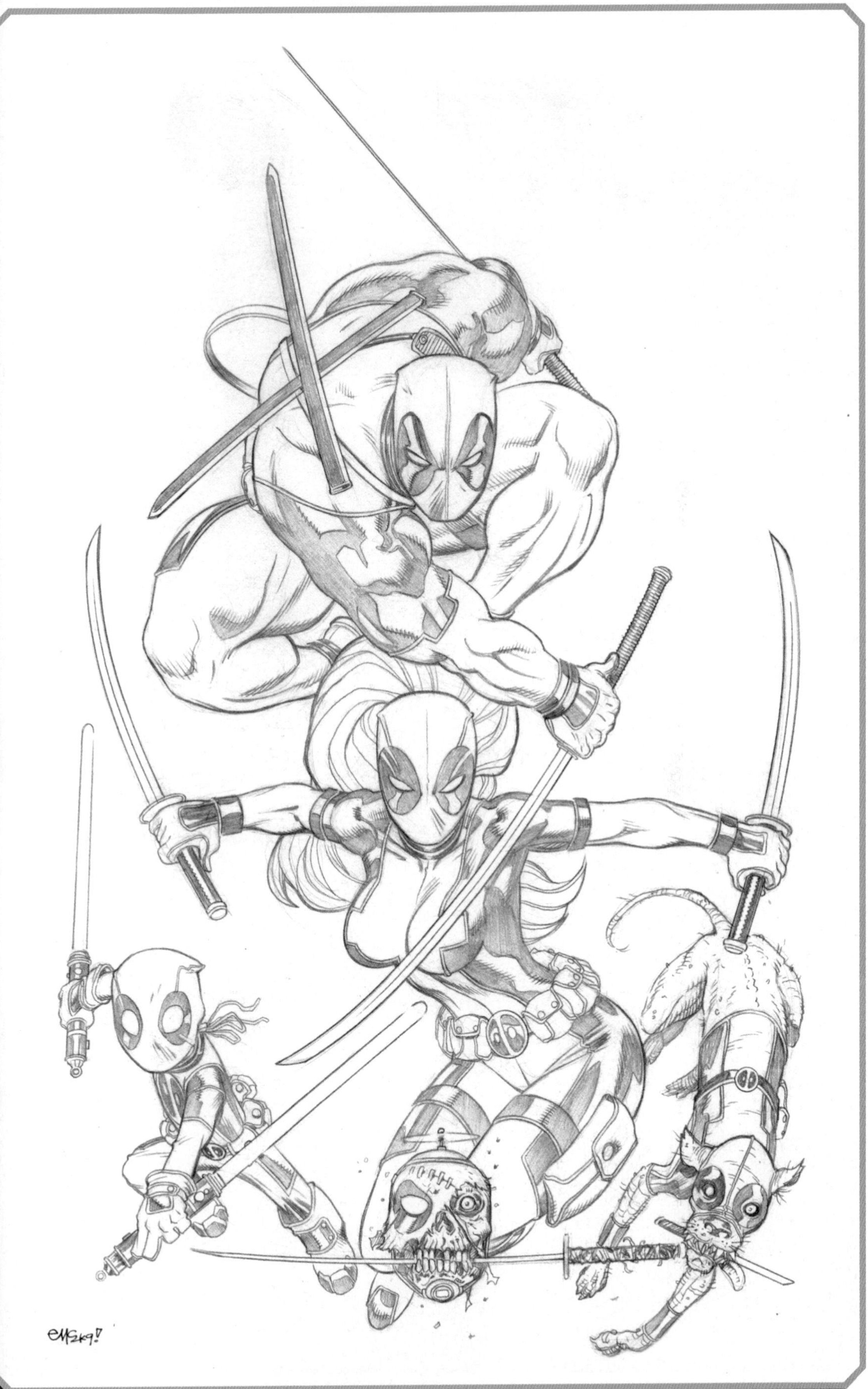

DEADPOOL CORPS #1 Variant by ED MCGUINNESS

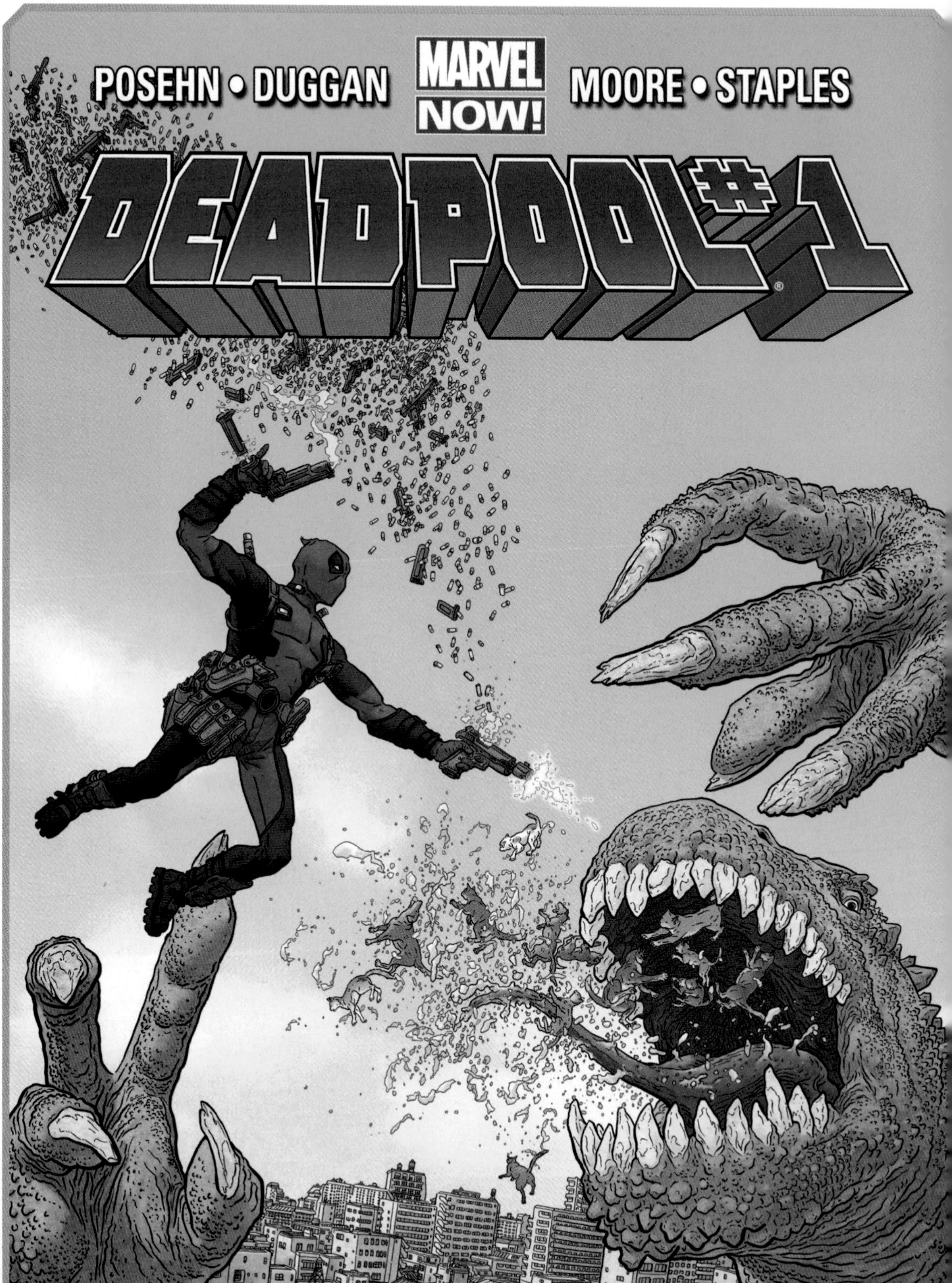

POSEHN • DUGGAN
MARVEL
NOW!
MOORE • STAPLES
DEADPOOL #1

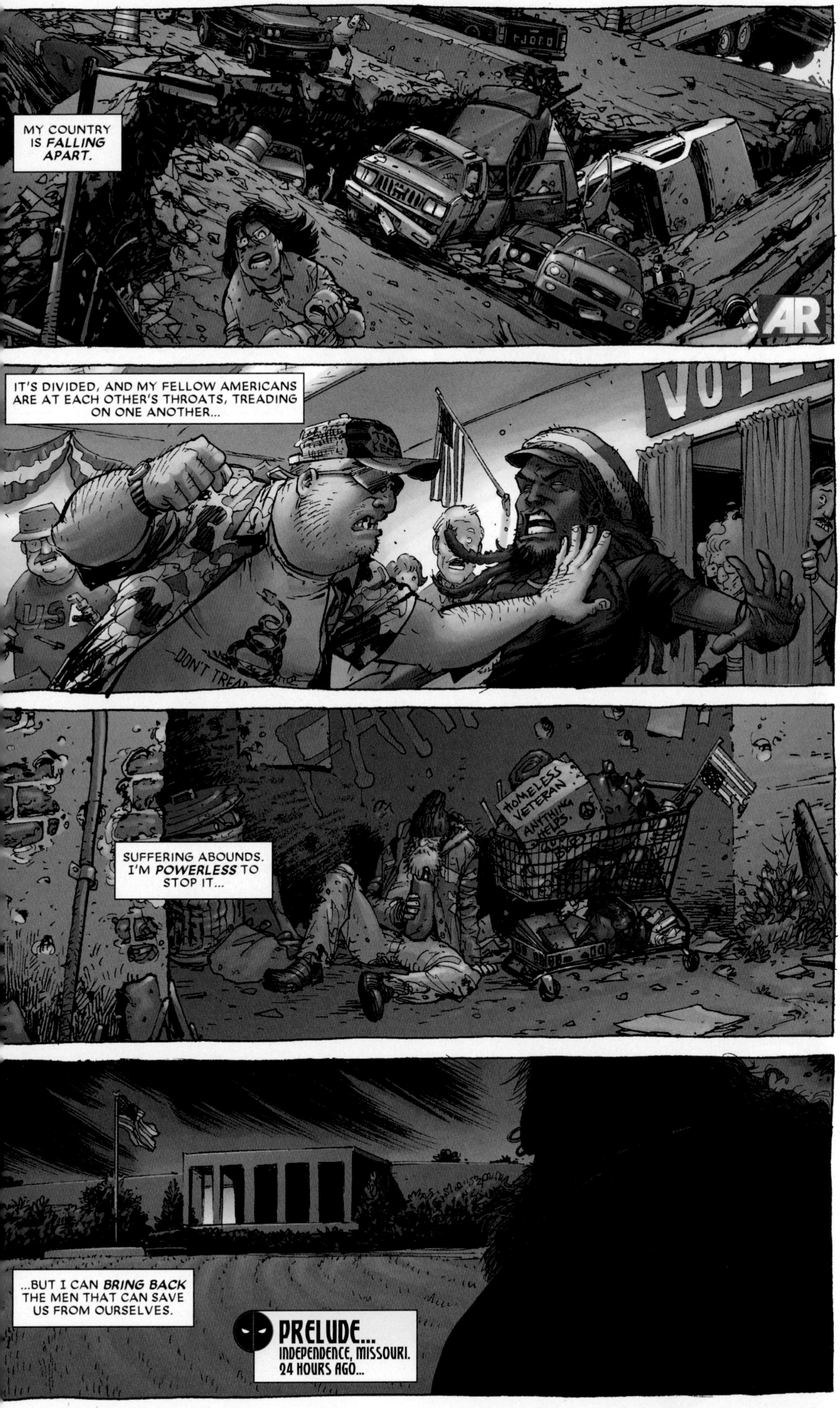
MY COUNTRY IS FALLING APART.
IT'S DIVIDED, AND MY FELLOW AMERICANS ARE AT EACH OTHER'S THROATS, TREADING ON ONE ANOTHER...
VOTE
DON'T TREAD
HOMELESS VETERAN ANYTHING HELPS.
SUFFERING ABOUNDS. I'M POWERLESS TO STOP IT...
...BUT I CAN BRING BACK THE MEN THAT CAN SAVE US FROM OURSELVES.
PRELUDE...
INDEPENDENCE, MISSOURI.
24 HOURS AGO...

GREAT MEN. *PRINCIPLED* MEN THAT KNEW HOW TO COMPROMISE, AND LEAD.

AMERICA NEEDS ITS *HEROES.*

ᛞᛗᛈᚾᛗ
ᛗᚦᛉᛉᛏᛏᚴ ᚻᛗ ᚤᛏᛗᛗ
ᛗᚾᛒᚠᛖᚷᛉ ᛒᚾᛖᛉᛗᛞ

HAIL TO THE CHIEF!

UGH!

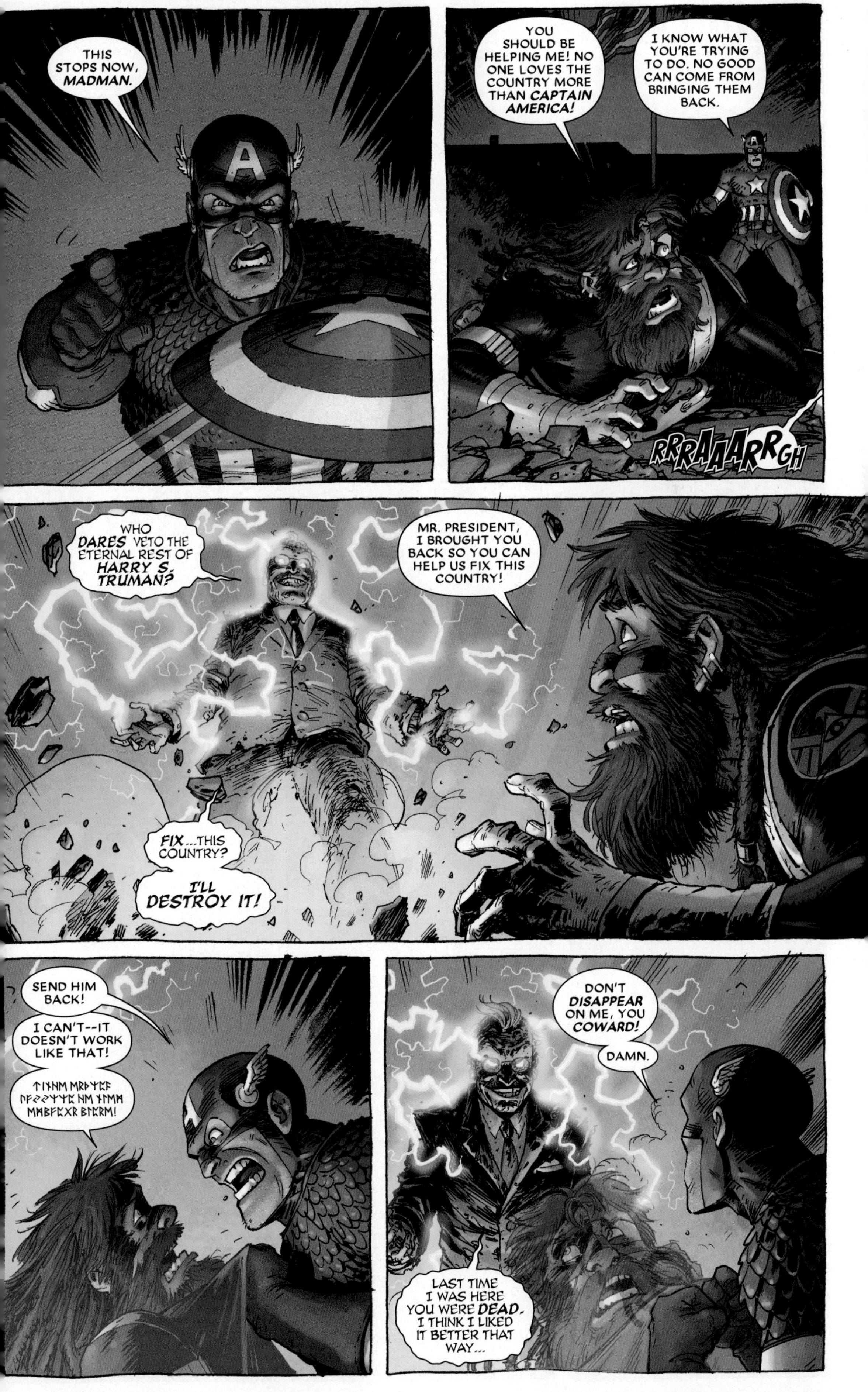
THIS STOPS NOW, MADMAN.
YOU SHOULD BE HELPING ME! NO ONE LOVES THE COUNTRY MORE THAN CAPTAIN AMERICA!
I KNOW WHAT YOU'RE TRYING TO DO. NO GOOD CAN COME FROM BRINGING THEM BACK.
RRRAAAARRGH
WHO DARES VETO THE ETERNAL REST OF HARRY S. TRUMAN?
MR. PRESIDENT, I BROUGHT YOU BACK SO YOU CAN HELP US FIX THIS COUNTRY!
FIX...THIS COUNTRY?
I'LL DESTROY IT!
SEND HIM BACK!
I CAN'T--IT DOESN'T WORK LIKE THAT!
DON'T DISAPPEAR ON ME, YOU COWARD!
DAMN.
LAST TIME I WAS HERE YOU WERE DEAD. I THINK I LIKED IT BETTER THAT WAY...

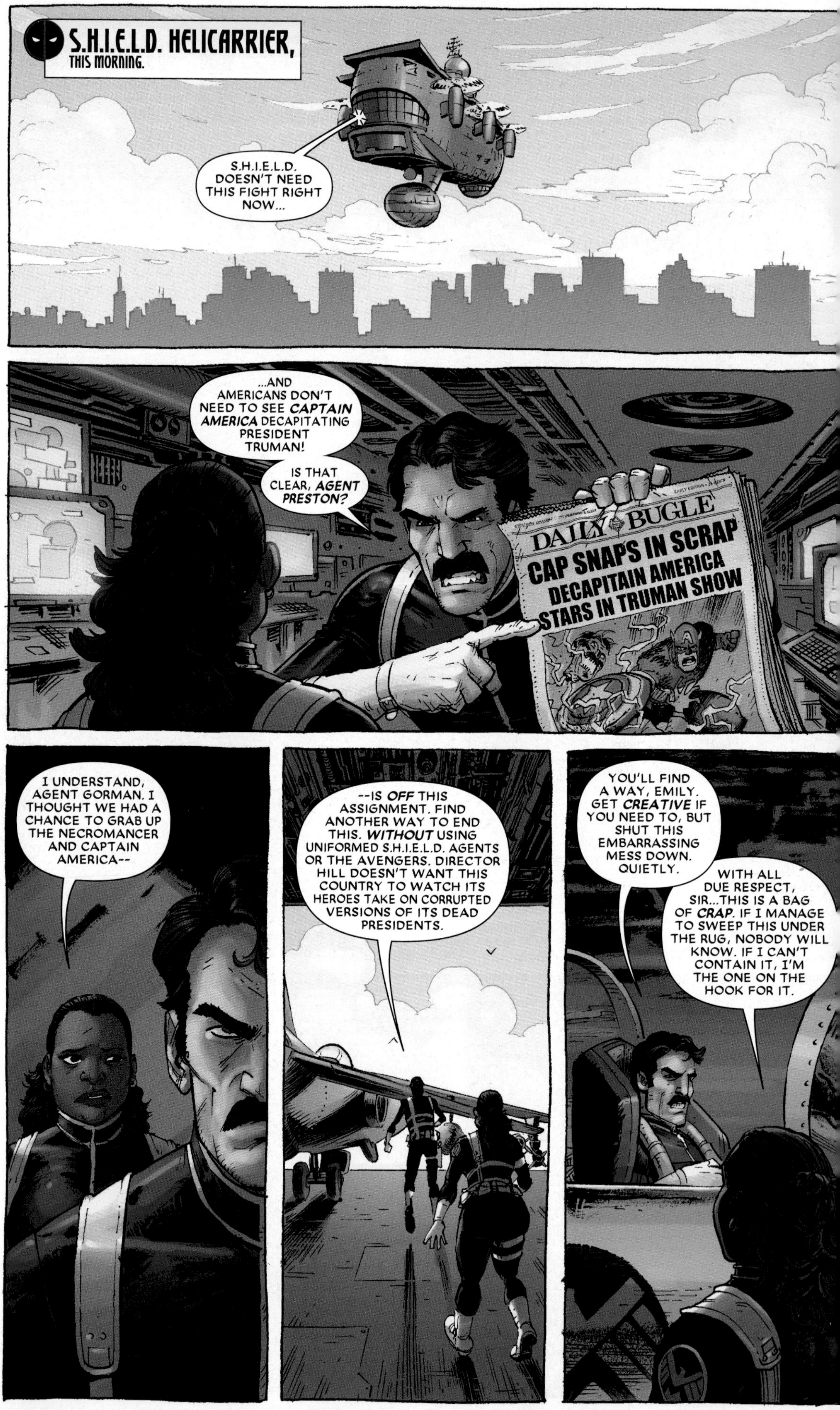
S.H.I.E.L.D. HELICARRIER, THIS MORNING.
S.H.I.E.L.D. DOESN'T NEED THIS FIGHT RIGHT NOW...
...AND AMERICANS DON'T NEED TO SEE CAPTAIN AMERICA DECAPITATING PRESIDENT TRUMAN!
IS THAT CLEAR, AGENT PRESTON?
DAILY BUGLE
CAP SNAPS IN SCRAP
DECAPITAIN AMERICA STARS IN TRUMAN SHOW
I UNDERSTAND, AGENT GORMAN. I THOUGHT WE HAD A CHANCE TO GRAB UP THE NECROMANCER AND CAPTAIN AMERICA--
--IS OFF THIS ASSIGNMENT. FIND ANOTHER WAY TO END THIS. WITHOUT USING UNIFORMED S.H.I.E.L.D. AGENTS OR THE AVENGERS. DIRECTOR HILL DOESN'T WANT THIS COUNTRY TO WATCH ITS HEROES TAKE ON CORRUPTED VERSIONS OF ITS DEAD PRESIDENTS.
YOU'LL FIND A WAY, EMILY. GET CREATIVE IF YOU NEED TO, BUT SHUT THIS EMBARRASSING MESS DOWN. QUIETLY.
WITH ALL DUE RESPECT, SIR...THIS IS A BAG OF CRAP. IF I MANAGE TO SWEEP THIS UNDER THE RUG, NOBODY WILL KNOW. IF I CAN'T CONTAIN IT, I'M THE ONE ON THE HOOK FOR IT.

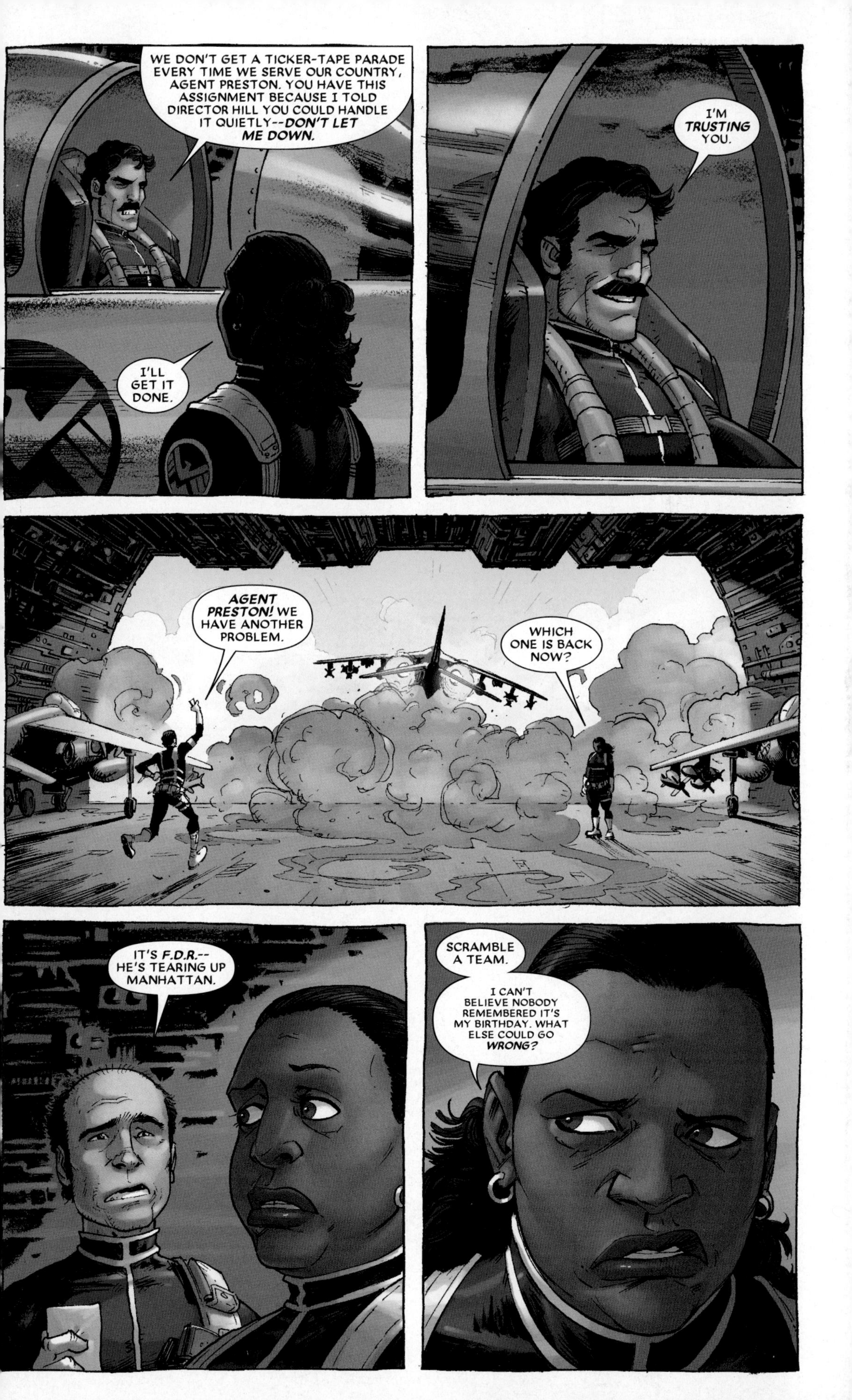
WE DON'T GET A TICKER-TAPE PARADE EVERY TIME WE SERVE OUR COUNTRY, AGENT PRESTON. YOU HAVE THIS ASSIGNMENT BECAUSE I TOLD DIRECTOR HILL YOU COULD HANDLE IT QUIETLY--DON'T LET ME DOWN.
I'LL GET IT DONE.
I'M TRUSTING YOU.
AGENT PRESTON! WE HAVE ANOTHER PROBLEM.
WHICH ONE IS BACK NOW?
IT'S F.D.R.-- HE'S TEARING UP MANHATTAN.
SCRAMBLE A TEAM.
I CAN'T BELIEVE NOBODY REMEMBERED IT'S MY BIRTHDAY. WHAT ELSE COULD GO WRONG?

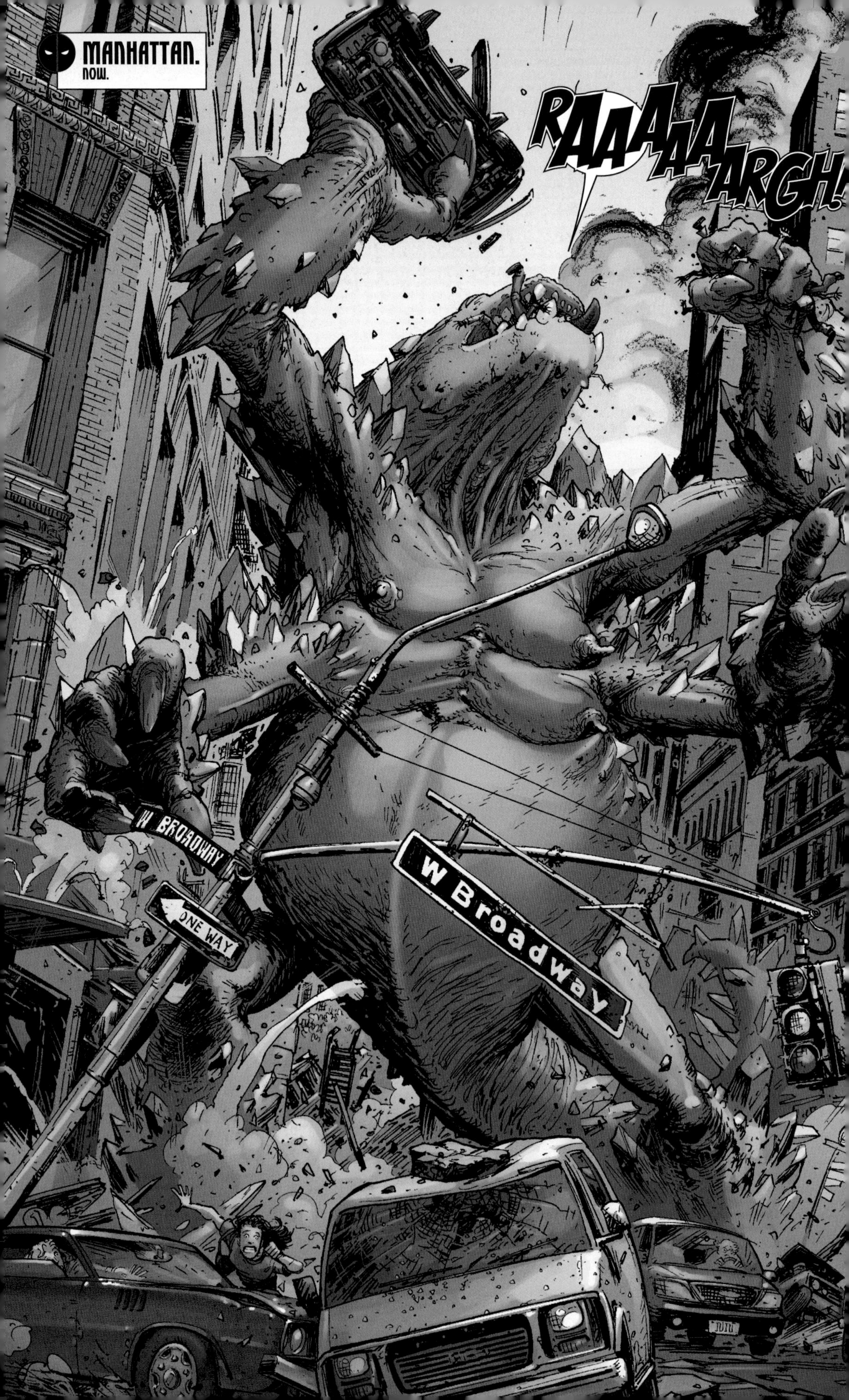
MANHATTAN.
NOW.
RAAAAAAARGH!
W BROADWAY
ONE WAY
W Broadway

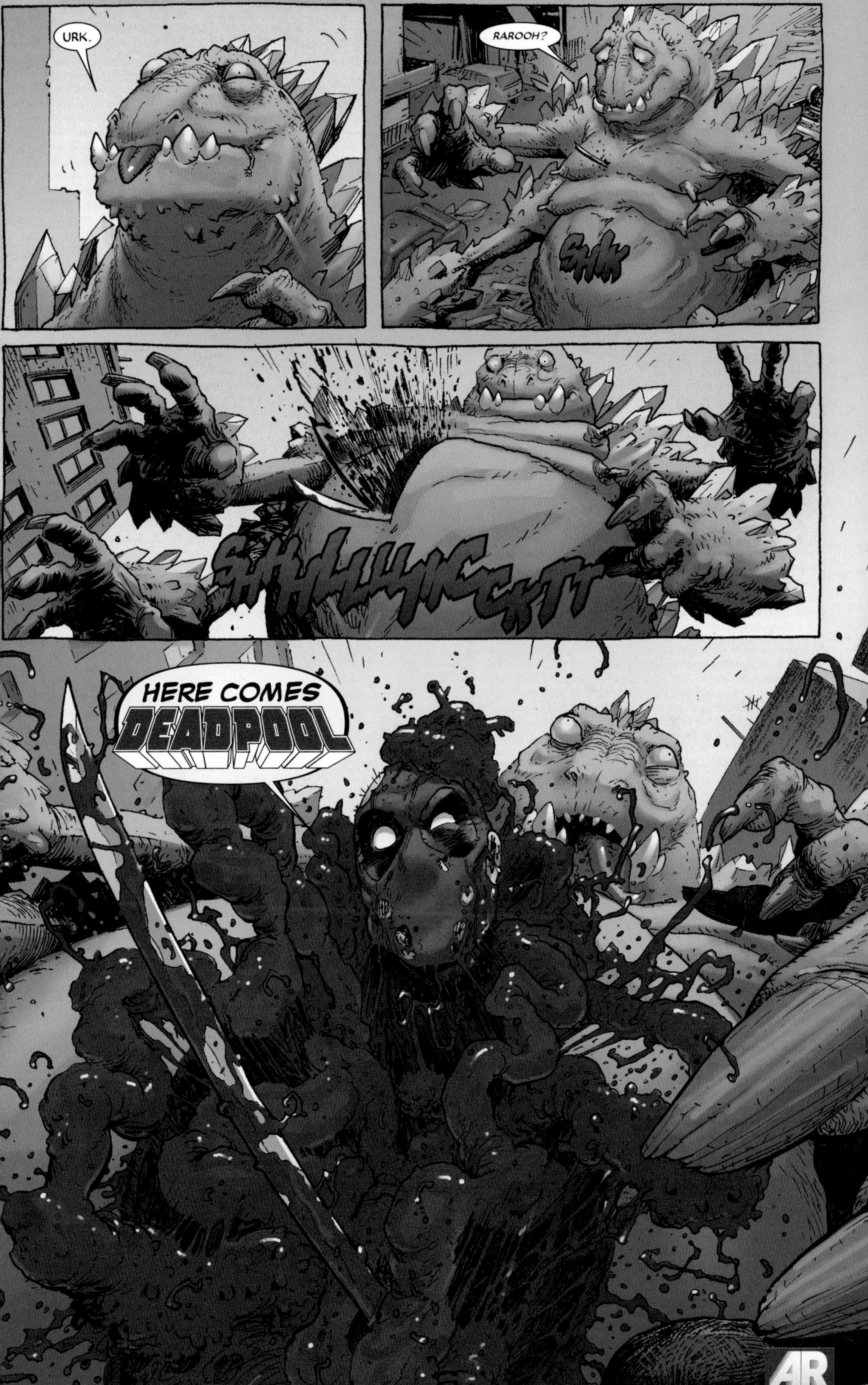
URK.
RAROOH?
SHK
SHHLLLLLKCKTT
HERE COMES DEADPOOL
AR

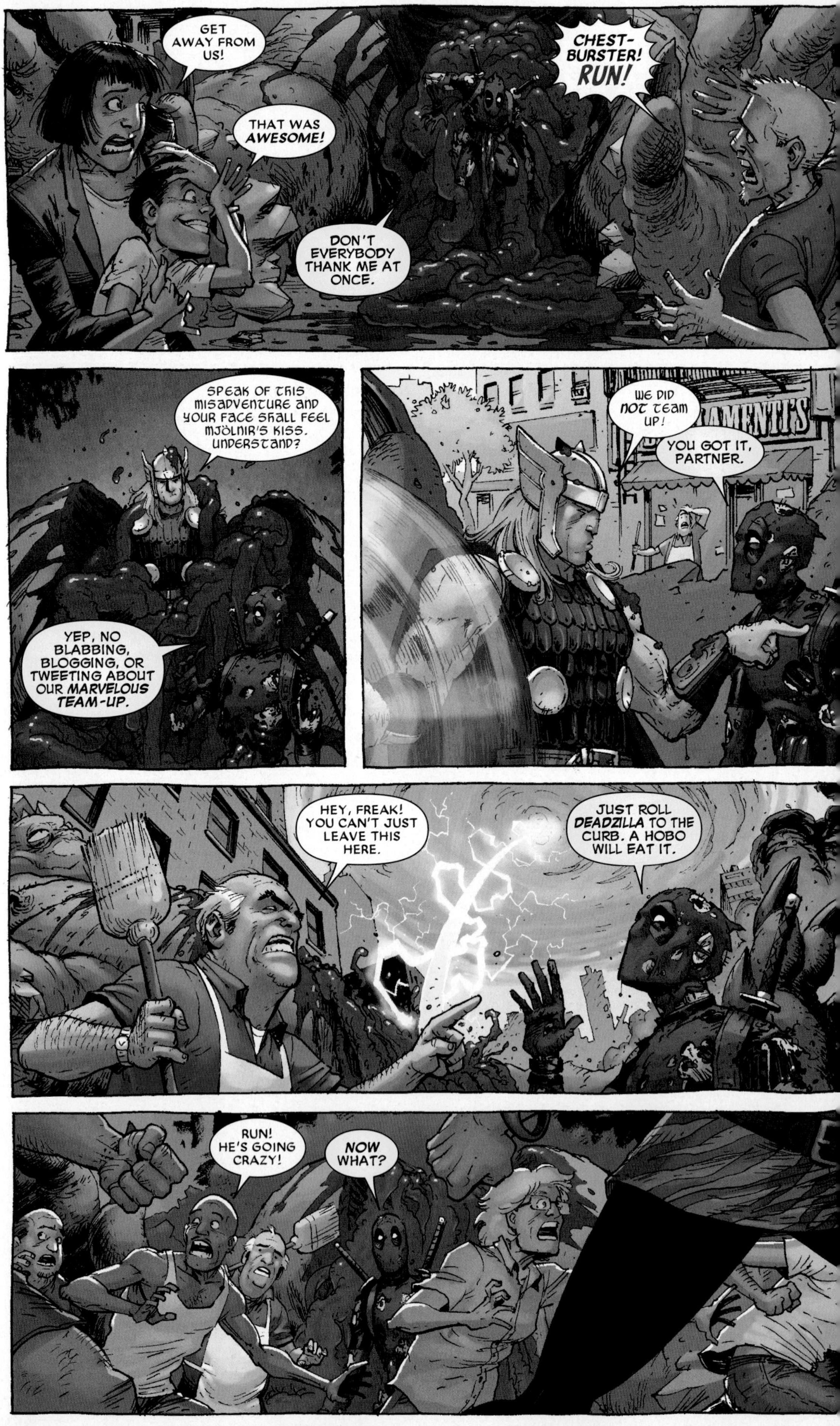
GET AWAY FROM US!
THAT WAS AWESOME!
CHEST-BURSTER! RUN!
DON'T EVERYBODY THANK ME AT ONCE.
SPEAK OF THIS MISADVENTURE AND YOUR FACE SHALL FEEL MJÖLNIR'S KISS. UNDERSTAND?
YEP, NO BLABBING, BLOGGING, OR TWEETING ABOUT OUR MARVELOUS TEAM-UP.
WE DID NOT TEAM UP!
YOU GOT IT, PARTNER.
HEY, FREAK! YOU CAN'T JUST LEAVE THIS HERE.
JUST ROLL DEADZILLA TO THE CURB. A HOBO WILL EAT IT.
RUN! HE'S GOING CRAZY!
NOW WHAT?

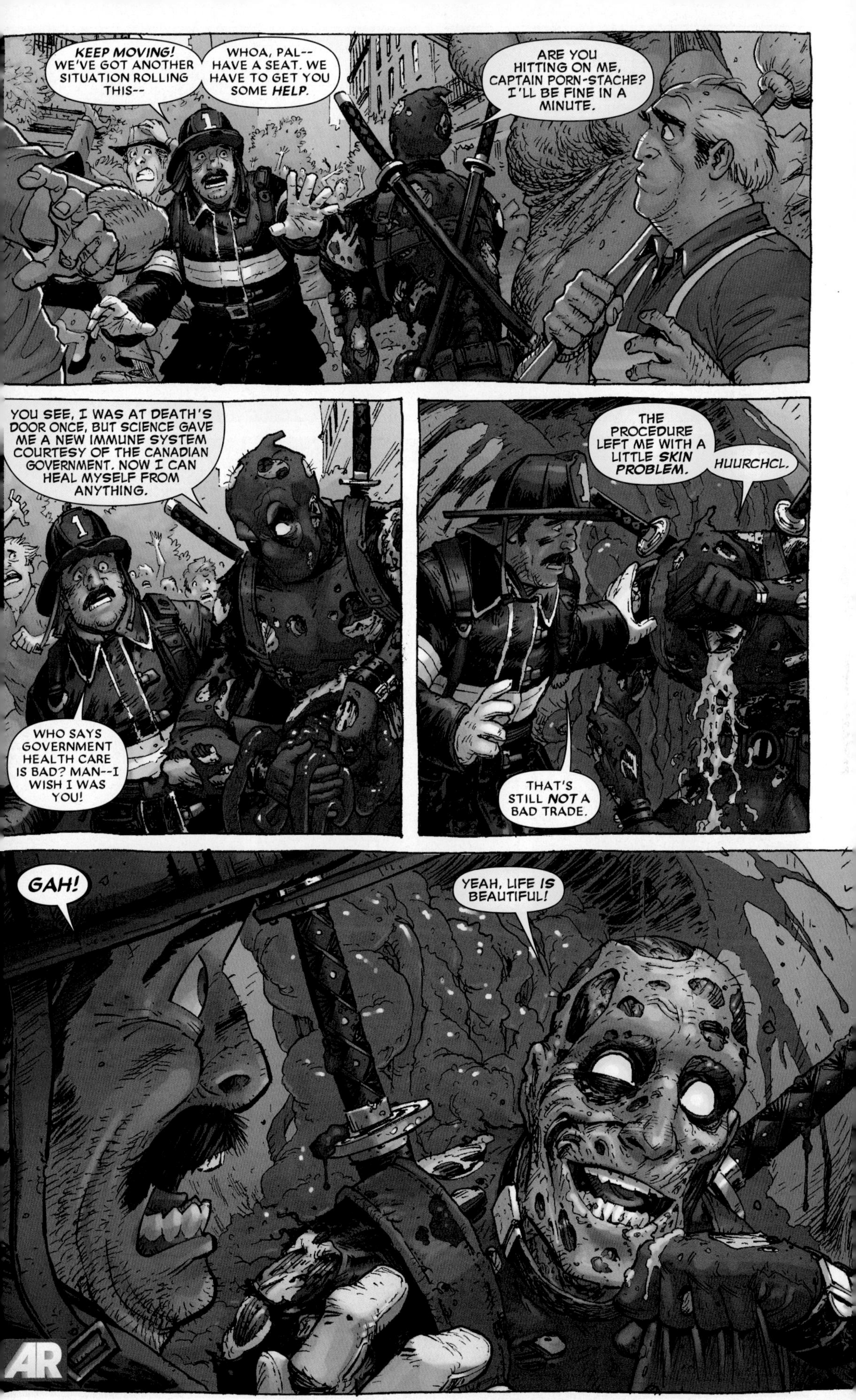

KEEP MOVING! WE'VE GOT ANOTHER SITUATION ROLLING THIS--
WHOA, PAL-- HAVE A SEAT. WE HAVE TO GET YOU SOME HELP.
ARE YOU HITTING ON ME, CAPTAIN PORN-STACHE? I'LL BE FINE IN A MINUTE.
YOU SEE, I WAS AT DEATH'S DOOR ONCE, BUT SCIENCE GAVE ME A NEW IMMUNE SYSTEM COURTESY OF THE CANADIAN GOVERNMENT. NOW I CAN HEAL MYSELF FROM ANYTHING.
WHO SAYS GOVERNMENT HEALTH CARE IS BAD? MAN--I WISH I WAS YOU!
THE PROCEDURE LEFT ME WITH A LITTLE SKIN PROBLEM.
HUURCHCL.
THAT'S STILL NOT A BAD TRADE.
GAH!
YEAH, LIFE IS BEAUTIFUL!
AR

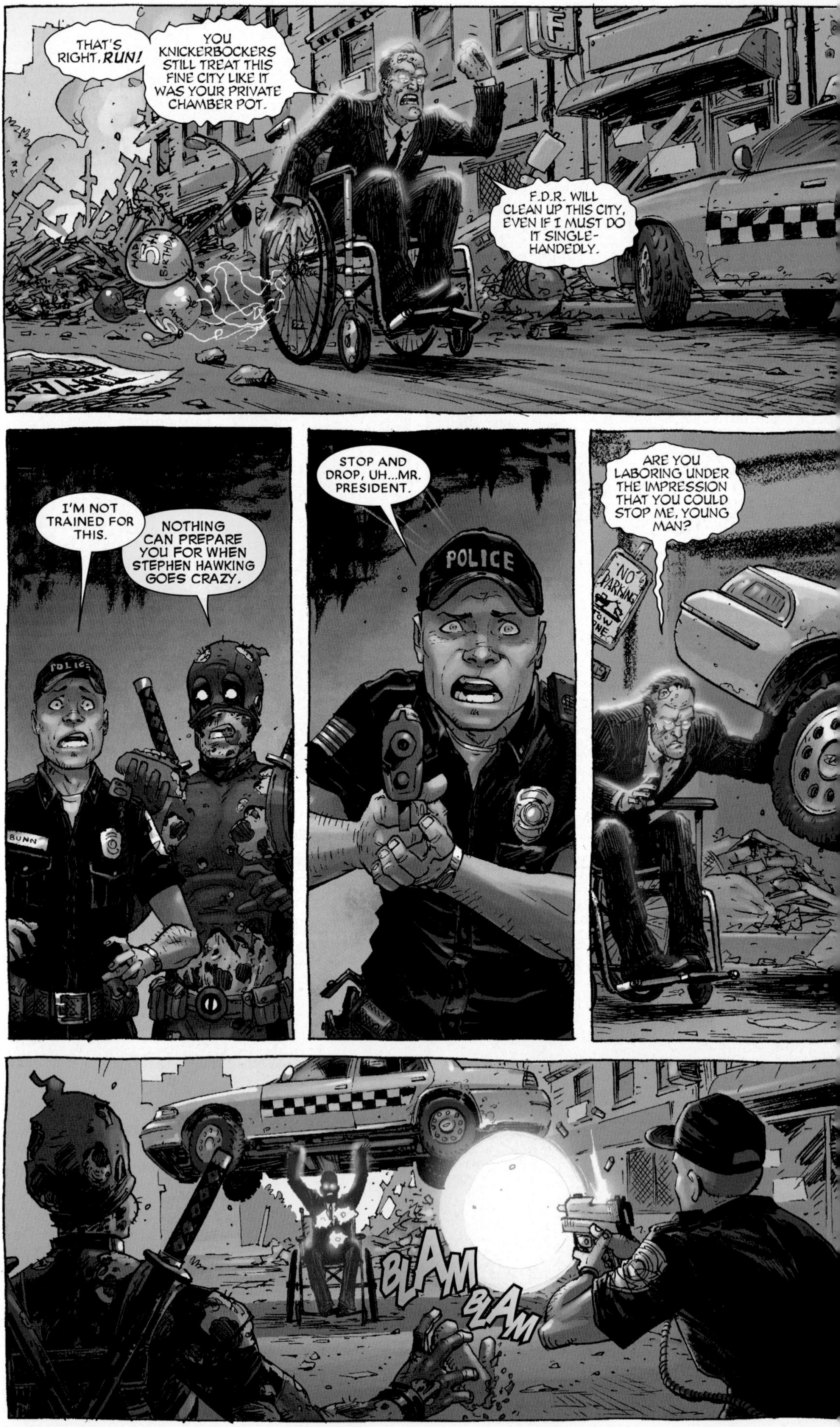
THAT'S RIGHT, RUN!
YOU KNICKERBOCKERS STILL TREAT THIS FINE CITY LIKE IT WAS YOUR PRIVATE CHAMBER POT.
F.D.R. WILL CLEAN UP THIS CITY, EVEN IF I MUST DO IT SINGLE-HANDEDLY.
I'M NOT TRAINED FOR THIS.
NOTHING CAN PREPARE YOU FOR WHEN STEPHEN HAWKING GOES CRAZY.
STOP AND DROP, UH...MR. PRESIDENT.
POLICE
ARE YOU LABORING UNDER THE IMPRESSION THAT YOU COULD STOP ME, YOUNG MAN?
NO PARKING
BLAM
BLAM

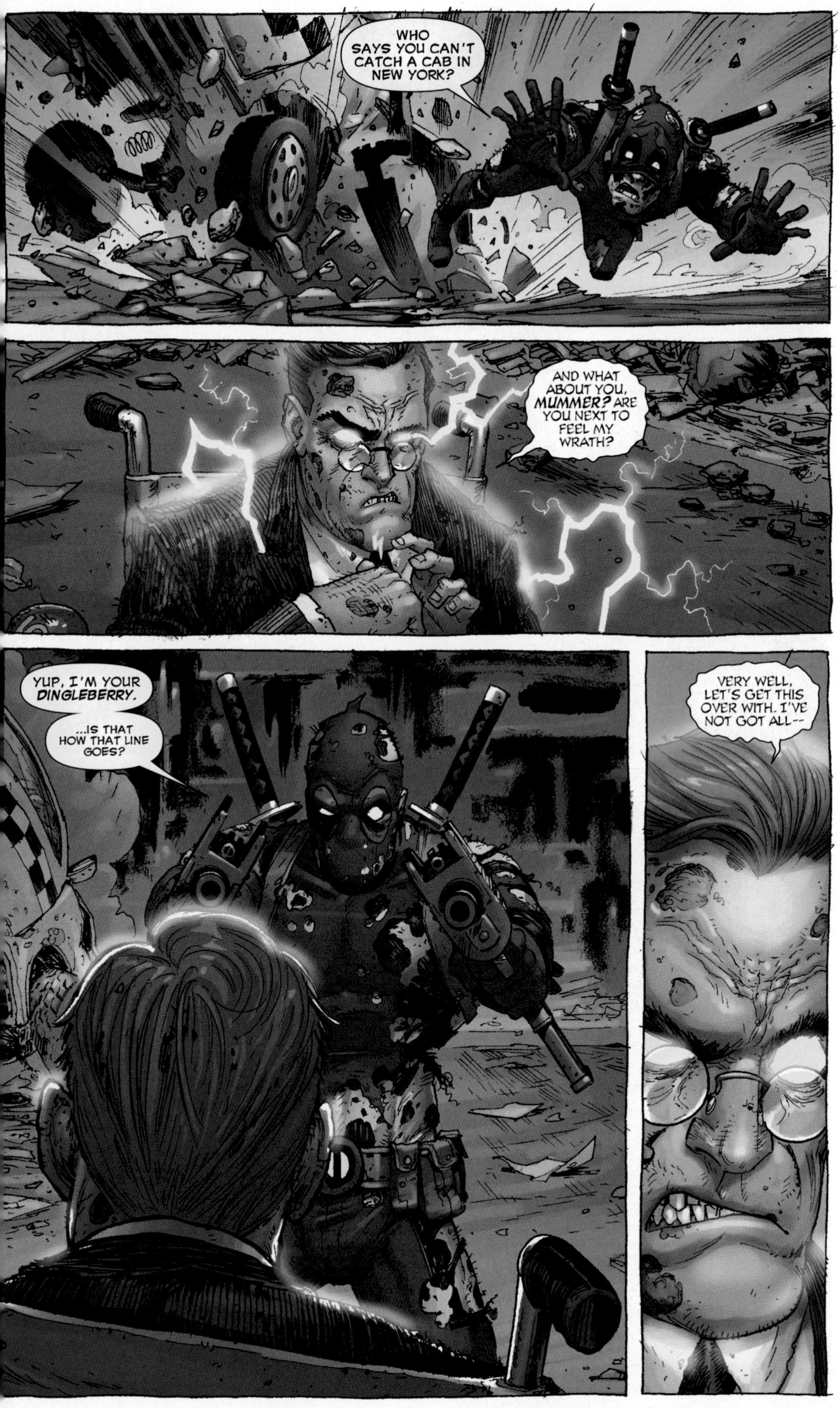
WHO SAYS YOU CAN'T CATCH A CAB IN NEW YORK?
AND WHAT ABOUT YOU, MUMMER? ARE YOU NEXT TO FEEL MY WRATH?
YUP, I'M YOUR DINGLEBERRY.
...IS THAT HOW THAT LINE GOES?
VERY WELL, LET'S GET THIS OVER WITH. I'VE NOT GOT ALL--

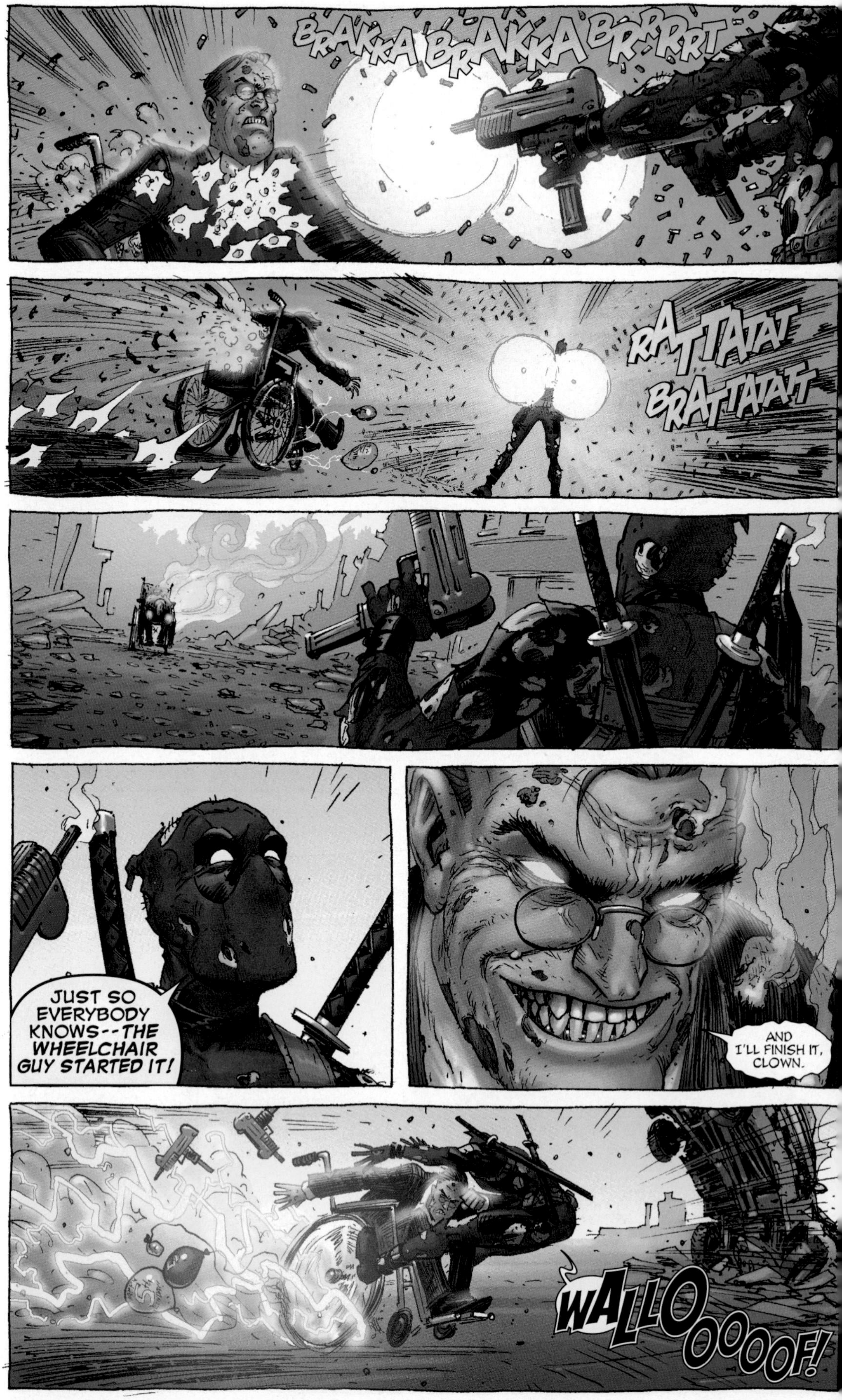
BRAKKA BRAKKA BRRRRRT
RATTATAT BRATTATAT
JUST SO EVERYBODY KNOWS--THE WHEELCHAIR GUY STARTED IT!
AND I'LL FINISH IT, CLOWN.
WALLOOOOOF!

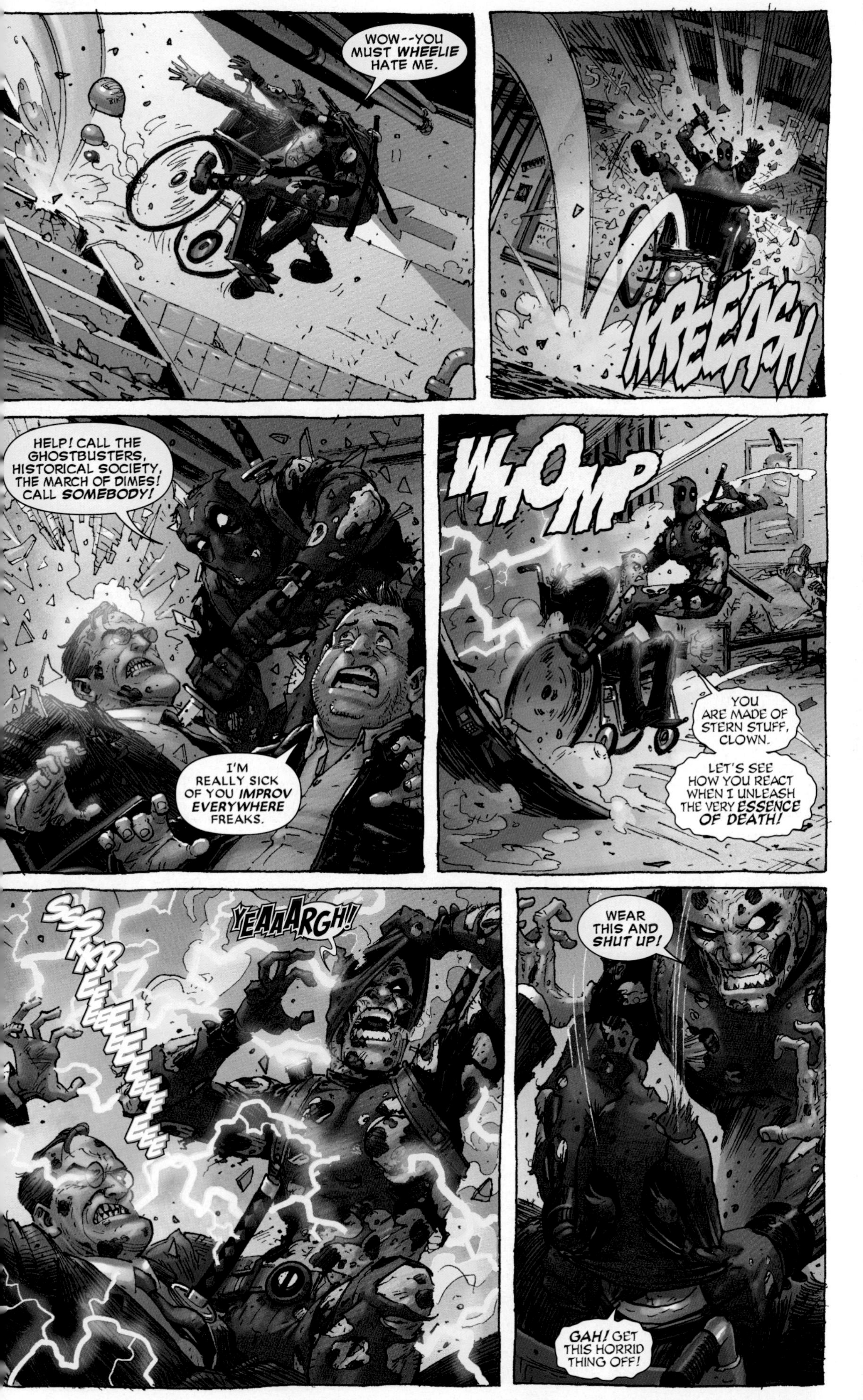
WOW--YOU MUST *WHEELIE* HATE ME.
KREEASH
HELP! CALL THE GHOSTBUSTERS, HISTORICAL SOCIETY, THE MARCH OF DIMES! CALL *SOMEBODY!*
I'M REALLY SICK OF YOU *IMPROV EVERYWHERE* FREAKS.
WHOMP
YOU ARE MADE OF STERN STUFF, CLOWN.
LET'S SEE HOW YOU REACT WHEN I UNLEASH THE VERY *ESSENCE OF DEATH!*
SSSKKREEEEEEEEEEEEEE
YEAAAARGH!
WEAR THIS AND *SHUT UP!*
GAH! GET THIS HORRID THING OFF!

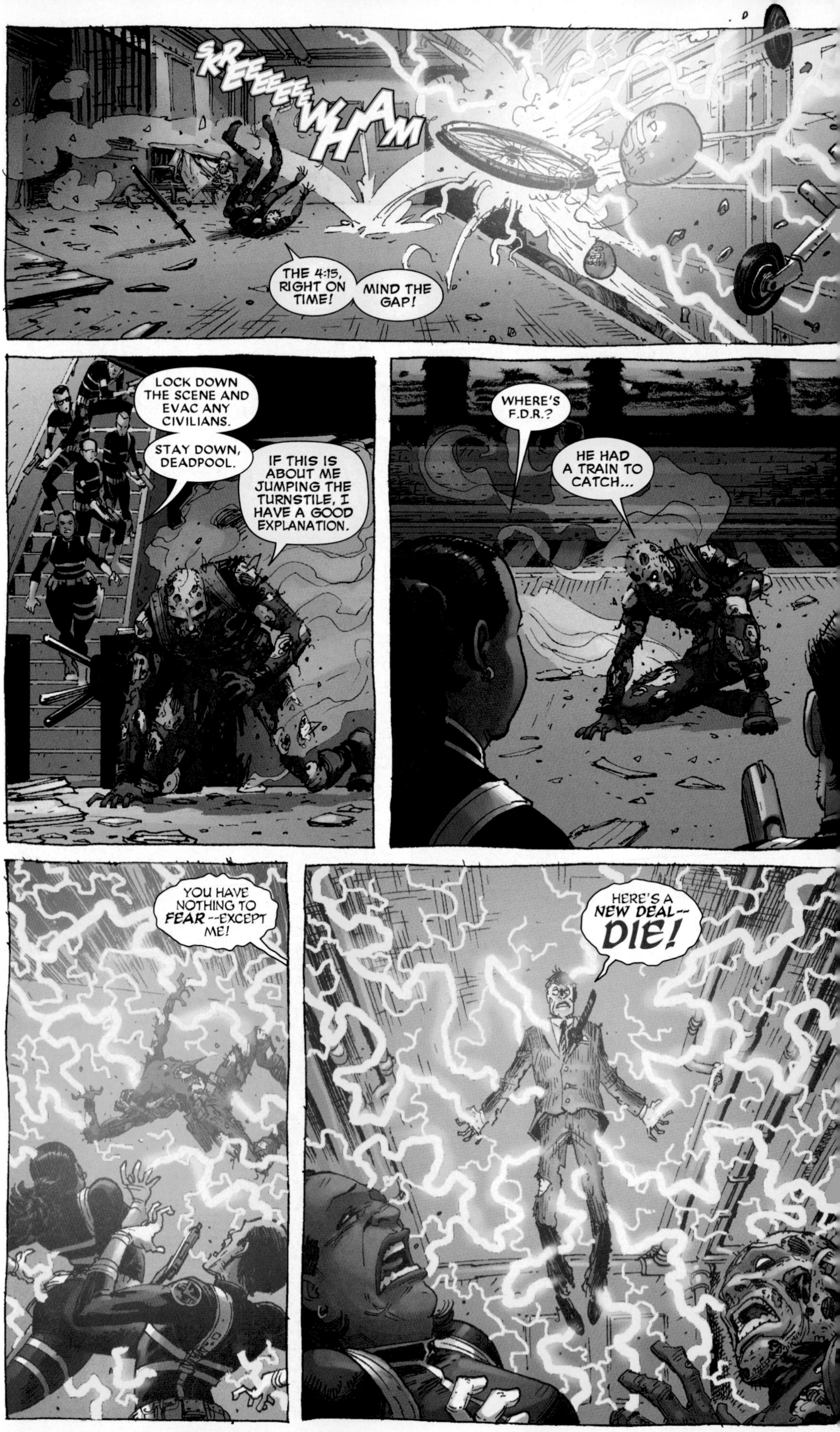
SKREEEEEEWHAM
THE 4:15, RIGHT ON TIME!
MIND THE GAP!
LOCK DOWN THE SCENE AND EVAC ANY CIVILIANS.
STAY DOWN, DEADPOOL.
IF THIS IS ABOUT ME JUMPING THE TURNSTILE, I HAVE A GOOD EXPLANATION.
WHERE'S F.D.R.?
HE HAD A TRAIN TO CATCH...
YOU HAVE NOTHING TO FEAR--EXCEPT ME!
HERE'S A NEW DEAL--DIE!

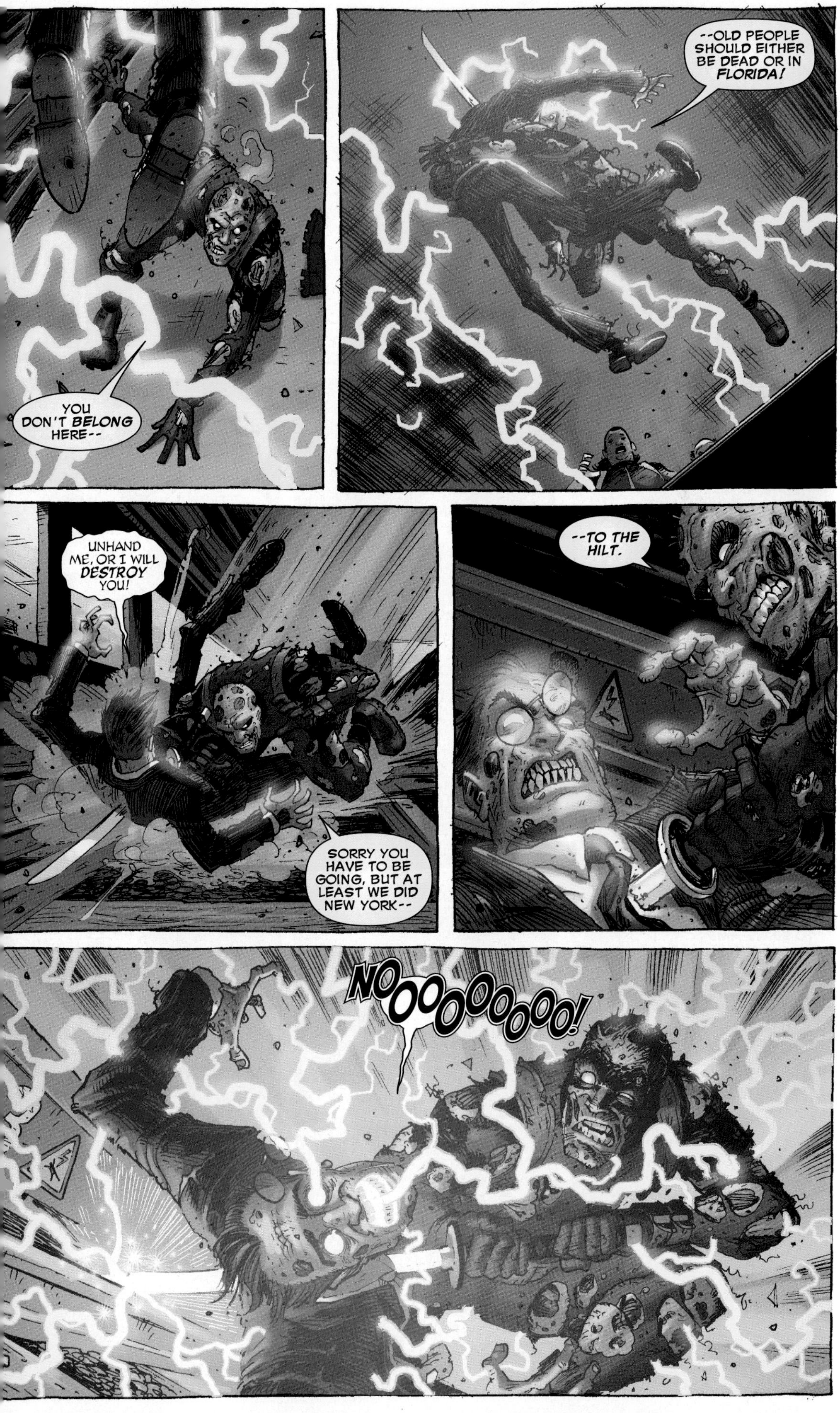
YOU DON'T BELONG HERE--
--OLD PEOPLE SHOULD EITHER BE DEAD OR IN FLORIDA!
UNHAND ME, OR I WILL DESTROY YOU!
SORRY YOU HAVE TO BE GOING, BUT AT LEAST WE DID NEW YORK--
--TO THE HILT.
NOOOOOOOOOO!

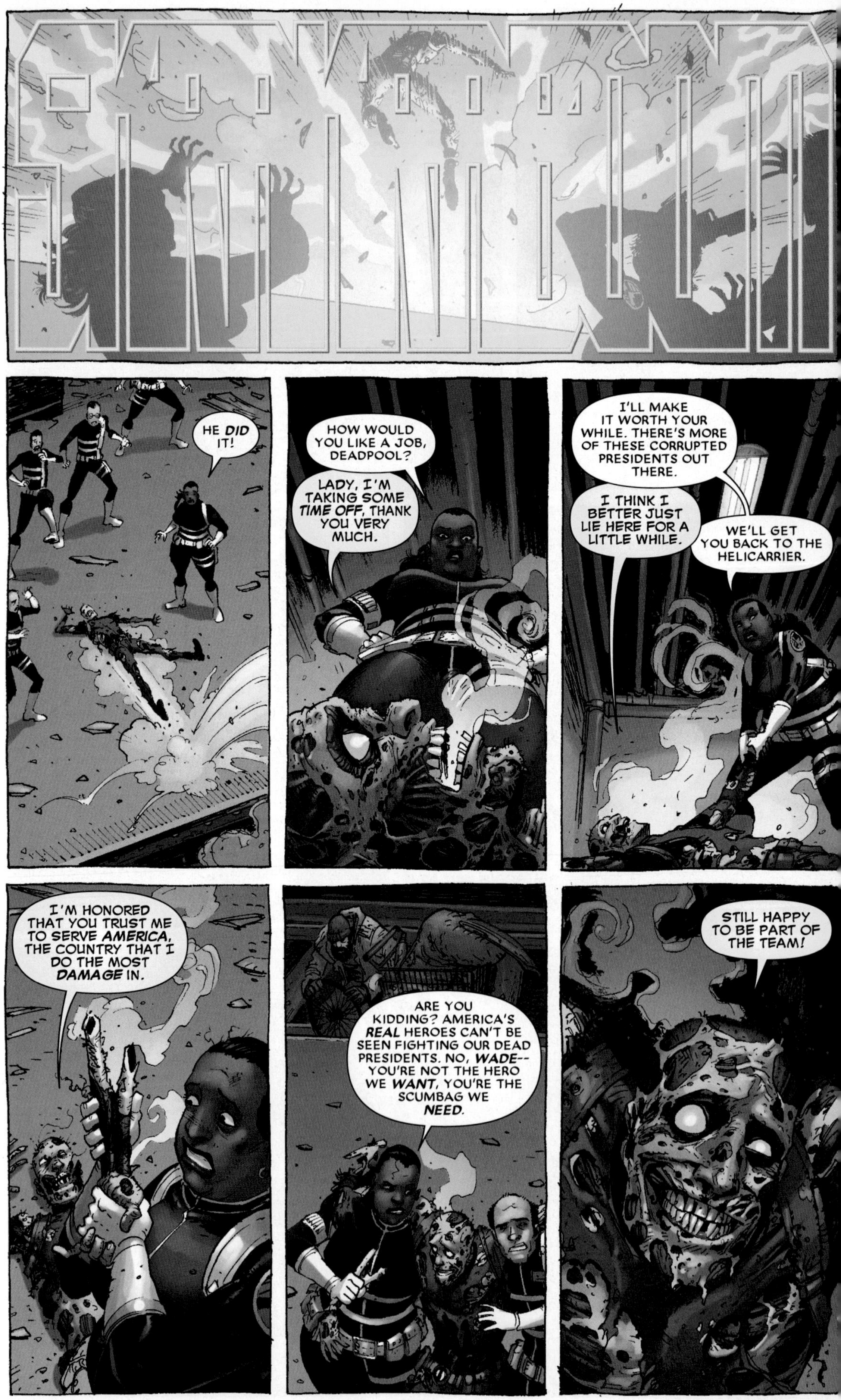
HE DID IT!
HOW WOULD YOU LIKE A JOB, DEADPOOL?
LADY, I'M TAKING SOME TIME OFF, THANK YOU VERY MUCH.
I'LL MAKE IT WORTH YOUR WHILE. THERE'S MORE OF THESE CORRUPTED PRESIDENTS OUT THERE.
I THINK I BETTER JUST LIE HERE FOR A LITTLE WHILE.
WE'LL GET YOU BACK TO THE HELICARRIER.
I'M HONORED THAT YOU TRUST ME TO SERVE AMERICA, THE COUNTRY THAT I DO THE MOST DAMAGE IN.
ARE YOU KIDDING? AMERICA'S REAL HEROES CAN'T BE SEEN FIGHTING OUR DEAD PRESIDENTS. NO, WADE-- YOU'RE NOT THE HERO WE WANT, YOU'RE THE SCUMBAG WE NEED.
STILL HAPPY TO BE PART OF THE TEAM!

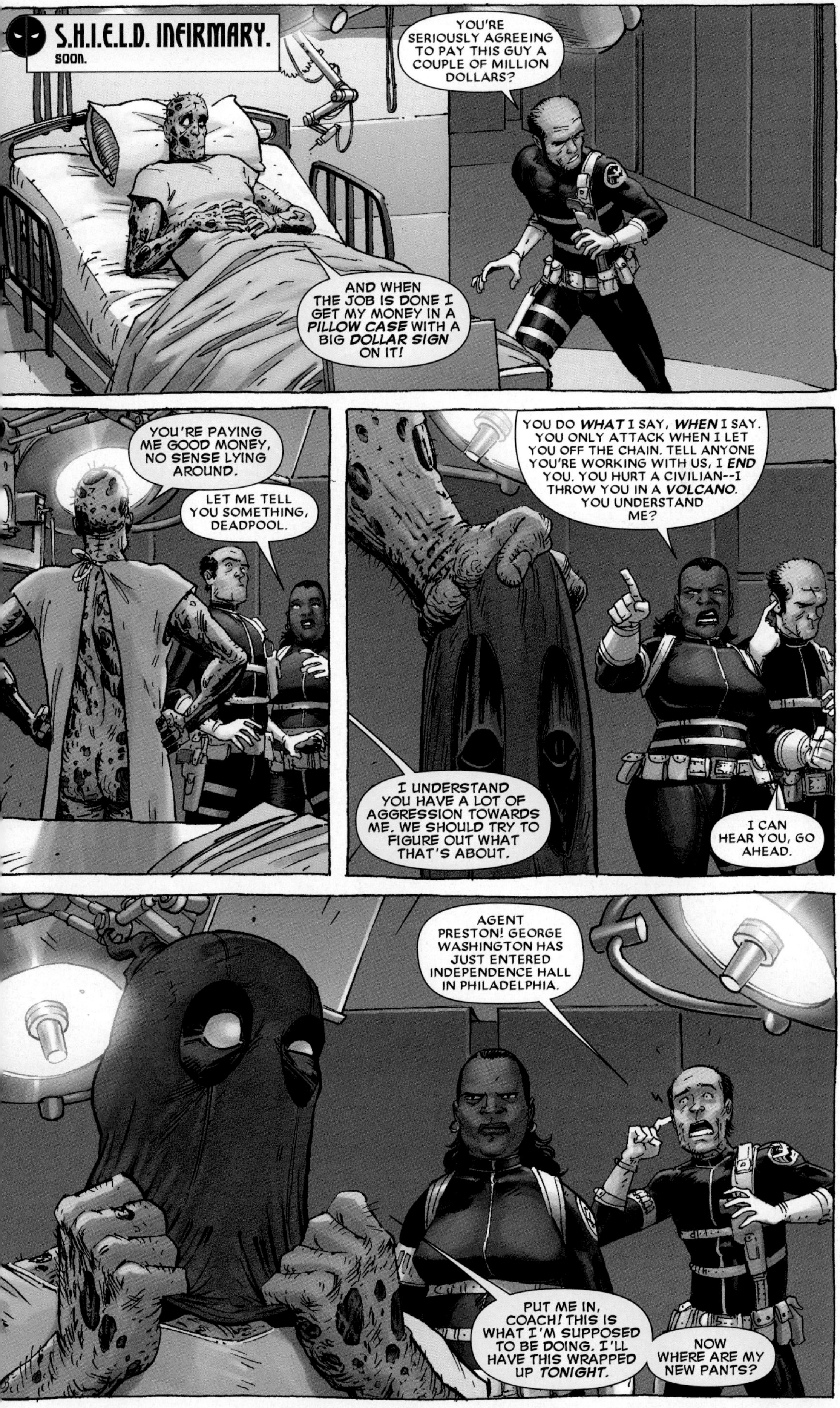
S.H.I.E.L.D. INFIRMARY.
SOON.
YOU'RE SERIOUSLY AGREEING TO PAY THIS GUY A COUPLE OF MILLION DOLLARS?
AND WHEN THE JOB IS DONE I GET MY MONEY IN A PILLOW CASE WITH A BIG DOLLAR SIGN ON IT!
YOU'RE PAYING ME GOOD MONEY, NO SENSE LYING AROUND.
LET ME TELL YOU SOMETHING, DEADPOOL.
YOU DO WHAT I SAY, WHEN I SAY. YOU ONLY ATTACK WHEN I LET YOU OFF THE CHAIN. TELL ANYONE YOU'RE WORKING WITH US, I END YOU. YOU HURT A CIVILIAN--I THROW YOU IN A VOLCANO. YOU UNDERSTAND ME?
I UNDERSTAND YOU HAVE A LOT OF AGGRESSION TOWARDS ME. WE SHOULD TRY TO FIGURE OUT WHAT THAT'S ABOUT.
I CAN HEAR YOU, GO AHEAD.
AGENT PRESTON! GEORGE WASHINGTON HAS JUST ENTERED INDEPENDENCE HALL IN PHILADELPHIA.
PUT ME IN, COACH! THIS IS WHAT I'M SUPPOSED TO BE DOING. I'LL HAVE THIS WRAPPED UP TONIGHT.
NOW WHERE ARE MY NEW PANTS?

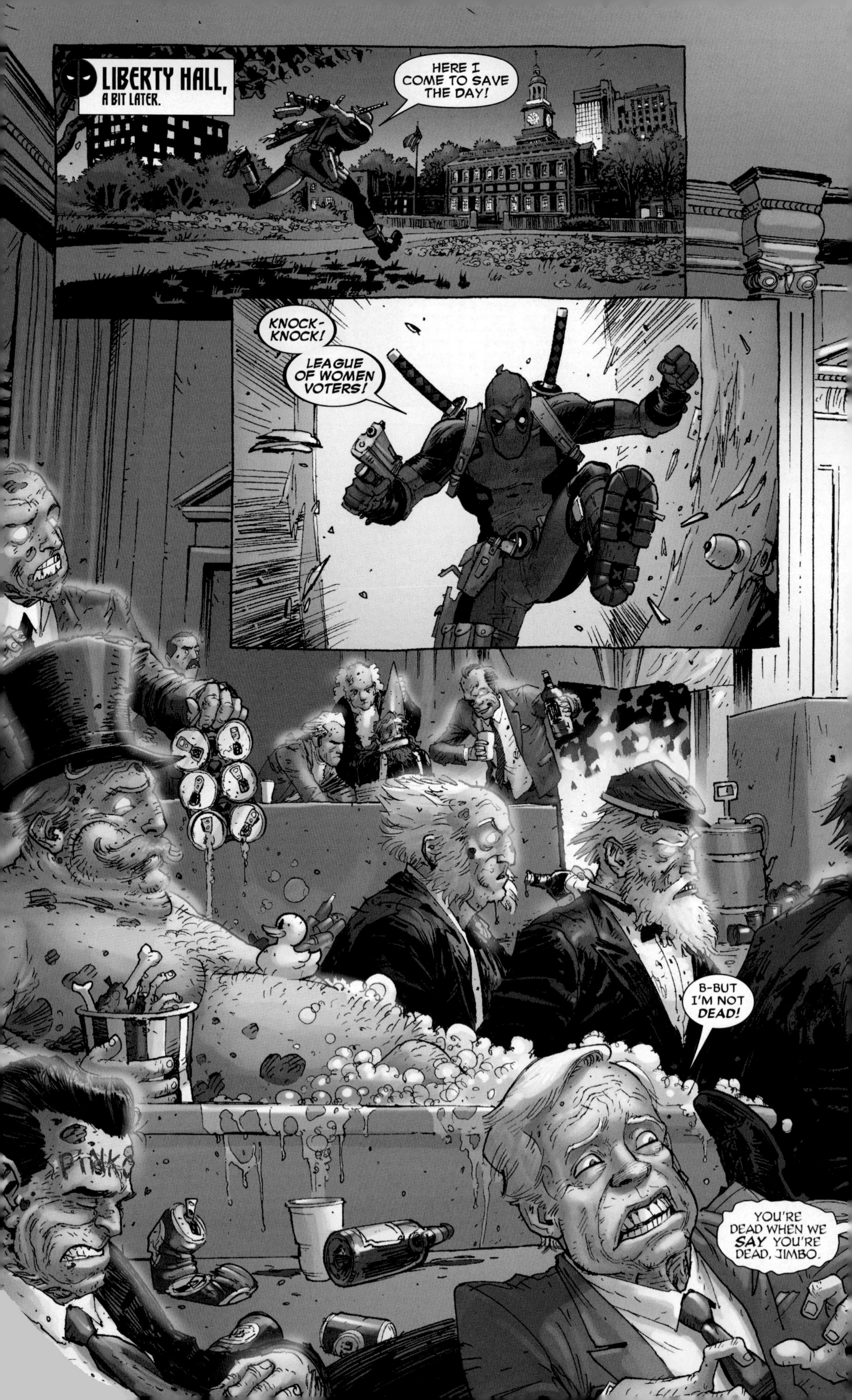
LIBERTY HALL,
A BIT LATER.
HERE I COME TO SAVE THE DAY!
KNOCK-KNOCK!
LEAGUE OF WOMEN VOTERS!
B-BUT I'M NOT DEAD!
YOU'RE DEAD WHEN WE SAY YOU'RE DEAD, JIMBO.

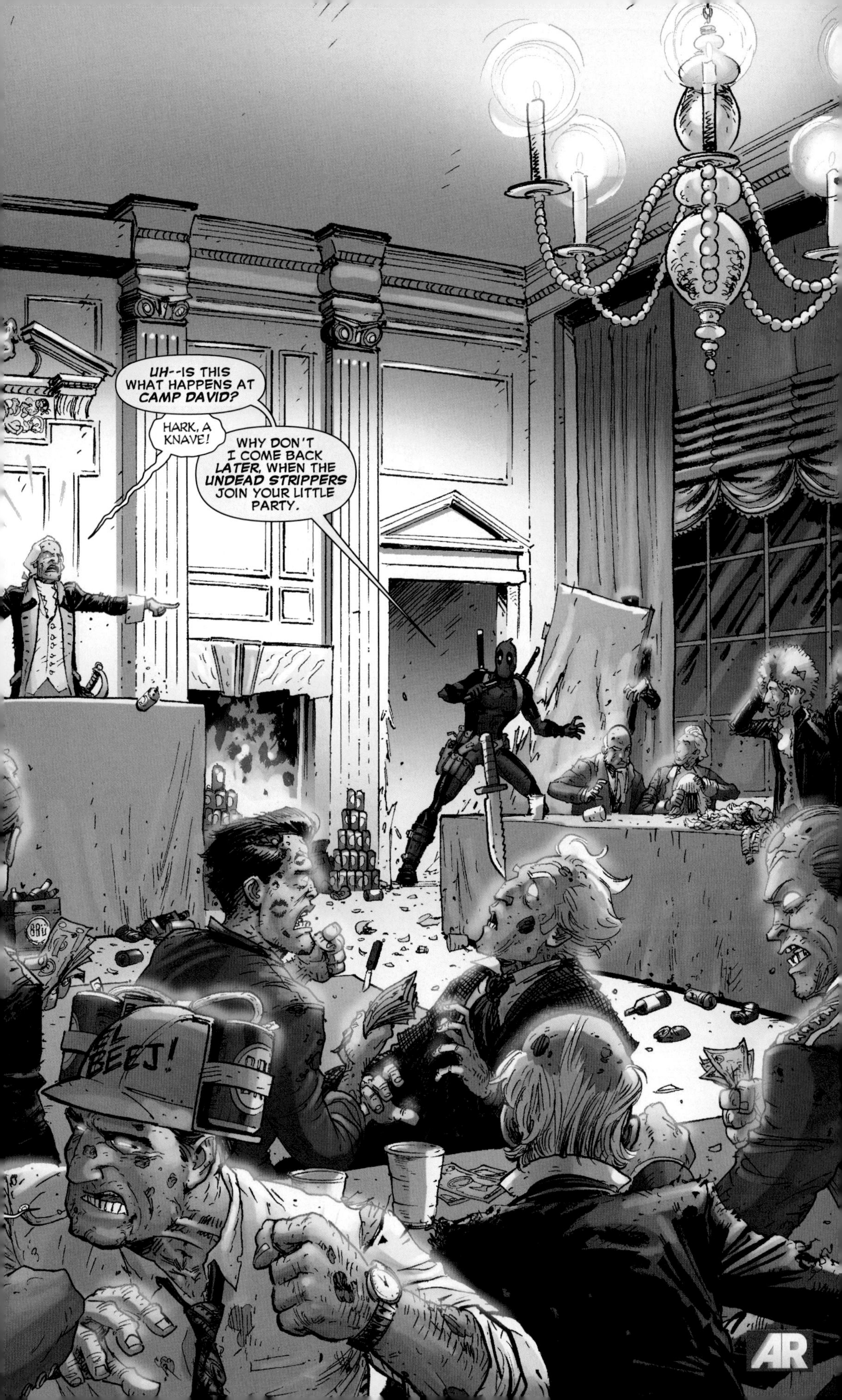
UH--IS THIS WHAT HAPPENS AT CAMP DAVID?
HARK, A KNAVE!
WHY DON'T I COME BACK LATER, WHEN THE UNDEAD STRIPPERS JOIN YOUR LITTLE PARTY.
EL BEEJ!

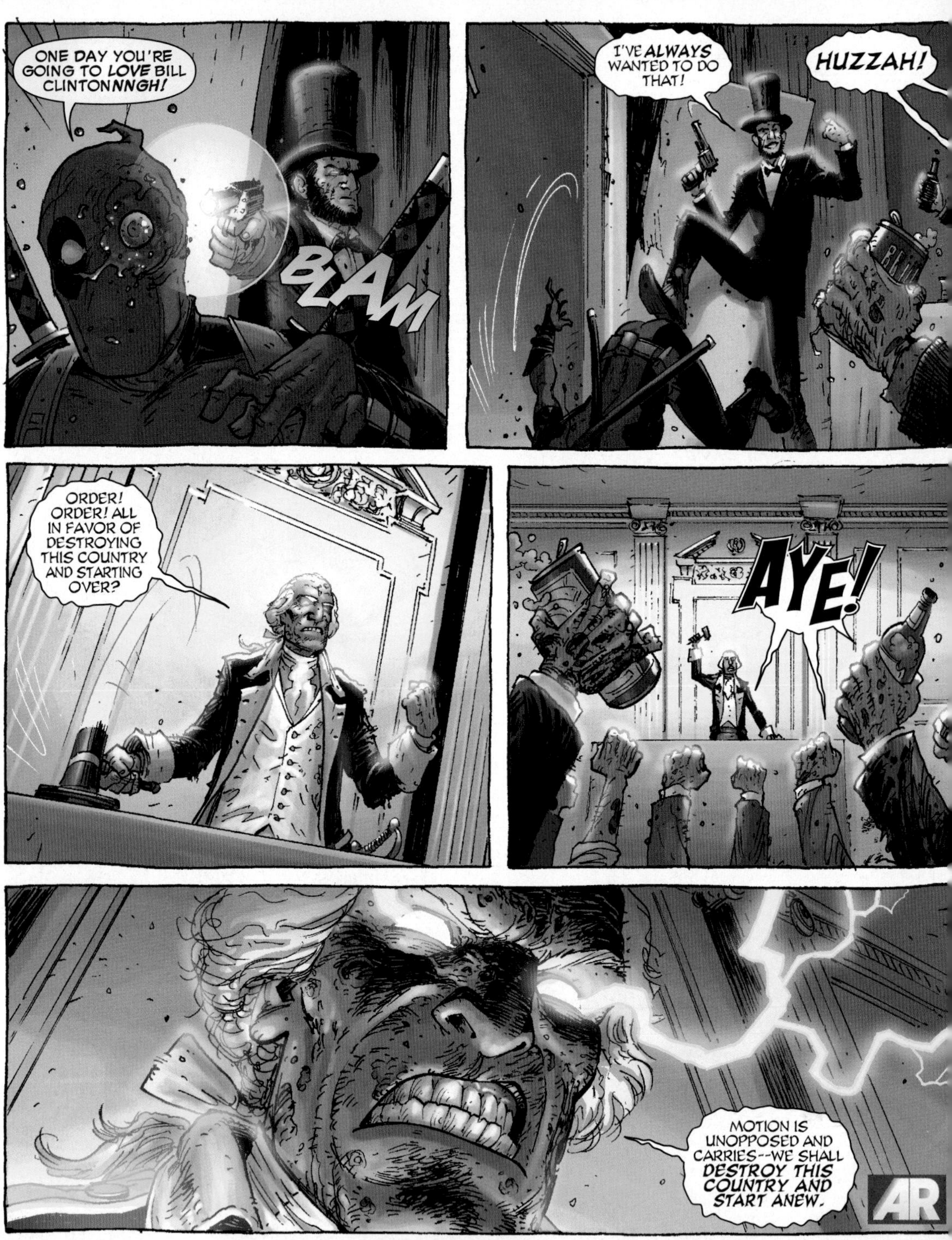
ONE DAY YOU'RE GOING TO LOVE BILL CLINTONNNGH!
BLAM
I'VE ALWAYS WANTED TO DO THAT!
HUZZAH!
ORDER! ORDER! ALL IN FAVOR OF DESTROYING THIS COUNTRY AND STARTING OVER?
AYE!
MOTION IS UNOPPOSED AND CARRIES--WE SHALL DESTROY THIS COUNTRY AND START ANEW.
AR

In Wade We Trust

Written by Gerry Duggan & Brian Posehn   Art by Tony Moore

Colors by Val Staples   Cover by Geof Darrow & Peter Doherty

Letters by VC's Joe Sabino   Edited by Jordan D. White

Nick Lowe — *Senior Editor*
Axel Alonso — *Editor in Chief*
Joe Quesada — *Chief Creative Officer*
Dan Buckley — *Publisher*
Alan Fine — *Executive Producer*

Stolen **FROM THE DESK OF CAPTAIN AMERICA**

135 W 50TH STREET, 7TH FLOOR
NEW YORK, NY 10020

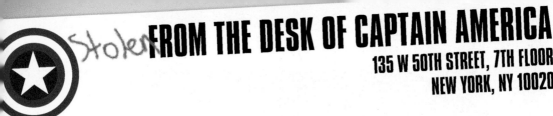

Welcome to the Marvel Now's ***Deadpool #1***. I know what you're thinking ut--IT'S NOT A REBOOT! How do I know this? Because I'm still shooting, unching, and stabbing my way through this crazy universe. I'm still the best hing that's happened to a healing factor...and also, it's not a reboot because xel Alonso said so.

Before I get to the new *"talent"* how about we pour one out for Dan Way? Ie survived sharing his head with me years longer than I thought he would. 3ut I'm not through with Dan yet. I'm the star of his new Thunderbolts book.

I'll kill him yet.

Which brings us to the new guys. I've starred in hundreds of comics, a movie, and soon a video game. If Gerry Duggan & Brian Posehn don't screw this up, they'll be able to coast on the Deadpool gravy-train for years. It's all their fault if you don't see *West Coast Deadpool*, *Great Lakes Deadpool*, *Web Of Deadpool* and many more that I can't announce just yet.

The two dummies *"writing"* this book are Brian Posehn & Gerry Duggan. What a coup for Marvel! I guess the *According To Jim* writers weren't available? When they're together they look like a *MythBuster* episode about Orson Welles' death. The poor bastard in charge of this train wreck is editor, Jordan D. White. He looks like the piano player that gets hit over the head with a bottle in every Western ever. The hillbilly drawing it is Tony Moore. He's pretty OK, I reckon. I don't know Val Staples, but she put some really nice colors on Tony's scribbles.

I'm supposed to tell you that I want to hear from you, and I give a care what you think about my new book, but...I don't. Luckily for you, Marvel cares. So do the creators. So drop them a line at officex@marvel.com if you want to make it onto a future letters page and get berated by me. Don't forget to mark the letter *"OK to print."*

Suck it,

Deadpool

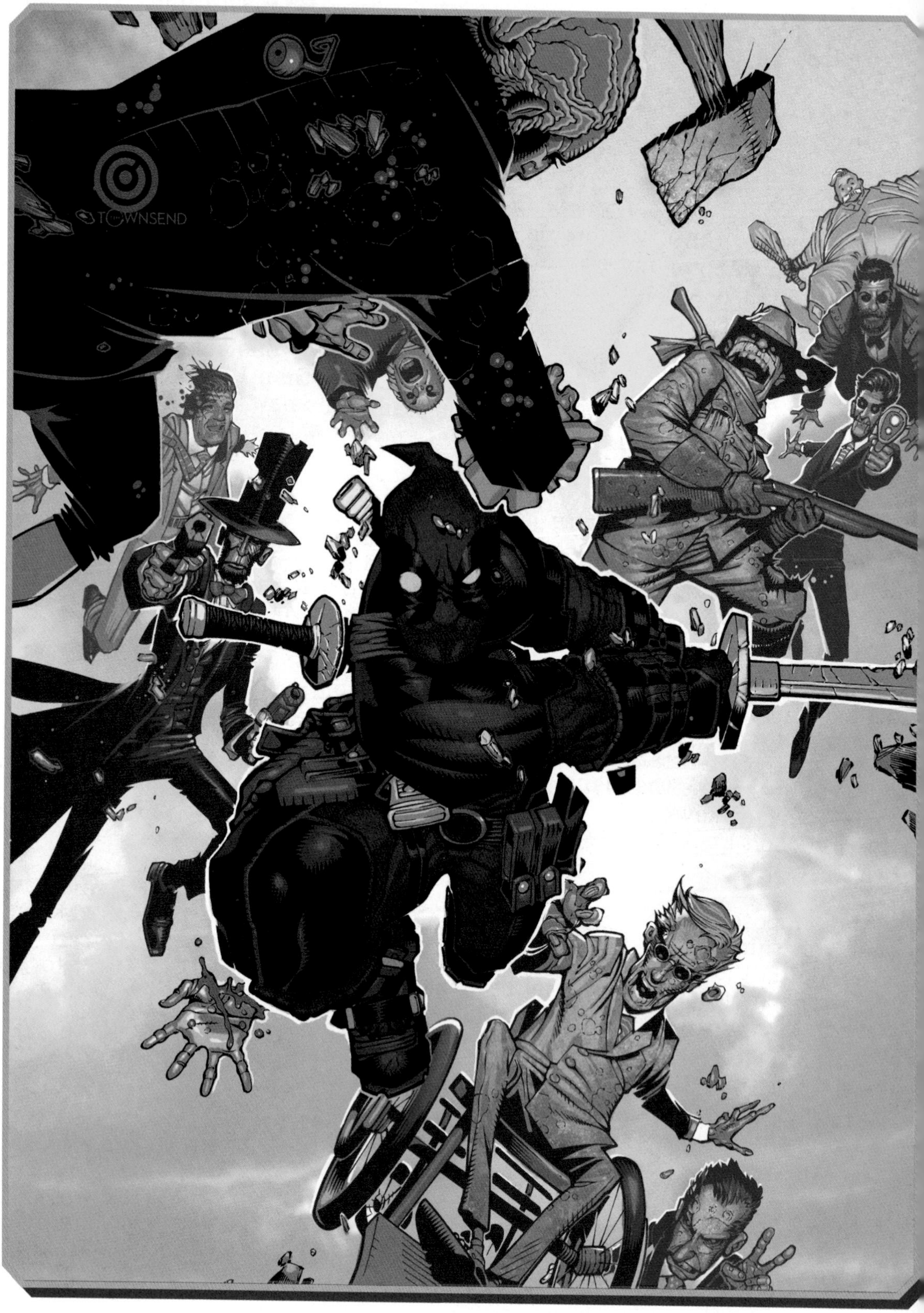
TOWNSEND

DEADPOOL (2012) #1 Variant by CHRIS BACHALO & TIM TOWNSEND

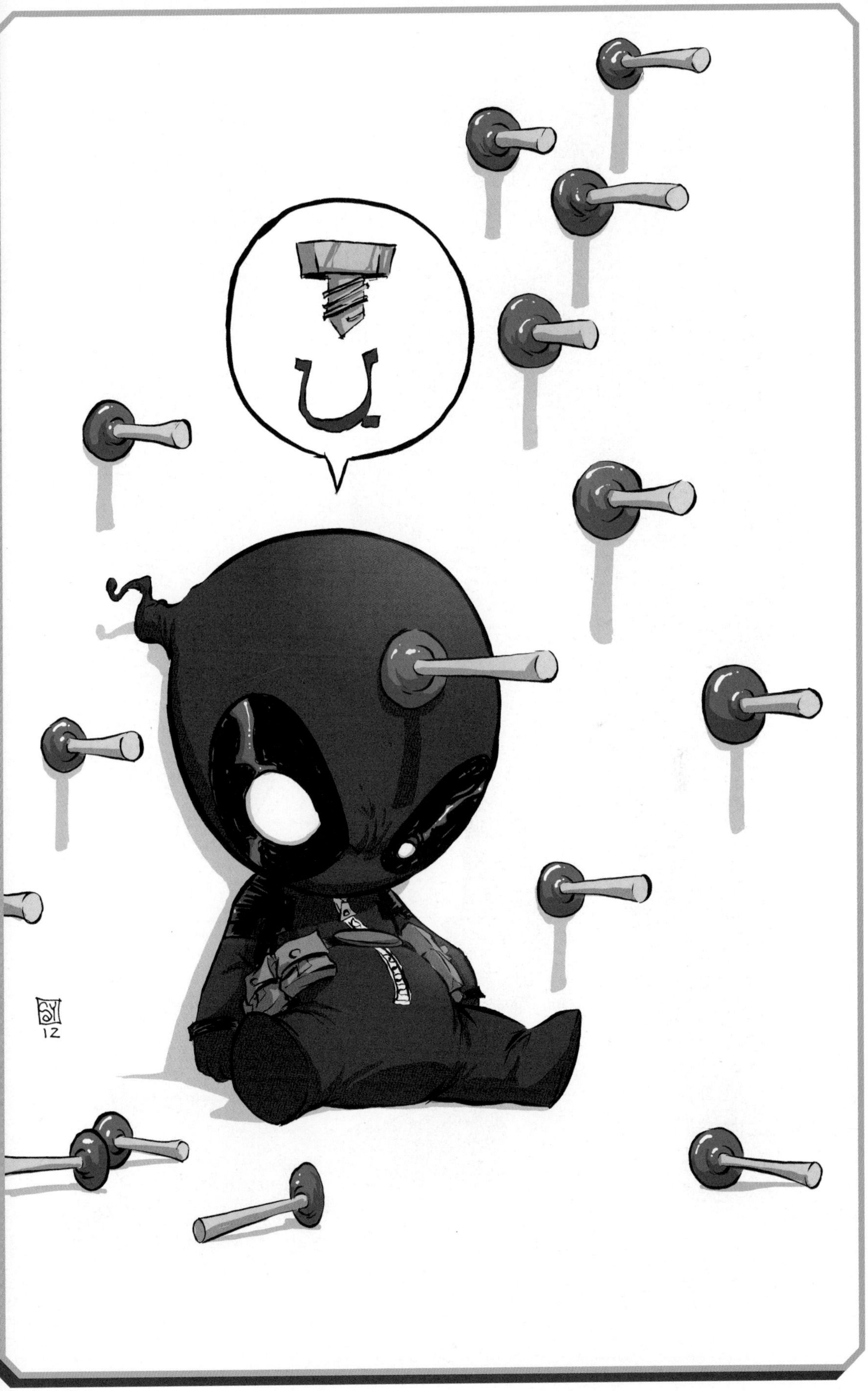
U

DEADPOOL (2012) #1 Variant by SKOTTIE YOUNG

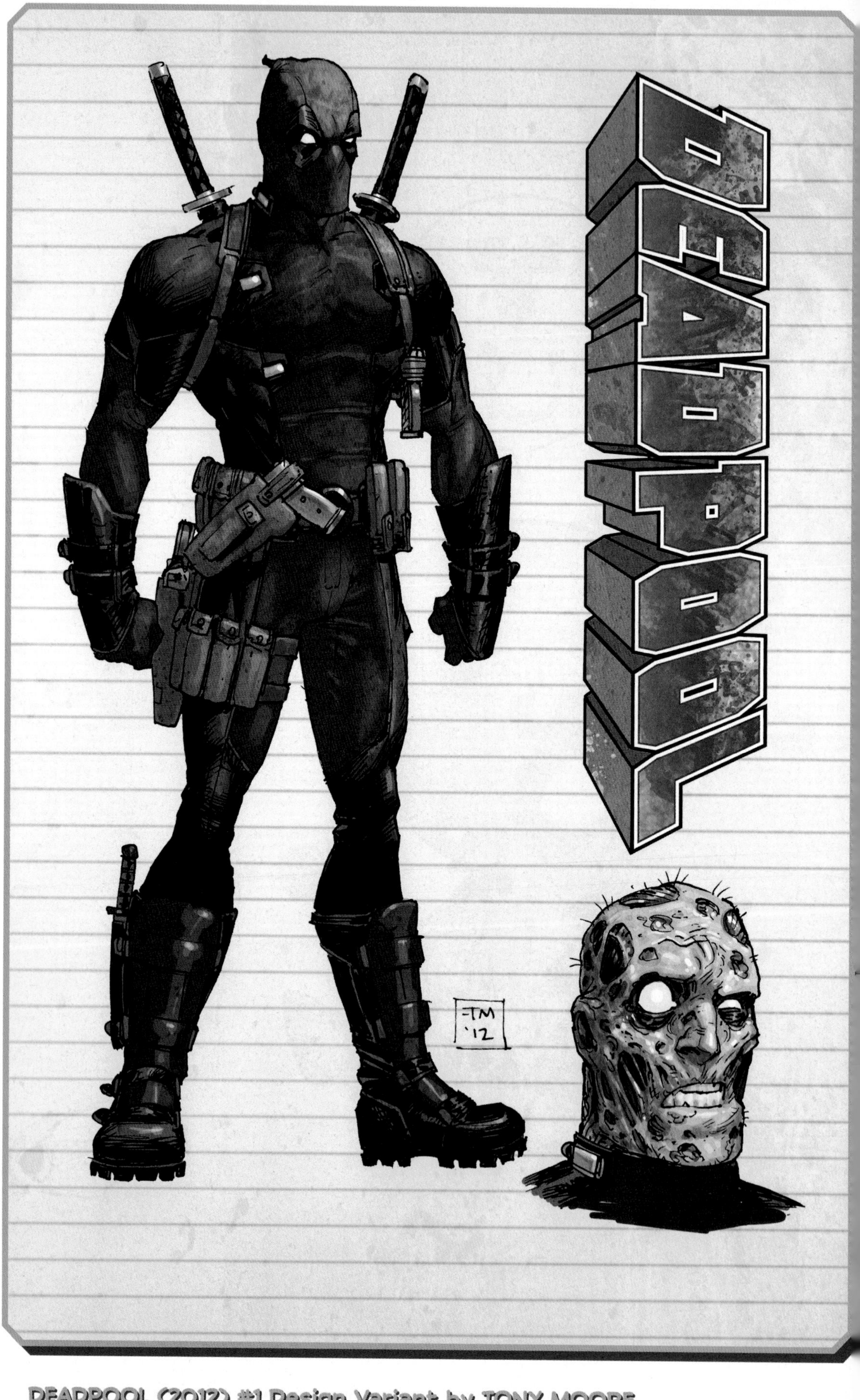
DEADPOOL
TM '12

DEADPOOL (2012) #1 Design Variant by TONY MOORE

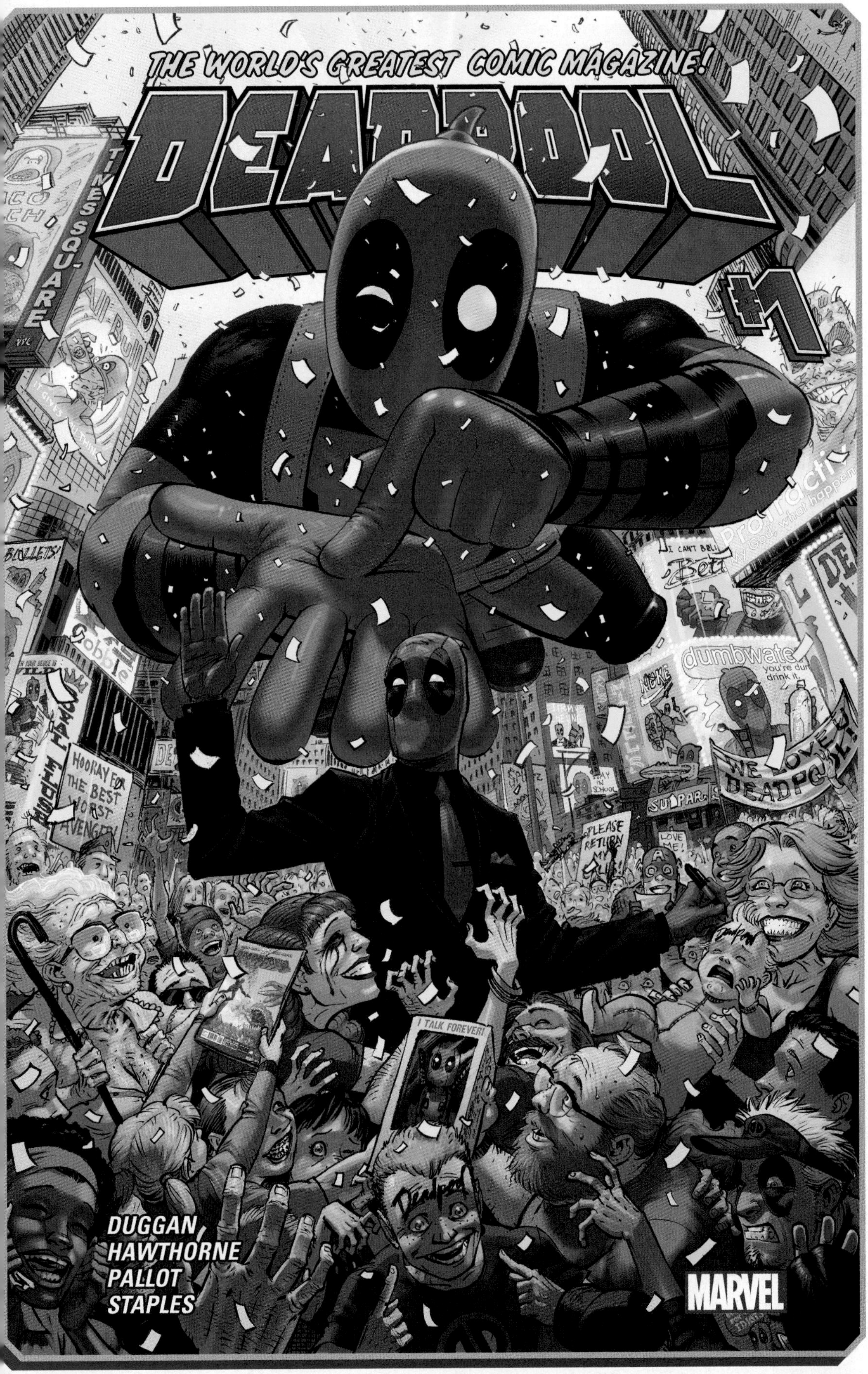
THE WORLD'S GREATEST COMIC MAGAZINE!
DEADPOOL
#1
TIMES SQUARE
HOORAY FOR THE BEST WORST AVENGER!
WE LOVE DEADPOOL!
PLEASE RETURN
LOVE ME!
I TALK FOREVER!
dumbwater
you're dum drink it.
SUPPAR
DUGGAN
HAWTHORNE
PALLOT
STAPLES
MARVEL

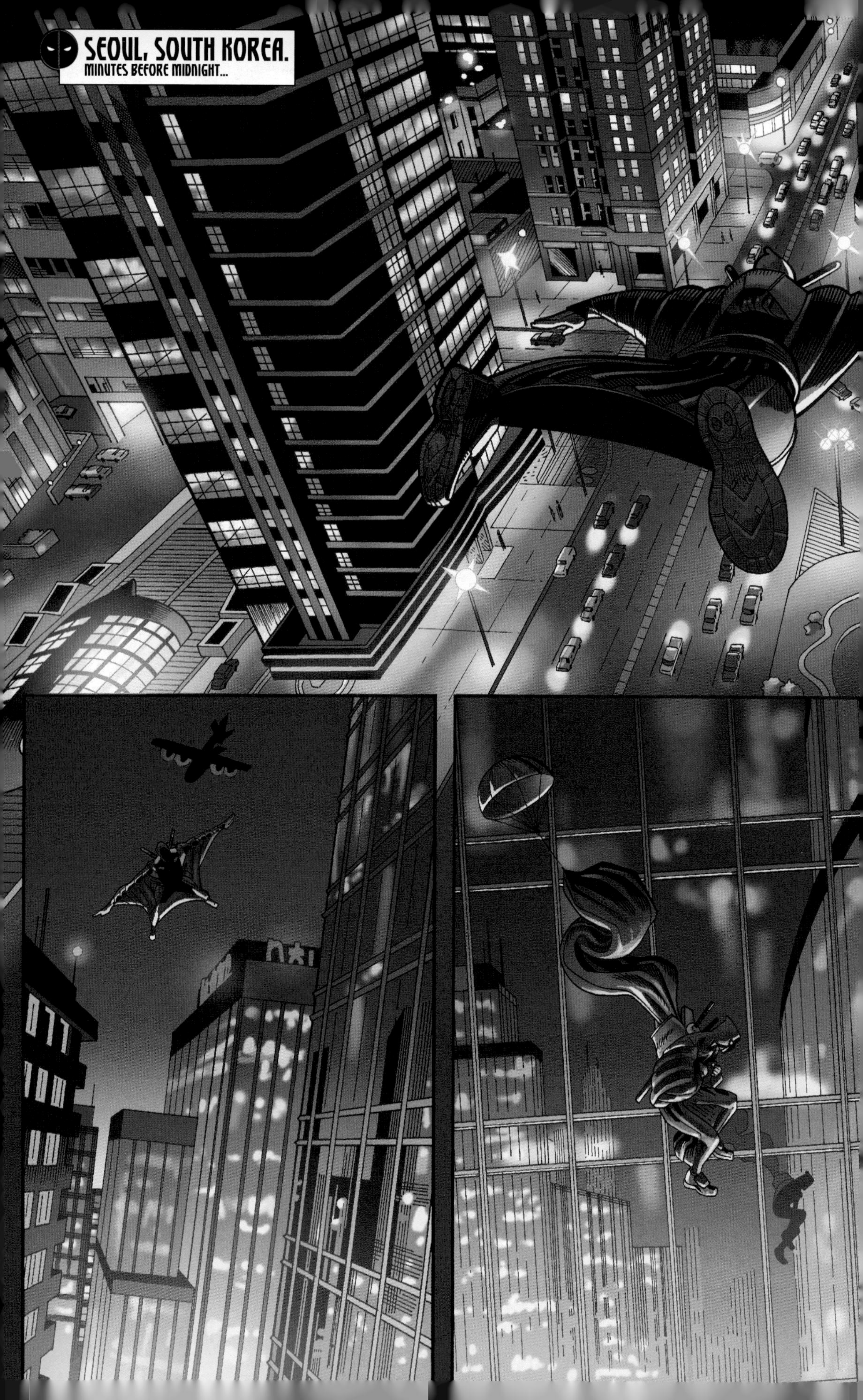
SEOUL, SOUTH KOREA.
MINUTES BEFORE MIDNIGHT...

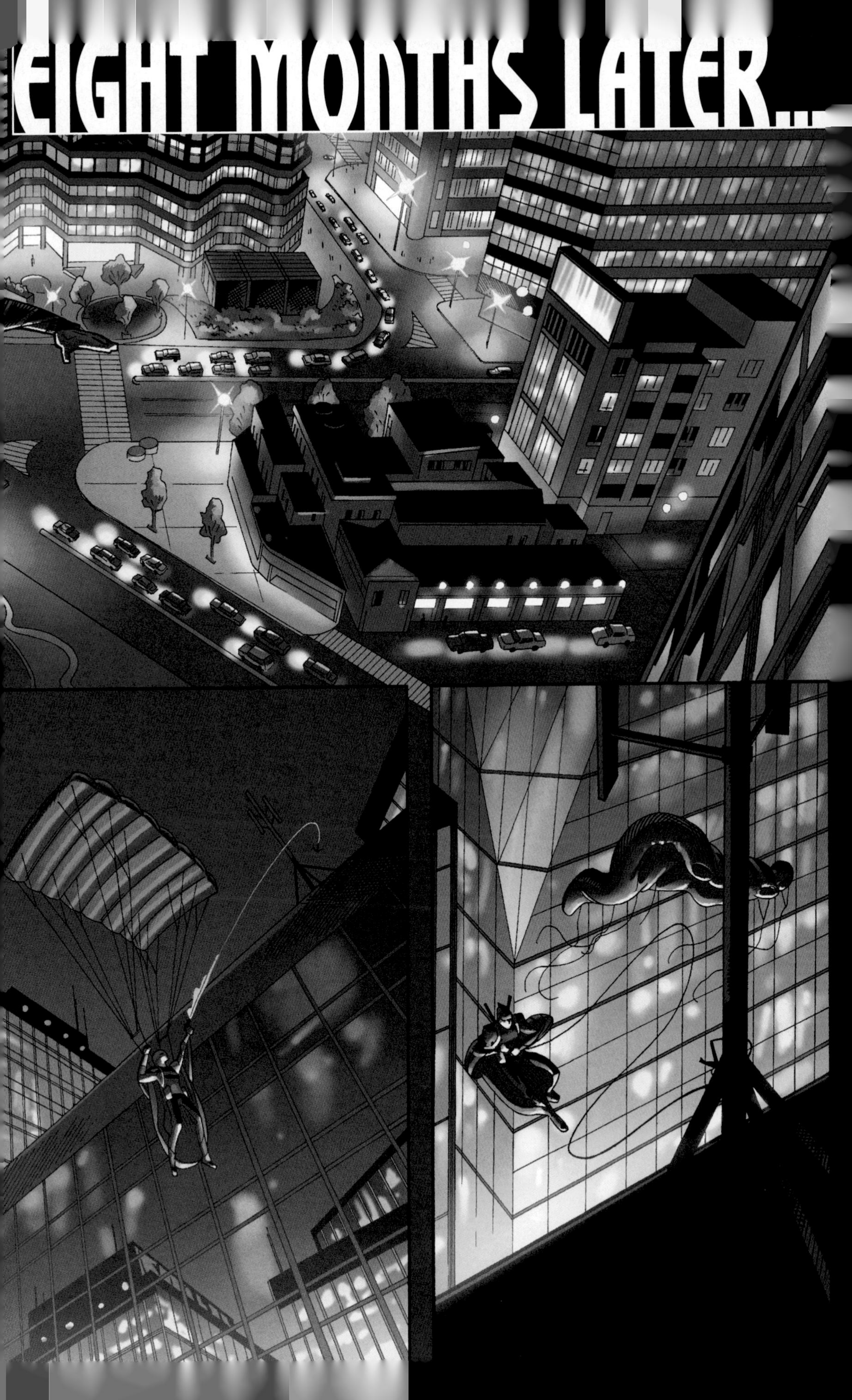
EIGHT MONTHS LATER...

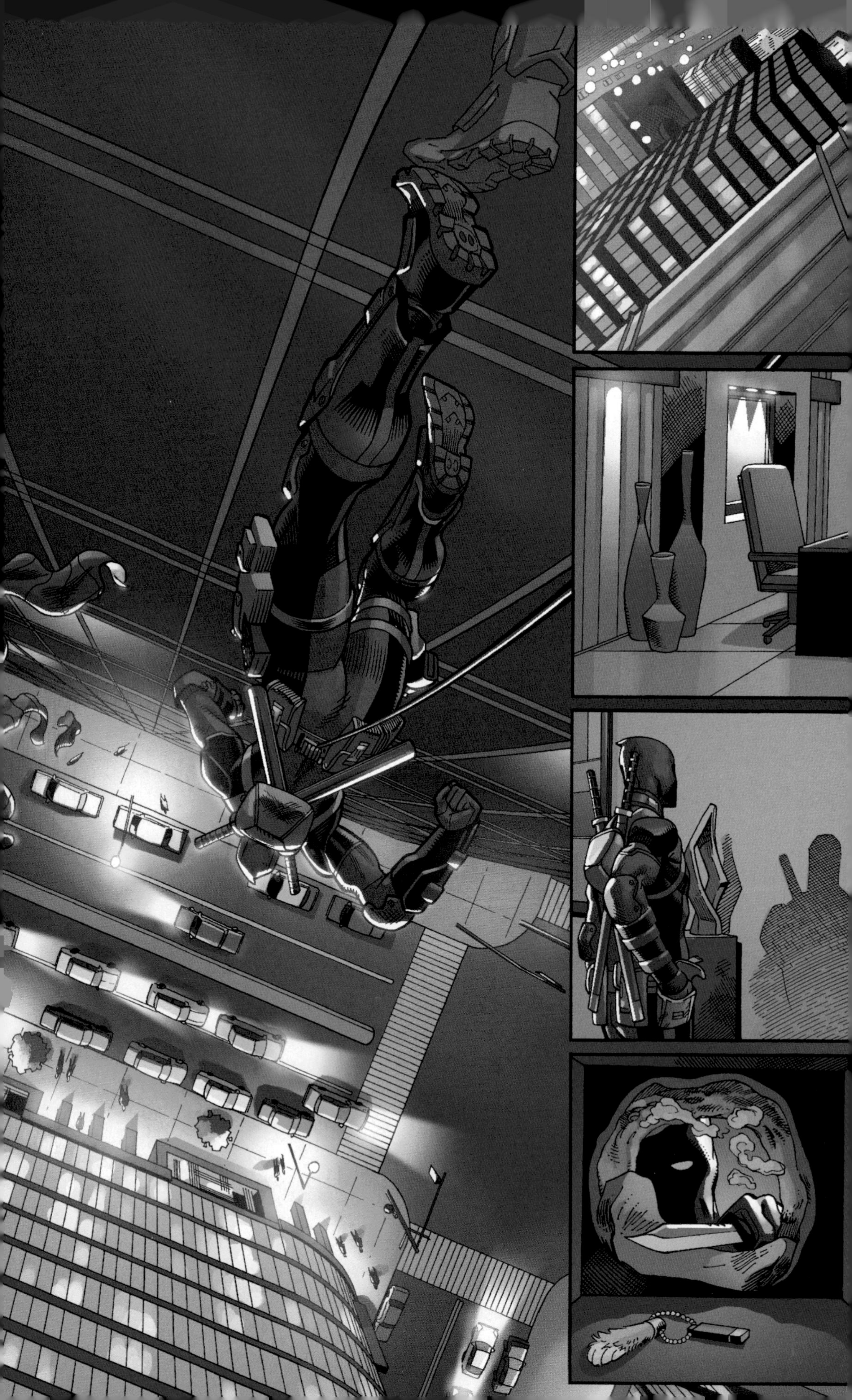

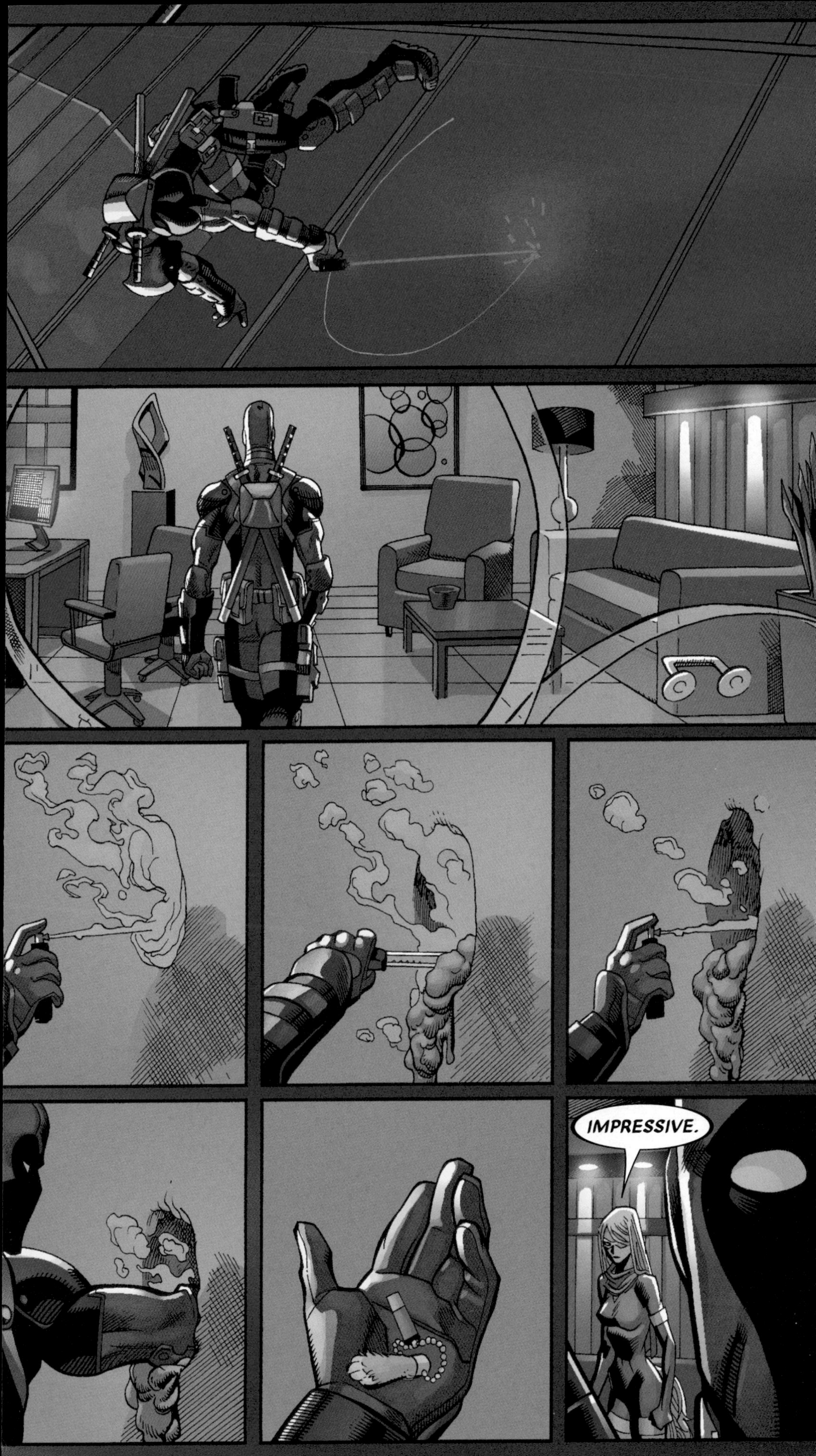
IMPRESSIVE.

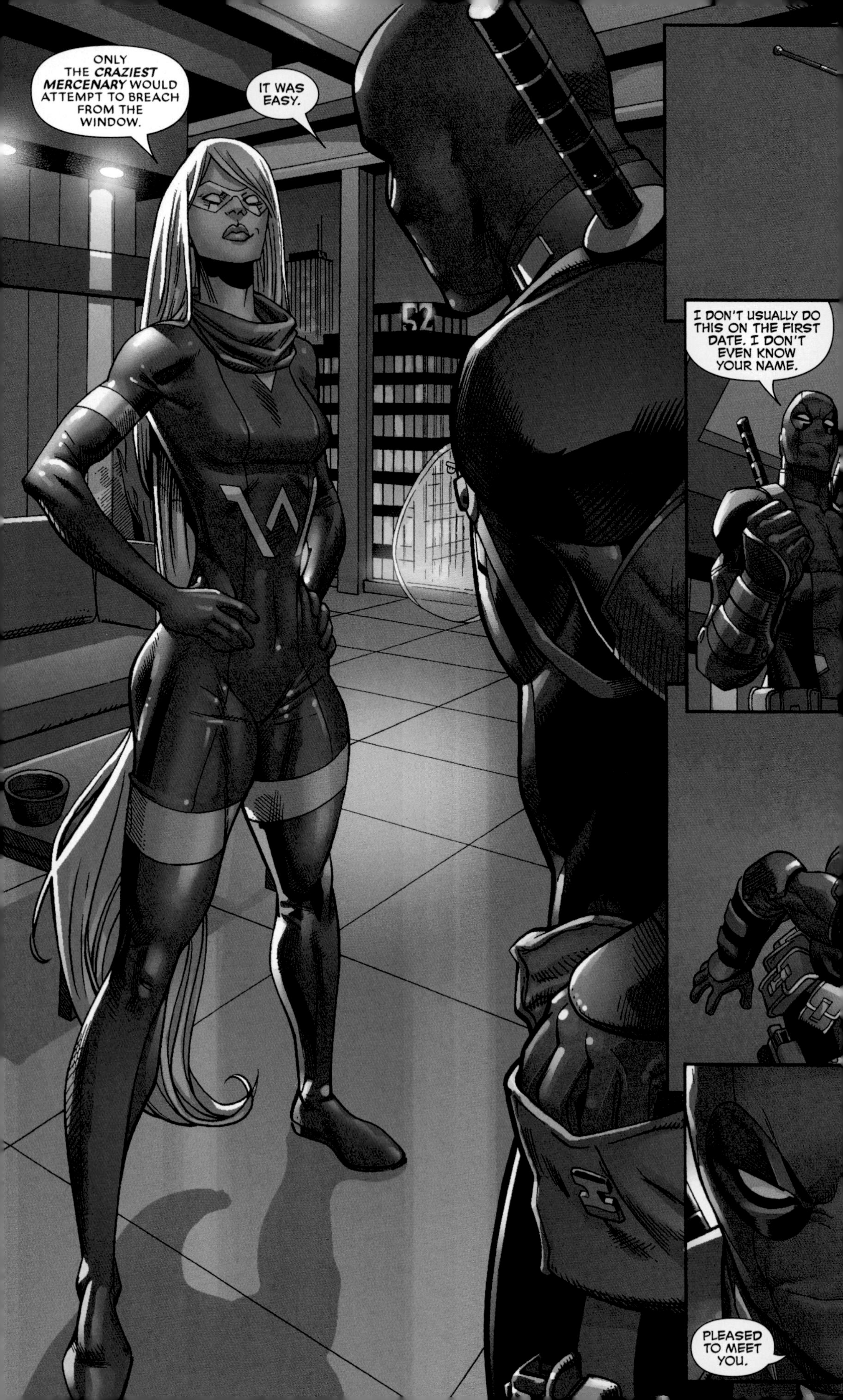
ONLY THE *CRAZIEST MERCENARY* WOULD ATTEMPT TO BREACH FROM THE WINDOW.
IT WAS EASY.
52
I DON'T USUALLY DO THIS ON THE FIRST DATE. I DON'T EVEN KNOW YOUR NAME.
PLEASED TO MEET YOU.

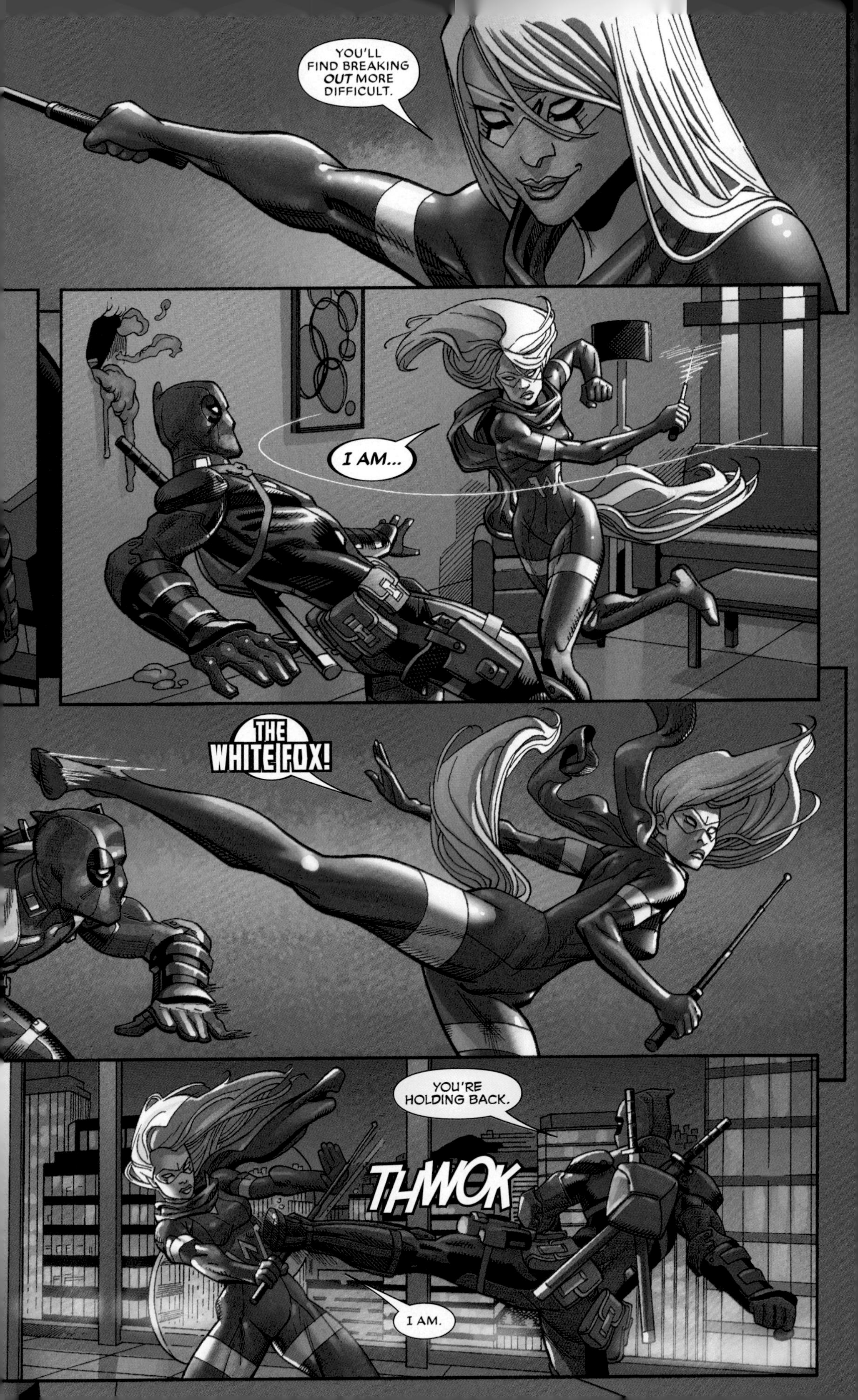
YOU'LL FIND BREAKING *OUT* MORE DIFFICULT.
I AM...
THE WHITE FOX!
YOU'RE HOLDING BACK.
THWOK
I AM.

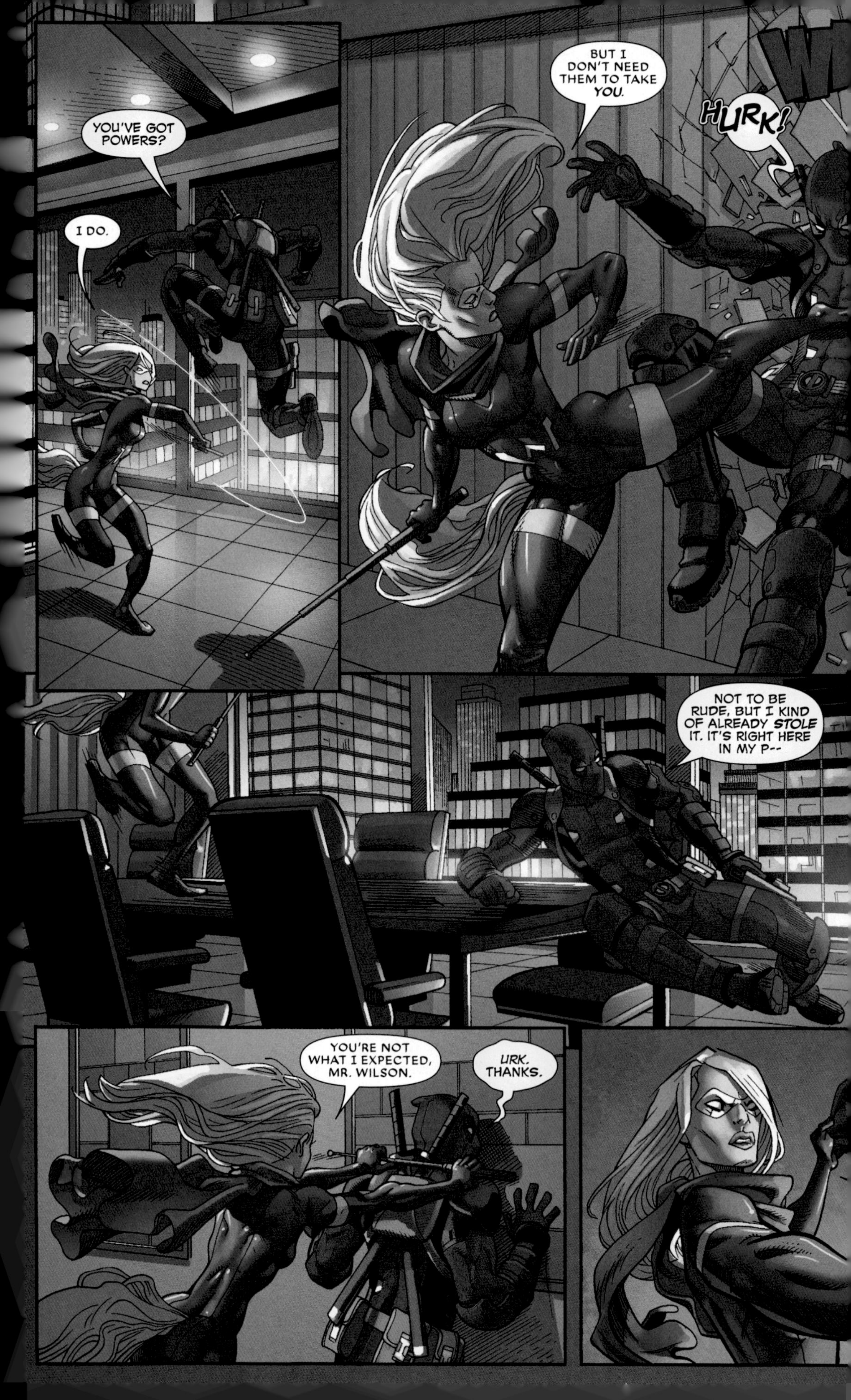
YOU'VE GOT POWERS?
I DO.
BUT I DON'T NEED THEM TO TAKE YOU.
HURK!
NOT TO BE RUDE, BUT I KIND OF ALREADY STOLE IT. IT'S RIGHT HERE IN MY P--
YOU'RE NOT WHAT I EXPECTED, MR. WILSON.
URK. THANKS.

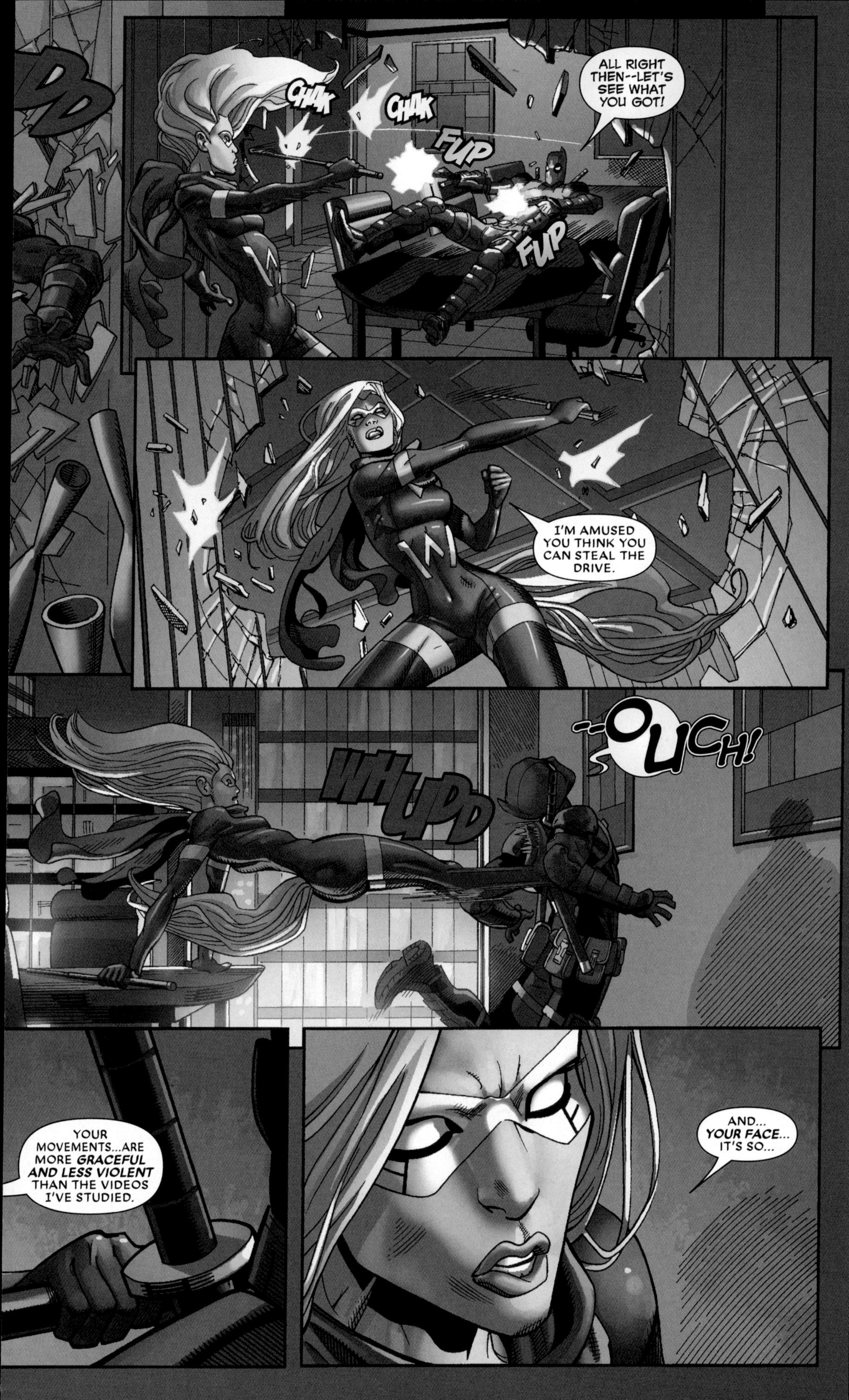

CHAK
CHAK
ALL RIGHT THEN--LET'S SEE WHAT YOU GOT!
FUP
FUP
I'M AMUSED YOU THINK YOU CAN STEAL THE DRIVE.
WHUDD
--OUCH!
YOUR MOVEMENTS...ARE MORE GRACEFUL AND LESS VIOLENT THAN THE VIDEOS I'VE STUDIED.
AND... YOUR FACE... IT'S SO...

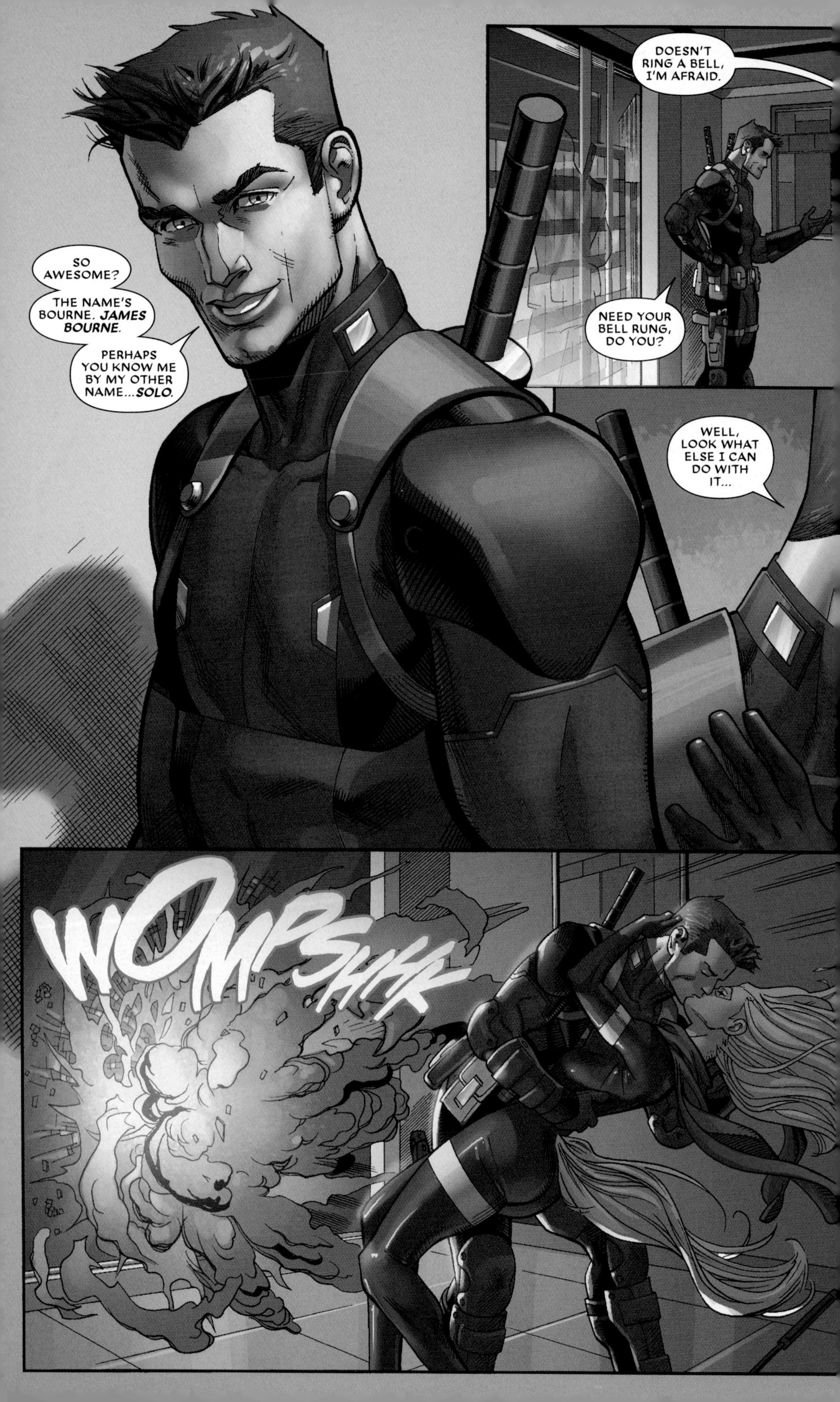
SO AWESOME?
THE NAME'S BOURNE. ***JAMES BOURNE.***
PERHAPS YOU KNOW ME BY MY OTHER NAME...***SOLO.***
DOESN'T RING A BELL, I'M AFRAID.
NEED YOUR BELL RUNG, DO YOU?
WELL, LOOK WHAT ELSE I CAN DO WITH IT...
WOMPSHKR

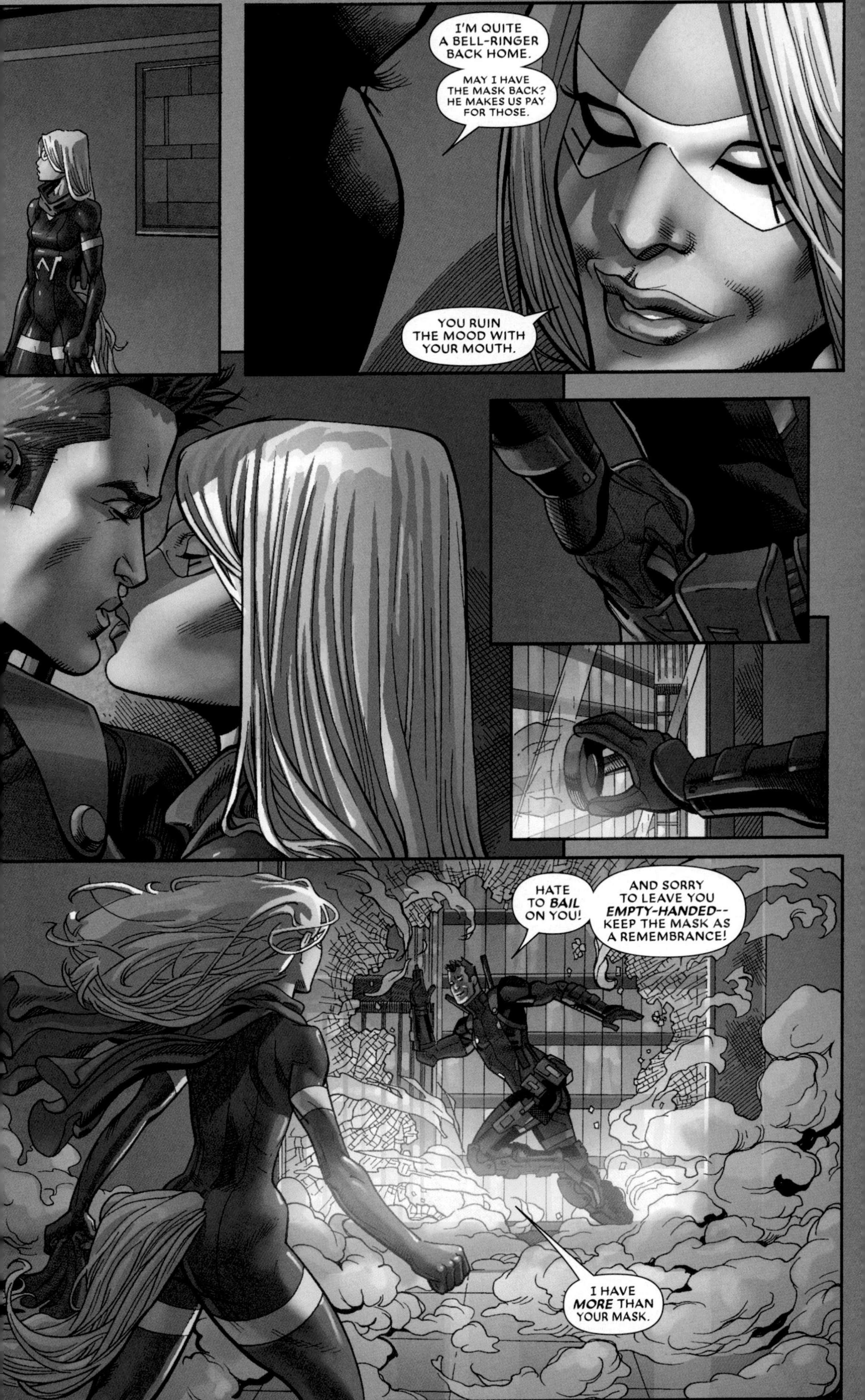
I'M QUITE A BELL-RINGER BACK HOME.
MAY I HAVE THE MASK BACK? HE MAKES US PAY FOR THOSE.
YOU RUIN THE MOOD WITH YOUR MOUTH.
HATE TO *BAIL* ON YOU!
AND SORRY TO LEAVE YOU *EMPTY-HANDED*-- KEEP THE MASK AS A REMEMBRANCE!
I HAVE *MORE* THAN YOUR MASK.

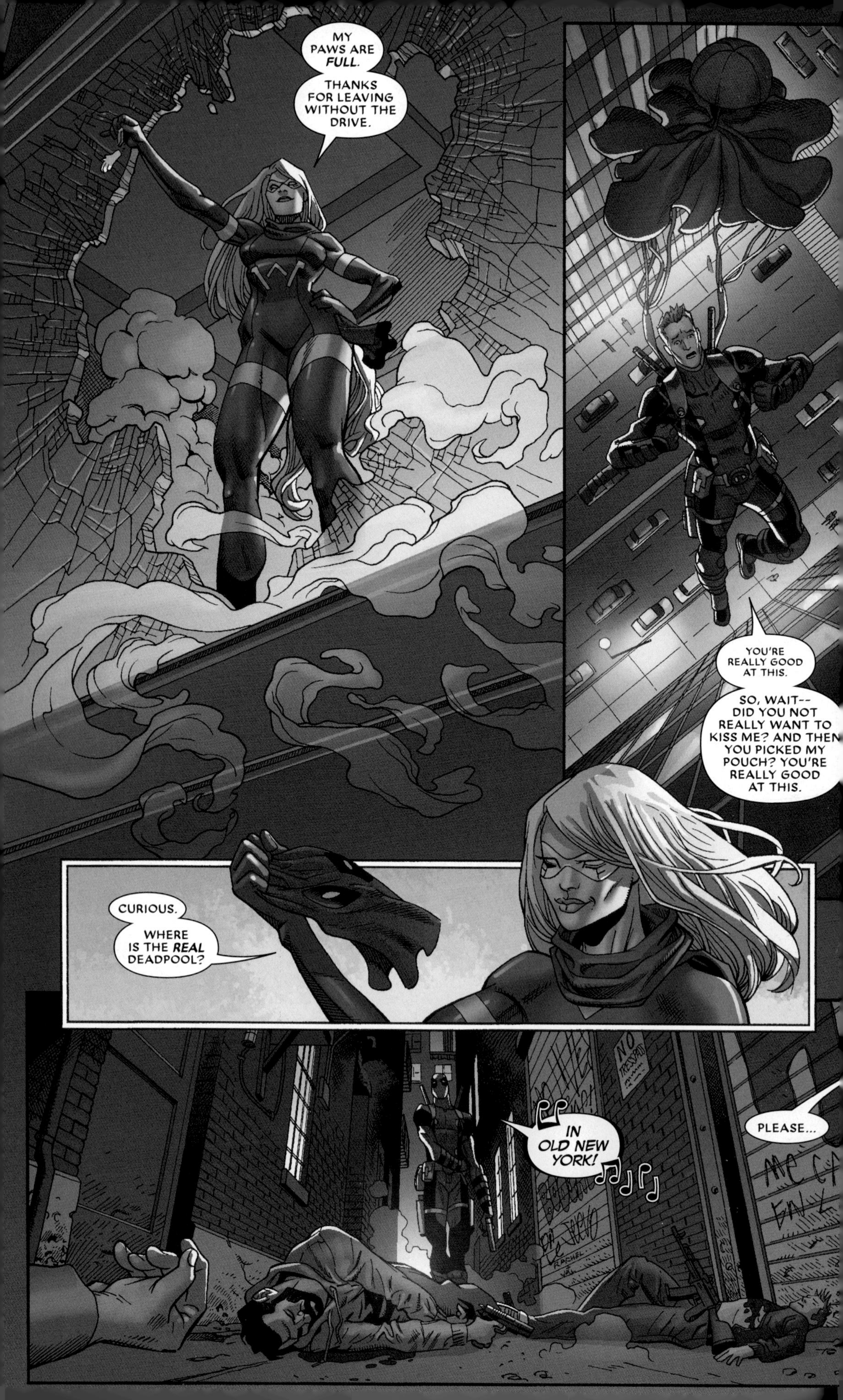

MY PAWS ARE *FULL*.
THANKS FOR LEAVING WITHOUT THE DRIVE.
YOU'RE REALLY GOOD AT THIS.
SO, WAIT-- DID YOU NOT REALLY WANT TO KISS ME? AND THEN YOU PICKED MY POUCH? YOU'RE REALLY GOOD AT THIS.
CURIOUS.
WHERE IS THE *REAL* DEADPOOL?
IN OLD NEW YORK!
PLEASE...
NO TRESPASSING

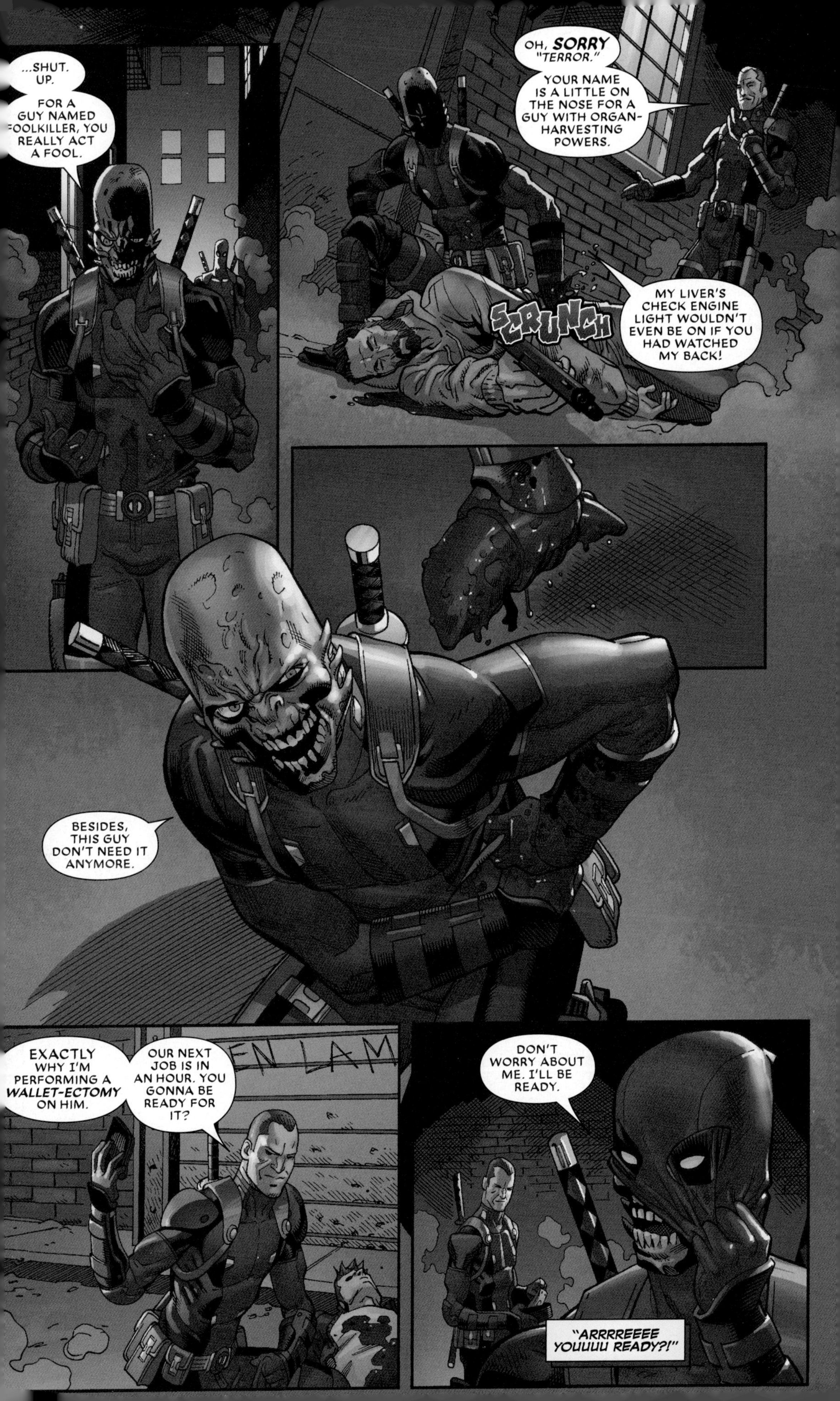
...SHUT. UP.
FOR A GUY NAMED FOOLKILLER, YOU REALLY ACT A FOOL.
OH, SORRY "TERROR."
YOUR NAME IS A LITTLE ON THE NOSE FOR A GUY WITH ORGAN-HARVESTING POWERS.
SCRUNCH
MY LIVER'S CHECK ENGINE LIGHT WOULDN'T EVEN BE ON IF YOU HAD WATCHED MY BACK!
BESIDES, THIS GUY DON'T NEED IT ANYMORE.
EXACTLY WHY I'M PERFORMING A WALLET-ECTOMY ON HIM.
OUR NEXT JOB IS IN AN HOUR. YOU GONNA BE READY FOR IT?
DON'T WORRY ABOUT ME. I'LL BE READY.
"ARRRREEEE YOUUUU READY?!"

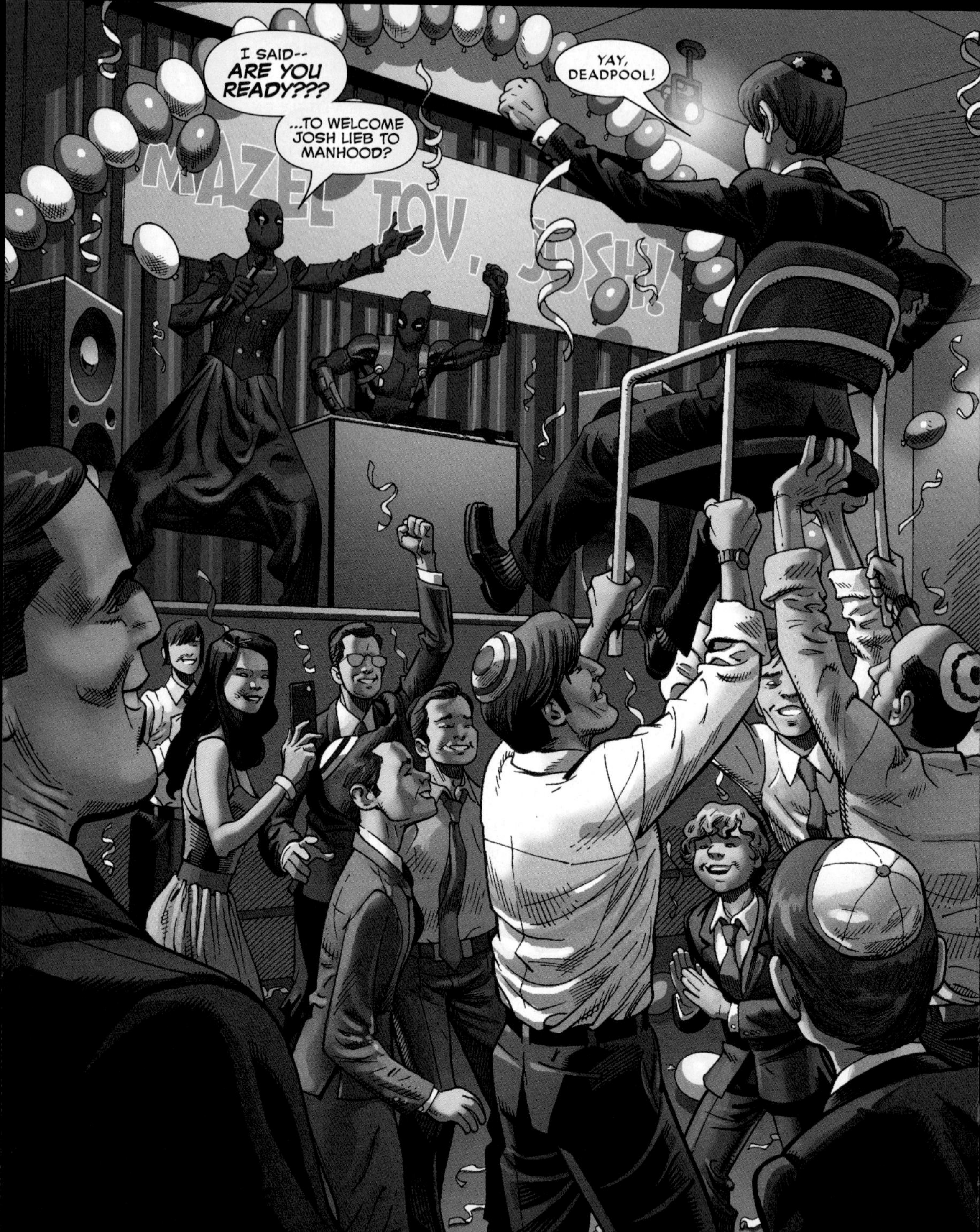
I SAID--
ARE YOU READY???
...TO WELCOME JOSH LIEB TO MANHOOD?
YAY, DEADPOOL!
MAZEL TOV, JOSH!

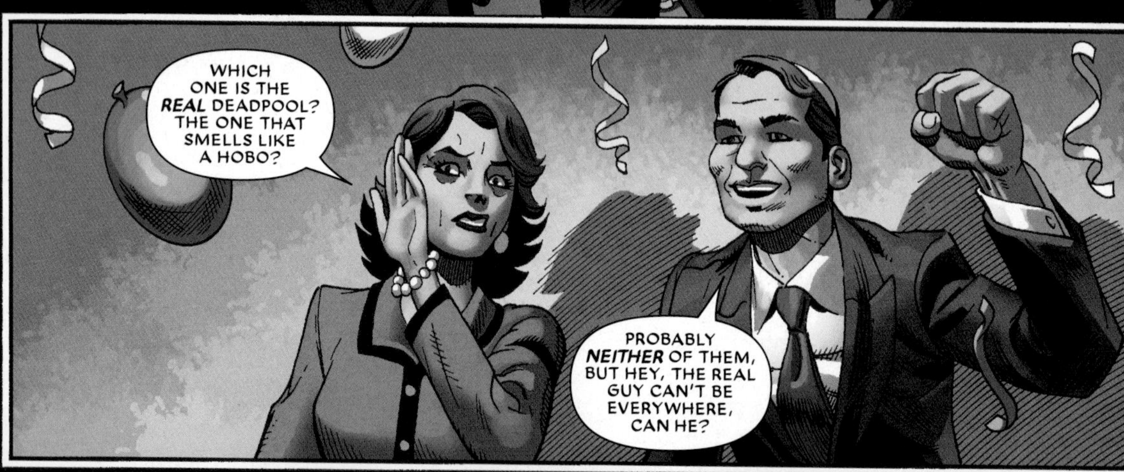
WHICH ONE IS THE REAL DEADPOOL? THE ONE THAT SMELLS LIKE A HOBO?
PROBABLY NEITHER OF THEM, BUT HEY, THE REAL GUY CAN'T BE EVERYWHERE, CAN HE?

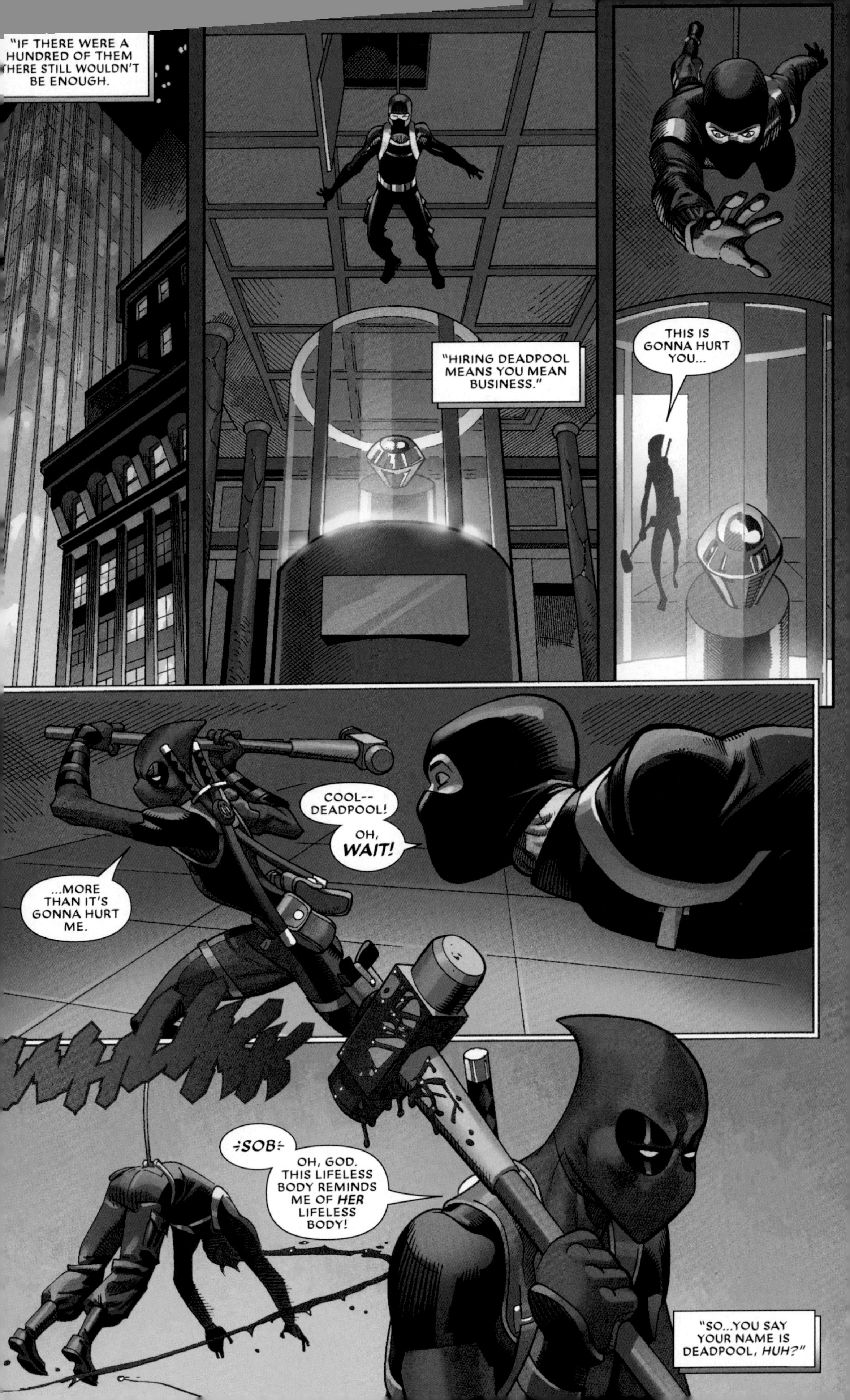
"IF THERE WERE A HUNDRED OF THEM THERE STILL WOULDN'T BE ENOUGH.
"HIRING DEADPOOL MEANS YOU MEAN BUSINESS."
THIS IS GONNA HURT YOU...
COOL-- DEADPOOL!
OH, *WAIT!*
...MORE THAN IT'S GONNA HURT ME.
SOB
OH, GOD. THIS LIFELESS BODY REMINDS ME OF *HER* LIFELESS BODY!
"SO...YOU SAY YOUR NAME IS DEADPOOL, *HUH?*"

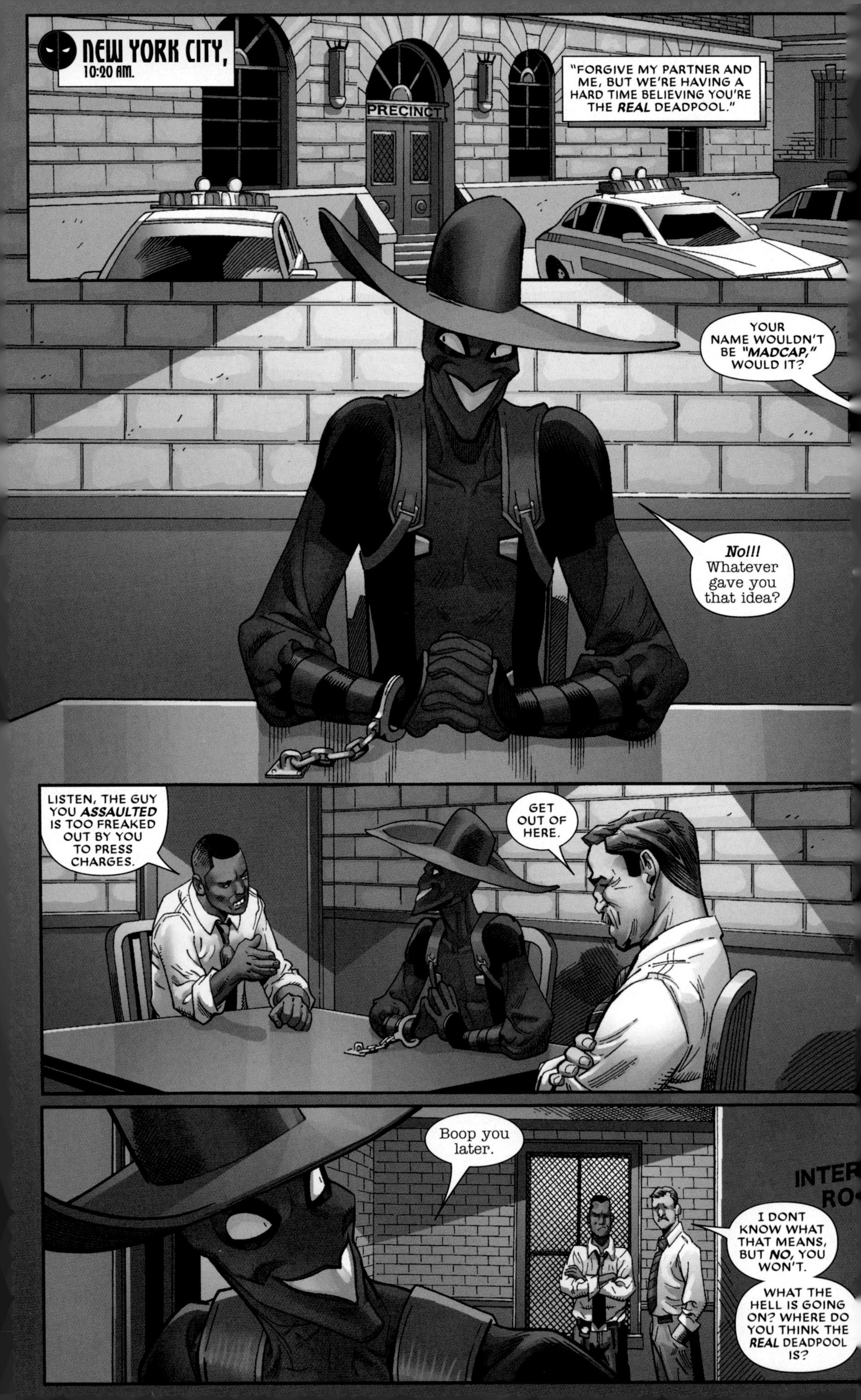
NEW YORK CITY, 10:20 AM.
PRECINCT
"FORGIVE MY PARTNER AND ME, BUT WE'RE HAVING A HARD TIME BELIEVING YOU'RE THE *REAL* DEADPOOL."
YOUR NAME WOULDN'T BE *"MADCAP,"* WOULD IT?
No!!! Whatever gave you that idea?
LISTEN, THE GUY YOU *ASSAULTED* IS TOO FREAKED OUT BY YOU TO PRESS CHARGES.
GET OUT OF HERE.
Boop you later.
I DONT KNOW WHAT THAT MEANS, BUT *NO,* YOU WON'T.
WHAT THE HELL IS GOING ON? WHERE DO YOU THINK THE *REAL* DEADPOOL IS?

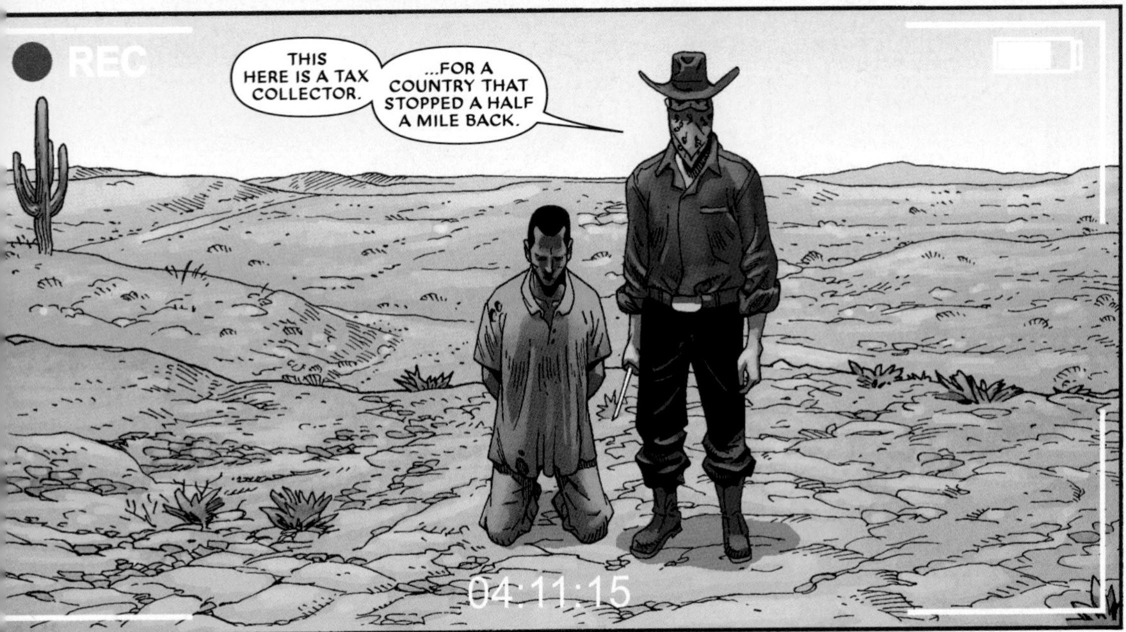
REC
THIS HERE IS A TAX COLLECTOR.
...FOR A COUNTRY THAT STOPPED A HALF A MILE BACK.
04:11:15

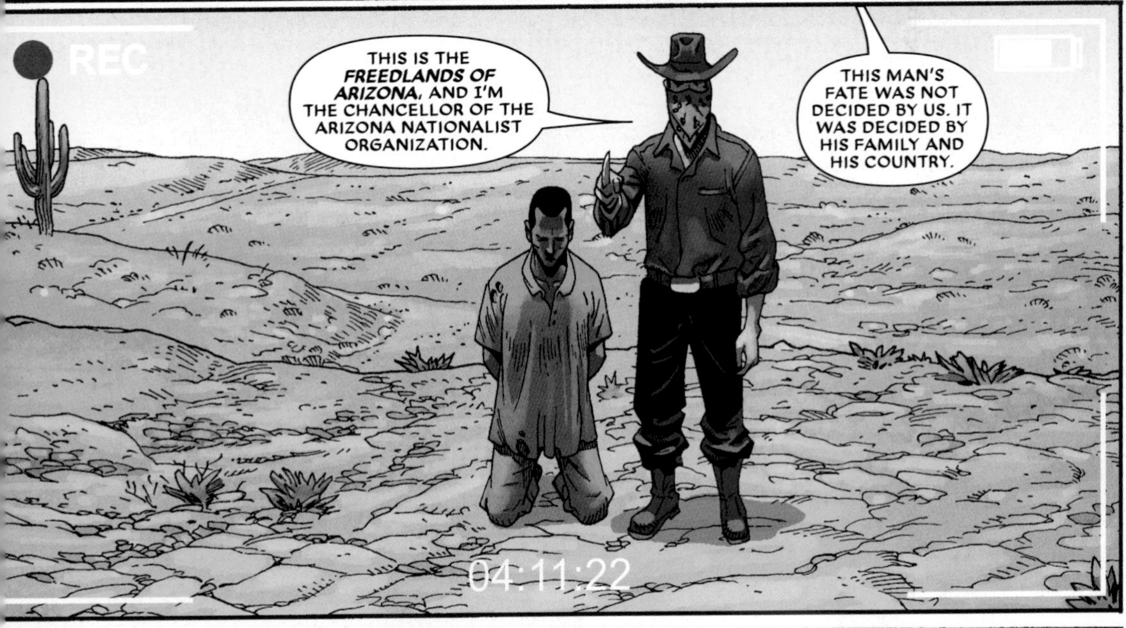
REC
THIS IS THE FREEDLANDS OF ARIZONA, AND I'M THE CHANCELLOR OF THE ARIZONA NATIONALIST ORGANIZATION.
THIS MAN'S FATE WAS NOT DECIDED BY US. IT WAS DECIDED BY HIS FAMILY AND HIS COUNTRY.
04:11:22

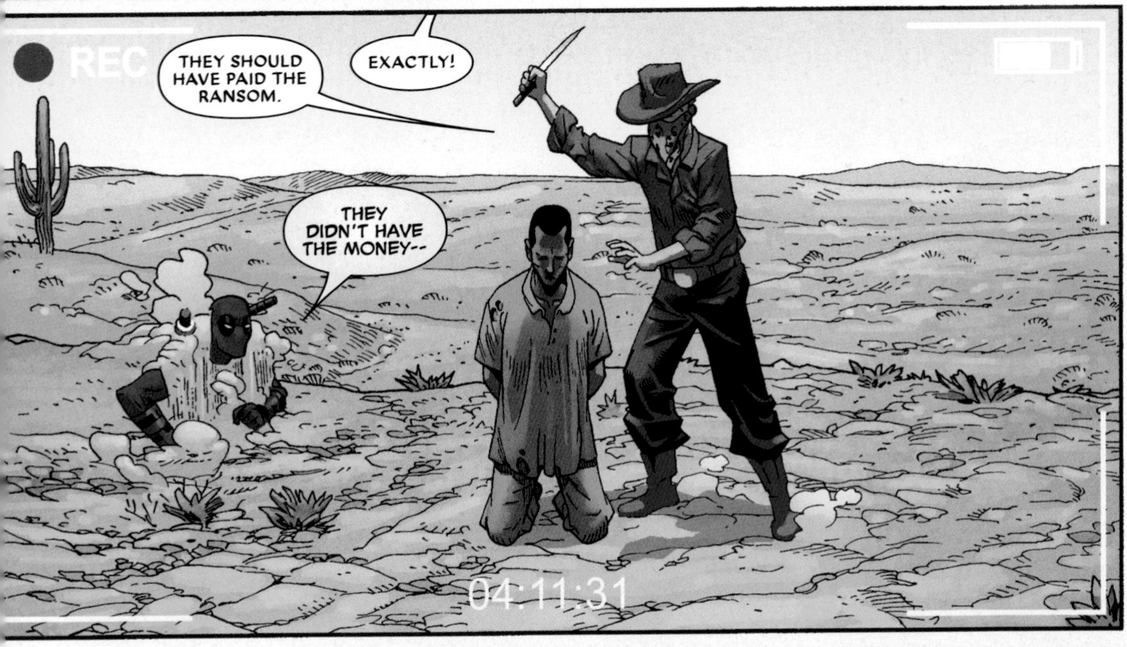
REC
THEY SHOULD HAVE PAID THE RANSOM.
EXACTLY!
THEY DIDN'T HAVE THE MONEY--
04:11:31

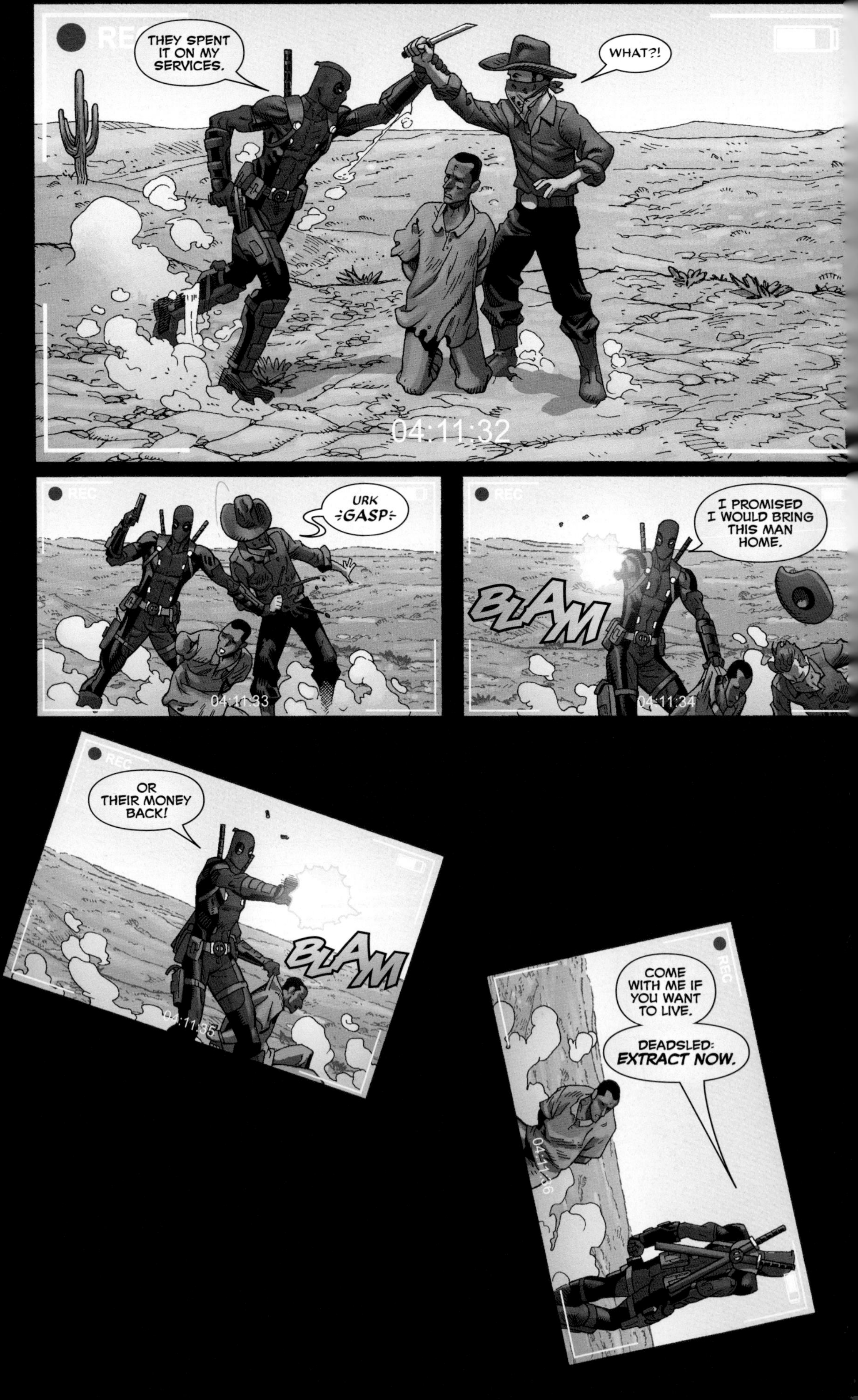
REC
THEY SPENT IT ON MY SERVICES.
WHAT?!
04:11:32
REC
URK GASP
04:11:33
REC
I PROMISED I WOULD BRING THIS MAN HOME.
BLAM
04:11:34
REC
OR THEIR MONEY BACK!
BLAM
04:11:35
REC
COME WITH ME IF YOU WANT TO LIVE.
DEADSLED: EXTRACT NOW.
04:11:36

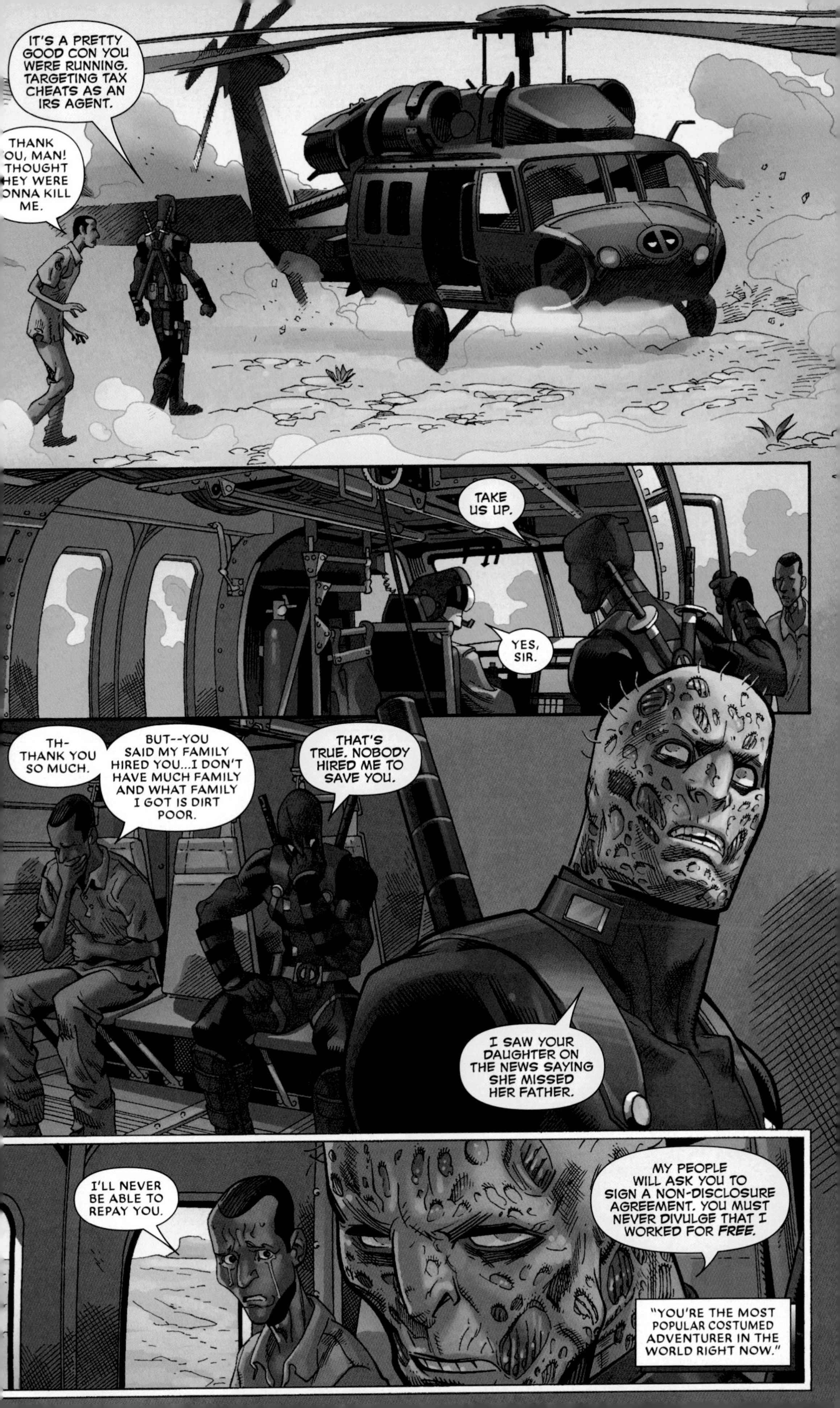
IT'S A PRETTY GOOD CON YOU WERE RUNNING. TARGETING TAX CHEATS AS AN IRS AGENT.
THANK OU, MAN! THOUGHT HEY WERE ONNA KILL ME.
TAKE US UP.
YES, SIR.
TH- THANK YOU SO MUCH.
BUT--YOU SAID MY FAMILY HIRED YOU...I DON'T HAVE MUCH FAMILY AND WHAT FAMILY I GOT IS DIRT POOR.
THAT'S TRUE. NOBODY HIRED ME TO SAVE YOU.
I SAW YOUR DAUGHTER ON THE NEWS SAYING SHE MISSED HER FATHER.
I'LL NEVER BE ABLE TO REPAY YOU.
MY PEOPLE WILL ASK YOU TO SIGN A NON-DISCLOSURE AGREEMENT. YOU MUST NEVER DIVULGE THAT I WORKED FOR FREE.
"YOU'RE THE MOST POPULAR COSTUMED ADVENTURER IN THE WORLD RIGHT NOW."

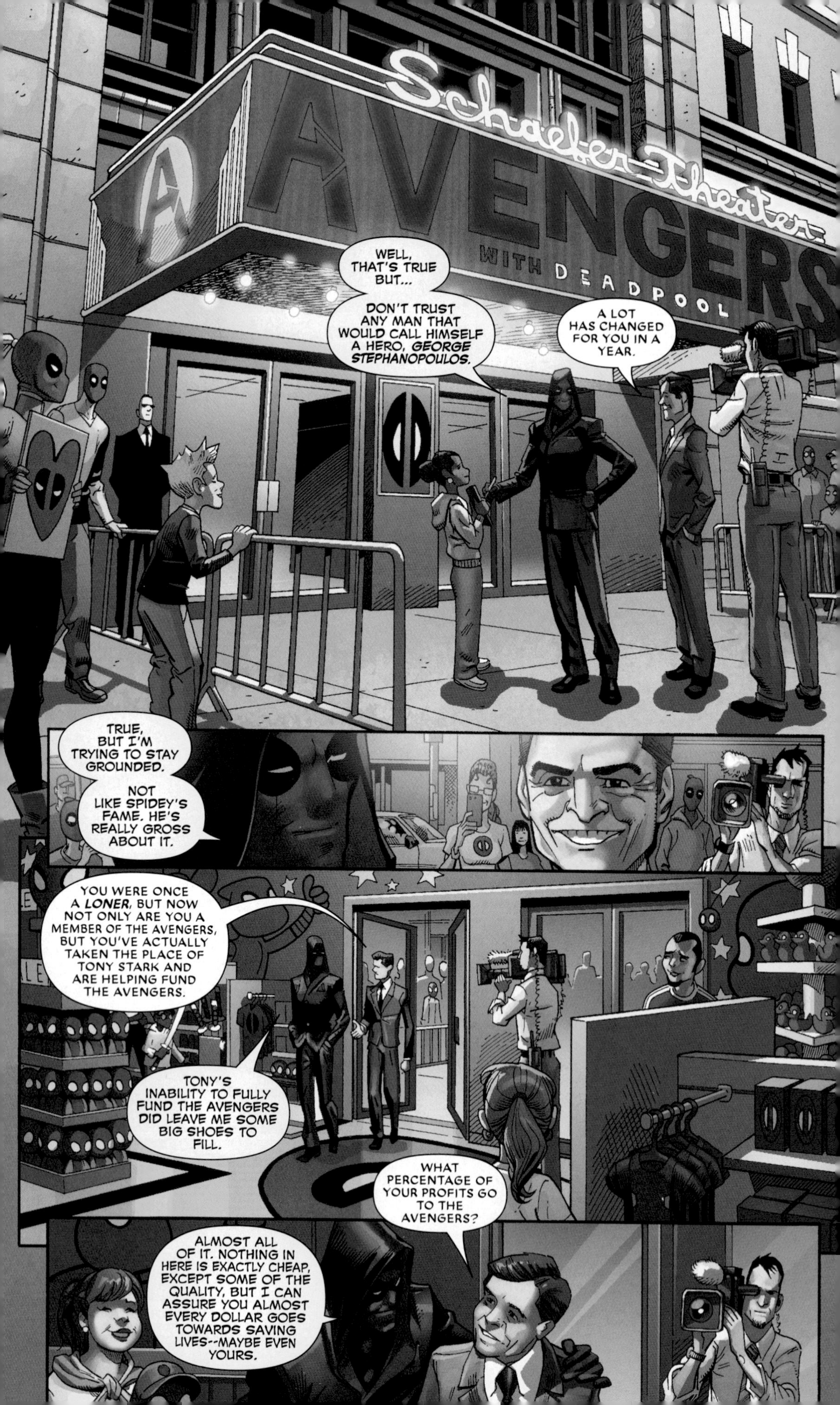
Schaefer Theater
AVENGERS
WITH DEADPOOL
WELL, THAT'S TRUE BUT...
DON'T TRUST ANY MAN THAT WOULD CALL HIMSELF A HERO, *GEORGE STEPHANOPOULOS.*
A LOT HAS CHANGED FOR YOU IN A YEAR.
TRUE, BUT I'M TRYING TO STAY GROUNDED.
NOT LIKE SPIDEY'S FAME. HE'S REALLY GROSS ABOUT IT.
YOU WERE ONCE A *LONER*, BUT NOW NOT ONLY ARE YOU A MEMBER OF THE AVENGERS, BUT YOU'VE ACTUALLY TAKEN THE PLACE OF TONY STARK AND ARE HELPING FUND THE AVENGERS.
TONY'S INABILITY TO FULLY FUND THE AVENGERS DID LEAVE ME SOME BIG SHOES TO FILL.
WHAT PERCENTAGE OF YOUR PROFITS GO TO THE AVENGERS?
ALMOST ALL OF IT. NOTHING IN HERE IS EXACTLY CHEAP, EXCEPT SOME OF THE QUALITY, BUT I CAN ASSURE YOU ALMOST EVERY DOLLAR GOES TOWARDS SAVING LIVES--MAYBE EVEN YOURS.

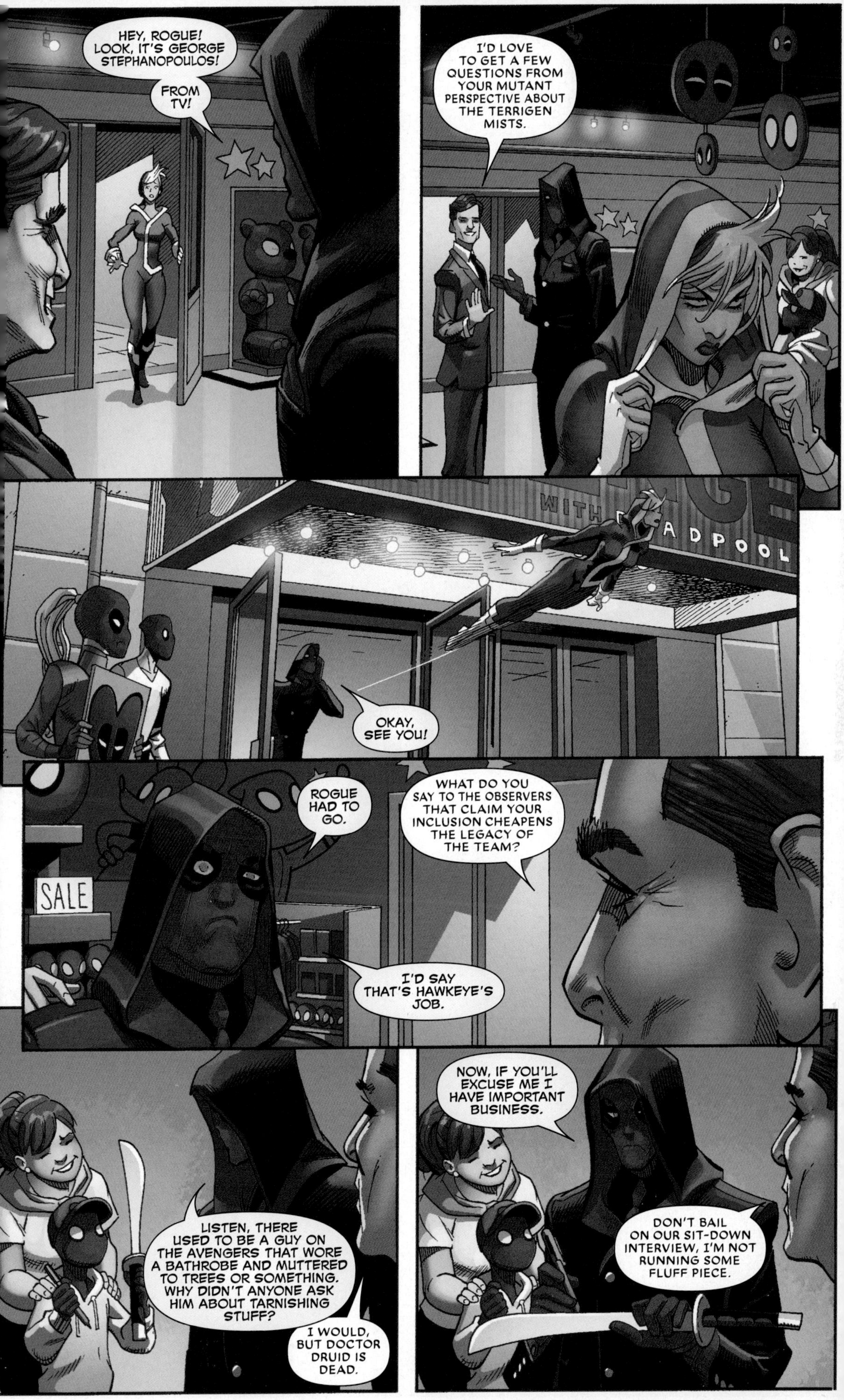

HEY, ROGUE! LOOK, IT'S GEORGE STEPHANOPOULOS!
FROM TV!
I'D LOVE TO GET A FEW QUESTIONS FROM YOUR MUTANT PERSPECTIVE ABOUT THE TERRIGEN MISTS.
WITH
ADPOOL
OKAY, SEE YOU!
SALE
ROGUE HAD TO GO.
WHAT DO YOU SAY TO THE OBSERVERS THAT CLAIM YOUR INCLUSION CHEAPENS THE LEGACY OF THE TEAM?
I'D SAY THAT'S HAWKEYE'S JOB.
LISTEN, THERE USED TO BE A GUY ON THE AVENGERS THAT WORE A BATHROBE AND MUTTERED TO TREES OR SOMETHING. WHY DIDN'T ANYONE ASK HIM ABOUT TARNISHING STUFF?
I WOULD, BUT DOCTOR DRUID IS DEAD.
NOW, IF YOU'LL EXCUSE ME I HAVE IMPORTANT BUSINESS.
DON'T BAIL ON OUR SIT-DOWN INTERVIEW, I'M NOT RUNNING SOME FLUFF PIECE.

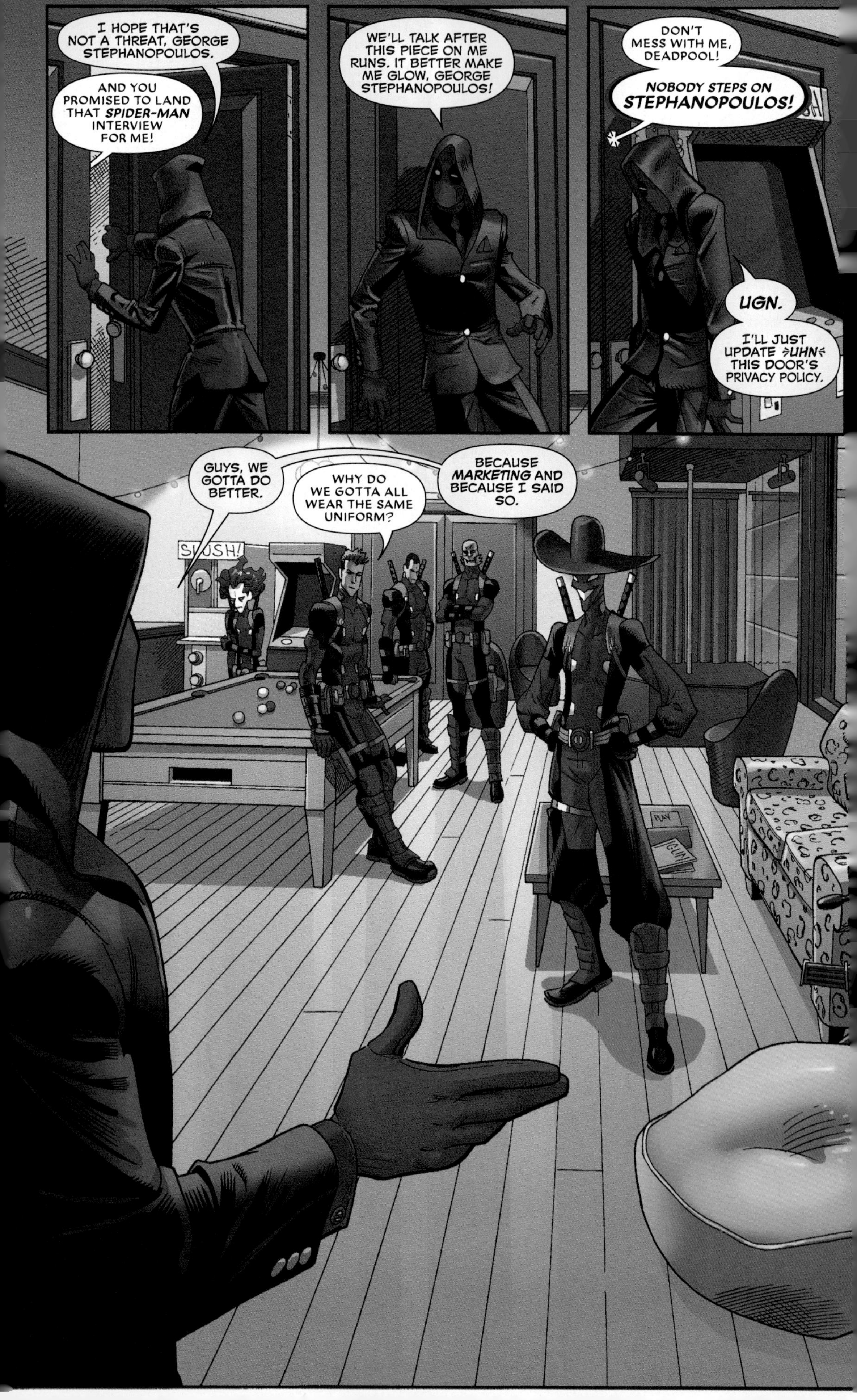
I HOPE THAT'S NOT A THREAT, GEORGE STEPHANOPOULOS.
AND YOU PROMISED TO LAND THAT SPIDER-MAN INTERVIEW FOR ME!
WE'LL TALK AFTER THIS PIECE ON ME RUNS. IT BETTER MAKE ME GLOW, GEORGE STEPHANOPOULOS!
DON'T MESS WITH ME, DEADPOOL!
NOBODY STEPS ON STEPHANOPOULOS!
UGN.
I'LL JUST UPDATE ≈UHN≈ THIS DOOR'S PRIVACY POLICY.
GUYS, WE GOTTA DO BETTER.
WHY DO WE GOTTA ALL WEAR THE SAME UNIFORM?
BECAUSE MARKETING AND BECAUSE I SAID SO.
SLUSH!
PLAY
GUN

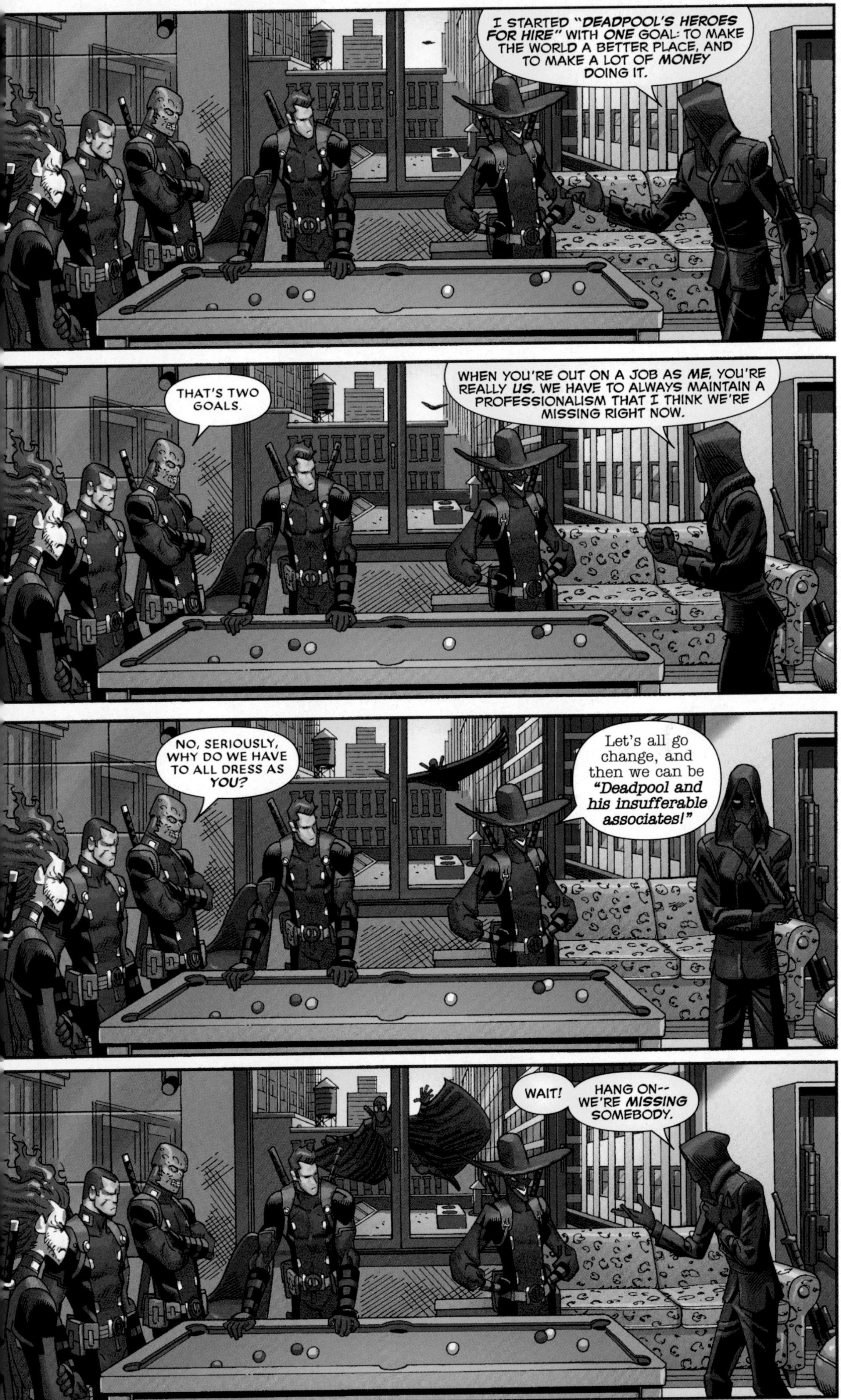

I STARTED "DEADPOOL'S HEROES FOR HIRE" WITH ONE GOAL: TO MAKE THE WORLD A BETTER PLACE, AND TO MAKE A LOT OF MONEY DOING IT.
THAT'S TWO GOALS.
WHEN YOU'RE OUT ON A JOB AS ME, YOU'RE REALLY US. WE HAVE TO ALWAYS MAINTAIN A PROFESSIONALISM THAT I THINK WE'RE MISSING RIGHT NOW.
NO, SERIOUSLY, WHY DO WE HAVE TO ALL DRESS AS YOU?
Let's all go change, and then we can be "Deadpool and his insufferable associates!"
WAIT!
HANG ON-- WE'RE MISSING SOMEBODY.

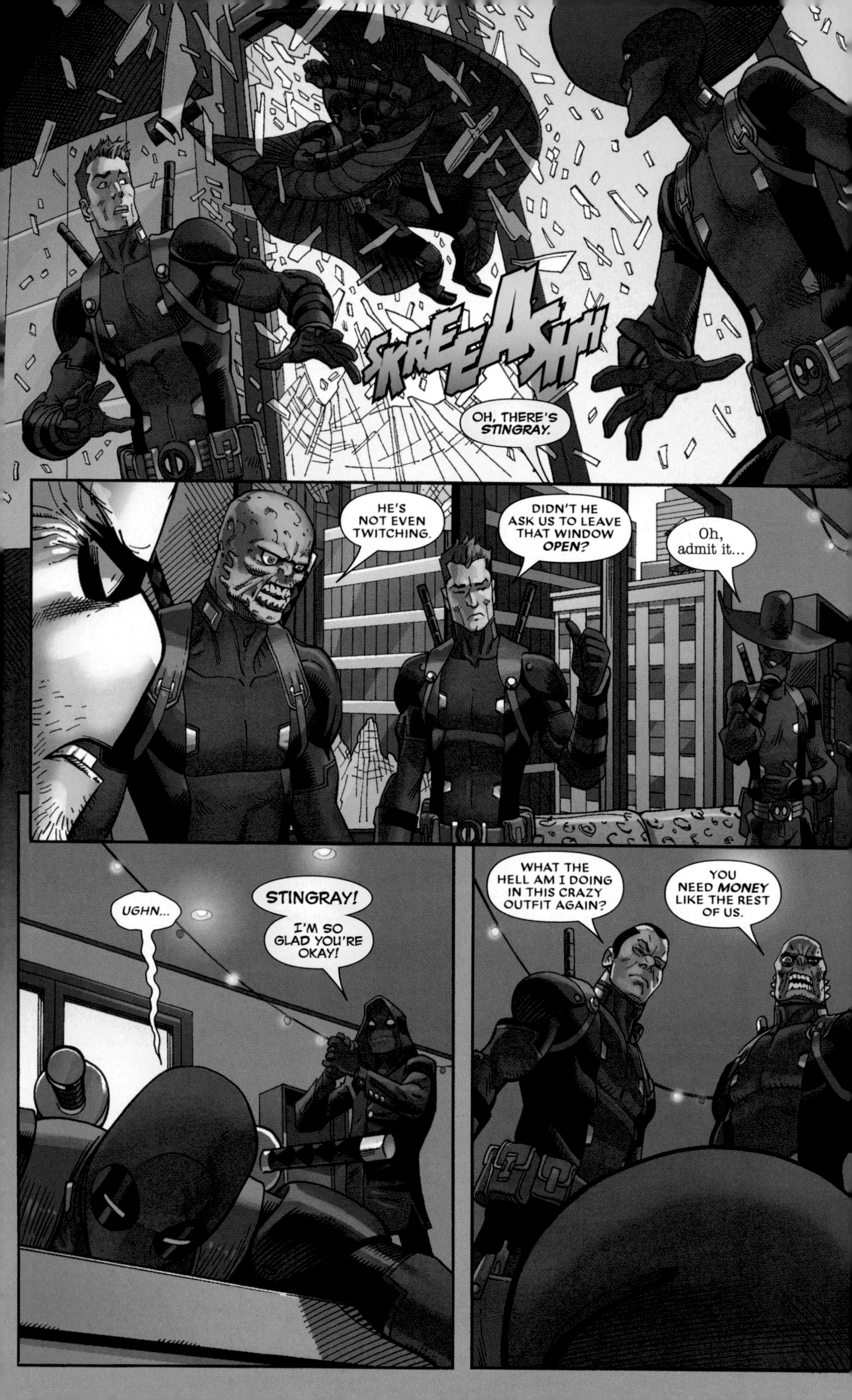
SKREEASHH
OH, THERE'S STINGRAY.
HE'S NOT EVEN TWITCHING.
DIDN'T HE ASK US TO LEAVE THAT WINDOW OPEN?
Oh, admit it...
UGHN...
STINGRAY!
I'M SO GLAD YOU'RE OKAY!
WHAT THE HELL AM I DOING IN THIS CRAZY OUTFIT AGAIN?
YOU NEED MONEY LIKE THE REST OF US.

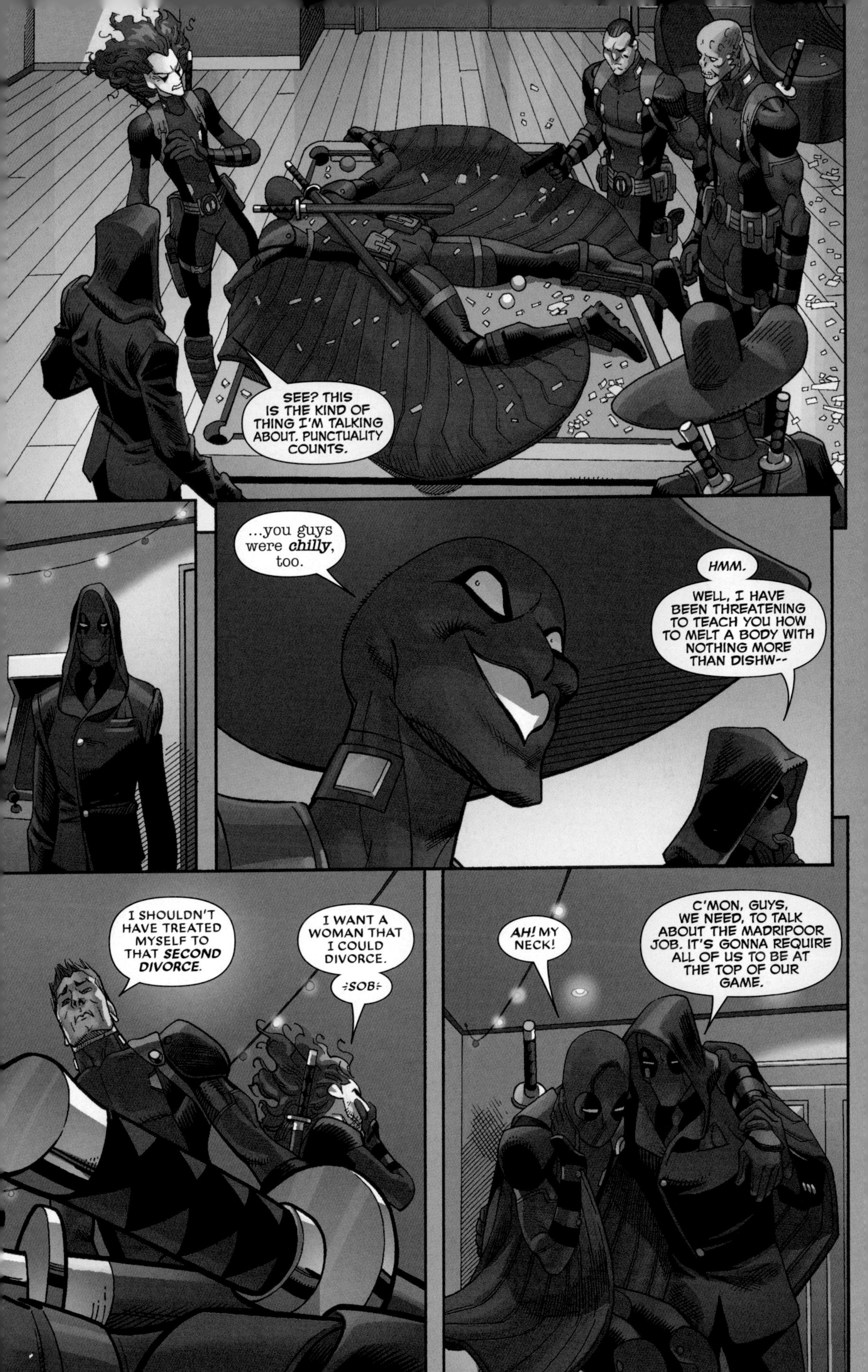
SEE? THIS IS THE KIND OF THING I'M TALKING ABOUT. PUNCTUALITY COUNTS.
...you guys were chilly, too.
HMM.
WELL, I HAVE BEEN THREATENING TO TEACH YOU HOW TO MELT A BODY WITH NOTHING MORE THAN DISHW--
I SHOULDN'T HAVE TREATED MYSELF TO THAT SECOND DIVORCE.
I WANT A WOMAN THAT I COULD DIVORCE.
SOB
AH! MY NECK!
C'MON, GUYS, WE NEED, TO TALK ABOUT THE MADRIPOOR JOB. IT'S GONNA REQUIRE ALL OF US TO BE AT THE TOP OF OUR GAME.

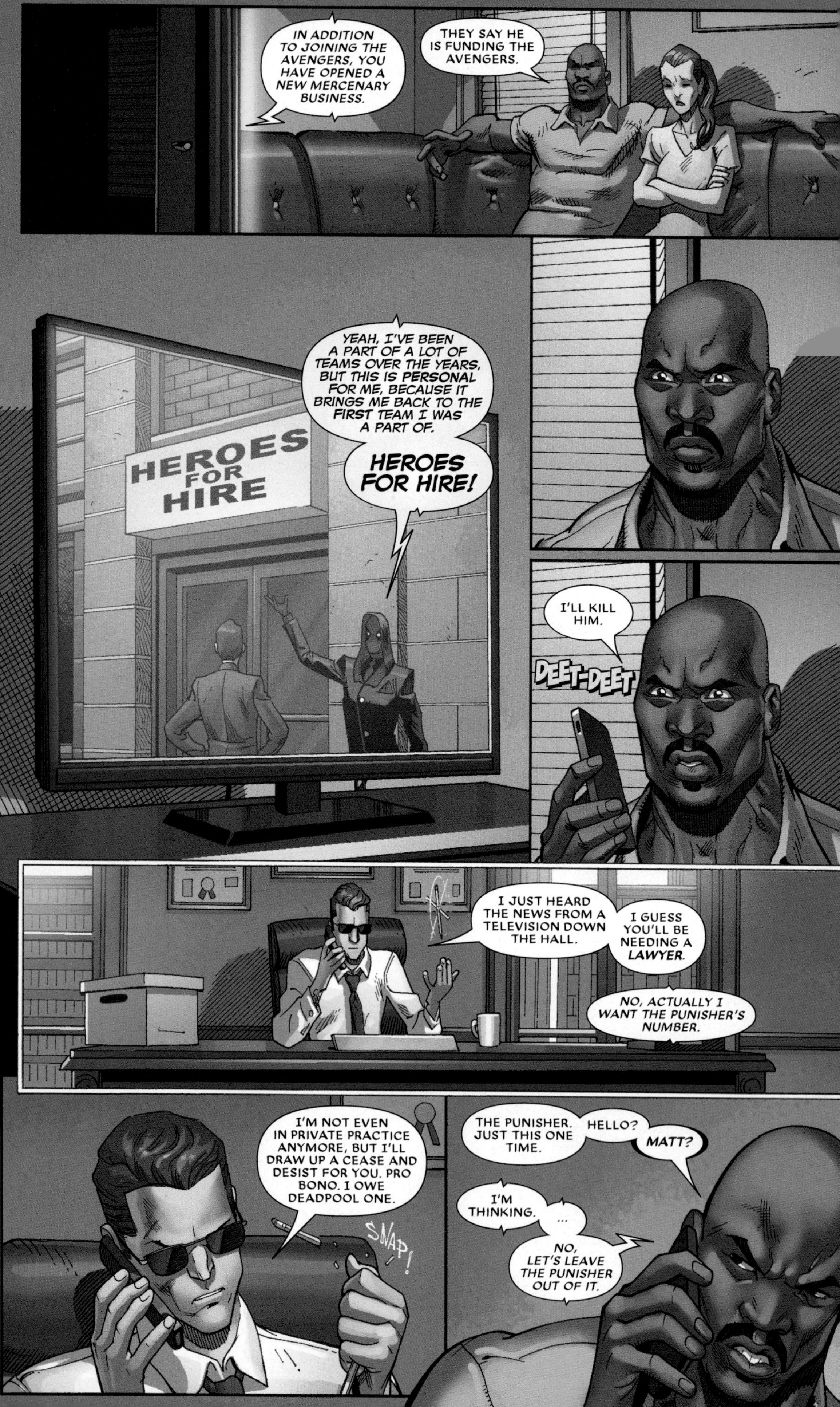

IN ADDITION TO JOINING THE AVENGERS, YOU HAVE OPENED A NEW MERCENARY BUSINESS.
THEY SAY HE IS FUNDING THE AVENGERS.
YEAH, I'VE BEEN A PART OF A LOT OF TEAMS OVER THE YEARS, BUT THIS IS PERSONAL FOR ME, BECAUSE IT BRINGS ME BACK TO THE FIRST TEAM I WAS A PART OF.
HEROES FOR HIRE!
HEROES FOR HIRE
I'LL KILL HIM.
DEET-DEET
I JUST HEARD THE NEWS FROM A TELEVISION DOWN THE HALL.
I GUESS YOU'LL BE NEEDING A LAWYER.
NO, ACTUALLY I WANT THE PUNISHER'S NUMBER.
I'M NOT EVEN IN PRIVATE PRACTICE ANYMORE, BUT I'LL DRAW UP A CEASE AND DESIST FOR YOU. PRO BONO. I OWE DEADPOOL ONE.
SNAP!
THE PUNISHER. JUST THIS ONE TIME.
HELLO?
MATT?
I'M THINKING.
...
NO, LET'S LEAVE THE PUNISHER OUT OF IT.

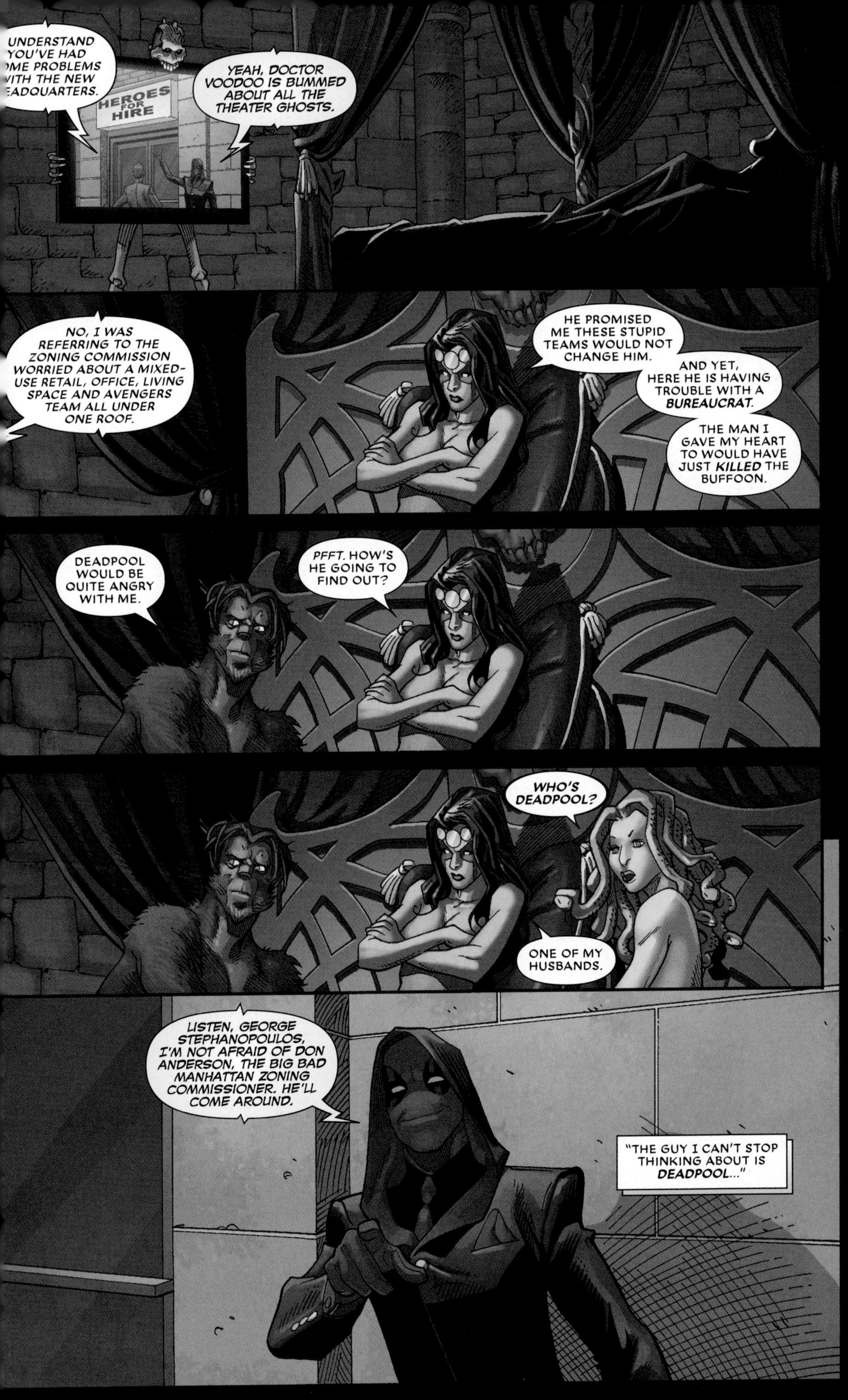
UNDERSTAND YOU'VE HAD OME PROBLEMS VITH THE NEW EADQUARTERS.
HEROES FOR HIRE
YEAH, DOCTOR VOODOO IS BUMMED ABOUT ALL THE THEATER GHOSTS.
NO, I WAS REFERRING TO THE ZONING COMMISSION WORRIED ABOUT A MIXED-USE RETAIL, OFFICE, LIVING SPACE AND AVENGERS TEAM ALL UNDER ONE ROOF.
HE PROMISED ME THESE STUPID TEAMS WOULD NOT CHANGE HIM.
AND YET, HERE HE IS HAVING TROUBLE WITH A BUREAUCRAT.
THE MAN I GAVE MY HEART TO WOULD HAVE JUST KILLED THE BUFFOON.
DEADPOOL WOULD BE QUITE ANGRY WITH ME.
PFFT. HOW'S HE GOING TO FIND OUT?
WHO'S DEADPOOL?
ONE OF MY HUSBANDS.
LISTEN, GEORGE STEPHANOPOULOS, I'M NOT AFRAID OF DON ANDERSON, THE BIG BAD MANHATTAN ZONING COMMISSIONER. HE'LL COME AROUND.
"THE GUY I CAN'T STOP THINKING ABOUT IS DEADPOOL..."

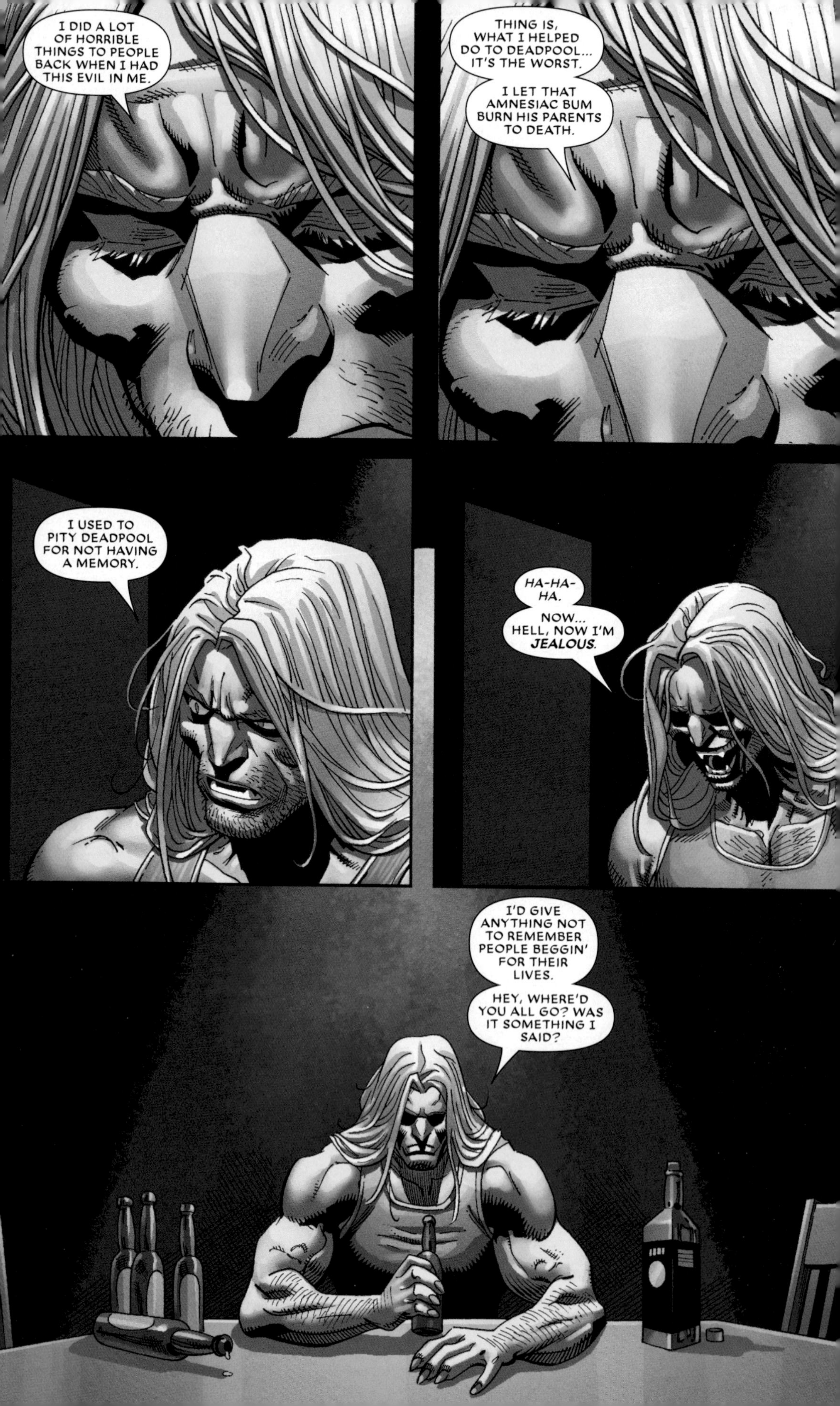
I DID A LOT OF HORRIBLE THINGS TO PEOPLE BACK WHEN I HAD THIS EVIL IN ME.
THING IS, WHAT I HELPED DO TO DEADPOOL... IT'S THE WORST.
I LET THAT AMNESIAC BUM BURN HIS PARENTS TO DEATH.
I USED TO PITY DEADPOOL FOR NOT HAVING A MEMORY.
HA-HA-HA.
NOW... HELL, NOW I'M *JEALOUS*.
I'D GIVE ANYTHING NOT TO REMEMBER PEOPLE BEGGIN' FOR THEIR LIVES.
HEY, WHERE'D YOU ALL GO? WAS IT SOMETHING I SAID?

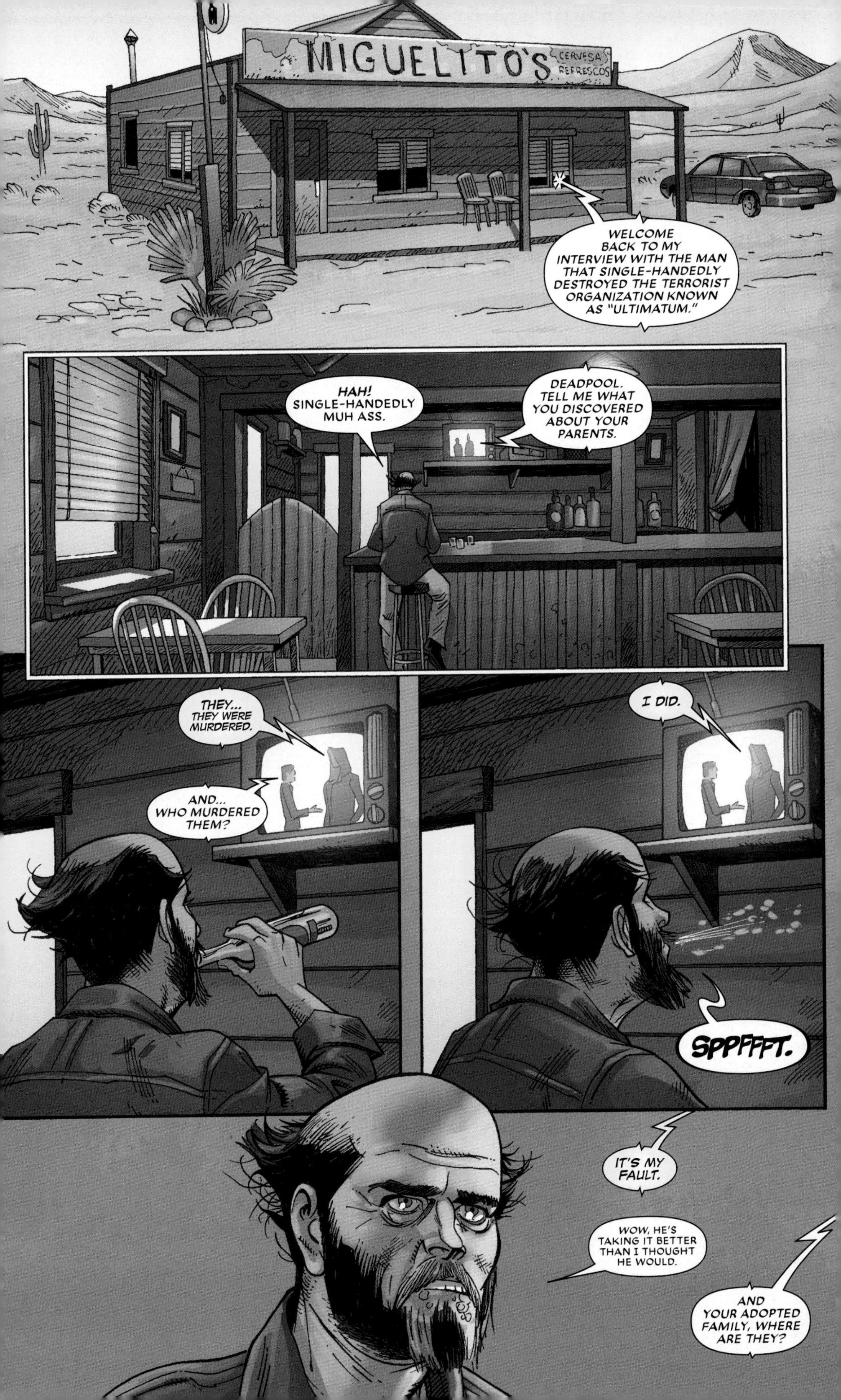
MIGUELITO'S
CERVESA
REFRESCOS
WELCOME BACK TO MY INTERVIEW WITH THE MAN THAT SINGLE-HANDEDLY DESTROYED THE TERRORIST ORGANIZATION KNOWN AS "ULTIMATUM."
HAH! SINGLE-HANDEDLY MUH ASS.
DEADPOOL. TELL ME WHAT YOU DISCOVERED ABOUT YOUR PARENTS.
THEY... THEY WERE MURDERED.
AND... WHO MURDERED THEM?
I DID.
SPPFFFT.
IT'S MY FAULT.
WOW, HE'S TAKING IT BETTER THAN I THOUGHT HE WOULD.
AND YOUR ADOPTED FAMILY, WHERE ARE THEY?

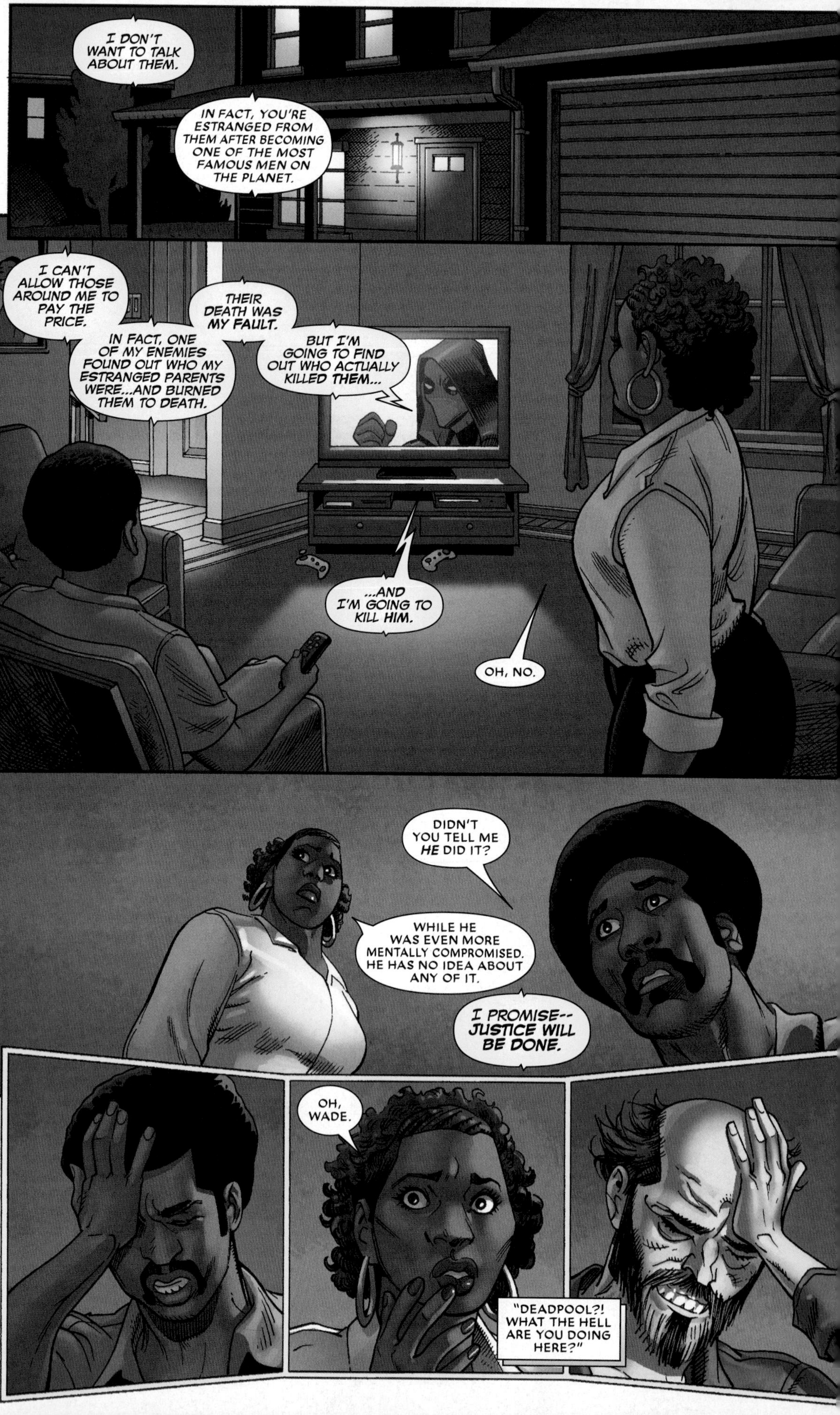
I DON'T WANT TO TALK ABOUT THEM.
IN FACT, YOU'RE ESTRANGED FROM THEM AFTER BECOMING ONE OF THE MOST FAMOUS MEN ON THE PLANET.
I CAN'T ALLOW THOSE AROUND ME TO PAY THE PRICE.
IN FACT, ONE OF MY ENEMIES FOUND OUT WHO MY ESTRANGED PARENTS WERE...AND BURNED THEM TO DEATH.
THEIR DEATH WAS MY FAULT.
BUT I'M GOING TO FIND OUT WHO ACTUALLY KILLED THEM...
...AND I'M GOING TO KILL HIM.
OH, NO.
DIDN'T YOU TELL ME HE DID IT?
WHILE HE WAS EVEN MORE MENTALLY COMPROMISED. HE HAS NO IDEA ABOUT ANY OF IT.
I PROMISE-- JUSTICE WILL BE DONE.
OH, WADE.
"DEADPOOL?! WHAT THE HELL ARE YOU DOING HERE?"

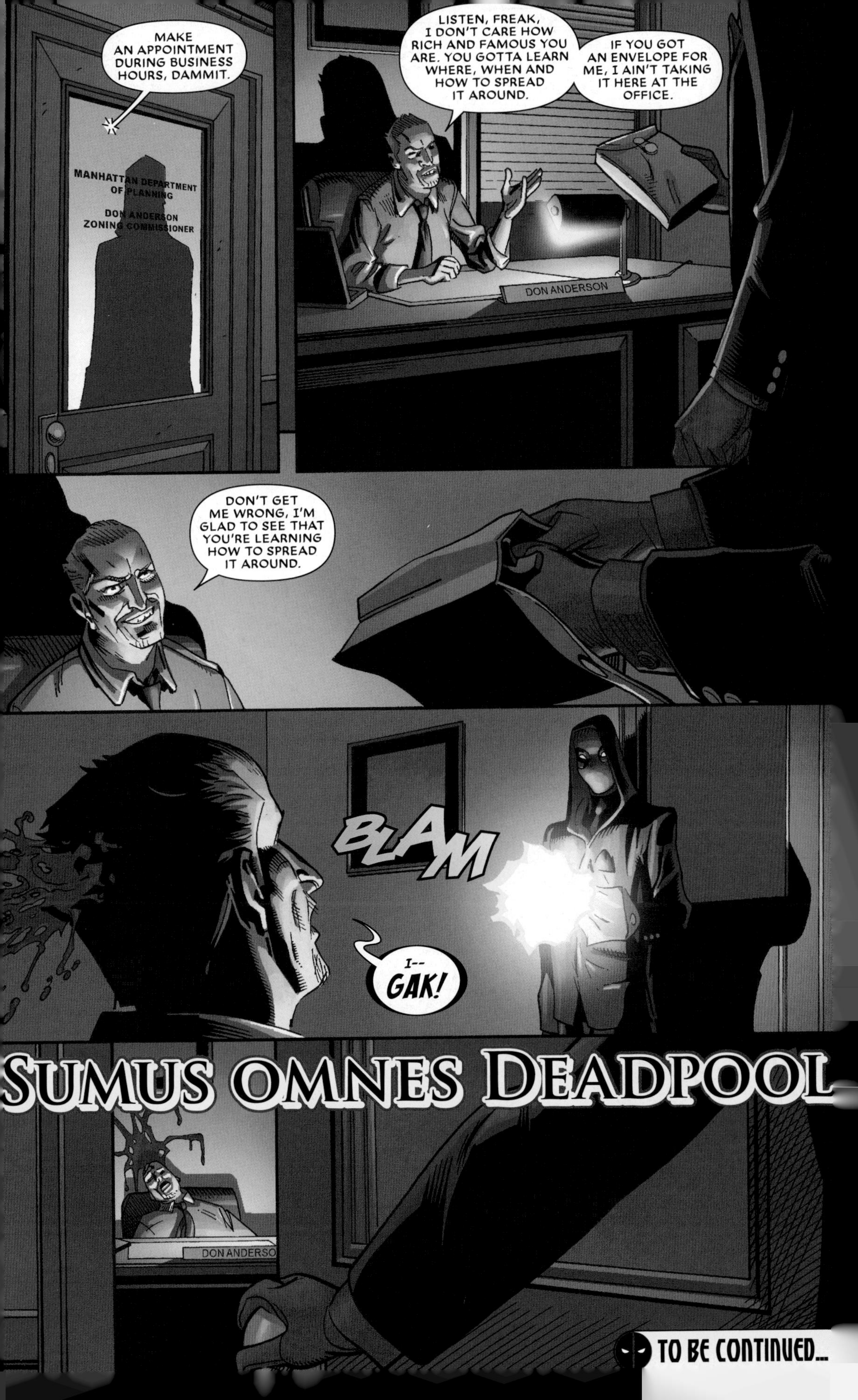
MAKE AN APPOINTMENT DURING BUSINESS HOURS, DAMMIT.
MANHATTAN DEPARTMENT OF PLANNING
DON ANDERSON ZONING COMMISSIONER
LISTEN, FREAK, I DON'T CARE HOW RICH AND FAMOUS YOU ARE. YOU GOTTA LEARN WHERE, WHEN AND HOW TO SPREAD IT AROUND.
IF YOU GOT AN ENVELOPE FOR ME, I AIN'T TAKING IT HERE AT THE OFFICE.
DON ANDERSON
DON'T GET ME WRONG, I'M GLAD TO SEE THAT YOU'RE LEARNING HOW TO SPREAD IT AROUND.
BLAM
I-- GAK!
SUMUS OMNES DEADPOOL
DON ANDERSON
TO BE CONTINUED...

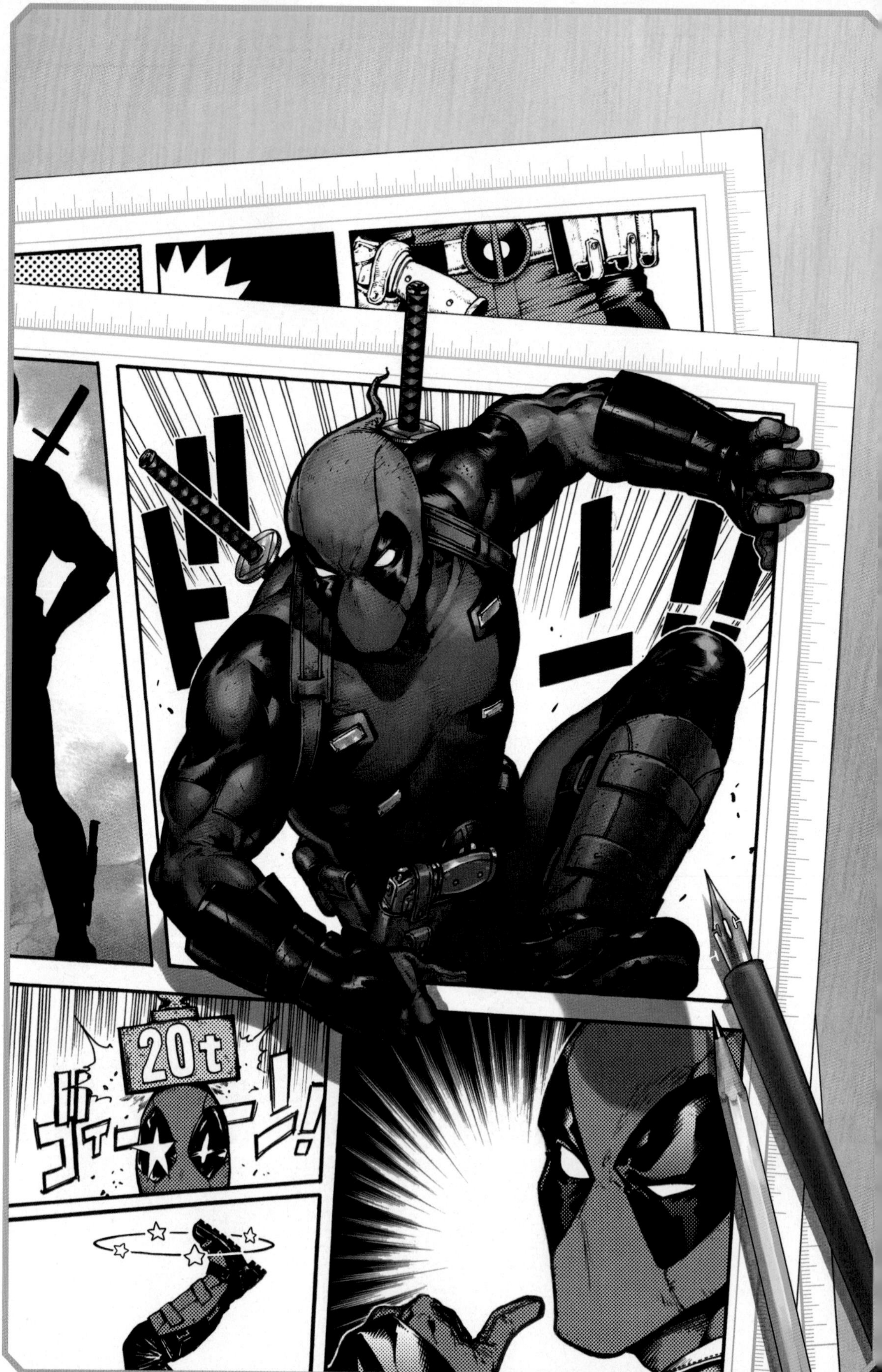
ドーン!!
20t

DEADPOOL (2015) #1 Variant by KAMOME SHIRAHAMA

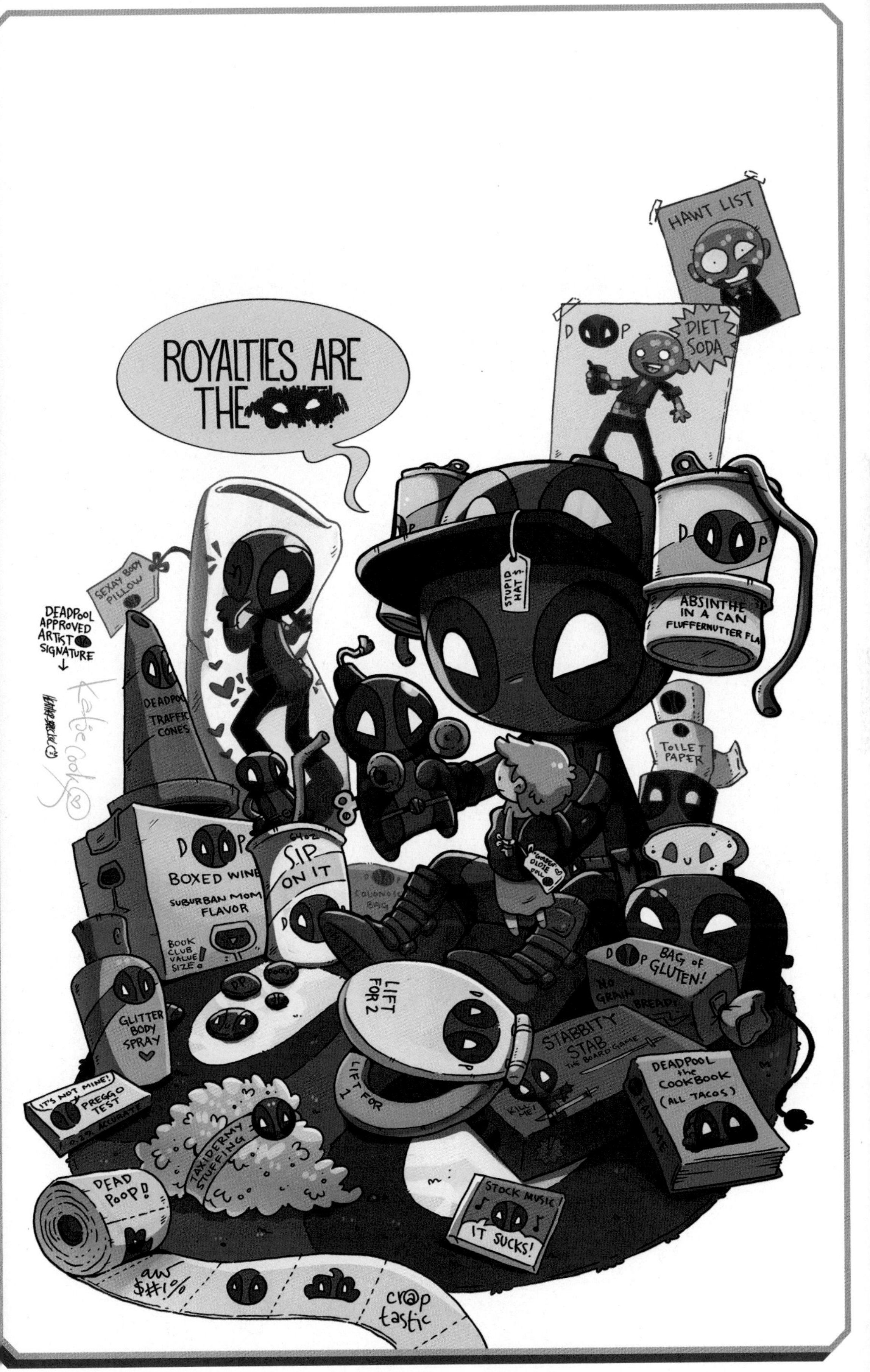

ROYALTIES ARE THE [redacted]!
HAWT LIST
DIET SODA
SEXAY BODY PILLOW
DEADPOOL APPROVED ARTIST SIGNATURE
STUPID HAT $
ABSINTHE IN A CAN
FLUFFERNUTTER FLA
DEADPOOL TRAFFIC CONES
TOILET PAPER
BOXED WINE
SUBURBAN MOM FLAVOR
BOOK CLUB VALUE SIZE!
64oz S.I.P. ON IT
COLONOSC BAG
BAG of GLUTEN!
NO GRAIN BREAD!
LIFT FOR 2
LIFT FOR 1
GLITTER BODY SPRAY
STABBITY STAB
THE BOARD GAME
KILL ME!
DEADPOOL the COOKBOOK
(ALL TACOS)
EAT ME
IT'S NOT MINE!
PREGGO TEST
0.2% ACCURATE
TAXIDERMY STUFFING
DEAD POOP!
STOCK MUSIC
IT SUCKS!
aw $#!%
cr@p tastic

DEADPOOL (2015) #1 Variant by KATIE COOK & HEATHER BRECKEL

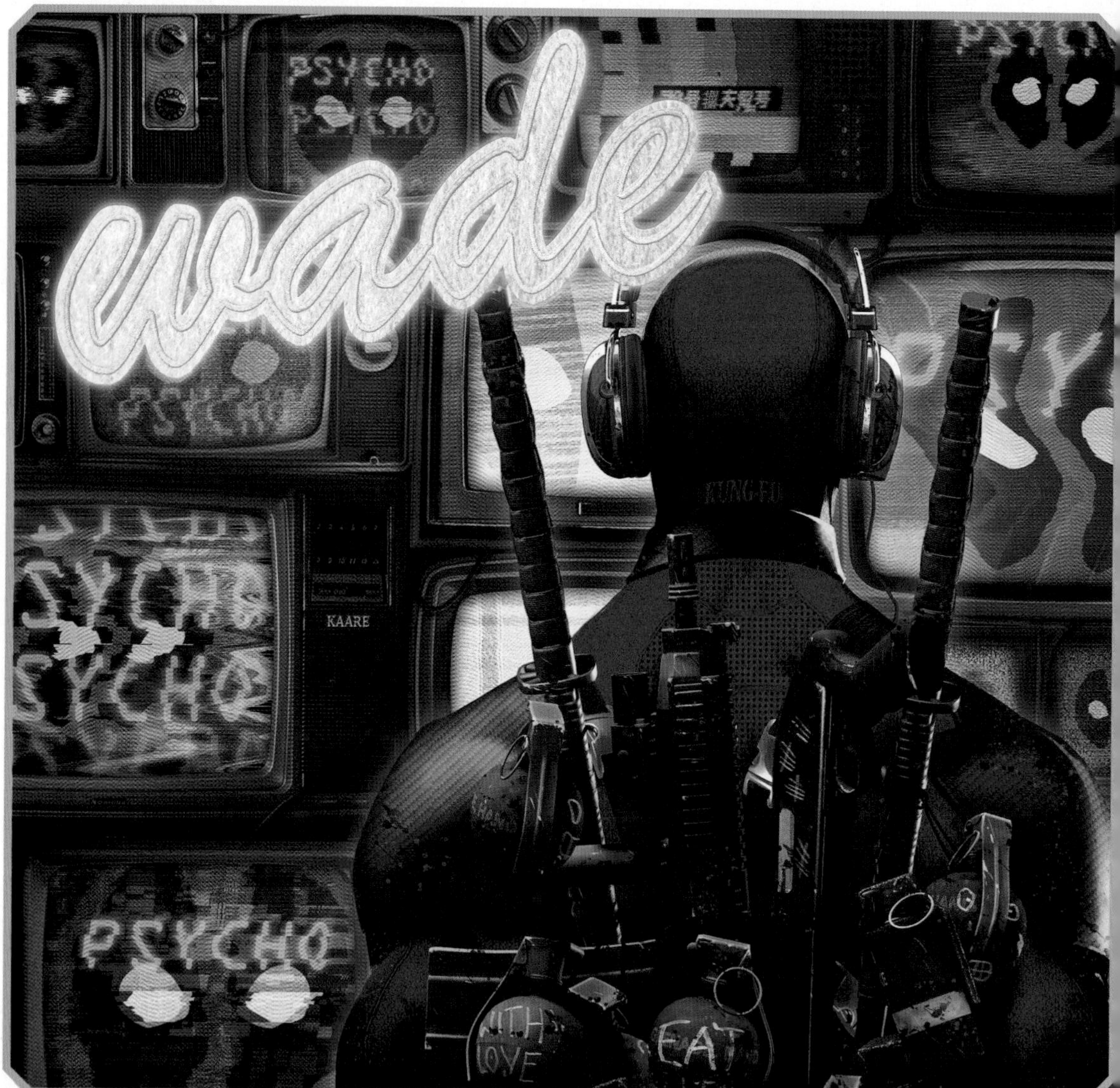
wade
PSYCHO
PSYCHO
PSYCHO
PSYCHO
PSYCHO
KAARE
KUNG-FU
PSYCHO
WITH LOVE
EAT

DEADPOOL (2015) #1 Hip-Hop Variant by KAARE ANDREWS

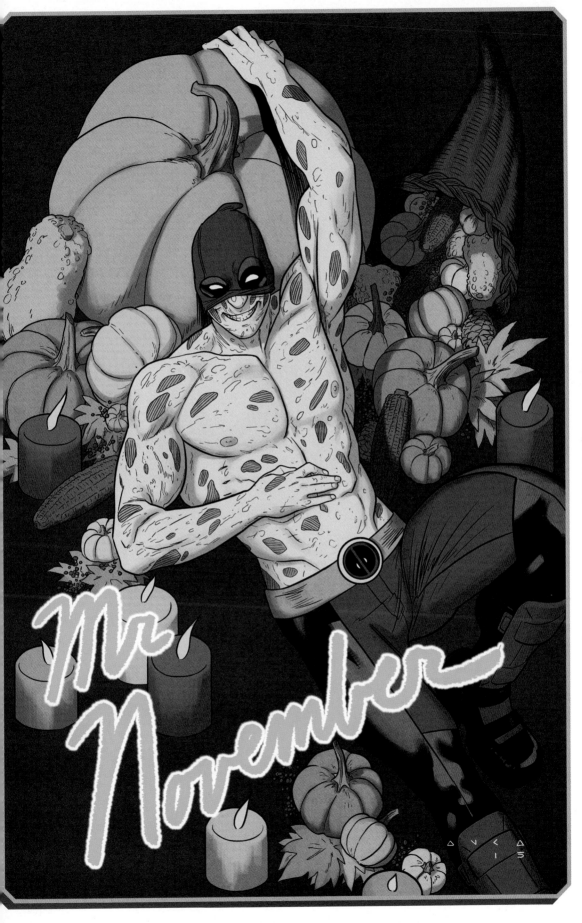

Mr November

DEADPOOL (2015) #1 Beefcake Variant by KRIS ANKA

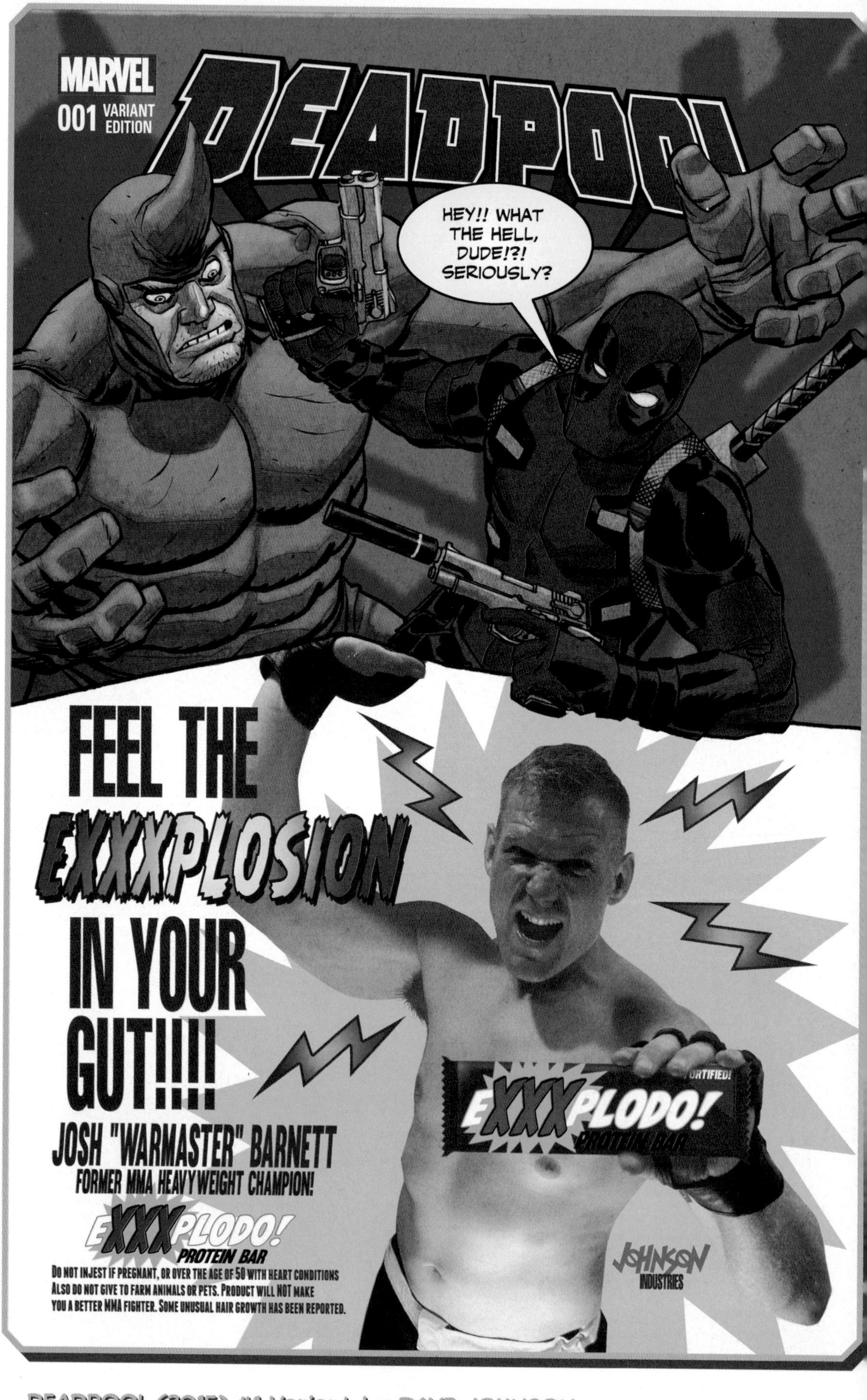
MARVEL
001 VARIANT EDITION
DEADPOOL
HEY!! WHAT THE HELL, DUDE!?! SERIOUSLY?
FEEL THE EXXXPLOSION IN YOUR GUT!!!!
JOSH "WARMASTER" BARNETT
FORMER MMA HEAVYWEIGHT CHAMPION!
EXXXPLODO! PROTEIN BAR
DO NOT INJEST IF PREGNANT, OR OVER THE AGE OF 50 WITH HEART CONDITIONS
ALSO DO NOT GIVE TO FARM ANIMALS OR PETS. PRODUCT WILL NOT MAKE
YOU A BETTER MMA FIGHTER. SOME UNUSUAL HAIR GROWTH HAS BEEN REPORTED.
EXXXPLODO!
JOHNSON INDUSTRIES

DEADPOOL (2015) #1 Variant by DAVE JOHNSON

COVER GALLERY: DEADPOOL'S OTHER FIRSTS – *COLLECT 'EM ALL, FANBOY!*

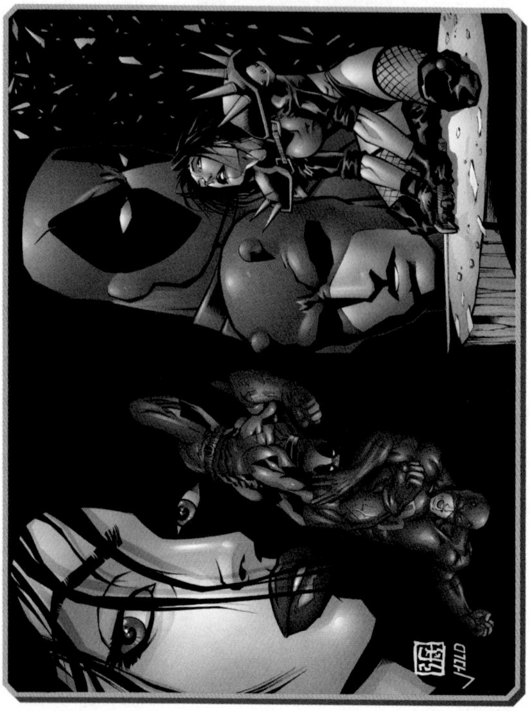

DAREDEVIL/DEADPOOL ANNUAL '97
July 1997

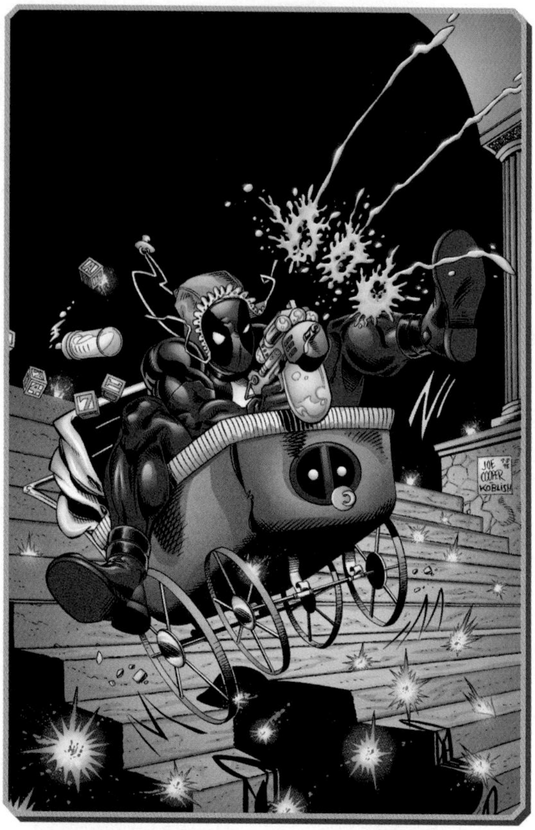

BABY'S FIRST DEADPOOL BOOK
(frst one-shot) December 1998

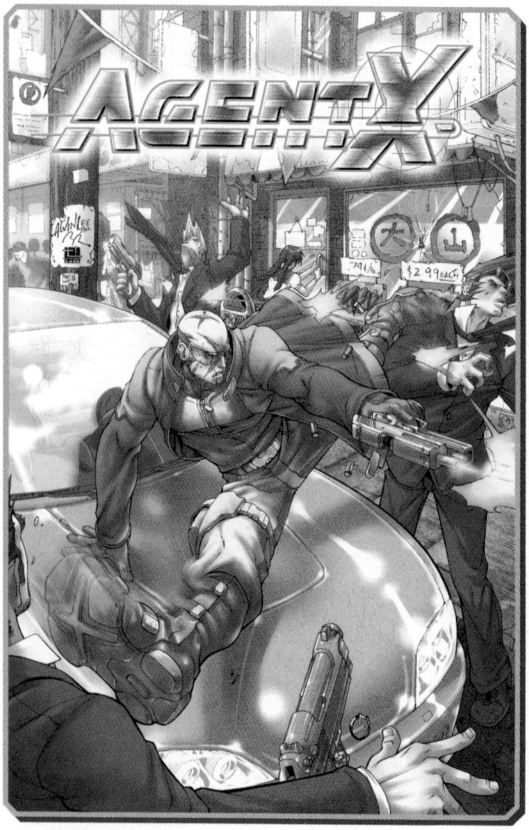
AGENT X

AGENT X #1
September 2002

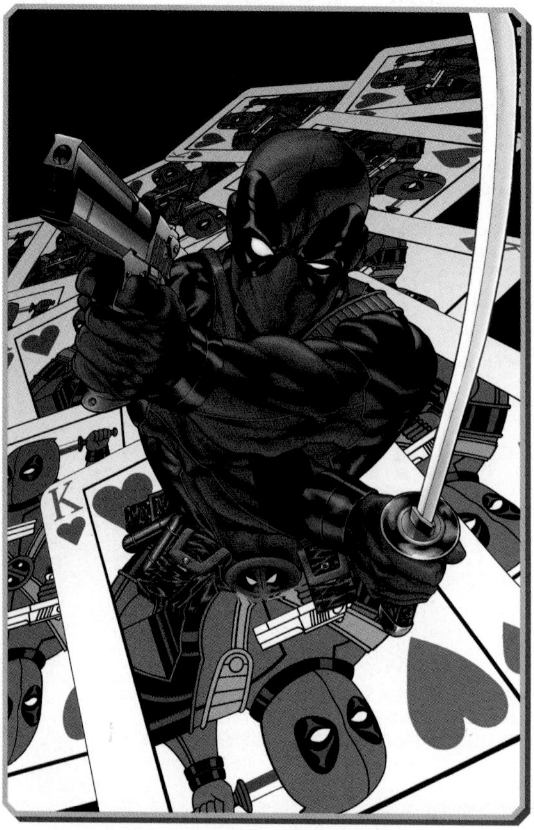

DEADPOOL: SUICIDE KINGS #1
June 2009

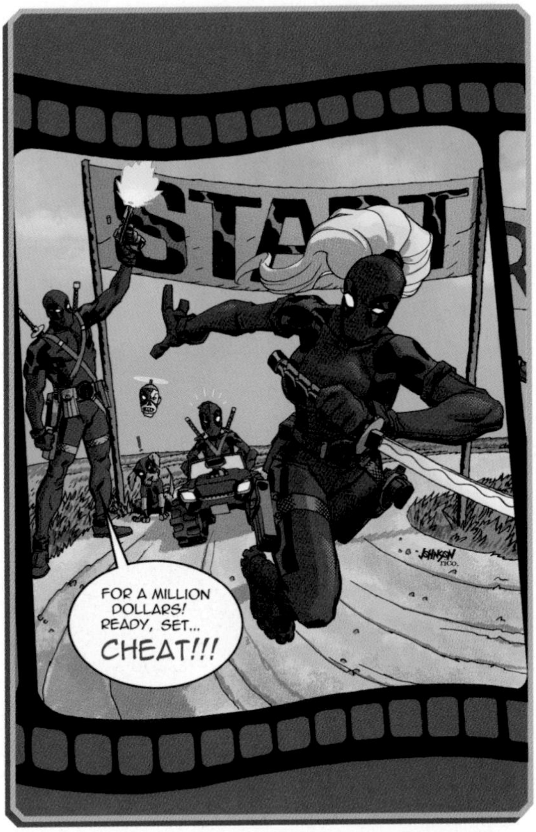
START
FOR A MILLION DOLLARS! READY, SET...
CHEAT!!!

PRELUDE TO DEADPOOL CORPS #1
May 2010

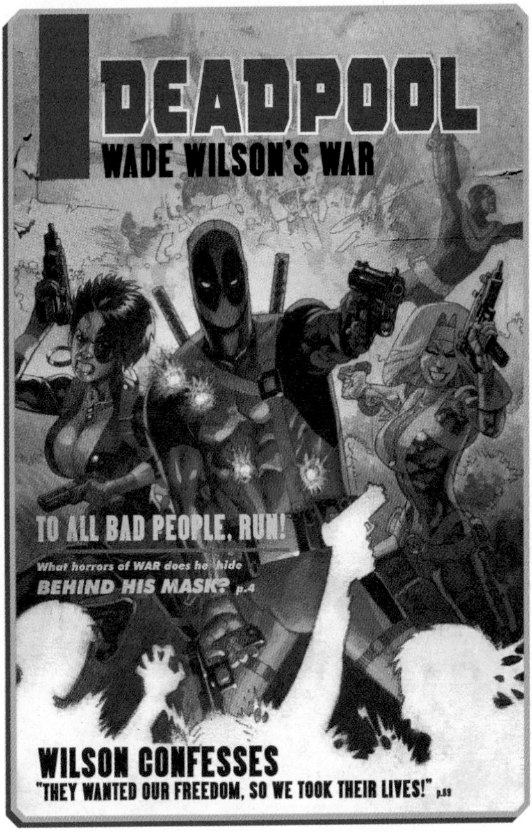
DEADPOOL
WADE WILSON'S WAR
TO ALL BAD PEOPLE, RUN!
What horrors of WAR does he hide
BEHIND HIS MASK? p.4
WILSON CONFESSES
"THEY WANTED OUR FREEDOM, SO WE TOOK THEIR LIVES!"

DEADPOOL: WADE WILSON'S WAR #1
August 2010

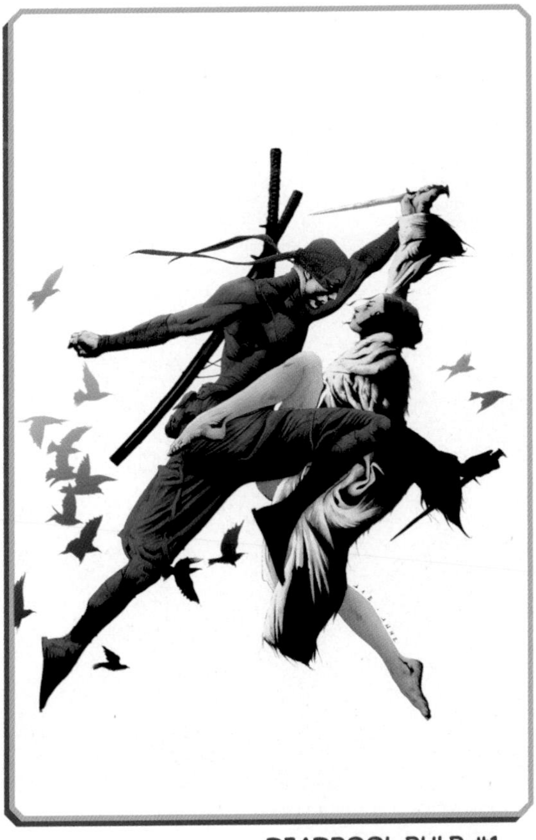

DEADPOOL PULP #1
November 2010

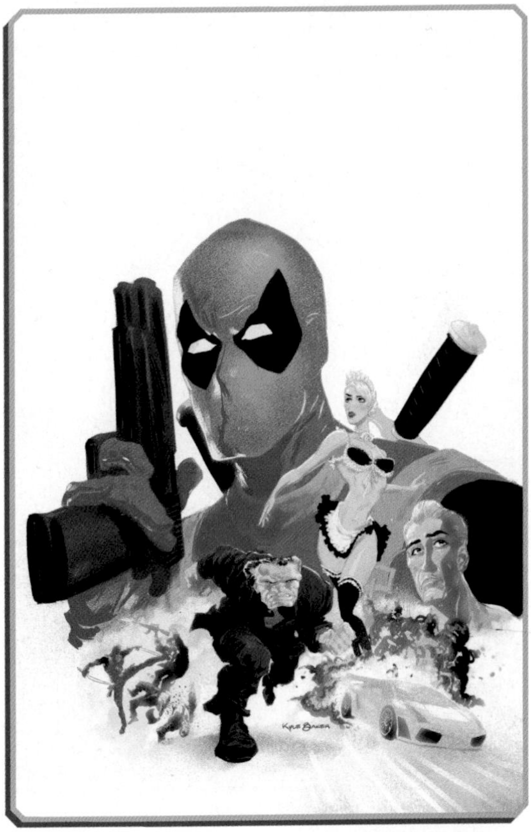

DEADPOOL MAX #1
December 2010

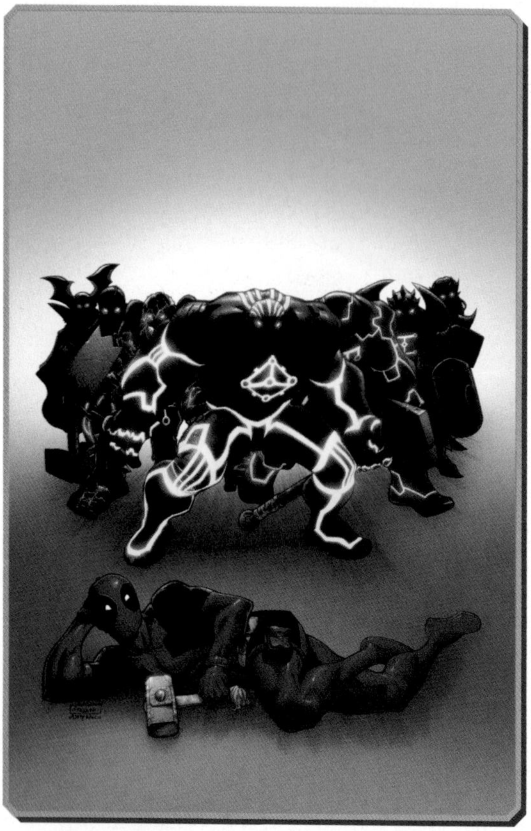

FEAR ITSELF: DEADPOOL #1
August 2011

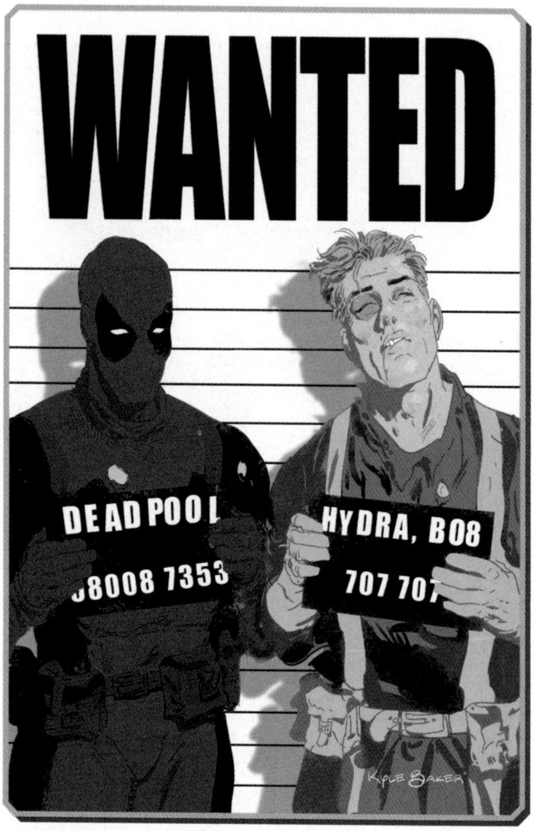
WANTED
DEADPOOL
8008 7353
HYDRA, BOB
707 707
KYLE BAKER

DEADPOOL MAX 2 #1
December 2011

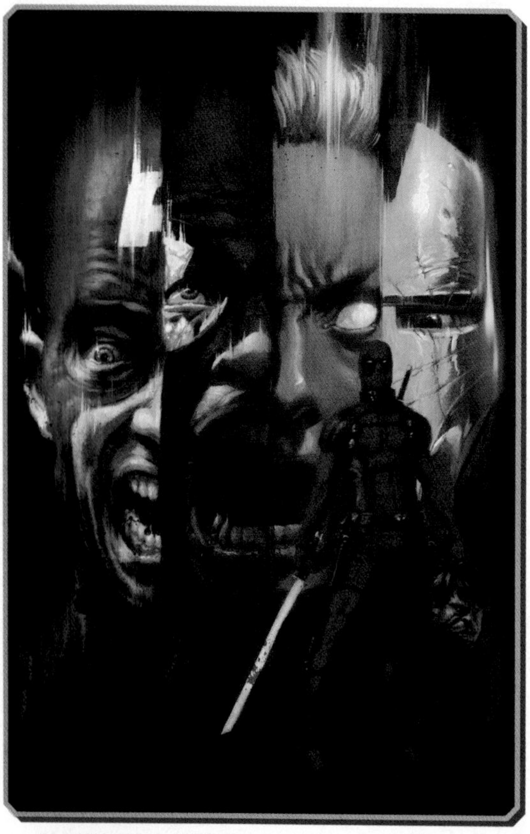

DEADPOOL KILLS
THE MARVEL UNIVERSE #1
October 2012

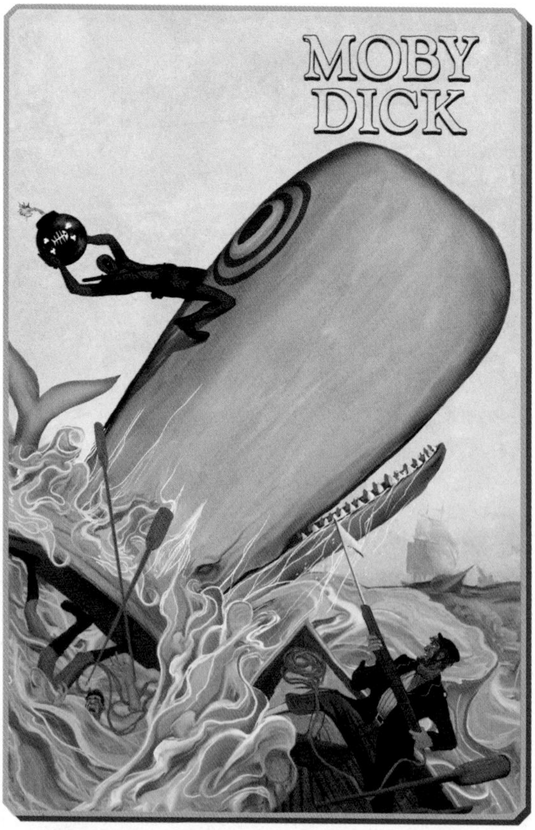
MOBY
DICK

DEADPOOL KILLUSTRATED #1
March 2013

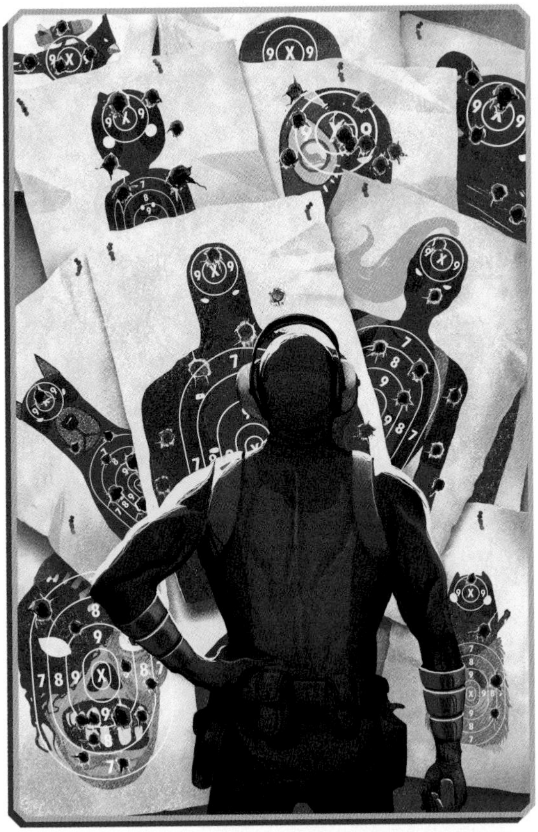

DEADPOOL KILLS DEADPOOL #1
September 2013

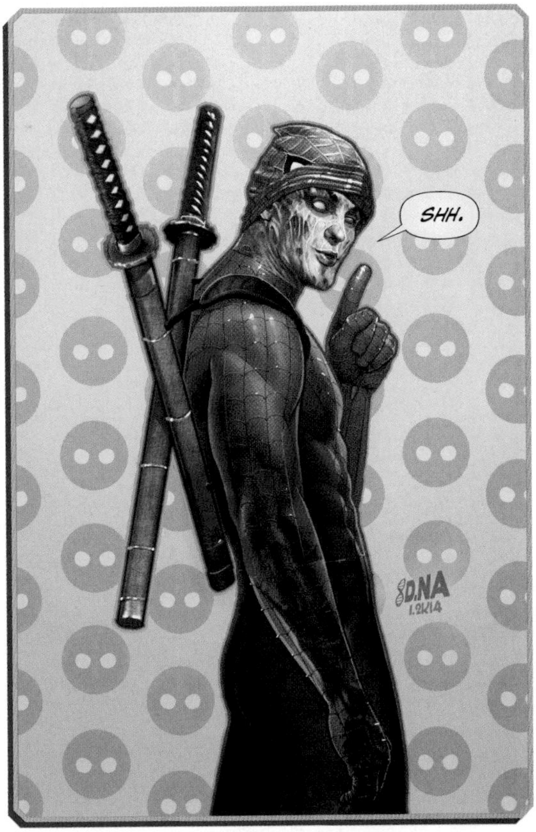
SHH.

DEADPOOL ANNUAL #1
January 2014

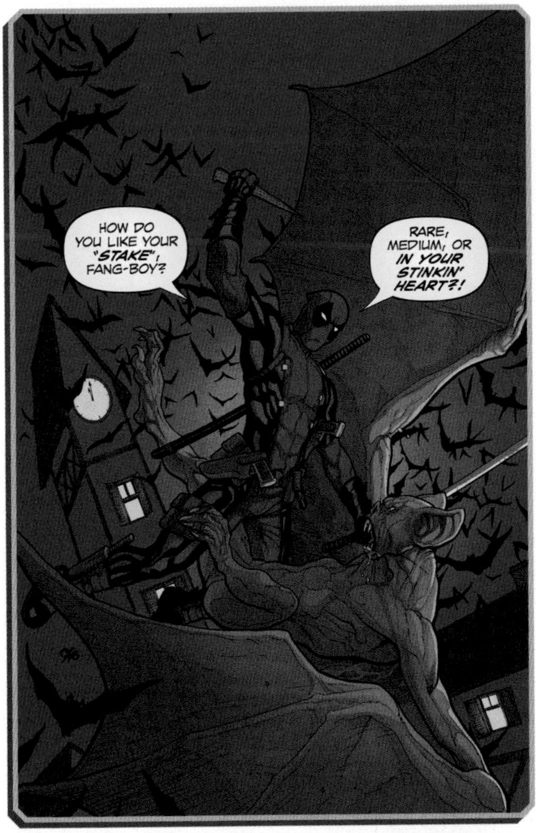
HOW DO YOU LIKE YOUR "STAKE", FANG-BOY?
RARE, MEDIUM, OR IN YOUR STINKIN' HEART?!

DEADPOOL:
THE GAUNTLET INFINITE COMIC #1
March 2014

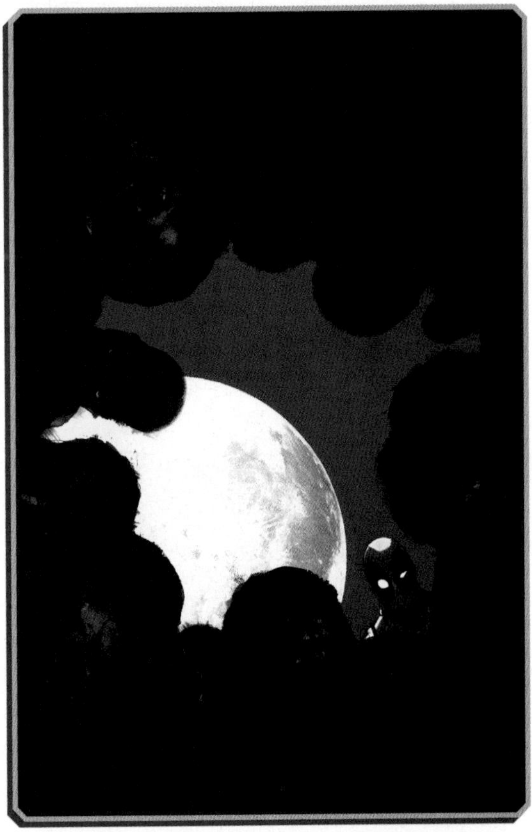

NIGHT OF THE LIVING DEADPOOL #1
March 2014

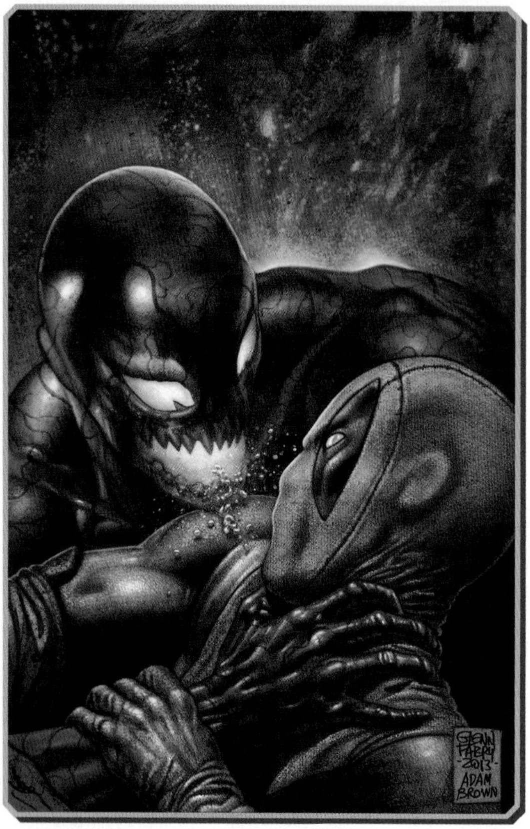
GLENN FABRY
2013
ADAM BROWN

DEADPOOL VS. CARNAGE #1
June 2014

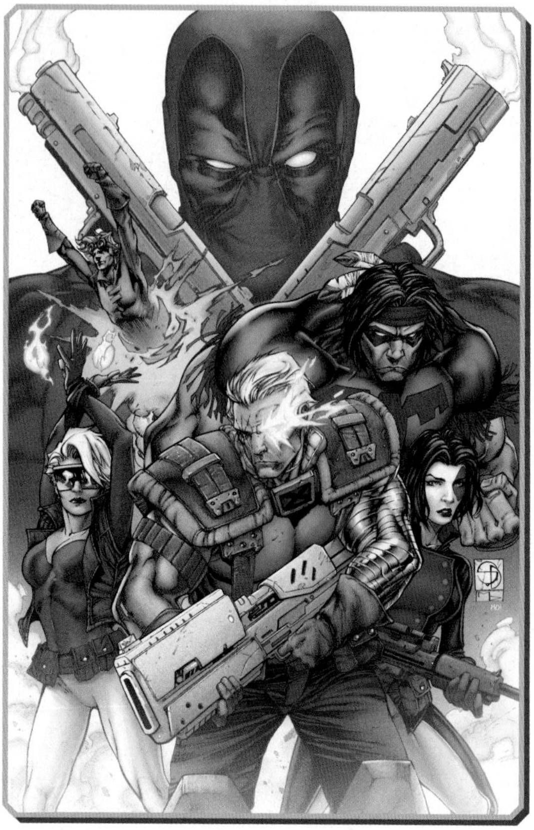

DEADPOOL VS. X-FORCE #1
September 2014

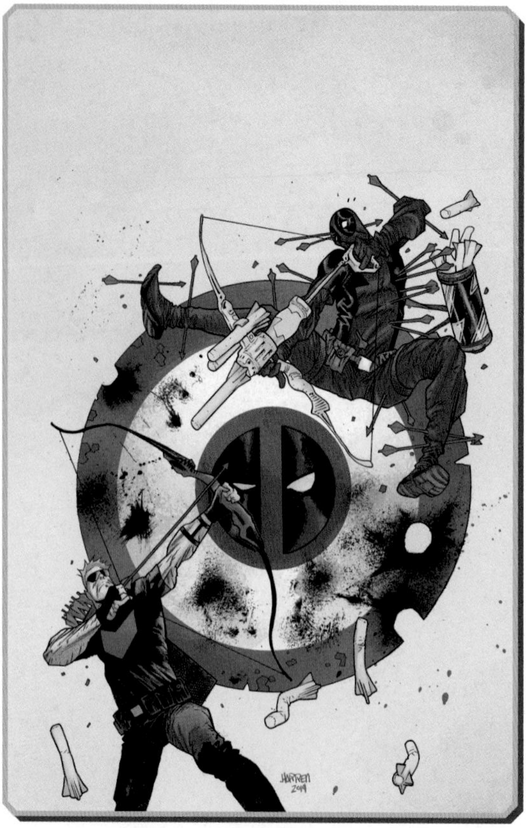

HAWKEYE VS. DEADPOOL #0
November 2014

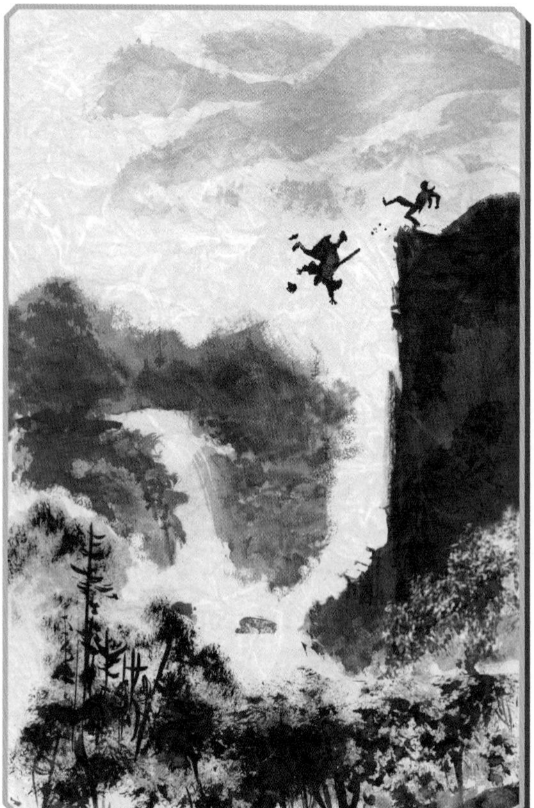

DEADPOOL'S ART OF WAR #1
December 2014

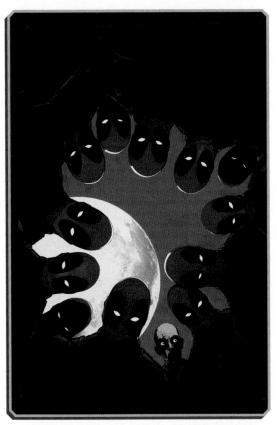

RETURN OF THE LIVING DEADPOOL #1
April 2015

DEADPOOL'S SECRET SECRET WARS #1
July 2015

MRS. DEADPOOL AND
THE HOWLING COMMANDOS #1
August 2015

DEADPOOL: PAWS HC
(frst prose novel) October 2015

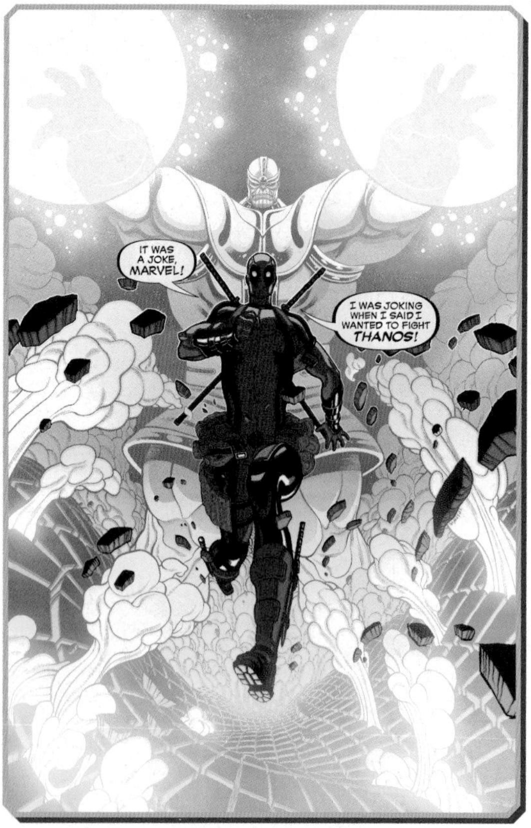
IT WAS A JOKE, MARVEL!
I WAS JOKING WHEN I SAID I WANTED TO FIGHT THANOS!

DEADPOOL VS. THANOS #1
November 2015

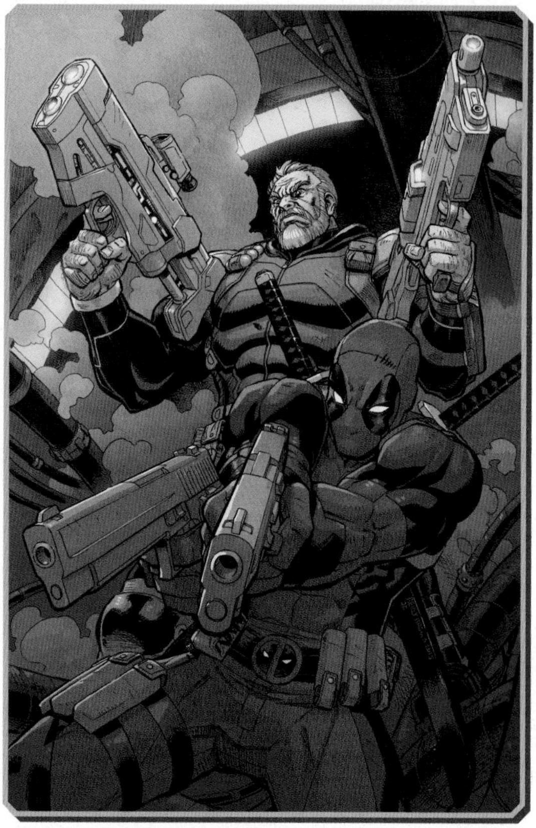

DEADPOOL & CABLE:
SPLIT SECOND INFINITE COMIC #1
December 2015

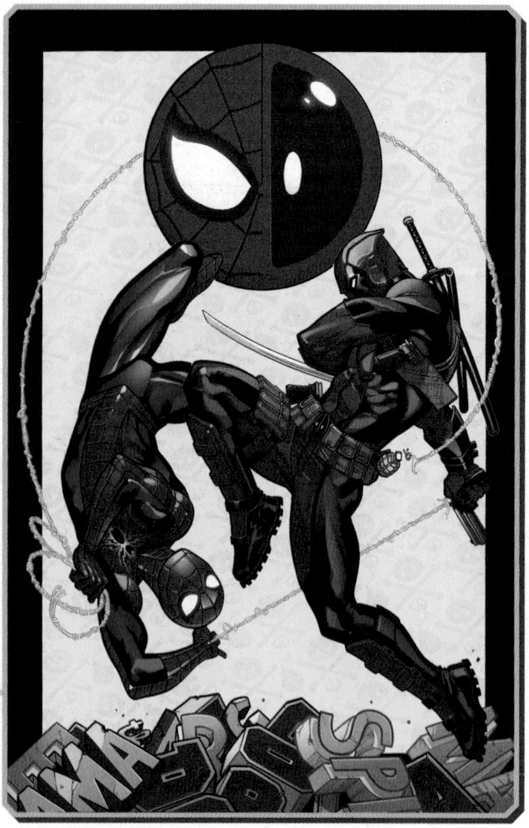

SPIDER-MAN/DEADPOOL #1
March 2016

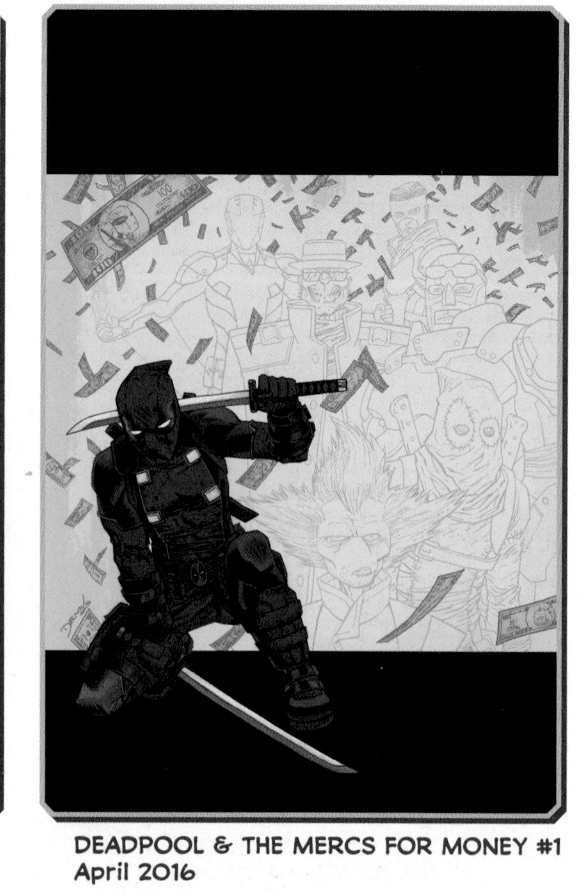

DEADPOOL & THE MERCS FOR MONEY #1
April 2016